Three

Renaissance Classics

THE MODERN STUDENT'S LIBRARY

Three Renaissance Classics

MACHIAVELLI
The Prince

MORE
Utopia

CASTIGLIONE
The Courtier

with INTRODUCTION and NOTES
by BURTON A. MILLIGAN

New York
CHARLES SCRIBNER'S SONS

INTRODUCTION

The Prince, Utopia and *The Courtier,* three of the most important books in Renaissance literature, were all written during the first third of the sixteenth century. They have brought down to us through more than four centuries an important part of the whole picture of the Renaissance. Together, they show us the Renaissance in its many-sidedness: its thirst for knowledge and beauty, its cynicism and idealism, its attitude toward human perfectibility and imperfectibility, its views concerning morality and manners. But what these three books have most in common is an intense interest in government and political theory. All three of the writers—Machiavelli, More, and Castiglione—looked upon the same European scene, in which tyranny, conquest, and political treachery were common. One of them, Machiavelli, accepted these evils as inevitable, and built a cynical but, as he felt, practicable political philosophy upon their inevitability. The other two, More and Castiglione, not blind to the faults that Machiavelli saw, but believing in man's potentialities for goodness and progress, built idealistic political philosophies.

Niccolò Machiavelli (1469–1527) made his reputation as a writer rather than as a statesman, but his career as a statesman gave authority to his writing. He served for a time as secretary to the Florentine republic and was sent on diplomatic missions that gave him a personal acquaintance with such personages as Caterina Sforza, Cesare Borgia, Louis XII of France, and the Emperor Maximilian. After the restoration of the Medici in 1512, Machiavelli was accused of conspiracy against them and was imprisoned, but was soon released. He retired to San Casciano,

near Florence, where the next year he wrote *The Prince,*
hopefully dedicated to Lorenzo de' Medici, but not successful in gaining the favor that Machiavelli sought. During his remaining years, in which he devoted himself
principally to writing, he produced, among other works,
The Art of War (1520) and his *History of Florence*
(1525).

Although written in 1513, *The Prince* was not published
until 1532. The first English translation, published in 1640,
was that of Edward Dacres, whose text is used in the present volume; but Machiavelli's book was known in England
earlier through a sixteenth-century French translation by
Gentillet of selections from it and, in turn, through the
English translation, in 1602, of this French work. Long
before Dacres' translation, Machiavelli's name had become
anathema in Elizabethan England, but he had defenders
and admirers, too, notably Francis Bacon.

The Prince is in essence a handbook on war, conquest,
and government. Its precepts are practical, based upon
ruthless realism and upon experience as revealed by history; and its purpose is practical, the liberating and uniting
of Italy. This purpose, although it is not fully stated until
the final chapter, which exhorts Lorenzo de' Medici to free
Italy from the barbarians by applying Machiavelli's precepts, must not be neglected if one is to understand
Machiavelli and his book. It is to the end of a united Italy
that the duplicity and expediency recommended throughout the book are directed. Recognizing this end, one may
convict Machiavelli of cold and ruthless unmorality, but
not make the mistake of believing that he loved evil for
its own sake. Rather, one will understand that his interest
was in the state, particularly in his own Italy, and that he
admired power and believed in fighting evil with evil. His
heroes are princes like Cesare Borgia and Ferdinand of
Aragon, heroic not because of their goodness, but because
of their strength and success.

iv

Machiavelli deals first with the particular problems of the prince who is a usurper or a conqueror. Both the usurper and the conqueror, he points out, face enemies in the old regime, and the usurper is confronted with the additional difficulty of trying to please the friends who have put him into power. Among the methods of establishing power that Machiavelli recommends—some ruthless, some benevolent, but all calculated to serve the new prince's interests—are extermination of the former ruling family; changing laws and systems of taxation as little as possible, and thus avoiding friction with the new subjects; either treating people well or crushing them, on the theory that timidity and half-measures are always ineffective; establishing colonies, as the successful Roman conquerors did, and thus gaining most satisfactory control of the invaded state; having the prince reside in the conquered country, where he may look closely to his own interests. Analyzing further the rule of conquered states, Machiavelli asserts that absolute monarchies are most easily ruled by new princes, because one absolute ruler is replaced by another; that limited monarchies are harder to rule, because the nobles in them once shared the power taken over by the conqueror and are jealous of regaining their places; and that republics are the hardest of all, because the whole people are usually the conqueror's enemies.

The obvious corollary to the stress upon conquest is Machiavelli's stress upon the importance of war. As Machiavelli puts it:

> A prince then ought to have no other ayme, nor other thought, nor take any thing else for his proper arte, but warr, and the orders and discipline thereof; for that is the sole arte which belongs to him that commands, and is of so great excellency, that not only those that are borne Princes, it maintains so; but many times rayses men from a private fortune to that dignity.

And war, so essential to the prince's accession to power and to his extension of it, must be the first consideration of the people as well as of the prince. Machiavelli rejects mercenary troops because their pay does not buy their loyalty. He disapproves of auxiliaries and allies, because "in losing, thou art left defeated; and conquering, thou becomest their prisoner." The prince himself must fight, followed by a united people. He must depend upon the people's military prowess and loyalty, rather than upon fortresses. He must keep his men well organized, well drilled, and physically fit.

In considering rules for the conduct of the prince in matters other than war and conquest, Machiavelli starts with the assumption that in an imperfect world a prince cannot be morally perfect without effecting his own destruction: "for that man who will professe honesty in all his actions, must needs go to ruine, among so many that are dishonest. Whereupon it is necessary for a Prince, desiring to preserve himselfe, to be able to make use of that honestie, and to lay it aside againe, as need shall require." But this does not mean that the prince should do wrong flagrantly, even under the spur of necessity. He must, rather, always strive for the appearance of rectitude, which the world values, however little it cares for actual rectitude. Thus, Machiavelli urges that prince to be niggardly, but to be esteemed liberal. Similarly, Machiavelli believes that the prince must not hesitate to be cruel, because cruelty makes people fear him, and "it is much safer to be feard, than to be lov'd." But the prince must not be a sadist; he must employ cruelty judiciously, in a paradoxical sense, almost humanely—for example, to discourage or prevent disorders in the state harmful to the majority of the people. Machiavelli disavows purposeless cruelty, not for humanitarian reasons, but because it incites the people's hatred, which is always dangerous. In short, although the prince must lie, cheat, break his word, and repudiate his religion whenever doing so is advantageous to the state, he must do none of these things needlessly. As the following quotation shows, Machiavelli, if not the very ardent friend of morality, is at least not its enemy unless it gets in his way!

> And it suffices to conceive this, that a Prince, and especially a new Prince, cannot observe all those things, for which men are held good; he being often forc'd, for the maintenance of his State, to do contrary to his faith, charity, humanity, and religion; and therefore it behooves him to have a mind so dispos'd as to turne and take the advantage of all winds and fortunes; and as formerly I said, not forsake the good, while he can; but to know how to make use of the evill upon necessity.

We in the modern world should be able at least to understand Machiavelli's viewpoints, whether we admire them or not, because in our times, in the totalitarian countries, we have often seen such zeal for the state and for the leader of the state put ahead of truth, humanitarianism, and moral values.

Sir Thomas More (1478–1535) stood in the front rank of the English humanists at the very beginning of the English Renaissance. Educated at Oxford under Linacre and Grocyn, brought up in the household of Cardinal Morton, who figures as a character in Book One of *Utopia*, More belonged, along with Erasmus and Colet, to the group known as the Oxford Reformers, who sought to apply humanistic principles to reforms in the Church and in education. From success in the practice of law, More passed to a brilliant career in public life under Henry VIII, which culminated with his becoming Lord Chancellor in 1529. His retirement from this high office, in 1532, was followed in 1534 by his break with Henry VIII over the King's claims to supremacy in the Church and over the validity of the King's divorce from Catherine of Aragon. Because More refused to compromise with his conscience, he was accused of high treason and, in 1535, was executed. As even these bare details of his life show, More wrote with authority about kings, government, education, religion, and law, the subjects which most concern him in *Utopia*.

Utopia, written in Latin, was first published at Louvain in 1516, and was reprinted in several other European cities within the next few years. The first English translation, by Ralphe Robynson, was published in 1551. It is the text used in the present volume. Sir Thomas More produced other works in Latin and in English, but they are of minor importance. His fame in literature rests upon *Utopia*.

The First Book of *Utopia* tells us what was wrong with the England, and for that matter the Europe generally, of More's time. The Second Book shows us an ideal commonwealth in which the social evils described in the First Book are corrected. Also, in a very important sense the Second Book is a continuation of the indictment of society in the First, because every wise and humane provision regulating government and society in More's Utopian state is a reminder of the foolish or inhumane conduct of affairs in the real world. No doubt More feared that the story of the Utopians would be regarded as an idle and pleasant fiction, and that his serious intention, his social satire, would be overlooked or only partly comprehended. At any rate, having written the Second Book, in 1515, he afterwards wrote the First. Its importance in providing verisimilitude is great, but its importance in providing explicit contrast between the real and the ideal is greater.

Although More was sufficiently politic to begin *Utopia* with a compliment to Henry VIII, a considerable part of the attack in Book One is directed against kings. The chief interests of most kings, according to More's spokesman, Hythloday, are war and conquest. Kings, he says, do not want the advice of philosophers, and they never will want it until they have followed Plato's advice and become philosophers themselves. Their greed for wealth is as insatiable as their lust for power.

Book One is also a penetrating study of the English penal system and of the basic economic and social evils underlying crime and poverty in More's England. In the conversations at Cardinal Morton's house, Hythloday sweeps aside the assumptions of some of the Cardinal's guests that people steal or beg because they are by nature dishonest or shiftless, and that the only preventive of crime is punishment. More's contentions are that the conditions that give rise to destitution and, consequently, to crime must be eliminated, and that punishment, however cruel, will not in itself prevent crime. The conditions in England leading to destitution and crime, Hythloday argues, are the unequal distribution of wealth and the denial to many people of an opportunity to make an honest living. Among these people are: the veterans maimed in war, unable to work at their old crafts or to learn new ones, and deserted by society; the serving men of the idle rich, untrained in useful work and left destitute at their masters' deaths; small farmers ejected from land enclosed for sheep-grazing, who, having no trade other than farming, can only wander through the countryside and become thieves or vagabonds. Most of these evils More blames upon "the unreasonable covetousnes of a few." The Church itself shares part of the guilt, through its own policy of land enclosure and through turning loose its hordes of begging friars upon the country, idle and sometimes mischievous churchmen, who are regarded by More much as Chaucer regarded their earlier counterparts. Severe punishments, such as capital punishment for thievery, are, More argues, not only morally reprehensible, but also impracticable: "Neither ther is any punishment so horrible, that it can kepe them from stealynge, which have no other craft, wherby to get their

living." And, says More, a thief facing capital punishment
for his stealing has every practical motive for committing
murder to cover up his theft.

For some of the social evils, however, More blames the
people themselves. Joined to the miserable poverty not of
their own making are "great wantonnes, importunate
superfluitie and excessive riote." The people are guilty of
moral laxity, thriftlessness, and dissipation of their time
and talents. They spend their time, says More, in "stewes,
wynetavernes, ale houses and tiplinge houses," or in playing "noughtie, lewde and unlawfull games," among which
he includes card playing, dice play, and bowling.

In the Second Book, More is concerned not merely with
correction of the evils examined in the First Book, but also
with a larger consideration of what would be ideal in government, social organization, law, education, and religion.

In devising his Utopian government, More rejects kings,
whose faults he has pointed out in Book One, and, like
Plato, adopts a republic. Of the federal government all
that More says is that there come yearly to Amaurote, the
capital city of Utopia, from each of the cities three wise,
experienced old men, "there to entreate and debate of the
common matters of the land." In the chapter "Of the
magistrates" More describes briefly the local governments,
republican in form, carefully controlled by checks and bal-
ances, open to public scrutiny. The attitudes toward government that lie behind these meagre details are obvious,
although not stated: distrust of great centralized power in
a national government, fear of hasty or secret action by
legislators, trust in the people acting through elected rep-
resentatives.

More's position in regard to communism in Utopia is
enigmatic, all the more so because, although Hythloday,
usually his spokesman, praises it, More himself condemns
it. Perhaps More held up the idea of common ownership
as a warning to those who abused private wealth; perhaps

he considered Utopian communism, whatever support he found for it in Plato's republic or in biblical teachings about wealth, to be an ideal, but not a practicable system. Whatever the fact, More makes every effort to make the Utopian system of communism seem practicable. It is no share-the-wealth plan for idlers. Every man may have his share, but only by working for it. Incidentally, More is greatly interested not only in the distribution of wealth, but also in the very nature of wealth, which he examines from the viewpoint of whether the scarcity of a thing, rather than its utility, should be the measure of its value.

Although More assumes that his communistic system will eliminate thievery, he does not assume that all crimes will be eliminated in his ideal state. He provides a legal and penal system of special interest when one recalls his criticisms of English law in Book One and remembers More's own unusual knowledge of law. In Utopia there are few laws, and they are so clearly stated that they are understandable to every man. There are no lawyers, for every man is able to plead his own cause. Capital punishment is employed as a last resort with only the most intractable criminals. Ordinarily the most severe punishment is bondage, itself inflicted upon only serious offenders. Bondmen are not shut uselessly in prisons, but are set to doing hard, useful work for the commonwealth. Thus, More gets the unpleasant work of his commonwealth done not by slaves, as in Plato's republic, but by convicted criminals. One of his most interesting conceptions is that the state should reward those who observe the laws as well as punish those who break them.

More's provisions regarding labor and agriculture offer reforms for the conditions exposed in the First Book. Not pointlessly, but recalling the plight of English workers deprived of their single trade or craft, More makes his Utopians learn both farming and a trade or craft. He provides for a six-hour working day, visionary indeed in the early sixteenth century, when the actual legal working day could extend to fourteen or fifteen hours; and he argues that it is feasible in a country where everyone—man and woman, priest and layman—works, and where no labor is wasted on the production of luxuries.

It is More the humanist who dreams of this six-hour working day. The many hours freed from drudgery are to be used for education and self-improvement, not for vain or harmful recreations. In Utopia "there be neither wine-tavernes, nor ale houses, nor stewes, nor anye occasion of vice or wickednes." Games are intellectually or morally improving; the Utopians spend leisure time in hearing lectures, in listening to readings pertaining to good manners and virtue, in hearing music, or in conversing with the wise. But all this is aside from formal education, which resembles that in a somewhat idealized sixteenth-century England, in which medieval education had been enriched by the Renaissance. Before Hythloday brings the Renaissance to Utopia by bringing classical learning, the principal subjects studied there correspond closely to the seven liberal arts of the medieval trivium (grammar, logic, and rhetoric) and quadrivium (music, geometry, arithmetic, and astronomy). But the subject of most interest to the Utopians, since they are a virtuous people, is moral philosophy, which they esteem as much as they despise the subtleties and fruitlessness of scholastic philosophy. When Hythloday brings Latin and Greek learning to Utopia, the people respond to it as the humanists that they are would be expected to do.

In his concepts of the ideal in family life and in marriage, More exhibits a curious combination of unconventionality and of great conservativeness. His program of pre-marital physical inspections, his attempts to liberalize divorce while guarding against its abuse, and his provisions for euthanasia are often hailed as ideas far ahead of their time. On the other hand, the patriarchal family life is likely to repel or disappoint modern readers, even when they realize that More lived in a world in which women had not been emancipated, and even when they understand that to More age meant wisdom.

More's ideas concerning war and international relations are midway between idealism and cautious realism, even cynicism. He can conceive of an ideal state, but not of an ideal world; and the ideal state will always be threatened by the imperfect outsiders. He accepts wars as inevitable and merely tries to restrain them and to perfect the waging of them. Utopians fight wars only for what they regard as just purposes: defense of their country, liberation of friendly countries from invaders, destruction of tyrants, seizure of unused territory of neighboring countries when it is needed for their own expanding population and is denied to them. They prevent war when they can, by means of what we would call economic sanctions. They protect their own citizens as much as possible from the horrors of war by employing mercenaries except in extreme emergencies. They pride themselves upon using every device of bribery, propaganda, and deceit instead of fighting stupidly and brutally, like bears or dogs. They are, in short, More's humanists, in war as in everything else. Impelled by their distrust of other countries, they form no leagues or confederations. There is almost Swiftian satire in More's condemnation of the treaty-breaking habits of the benighted countries near Utopia and his ironical praise of the scrupulous adherence to treaties of the Christian countries of Europe.

Perhaps nothing in *Utopia* is more enlightened than More's treatment of religion. Complete freedom of religious views prevails in his ideal commonwealth. Only atheism crosses the boundary of the Utopians' tolerance, and even it is not as severely condemned as bigotry, for the atheist is deprived of some of his civil rights, but the bigot is exiled. The priests, contrasting with those in the

Christian countries of More's time, are few in number and exceedingly holy. The religion is a religion of good works and of cheerfulness, like More's own.

Baldassare Castiglione (1478–1529), the author of *The Courtier,* was himself a courtier and was to some extent a model for his own book, although with characteristic modesty he did not make himself a character in it. He was a scholar, minor poet, courtier for many years at the brilliant court of Urbino, whose real personages are the characters of *The Courtier,* later ambassador at Rome for the Marquis of Mantua, and, finally, in his last years, diplomatic representative of Pope Clement VII at the court of Charles V in Spain. *The Courtier,* written between 1508 and 1516, was published at Venice in 1528. It was first translated into English in 1561 by Sir Thomas Hoby, whose famous translation is the text used in the present volume.

In describing the soldier, courtier, scholar, the versatile and graceful Renaissance man, Castiglione created a pattern for Elizabethan courtiers like Sir Philip Sidney and Sir Walter Ralegh, influenced English courtesy books like Ascham's *The Scholemaster,* helped shape the courtly ideals of Spenser's *Faerie Queene,* gave Elizabethan England the concept of the non-professional literary man writing for a court circle rather than for publication, and influenced prose fiction like Lyly's *Euphues* in the witty and sophisticated treatment of problems of morality, etiquette, education, and love.

Sometimes *The Courtier* is regarded as primarily a manual of courtesy and etiquette, but this view ignores its more serious purposes. Manners and courtesy are not stressed at the expense of more substantial attributes of the ideal courtier: skill in warfare, wisdom and integrity in advising his prince, excellence and versatility in learning and the arts, and refinement and idealism in love.

"I judge the principall and true profession of a Courtier

ought to be in feates of arms," says Count Lewis of Canossa, stating one of the viewpoints of *The Courtier* with which Machiavelli would have agreed. To develop grace, stamina, and the skills valuable in war, the courtier must learn how to handle weapons and how to ride well, and must engage in sports such as hunting, swimming, wrestling, leaping, running, and casting the stone. He must be imbued in war, as in everything else, with chivalry and modesty: "How much more doe we take pleasure in a Gentleman that is man at armes, and how much more worthy praise is he if he bee modest, of few words, and no bragger."

In Castiglione's view, the principal obligation of the courtier besides his duties in war is to serve as the wise counselor of his prince. Castiglione sees him not as a self-seeker or flatterer, but as a man of integrity furthering the prince's and the state's interests by honest and forthright counsel. When one of the speakers raises the question "whether a gentleman be bound or no, while he is in his prince's service, to obey him in all things which he shall command, though they were dishonest and shameful matters," Sir Frederick Fregoso delivers what we may be sure is Castiglione's answer: "In dishonest matters we are not bound to obey any bodie." Castiglione's very serious interest in good government, and the relative unimportance that he attached to the polite personal accomplishments of the courtier may be judged from the following passage: "You may see that ignorance in musicke, in dancing, in riding, hurteth no man. . . . But of the unskilfulnesse to governe people arise so many evils, deaths, destructions, mischiefes, and confusions, that it may be called the deadlyest plague upon the earth."

The courtier's learning and his attainments in the arts are those of neither the modern specialist nor the modern dilettante, but of the Renaissance gentleman, our conception of whom springs in large measure from Castiglione's book. The courtier, Castiglione felt, must be well read, for letters are "beside goodnesse the true and principall ornament of the minde in every man." To the humanist Castiglione, letters mean particularly the Greek and Roman classics, the orators and the historians as well as the poets; but he expects the courtier to know the best Italian writers, too—Dante, Petrarch, and Boccaccio. The courtier must be skilled, also, in speaking and writing. In his speech he must avoid affectation and singularity. He must write both verse and prose well, taking Petrarch and Boccaccio as models. He must not overvalue his writing and must not, unless he can attain perfection in it, allow anyone except trusted friends to see it—an injunction against publication that was taken very seriously by Elizabethan court poets. Other arts in which Castiglione recommends that the courtier be proficient are music, dancing, drawing, and painting.

Throughout the book Castiglione stresses the desirability of decorum, modesty, and courtesy. Even in sports the courtier must observe decorum, avoiding those unbecoming to a gentleman—for example, tumbling, rope-climbing, or wrestling with men of inferior station. Decorum in dress also is emphasized: the courtier's dress must never be extreme, must be black or dark-colored for ordinary occasions, "rather somewhat grave and auncient than garish." In jesting he must "have respect to the time, to the persons, to his degree." He must choose his friends with care, because others will judge him by them. He must be clean and neat. He must not be a glutton or a drunkard, must never be riotous, boisterous, or rude, must not be stubborn, ill-tempered, or contentious. Always he must be modest, even deprecatory, concerning his own talents and achievements.

As part of the counsel of perfection for the courtier, good birth is recommended, although Castiglione's spokesmen in the dialogues admit that this is desirable rather than imperative. Even the courtier's physical appearance is prescribed: "a comely shape of person and countenance." With this must be manliness and forcefulness. Wit is highly valued, too, and many pages of *The Courtier* are devoted to examples of the kinds of jests and witicisms with which the courtier may properly entertain his hearers.

As a lover, Castiglione's courtier is urged, in Bembo's famous speech in the Fourth Book, to rise from physical love to neo-Platonic love, "this so happie a love, which bringeth with it neither slaunder, nor any inconveniencie." Sensual love, instead of being denied or utterly condemned, is seen as the lowest step of the stairway of love—as a natural seeking for beauty, which all love is, but as a limited seeking for it on the physical plane only. In the youthful courtier sensual love is understandable, but the older courtier, controlled more by reason than by the senses, should mount the stirway of love toward the ideal: "And thus shall he beholde no more the particular beautie of one woman, but an universall, that decketh out all bodies." Bembo's discussion of love, attempting to reconcile idealism and worldliness, morality and courtly manners, was deservedly one of the most popular and influential statements of neo-Platonism in the Renaissance.

Castiglione's book gives some attention to the characterization of the ideal court lady. As manliness is one of the first requisites of the courtier, womanly sweetness is required of the court lady. Virtues of the mind are as necessary for her as for him, a requirement certainly fulfilled by the intelligent and witty ladies of the court of Urbino. The court lady must "have a sight in letters, in musicke, in drawing, or painting." She must be skillful in dancing and in graceful and suitable sports. She must have good birth, grace, wit, good manners. She must be more circumspect morally than the male, for breach of chastity may be condoned in the courtier, but not in her. She must not praise herself, must avoid showiness, and must dress in a seemly and dignified way. In short, like the courtier, she must be compounded of virtue, grace, learning, and versatility.

Castiglione gives also a brief characterization of the ideal prince, prefaced by some cynical comments by Lord Octavian Fregoso concerning the shortcomings of most real princes. These comments, like the earlier remark of Sir Frederick Fregoso concerning the number of "Asseheades" among real courtiers, are a useful reminder that, although Castiglione concerned himself with the ideal, he was not blind to the real. "But in case a grave Philosopher," says the Lord Octavian, "shoulde come before any of our Princes, or who ever beside, that would shew them plainly and without anie circumstances the horrible face of true vertue, and teach them good manners, and what the life of a good Prince ought to be, I am assured they would abhorre him at the first sight, as a most venemous serpent, or els they woulde make him a laughing stocke, as a most vile matter." Even Hythloday in *Utopia* said nothing more bitter about the faults of most princes. Castiglione's ideal prince values virtue and good manners, considers it "not a matter lawful to be alwaies in war," strives for peace and justice, is devout in his religion, and loves his people. He is in most ways the direct opposite of Machiavelli's prince.

Part of the success of *The Courtier* as a piece of literature comes from Castiglione's characterizations of the speakers in his dialogues and from his making their conversations illustrate the very urbanity and wit that is being praised. Not all of the characters, it is true, emerge as clearly as Lady Emilia Pia and Lord Caspar Pallavicin, who are almost as vivid as the Beatrice and Benedick to whom they are often compared; but Castiglione manages to give considerable individuality to most of the other characters, especially to the gracious Lady Elizabeth Gonzaga. That so long and essentially artificial a dialogue as *The Courtier* should be a readable book is a tribute to

Castiglione's wit and to his characterizations, as well as to the interest of his ideas.

More and Castiglione were Christian humanists, as *Utopia* and *The Courtier* show; Machiavelli, as *The Prince* shows, belonged to what Hiram Haydn has called the Counter-Renaissance. In other words, More and Castiglione saw classical moral philosophy and Christian ethics as guides to life; Machiavelli rebelled against the practicability of moralism and Christianity. More and Castiglione were idealistic and speculative; Castiglione was naturalistic, pragmatic, and empirical. More and Castiglione believed in the perfectibility of man; Machiavelli, to all practical purposes, believed in man's depravity. With all of their differences and incompatibilities in religion and ethics, the three writers were alike in their free inquiry into truth and their departure from narrow authoritarianism, attitudes of mind which led them to arrive at various concepts new to the world and of continuing interest to it.

B. A. M.

CONTENTS

CONTENTS

THE PRINCE

written by

Niccolò Machiavelli

Secretary and Citizen of Florence

1640

Ed. Dacres

Niccolò Machiavelli

TO THE MAGNIFICENT LAURENCE,

SONNE TO PETER OF MEDICIS,

HEALTH.

THEY, that desire to ingratiate themselves with a Prince, commonly use to offer themselves to his view, with things of that nature, as such persons take most pleasure and delight in: whereupon wee see they are many times presented with Horses and Armes, cloth of gold, pretious stones, and such like ornaments, worthy of their greatnesse. Having then a mind to offer my selfe to your Magnificence, with some testimony of my service to you, I found nothing in my whole Inventory, that I thinke better of, or more esteeme, than the knowledge of great mens actions, which I have learnd by a long experience of moderne affaires, and a continuall reading of those of the Ancients. Which, now that I have with great diligence long workt it out, and thoroughly sifted, I commend to your Magnificence.

And however I may well think this work unworthy of your view; yet such is your humanity, that I doubt not but it shall find acceptance, considering, that for my part I am not able to tender a greater gift, than to present you with the meanes, whereby in a very short time you may be able to understand all that, which I, in the space of many yeares, and with many sufferances and dangers, have made proofe and gaind the knowledge of.

3

And this worke I have not set forth either with elegancy of discourse or stile, nor with any other ornament whereby to captivate the reader, as others use, because I would not have it gaine its esteeme from elsewhere, than from the truth of the matter, and the gravity of the subject. Nor can this be thought presumption; if a man of humble and low condition venture to dilate and discourse upon the governments of Princes; for even as they that with their pensills designe out countreys, get themselves into the plaines below to consider the nature of the mountaines, and other high places above; and againe to consider the plaines below, they get up to the tops of the mountaines; in like manner to understand the nature of the people, it is fit to be a Prince; and to know well the dispositions of Princes, sutes best with the understanding of a subject.

Your Magnificence then may be pleasd, to receive this small present, with the same mind that I send it; which if you shall throughly peruse and consider, you shall perceive therein that I exceedingly wish, that you may attaine to that greatnesse, which your own Fortune, and your excellent endowments promise you: and if your Magnificence from the very point of your Highnesse shall sometime cast your eyes upon these inferiour places, you shall see how undeservedly I undergoe an extreame and continuall despight of Fortune.

CHAPTER I

How Many Sorts of Principalities There Are, and How Many Wayes They Are Attained To

All States, all Dominions that have had, or now have rule over men, have been, and are, either Republiques, or Principalities. Principalities are either hereditary, whereof they of the bloud of the Lord thereof have long time been Princes; or else they are new; and those that are new, are either all new, as was the Dutchy of Millan to Francis Sforce; or are as members adjoyned to the hereditary State of the Prince that gaines it; as the kingdome of Naples is to the King of Spain. These Dominions so gotten, are accustomed either to live under a Prince, or to enjoy their liberty; and are made conquest of, either with others forces, or ones owne, either by fortune, or by valour.

CHAPTER II

Of Hereditary Principalities

I will not here discourse of Republiques, because I have otherwhere treated of them at large [1]: I will apply my selfe only to a Principality, and proceed, while I weave this web, by arguing thereupon, how these Principalities can be governed and maintained.

I say then that in States of inheritance, and accustomed to the bloud of their Princes, there are far fewer difficulties to keep them, than in the new: for it suffices only not to transgresse the course his Ancestors took, and so afterwards to temporize with those accidents that can happen; that if such a Prince be but of ordinary industry, he shall alwayes be able to maintain himselfe in his State, unlesse by some extraordinary or excessive power he be deprived thereof; and when he hath lost it, upon the least sinister chance that befals the usurper, he recovers it again.

We have in Italy the Duke of Ferrara for example hereof, who was of ability to resist the Venetians, in the yeer 84, and to withstand Pope Julius in the tenth for no other reason, than because he had of old continued in that rule; for the naturall Prince hath fewer occasions, and lesse heed to give offence, whereupon of necessity he must be more beloved; and unlesse it be that some extravagant vices of his bring him into hatred, it is agreeable to reason, that naturally he should be well beloved by his own subjects: and in the antiquity and continuation of the Dominion, the remembrances and occasions of innovations are quite extinguished: for evermore one change leaves a kinde of breach or dent, to fasten the building of another.

CHAPTER III

Of Mixt Principalities

But the difficulties consist in the new Principality; and first, if it be not all new, but as a member, so that it may be termed altogether as mixt; and the variations thereof proceed in the first place, from a naturall difficulty, which we commonly finde in all new Principalities; for men do willingly change their Lord, beleeving to better their condition; and this beliefe causes them to take armes against him that rules over them, whereby they deceive themselves; because they finde after by experience, they have made it worse: which depends upon another naturall and ordinary necessity, forcing him alwayes to offend those, whose Prince he newly becomes, as well by his souldiers he is put to entertain upon them, as by many other injuries, which a new conquest draws along with it; in such manner as thou findest all those thine enemies, whom thou hast endammaged in the seizing of that Principality, and afterwards canst not keep them thy friends that have seated thee in it, for not being able to satisfie them according to their expectations, nor put in practise strong remedies against them, being obliged to them. For however one bee very well provided with strong armies, yet hath he alwayes need of the favour of the inhabitants in the countrey, to enter thereinto.

For these reasons, Lewis the twelfth, King of France, suddenly tooke Milan, and as soone lost it; and the first time Lodwick his owne forces served well enough to wrest it out of his hands; for those people that had opened him the gates, finding themselves deceived of their opinion, and of that future good which they had promised themselves, could not endure the distastes the new Prince gave them.

True it is, that countreyes that have rebelled again the second time, being recovered, are harder lost; for their Lord taking occasion from their rebellion, is lesse respective of persons, but cares only to secure himselfe, by punishing delinquents, to clear all suspicions, and to provide for himselfe where he thinks he is weakest: so that if to make France lose Millan the first time, it was enough for Duke Lodwick to make some small stir only upon the confines; yet afterwards, before they could make him lose it the second time, they had neede of the whole world together against him, and that al his armies should be wasted and driven out of Italy; which proceeded from the forenamed causes: however though, both the first and second time it was taken from him.

The generall causes of the first we have treated of; it remaines now that we see those of the second, and set down the remedies that he had, or any one else can have, that should chance to be in those tearmes he was, whereby he might be able to maintaine himselfe better in his conquest, than the King of France did.

I say therefore, that these States which by conquest are annexed to the ancient states of their Conquerour, are either of the same Province, and the same language, or otherwise; and when they are, it is very easie to hold them, especially when they are not used to live free: and to enjoy them securely, it is enough to have extinguished the Princes line who ruled over them: for in other matters, allowing them their ancient conditions, and there being not much difference of manners betwixt them, men ordinarily live quiet enough; as we have seene that Burgundy did, Britany, Gascony, and Normandy, which so long time continued with France: for however there be some difference of language betweene them, yet can they easily comport one with another; and whosoever makes the conquest of them, meaning to hold them, must have two regards; the first, that the race of their former Prince be quite extinguished; the other, that he change nothing, neither in their lawes nor taxes, so that in a very short time they become one entire body with their ancient Principality.

But when any States are gaind in a Province disagreeing in language, manners, and orders, here are the difficulties, and here is there need of good fortune, and great industry to maintain them; and it would be one of the best and liveliest remedies, for the Conquerour to goe in person and dwell there; this would make the possession hereof more secure and durable; as the Turke hath done in Greece, who among al the other courses taken by him for to hold that State, had he not gone thither himselfe in person to dwell, it had never beene possible for him to have kept it: for abiding there, he sees the disorders growing in their beginnings, and forthwith can remedy them; whereas, being not there present, they are heard of when they are growne to some height, and then is there no help for them. Moreover, the Province is not pillaged by the officers thou sendest thither: the subjects are much satisfied, of having recourse to the Prince neere at hand, whereupon have they more reason to love him, if they meane to be good; and intending to doe otherwise, to feare him: and forrein Princes will be well aware how they invade that State; insomuch, that making his abode there, he can very hardly lose it.

Another remedy, which is also a better, is to send Colonies into one or two places, which may be as it were the keyes of that State; for it is necessary either to doe this, or to maintaine there many horse and foot. In these colonies the Prince makes no great expence, and either without his charge, or at a very small rate, he may both send and maintaine them; & gives offence only to them from whom he takes their fields and houses, to bestow them on those new inhabitants, who are but a very small part of that State; and those that he offends, remaining dispersed and poore, can never hurt him: and all the rest on one part, have no offence given them, and therefore a small matter keeps them in quiet: on the other side, they are wary not to erre, for feare it befals not them, as it did those that were dispoyld. I conclude then, that those colonies that are not chargeable, are the more trusty, give the lesse offence; and they that are offended, being but poor and scattered, can do but little harme, as I have said; for it is to be noted, that men must either be dallied and flatterd withall, or else be quite crusht; for they revenge themselves of small dammages; but of great ones they are not able; so that when wrong is done to any man, it ought so to be done, that it need feare no returne of revenge againe. But in lieu of colonies, by maintaining souldiers there, the expence is great; for the whole revenues of that State are to be spent in the keeping of it; so the conquest proves but a losse to him that hath got it, and endammages him rather; for it hurts that whole State, to remove the army from place to place, of which annoyance, every one hath a feeling, and so becomes enemie to thee; as they are enemies, I wis, who are outraged by thee in their own houses, whensoever they are able to do thee mischief. Every way then is this guard unprofitable, as that of the colonies is profitable.

Besides, he that is in a different Province, (as it is said) should make himself Head and defender of his lesse powerfull neighbours, and devise all wayes to weaken those that are more mighty therein, and take care, that upon no chance there enter not any forreiner as mighty as himselfe; for it will alwayes come to passe, that they shall be brought in by those, that are discontented, either upon ambition, or feare; as the Etolians brought the Romans into Greece; and they were brought into every countrey they came, by the Natives; and the course of that matter is, that so soone as a powerfull Stranger enters a countrey, all those that are the lesse powerfull there, cleave to him, provoked by an envie they beare him that is more mighty than they: so that, for these of the weaker sort, he may easily gaine them without any paines: for presently all of them together very willingly make one lump with that hee hath gotten: Hee hath only to beware that these increase not their strengths, nor their authorities, and so he shall easily be able by his own forces, and their assistances, to take down those that are mighty, and remain himselfe absolute arbitre of that countrey. And he that playes not well this part, shall quickly lose what hee hath gotten; and while hee holds it, shall find therein a great many troubles and vexations.

The Romans in the Provinces they seiz'd on, observed well these points, sent colonies thither, entertained the weaker sort, without augmenting any thing their power, abated the forces of those that were mighty, and permitted not any powerfull forreiner to gaine too much reputation there. And I will content my self only with the countrey of Greece for example hereof. The Achayans and Etolians were entertained by them, the Macedons kingdome was brought low, Antiochus was driven thence, nor ever did the Achayans or Etolians deserts prevaile so farre for them, that they would ever promise to enlarge their State, nor the perswasions of Philip induce them ever to bee his friends, without bringing him lower: nor yet could Antiochus his power make them ever consent that hee should hold any state in that country: for the Romans did in these cases that, which all judicious Princes ought to doe, who are not only to have regard unto all present mischiefes, but also to the future, and to provide for those with all industry; for by taking order for those when they are afarre off, it is easie to prevent them; but by delaying till they come neare hand to thee, the remedy comes too late: for this malignity is grown incurable, and it befals this, as the physicians say of the Hectique feaver, that in the beginning it is easily cur'd, but hardly known: but in the course of time, not having been known in the beginning, nor cured, it becomes easie to know, but hard to cure.

Even so falls it out in matters of State; for by knowing it aloofe off (which is given only to a wise man to doe) the mischiefs that then spring up, are quickly helped; but when, for not having been perceived, they are sufferd to increase, so that every one sees them; there is then no cure for them: therefore the Romans, seeing these inconvenients afarre off, alwayes prevented them, and never sufferd them to follow, for to escape a warre; because they knew that a warre is not undertaken, but deferrd for anothers advantage; therfore would they rather make warre with Philip, and Antiochus in Greece, to the end it should not afterwards be made with them in Italy, though for that time they were able to avoyd both the one and the other, which they thought not good to doe: nor did they approve of that saying that is ordinarily in the mouths of the Sages of our dayes, *to enjoy the benefits of the present time;* but that rather, to take the benefit of their valour and wisdome; for time drives forward every thing, and may bring with it as well good as evill, and evill as good.

But let us return to France, and examine if any of the things prescribed have been done by them: and we will speak of Lewis, and not of Charles, as of whom by reason of the long possession he held in Italy wee better knew the wayes hee went: and you shall see hee did the clean contrary to what should have been done by him that would maintain a State of different Language and conditions.

King Lewis was brought into Italy by the Venetians ambition, who would have gotten for their shares half the State of Lombardy: I will not blame his comming, or the course hee took, because hee had a mind to begin to set a foot in Italy; but having not any friends in the country, all gates being barrd against him, by reason of King Charles his carriage there; he was constrain to joyne friendship with those hee could; and this consideration well taken, would have proved lucky to him, when in the rest of his courses he had not committed any errour. The King then having conquerd Lombardy, recoverd presently all that reputation, that Charles had lost him; Genua yeelded to him, the Florentines became friends with him; the Marquesse of Mantua the Duke of Ferrara, the Bentivolii, the Lady of Furli, the Lord of Faenza, Pesaro, Rimino, Camerino, and Piombino, the Luccheses, Pisans, and Sieneses, every one came and offered him friendship: then might the Venetians consider the rashnesse of the course they had taken, who, only to get into their hands two Townes in Lombardy, made the King Lord of two thirds in Italy.

Let any man now consider with how small difficulty could the King have maintained his reputation in Italy, if he had followed these afornamd rules, and secured & defended those his friends; who because their number was great, and they weak and fearefull, some of the Church, and others of the Venetians, were alwayes forced to hold with him, and by their meanes he might easily have been able to secure himself against those that were mightiest: but hee was no sooner got into Milan, than hee took a quite wrong course, by giving ayd to Pope Alexander, to seize upon Romania,[2] and perceivd not that by this resolution he weakned himself, ruining his own friends, and those that had cast themselves into his bosome, making the Church puissant, by adding to their Spirituall power, whereby they gaind their authority, and so much temporall estate.

And having once got out of the way, hee was constrained to goe on forward; insomuch as to stop Alexanders ambition, and that he should not become Lord of all Tuscany, of force he was to come into Italy: and this sufficed him not, to have made the Church mighty, and taken away his own friends; but for the desire hee had to get the kingdome of Naples, he divided it with the King of Spain:[3] and where before he was the sole arbitre of Italy; he brought in a competitour, to the end that all the ambitious persons of that country, and all that were ill-affected to him, might have otherwhere to make their recourse: and whereas he might have left in that Kingdome some Vice-King of his owne, hee took him from thence, to place another there, that might afterward chace him thence.

It is a thing indeed very naturall and ordinary, to desire to be of the getting hand: and alwayes when men undertake it, if they can effect it, they shall bee prais'd for't, or at least not blam'd: but when they are not able, and yet will undertake it, here lies the blame, here is the errour committed. If France then was able with her own power to assaile the Kingdome of Naples: she might well have done it; but not being able, she should not have divided it: and if the division she made of Lombardy with the Venetians, deserv'd some excuse, thereby to set one foot

13

in Italy; yet this merits blame, for not being excus'd by that necessity.

Lewis then committed these five faults; extinguish't the feebler ones, augmented the State of another that was already powerfull in Italy, brought thereinto a very puissant forreiner, came not thither himself to dwell there, nor planted any colonies there: which faults while he liv'd, he could not but be the worse for; yet all could not have gone so ill, had he not committed the sixt, to take from the Venetians their State; for if he had not enlarg'd the Churches territories, nor brought the Spaniard into Italy, it had been necessary to take them lower; but having first taken those other courses, he should never have given way to their destruction; for while they had been strong, they would alwayes have kept the others off from venturing on the conquest of Lombardy. For the Venetians would never have given their consents thereto, unlesse they should have been made Lords of it themselves; and the others would never have taken it from France, to give it them; & then they would never have dar'd to goe and set upon them both together.

And if any one should say, that King Lewis yeelded Romania to Alexander, and the Kingdome of Naples to Spain, to avoyd a warre; I answer with the reasons above alleaged, that one should never suffer any disorder to follow, for avoyding of a warre; for that warre is not sav'd, but put off to thy disadvantage. And if any others argue, that the King had given his word to the Pope, to doe that exploit for him, for dissolving of his marriage, and for giving the Cardinalls Cap to him of Roan; I answer with that, which hereafter I shall say, touching Princes words, how they ought to bee kept.

King Lewis then lost Lombardy, for not having observed some of those termes, which others us'd, who have possessed themselves of countries, and desir'd to keep them. Nor is this any strange thing, but very ordinary and reasonable: and to this purpose I spake at Nantes with that French Cardinall, when Valentine (for so ordinarily was Cæsar Borgia Pope Alexanders sonne call'd) made himself master of Romania; for when the Cardinall said to mee, that the Italians understood not the feates of warre, I answered, the Frenchmen understood not matter of State: for had they bin wel vers'd therein, they would never have suffer'd the Church to have grown to that greatnesse. And by experience wee have seen it, that the power hereof in Italy, and that of Spain also, was caused by France, and their own ruine proceeded from themselves.

From whence a generall rule may bee taken, which never, or very seldome fails: *That hee that gives the meanes to another to become powerfull, ruines himselfe;* for that power is caus'd by him either with his industry, or with his force; and as well the one as the other of these two is suspected, by him that is grown puissant.

CHAPTER IV

Wherefore Darius His Kingdome Taken by Alexander, Rebell'd Not Against Alexanders Successours After His Death

The difficulties being consider'd, which a man hath in the maintaining of a State new gotten, some might marvaile how it came to passe, that Alexander the Great subdued all Asia in a few yeeres; and having hardly possessed himselfe of it, died; whereupon it seem'd probable that all that State should have rebell'd; nevertheless his Successours kept the possession of it, nor found they other difficulty in holding it, than what arose among themselves through their own ambition.

15

I answer, that all the Principalities, whereof wee have memory left us, have been governed in two severall manners; either by a Prince, and all the rest Vassalls, who as ministers by his favour and allowance, doe help to govern that Kingdom; or by a Prince and by Barons, who not by their Princes favour, but by the antiquity of blood hold that degree. And these kinds of Barons have both states of their own, and Vassalls who acknowledge them for their Lords; and beare them a true naturall affection. Those States that are govern'd by a Prince and by Vassalls, have their Prince ruling over them with more authority: for in all his country, there is none acknowledg'd for superiour, but himselfe: and if they yeeld obedience to any one else, it is but as to his minister and officer, nor beare they him any particular good will.

The examples of these two different Governments now in our dayes, are, the Turk, and the King of France. The Turks whole Monarchy is govern'd by one Lord, and the rest are all his Vassalls; and deviding his whole Kingdom into divers Sangiacques or Governments, he sends severall thither: and those hee chops and changes, as hee pleases. But the King of France is seated in the midst of a multitude of Lords, who of old have been acknowledg'd for such by their subjects, and being belov'd by them, injoy their preheminencies; nor can the King take their States from them without danger.

Hee then that considers the one and the other of these two States, shall find difficulty in the conquest of the Turks State; but when once it is subdu'd, great facility to hold it. The reasons of these difficulties in taking of the Turks Kingdom from him, are, because the Invader cannot be call'd in by the Princes of that Kingdom, nor hope by the rebellion of those which hee hath about him, to bee able to facilitate his enterprize: which proceeds from the reasons aforesaid; for they being all his slaves, and oblig'd to him, can more hardly bee corrupted; and put case they were corrupted, little profit could hee get by it, they not being able to draw after them any people, for the reasons wee have shewed: whereupon hee that assailes the Turk, must think to find him united; and must rather relie upon his own forces, than in the others disorders: but when once he is overcome and broken in the field, so that hee cannot repaire his armies, there is nothing else to bee doubted, than the Royall blood, which being once quite out, there is none else left to bee fear'd, none of the others having any credit with the people. And as the conquerour before the victory could not hope in them; so after it, ought he not to feare them.

The contrary falls out in Kingdoms govern'd as is that of France: for it is easie to be enter'd, by the gaining of any Baron in the Kingdom; for there are always some malecontents to be found, and those that are glad of innovation. Those for the reasons alleag'd are able to open thee a way into that State, and to further thy victory, which afterwards to make good to thee, draws with it exceeding many difficulties, as well with those that have ayded thee, as those thou hast supprest. Nor is it enough for thee to root out the Princes race: for there remaine still those Lords who quickly will bee the ring-leaders of new changes; and in case thou art not able to content these, nor extinguish them, thou losest that State, whensoever the occasion is offer'd.

Now if thou shalt consider what sort of government that of Darius was, thou shalt find it like to the Turks dominions, and therefore Alexander was necessitated first to defeat him utterly, and drive him out of the field; after which victory, Darius being dead, that State was left secure to Alexander, for the reasons we treated of before: and his successors had they continued in amity, might have injoy'd it at ease: nor ever arose there in that Kingdome other tumults, than those they themselves stir'd up.

But of the States that are order'd and grounded as that of France, it is impossible to become master at such ease: and from hence grew the frequent rebellions of Spain,

France, and Greece against the Romans, by reason of the many Principalities those States had: whereof while the memory lasted, the Romans were alwayes doubtfull of the possession of them; but the memory of them being quite wip't out, by the power and continuance of the Empire, at length they injoy'd it securely; and they also were able afterwards fighting one with another, each one of them to draw after them the greater part of those provinces, according as their authority had gain'd them credit therein: and that because the blood of their ancient Lord was quite spent, they acknowledg'd no other but the Romans.

By the consideration then of these things, no man will marvaile that Alexander had so little trouble to keep together the State of Asia; and that others have had such great difficulties to maintain their conquest, as Pyrrhus, and many others; which proceeds not from the small or great valour of the conquerour, but from the difference of the subject.

CHAPTER V

In What Manner Cities and Principalities Are to be Govern'd, Which, Before They Were Conquer'd, Liv'd Under Their Own Laws

When those States, that are conquered, as it is said, have been accustomed to live under their own Laws, and in liberty, there are three wayes for a man to hold them. The first is to demolish all their strong places; the other, personally to goe and dwell there; the third, to suffer them to live under their own Laws, drawing from them some tribute, and creating therein an Oligarchy, that may continue it in thy service: for that State being created

18

by that Prince, knowes it cannot consist, without his aid and force, who is like to doe all he can to maintain it, and with more facility is a City kept by meanes of her own Citizens, which hath been us'd before to live free, than by any other way of keeping. We have for example the Spartans, and the Romans; the Spartans held Athens and Thebes, creating there an Oligarchy: yet they lost it. The Romans to be sure of Capua, Carthage, and Numantia, dismantell'd them quite, and so lost them not: they would have kept Greece as the Spartans had held them, leaving them free, & letting them injoy their own Lawes; and it prospered not with them: so that they were forc'd to deface many Cities of that province to hold it.

For in truth there is not a surer way to keep them under, than by demolishments; and whoever becomes master of a City us'd to live free, and dismantells it not; let him look himselfe to bee ruin'd by it: for it alwayes in time of rebellion takes the name of liberty for refuge, and the ancient orders it had; which neither by length of time, nor for any favours afforded them, are ever forgotten; and for any thing that can bee done, or order'd, unlesse the inhabitants be disunited and dispers'd, that name is never forgotten, nor those customes: but presently in every chance resource is thither made: as Pisa did after so many yeeres, that she had been subdu'd by the Florentines.

But when the Cities or the Provinces are accustomed to live under a Prince, and that whole race is quite extirpated; on one part being us'd to obey; on the other, not having their old Prince; they agree not to make one from among themselves: they know not how to live in liberty; in such manner that they are much slower to take armes, and with more facility may a Prince gaine them, and secure himselfe of them. But in Republiques there is more life in them, more violent hatred, more earnest desire of revenge; nor does the remembrance of the ancient liberty ever leave them, or suffer them to rest: so that the safest way, is, either to ruine them, or dwell among them.

CHAPTER VI

Of New Principalities, That Are Conquer'd by Ones Own Armes, and Valour

Let no man marvaile, if in the discourse I shall make of new Principalities, both touching a Prince, and touching a State, I shall alleadge very famous examples: for seeing men almost alwayes walk in the pathes beaten by others, and proceed in their actions by imitation, and being that others wayes cannot bee exactly follow'd, nor their vertues, whose patterne thou set'st before thee, attain'd unto; a wise man ought alwayes to tread the footsteps of the worthiest persons, and imitate those that have been the most excellent: to the end that if his vertue arrive not thereto, at least it may yeeld some savour thereof, and doe as good Archers use, who thinking the place they intend to hit, too farre distant, & knowing how farr the strength of their bow will carry, they lay their ayme a great deale higher than the mark; not for to hit so high with their arrow, but to bee able with the help of so high an aime to reach the place they shoot at.

I say, that in Principalities wholly new, where there is a new Prince; there is more and lesse difficulty in maintaining them, as the vertue of their Conquerour is greater or lesser. And because this successe, to become a Prince of a private man, presupposes either vertue, or fortune; mee thinks the one and the other of these two things in part should mitigate many difficulties; however he that hath lesse stood upon fortune, hath maintain'd himselfe the better. Moreover it some what facilitates the matter in that the Prince is constrain'd, because hee hath not other dominions, in person to come and dwell there.

But to come to these, who by their own vertues, and not by fortune, attain'd to be Princes; the excellentest of these are, Moyses, Cyrus, Romulus, Theseus, and such like; and though of Moyses we are not to reason, he onely executing the things that were commanded him by God; yet merits hee well to be admir'd, were it only for that grace, that made him worthy to converse with God. But considering Cyrus, and the others, who either got or founded Kingdomes, wee shall find them all admirable; and if their particular actions, and Lawes bee throughly weigh'd, they will not appeare much differing from those of Moyses, which hee receiv'd from so Soveraigne an instructer.

And examining their lives and actions, it will not appeare, that they had other help of fortune, than the occasion, which presented them with the matter wherein they might introduce what forme they then pleas'd; and without that occasion, the vertue of their mind had been extinguish'd; and without that vertue, the occasion had been offer'd in vaine. It was then necessary for Moyses to find the people of Israel slaves in Ægypt, and oppress'd by the Ægyptians: to the end that they to get out of their thraldome, should bee willing to follow him. It was fit that Romulus should not bee kept in Albia, but expos'd presently after his birth that hee might become King of Rome, and founder of that City. There was need that Cyrus should find the Persians discontented with the Medes government, and the Medes delicate and effeminate through their long peace. Theseus could not make proof of his vertue, had not he found the Athenians dispers'd. These occasions therefore made these men happy, and their excellent vertue made the occasion be taken notice of, whereby their country became ennobled, and exceeding fortunate.

They, who by vertuous wayes, like unto these, become Princes, attain the Principality with difficulty, but hold it with much ease; and the difficulties they find in gayning the Principality, arise partly from the new orders and courses they are forc'd to bring in, to lay the foundation of their State, and worke their own security. And it is to be consider'd, how there is not any thing harder to take in hand, nor doubtfuller to succeed, nor more dangerous to mannage, than to be the chiefe in bringing in new orders; for this Chiefe finds all those his enimies, that thrive upon the old orders, and hath but lukewarme defenders of all those that would doe well upon the new orders, which lukewarme temper proceeds partly from feare of the opposers, who have the lawes to their advantage; partly from the incredulity of the men, who truly beleeve not a new thing, unlesse there bee some certain proofe given them thereof. Whereupon it arises, that whensoever they that are adversaries take the occasion to assayle, they doe it factiously; and these others defend but cooly, so that their whole party altogether runs a hazzard.

Therefore it is necessary, being we intend throughly to discourse this part, to examine, if these innovators stand of themselves, or if they depend upon others; that is, if to bring their worke to effect, it bee necessary they should intreat, or be able to constrain. In the first case they alwayes succeed ill, and bring nothing to passe; but when they depend of themselves, and are able to force, then seldome it is that they hazzard.

Hence came it that all the Prophets that were arm'd, prevail'd; but those that were unarm'd, were too weak: for besides what wee have alleadg'd, the nature of the people is changeable, and easie to bee perswaded to a matter; but it is hard also to settle them in that perswasion. And therefore it behooves a man to be so provided, that when they beleeve no longer, hee may be able to compell them thereto by force. Moyses, Cyrus, Theseus, and Romulus would never have been able to cause their Lawes long to be obey'd, had they been disarm'd; as in our times it befell Fryer Jerome Savonarola, who perish'd in his new constitutions, when the multitude began not to beleeve him;

neither had hee the meanes to keep them firme, that had beleev'd; nor to force beleefe in them that had not beleev'd him. Wherefore such men as these, in their proceedings find great difficulty, and all their dangers are in the way, and these they must surmount by their vertue: but having once masterd them, and beginning to bee honourd by all, when they have rooted those out that envy'd their dignities, they remain powerfull, secure, honourable, and happy. To these choice Examples, I will adde one of lesse remarque; but it shall hold some proportion with them and this shall suffice me for all others of this kind, which is Hiero the Siracusan. He of a private man, became Prince of Siracusa,[4] nor knew hee any other ayd of fortune, than the occasion: for the Siracusans being oppress'd, made choyce of him for their Captaine, whereupon hee deserv'd to be made their Prince: and he was of such vertue even in his private fortune, that hee who writes of him, sayes, he wanted nothing of reigning, but a Kingdome. This man extinguish'd all the old souldiery, ordein'd the new; left the old allyances, entertain'd new; and as he had friendship, and souldiers that were his own, upon that ground he was able to build any edifice; so that hee indur'd much trouble in gaining, and suffered but little in maintaining.

CHAPTER VII

Of New Principalities, Gotten by Fortune, and Other Mens Forces

They, who by fortune only become Princes of private men, with small paines attain to it; but have much adoe to maintain themselves in it, and find no difficulty at all in the way, because they are carried thither with wings: but all the difficulties arise there, after they are plac'd in them. And of such sort are those, who have an estate given them for money, by the favour of some one that grants it them: as it befell many in Greece, in the cities of Jonia, and Hellespont; where divers Princes were made by Darius, as well for his own safety, as his glory; as also them that were made Emperours; who from private men by corrupting the souldiers, attaind to the Empire.

These subsist meerly upon the will, and fortune of those that have advanc'd them; which are two voluble and unsteady things; and they neither know how, nor are able to continue in that dignity: they know not how, because unlesse it be a man of great understanding and vertue, it is not probable, that hee who hath alwayes liv'd a private life, can know how to command: neyther are they able, because they have not any forces that can be freindly or faythfull to them.

Moreover those States that suddenly fall into a mans hands, as all other things in nature that spring and grow quickly, cannot well have taken roote, nor have made their correspondencyes so firme, but that the first storme that takes them, ruines them; in case these, who (as it is sayd) are thus on a suddain clamberd up to be Princes, are not of that worth and vertue as to know how to prepare themselves to maintain that, which Chance hath cast into their bosomes, and can afterwards lay those foundations, which others have cast before they were Princes.

For the one and the other of these wayes about the attaining to be a Prince, by Vertue, or by Fortune, I will alleage you two examples which have been in the days of our memory. These were Francis Sforza and Cæsar Borgia; Francis by just meanes and with a great deal of vertue, of a private man got to be Duke of Millan; and that which with much payns he had gaind, he kept with small adoe.

On the other side Cæsar Borgia (commonly termd Duke

Valentine) gott his state by his Fathers fortune, and with the same lost it; however that for his owne part no paynes was spard, nor any thing omitted, which by a discreet and valorous man ought to have been done, to fasten his roots in those Estates, which others armes or fortune had bestowed on him; for (as it was formerly sayd) he that lays not the foundations first, yet might be able by means of his extraordinary vertues to lay them afterwards, however it be with the great trouble of the architect, and danger of the ædifice.

If therfore we consider all the Dukes progresses, we may perceive how great foundations he had cast for his future power, which I judge a matter not superfluous to runne over; because I should not well know, what better rules I might give to a new Prince, than the patterne of his actions; and however the courses he took, availd him not, yet was it not his fault, but it proceeded from an extraordinary and extreame malignity of fortune.

Pope Alexander the sixt, desiring to make the Duke his sonne a great man, had a great many difficulties, present and future: First hee saw no way there was whereby hee might be able to make him Lord of any State, that was not the Churches; and if hee turnd to take that from the Church, hee knew that the Duke of Milan, and the Venetians would never agree to it; for Faenza and Riminum were under the Venetians protection. Moreover, hee saw that the armes of Italy, and those whereof in particular hee might have been able to make some use, were in their hands, who ought to feare the Popes greatnesse: and therefore could not any wayes rely upon them: being all in the Orsins and Colonnies hands, and those of their faction. It was necessary then, that those matters thus appointed by them, should bee disturb'd, and the States of Italy disorder'd, to bee able safely to master part of them, which he then found easie to doe, seeing the Venetians upon three considerations had us'd the meanes to bring the French men back again into Italy: which hee not only did not withstand, but further'd, with a resolution of King Lewis his ancient marriage. The King then past into Italy with the Venetians ayd, and Alexanders consent; nor was hee sooner arriv'd in Milan, than the Pope had souldiers from him for the service of Romania, which was quickly yeelded up to him upon the reputation of the Kings forces.

The Duke then having made himselfe master of Romania, and beaten the Colonnies; desiring to hold it, and proceed forward, two things hinder'd him: the one, his owne souldiers, which hee thought were not true to him; the other, the French mens good wills; that is to say, hee fear'd that the Princes souldiers, whereof he had serv'd himselfe, would faile him, and not only hinder his conquest, but take from him what hee had gotten; and that the King also would serve him the same turne. Hee had experience of the Orsini upon an occasion, when after the taking of Faenza, hee assaulted Bolonia, to which assault he saw them goe very cold. And touching the King, he discoverd his mind, when having taken the Dutchy of Urbin, he invaded Tuscany; from which action the King made him retire; whereupon the Duke resolv'd to depend no more upon fortune, and other mens armes.

And the first thing hee did, was, to weaken the Orsini and Colonnies factions in Rome: for hee gain'd all their adherents that were gentlemen, giving them large allowances, and honouring them according to their qualities with charges and governments: so that in a few months the good will they bare to the parties was quite extinguisht, and wholly bent to the Duke.

After this, hee waited an occasion to root out the Orsini, having before dispersd those of the family of Colonna, which fell out well to his hand; and he us'd it better. For the Orsini being too late aware, that the Dukes and the Churches greatnesse was their destruction; held a Counsell together in a dwelling house of theirs in the country adjoyning to Perusia. From thence grew the

rebellion of Urbin, and the troubles of Romania, and many
other dangers befell the Duke, which he overcame all
with the help of the French: and having regaind his
reputation, trusting neither France, nor any forreine
forces, to the end hee might not bee put to make triall of
them again, he betook himselfe to his sleights; and he
knew so well to disguise his intentions, that the Orsins,
by the mediation of Paul Orsini, were reconciled to him,
to whom the Duke was no way wanting in all manner
of courtesies whereby to bring them into security, giving
them rich garments, mony, and horses, till their owne
simplicities led them all to Sinigallia, into his hands. These
heads being then pluck'd off, and their partisans made his
friends, the Duke had laid very good foundations, to
build his owne greatnesse on, having in his power all Romania with the Dutchy of Urbin, and gaind the hearts
of those people, by beginning to give them some rellish
of their well being.

And because this part is worthy to bee taken notice
of, and to be imitated by others, I will not let it scape.
The Duke, when he had taken Romania, finding it had
been under the hands of poor Lords, who had rather pil-
lag'd their subjects, than chastis'd or amended them,
giving them more cause of discord, than of peace and
union, so that the whole country was fraught with robberies, quarrells, and all other sorts of insolencies; thought
the best way to reduce them to termes of pacification, and
obedience to a Princely power, was, to give them some
good government: and therefore hee set over them one
Remiro D'Orco, a cruell, hasty man, to whom he gave an
absolute power. This man in a very short time setled peace
and union amongst them with very great reputation.

Afterwards the Duke thought such excessive authority
serv'd not so well to his purpose, and doubting it would
grow odious, he erected a Civill Iudicature in the midst
of the countrey, where one excellent Iudge did preside,
and thither every City sent their Advocate: and because

he knew the rigours past had bred some hatred against him, to purge the mindes of those people, and to gaine them wholly to himselfe, he purpos'd to shew, that if there was any cruelty used, it proceeded not from any order of his, but from the harsh disposition of his Officer. Whereupon laying hold on him, at this occasion, hee causd his head to bee struck off one morning early in the market place at Cesena, where hee was left upon a gibbet, with a bloodie sword by his side; the cruelty of which spectacle for a while satisfied and amaz'd those people.

But to returne from whence wee have digressd: I say, that the Duke finding himselfe very strong, and in part out of doubt of the present dangers, because hee was armd after his owne manner, and had in some good measure suppressd those forces, which, because of their vicinity, were able to annoy him, hee wanted nothing else to goe on with his Conquest, but the consideration of France: for hee knew, that the King, who now, though late, was advisd of his errour, would never suffer him: and hereupon hee began to seeke after new allyances, and to waver with France, when the French came towards Naples against the Spaniards, who then besiegd Gagetta; and his designe was onely to be out of their danger, which had been effected for him, had Pope Alexander liv'd.

And thus were his businesses carried touching his present estate. As for the future, hee had reason to doubt, least the new successor to the Papacy would not bee his friend, and would indeavour to take that from him that Alexander had bestowd on him: and hee thought to provide for this fowre wayes: first by rooting out the races of all those Lords hee had dispoyled, whereby to take those occasions from the Pope. Secondly, by gaining all the gentlemen of Rome, whereby he might be able with those to keep the Pope in some awe. Thirdly, to make the Colledge of Cardinals as much at his devotion as possibly might bee. Fourthly, by making of so large Conquests, before the Popes death, as that hee might be able of himselfe to withstand the first fury of his enemies.

Three of these fowre at Pope Alexanders death hee had effected, and the fourth hee had neare brought to a point. For of those Lords he had stripd hee put to death as many as hee could come at, and very few scap'd him: hee gaind him the Romane gentlemen: and in the Colledge hee had made a great faction. And touching his new Conquest, hee had a designe to become Lord of Tuscany. And he had possessed himselfe already of Perusia, and Piombin, and taken protection of Pisa: and so soone as hee should have cast of his respect to France (which now hee meant to hold no longer) being the French were now driven out of the Kingdome of Naples by the Spanyards, so, that each of them was forc'd to buy his friendship at any termes; he was then to leape into Pisa. After this Lucca and Siena, were presently to fall to him, partly for envy to the Florentines, and partly for feare. The Florentines had no way to escape him: all which had it succeeded with him, as without question it had, the very same yeere that Alexander dy'd, he had made himselfe master of so great forces, and such reputation, that hee would have been able to have stood upon his own bottome, without any dependance of fortune, or resting upon others helps; but only upon his own strength and valour.

But Alexander dy'd five yeeres after that hee had begun to draw forth his sword: and left him settled only in the State of Romania, with all his other designes in the ayre, sick unto death, between two very strong armies of his enemies: and yet was there in this Duke such a spirit and courage, and hee understood so well, how men are to be gaind, and how to be lost, and so firme were the grounds hee had laid in a short time, that, had he not had those armies upon his back, or had hee been in health, hee would have carried through his purpose in spight of all opposition: and that the foundations hee grounded upon, were good, it appeard in that Romania held for him above a month, and hee remaind secure in Rome, though even at deaths doore: and however the Baglioni, Vitelli, and Orsini came into Rome; yet found they none would take their parts against him. And this hee was able to have effected, that if hee could not have made him Pope whom hee would, he could have hindred him that hee would not should bee Pope.

But had hee been in health when Alexander dy'd, every thing had gone easily with him; and hee told mee on that day that Julius the second was created Pope, that hee had fore-thought on all that which could happen, in case his father chanc'd to dye, and for every thing provided its remedy: this onely excepted, that hee foresaw not that hee himselfe should at the same time be brought unto deaths dore also.

Having then collected all the Dukes actions, me thinks I could not well blame him, but rather (as I have here done) set him as a patterne to be followd by all those, who by fortune and others armes have been exalted to an Empire. For hee being of great courage, and having lofty designes, could not carry himselfe otherwise; and the only obstacle of his purposes was the brevity of Alexanders life, and his own sicknesse.

Whoever therefore deemes it necessary in his entrance into a new Principality, to secure himselfe of his enemies, and gaine him friends, to overcome either by force, or by cunning, to make himselfe be belovd, or feard of his people, be follow'd and reverenc'd by his souldiers, to root out those that can, or owe thee any hurt, to change the ancient orders with new wayes, to bee severe, and yet acceptable, magnanimous, and liberall, to extinguish the unfaithfull souldiery, and create new, to maintaine to himselfe the amities of Kings and Princes, so that they shall either with favour benefit thee, or bee wary how to offend thee; cannot find more fresh and lively examples than the actions of this man.

Hee deserves to bee found fault withall for the creation of Julius the second, wherein an evill choice was made for him: for, as it is said, not being able to make a Pope to his mind, hee could have with-held any one from being Pope; and should never have consented that any one of those Cardinals, should have got the Papacy, whom hee had ever done harme to; or who having attaind the Pontificate were likely to be afraid of him: because men ordinarily doe hurt either for feare, or hatred. Those whom hee had offended, were among others, hee who had the title of St. Peter ad Vincula, Colonna, St. George, and Ascanius; all the others that were in possibility of the Popedome, were such as might have feard him rather, except the Cardinall of Roan,[5] and the Spanyards; these by reason of their alliance and obligation with him, the other, because of the power they had, having the Kingdome of France on their party.

Wherefore the Duke above all things should have created a Spanyard Pope, and in case hee could not have done that, hee should have agreed that Roan should have been, and not St. Peter ad Vincula. And whoever beleeves, that with great personages new benefits blot out the remembrance of old injuries, is much deceiv'd. The Duke therefore in this election, was the cause of his own ruine at last.

CHAPTER VIII

Concerning Those Who by Wicked Meanes Have Attaind to a Principality

But because a man becomes a Prince of a private man two wayes, which cannot wholly be attributed eyther to Fortune or Vertue, I think not fit to let them passe me: howbeit the one of them may be more largely discoursed upon, where the Republicks are treated of. These are,

31

when by some wicked and unlawfull meanes a man rises to the Principality; or when a private person by the favour of his fellow Citizens becomes Prince of his countrey. And speaking of the first manner, it shall be made evident by two Examples, the one ancient, the other moderne, without entring otherwise into the justice or merit of this part; for I take it that these are sufficient for any body that is forc'd to follow them.

Agathocles the Sicilian, not of a private man only, but from a base and abject fortune got to be King of Siracusa. This man borne but of a Potter, continued always a wicked life throughout all the degrees of his fortune: neverthelesse he accompanied his lewdnesse with such a courage and resolution, that applying himselfe to military affaires, by the degrees thereof he attain to bee Prætour of Siracusa, and being setled in that degree, and having determind that he would become Prince, and hold that by violence and without obligation to any other, which by consent had been granted him; and to this purpose having had some private intelligence touching his designe with Amilcar [6] the Carthaginian, who was imployd with his army in Sicily, one morning gatherd the people together and the Senate of Siracusa, as if he had somewhat to advise with them of matters belonging to the Commonwealth, and upon a signe given, caus'd his souldiers to kill all his Senatours, and the richest of the people; who being slaine, he usurp'd the Principality of that City without any civill strife: and however he was twice broken by the Carthaginians, and at last besiegd, was able not only to defend his own City, but leaving part of his own army at the defence thereof, with the other invaded Affrique, and in a short time freed Siracusa from the siege, and brought the Carthaginians into extreme necessity, who were constraind to accord with him, be contented with the possession of Affrique, and quitt Sicily to Agathocles.

He then that should consider the actions and valour of this man, would not see any, or very few, things to be attributed unto Fortune; seeing that as is formerly sayd, not by any ones favour, but by the degrees of service in warre with many sufferings and dangers, to which he had risen, he came to the Principality; and that hee maintaind afterwards with so many resolute and hazardous undertakings. Yet cannot this be term'd verture or valour to slay his own Citizens, betray his friends, to be without faith, without pitty, without religion, which wayes are of force to gaine dominion, but not glory: for if Agathocles his valour bee well weighd, in his venturing upon, and comming off from dangers, and the greatnesse of his courage, in supporting and mastering of adversities, no man can see why he should be thought any way inferiour even to the ablest Captaines. Notwithstanding his beastly cruelty and inhumanity with innumerable wickednesses, allow not that he should be celebrated among the most excellent men. That cannot then be attributed to Fortune or Vertue, which without the one or th' other was attaind to by him.

In our dayes, while Alexander the sixth held the sea, Oliverotto of Fermo, who some few yeeres before had been left young by his parents, was brought up under the care of an uncle of his on the mothers side, calld John Foliani, and in the beginning of his youth given by him to serve in the warres under Paulo Vitelli: to the end that being well instructed in that discipline, hee might rise to some worthy degree in the warrs. Afterwards when Paulo was dead, hee served under Vitelozzo his brother, and in very short time, being ingenious, of a good personage, and brave courage, he became one of the prime men among the troops he served in: but thinking it but servile to depend upon another; hee plotted by the ayd of some Citizens of Fermo (who lik'd rather the thraldome of their City than the liberty of it) and by the favour of the Vitelli, to make himselfe master of Fermo; and writ to John Foliani, that having been many yeeres from home, he had a mind to come and see him and the City, and in some part take notice of his own patrimony; and because he had not imployd himselfe but to purchase honour, to the end his Citizens might perceive, that he had not vainely spent his time, he had a desire to come in good equipage and accompanied with a hundred horse of his friends and servants; and he intreated him that he would be pleasd so to take order, that he might be honourably receivd by the inhabitants of Fermo; which turnd as well to his honour that was his uncle, as his that was the nephew.

In this, John faild not in any office of courtesie due to his nephew: and caus'd him to be well receivd by them of Fermo, and lodgd him in his own house: where having passd some dayes, and stayd to put in order somewhat that was necessary for his intended villany, he made a very solemne feast, whether he invited John Foliani, and all the prime men of Fermo: and when all their cheare was ended, and all their other entertainments, as in such feasts it is customary, Oliverotto of purpose mov'd some grave discourses; speaking of the greatnesse of Pope Alexander, and Cæsar his son, and their undertakings; whereunto John and the others making answer: he of a sudden stood up, saying, that those were things to be spoken of in a more secret place, and so retir'd into a chamber, whether John and all the other Citizens followd him; nor were they sooner set down there, than from some secret place therein came forth diverse souldiers, who slew John and all the others: after which homicide Oliverotto got a horsebacke and ravagd the whole towne, and besiegd the supreme Magistrate in the palace, so that for feare they were all constraind to obey him, and to settle a government, whereof hee made himselfe Prince; and they being all dead, who, had they been discontented with him, could have hurt him; he strengthned himselfe with new civill and military orders, so that in the space of a yeere that he held the Principality, he was not only secure in the City of Fermo, but became fearefull to all his neighbours; and the conquest of him would have prov'd difficult, as that of Agathocles, had he not let himselfe been deceivd by Cæsar Borgia; when at Sinigallia, as before was said, he took the Orsini and Vitelli: where he also being taken a yeere after he had committed the parricide, was strangled together with Vitellozzo (whom he had had for master both of his vertues and vices).

Some man might doubt from whence it should proceed, that Agathocles, and such like, after many trecheryes and crueltyes, could possibly live long secure in his own countrey, and defend himselfe from his forren enemyes, and that never any of his own Citizens conspir'd against him; seeing that by means of cruelty, many others have never been able even in peaceable times to maintaine their States, much lesse in the doubtfull times of warre. I beleeve that this proceeds from the well, or ill using of those crueltyes: they may bee termd well us'd (if it bee lawfull to say well of evill) that are put in practise only once of necessity for securities sake, not insisting therein afterwards, but there is use made of them for the subjects profit, as much as may be. But those that are ill usd, are such as though they bee but few in the beginning, yet they multiply rather in time, than deminish. They that take that first way, may with the help of God, and mens care, find some remedy for their State, as Agathocles did: for the others, it is impossible they should continue.

Whereupon it is to be noted, that in the laying hold of a State, the usurper thereof ought to runne over and execute all his cruellties at once, that hee bee not forcd often to returne to them, and that hee may be able, by not renewing of them, to give men some security, and gaine their affections by doing them some courtesies. Hee that carries it otherwise, either for fearefullnesse, or upon evill advice, is alwayes constraind to hold his sword drawne in his hand; nor ever can hee rely upon his subjects, there being no possibility for them, because of his daily and continuall injuries, to live in any safety: for his injuries should bee done altogether, that being seldomer tasted, they might lesse offend: his favours should bee bestowd by little and little, to the end they might keep their taste the better; and above all things a Prince must live with his subjects in such sort, that no accident either of good or evill can make him vary: for necessity comming upon him by reason of adversities, thou hast not time given thee to make advantage of thy cruellties; and the favours which then thou bestowest, will little help thee, being taken, as if they came from thee perforce, and so yeeld no returne of thanks.

CHAPTER IX

Of the Civill Principality

But comming to the other part, when a principall Citizen, not by villany, or any other insufferable violence, but by the favour of his fellow-citizens becomes Prince of his native countrey: which we may terme a Civill Principality; not to attaine hereunto is Vertue wholly, or Fortune wholly necessary, but rather a fortunate cunning. I say, this Principality is climb'd up to, either by the peoples help, or the great mens. For, in every City we finde these two humours differ; and they spring from this, that the people desire not to be commanded nor oppressed by the great ones, and the great ones are desirous to command and oppresse the people: and from these two several appetites, arises in the City one of these three effects, either a Principality, or Liberty, or Tumultuary licientiousnesse.

The Principality is caused either by the people, or the great ones; according as the one or the other of these factions have the occasion offerd; for the great ones seeing themselves not able to resist the people, begin to turne the whole reputation to one among them, and make him Prince, whereby they may under his shadow vent their spleenes. The people also, not being able to support the great mens insolencies, converting the whole reputation to one man, create him their Prince, to be protected by his authority.

He that comes to the Principality by the assistance of the great ones, subsists with more difficulty, than he that attaines to it by the peoples favour; for he being made Prince, hath many about him, who account themselves his equalls, and therefore cannot dispose nor command them at his pleasure. But he that gaines the Principality by the peoples favor, finds himselfe alone in his throne, and hath none or very few neare him, that are not very supple to bend: besides this, the great ones cannot upon easie termes be satisfied, or without doing of wrong to others, whereas a small matter contents the people: for the end which the people propound to themselves, is more honest than that of the great men, these desiring to oppresse, they only not to be oppressed. To this may be added also, that the Prince which is the peoples enemy, can never well secure himselfe of them, because of their multitude; well may hee bee sure of the Nobles, they being but a few.

The worst that a Prince can look for of the people become his enemy, is, to be abandoned by them: but when the great ones once grow his enemyes, he is not only to feare their abandoning of him, but their making of a party against him also: for there being in them more forecast and craft, they alwayes take time by the forelocks whereby to save themselves, and seeke credit with him, who they hope shall get the mastery. The Prince likewise is necessitated alwayes to live with the same people, but can doe well enough without the same great men, he being able to create new ones, and destroy them againe every day, and to take from them, and give them credit as he pleases: and to cleare this part, I say, that great men ought to be considered two wayes principally, that is, if they take thy proceedings so much to heart, as to ingage their for-

tunes wholly in thine, in case they lye not alwayes catch-
ing at spoyle, they ought to bee well honoured and
esteem'd: those that bind themselves not to thy fortune,
are to be considered also two wayes; either they doe it
for lack of courage, and naturall want of spirit, and then
shouldst thou serve thy selfe of them, and of them especially that are men of good advice; for if thy affaires prosper, thou dost thy self honor thereby; if crost, thou needst
not feare them: but when they oblige not themselves to
thee of purpose, and upon occasion of ambition, it is a
signe they think more of themselves than of thee: and
of these the Prince ought to beware, and account of them
as his discovered enemyes: for alwayes in thy adversity
they will give a hand too to ruine thee.

Therefore ought hee that comes to be Prince by the
peoples favour, keepe them his friends: which he may
easily doe, they desiring only to live free from oppression:
but he that becomes Prince by the great mens favour,
against the will of the people, ought above all things to
gaine the people to him, which he may easily effect, when
he takes upon him their protection: And because men
when they find good, where they look for evill, are therby
more endeard to their benefactour, therefore growes the
people so pliant in their subjection to him, as if by their
favours he had attaind his dignity. And the Prince is able
to gaine them to his side by many wayes, which because
they vary according to the subject, no certaine rule can
bee given thereupon, wherefore we shall let them passe;
I will only conclude, that it is necssary for a Prince to have
the people his friend, otherwise in his adversities he hath
no helpe.

Nabis Prince of the Spartans supported the siege of all
Greece, and an exceeding victorious army of the Romans,
and against those defended his native countrey and State,
and this suffic'd him alone, that as the danger came upon
him, he secur'd himselfe of a few: whereas if the people
had been his enemy, this had nothing availd him.

And let no man think to overthrow this my opinion with that common proverb, that he who relyes upon the people, layes his foundation in the dirt; for that is true, where a private Citizen grounds upon them, making his account that the people shall free him, when either his enemyes or the Magistrates oppresse him. In this case he should find himselfe often deceiv'd, as it befell the Gracchyes [7] in Rome, and in Florence George Scali: [8] but he being a Prince that grounds thereupon, who can command, and is a man of courage, who hath his wits about him in his adversityes, and wants not other preparations, and holds together the whole multitude animated with his valour and orders, shall not prove deceiv'd by them, and shall find he hath layd good foundations.

These Principalityes are wont to be upon the point of falling when they goe about to skip from the civill order, to the absolute: for these Princes either command of themselves, or by the Magistrats; in this last case their State is more weak and dangerous: because they stand wholly at the will and pleasure of these Citizens, who then are set over the Magistrates, who especially in adverse times are able with facility to take their State from them, either by rising up against them, or by not obeying them; and then the Prince is not at hand in those dangers to take the absolute authority upon him: for the Citizens and subjects that are accustomed to receive the commands from the Magistrates, are not like in those fractions to obey his: and in doubtfull times hee shall alwayes have greatest penury of whom hee may trust; for such a Prince cannot ground upon that which he sees in peaceable times, when the Citizens have need of the State; for then every one runs and every one promises, and every one will venture his life for him, when there is no danger neare; but in times of hazzard, when the State hath need of Citizens, there are but few of them then, and so much the more is this experience dangerous, in that it can be but once made.

Therefore a prudent Prince ought to devise a way,

whereby his Citizens alwayes and in any case and quality of time may have need of his government, and they shall alwaies after proove faithfull to him.

CHAPTER X

In What Maner the Forces of Al Principalities Ought to Be Measured

It is requisite in examining the quality of those Principalities, to have another consideration of them, that is, if a Prince have such dominions, that hee is able in case of necessity to subsist of himselfe, or else whether hee hath alwaies need of another to defend him. And to cleer this point the better, I judge them able to stand of themselves, who are of power either for their multitudes of men, or quantity of money, to bring into the feild a compleat armie, and joyne battell with whoever comes to assaile them: and so I think those always to stand in need of others help, who are not able to appear in the feild against the enemy, but are forc'd to retire within their walls and guard them. Touching the first case, wee have treated already, and shall adde somewhat thereto as occasion shall require.

In the second case, wee cannot say other, save only to incourage such Princes to fortifie and guard their own Capitall city, and of the countrey about not to hold much account; and whoever shall have well fortifi'd that towne, and touching other matters of governments shall have behav'd himselfe towards his subjects, as hath been formerly said, and hereafter shall bee, shall never be assaild but with great regard; for men willingly undertake not enterprises, where they see difficulty to work them through;

nor can much facility bee there found, where one assailes him, who hath his towne strong and well guarded, and is not hated of his people.

The cities of Germany are very free; they have but very little of the countrey about them belonging to them, and they obey the Emperour, when they please, and they stand not in fear, neither of him nor any other potentate about them: for they are in such a manner fortifi'd, that every one thinks the siege of any of them would proove hard and tedious: for all of them have ditches and rampires, and good store of Artillery, and alwayes have their publick sellers well provided with meat and drink and firing for a yeere: besides this whereby to feed the common people, and without any losse to the publick, they have alwayes in common whereby they are able for a yeere to imploy them in the labour of those trades, that are the sinews and the life of that city, and of that industry, whereby the commons ordinarily supported themselves: they hold up also the mititary exercises in repute, and hereupon have they many orders to maintaine them.

A Prince then that is master of a good strong city, and causeth not himselfe to be hated, cannot bee assaulted; and in case hee were, he that should assaile him, would be faine to quitt him with shame: for the affayres of the world are so various, that it is almost impossible that an army can lye incampt before a towne for the space of a whole yeere: and if any should reply, that the people having their possessions abroad, in case they should see them afire, would not have patience, and the tedious siege and their love to themselves would make them forget their Prince: I answer that a Prince puissant and couragious, will easily master those difficulties, now giving his subjects hope, that the mischiefe will not bee of durance, sometimes affrighting them with the cruelty of their enemies, and otherwhiles cunningly securing himself of those, whom he thinks too forward to runne to the enemy.

Besides this by ordinary reason the enemy should burne

and waste their country upon his arrivall, and at those times while mens minds are yet warme, and resolute in their defence: and therefore so much the lesse ought a Prince doubt: for after some few dayes, that their courages grow coole, the dammages are all done, and mischiefes receivd, and there is no help for it, and then have they more occasion to cleave faster to their Prince; thinking hee is now more bound to them, their houses having for his defence been fir'd, and their possessions wasted; and mens nature is as well to hold themselves oblig'd for the kindnesses they doe, as for those they receive; whereupon if all be well weigh'd, a wise Prince shall not find much difficulty to keep sure and true to him his Citizens hearts at the beginning and latter end of the siege, when hee hath no want of provision for food and munition.

CHAPTER XI

Concerning Ecclesiasticall Principalities

There remains now only that wee treat of the Ecclesiasticall Principalities, about which all the difficulties are before they are gotten: for they are attain'd to either by Vertue or Fortune, and without the one or the other they are held: for they are maintaind by orders inveterated in the religion, all which are so powerfull and of such nature, that they maintaine their Princes in their dominions in what manner soever they proceed and live. These only have an Estate and defend it not; have subjects and governe them not; and yet their States because undefended, are not taken from them; nor their subjects, though not govern'd, care not, think not, neither are able to aliene themselves from them. These Principalities then are only happy and secure: but they being sustained by

42

superiour causes, whereunto humane understanding reaches not, I will not meddle with them: for being set up and maintaind by God; it would be the part of a presumptuous and rash man to enter into discourse of them.[9]

Yet if any man should aske mee whence it proceeds, that the Church in temporall power hath attaind to such greatnesse, seeing that till the time of Alexander the sixt, the Italian potentates, and not only they who are entitled potentates, but every Baron and Lord though of the meanest condition, in regard of the temporality made but small account of it, and now a King of France trembles at the power thereof, and it hath been able to drive him out of Italy, and ruine the Venetians; and however this bee well known, me thinks it is not superfluous in some part to recall it to memory.

Before that Charles King of France past into Italy, this countrey was under the rule of the Pope, the Venetians, the King of Naples, the Duke of Milan, and the Florentines. These potentates took two things principally to their care; the one, that no forreiner should invade Italy; the other, that no one of them should inlarge their State. They, against whom this care was most taken, were the Pope and the Venetians; and to restraine the Venetians, there needed the union of all the rest, as it was in the defence of Ferrara; and to keep the Pope low, they servd themselves of the Barons of Rome, who being devided into two factions, the Orsini and Collonnesi, there was alwayes occasion of offence between them, who standing ready with their armes in hand in the view of the Pope, held the Popedome weak and feeble: and however sometimes there arose a couragious Pope, as was Sextus; [10] yet either his fortune, or his wisdome was not able to free him of these incommodities, and the brevity of their lives was the cause thereof: for in ten yeers, which time one with another, the Popes ordinarily liv'd, with much adoe could they bring low one of the factions. And if, as we may say, one had near put out the Colonnesi, there arose another enemy to the Orsini, who made them grow againe, so that there was never time quite to root them out. This then was the cause, why the Popes temporall power was of small esteeme in Italy.

There arose afterwards Pope Alexander the sixt, who of all the Popes that ever were, shewd what a Pope was able to doe with money and forces: and hee effected by meanes of his instrument, Duke Valentine, and by the occasion of the French mens passage, all those things, which I have formerly discoursed upon in the Dukes actions: and however his purpose was nothing at all to inlarge the Church dominions, but to make the Duke great; yet what hee did, turnd to the Churches advantage; which after his death, when the Duke was taken away, was the heire of all his paines.

Afterwards succeeded Pope Julius, and found the Church great, having all Romania, and all the Barons of Rome being quite rooted out, and by Alexanders persecutions all their factions worne down; hee found also the way open for the heaping up of monyes, never practis'd before Alexanders time; which things Julius not only follow'd, but augmented; and thought to make himselfe master of Bolonia, and extinguish the Venetians, and chase the French men out of Italy: and these designes of his prov'd all lucky to him, and so much the more to his praise in that he did all for the good of the Church, and in no private regard: hee kept also the factions of the Orsini and Colonnesi, in the same State hee found them: and though there were among them some head whereby to cause an alteration; yet two things have held them quiet, the one the power of the Church, which somewhat affrights them; the other because they have no Cardinals of their factions, who are the primary causes of all the troubles amongst them: nor shall these parties ever bee at rest, while they have Cardinals; because they nourish the factions both in Rome, and abroad, and the Barons then are forc'd to undertake the defence of them: and thus from the Prelates ambitions arise the discords and tumults among the Barons.

And now hath Pope Leo his Holinesse found the Pope-dome exceeding puissant, of whome it is hop'd, that if they amplifi'd it by armes, hee by his goodnesse, and infinite other vertues, will much more advantage and dignifie it.

CHAPTER XII

How Many Sorts of Military Discipline There Are: and Touching Mercenary Souldiers

Having treated particularly of the qualities of those Principalities, which in the beginning I propounded to discourse upon, and considered in some part the reasons of their well and ill being, and shewed the wayes whereby many have sought to gaine, and hold them; it remaines now that I speak in generall of the offences and defences, that may chance in each of the forenamed.

We have formerly said that it is necessary for a Prince to have good foundations laid; otherwise it must needs bee that hee goe to wrack. The principall foundations that all States have, as well new, as old, or mixt, are good lawes, and good armes; and because there cannot bee good lawes, where there are not good armes, and where there are good armes, there must needs be good lawes, I will omit to discourse of the lawes, and speak of armes.

I say then that the armes, wherewithall a Prince defends his State, either are his own, or mercenary, or auxiliary, or mixt. Those that are mercenary, and auxiliary, are unprofitable, and dangerous; and if any one holds his State founded upon mercenary armes, hee shall never be quiet, nor secure: because they are never well united,

ambitious, and without discipline, treacherous, among their
friends stout, among their enemies cowardly, they have no
feare of God, nor keep any faith with men, and so long
only deferre they the doing of mischiefe, till the enemy
comes to assayle thee, and in time of peace thou art dispoyld by them, in warre by thy enemies: the reason hereof
is, because they have no other love, nor other cause to
keep them in the feild, but only a smal stipend, which is
not of force to make them willing to hazard their lives for
thee: they are willing indeed to be thy souldiers, til thou
goest to fight, but then they flye, or run away: which
thing would cost mee but small paines to perswade: for
the ruine of Italy hath not had any other cause now
adayes, than for that it hath these many yeers rely'd upon
mercenary armes; which a good while since perhaps may
have done some man some service, and among themselves
they may have been thought valiant: but so soone as any
forrein enemy appeard, they quickly shewd what they
were: Whereupon Charles the King of France, without
opposition made himself master of all Italy: and he that
said, that the cause thereof were our faults, said true; but
these were not those they beleevd, but what I have told;
and because they were the Princes faults, they also have
suffered the punishment.

I will fuller shew the infelicity of these armes. The
mercenary Captaines are either very able men, or not: if
they bee, thou canst not repose any trust in them: for
they will alwayes aspire unto their owne proper advance-
ments, either by suppressing of thee that art their Lord,
or by suppressing of some one else quite out of thy purpose: but if the Captaine bee not valourous, hee ordinarily
ruines thee: and in case it be answerd, that whoever
shall have armes in his hands, whether mercenary or not,
will doe so: I would reply, that armes are to be imployed
either by a Prince, or common-wealth.

The Prince ought to goe in person, and performe the
office of a commander: the Republick is to send forth her

Citizens: and when shee sends forth one that proves not of abilities, shee ought to change him then, and when hee does prove valourous, to bridle him so by the laws, that he exceed not his commissions.

And by experience wee see, that Princes and Republicks of themselves alone, make very great conquests; but that mercenary armes never doe other than harme: and more hardly falls a Republick armed with her owne armes under the obedience of one of her owne Citizens; than one that is armd by forrein armes. Rome and Sparta subsisted many ages armd and free. The Swissers are exceedingly well armd, and yet very free.

Touching mercenary armes that were of old, we have an example of the Carthagians, who neare upon were oppressd by their owne mercenary souldiers, when the first warre with the Romans was finishd, however the Carthagians had their owne Citizens for their Captaines. Philip of Macedon was made by the Thebans after Epaminondas his death, Generall of their Armies; and after the victory, he took from them their liberty. The Milaneses when Duke Philip was dead, entertaind Francis Sforza into their pay against the Venetians, who having vanquisht their enemies at Caravaggio, afterwards joyned with them, whereby to usurp upon the Milaneses his Masters. Sforza his father, being in Joane the Queen of Naples pay, left her on a sudden disarmd, whereupon she, to save her Kingdome, was constraind to cast her selfe into the King of Arragon's bosome.

And in case the Venetians and the Florentines have formerly augmented their State with these kinde of Armes, and their owne Captaines, and yet none of them have ever made themselves their Princes, but rather defended them: I answer, that the Florentines in this case have had Fortune much their friend: for of valorous Captains, which they might any way feare, some have not been victors, some have had opposition, and others have layd the ayme of their ambitions another way. Hee who overcame not, was John Acuto, of whose faith there could no proofe bee made, being he vanquisht not; but every one will acknowledge, that had he vanquisht, the Florentines were at his discretion. Sforza had alwayes the Bracceschi for his adversaries, so that they were as a guard one upon another. Francis converted all his ambition against Lombardy. Braccio against the Church, and the Kingdome of Naples.

But let us come to that, which followed a while agoe. The Florentines made Paul Vitelli their Generall, a throughly advisd man, and who from a private fortune had rose to very great reputation: had he taken Pisa, no man will deny but that the Florentines must have held fast with him; for had he been entertaind in their enemyes pay, they had had no remedy, and they themselves holding of him, of force were to obey him.

The Venetians, if wee consider their proceedings, wee shall see wrought both warily and gloriously, while they themselves made warre, which was before their undertakings by land, where the gentlemen with their own Commons in armes behav'd themselves bravely: but when they began to fight by land, they lost their valour, and follow'd the customes of Italy; and in the beginning of their inlargement by land, because they had not much territory, and yet were of great reputation, they had not much cause to feare their Captaines; but as they began to extend their bounds, which was under their Commander Carminiola, they had a taste of this error: for perceiving hee was exceeding valourous, having under his conduct beaten the Duke of Milan, and knowing on the other side, how hee was cold in the warre, they judg'd that they could not make any great conquest with him; and because they neither would, nor could not cashier him, that they might not lose what they had gotten, they were forc'd for their owne safeties to put him to death. Since they have had for their Generall Bartholomew of Berganio, Robert of St. Severin, the Count of Petilian, and such like: whereby they were to feare their losses, as well as to hope for gaine: as it fell out afterwards at Vayla, where in one day they lost that, which with so much paines they had gotten in eight hundred yeeres: for from these kind of armes grow slack and slow and weake gaines; but sudden and wonderfull losses.

And because I am now come with these examples into Italy, which now these many yeeres, hath been governd by mercenary armes, I will search deeper into them, to the end that their course and progresse being better discovered, they may be the better amended.

You have to understand, that so soone as in these later times the yoak of the Italian Empire began to be shaken off, and the Pope had gotten reputation in the temporalty, Italy was divided into severall States: for many of the great cities took armes against their Nobility; who under the Emperours protection had held them in oppression; and the Pope favourd these, whereby he might get himselfe reputation, in the temporalty; of many others, their Citizens became Princes, so that hereupon Italy being come into the Churches hands as it were, and some few Republicks, those Priests and Citizens not accustomed to the use of armes, began to take strangers to their pay.

The first that gave reputation to these souldiers was Alberick of Conio [11] in Romania. From his discipline among others descended Brachio and Sforza, who in their time were the arbitres of Italy. After these followd all the others, who even til our dayes have commanded the armes of Italy: and the successe of their valour hath been, that it was overrunne by Charles, pillagd by Lewis, forc'd by Ferdinand, and disgrac'd by the Swissers.

The order which they have held, hath been, first whereby to give reputation to their owne armes, to take away the credit of the infantrey. This they did, because they having no State of their owne, but living upon their industry, their few foot gave them no reputation, and many they were not able to maintaine, whereupon they reduc'd themselves to cavalery, and so with a supportable number they were intertaind and honourd: and matters were brought to such termes, that in an army of twenty thousand souldiers, you should not find two thousand foot.

They had moreover usd all industry to free themselves and their souldiers of all paines and feare, in their skirmishes, not killing, but taking one another prisoners, and without ransome for their freedomes; they repaird not all to their tents by night, nor made palizado, or trench thereabout, nor lay in the feild in the summer: and all these things were thus contrivd and agreed of among them in their military orders: whereby (as is sayd) to avoyd paines and dangers; insomuch as they have brought Italy into slavery and disgrace.

CHAPTER XIII

Of Auxiliary Souldiers, Mixt, and Natives

The Auxiliary forces, being the other kind of unprofitable armes, are, when any puissant one is cal'd in, who with his forces comes to assist and defend thee; such as in these later times did Pope Julius use, who having seen the evill proof of his mercenary souldiers in the enterprize of Ferrara, appli'd himselfe to the Auxiliaries, and agreed with Ferdinand King of Spain, that with his forces hee should ayd him. These armes may be profitable and advantagious for themselves; but for him that calls them in, hurtfull; because in losing, thou are left defeated; and conquering, thou becomest their prisoner.

And however that of these examples the ancient stories are full fraught, yet will I not part from this of Pope Julius the second, which is as yet fresh: [12] whose course could not have been more inconsiderate, for the desire hee had to get Ferrara, putting himselfe wholly into strangers hands: but his good fortune, causd another third cause to arise, that hindred him from receiving the fruit of his evill choice; for his Auxiliaries being broken at Ravenna, and the Swissers thereupon arriving, who put the Conquerours to flight, beyond all opinion even their owne and others, he chanc'd not to remaine his enemies prisoner, they being put to flight; nor prisoner to his Auxiliaries, having vanquishd by other forces, than theirs.

The Florentines being wholly disarmd, brought ten thousand French to Pisa for to take it: by which course they ran more hazzard, than in any time of their troubles.

The Emperour of Constantinople, to oppresse his neighbours, brought into Greece ten thousand Turks, who when the warre was ended, could not bee got out thence, which was the beginning of Greeces servitude under the Infidels.

He then that will in no case be able to overcome, let him serve himselfe of these armes; for they are much more dangerous than the mercenaries; for by those thy ruine is more suddenly executed; for they are all united, and all bent to the obedience of another. But for the mercenaries to hurt thee, when they have vanquishd, there is no more need of time, and greater occasion, they not being all united in a body, and being found out and paid by thee, wherein a third that thou mak'st their head, cannot suddenly gaine so great authority, that hee can endammage thee. In summe, in the mercenaries their sloth and lazinesse to fight is more dangerous: in the auxiliaries their valour.

Wherefore a wise Prince hath alwayes avoyded these kind of armes, and betaken himselfe to his owne, and desird rather to lose with his owne, than conquer with anothers, accounting that not a true victorie, which was gotten with others armes.

I will not doubt to alleadge Cæsar Borgia, and his actions. This Duke entred into Romania with auxiliarie armes, bringing with him all French souldiers: but after-

51

wards not accounting those armes secure, bent himselfe to mercenaries, judging lesse danger to be in those, and tooke in pay the Orsini and the Vetelli, which afterwards in the proof of them, finding wavering, unfaithfull, and dangerous, hee extinguishd, and betook himselfe to his owne; and it may easily be perceiv'd, what difference there is between the one and the other of these armes, considering the difference that was between the Dukes reputation, when he had the French men alone, and when he had the Orsini and Vetelli; but when he remaind with his own, and stood of himselfe, wee shall find it was much augmented: nor ever was it of great esteeme, but when every one saw, that hee wholly possesd his owne armes.

I thought not to have parted from the Italian examples of late memory; but that I must not let passe that of Hiero the Siracusan, being one of those I formerly nam'd. This man (as I said before) being made generall of the Siracusans forces, knew presently that that mercenary souldiery was nothing for their profit, in that they were hirelings, as our Italians are; and finding no way either to hold, or cashier them, made them all bee cut to peeces, and afterwards wag'd warre with his owne men, and none others.

I will also call to memory a figure of the old Testament serving just to this purpose. When David presented himselfe before Saul to goe to fight with Goliah the Philistims Champion; Saul to incourage him, clad him with his owne armes, which David when hee had them upon his back, refus'd, saying, he was not able to make any proofe of himselfe therein, and therefore would goe meet the enemy with his own sling and sword. In summe, others armes either fall from thy shoulders, or cumber or streighten thee.

Charles the seaventh,[13] Father of Lewis the eleventh, having by his good fortune & valour set France at liberty from the English, knew well this necessity of being arm'd with his owne armes, and settled in his Kingdome the ordinances of men at armes, and infantry. Afterwards King Lewis his sonne, abolishd those of the infantry, and began to take the Swissers to pay; which errour follow'd by the others, is (as now in deed it appeares) the cause of that Kingdomes dangers. For having given reputation to the Swissers, they have renderd all their own armes contemptible; for this hath wholly ruind their foot, and oblig'd their men at armes to forrein armes: for being accustomed to serve with the Swissers, they think they are not able to overcome without them. From whence it comes that the French are not of force against the Swissers, and without them also against others they use not to adventure. Therefore are the French armies mixt, part mercenaries, and part natives, which armes are farre better than the simple mercenaries or simple auxiliaries, and much inferiour to the natives; and let the said example suffice for that: for the Kingdome of France would have been unconquerable, if Charles his order had been augmented and maintaind: but men in their small wisdome begin a thing, which then because it hath some savour of good, discovers not the poyson, that lurkes there under, as I before said of the hectick feavers.

Wherefore that Prince which perceives not mischiefes, but as they grow up, is not truely wise; and this is given but to few: and if we consider the first ruine of the Romane Empire, wee shall find it was, from taking the Goths first into their pay; for from that beginning the forces of the Romane Empire began to grow weak, and all the valour that was taken hence was given to them.

I conclude then that without having armes of their owne, no Principality can be secure, or rather is wholly oblig'd to fortune, not having valour to shelter it in adversity. And it was alwayes the opinion and saying of wise men, that nothing is so weak and unsetled, as is the reputation of power not founded upon ones owne proper forces: which are those that are composed of thy subjects, or Citizens, or servants; all the rest are mercenary or auxiliary; and the manner how to order those well, is easie to find out, if those orders above nam'd by me, shall be but run over, and if it shall be but consider'd, how Philip Alexander the Great his Father, and in what manner many Republicks and Princes have armd and appointed themselves, to which appointments I referre my selfe wholly.

CHAPTER XIV

What Belongs to the Prince Touching Military Discipline

A Prince then ought to have no other ayme, nor other thought, nor take any thing else for his proper arte, but warr, and the orders and discipline thereof; for that is the sole arte which belongs to him that commands, and is of so great excellency, that not only those that are borne Princes, it maintains so; but many times rayses men from a private fortune to that dignity. And it is seene by the contrary, that when Princes have given themselves more to their delights, than to the warres, they have lost their States; and the first cause that makes thee lose it, is the neglect of that arte; and the cause that makes thee gaine it, is that thou art experienc'd and approv'd in that arte. Francis Sforza by being a man at armes, of a private man became Duke of Milan; and his sons by excusing themselves of the troubles and paines belonging to those imployments of Princes, became private men.

For among other mischiefes thy neglect of armes brings upon thee, it causes thee to be contemnd, which is one of those disgraces, from which a Prince ought to keep himselfe, as hereafter shall be sayd: for from one that is disarmd to one that is armd there is no proportion; and reason will not, that he who is in armes, should willingly yeeld obedience to him that is unfurnishd of them, & that he that is disarmd should be in security among his armed vassalls; for there being disdaine in the one, and suspicion in the other, it is impossible these should ever well co-operate.

And therefore a Prince who is quite unexperienc'd in matter of warre, besides the other infelicities belonging to him, as is said, cannot bee had in any esteeme among his souldiers, nor yet trust in them. Wherefore he ought never to neglect the practice of the arte of warre, and in time of peace should he exercise it more than in the warre; which he may bee able to doe two wayes, the one practically, and in his labours & recreations of his body, the other theorically.

And touching the practick part, hee ought besides the keeping of his own subjects well traind up in the discipline and exercise of armes, give himselfe much to the chase,[14] whereby to accustome his body to paines, and partly to understand the manner of situations, & to know how the mountaines arise, which way the vallyes open themselves, and how the plaines are distended flat abroad, and to con-ceive well the nature of the rivers, and marrish ground, and herein to bestow very much care, which knowledge is profitable in two kinds: first he learnes thereby to know his own countrey, and is the better enabled to understand the defence thereof, and afterwards by meanes of his knowledge and experience in these situations easily com-prehend any other situation, which a new hee hath need to view, for the little hillocks, vallies, plaines, rivers, and mar-rish places. For example, they in Tuscany are like unto those of other countries; so that from the knowledge of the site of one country, it is easie to attain to know that of others. And that Prince that wants this skill, failes of the principall part a Commander should be furnisht with: for this shows the way, how to discover the enemy, to pitch the camp, to lead their armies, to order their battells, and also to besiege a town at thy best advantage.

Philopomenes Prince of the Achayans, among other prayses writers give him, they say, that in time of peace, he thought not upon any thing so much as the practise of warre; and whensoever he was abroad in the field to disport himselfe with his friends, would often stand still, and discourse with them, in case the enemies were upon the top of that hill, and we here with our army, whether of us two should have the advantage, and how might wee safely goe to find them, keeping still our orders? and if we would retire our selves, what course should we take? if they retir'd, how should wee follow them? and thus on the way propounded them all such accidents could befall in an army; would heare their opinions, and tell his own, and confirme it by argument, so that by his continuall thought hereupon, whenever he led any army, no chance could happen, for which he had not a remedy.

But touching the exercise of the mind, a Prince ought to reade Histories, and in them consider the actions of the worthiest men, marke how they have behav'd themselves in the warrs, examine the occasions of their victories, and their losses; whereby they may be able to avoyd these, and obtaine those; and above all, doe as formerly some excellent man hath done, who hath taken upon him to imitate, if any one that hath gone before him, hath left his memory glorious; the course he took, and kept alwaies neare unto him the remembrances of his actions and worthy deeds: as it is said, that Alexander the great imitated Achilles; Cæsar Alexander; and Scipio Cyrus. And whoever reads the life of Cyrus, written by Xenophon, may easily perceive afterwards in Scipio's life, how much glory his imitation gaind him, and how much Scipio did conforme himselfe in his chastity, affability, humanity, and liberality with those things, that are written by Xenophon of Cyrus.

Such like wayes ought a wise Prince to take, nor ever

be idle in quiet times: but by his paines then, as it were provide himselfe of store, whereof he may make some use in his adversity, to the end that when the times change, he may be able to resist the stormes of his hard fortune.

CHAPTER XV

Of Those Things, in Respect Whereof, Men,
and Especially Princes, Are Praised,
or Dispraised

It now remaines that we consider, what the conditions of a Prince ought to be, and his termes of government over his subjects, and towards his friends. And because I know that many have written hereupon; I doubt, lest I venturing also to treat thereof, may be branded with presumption, especially seeing I am like enough to deliver an opinion different from others. But my intent being to write for the advantage of him that understands mee, I thought it fitter to follow the effectuall truth of the matter, than the imagination thereof: And many Principalities and Republiques, have been in imagination, which neither have been seen nor knowne to be indeed: for there is such a distance between how men doe live, and how men ought to live; that hee who leaves that which is done, for that which ought to bee done, learnes sooner his ruine, than his preservation: for that man who will professe honesty in all his actions, must needs goe to ruine, among so many that are dishonest. Whereupon it is necessary for a Prince, desiring to preserve himselfe, to be able to make use of that honestie, and to lay it aside againe, as need shall require.

Passing by then things that are only in imagination belonging to a Prince, to discourse upon those that are really true; I say that all men, whensoever mention is made of them, and especially Princes, because they are placd aloft in the view of all, are taken notice of, for some of these qualities, which procure them either commendations, or blame: & this is, that some one is held liberall, some miserable, (miserable I say, not covetous, for the covetous desire to have, though it were by rapine, but a miserable man is he, that too much forbears to make use of his owne) some free givers, others extortioners; some cruell, others pittious; the one a League breaker, another faithfull; the one effeminate and of small courage, the other fierce and couragious; the one courteous, the other proud; the one lascivious, the other chaste; the one of faire dealing, the other wily and crafty; the one hard, the other easie; the one grave, the other light; the one religious, the other incredulous, and such like.

I know that every one will confesse, it were exceedingly praiseworthy for a Prince to be adorned with all these above nam'd qualities that are good: but because this is not possible, nor doe humane conditions admit such perfection in vertues, it is necessary for him to be so discreet, that he know how to avoid the infamie of those vices, which would thrust him out of his State; and if it be possible; beware of those also which are not able to remove him thence; but where it cannot bee, let them passe with lesse regard.

And yet, let him not stand much upon it, though he incurre the infamie of those vices, without which hee can very hardly save his State: for if all bee throughly considerd, some things we shall find which will have the colour and very face of Vertue, and following them, they will lead thee to thy destruction; whereas some others, that shall as much seeme vice, if we take the course they lead us, shall discover unto us the way to our safety and well-being.

CHAPTER XVI

Of Liberality, and Miserablenesse

Beginning then at the first of the above mentioned qualities, I say, that it would be very well to be accounted
liberall: nevertheless, liberality used in such a manner, as
not [15] to make thee be accounted so, wrongs thee: for in
case it be used vertuously, and as it ought to be, it shall
never come to be taken notice of, so as to free thee from
the infamie of its contrary.

And therefore for one to hold the name of liberall among
men, it were needfull not to omit any sumptuous quality,
insomuch that a Prince alwayes so disposd, shall waste all
his revenues, and at the end shall be forc'd, if he will still
maintaine that reputation of liberality, heavily to burthen
his subjects, and become a great exactour; and put in practise all those things, that can be done to get mony. Which
begins to make him hatefull to his subjects, and fall into
every ones contempt, growing necessitous: so that having
with this his liberality wrong'd many, and imparted of his
bounty but to a few, he feeles every first mischance, and
runnes a hazzard of every first danger. Which he knowing,
and desiring to withdraw himselfe from, incurrs presently
the disgrace of being termd miserable. [16]

A Prince therefore not being able to use this vertue of
liberality, without his owne dammage, in such a sort, that
it may be taken notice of, ought, if he be wise, not to
regard the name of Miserable; for in time he shall alwayes
be esteemed the more liberall, seeing that by his parsimony
his owne revenues are sufficient for him, as also he can
defend himselfe against whoever makes warre against him,
and can doe some exploits without grieving his subjects:
so that he comes to use his liberality to all those, from

whom he takes nothing, who are infinite in number; and his miserablenesse towards those, to whom hee gives nothing, who are but a few.

In our dayes wee have not seen any, but those who have been held miserable, doe any great matters, but the others all quite ruind. Pope Julius the second, however he serv'd himselfe of the name of Liberall, to get the Papacy, yet never intended he to continue it, to the end he might bee able to make warre against the King of France; and hee made so many wars without imposing any extraordinary taxe; because his long thrift supplyd his large expenses. This present King of Spain could never have undertaken, nor gone through with so many exployts, had he been accounted liberall.

Wherefore a Prince ought little to regard (that he may not be driven to pillage his subjects, that he may be able to defend himselfe, that he may not fall into poverty and contempt, that he be not forcd to become an extortioner) though he incurre the name of Miserable; for this is one of those vices, which does not pluck him from his throne.

And if any one should say; Cæsar by his liberality obtaind the Empire, and many others (because they both were, and were esteemd liberall) attaind to exceeding great dignities. I answer, either thou art already come to be a Prince, or thou art in the way to it: in the first case this liberality is hurtfull; in the second it is necessary to be accounted so; and Cæsar was one of those that aspird to the Principality of Rome. But if after he had gotten it, he had survivd, and not forborne those expences, hee would quite have ruind that Empire.

And if any one should reply; many have been Princes, and with their armies have done great exploits, who have been held very liberall. I answer, either the Prince spends of his owne and his subjects, or that which belongs to others: in the first, hee ought to be sparing, in the second hee should not omit any part of liberality.

And that Prince, that goes abroad with his army, and

feeds upon prey, and spoyle, and tributes, and hath the disposing of that which belongs to others, necessarily should use this liberality; otherwise would his souldiers never follow him; and of that which is neither thine, nor thy subjects, thou mayest well be a free giver, as were Cyrus, Cæsar, and Alexander; for the spending of that which is anothers, takes not away thy reputation, but rather addes to it, only the wasting of that which is thine owne, hurts thee; nor is there any thing consumes it selfe so much as liberality, which whilst thou usest, thou losest the meanes to make use of it, and becom'st poore and abject, or to avoyd this poverty an extortioner and hatefull person. And among all those things which a Prince ought to beware of, is, to be dispisd, and odious; to one and the other of which, liberality brings thee.

Wherefore there is more discretion to hold the stile of Miserable, which begets an infamy without hatred, than to desire that of Liberall, whereby to incurre the necessity of being thought an extortioner, which procures an infamy with hatred.

CHAPTER XVII

Of Cruelty, and Clemency, and Whether It Is Better to Be Belov'd, or Feard

Descending afterwards unto the other forealleadged qualities, I say, that every Prince should desire to be held pittifull, and not cruell. Neverthelesse ought hee beware that he ill uses not this pitty. Cæsar Borgia was accounted cruell, yet had his cruelty redrest the disorders in Romania, settled it in union, and restord it to peace, and fidelity: which, if it be well weighd, we shall see was an act of more pitty, than that of the people of Florence, who to avoyd the terme of cruelty, sufferd Pistoya to fall to destruction.[17]

Wherefore a Prince ought not to regard the infamy of cruelty, for to hold his subjects united and faithfull: for by giving a very few proofes of himselfe the other way, hee shall be held more pittifull than they, who through their too much pitty, suffer disorders to follow, from whence arise murthers and rapines: for these are wont to hurt an intire universality, whereas the executions practisd by a Prince, hurt only some particular.

And among all sorts of Princes, it is impossible for a new Prince to avoyd the name of cruell, because all new States are full of dangers: Whereupon Virgil by the mouth of Dido excuses the inhumanity of her Kingdome, saying,

Res dura & Regni novitas me talia cogunt
Moliri et late fines custode tueri.

My hard plight and new State force me to guard
My confines all about with watch and ward.

Neverthelesse ought he be judicious in his giving beleefe to any thing, or moving himselfe thereat, nor make his people extreamly affraid of him; but proceed in a moderate way with wisdome, and humanity, that his too much confidence make him not unwary, and his too much distrust intolerable.

From hence arises a dispute, whether it is better to be belov'd or feard: I answer, a man would wish hee might bee the one and the other: but because hardly can they subsist both together, it is much safer to be feard, than be lov'd; being that one of the two must needs faile; for touching men, wee may say this in generall, they are unthankfull, unconstant, dissemblers, they avoyd dangers, and are covetous of gaine; and whilst thou doest them good, they are wholly thine; their blood, their fortunes, lives and children are at thy service, as is said before, when the danger is remote; but when it approaches, they revolt. And that Prince; who wholly relyes upon their words, unfurnishd of all other preparations, goes to wrack: for the friendships that are gotten with rewards, and not by the magnificence and worth of the mind, are dearely bought indeed; but they will neither keep long, nor serve well in time of need: and men doe lesse regard to offend one that is supported by love, than by feare. For love is held by a certainty of obligation, which, because men are mischeivous, is broken upon any occasion of their owne profit. But feare restrains with a dread of punishment which never forsaks a man.

Yet ought a Prince cause himselfe to be belovd in such a manner, that if hee gaines not love, he may avoyd hatred: for it may well stand together, that a man may bee feard and not hated; which shall never faile, if hee abstaine from his subjects goods, and their wives; and whensoever hee should be forc'd to proceed against any of their lives, doe it when it is to be done upon a just cause, and apparent conviction; but above all things forbeare to lay his hands on other mens goods; for men forget sooner the death of their father, than the losse of their patrimony. Moreover the occasions of taking from men their goods, do never faile: and alwayes hee that begins to live by rapine, finds occasion to lay hold upon other mens goods: but against mens lives they are seldomer found, and sooner faile.

But when a Prince is abroad in the feild with his army and hath a multitude of souldiers under his government, then is it necessary that he stands not much upon it, though hee be termd cruell: for unlesse hee be so, hee shall never have his souldiers live in accord one with another, nor ever well disposed to any brave peece of service.

Among Hannibals actions of mervaile this is reckond for one, that having a very huge army, gatherd out of severall nations, and all led to serve in a strange countrey, there was never any dissention neither amongst themselves, nor against their Generall, as well in their bad fortune as their good. Which could not proceed from any thing else, than from that barbarous cruelty of his, which, together with his exceeding many vertues, renderd him to his souldiers both venerable and terrible; without which, to that effect his other vertues had servd him to little purpose: and some writers, though not of the best advised, on one side admire these his worthy actions, and on the other side, condemne the principall causes thereof.

And that it is true, that his other vertues would not have suffis'd him, wee may consider in Scipio, the rarest man not only in the dayes he liv'd, but even in the memory of man; from whom his army rebell'd in Spain: which grew only from his too much clemency, which had given way to his souldiers to become more licentious, than was well tolerable by military discipline: for which hee was reprov'd by Fabius Maximus in the Senate, who termd him the corrupter of the Romane souldiery. The Locrensians having been destroyed by a Lieftenant of Scipio's, were never reveng'd by him, nor the insolence of that Lieftenant punisht, all this arising from his easie nature: so that one desiring to excuse him in the Senate, said, that there were many men knew better how to keep themselves from faults, than to correct the faults of other men: which disposition of his in time would have wrong'd Scipio's reputation & glory, had he therewith continu'd in his commands: but living under the government of the Senate, this quality of his that would have disgrac'd him, not only was conceal'd, but prov'd to the advancement of his glory.

I conclude then, returning to the purpose of being feard, and belov'd; insomuch as men love at their owne pleasure and to serve their owne turne, and their feare depends upon the Princes pleasure, every wise Prince ought to ground upon that which is of himselfe, and not upon that which is of another: only this, he ought to use his best wits to avoid hatred, as was said.

CHAPTER XVIII

In What Manner Princes Ought to Keep Their Words

How commendable in a Prince it is to keepe his word, and live with integrity, not making use of cunning and subtlety, every one knows well: yet wee see by experience in these our dayes, that those Princes have effected great matters, who have made small reckoning of keeping their words, and have known by their craft to turne and wind men about, and in the end have overcome those who have grounded upon the truth.

You must then know there are two kinds of combating or fighting; the one by right of the laws, the other meerly by force. That first way is proper to men, the other is also common to beasts: but because the first many times suffices not, there is a necessity to make recourse to the second; wherefore it behooves a Prince to know how to make good use of that part which belongs to a beast, as well as that which is proper to a man.

This part hath been covertly shew'd to Princes by ancient writers; who say that Achilles and many others of those ancient Princes were intrusted to Chiron the Centaure, to bee brought up under his discipline: the morall of this, having for their teacher one that was halfe a beast and halfe a man, was nothing else, but that it was needfull for a Prince, to understand how to make his advantage of the one and the other nature, because neither could subsist without the other.

A Prince then being necessitated to know how to make use of that part belonging to a beast, ought to serve himselfe of the conditions of the Foxe and the Lion; for the

Lion cannot keep himself from snares, nor the Foxe defend himselfe against the Wolves. Hee had need then bee a Foxe, that hee may beware of the snares, and a Lion, that he may scarre the Wolves. Those that stand wholly upon the Lion, understand not well themselves.

And therefore a wise Prince cannot, nor ought not keep his faith given, when the observance thereof turnes to disadvantage, and the occasions that made him promise, are past. For if men were all good, this rule would not be allowable; but being they are full of mischiefe, and would not make it good to thee, neither art thou tyed to keep it with them: nor shall a Prince ever want lawfull occasions to give colour to this breach.

Very many moderne examples hereof might be alleadg'd, wherin might be shewd how many peaces concluded, and how many promises made, have bin violated and broken by the infidelity of Princes; and ordinarily things have best succeeded with him that hath been neerest the Foxe in condition. But it is necessary to understand how to set a good colour upon this disposition, and to bee able to faine and dissemble throughly; and men are so simple and yeeld so much to the present necessities, that hee who hath a mind to deceive, shall alwayes find another that will be deceivd.

I will not conceale any one of the examples that have been of late. Alexander the sixth, never did any thing else than deceive men, and never meant otherwise, and alwayes found whome to worke upon; yet never was there man would protest more effectually, nor averre any thing with more solemne oaths, and observe them lesse than he; neverthelesse, his coosenages all thriv'd well with him; for hee knew how to play this part cunningly.

Therefore is there no necessity for a Prince to bee endued with all these above written qualities, but it behooves well that he seeme to be so; or rather I will boldly say this, that having these qualities, and always regulating himselfe by them, they are hurtfull; but seeming to have them, they are advantagious; as to seeme pitifull, faithfull, mild, religious, and of integrity, and indeed to be so; provided withall thou beest of such a composition, that if need require thee to use the contrary, thou canst, and know'st how to apply thy selfe thereto.

And it suffices to conceive this, that a Prince, and especially a new Prince, cannot observe all those things, for which men are held good; he being often forc'd, for the maintenance of his State, to do contrary to his faith, charity, humanity, and religion: and therefore it behooves him to have a mind so disposd as to turne and take the advantage of all winds and fortunes; and as formerly I said, not forsake the good, while he can; but to know how to make use of the evill upon necessity.

A Prince then ought to have a speciall care, that he never let fall any words, but what are all season'd with the five above-written qualities, and let him seem to him that sees and heares him, all pitty, all faith, all integrity, all humanity, all religion; nor is there any thing more necessary for him to seeme to have, than this last quality: for all men in generall judge thereof, rather by the sight than by the touch; for every man may come to the sight of him, few come to the touch and feeling of him; every man may come to see what thou seemest, few come to perceive and understand what thou art; and those few dare not oppose the opinion of many, who have the majesty of State to protect them: And in all mens actions, especially those of Princes, wherein there is no judgement to appeale unto, men forbeare to give their censures till the events, and ends of things.

Let a Prince therefore take the surest courses he can to maintaine his life and State: the meanes shall alwaies be thought honorable, and commended by every one: for the vulgar is over-taken with the appearance and event of a thing: and for the most part of people, they are but the vulgar: the others that are but few, take place where the vulgar have no subsistence. A Prince there is in these dayes, whom I shall not do well to name, that preaches nothing else but peace and faith; [18] but had he keept the one and the other, severall times had they taken from him his State and reputation.

CHAPTER XIX

That Princes Should Take a Care, Not to Incurre Contempt or Hatred

But because among the qualities, whereof formerly mention is made, I have spoken of those of most importance; I will treat of the others more briefly under these qualities, that a Prince is to beware, as in part is above said, and that he fly those things which cause him to bee odious or vile: and when ever hee shall avoid this, he shall fully have playd his part, and in the other disgraces he shall find no danger at all.

There is nothing makes him so odious, as I said, as his extortion of his subjects goods, and abuse of their women, from which hee ought to forbeare: and so long as hee wrongs not his whole people neither in their goods, nor honors, they live content, and hee hath only to strive with the Ambition of some few: which many wayes & easily too, is restrain'd.

To be held various, light, effeminate, faint-harted, unresolv'd, these make him be contemnd and thought base, which a Prince should shun like rocks, and take a care that in all his action there appeare magnanimity, courage, gravity, and valour; and that in all the private affaires of his subjects, he orders it so, that his word stand irrevocable: and maintaines himselfe in such repute, that no man may think neither to deceive, nor wind and turn him about; that Prince that gives such an opinion of himself, is much esteemd: and against him, who is so well esteemd, hardly are any conspiracies made by his subjects, or by forreiners any invasion, when once notice is taken of his worth, and how much hee is reverenced by his subjects.

For a Prince ought to have two feares, the one from within, in regard of his subjects; the other from abroad, in regard of his mighty neighbours; from these he defends himselfe by good armes and good friends, and alwayes he shall have good friends if he have good armes; and all things shall always stand sure at home, when those abroad are firme; in case some conspiracy have not disturb'd them, and however the forraine matters stand but ticklishly; yet if hee have taken such courses at home, and liv'd as we have prescrib'd, he shall ever be able (in case he forsake not himselfe) to resist all possible force and violence, as I said Nabis the Spartan did: but touching his subjects, even when his affaires abroad are setled, it is to be fear'd, they may conspire privily; from which a Prince sufficiently secures himselfe by shunning to be hated or contemnd, and keeping himself in his peoples good opinion, which it is necessary for him to compasse, as formerly we treated at large. And one of the powerfullest remedies a Prince can have against conspiracies, is, not to bee hated nor despisd by the universality; for alwaies he that conspires, beleevs the Princes death is acceptable to the subject: but when he thinks it displeases them, he hath not the heart to venture on such a matter; for the difficulties that are on the conspirators side, are infinite.

By experience it is plaine, that many times plots have been laid, but few of them have succeeded luckily; for hee that conspires, cannot be alone, nor can he take the company of any but of those, who, he beleevs are malecontents; and so soon as thou hast discover'd thy self to a malecontent, thou giv'st him meanes to work his own content: for by revealing thy treason, hee may well hope for all manner of favour: so that seeing his gaine certaine of one side; and on the other, finding only doubt and danger, either hee had need be a rare friend, or that he be an exceeding obstinate enemy to the Prince, if he keeps his word with thee.

And to reduce this matter into short termes: I say, there is nothing but jealousie, feare, and suspect of punishment on the conspirators part to affright him; but on the Princes part, there is the majesty of the principality, the lawes, the defences of his friends and the State, which do so guard him; that to all these things the peoples good wills being added, it is unpossible, any one should be so head-strong, as to conspire; for ordinarily where a traytor is to feare before the execution of his mischiefe; in this case he is also to feare afterwards, having the people for his enemy, when the fact is committed; and therefore for this cause, not being able to hope for any refuge.

Touching this matter, many examples might be brought, but I will content my selfe to name one which fell out in the memory of our Fathers. Annibal Bentivolii, grand-father of this Anniball who now lives, that was Prince in Bolonia, being slaine by the Canneschi, that conspir'd against him, none of his race being left, but this John, who was then in swadling clouts; presently the people rose, upon this murder, and slew all the Canneschi; which proceeded from the popular affection, which the family of the Bentivolii held then in Bolonia: which was so great, that being there remain'd not any, now Anniball was dead, that was able to manage the State; and having notice that in Florence there was one borne of the Bentivolii, who till then was taken for a Smiths sonne: the citizens of Bolonia went to Florence for him, and gave the government of their City to him, which was rul'd by him, untill John was of fit yeares to governe.

I conclude then that a Prince ought to make smal account of treasons, whiles he hath the people to friend: but if they be his enemies and hate him, he may well feare every thing, and every one. And well orderd States, and discreet Princes have taken care with all diligence, not to cause their great men to fall into desperation, and to content the people, and so to maintaine them: for this is one of the most important businesses belonging to a Prince.

Among the Kingdomes that are well orderd and governd in our dayes, is that of France, and therein are found exceeding many good orders; whereupon the Kings liberty and security depends: of which the chiefe is the Parliament, and the authority thereof: for hee that founded that Kingdome, knowing the great mens ambition and insolence; and judgeing it necessary there should bee a bridle to curbe them; and on the other side knowing the hatred of the Commonalty against the great ones, grounded upon feare, intending to secure them, would not lay this care wholly upon the King; but take this trouble from him, which hee might have with the great men, in case hee favourd the Commonalty, or with the Commonalty, in case hee favourd the great men: and thereupon set up a third judge, which was that, to the end it should keep under the great ones, and favour the meaner sort, without any imputation to the King. It was not possible to take a better, nor wiser course than this, nor a surer way to secure the King, and the Kingdome. From whence we may drawe another conclusion worthie of note, that Princes ought to cause others to take upon them the matters of blame and imputation; and upon themselves to take only those of grace and favour.

Here againe I conclude, that a Prince ought to make good esteeme of his Nobility; but not thereby to incurre the Commons hatred: It would seem perhaps to many, considering the life and death of many Romane Emperours, that they were examples contrary to my opinion, finding that some have liv'd worthily, and shewd many rare vertues of the minde, and yet have lost the Empire, and been put to death by their owne subjects, conspiring against them. Intending then to answer these objections; I shall discourse upon the qualities of some Emperours, declaring the occasions of their ruine, not disagreeing from that

which I have alleagd: and part thereof I will bestow on
the consideration of these things; which are worthy to be
noted by him that reads the actions of those times: and it
shall suffice mee to take all those Emperours that succeeded in the Empire from Marcus the Philosopher to
Maximinus, who were Marcus and Commodus his sonne,
Pertinax, Julian, Severus, Antonius, Caracalla his sonne,
Macrinus, Heliogabalus, Alexander, and Maximin.

And first it is to be noted, that where in the other Principalities, they are to contend only with the ambition of
the Nobles, and the insolence of the people; the Romane
Emperours had a third difficulty, having to support the
cruelty and covetousnesse of the souldiers, which was so
hard a thing, that it causd the ruine of many, being hard
to satisfy the souldiers, and the people: for the people love
their quiet, and therefore affect modest Princes; and the
souldiers love a Prince of a warlike courage, that is insolent,
cruell and plucking from every one: which things they
would have them exercise upon the people, whereby they
might bee able to double their stipends, and satisfie their
avarice and cruelty: whence it proceeded, that those Emperours who either by Nature or by Art had not such a
reputation, as therewith they could curbe the one and the
other, were alwayes ruind: and the most of them, specially
those, who as new men came to the principality, finding
the difficulty of those two different humours, applyd themselves to content the souldiers, making small account of
wronging the people: which was a course then necessary;
for the Princes not being able to escape the hatred of every
one, ought first endeavour that they incurre not the hatred
of any whole universality; and when they cannot attaine
therunto, they are to provide with all industry, to avoyd
the hatred of those universalities, that are the most mighty.
And therefore those Emperours, who because they were
but newly call'd to the Empire, had need of extraordinary
favours, more willingly stuck to the souldiers, than to the
people; which neverthelesse turnd to their advantage, or

otherwise, according as that Prince knew how to maintaine his repute with them.

From these causes aforesayd proceeded it, that Marcus, Pertinax, and Alexander, though all living modestly, being lovers of justice, and enemies of cruelty, courteous, and bountifull, had all from Marcus onward, miserable ends; Marcus only liv'd and dy'd exceedingly honoured: for hee came to the Empire by inheritance, and was not to acknowledge it neither from the souldiers, nor from the people: afterwards being accompanyed with many vertues, which made him venerable, hee held alwayes whilst he liv'd, the one and the other order within their limits, and was never either hated, or contemnd. But Pertinax was created Emperour against the souldiers wills, who being accustomed to live licentiously under Commodus, could not endure that honest course, that Pertinax sought to reduce them to: Whereupon having gotten himself hatred, and to this hatred added contempt, in that he was old, was ruind in the very beginning of his government.

Whence it ought to be observed, that hatred is gaind as well by good deeds as bad; and therefore as I formerly said, when a Prince would maintaine the State, hee is often forcd not to be good: for when that generalty, whether it be the people, or souldiers, or Nobility, whereof thou thinkst thou standst in need to maintain thee, is corrupted, it behooves thee to follow their humour, and content them, and then all good deeds are thy adversaries.

But let us come to Alexander, who was of that goodnesse, that among the prayses given him, had this for one, that in fourteen yeers wherein he held the Empire, he never put any man to death but by course of justice; neverthelesse being held effeminate, and a man that suffered himselfe to be ruld by his mother, and thereupon fallen into contempt; the army conspird against him.

Now on the contrary discoursing upon the qualities of Commodus, Severus, Antonius, Caracalla, and Maximinus, you shall find them exceeding cruell, and ravinous, who to satisfie their souldiers, forbeare no kinde of injury, that could be done upon the people; and all of them, except Severus, came to evill ends: for in Severus there was such extraordinary valour, that while hee held the souldiers his friends, however the people were much burthend by him, he might alwayes reigne happily: for his valour rendred him so admirable in the souldiers and peoples sights; that these in a manner stood amazd and astonishd, and those others reverencing, and honoring him.

And because the actions of this man were exceeding great being in a new Prince, I will briefly shew, how well hee knew to act the Foxes and the Lions parts; the conditions of which two, I say, as before, are very necessary for a Prince to imitate. Severus having had experience of Julian the Emperours sloth, perswaded his army (whereof hee was commander in Sclavonia) that they should doe well to goe to Rome, to revenge Pertinax his death, who was put to death by the Imperiall guard; and under this pretence, not making any shew that hee aspird unto the Empire, set his army in march directly towards Rome, and was sooner come into Italy, than it was knowne hee had mov'd from his station. Being arriv'd at Rome, hee was by the Senate chosen Emperour for feare; and Julian slaine.

After this beginning, two difficulties yet remaind to Severus, before hee could make himselfe Lord of the whole State; the one in Asia, where Niger the Generall of those armies had gotten the title of Emperour; the other in the West with Albinus, who also aspird to the Empire: and because hee thought there might be some danger to discover himselfe enemy to them both; he purposd to set upon Niger, and cozen Albinus, to whom hee writ, that being elected Emperour by the Senate hee would willingly communicate it with him; and thereupon sent him the title of Cæsar, and by resolution of the Senate, tooke him to him for his Collegue; which things were taken by Albinus in true meaning. But afterwards when Severus had overcome and slaine Niger, and pacified the affaires in the East, being returnd to Rome, hee complaind in the Senate of Albinus, how little weighing the benefits received from him, hee had sought to slay him by treason, and therefore was hee forc'd to goe punish his ingratitude: afterwards hee went into France, where hee bereft him, both of his State, and life.

Whoever then shall in particular examine his actions, shall finde he was a very cruell Lion, and as crafty a Foxe: and shall see that hee was alwayes feard and reverenc'd by every one, and by the armies not hated; and shall nothing marvell that hee being a new man, was able to hold together such a great Empire: for his extraordinary reputation defended him alwayes from that hatred, which the people for his extortions might have conceiv'd against him.

But Antonius his sonne, was also an exceeding brave man, and endued with most excellent qualities, which causd him to be admird by the people, and acceptable to the souldiers; because hee was a warrlike man, enduring all kind of travell and paines, despising all delicate food, and all kinde of effeminacy; which gaind him the love of all the armies: neverthelesse his fiercenesse and cruelty were such and so hideous, having upon many particular occasions put to death a great part of the people of Rome, and all those of Alexandria, that hee grew odious to the world: and began to bee feard by those also, that were neare about him; so that he was slaine by a Centurion in the very midst of his army.

Where it is to be noted, that these kinde of deaths, which follow upon the deliberation of a resolv'd and obstinate minde, cannot by a Prince be avoyded: for every one that feares not to dye, is able to doe it; but a Prince ought to be lesse afraid of it; because it very seldome falls out. Only should he beware not to doe any extreame injury, to any of those of whom he serves himselfe, or that hee hath near about him in any imployment of his Principality; as Antonius did: who had reproachfully slaine a brother of that Centurion, also threatned him every day, and neverthelesse entertaind him still as one of the guards of his body: which was a rash course taken, and the way to destruction, as befell him.

But let us come to Commodus, for whom it was very easie to hold the Empire, by reason it descended upon him by inheritance, being Marcus his sonne; and it had been enough for him to follow his fathers footsteps, and then had hee contented both the people and the souldiers: but being of a cruell and savage disposition, whereby to exercise his actions upon the people, hee gave himselfe to entertaine armies, and those in all licentiousnesse. On the other part not maintaining his dignity, but often descending upon the stages to combate with fencers, and doing such other like base things, little worthy of the Imperiall majesty, hee became contemptible in the souldiers sight, and being hated of one part, and dispisd of the other, he was conspird against, and slaine.

It remaines now that wee declare Maximinus his conditions: who was a very warrlike man; and the armies loathing Alexanders effeminacy, whereof I spake before, when they had slain him, chose this man Emperour; who not long continu'd so, because two things there were that brought him into hatred and contempt; the one because hee was very base, having kept cattell in Thrace, which was well knowne to every one, and made them to scorne him; the other, because in the beginning of his Principality having delayd to goe to Rome, and enter into possession of the Imperiall throne, he had gaind the infamy of being thought exceding cruell, having by his Prefects in Rome, and in every place of the Empire exercis'd many cruelties, insomuch that the whole world being provok'd against him to contempt for the basenesse of his blood. on the other side upon the hatred conceiv'd against him for feare of his cruelty; first Affrica, afterwards the Senate with all the people of Rome, and all Italy conspird against him, with whom his own army took part; which incamping before Aquileya, and finding some difficulty to take the town, being weary of his cruelties, & because they saw he had so many enemies, fearing him the lesse, slew him.

I purpose not to say any thing either of Heliogabalus, Macrinus, or Julian, who because they were throughly base, were suddenly extinguishd; but I will come to the conclusion of this discourse; and I say, that the Princes of our times have lesse of this difficulty to satisfie the Souldiers extraordinarily in their governments; for notwithstanding that there be some consideration to bee had of them; yet presently are those armies dissolv'd, because none of these Princes do use to maintaine any armies together, which are annex'd and inveterated with the governments of the provinces, as were the armies of the Romane Empire.

And therefore if then it was necessary rather to content the souldiers than the people, it was because the souldiers were more powerfull than the people: now is it more necessary for all Princes, (except the Turk and the Souldan) to satisfie their people than their souldiers: because the people are more mighty than they; wherein I except the Turk, he alwayes maintaining about his person 12000 foot, and 15000 horse, upon which depends the safety and strength of his Kingdome, and it is necessary that laying aside all other regard of his people, hee maintaine these his friends.

The Souldans Kingdome is like hereunto, which being wholly in the souldiers power, hee must also without respect of his people keep them his friends. And you are to consider, that this State of the Souldans differs much from all the other Principalities: for it is very like the Papacy, which cannot be termd a hereditary Principality, nor a new Principality: for the sonns of the deceasd Prince are not heires and Lords thereof; but hee that is chosen, receives that dignity from those, who have the authority in them. And this order being of antiquity, cannot be termd a new Principality, because therein are none of those difficulties, that are in the new ones: for though the Prince

77

be new; yet are the orders of that State ancient, and ordaind to receive him, as if hee were their hereditary Prince.

But let us returne to our matter; whosoever shall consider our discourse before, shall perceive that either hatred, or comtempt have causd the ruine of the aforenamd Emperours; and shall know also, from it came that part of them proceeding one way, and part a contrary; yet in any of them the one had a happy successe, and the others unhappy: for it was of no availe, but rather hurtfull, for Pertinax and Alexander, because they were new Princes, to desire to imitate Marcus, who by inheritance came to the Principality: and in like manner it was a wrong to Caracalla, Commodus, and Maximinus to imitate Severus, because none of them were endued with so great valour as to follow his stepps therein.

Wherefore a new Prince in his Principality cannot well imitate Marcus his actions; nor yet is it necessary to follow those of Severus: but he ought make choyce of those parts in Severus which are necessary for the founding of a State; and to take from Marcus those that are fitt and glorious to preserve a State which is already establishd and setled.

CHAPTER XX

Whether the Citadels and Many Other Things, Which Princes Often Make Use of, Are Profitable or Dammageable

Some Princes, whereby they might safely keep their State, have disarmd their subjects; some others have held the townes under their dominion, devided into factions; others have maintain'd enmities against themselves; others have

apply'd themselves to gaine them, where they have suspected at their entrance into the government; others have
built Fortresses; and others again have ruind and demol-
ishd them: and however that upon all these things, a man
cannot well passe a determinate sentence, unlesse one
comes to the particulars of these States, where some such
like determinations were to be taken; yet shall I speake of
them in so large a manner, as the matter of it selfe will
beare.

It was never then that a new Prince would disarme his
own subjects; but rather when hee hath found them disarmd, hee hath alwayes armd them. For being belov'd,
those armes become thine; those become faithfull, which
thou hadst in suspicion; and those which were faithfull,
are maintaind so; and thy subjects are made thy partisans:
and because all thy subjects cannot be put in armes, when
thou bestowst favours on those thou armest, with the
others thou canst deale more for thy safety; and that difference of proceding which they know among them, obliges
them to thee; those others excuse thee, judgeing it necessary that they have deservd more, who have undergon
more danger, and so have greater obligation: but when
thou disarmst them, thou beginst to offend them, that
thou distrusts them, either for cowardise, or small faith;
and the one or the other of those two opinions provokes
their hatred against thee: and because thou canst not
stand disarmd, thou must then turne thy selfe to mercenary Souldiery, whereof wee have formerly spoken what it
is: and when it is good, it can never bee so much as to
defend thee from powerfull enemies, and suspected subjects; therefore as I have said, a new Prince in a new
Principality hath always ordaind them armes. Of examples
to this purpose, Histories are full.

But when a Prince gaines a new State, which as a
member hee addes to his ancient dominions; then it is
necessary to disarme that State, unlesse it be those whom
thou hast discoverd to have assisted thee in the conquest

thereof; and these also in time and upon occasions, it is necessary to render delicate and effeminate, and so order them, that all the armes of thy State be in the hands of thy own Souldiers, who live in thy ancient State neare unto thee.

Our ancestors and they that were accounted sages, were wont to say, that it was necessary to hold Pistoya in factions, and Pisa with Fortresses; and for this cause maintaind some towne subject to them in differences, whereby to hold it more easily. This, at what time Italy was ballanc'd in a certaine manner, might be well done; but me thinks it cannot now adayes bee well given for a precept; for I do not beleeve, that divisions made can do any good; rather it must needs bee, that when the enemy approaches them, Cities divided are presently lost; for alwayes the weaker part will cleave to the forreine power, and the other not be able to subsist.

The Venetians (as I think) mov'd by the aforesaid reasons, maintaind the factions of the Guelfes and Gibellins, in their townes; and however they never suffer'd them to spill one anothers blood, yet they nourishd these differences among them, to the end that the citizens imployd in these quarrels, should not plot any thing against them: which as it prov'd, never serv'd them to any great purpose: for being defeated at Vayla, presently one of those two factions tooke courage and seizd upon their whole State.

Therefore such like wayes argue the Princes weakenesse; for in a strong principality they never will suffer such divisions; for they shew them some kind of profit in time of peace, being they are able by meanes thereof more easily to manage their subjects; but war comming, such like orders discover their fallacy.

Without doubt, Princes become great, when they overcome the difficulties and oppositions that are made against them; and therefore Fortune especially when she hath to make any new Prince great, who hath more need to gaine reputation, than a hereditary Prince, causes enemies to rise against him, and him to undertake against them; to the end he may have occasion to master them, and know that ladder, which his enemies have set him upon, whereby to rise yet higher. And therefore many think, that a wise Prince, when hee hath the occasion, ought cunningly to nourish some enmity, that by the suppressing thereof, his greatnesse may grow thereupon.

Princes, especially those that are new, have found more faith and profit in those men, who in the beginning of their State, have been held suspected, than in those who at their entrance have been their confidents. Pandulphus Petrucci, Prince of Siena, governd his State more with them that had bin suspected by him, than with the others. But of this matter we cannot speak at large, because it varies according to the subject; I will only say this, that those men, who in the beginning of a principality were once enemies, if they be of quality, so that to maintain themselves they have need of support, the Prince might alwayes with the greatest facility gaine for his; and they are the rather forc'd to serve him faithfully, insomuch as they know it is more necessary for them by their deeds to cancell that sinister opinion, which was once held of them; and so the Prince ever draws from these more advantage, than from those, who serving him too supinely, neglects his affaires.

And seing the matter requires it, I will not omit, to put a Prince in mind, who hath anew made himselfe master of a State, by meanes of the inward helpes he had from thence, that he consider well, the cause that mov'd them that favour'd him to favour him, if it be not a naturall affection towards him; for if it be only because they were not content with their former government, with much paines and difficulties shall he be able to keep them long his friends, because it will bee impossible for him to content them. By these examples then, which are drawn out of ancient and moderne affaires, searching into the cause

hereof, wee shall find it much more easie to gaine those
men for friends, who formerly were contented with the
State, and therefore were his enemies: than those, who
because they were not contented therewith, became his
friends, and favour him in getting the mastery of it.

It hath been the custome of Princes, wherby to hold
their States more securely, to build Citadels, which might
bee bridles and curbs to those that should purpose any
thing against them, and so to have a secure retraite from
the first violences. I commend this course, because it hath
been usd of old; notwithstanding Nicolas Vitelli in our
dayes hath been knowne to demolish two Citadels in the
towne of Castello, the better to keep the State. Guidubaldo Duke of Urbin being to returne into his State, out
of which hee was driven by Cæsar Borgia, raz'd all the
Fortresses of that Country, and thought he should hardlyer
lose that State againe without them. The Bentivolii returning into Bolonia, usd the like courses.

Citadels then are profitable, or not, according to the
times, and if they advantage thee in one part, they do
thee harme in another, and this part may be argued thus.
That Prince, who stands more in feare of his owne people
than of strangers, ought to build Fortresses: but hee that
is more afraid of strangers than of his people, should let
them alone. Against the house of Sforza, the Castle of
Milan, which Francis Sforza built, hath and will make
more war, than any other disorder in that State: and
therefore the best Citadell that may be, is not to incurre
the peoples hatred; for however thou holdst a Fortresse,
and the people hate thee, thou canst hardly scape them:
for people, when once they have taken armes, never want
the help of strangers at their need, to take their parts.

In our dayes we never saw, that they ever profited any
Prince, unlesse it were the Countesse of Furli,[19] when
Count Hieronimo of Furli her husband was slaine; for by
meanes thereof she escap'd the peoples rage, and attended
aid from Milan, and so recoverd her State: and then such

were the times that the stranger could not assist the people: but afterwards they servd her to little purpose, when Cæsar Borgia assaild her,[20] and that the people which was her enemy, sided with the stranger. Therefore both then, and at first, it would have been more for her safety, not to have been odious to the people, than to have held the Fortresses.

These things being well weigh'd then, I will commend those that shall build up Fortresses, and him also that shall not; and I will blame him, howsoever he be that relying upon those, shall make small account of being hated by his people.

CHAPTER XXI

How a Prince Ought to Behave Himselfe to Gaine Reputation

THERE is nothing gaines a Prince such repute, as great exployts, and rare trialls of himselfe in Heroicke actions.

We have now in our dayes Ferdinand King of Arragon the present King of Spain: hee in a manner may be termd a new Prince, for from a very weak King, hee is now become for fame and glory, the first King of Christendome, and if you shall well consider his actions, you shall find them all illustrious, and every one of them extraordinary.

Hee in the beginning of his reigne assaild Granada, and that exployt was the ground of his State. At first hee made that warre in security and without suspicion he should be any wayes hindred, and therein held the Barons of Castiglias minds busied, who thinking upon that warre, never minded any innovation; and in this while he gaind credit and authority with them, they not being aware of

83

it; was able to maintaine with the Church, and the peoples
mony all his souldiers, and to lay a foundation for his
military ordinances with that long warre: which afterwards
gaind him exceeding much honour.

Besides this, to the end hee might be able here-among
to undertake greater matters, serving himselfe alwaies of
the colour of religion; hee gave himselfe to a kind of
religious cruelty, chasing and dispoyling those Jewes out
of the Kingdome; nor can this example bee more admirable and rare: under the same cloke hee invaded Affrick
and went through with his exployt in Italy: and last of
all hath he assaild France, and so alwaies proceeded on
forwards contriving of great matters: which always have
held his subjects minds in peace and admiration, and
busied in attending the event what it should bee: and
these his actions have thus grown, one upon another, that
they have never given leysure to men so to rest, as that
they might ever plot any thing against them.

Moreover it much availes a Prince to give extraordinary
proofes of himselfe touching the government within, such
as those wee have heard of Bernard of Milan; whensoever
occasion is given by any one, that may effectuate some
great thing either of good or evill, in the civill government;
and to finde out some way either to reward or punish it,
whereof in the world much notice may be taken.

And above all things a Prince ought to endeavour in
all his actions to spread abroad a fame of his magnificence
and worthinesse.

A Prince also is well esteemd, when hee is a true friend,
or a true enemy, when without any regard hee discovers
himselfe in favour of one against another; which course
shall bee alwayes more profit, than to stand neuter: for if
two mighty ones that are thy neighbours come to fall out,
or are of such quality, that one of them vanquishing, thou
art like to be in feare of the vanquisher; or not; in either
of these two cases, it will ever prove more for thy profit
to discover thy selfe, and make a good war of it: for in

the first case, if thou discoverst not thy selfe, thou shalt alwayes bee a prey to him that overcomes, to the contentment and satisfaction of the vanquisht; neither shalt thou have reason on thy side, nor any thing else to defend or receive thee.

For hee that overcomes, will not have any suspected freinds, that give him no assistance in his necessity: and hee that loses, receives thee not, because thou wouldst not with thy armes in hand runne the hazzard of his fortune. Antiochus passd into Greece thereunto induc'd by the Etolians, to chace the Romans thence: and sent his Ambassadors to the Achayans, who were the Romans friends, to perswade them to stand neuters; on the other side the Romans mov'd them to joyne armes with theirs: this matter came to bee deliberated on in the counsell of the Achayans, where Antiochus his Ambassadour encouragd them to stand neuters, whereunto the Romans Ambassadour answerd. Touching the course, that is commended to you, as best and profitablest for your State, to wit, not to intermeddle in the warre between us, nothing can be more against you: because, not taking either part, you shall remaine without thanks, and without reputation a prey to the Conquerour.

And it will alwayes come to passe that hee who is not thy freind, will require thy neutrality, and hee that is thy friend, will urge thee, to discover thy selfe by taking armes for him: and evill advisd Princes, to avoyd the present dangers, follow often times that way of neutrality, and most commonly goe to ruine: but when a Prince discovers himselfe strongly in favour of a party, if hee to whom thou cleavest, overcomes, however that hee be puissant, and thou remainst at his disposing, hee is oblig'd to thee, and there is a contract of friendship made; and men are never so openly dishonest, as with such a notorious example of dishonesty to oppresse thee. Besides victories are never so prosperous, that the conquerour is like to neglect all respects, and especially of justice. But if he to whom thou stickst, loses, thou art receivd by him; and, while hee is able, he aydes thee, and so thou becomst partner of a fortune that may arise againe.

In the second case, when they that enter into the lists, together, are of such quality, that thou needst not feare him that vanquisheth, so much the more is it discretion in thee to stick to him; for thou goest to ruine one with his assistance, who ought to doe the best hee could to save him, if he were well advisd; and hee overcomming, is left at thy discretion, and it is unpossible but with thy ayd he must overcome.

And here it is to be noted, that a Prince should bee well aware never to joyne with any one more powerfull than himselfe, to offend another, unlesse upon necessity as formerly is said. For when he overcomes, thou art left at his discretion; and Princes ought avoid as much as they are able, to stand at anothers discretion. The Venetians took part with France against the Duke of Milan, and yet could have avoided that partakeing, from which proceeded their ruine. But when it cannot bee avoyded, as it befell the Florentines, when the Pope and the King of Spain went both with their armies to assaile Lombardy, there the Prince ought to side with them for the reasons aforesaid. Nor let any State think they are able to make such sure parties; but rather that they are all doubtfull; for in the order of things wee find it alwayes, that whensoever a man seeks to avoid one inconvenient; hee incurres another. But the principall point of judgement, is in discerning between the qualities of inconvenients, and not taking the bad for the good.

Moreover a Prince ought to shew himself a lover of vertue, and that he honours those that excell in every Art.

Afterwards ought hee incourage his Citizens, whereby they may bee enabled quickly to exercise their faculties as well in merchandise, and husbandry, as in any other kind of traffick, to the end that no man forbeare to adorne and cultivate his possessions for feare, that hee be despoyld of them; or any other to open the commerce upon the danger of heavy impositions: but rather to provide rewards for those that shall set these matters afoot, or for any one else that shall any way amplifie his City or State.

Besides hee ought in the fit times of the yeare entertain the people with Feasts and Maskes; and because every City is devided into Companyes, and Arts, and Tribes; hee ought to take speciall notice of those bodies, and some times afford them a meeting, and give them some proofe of his humanity, and magnificence; yet withall holding firme the majestie of his State, for this must never faile in any case.

CHAPTER XXII

Touching Princes Secretaries

IT is no small importance to a Prince, the choyce he makes of servants, being ordinarily good, or bad, as his wisdome is. And the first conjecture one gives of a great man, and of his understanding, is upon the sight of his followers and servants hee hath about him, when they prove able and faithfull, and then may hee alwayes be reputed wise; because hee hath knowne how to discerne those that are able, and to keepe them true to him. But when they are otherwise, there can be no good conjecture made of him, for the first errour hee commits, is in this choyce.

There was no man, that had any knowledge of Antony of Vanafro, the servant of Pandulfus Petrucci Prince of Siena, who did not esteeme Pandulfus for a very discreet man, having him for his servant. And because there are three kinds of understandings, the one that is advisd by it selfe; the other that understands when it is informd by another; the third that neither is advisd by it selfe, nor

by the demonstration of another; the first is best, the
second is good, and the last quite unprofitable. Therefore
it was of necessity, that if Pandulfus attain not the first
degree, yet hee got to the second; for whenever any one
hath the judgement to discerne between the good and the
evill, that any one does and sayes, however that hee hath
not this invention from himselfe, yet still comes hee to
take notice of the good or evill actions of that servant;
and those hee cherishes, and these hee suppresses; insomuch that the servant finding no meanes to deceive his
master, keeps himselfe upright and honest.

But how a Prince may throughly understand his servant,
here is the way that never failes. When thou seest, the
servant study more for his owne advantage than thine,
and that in all his actions, hee searches most after his
owne profit; this man thus qualified, shall never prove
good servant, nor canst thou ever relie upon him: for he
that holds the sterne of the State in hand, ought never
call home his cares to his owne particular, but give himselfe wholly over to his Princes service, nor ever put him
in mind of any thing not appertaining to him.

And on the other side the Prince to keepe him good to
him, ought to take a care for his servant, honouring him,
enriching, and obliging him to him, giving him part both
of dignities and offices, to the end that the many honors
and much wealth bestowd on him, may restraine his desires from other honours, and other wealth, and that those
many charges cause him to feare changes that may fall,
knowing hee is not able to stand without his master.

And when both the Princes and the servants are thus
disposd, they may rely the one upon the other: when
otherwise, the end will ever prove hurtfull for the one as
well as for the other.

CHAPTER XXIII

That Flatterers Are to Bee Avoyded

I WILL not omit one principle of great importance, being an errour from which Princes with much difficulty defend themselves, unlesse they be very discreet, and make a very good choice; and this is concerning flatterers, whereof all writings are full: and that because men please themselves so much in their owne things, and therein cozen themselves, that very hardly can they escape this pestilence; and desiring to escape it, there is danger of falling into contempt; for there is no other way to bee secure from flattery, but to let men know, that they displease thee not in telling thee truth: but when every one hath this leave, thou losest thy reverence.

Therefore ought a wise Prince take a third course, making choyce of some understanding men in his State, and give only to them a free liberty of speaking to him the truth: and touching those things only which hee inquires of, and nothing else; but hee ought to be inquisitive of every thing, and heare their opinions, and then afterwards advise himselfe after his owne manner, and in these deliberations, and with every one of them so carry himselfe, that they all know, that the more freely they shall speake, the better they shall be lik'd of: and besides those, not give eare to any one, and thus pursue the thing resolvd on, and thence continue obstinate in the resolution taken. Hee who does otherwise, either falls upon flatterers, or often changes upon the varying of opinions, from whence proceeds it that men conceive but slightly of him. To this purpose I will alleadge you a modern example.

Pre' [21] Lucas a servant of Maximilians the present Emperour,[22] speaking of his Majesty, said that hee never advisd with any body, nor never did any thing after his owne way: which was because he took a contrary course to what wee have now said: for the Emperour is a close man, who communicates his secrets to none, nor takes counsaile of any one: but as they come to be put in practise, they begin to be discoverd and knowne, and so contradicted by those that are neare about him, and hee as being an easie man, is quickly wrought from them. Whence it comes, that what hee does to day, hee undoes on the morrow; and that hee never understands himself what he would, nor what hee purposes, and that there is no grounding upon any of his resolutions.

A Prince therefore ought alwayes to take counsell, but at his owne pleasure, and not at other mens; or rather should take away any mans courage to advise him of any thing, but what hee askes: but hee ought well to aske at large; and then touching the things inquird of, be a patient hearer of the truth, and perceiving that for some respect the truth were conceald from him, be displeasd thereat.

And because some men have thought, that a Prince that gaines the opinion to bee wise, may be held so, not by his owne naturall indowments, but by the good counsells hee hath about him; without question they are deceivd; for this is a generall rule and never failes, that a Prince who of himselfe is not wise, can never bee well advisd, unlesse he should light upon one alone, wholly to direct and governe him, who himselfe were a very wise man. In this case it is possible hee may bee well governd: but this would last but little: for that governour in a short time would deprive him of his State; but a Prince not having any parts of nature, being advisd of more than one, shall never bee able to unite these counsells: of himselfe shall hee never know how to unite them, and each one of the counsellers, probably will follow that which is most properly his owne; and hee shall never finde the meanes to amend or discerne these things, nor can they fall out otherwise, because men always prove mischievous, unlesse upon some necessity they be forc'd to become good: wee conclude therefore, that counsells from whencesoever they proceed, must needs take their beginning from the Princes wisdome, and not the wisdome of the Prince from good counsells.

CHAPTER XXIV

Wherefore the Princes of Italy Have Lost Their States

WHEN these things above said are well observ'd, they make a new Prince seeme as if he had been of old, and presently render him more secure and firme in the State, than if he had already grown ancient therein: for a new Prince is much more observd in his actions, than a Prince by inheritance, and when they are known to bee vertuous, men are much more gaind and oblig'd to them thereby, than by the antiquity of their bloud: for men are much more taken by things present, than by things past; and when in the present they find good, they content themselves therein, and seeke no further, or rather they undertake the defence of him to their utmost, when the Prince is not wanting in other matters to himselfe; and so shall he gaine double glory to have given a beginning to a new Principality, adorn'd, and strengthnd it with good lawes, good arms, good friends, and good examples; as hee shall have double shame, that is borne a Prince, and by reason of his small discretion hath lost it.

And if we shall consider those Lords, that in Italy have lost their States in our dayes, as the King of Naples, the Duke of Milan, and others; first we shall find in them a common defect, touching their armes, for the reasons which have been above discoursd, at length, Afterwards we shall see some of them, that either shall have had the people for their enemies; or be it they had the people to friend, could never know how to assure themselves of the great ones: for without such defects as these, States are not lost, which have so many nerves, that they are able to maintaine an army in the field.

Philip of Macedon, not the father of Alexander the Great, but he that was vanquishd by Titus Quintius, had not much State in regard of the greatnesse of the Romanes and of Greece that assail'd him, neverthelesse in that he was a warlike man and knew how to entertaine the people and assure himselfe of the Nobles, for many yeares he made the warre good against them: and though at last some town perhaps were taken from him, yet the King-dome remaind in his hands still.

Wherefore these our Princes who for many yeares had continued in their Principalities, for having afterwards lost them, let them not blame Fortune, but their own sloth; because they never having thought during the times of quiet, that they could suffer a change (which is the common fault of men, while faire weather lasts, not to provide for the tempest) when afterwards mischiefes came upon them, thought rather upon flying from them, than upon their defence, and hop'd that the people, weary of the vanquishers insolence, would recall them: which course when the others faile, is good: but very ill is it to leave the other remedies for that: for a man would never go to fall, beleeving another would come to take him up: which may either not come to passe, or if it does, it is not for thy security, because that defence of his is vile, and de-pends not upon thee; but those defences only are good, certaine, and durable, which depend upon thy owne selfe, and thy owne vertues.

CHAPTER XXV

How Great Power Fortune Hath in Humane
Affaires, and What Meanes There Is
to Resist It

IT is not unknown unto me, how that many have held opinion, and still hold it, that the affaires of the world are so governd by fortune, and by God, that men by their wisdome cannot amend or alter them; or rather that there is no remedy for them: and hereupon they would think that it were of no availe to take much paines in any thing, but leave all to be governd by chance.

This opinion hath gain'd the more credit in our dayes, by reason of the great alteration of things, which wee have of late seen, and do every day see, beyond all humane conjecture: upon which, I some times thinking, am in some part inclind to their opinion: neverthelesse not to extinguish quite our own free will, I think it may be true, that Fortune is the mistresse of one halfe of our actions; but yet that she lets us have rule of the other halfe, or little lesse. And I liken her to a precipitous torrent, which when it rages, over-flows the plaines, overthrowes the trees, and buildings, removes the earth from one side, and laies it on another, every one flyes before it, every one yeelds to the fury thereof, as unable to withstand it; and yet however it be thus, when the times are calmer, men are able to make provision against these excesses, with banks and fences so, that afterwards when it swels again, it shall all passe smoothly along, within its channell, or else the violence thereof shall not prove so licentious and hurtfull. In like manner befals it us with fortune, which there shewes her power where vertue is not ordeind to resist her, and thither turnes she all her forces, where shee perceives that no provisions nor resistances are made to uphold her.

And if you shall consider Italy, which is the seat of these changes, and that which hath given them their motion, you shall see it to be a plaine field, without any trench or banck; which had it been fenc'd with convenient vertue, as was Germany, Spaine, or France; this inundation would never have causd these great alterations it hath, or else would it not have reach'd to us: and this shall suffice to have said, touching the opposing of fortune in generall.

But restraining my selfe more to particulars: I say, that to day we see a Prince prosper and flourish, and to morrow utterly go to ruine; not seeing that he hath alterd any condition or quality; which I beleeve arises first from the causes which wee have long since run over, that is because that Prince that relies wholly upon fortune, ruines, as her wheele turnes.

I beleeve also, that he proves the fortunate man, whose manner of proceeding meets with the quality of the times: and so likewise he unfortunate, from whose course of proceeding the times differ: for we see that men, in the things that induce them to the end, (which every one propounds to himselfe, as glory and riches) proceed therein diversly; some with respects, others more bold, and rashly; one with violence, and th'other with cunning; the one with patience, th'other with its contrary; and every one by severall ways may attaine thereto.

We see also two very respective and wary men, the one come to his purpose, and th'other not; and in like manner two equally prosper taking divers courses, th'one being wary, th'other headstrong; which proceeds from nothing else, but from the quality of the times, which agree, or not, with their proceedings. From hence arises that which I said, that two working diversly, produce the same effect;

and two equally working, th'one attaines his end, th'other not.

Hereupon also depends the alteration of the good; for if to one that behaves himself with warinesse and patience, times and affaires turne so favourably, that the carriage of his businesse prove well, hee prospers; but if the times and affaires change, he is ruind; because he changes not his manner of proceeding: nor is there any man so wise, that can frame himselfe hereunto; as well because he cannot go out of the way, from that whereunto Nature inclines him: as also, for that one having alwayes prosperd, walking such a way cannot be perswaded to leave it: and therefore the respective and wary man, when it is fit time for him to use violence and force, knows not how to put it in practise, wherupon hee is ruind: but if he could change his disposition with the times and the affaires, he should not change his fortune.

Pope Julius the second, proceeded in all his actions with very great violence, and found the times and things so conformable to that his manner of proceeding, that in all of them he had happy successe. Consider the first exploit he did at Bolonia, even while John Bentivolio liv'd: the Venetians were not well contented therewith; the King of Spaine likewise with the French, had treated of that enterprise; and notwithstanding all this, hee stirrd up by his own rage and fiercenesse, personally undertook that expedition: which action of his put in suspence and stopt Spaine and the Venitians, those for feare, and th'others for desire to recover the Kingdome of Naples; and on th'other part drew after him the King of France: for that King seeing him already in motion, and desiring to hold him his friend, whereby to humble the Venetians, thought he could no way deny him his souldiers, without doing him an open injury.

Julius then effected that with his violent and heady motion, which no other Pope with all humane wisdome could ever have done; for if hee had expected to part from

95

Rome with his conclusions settled, and all his affaires
ordered before hand, as any other Pope would have done,
hee had never brought it to passe: For the King of France
would have devisd a thousand excuses, and others would
have put him in as many feares.

I will let passe his other actions, for all of them were
alike, and all of them prov'd lucky to him; and the brevity
of his life never sufferd him to feele the contrary: for had
he litt upon such times afterwards, that it had been necessary for him to proceed with respects, there had been his
utter ruine; for hee would never have left those wayes, to
which he had been naturally inclind.

I conclude then, fortune varying, and men continuing
still obstinate to their own wayes, prove happy, while
these accord together: and as they disagree, prove unhappy: and I think it true, that it is better to be heady,
than wary: because Fortune is a mistresse; and it is necessary, to keep her in obedience, to ruffle and force her: and
we see, that she suffers her selfe rather to be masterd by
those, than by others that proceed coldly. And therefore,
as a mistresse, shee is a friend to young men, because
they are lesse respective, more rough, and command her
with more boldnesse.

CHAPTER XXVI

An Exhortation to Free Italy from the Barbarians

HAVING then weigh'd all things above discoursd, and devising with my selfe, whether at this present in Italy the
times might serve to honour a new Prince, and whether
there were matter, that might minister occasion to a wise

and valourous Prince, to introduce such a forme, that might doe honour to him, and good to the whole generalty of the people in the countrey: me thinks so many things concurre in favour of a new Prince, that I know not whether there were ever any time more proper for this purpose.

And if as I said, it was necessary, desiring to see Moyses his vertue, that the children of Israel should bee inthrald in Ægypt; and to have experience of the magnanimity of Cyrus his minde, that the Persians should be oppresd by the Medes; and to set forth the excellency of Theseus, that the Athenians should bee dispersd: so at this present now wee are desirous to know the valour of an Italian spirit, it were necessary Italy should bee reduc'd to the same termes it is now in, and were in more slavery, than the Hebrews were; more subject than the Persians; more scatterd than the Athenians; without head, without order, batterd, pillagd, rent asunder, overrunne, and had undergone all kind of destruction.

And however even in these later dayes, wee have had some kinde of shew of hope in some one,[23] whereby wee might have conjectur'd, that hee had been ordeind for the deliverance hereof, yet it prov'd afterwards, that in the very height of all his actions hee was curb'd by fortune, insomuch that this poore countrey remaining as it were without life, attends still for him that shall heale her wounds, give an end to all those pillagings and sackings of Lombardy, to those robberies and taxations of the Kingdome, and of Tuscany, and heale them of their soares, now this long time gangren'd.

We see how she makes her prayers to God, that he send some one to redeem her from these Barbarous cruelties and insolences.

Wee see her also wholly ready and disposd to follow any colours, provided there bee any one to take them up.

Nor doe wee see at this present, that shee can look for other, than your Illustrious Family,[24] to become Cheiftaine

97

of this deliverance, which hath now by its owne Vertue and Fortune been so much exalted, and favour by God and the Church, whereof it now holds the Principality: and this shall not be very hard for you to doe, if you shall call to minde the former actions, and lives of those that are above named. And though those men were very rare and admirable, yet were they men, and every one of them began upon lesse occasion than this; for neither was their enterprise more just than this, nor more easie; nor was God more their friend, than yours.

Here is very great justice: for that warre is just, that is necessary; and those armes are religious, when there is no hope left otherwere, but in them.

Here is an exceeding good disposition thereto: nor can there be, where there is a good disposition, a great difficulty, provided that use bee made of those orders, which I propounded for ayme and direction to you.

Besides this, here we see extraordinary things without example effected by God; the sea was opened, a cloud guided the way, devotion powrd forth the waters, and it raind downe manna; all these things have concurrd in your greatnesse, the rest is left for you to doe. God will not doe every thing himself, that he may not take from us our free will, and part of that glory that belongs to us.

Neither is it a marvell, if any of the aforenamd Italians have not been able to compasse that, which wee may hope your Illustrious family shall: though in so many revolutions of Italy, and so many feats of warr, it may seeme that the whole military vertue therein be quite extinguisht; for this arises from that the ancient orders thereof were not good; and there hath since been none that hath knowne how to invent new ones.

Nothing can so much honour a man rising anew, as new lawes and new ordinances devisd by him: these things when they have a good foundation given them, and containe in them their due greatnesse, gaine him reverence and admiration; and in Italy their wants not the matter wherein to introduce any forme. Here is great vertue in the members, were it not wanting in the heads.

Consider in the single fights that have been, and duells, how much the Italians have excell'd in their strength, activity and adresse; but when they come to armies, they appeare not, and all proceeds from the weaknesse of the Chieftaines; for they that understand the managing of these matters, are not obeyd, and every one presumes to understand; hitherto there having not been any one so highly raisd either by fortune or vertue, as that others would submit unto him. From hence proceeds it, that in so long time, and in so many battles fought for these last past 20 yeers, when there hath been an army wholly Italian, it alwayes hath had evill successe; whereof the river Tarus first was witnesse, afterwards Alexandria, Capua, Genua, Vayla, Bolonia, Mestri.

Your Illustrious family then being desirous to tread the footsteps of these Worthyes, who redeemed their countryes, must above all things as the very foundation of the whole fabrick, be furnished with souldiers of your owne natives: because you cannot have more faithfull, true, nor better souldiers; and though every one of them be good, all together they will become better when they shall find themselves entertaind, commanded, and honourd by their owne Prince. Wherefore it is necessary to provide for those armes, whereby to be able with the Italian valour to make a defence against forreiners.

And however the Swisse infantery and Spanish bee accounted terrible; yet is there defect in both of them, by which a third order might not only oppose them, but may bee confident to vanquish them: for the Spanyards are not able to indure the Horse, and the Swisse are to feare the Foot, when they incounter with them as resolute in the fight as they. Whereupon it hath been seene, and upon experience shall bee certaine, that the Spaniards are not able to beare up against the French Cavalery, and the Swisses have been routed by the Spanish Foot. And though touching this last, there hath not been any entire experience had, yet was there some proofe thereof given in the battell of Ravenna, when the Spanish Foot affronted the Dutch batallions, which keepe the same ranke the Swisses doe, where the Spanyards with their nimblenesse of body, and the help of their targets entred in under their Pikes, and there stood safe to offend them; the Dutch men having no remedy: and had it not been for the Cavalery that rushd in upon them, they had quite defeated them.

There may then (the defect of the one and the other of these two infanteries being discoverd) another kind of them bee anew ordaind, which may bee able to make resistance against the Horse, and not feare the Foot, which shall not be a new sort of armes, but a change of orders. And these are some of those things which ordaind anew, gaine reputation and greatnesse to a new Prince.

Therefore this occasion should not bee let passe, to the end that Italy after so long a time may see some one redeemer of hers appeare. Nor can I expresse with what dearnesse of affection hee would be receiv'd in all those countryes which have sufferd by those forrein scumms, with what thirst of revenge, with what resolution of fidelity, with what piety, with what teares. Would any gates bee shut against him? Any people deny him obedience? Any envy oppose him? Would not every Italian fully consent with him? This government of the Barbarians stinks in every ones nostrills.

Let your Illustrious Family then undertake this worthy exployt with that courage and those hopes wherewith such just actions are to be attempted; to the end that under your colours, this country may be ennobled, and under the protection of your Fortune that saying of Petrarch bee verifyd.

> *Vertu contr' al furore*
> *Prendera l'arme, & fia il combatter corto:*
> *Che l'antico valore*
> *Ne gli Italici cor non è anchor morto.*

Vertue 'gainst fury shall advance the fight,
And it i'th' combate soone shall put to flight:
For th'old Romane valour is not dead,
Nor in th' Italians brests extinguished.

FINIS

UTOPIA

Sir Thomas More

Thomas More

TO PETER GILES,

SENDETH GRETYNGE.

I AM almoste ashamed, righte welbeloved Peter Giles,[1] to send unto you this boke of the Utopian commen wealth, welniegh after a yeres space, whiche I am sure you looked for within a moneth and a halfe. And no marveil. For you knewe well ynough that I was alreadye disbourdened of all the laboure and studye belongynge to the invention in this worke, and that I had no nede at al to trouble my braines about the disposition or conveiaunce of the matter: and therfore had herein nothing els to do, but only to rehearse those thinges, whiche you and I togethers hard maister Raphael tel and declare. Wherefore there was no cause why I shuld study to set forth the matter with eloquence: for as much as his talke could not be fine and eloquent, beynge firste not studied for, but suddein and unpremeditate, and then, as you know, of a man better sene in the Greke language, then in the Latin tonge. And my writynge, the niegher it should approche to his homely plaine, and simple speche, somuche the niegher shuld it go to the trueth: which is the onelye marke, wherunto I do and ought to directe all my travail and study herin.

I graunte and confesse, frende Peter, myselfe discharged of so muche laboure, havinge all these thinges ready done to my hande, that almooste there was nothinge left for me to do. Elles either the invention, or the disposition of this matter myghte have required of a witte neither base,

105

neither at all unlearned, both some time and leasure and also some studie. But if it were requisite and necessarie, that the matter shoulde also have bene wrytten eloquentlie, and not alone truelye: of a sueretie that thynge coulde I have perfourmed by no tyme nor studye. But now seynge all these cares, stayes and lettes were taken awaye, wherin elles so muche laboure and studye shoulde have bene employed, and that there remayned no other thynge for me to do, but onelye to write playnelie the matter as I hard it spoken: that in deede was a thynge lighte and easye to be done. Howbeit to the dispatchynge of thys so lytle busynesse, my other cares and troubles did leave almost lesse then no leasure. Whiles I doo dayelie bestowe my time aboute lawe matters: some to pleade, some to heare, some as an arbitratoure with myne awarde to determine, some as an umpier or a judge, with my sentence finallye to discusse. Whiles I go one waye to see and visite my frende: another waye about myne owne privat affaires. Whiles I spende almost al the day abrode emonges other, and the residue at home among mine owne; I leave to my self, I meane to my booke, no time.

For when I am come home, I muste commen with my wife, chatte with my children and talke wyth my servauntes. All the whiche thinges I recken and accompte amonge businesse, forasmuche as they muste of necessitie be done: and done muste they nedes be, onelesse a man wyll be straunger in his owne house. And in any wyse a man muste so fashyon and order hys conditions, and so appoint and dispose himselfe, that he be merie, jocunde and pleasaunt amonge them, whom eyther nature hathe provided, or chaunce hath made, or he hym selfe hath chosen to be the felowes and companyons of hys life: so that with to muche gentle behavioure and familiaritie, he do not marre them, and by to muche sufferaunce of his servauntes make them his maysters. Emonge these thynges now rehearsed, stealeth awaye the daye, the moneth, the yeare. When do I write then? And all this while have I

spoken no worde of slepe, neyther yet of meate, which
emong a great number doth wast no lesse tyme then doeth
slepe, wherein almoste halfe the life tyme of man crepeth
awaye. I therefore do wynee and get onelye that tyme,
whiche I steale from slepe and meate. Whiche tyme because it is very litle, and yet somwhat it is, therefore have I
ones at the laste, thoughe it be longe first, finished Utopia;
and have sent it to you, frende Peter, to reade and peruse:
to the intente that yf anye thynge have escaped me, you
might put me in remembraunce of it.

For thoughe in this behalfe I do not greatlye mistruste
my selfe (whiche woulde God I were somwhat in wit
and learninge, as I am not all of the worste and dullest
memorye) yet have I not so great truste and confidence
in it, that I thinke nothinge coulde fall out of my mynde.
For John Clement [2] my boye, who as you know was there
presente with us, whome I suffer to be awaye frome no
talke, wherein maye be any profyte or goodnes (for oute
of this yonge bladed and new shotte up corne, whiche
hathe alreadye begon to spring up both in Latin and Greke
learnyng, I loke for plentifull increase at length of goodly
rype grayne) he, I saye, hathe broughte me into a greate
doubte. For wheras Hythlodaye (onelesse my memorye
fayle me) sayde that the bridge of Amaurote, whyche
goethe over the river of Anyder is fyve hundreth paseis,
that is to saye, halfe a myle in lengthe: my John sayeth
that two hundred of those paseis muste be plucked away,
for that the ryver conteyneth there not above three hundreth paseis in breadthe, I praye you hartelye call the
matter to youre remembraunce. For yf you agree wyth
hym, I also wyll saye as you saye, and confesse myselfe
deceaved. But if you cannot remember the thing, then
surelye I wyll write as I have done and as myne owne
remembraunce serveth me.

For as I wyll take good hede, that there be in my booke
nothing false, so yf there be anye thynge doubtefull, I
wyll rather tell a lye, then make a lie: bycause I had

rather be good, then wilie. Howebeit thys matter maye
easelye be remedied, yf you wyll take the paynes to aske
the question of Raphael him selfe by woorde of mouthe,
if he be nowe with you, or elles by youre letters. Whiche
you muste nedes do for another doubte also, that hathe
chaunced, throughe whose faulte I cannot tel: whether
through mine, or yours, or Raphaels. For neyther we re-
membred to enquire of him, nor he to tel us in what part
of the newe world Utopia is situate. The whiche thinge,
I had rather have spent no small somme of money, then
that it should thus have escaped us: as well for that I am
ashamed to be ignoraunt in what sea that ylande standeth,
wherof I write so long a treatise, as also because there be
with us certen men, and especiallie one vertuous and
godly man, and a professour of divinitie, who is excedynge
desierous to go unto Utopia: not for a vayne and curious
desyre to see newes, but to the intente he maye further
and increase oure religion, whiche is there alreadye luck-
elye begonne. And that he maye the better accomplyshe
and perfourme this hys good intente, he is mynded to
procure that he maye be sente thether by the hieghe
byshoppe: yea, and that he himselfe may be made
bishoppe of Utopia, beynge nothynge scrupulous herein,
that he muste obteyne this byshopricke with suete. For he
counteth that a godly suete, which procedeth not of the
desire of honoure or lucre, but onelie of a godlie zeale.

Wherfore I moste earnestly desire you, frende Peter, to
talke with Hythlodaye, yf you can, face to face, or els to
wryte youre letters to hym, and so to woorke in thys
matter, that in this my booke there maye neyther anye
thinge be founde, whyche is untrue, neyther any thinge
be lacking, whiche is true. And I thynke verelye it shal be
well done, that you shewe unto him the book it selfe. For
yf I have myssed or fayled in anye poynte, or if anye faulte
have escaped me, no man can so well correcte and amende
it, as he can: and yet that can he not do, oneles he peruse
and reade over my booke written. Moreover by this

meanes shall you perceave, whether he be well wyllynge
and content, that I shoulde undertake to put this woorke in
writyng. For if he be mynded to publyshe, and put forth
his owne laboures, and travayles himselfe, perchaunce he
woulde be lothe, and so woulde I also, that in publishynge
the Utopiane weale publyque, I shoulde prevent him, and
take frome him the flower and grace of the noveltie of this
his historie.

Howbeit, to saye the very trueth, I am not yet fullye
determined with my selfe, whether I will put furth my
booke or no. For the natures of man be so divers, the
phantasies of some so waywarde, their myndes so unkynde,
their judgementes so corrupte, that they which leade a
merie and a jocounde lyfe, folowynge theyr owne sensuall
pleasures and carnall lustes, maye seme to be in a muche
better state or case, then they that vexe and unquiete
themselves with cares and studie for the puttinge forthe
and publishynge of some thynge, that maye be either
profeit or pleasure to others: whiche others nevertheles
will disdainfully, scornefully, and unkindly accepte the
same. The moost part of al be unlearned. And a greate
number hathe learning in contempte. The rude and barbarous alloweth nothing, but that which is verie barbarous
in dede. If it be one that hath a little smacke of learnynge,
he rejecteth as homely geare and commen ware, whatsoever is not stuffed full of olde moughteaten termes, and
that be worne out of use.

Some there be that have pleasure onelye in olde rustie
antiquities. And some onelie in their owne doynges. One
is so sowre, so crabbed, and so unpleasaunte, that he can
awaye with no myrthe nor sporte. An other is so narrowe
betwene the shulders, that he can beare no jestes nor
tauntes. Some seli poore soules be so afearde that at everye
snappishe woorde their nose shall be bitten of, that they
stande in no lesse drede of everye quicke and sharpe
woorde, then he that is bitten of a madde dogge feareth
water. Some be so mutable and waverynge, that every

109

houre they be in a newe mynde, sayinge one thinge syttinge and an other thynge standynge. An other sorte sytteth
upon their allebencheis, and there amonge their cuppes
they geve judgement of the wittes of writers, and with
greate authoritie they condempne, even as pleaseth them,
everye writer accordynge to his writinge, in moste spitefull
maner mockynge, lowtinge and flowtinge them; beyng
them selves in the meane season sauffe and, as sayeth the
proverbe, oute of all daunger of gonneshotte. For why,
they be so smugge and smothe, that they have not so much
as one hearre of an honeste man, wherby one may take
holde of them. There be moreover some so unkynde and
ungentle, that thoughe they take great pleasure, and delectation in the worke, yet for all that, they can not fynde
in their hertes to love the author therof, nor to aforde him
a good woorde: beynge much like uncourteous, unthankfull, and chourlish gestes. Whiche when they have with
good and daintie meates well fylled theire bellyes, departe
home, gevyng no thankes to the feaste maker. Go your
wayes now and make a costlye feaste at youre owne
charges for gestes so dayntie mouthed, so divers in taste,
and besides that of so unkynde and unthankfull natures.
But nevertheles (frende Peter) doo, I pray you, with
Hithloday, as I willed you before. And as for this matter
I shall be at my libertie, afterwardes to take newe advisement. Howbeit, seeyng I have taken great paynes and
laboure in writyng the matter, if it may stande with his
mynde and pleasure, I wyll as touchyng the edition or
publishyng of the booke, followe the counsell and advise
of my frendes, and speciallye yours. Thus fare you well

right hertely beloved frende Peter,

with your gentle wife: and

love me as you have ever

done, for I love you

better then

ever I

dyd.

THE FIRST BOOKE

of the Communication of RAPHAEL HYTHLODAY,

Concernyng

the Best State of a Commen Welth.

THE moste victorious and triumphant kyng of Englande Henrye the eyght of that name, in al roial vertues, a prince most perelesse, hadde of late in controversie with Charles, the right highe and mightye kyng of Castell, weighty matters and of great importaunce. For the debatement and final determinatioñ wherof, the kinges Majesty sent me ambassadour into Flaunders, joyned in commission with Cuthbert Tunstall,[3] a man doutlesse out of comparison, and whom the kynges Majestie of late, to the great rejoysynge of all men, dyd preferre to the office of Maister of the Rolles.

But of this mannes prayses I wyll saye nothyng, not bicause I doo feare that small credence shal be geven to the testimonye that cometh out of a frendes mouthe: but bicause his vertue and lernyng be greater, and of more excellency, then that I am able to praise them: and also in all places so famous and so perfectly well knowne, that they neede not, nor oughte not of me to bee praysed, unlesse I woulde seeme to shew and set furth the brightnes of the sonne with a candell, as the proverbe saieth. There mette us at Bruges (for thus it was before agreed) thei whom their Prince hadde for that matter appoynted commissioners: excellent men all. The chiefe and the head of theym was the Maregrave (as thei call him) of Bruges, a right honorable man: but the wisest and the best spoken of them was George Temsice, provost of Casselses, a man,

111

not only by lernyng, but also by nature of singular eloquence, and in the lawes profoundly learned: but in rea-
sonynge and debatyng of matters, what by his naturall
witte, and what by daily exercise, surely he hadde few
fellowes. After that we had once or twise mette, and upon
certayne poyntes or articles coulde not fully and throughly
agree, they for a certayne space tooke their leave of us,
and departed to Bruxelle, there to know their Princes
pleasure. I in the meane time (for so my busines laye)
wente streighte thence to Antwerpe. Whiles I was there
abidynge, often times amonge other, but whiche to me was
more welcome then annye other, dyd visite me one Peter
Giles, a citisen of Antwerpe, a man there in his countrey
of honest reputation, and also preferred to high promotions, worthy truly of the hyghest. For it is hard to say,
whether the yong man be in learnyng, or in honestye
more excellent. For he is bothe of wonderfull vertuous conditions, and also singularly wel learned, and towardes all
sortes of people excedyng gentyll: but towardes his frendes
so kynde herted, so lovyng, so faithfull, so trustye, and of
so earnest affection, that it were verye harde in any place to
fynde a man, that with him in all poyntes of frendshippe
maye be compared. No man can be more lowlye or courteous. No man useth lesse simulation or dissimulation, in
no man is more prudent simplicitie. Besides this, he is in
his talke and communication so merye and pleasaunte, yea
and that withoute harme, that throughe his gentyll inter-
taynement, and his sweete and delectable communication,
in me was greatly abated and diminished the fervente desyre, that I had to see my native countrey, my wyfe and
my chyldren, whom then I dyd muche longe and covete to
see, because that at that time I had been more than iiii.
monethes from them. Upon a certayne daye when I hadde
herde the divine service in our Ladies churche, which is
the fayrest, the most gorgeous and curious churche of
buyldyng in all the citie and also most frequented of
people and, the service beynge doone, was readye to go

home to my lodgynge, I chaunced to espye this foresayde Peter talkynge with a certayne straunger, a man well stricken in age, with a blacke sonneburned face, a longe bearde, and a cloke cast homly about his shoulders, whome by his favoure and apparell furthwith I judged to bee a mariner. But the sayde Peter seyng me, came unto me and saluted me.

And as I was aboute to answere him: see you this man, sayth he (and therewith he poynted to the man, that I sawe hym talkynge with before) I was mynded, quod he, to brynge him strayghte home to you.

He should have ben very welcome to me, sayd I, for your sake.

Nay (quod he) for his owne sake, if you knewe him: for there is no man thys day livyng, that can tell you of so many estraunge and unknowen peoples, and countreyes, as this man can. And I know wel that you be very desirous to heare of such newes.

Then I conjectured not farre a misse (quod I) for even at the first syght I judged him to be a mariner.

Naye (quod he) there ye were greatly deceyved, he hath sailed in deede, not as the mariner Palinure, but as the experte and prudent prince Ulisses: yea, rather as the auncient and sage philosopher Plato. For this same Raphaell Hythlodaye [4] (for this is his name) is very well lerned in the Latine tongue: but profounde and excellent in the Greke language. Wherin he ever bestowed more studye then in the Latine, bycause he had geven him-selfe wholy to the study of philosophy. Wherof he knew that ther is nothyng extante in Latine, that is to anye purpose, savynge a fewe of Senecaes, and Ciceroes doo-ynges. His patrimonye that he was borne unto, he lefte to his brethern (for he is a Portugall borne) and for the desire that he had to see, and knowe the farre countreyes of the worlde, he joyned himselfe in company with Amerike Vespuce, and in the iii. last voyages of those iiii. that be nowe in printe and abrode in every mannes handes, he

113

continued styll in his company, savyng that in the last
voyage he came not home agayne with him. For he made
suche meanes and shift, what by intretaunce, and what by
importune sute, that he gotte licence of mayster Americke
(though it were sore against his wyll) to be one of the
xxiiii whiche in the ende of the last voyage were left in
the countrey of Gulike. He was therefore lefte behynde
for hys mynde sake, as one that tooke more thoughte and
care for travailyng then dyenge: havyng customably in
his mouth these saiynges: he that hathe no grave, is covered with the skye: and, the way to heaven out of all
places is of like length and distaunce. Which fantasy of
his (if God had not ben his better frende) he had surely
bought full deare. But after the departynge of mayster
Vespuce, when he had travailed thorough and aboute
many countreyes with v. of his companions Gulikianes, at
the last by merveylous chaunce he arrived in Taprobane,
from whence he went to Caliquit, where he chaunced to
fynde certayne of hys countreye shippes, wherein he re-
tourned agayne into his countreye, nothynge lesse then
looked for.

All this when Peter hadde tolde me, I thanked him for
his gentle kindnesse, that he had vouchsafed to brynge me
to the speache of that man, whose communication he
thoughte shoulde be to me pleasaunte and acceptable.
And therewith I tourned me to Raphaell. And when wee
hadde haylsed eche other, and had spoken these commune
woordes, that bee customablye spoken at the first meting
and acquaintaunce of straungers, we went thence to my
house, and there in my gardaine upon a bench covered
with greene torves we satte downe talkyng together. There
he tolde us, how that after the departyng of Vespuce, he
and his fellowes, that taried behynde in Gulicke, began
by litle and litle, throughe fayre and gentle speache, to
wynne the love and favoure of the people of that countreye, insomuche that within shorte space, they dyd dwell
amonges them, not only harmlesse, but also occupiyng

114

with them verye familiarly. He tolde us also, that they were in high reputation and favour with a certayne great man (whose name and countreye is nowe quite out of my remembraunce) which of his mere liberalitie dyd beare the costes and charges of him and his fyve companions. And besides that gave theim a trustye guyde to conducte them in their journey (which by water was in botes, and by land in wagons) and to brynge theim to other princes with verye frendlye commendations.

Thus after manye dayes journeys, he sayd, they founde townes and cities and weale publiques, full of people, governed by good and holsome lawes. For under the line equinoctiall, and on bothe sydes of the same, as farre as the sonne doth extende his course, lyeth (quod he) great and wyde desertes and wildernesses, parched, burned and dryed up with continuall and intollerable heate. All thynges bee hideous, terrible, lothesome and unpleasaunt to beholde: all thynges out of fassyon and comelinesse, inhabited withe wylde beastes and serpentes, or at the leaste wyse, with people, that be no lesse savage, wylde and noysome, then the verye beastes theim selves be. But a little farther beyonde that, all thynges beginne by litle and lytle to waxe pleasaunte; the ayre softe, temperate and, gentle; the grounde covered with grene grasse; lesse wildnesse in the beastes. At the last shall ye come agayne to people, cities and townes wherein is continuall entercourse and occupiyng of merchaundise and chaffare, not only among themselves and with theire borderers, but also with merchauntes of farre countreyes, bothe by lande and water. There I had occasion (sayd he) to go to many countreyes on every syde. For there was no shippe ready to any voyage or journey, but I and my fellowes were into it very gladly receyved. The shippes that thei founde first were made playn, flatte and broade in the botome, trough wise. The sayles were made of great russhes, or of wickers, and in some places of lether. Afterwarde thei founde shippes with ridged kyeles, and sayles of canvasse, yea,

115

and shortly after, havyng all thynges lyke oures. The ship-
men also very experte and cunnynge, bothe in the sea and
in the wether. But he saide that he founde great favoure
and frendship amonge them, for teachynge them the feate
and the use of the lode stone, whiche to them before that
time was unknowne. And therfore they were wonte to be
verye timerous and fearfull upon the sea; nor to venter
upon it, but only in the somer time. But nowe they have
suche a confidence in that stone, that they feare not stormy
winter: in so dooynge farther from care then daunger; in
so muche, that it is greatly to be doubted, lest that thyng,
throughe their owne folish hardinesse, shall tourne them
to evyll and harme, which at the first was supposed shoulde
be to them good and commodious.

But what he tolde us that he sawe in everye countreye
where he came, it were very longe to declare; neither it is
my purpose at this time to make rehersall therof. But
peradventure in an other place I wyll speake of it, chiefly
suche thynges as shall be profitable too bee knowen, as in
speciall be those decrees and ordinaunces, that he marked
to be well and wittely provided and enacted amonge suche
peoples, as do live together in a civile policye and good
ordre. For of suche thynges dyd wee buselye enquire and
demaunde of him, and he likewise very willingly tolde us
of the same. But as for monsters, bycause they be no
newes, of them we were nothyng inquisitive. For nothyng
is more easye to bee founde, then bee barkynge Scyllaes,
ravenyng Celenes, and Lestrigones devourers of people, and
suche lyke great, and incredible monsters. But to fynde
citisens ruled by good and holsome lawes, that is an exceding rare, and harde thyng. But as he marked many fonde,
and folisshe lawes in those newe founde landes, so he
rehersed divers actes, and constitutions, whereby these oure
cities, nations, countreis, and kyngdomes may take example
to amende their faultes, enormities and errours. Wherof in
another place (as I sayde) I wyll intreate.

Now at this time I am determined to reherse only that

116

he tolde us of the maners, customes, lawes, and ordinaunces of the Utopians. But first I wyll repete oure
former communication by thoccasion, and (as I might
saye) the drifte wherof, he was brought into the mention
of that weale publique.

For, when Raphael had very prudentlye touched divers
thynges that be amisse, some here and some there, yea,
very many on bothe partes; and againe had spoken of suche
wise lawes and prudente decrees, as be established and
used, bothe here amonge us and also there amonge theym,
as a man so perfecte, and experte in the lawes, and customes of every severall countrey, as though into what place
soever he came geastwise,[5] there he had ledde al his life:
then Peter muche mervailynge at the man: Surely maister
Raphael (quod he) I wondre greatly, why you gette you not
into some kinges courte. For I am sure there is no prince
livyng, that wold not be very glad of you, as a man not
only hable highly to delite him with your profounde learnyng, and this your knowlege of countreis, and peoples, but
also mete to instructe him with examples, and helpe him
with counsell. And thus doyng, you shall bryng your selfe
in a verye good case, and also be of habilitie to helpe all
your frendes and kinsfolke.

As concernyng my frendes and kynsfolke (quod he) I
passe not greatly for them. For I thinke I have sufficiently
doone my parte towardes them already. For these thynges,
that other men doo not departe from, untyl they be olde
and sycke, yea, whiche they be then verye lothe to leave,
when they canne no longer keepe, those very same thynges
dyd I beyng not only lustye and in good helth, but also
in the floure of my youth, divide among my frendes and
kynsfolkes. Which I thynke with this my liberalitie ought
to holde them contented, and not to require nor to loke
that besydes this, I shoulde for their sakes geve myselfe in
bondage unto kinges.

Nay, God forbyd that (quod Peter) it is notte my mynde
that you shoulde be in bondage to kynges, but as a re-

tainour to them at your pleasure. Whiche surely I thinke is the nighest waye that you can devise howe to bestowe your time frutefully, not onlye for the private commoditie of your frendes and for the generall profite of all sortes of people, but also for thadvauncement of your self to a much welthier state and condition, then you be nowe in.

To a welthier condition (quod Raphael) by that meanes, that my mynde standeth cleane agaynst? Now I lyve at libertie after myne owne mynde and pleasure, whiche I thynke verye fewe of these great states and pieres of realmes can saye. Yea, and there be ynow of them that sue for great mens frendeshippes: and therfore thinke it no great hurte, if they have not me, nor iii. or iiii. suche other as I am.

Well, I perceive playnly frende Raphael (quod I) that you be desirous neither of richesse nor of power. And truly I have in no lesse reverence and estimation a man of your mynde, then anye of theim all that bee so high in power and authoritie. But you shall doo as it becometh you: yea, and accordyng to this wisdome, to this high and free courage of yours, if you can finde in your herte so to appoynt and dispose your selfe, that you mai applye your witte and diligence to the profite of the weale publique, thoughe it be somewhat to youre owne payne and hyndraunce. And this shall you never so wel doe, nor wyth so greate proffitte perfourme, as yf you be of some greate princes counsel, and put into his heade (as I doubte not but you wyl) honeste opinions and vertuous persuasions. For from the prince, as from a perpetual wel sprynge, commethe amonge the people the floode of al that is good or evell. But in you is so perfitte lernynge, that withoute anye experience, and agayne so greate experience, that wythoute anye lernynge you maye well be any kinges counsellour.

You be twyse deceaved, maister More, (quod he) fyrste in me, and agayne in the thinge it selfe. For neither is in me the habilitye that you force upon me, and yf it wer never so much, yet in disquieting myne owne quietnes I should nothing further the weale publique. For first of all, the moste parte of all princes have more delyte in warlike matters and feates of chivalrie (the knowlege wherof I neither have nor desire) than in the good feates of peace: and employe muche more study, how by right or by wrong to enlarge their dominions, than howe wel and peaceablie to rule and governe that they have alredie. Moreover, they that be counsellours to kinges, every one of them eyther is of him selfe so wise in dede, that he nedeth not, or elles he thinketh himself so wise, that he wil not allowe another mans counsel, saving that they do shamefully and flatteringly geve assent to the fond and folishe sayinges of certeyn great men. Whose favours, bicause they be in high authoritie with their prince, by assentation and flatterie they labour to obteyne. And verily it is naturally geven to all men to esteme their owne inventions best. So both the raven and the ape thincke their owne yonge ones fairest. Than if a man in such a company, where some disdayne and have despite at other mens inventions, and some counte their owne best, if among suche menne (I say) a man should bringe furth any thinge, that he hath redde done in tymes paste, or that he hath sene done in other places: there the hearers fare as though the whole existimation of their wisdome were in jeoperdye to be overthrowen, and that ever after thei shoulde be counted for verye diserdes, unles they could in other mens inventions pycke out matter to reprehend, and find fault at. If all other poore helpes fayle, then this is their extreame refuge. These thinges (say they) pleased our forefathers and auncestours; wolde God we coulde be so wise as thei were: and as though thei had wittely concluded the matter, and with this answere stopped every mans mouth, thei sitte downe againe. As who should sai, it were a very daungerous matter, if a man in any pointe should be founde wiser then his forefathers were. And yet bee we content to suffre the best and wittiest of their decrees to lye unexecuted: but if in any thing a better ordre might have ben taken, then by them was, there we take fast hold, findyng therin many faultes. Manye tymes have I chaunced upon such proude, leude, over-thwarte and waywarde judgementes, yea, and once in England:

I prai you Syr (quod I) have you ben in our countrey?

Yea forsoth (quod he) and there I taried for the space of iiii. or v. monethes together, not longe after the insurrec-tion, that the westerne English men made agaynst their kyng, which by their owne miserable and pitiful slaughter was suppressed and ended.[6] In the meane season I was muche bounde and beholdynge to the righte reverende father, Jhon Morton, Archebishop and Cardinal of Canter-bury,[7] and at that time also lorde Chauncelloure of Eng-lande: a man, Mayster Peter, (for Mayster More knoweth already that I wyll saye) not more honorable for his autho-ritie, then for his prudence and vertue. He was of a meane stature, and though stricken in age, yet bare he his bodye upright. In his face did shine such an amiable reverence, as was pleasaunte to beholde, gentill in communication, yet earnest, and sage. He had great delite manye times with roughe speache to his sewters, to prove, but withoute harme, what prompte witte and what bolde spirite were in every man. In the which, as in a vertue much agreinge with his nature, so that therewith were not joyned impudency, he toke greate delectatyon. And the same person, as apte and mete to have an administratyon in the weale publique, he dyd lovingly embrace. In his speche he was fyne, elo-quent and pytthye. In the lawe he had profounde knowl-edge, in witte he was incomparable, and in memory won-derful excellente. These qualityes, which in hym were by nature singular, he by learnynge and use had made per-fecte. The kynge put muche truste in his counsel, the weale publyque also in a maner leaned unto hym, when I was there. For even in the chiefe of his youth he was taken from schole into the courte, and there passed all his tyme in much trouble and busines, beyng continually tumbled

and tossed in the waves of dyvers mysfortunes and adversities. And so by many and greate daungers he lerned the
experience of the worlde, whiche so beinge learned can not
easely be forgotten. It chaunced on a certayne daye, when
I sate at his table, there was also a certayne laye man
cunnynge in the lawes of youre realme. Who, I can not tell
wherof takynge occasion, began diligently and earnestly
to prayse that strayte and rygorous justice, which at that
tyme was there executed upon fellones, who, as he sayde,
were for the moste parte xx. hanged together upon one
gallowes. And, seyng so fewe escaped punyshement, he
sayde he coulde not chuse, but greatly wonder and marvel,
howe and by what evil lucke it shold so come to passe, that
theves nevertheles were in every place so ryffe and so
rancke. Naye, Syr, quod I (for I durst boldely speake my
minde before the Cardinal) marvel nothinge hereat: for
this punyshment of theves passeth the limites of justice,
and is also very hurtefull to the weale publique. For it is to
extreame and cruel a punishment for thefte, and yet not
sufficient to refrayne and withhold men from thefte. For
simple thefte is not so great an offense, that it owght to be
punished with death. Neither ther is any punishment so
horrible, that it can kepe them from stealynge, which have
no other craft, wherby to get their living. Therfore in this
poynte, not you onlye, but also the most part of the world,
be like evyll scholemaisters, which be readyer to beate, then
to teache their scholers. For great and horrible punish-
mentes be appointed for theves, whereas much rather
provision should have ben made, that there were some
meanes, whereby they myght get their livyng, so that no
man shoulde be dryven to this extreme necessitie, firste to
steale, and then to dye. Yes (quod he) this matter is wel
ynough provided for already. There be handy craftes, there
is husbandrye to gette their livynge by, if they would not
willingly be nought. Nay, quod I, you shall not skape so:
for first of all, I wyll speake nothynge of them, that come
home oute of the warres, maymed and lame, as not longe

ago, oute of Blackeheath fielde, and a litell before that, out
of the warres in Fraunce: suche, I saye, as put their lives
in jeoperdye for the weale publiques or the kynges sake,
and by reason of weakenesse and lamenesse be not hable
to occupye their olde craftes, and be to aged to lerne new:
of them I wyll speake nothing, forasmuch as warres have
their ordinarie recourse. But let us considre those thinges
that chaunce daily before our eyes.

First there is a great numbre of gentlemen, which can
not be content to live idle themselves, lyke dorres, of that
whiche other have laboured for: their tenauntes I meane,
whom they polle and shave to the quicke, by reisyng their
rentes (for this onlye poynte of frugalitie do they use,
men els through their lavasse and prodigall spendynge,
hable to brynge theymselfes to verye beggerye) these
gentlemen, I say, do not only live in idlenesse themselves,
but also carrye about with them at their tailes a great
flocke or traine of idle and loyterynge servyngmen, which
never learned any craft wherby to gette their livynges.
These men as sone as their mayster is dead, or be sicke
themselfes, be incontinent thrust out of dores. For gentlemen hadde rather keepe idle persones, then sicke men, and
many times the dead mans heyre is not hable to mainteine
so great a house, and kepe so many serving men as his
father dyd. Then in the meane season they that be thus
destitute of service, either starve for honger, or manfullye
playe the theves. For what would you have them to do?
When they have wandred abrode so longe, untyl they have
worne thredebare their apparell, and also appaired their
helth, then gentlemen because of their pale and sickely
faces, and patched cotes, will not take them into service.
And husbandmen dare not set them a worke, knowynge
wel ynoughe that he is nothing mete to doe trewe and
faythful service to a poore man wyth a spade and a mattoke
for small wages and hard fare, whyche beynge deyntely
and tenderly pampered up in ydilnes and pleasure, was
wont with a sworde and a buckler by hys syde to jette

122

through the strete with a bragginge loke, and to thynke hym selfe to good to be anye mans mate.

Naye, by saynt Mary, sir (quod the lawier) not so. For this kinde of men muste we make moste of. For in them as men of stowter stomackes, bolder spirites, and manlyer courages then handycraftes men and plowemen be, doth consiste the whole powre, strength and puissaunce of oure army, when we muste fight in battayle.

Forsothe, sir, as well you myghte saye (quod I) that for warres sake you muste cheryshe theves. For suerly you shall never lacke theves, whyles you have them. No, nor theves be not the most false and faynt harted soldiers, nor souldiours be not the cowardleste theves: so wel thees ii. craftes agree together. But this faulte, though it be much used amonge you, yet is it not peculiar to you only, but commen also almoste to all nations. Yet Fraunce besides this is troubled and infected with a much sorer plage. The whole royalme is fylled and besieged with hiered souldiours in peace tyme (yf that bee peace) whyche be brought in under the same colour and pretense, that hath persuaded you to kepe these ydell servynge men. For thies wyse fooles and verye archedoltes thought the wealthe of the whole countrey herin to consist, if there were ever in a redinesse a stronge and sure garrison, specially of old practised souldiours, for they put no trust at all in men unexercised. And therfore they must be forced to seke for warre, to the ende thei may ever have practised souldiours and cunnyng mansleiers, lest that (as it is pretely sayde of Salust) their handes and their mindes through idlenes or lacke of exercise, should waxe dul. But howe pernitious and pestilenet a thyng it is to maintayne suche beastes, the Frenche men, by their owne harmes have learned, and the examples of the Romaynes, Carthaginiens, Syriens and of manye other countreyes doo manifestly declare. For not onlye the empire, but also the fieldes and cities of all these, by divers occasions have been overrunned and destroyed of their owne armies before hande had in a redinesse. Now how unnecessary a thinge this is, hereby it maye appeare: that the French souldiours, which from their youth have ben practised and inured in feates of armes, do not cracke nor advaunce themselfes to have very often gotte the upper hand and maistry of your new made and unpractised souldiours.

But in this poynte I wyll not use many woordes, leste perchaunce I maye seeme to flatter you. No, nor those same handy crafte men of yours in cities, nor yet the rude and uplandish plowmen of the countrye, are not supposed to be greatly affrayde of your gentlemens idle servyngmen, unlesse it be suche as be not of body or stature correspondent to their strength and courage, or els whose bolde stomakes be discouraged throughe povertie. Thus you may see, that it is not to be feared lest they shoulde be effeminated, if thei were brought up in good craftes and laboursome woorkes, whereby to gette their livynges, whose stoute and sturdye bodyes (for gentlemen vouchsafe to corrupte and spill none but picked and chosen men) now either by reason of rest and idlenesse be brought to weakenesse: or els by easy and womanly exercises be made feble and unhable to endure hardnesse. Truly howe so ever the case standeth, thys me thinketh is nothing avayleable to the weale publique, for warre sake, which you never have, but when you wyl your selfes, to kepe and mainteyn an unnumerable flocke of that sort of men, that be so troublesome and noyous in peace, wherof you ought to have a thowsand times more regarde, then of warre. But yet this is not only the necessary cause of stealing. There is an other, whych, as I suppose, is proper and peculiar to you Englishmen alone.

What is that, quod the Cardinal? forsoth my lorde (quod I) your shepe that were wont to be so meke and tame, and so smal eaters, now, as I heare say, be become so great devowerers and so wylde, that they eate up, and swallow downe the very men them selfes. They consume, destroye, and devoure whole fieldes, howses, and cities.

For looke in what partes of the realme doth growe the fynest and therfore dearest woll, there noblemen and gentlemen, yea and certeyn abbottes, holy men no doubt, not contenting them selfes with the yearely revenues and profytes, that were wont to grow to theyr forefathers and predecessours of their landes, nor beynge content that they live in rest and pleasure nothinge profiting, yea much noyinge the weale publique, leave no grounde for tillage, thei inclose al into pastures; thei throw doune houses; they plucke downe townes, and leave nothing standynge, but only the churche to be made a shepehowse. And as thoughe you loste no small quantity of grounde by forestes, chases, laundes and parkes, those good holy men turne all dwellinge places and all glebeland into desolation and wildernes.

Therfore that one covetous and unsatiable cormaraunte and very plage of his natyve contrey maye compasse aboute and inclose many thousand akers of grounde together within one pale or hedge, the husbandmen be thrust owte of their owne, or els either by coveyne and fraude, or by violent oppression they be put besydes it, or by wronges and injuries thei be so weried, that they be compelled to sell all: by one meanes therfore or by other, either by hooke or crooke they muste needes departe awaye, poore, selye, wretched soules, men, women, husbands, wives, fatherlesse children, widowes, wofull mothers, with their yonge babes, and their whole houshold smal in substance and muche in numbre, as husbandrye requireth manye handes. Awaye thei trudge, I say, out of their knowen and accustomed houses, fyndynge no place to reste in. All their housholdestuffe, whiche is verye litle woorthe, thoughe it myght well abide the sale: yet beeynge sodainely thruste oute, they be constrayned to sell it for a thing of nought. And when they have wandered abrode tyll that be spent, what can they then els doo but steale, and then justly pardy be hanged, or els go about a beggyng. And yet then also they be caste in prison as vagaboundes, because they go aboute and worke not: whom no man wyl set a worke, though thei never so willyngly profre themselves therto.

For one shephearde or heardman is ynoughe to eate up that grounde with cattel, to the occupiyng wherof aboute husbandrye manye handes were requisite. And this is also the cause why victualles be now in many places dearer. Yea, besides this the price of wolle is so rysen, that poore folkes, which were wont to worke it and make cloth therof, be nowe hable to bye none at all. And by thys meanes verye manye be forced to forsake worke, and to geve them selves to idelnesse. For after that so much grounde was inclosed for pasture, an infinite multitude of shepe dyed of the rotte, suche vengeaunce God toke of their inordinate and unsaciable covetousnes, sendinge amonge the shepe that pestiferous morrein, whiche much more justely shoulde have fallen on the shepemasters owne heades. And though the number of shepe increase never so faste, yet the price falleth not one myte, because there be so fewe sellers. For they be almooste all comen into a fewe riche mennes handes, whome no neade forceth to sell before they lust, and they luste not before they maye sell as deare as they luste.

Now the same cause bringeth in like dearth of the other kindes of cattell, yea and that so much the more, bicause that after fermes plucked downe and husbandry decaied, there is no man that passethe for the breadynge of younge stoore. For these riche men brynge not up the yonge ones of greate cattel as they do lambes. But first they bie them abrode verie chepe and afterward, when they be fatted in their pastures, they sell them agayne excedynge deare. And therefore (as I suppose) the whole incommoditie hereof is not yet felte. For yet they make dearth onely in those places where they sell. But when they shall fetche them away from thence wheare they be bredde faster then they can be broughte up: then shall there also be felte greate dearth, stoore beginning there to faile, where the ware is boughte. Thus the unreasonable covetousnes of a few hath turned that thing to the utter undoing of your ylande, in the whiche thynge the cheife felicitie of your realme did consist. For this greate dearth of victualles causeth men to kepe as litle houses and as smale hospitalitie as they possible maye, and to put away their servauntes: whether, I pray you, but a beggynge: or elles (whyche these gentell bloudes and stoute stomackes wyll sooner set their myndes unto) a stealing?

Nowe to amende the matter, to this wretched beggerye and miserable povertie is joyned great wantonnes, importunate superfluitie and excessive riote. For not only gentle mennes servauntes, but also handicrafe men: yea and almooste the ploughmen of the countrey, with al other sortes of people, use muche straunge and proude newefanglenes in their apparell, and to muche prodigall riotte and sumptuous fare at their table. Nowe bawdes, queines, whoores, harlottes, strumpettes, brothelhouses, stewes, and yet another stewes, wynetavernes, ale houses and tiplinge houses, with so manye noughtie, lewde and unlawfull games, as dyce, cardes, tables, tennis, boules, coytes, do not all these sende the haunters of them streyghte a stealynge when theyr money is gone? Caste oute these pernicyous abhominations, make a lawe, that they, whiche plucked downe fermes and townes of husbandrie, shal reedifie them, or els yelde and uprender the possession therof to suche as wil go to the cost of buylding them anewe. Suffer not these riche men to bie up al, to ingrosse and forstalle, and with their monopolie to kepe the market alone as please them. Let not so many be brought up in idelnes, let husbandry and tillage be restored, let clotheworkinge be renewed, that ther may be honest labours for this idell sort to passe their tyme in profitablye, whiche hitherto either povertie hath caused to be theves, or elles nowe be either vagabondes, or idel serving men, and shortelye wilbe theves. Doubtles onles you finde a remedy for these enormities, you shall in vaine advaunce your selves of executing justice upon fellons. For this

justice is more beautiful in apperaunce, and more florish-
ynge to the shewe, then either juste or profitable. For by
suffring your youthe wantonlie and viciously to be brought
up, and to be infected, even frome theyr tender age, by
litle and litle with vice: then a Goddes name to be punished, when they commit the same faultes after being come
to mans state, which from their youthe they were ever
like to do: In this pointe, I praye you, what other thing do
you, then make theves and then punish them?

Now as I was thus speakinge, the lawier began to make
hym selfe readie to answere, and was determined with him
selfe to use the common fashion and trade of disputers,
whiche be more diligent in rehersinge, then answering, as
thinking the memorie worthy of the chief praise. In dede
sir, quod he, you have said wel, being but a straunger and
one that myghte rather heare some thing of these matters,
then have any exacte or perfecte knowledge of the same,
as I wil incontinent by open proffe make manifest and
plaine. For firste I will reherse in order all that you have
sayde: then I wyll declare wherein you be deceaved,
through lacke of knowledge, in all oure fashions, maners
and customes: and last of all I will aunswere youre argu-
mentes and confute them every one. Firste therefore I wyll
begynne where I promysed. Foure thynges you semed to
me. Holde youre peace, quod the Cardinall: for it appeareth that you will make no shorte aunswere, which make
suche a beginnynge. Wherefore at this time you shall not
take the paynes to make youre aun[s]were, but kepe it
to youre nexte meatynge, which I woulde be righte glad,
that it might be even to morrowe next, onles either you or
mayster Raphael have any earnest let. But nowe, mayster
Raphael, I woulde verye gladlye heare of you, why you
thinke thefte not worthye to be punished with deathe, or
what other punishemente you can devise more expedient
to the weale publique. For I am sure you are not of that
minde, that you woulde have thefte escape unpunished.
For yf nowe the extreme punishemente of deathe can not

cause them to leave stealinge, then yf ruffians and robbers shoulde be suer of their lyves; what violence, what feare were hable to holde their handes from robbinge, whiche woulde take the mitigation of the punishmente, as a verye provocation to the mischiefe?

Suerlye my lorde, quod I, I thinke it not ryght nor justice, that the losse of money should cause the losse of mans life. For myne opinion is, that all the goodes in the worlde are not hable to countervayle mans life. But if they would thus say; that the breakynge of justice, and the transgression of the lawes is recompensed with this punishment, and not the losse of the money, then why maye not this extreme and rigorous justice wel be called plaine injurie? For so cruell governaunce, so streite rules, and unmercyful lawes be not allowable, that if a small offense be committed, by and by the sword should be drawen: nor so stoical ordinaunces are to be borne withall, as to counte al offenses of suche equalitie, that the killing of a man, or the takyng of his money from him were both a matter, and the one no more heinous offense then the other: betwene the whyche two, yf we have anye respecte to equitie, no similitude or equalitie consisteth. God commaundeth us that we shall not kill. And be we then so hastie to kill a man for takinge a litle money? And if any man woulde understande killing by this commaundement of God to be forbidden after no larger wise, then mans constitutions define killynge to be lawfull, then whye maye it not lykewise by mans constitutions be determined after what sort whordome, fornication and perjurie may be lawfull? For whereas, by the permission of God, no man hath power to kil neither himself, nor yet anye other man: then yf a lawe made by the consent of men, concerninge slaughter of men, oughte to be of suche strengthe, force and vertue, that they which contrarie to the commaundement of God have killed those, whom this constitution of man commaunded to be killed, be cleane quite and exempte out of the bondes and daunger of Gods commaundement: shall it not then by this reason folow, that the power of Gods commaundemente shall extende no further, then mans lawe doeth define, and permitte? And so shall it come to passe, that in like maner mans constitutions in al thinges shal determine how farre the observation of all Gods commaundementes shall extende.

To be shorte Moyses law, though it were ungentle and sharpe, as a law that was geven to bondmen; yea, and them very obstinate, stubborne, and styfnecked; yet it punished thefte by the purse, and not wyth death. And let us not thinke that God in the newe law of clemencie and mercye, under the whiche he ruleth us with fatherlie gentlenes, as his deare children, hathe geven us greater scoupe and licence to the execution of cruelte, one upon another. Nowe ye have heard the reasons whereby, I am persuaded that this punishement is unlawful. Furthermore I thinke ther is no body that knoweth not, how unreasonable, yea, how pernitious a thinge it is to the weale publike, that a thefe and an homicide or murderer, should suffer equall and like punishment. For the thefe seynge that man, that is condempned for thefte in no less jeoperdie, nor judged to no lesse punishment, then him that is convicte of manslaughter; throughe this cogitation onelye he is strongly and forciblye provoked, and in a maner constreined to kill him whome els he woulde have but robbed. For the murder beynge ones done, he is in lesse feare, and in more hoope that the deede shall not be bewrayed or knowen, seynge the partye is nowe deade and rydde oute of the waye, which onelye mighte have uttered and disclosed it. But if he chaunce to be taken and discrived, yet he is in no more daunger and jeoperdie, then if he had committed but single fellonye. Therfore whiles we go about with suche crueltie to make theves aferd, we provoke them to kil good men.

Now as touchinge this question, what punishmente were more commodious and better; that truelye in my judgemente is easier to be founde, then what punishment might be wurse. For why should we doubt that to be a good and a profytable waye for the punishemente of offendours, whiche we knowe did in tymes paste so longe please the Romaines, men in the administration of a weale publique mooste experte, politique, and cunnynge? Suche as amonge them were convicte of great and heynous trespaces, them they condempned into stone quarries, and into mienes to digge mettalle, there to be kepte in cheynes all the dayes of their life. But as concernyng this matter, I allow the ordinaunce of no nation so wel as that which I sawe, whiles I travailed abroade aboute the worlde, used in Persia amonge the people that commenly be called the Polylerites.[8] Whose land is both large and ample, and also well and wittelye governed: and the people in all conditions free and ruled by their owne lawes, saving that they paye a yearelye tribute to the great kinge of Persia. But bicause they be farre from the sea, compassed and inclosed almoste rounde aboute with hyghe mountaines, and do content them selves with the fruites of their owne lande, which is of it selfe verye fertile and frutfull: for this cause neither they go to other countreis, nor other come to them. And accordynge to the olde custome of the land, they desire not to enlarge the boundes of their dominions: and those that they have by reason of the highe hilles be easely defended: and the tribute whiche they paye to their chiefe lord and kinge setteth them quite and free from warfare. Thus their life is commodious rather then gallante, and may better be called happie or welthy, then notable or famous. For they be not knowen as much as by name, I suppose saving only to theyr next neighbours and borderes. They that in this lande be atteinted and convict of felony, make restitution of that which they stole, to the right owner, and not (as they do in other landes) to the kinge: whome they thinke to have no more righte to the thiefe-stolen thinge, then the thiefe him selfe hathe. But if the thing be loste or made away, then the value of it is paide of the gooddes of such offenders, which els remaineth all

131

whole to their wives and children. And they them selves
be condempned to be common laborers, and, oneles the
thefte be verie heinous, they be neyther locked in prison,
nor fettered in gives, but be untied and go at large, labor-
ing in the common workes. They that refuse labour, or go
slowly and slacklye to their worke; be not onelye tied in
cheynes, but also pricked forward with stripes. But beinge
diligente aboute theyr worke they live without checke or
rebuke. Every night they be called in by name, and be
locked in theyr chambers. Beside their dayly labour, their
life is nothing hard or incommodious. Their fare is indifferent good, borne at the charges of the weale publike,
bicause they be commen servauntes to the commen wealth.
But their charges in all places of the lande is not borne
alike. For in some partes that which is bestowed upon
them is gathered of almes. And thoughe that waye be un-
certein, yet the people be so ful of mercy and pitie, that
none is found more profitable or plentifull. In some places
certein landes be appointed hereunto, of the revenewes
whereof they be mainteined. And in some places everye
man geveth a certein tribute for the same use and purpose.
Againe in some partes of the land these serving men (for
so be these dampned persons called) do no common worke,
but as everye private man nedeth laborours, so he commeth
into the markette place, and there hierethe some of them
for meate and drinke, and a certeine limitted waiges by the
daye, sumwhat cheper then he shoulde hire a free man. It
is also lawefull for them to chastice the slouthe of these
servinge men with stripes.

By this meanes they never lacke worke, and besides the
gayninge of their meate and drinke, everye one of them
bringeth dailie some thing into the common treasourie. All
and every one of them be apparailed in one coloure. Their
heades be not polled or shaven, but rounded a lytle above
the eares. And the typpe of the one eare is cut of. Every
one of them maye take meate and drinke of their frendes,
and also a coate of their owne colloure: but to receive

money is deathe, as well to the gever, as to the receivoure.
And no lesse jeoperdie it is for a free man to receive
moneye of a seruynge manne for anye maner of cause:
and lykewise for servinge men to touche weapons. The
servinge men of every severall shire be distincte and
knowen frome other by their severall and distincte badges:
whiche to caste awaye is death: as it is also to be sene oute
of the precincte of their owne shire, or to talke with a
servinge man of another shyre. And it is no lesse daunger
to them, for to intende to runne awaye, then to do it in
dede. Yea and to conceal suche an enterpries in a servinge
man it is deathe, in a free man servitude. Of the contrairie
parte, to him that openeth and uttereth suche counselles, be
decreed large giftes: to a free man of great some of money,
to a serving man freedome: and to them bothe forgevenes
and pardone of that they were of counsell in that pretence.
So that it can never be so good for them to go forewarde in
their evyll purpose, as by repentaunce to tourne backe.

This is the lawe and order in this behalfe, as I have
shewed you. Wherein what humanitie is used, howe farre it
is frome crueltie, and howe commodyous it is, you do
playnelye perceave: for asmuche as the ende of their
wrath and punyshemente intendeth nothynge elles, but the
destruction of vices, and savynge of menne: wyth so usynge
and ordering them, that they can not chuse but be good,
and what harme so ever they did before, in the residewe
of theyr life to make amendes for the same. Moreover it is
so litle feared, that they shoulde tourne againe to their
vicious conditions, that wayefaringe men wyll for their savegarde chuse them to theyr guydes before any other, in
every sheire chaunging and taking new. For if they would
committe robbery, they have nothinge aboute them meate
for that purpose. They may touch no weapons: money
founde aboute them shoulde betraie the robbery. They
shoulde be no sooner taken with the maner, but furthwith
they shoulde be punished. Neither they can have any
hope at all to skape awaye by flienge. For howe should

133

a man, that in no parte of his apparell is like other men,
flye prevelie and unknowen, onles he woulde runne awaye
naked? Howebeit so also flyinge he shoulde be discrived
by the roundyng of his heade, and his eare-marke. But
it is a thinge to be doubted, that they will laye theyr
heddes together, and conspire againste the weale publique.
No, no, I warrante you. For the servyng men of one sheire
alone coulde never hoope to bringe to passe such an enterprise, without sollicitinge, entysinge, and allurynge the
servinge men of manye other shieres to take their partes.
Whiche thinge is to them so impossible, that they maye not
as much as speake or talke togethers, or salute one an other.
No, it is not to be thoughte that they woulde make theyr
owne countreymen and companions of their counsell in
suche a matter, whiche they knowe well should be jeopardie
to the concelour thereof, and great commoditie and goodnes to the opener and detectour of the same. Whereas on
the other parte, there is none of them all hopeles or in dispaire to recover againe his former estate of fredome, by
humble obedience, by paciente suffringe and by geving
good tokens and likelyhoode of himselfe, that he wyll, ever
after that, lyve like a trewe and an honest man. For
everye yeare divers of them be restored to their freedome:
throughe the commendation of their patience.

Whan I had thus spoken, sayinge moreover that I
coulde see no cause why this ordre might not be had in
Englande with muche more profyte, then the justice
whiche the lawyer so heighly praysed: Naye, quod the
lawier, this coulde never be so stablyshed in Englande, but
that it must nedes bringe the weale publike into great
jeoperdie and hasarde. And as he was thus sayinge, he
shaked his heade, and made a wrie mouthe, and so he
helde his peace. And all that were there present, with one
assent agreed to his sayinge.

Well, quod the Cardinall, yet it were harde to judge
withoute a proffe, whether this order would do wel here or
no. But when the sentence of death is geven if than the

kinge shoulde commaunde execution to be defferred and spared, and would prove this order and fassion: takinge awaye the priviliges of all saintuaries: if then the profe shoulde declare the thinge to be good and profitable, than it were wel done that it were stablished: els the condempned and reprived persons may as wel and as justly be put to death after this profe, as when they were first cast. Neither any jeoperdie can in the meane space growe herof. Yea, and me thynketh that these vagaboundes may very wel be ordered after the same fashion, against whom we have hitherto made so many lawes, and so litle prevailed.

When the Cardinall had thus saide, than every man gave greate praise to my sayinges, whiche a litle before they had disallowed. But moost of al was estemed that which was spoken of vagaboundes, bicause it was the Cardinalles owne addition. I can not tell whether it were best to reherse the communication that folowed, for it was not very sad. But yet you shall heare it, for there was no evil in it, and partlye it parteined to the matter before saide. There chaunced to stand by a certein jesting parasite, or scoffer, which wold seme to resemble and counterfeit the foole. But he did in such wise counterfeit, that he was almost the very same in dede that he labored to represent: he so studied with wordes and sayinges brought furth so out of time and place to make sporte and move laughter, that he himselfe was oftener laughed at then his jestes were. Yet the foolishe fellowe brought out now and then such indifferent and reasonable stuffe, that he made the proverbe true, which saieth: he that shoteth oft at the last shal hit the mark.

So that when one of the company sayd, that throughe my communication a good order was founde for theves, and that the Cardinal also had wel provided for vagaboundes, so that only remained some good provision to be made for them that through sicknes and age were fallen into povertie, and were become so impotent and unweldie, that they were not hable to worke for their livinge: Tushe (quod he) let me alone with them: you shall se me do well ynough with them. For I had rather then any good, that this kinde of people were driven sumwher oute of my sight, they have so sore troubled me manye times and ofte, when they have wyth their lamentable teares begged money of me: and yet they coulde never to my mynde so tune their songe, that thereby they ever got of me one farthinge. For ever more the one of these two chaunced: either that I would not, or els that I could not, bicause I had it not. Therfore now they be waxed wise. For when they see me go by, bicause they will not leese theyr labour, they let me passe and saye not one worde to me. So they loke for nothinge of me, no in good sothe no more, then yf I were a priest, or a monke. But I will make a lawe, that all these beggers shall be distributed, and bestowed into houses of religion. The men shal be made laye brethren, as they call them, and the women nunnes.

Hereat the Cardinal smiled, and allowed it in jest, yea and all the residue in good earnest. But a certeine freare, graduate in divinitie, toke suche pleasure and delite in this jeste of priestes and monkes, that he also beynge elles a man of grislie and sterne gravitie, began merilie and wantonlye to jeste and taunt. Naye, quod he, you shall not so be ridde and dispatched of beggers, oneles you make some provision also for us frears. Why, quod the jester, that is done alreadie, for my lord him selfe set a verye good order for you, when he decreed that vagaboundes should be kept straite and set to worke: for you be the greatest and veriest vagaboundes that be. This jest also, when they sawe the Cardinall not disprove it, every man toke it gladly, savying onelye the frear. For he (and that no marveile) beynge thus touched on the quicke, and hit on the gaule, so fret, so fumed, and chafed at it, and was in such a rage, that he could not refraine himselfe from chidinge, skolding, railing and reviling. He called the fellow ribbalde, villaine, javel, backbiter, sclaunderer, and the childe of perdition: citinge therwith terrible threateninges out of holie scripture. Then the jestynge scoffer beganne to playe the scoffer in dede, and verely he was good at yt, for he could play a part in that play no man better. Patient youre selfe, good maister freare, quod he, and be not angrie, for scripture saieth: in youre patience you shall save your soules. Then the freare (for I will rehearse his own very woordes) No, gallous wretche, I am not angrie (quod he) or at the leaste wise, I do not sinne: for the Psalmiste saith, be you angrie, and sinne not.

Then the Cardinal spake gently to the freare, and desired him to quiete himselfe. No my lord, quod he, I speak not but of a good zeale as I oughte: for holye men had a good zeale. Wherefore it is sayd: the zeale of thy house hath eaten me. And it is songe in the church, the skorners of Helizeus, whiles he went up into the house of God, felte the zeale of the bald, as peradventure this skorning villaine ribaulde shall feele. You do it (quod the Cardinall) perchaunce of a good mynde and affection: but me thinketh you should do, I can not tell whether more holilie, certes more wisely, yf you woulde not set youre witte to a fooles witte, and with a foole take in hande a foolishe contention. No forsoeth, my lorde, (quod he) I shoulde not do more wyselye. For Salomon the wyse saieth: Answere a foole accordinge to his folye, like as I do nowe, and do shew him the pit that he shall fall into, yf he take not hede. For if many skorners of Helizeus,[9] whiche was but one bald man, felte the zeale of the balde, how muche more shall one skorner of many frears feele, amonge whom be manye balde men? [10] And we have also the popes bulles, whereby all that mocke and skorne us be excommunicate, suspended and acursed.

The Cardinal, seeing that none ende would be made, sent awaie the jester by a prevy becke, and turned the communication to an other matter. Shortly after, when he was risen from the table, he went to heare his sueters, and so dismissed us. Looke, maister More, wyth how longe and tedious a tale I have kept you, whiche surely I woulde have bene ashamed to have done, but that you so earnestly desired me, and did after such a sorte geve eare unto it, as though you would not that any parcel of that communication should be left out. Whiche thoughe I have done sumwhat briefely, yet could I not chuse but rehearse it, for the judgemente of them, whyche when they had improved and disallowed my sayinges, yet incontinent, hearynge the Cardinall allowe them, dyd themselves also approve the same: so impudently flattering him, that they wer nothing ashamed to admitte, yea almoste in good earnest, his jesters folish inventions: bicause that he him selfe by smiling at them did seme not to disprove them. So that herby you may right wel perceave how litle the courtiers woulde regarde and esteme me and my sayinges.

I ensure you, maister Raphael, quod I, I toke greate delectacion in hearing you: all thinges that you saide were spoken so wittilye and so pleasauntly. And me thought me selfe to be in the meanetime, not onelye at home in my countrei, but also through the pleasaunt remembraunce of the Cardinal, in whose house I was broughte up of a childe, to waxe a child againe. And, frend Raphael, though I did beare verye greate love towardes you before, yet seynge you do so earnestlye favoure this man you wyll not beleve howe muche my love towardes you is nowe increased. But yet, all this notwithstandinge, I can by no meanes chaunge my mind, but that I must nedes believe, that you, if you be disposed, and can fynde in youre hearte to followe some princes courte, shall with your good counselles greatlye helpe and further the commen wealthe. Wherfore there is nothynge more apperteining to youre dewty, that is to saye, to the dewtie of a good man. For where as your Plato judgeth that weale publiques shall by this meanes atteyne perfecte felicitie, eyther if philosophers be kynges, or elles if kynges geve themselves to the studie of philosophie, how farre I praye you, shall commen wealthes then be frome thys felicitie, yf philosophers wyll vouchesaufe to enstruct kinges with their good counsell?

They be not so unkinde (quod he) but they woulde gladlye do it, yea, manye have done it alreadye in bookes that they have put furthe, if kynges and princes would be willynge and readye to folowe good counsell. But Plato doubtlesse dyd well foresee, onelesse kynges themselves woulde applye their mindes to the studye of Philosophie, that elles they woulde never thoroughlye allowe the counsell of philosophers, beynge themselves before even from their tender age infected, and corrupt with perverse and evill opinions. Whiche thynge Plato hymselfe proved trewe in kinge Dionyse. If I shoulde propose to any kyng wholsome decrees, doynge my endevoure to plucke out of hys mynde the pernicious originall causes of vice and noughtines, thinke you not that I shoulde furthewith either be driven awaye, or elles made a laughyng stocke.

Well suppose I were with the French kynge, and there syttinge in his counsell, whiles in that mooste secrete consultation, the kynge him selfe there beynge presente in hys owne personne, they beate their braynes and serche the verye bottomes of their wittes to discusse by what crafte and meanes the kynge maye styl kepe Myllayne, and drawe to him againe fugitive Naples, and then howe to conquere the Venetians, and howe to bringe under his jurisdiction all Italie, then howe to win the dominion of Flaunders, Brabant, and of all Burgundie: with divers other landes, whose kingdomes he hath longe ago in mind and purpose invaded. Here whiles one counselleth to conclude a legue of peace with the Venetians, so longe to endure, as shall be thought mete and expedient for their purpose, and to make them also of their counsell, yea, and besides that to geve them part of the pray, whiche afterwarde, when they have brought theyr purpose about after their owne myndes, they maye require and clayme againe. Another thinketh best to hiere the Germaynes. Another woulde have the favoure of the Swychers wonne with money. Anothers advyse is to appease the puissaunte power of the Emperoures majestie wyth golde, as with a moste pleas-

aunte and acceptable sacrifice. Whiles another gyveth
counsell to make peace wyth the kynge of Arragone, and
to restoore unto him hys owne kyngedome of Navarra, as
a full assuraunce of peace. Another commeth in with his
five egges, and adviseth to hooke in the kynge of Castell
with some hope of affinitie or allyaunce, and to bringe to
their parte certeine pieers of his courte for greate pensions.
Whiles they all staye at the chiefeste doubte of all, what to
do in the meane time with Englande, and yet agree all in
this to make peace with the Englishmen, and with mooste
suer and stronge bandes to bynde that weake and feable
frendeshippe, so that they muste be called frendes, and
hadde in suspicion as enemyes. And that therfore the
Skottes muste be hadde in a readines, as it were in a
standynge, readie at all occasions, in aunters the Englishmen shoulde sturre never so lytle, incontinent to set upon
them. And moreover previlie and secretlye (for openlie it
maye not be done by the truce that is taken) privelie therefore I saye to make muche of some piere of Englande, that
is bannished hys countrey, whiche muste cleime title to the
crowne of the realme, and affirme hym selfe juste in-
herytoure thereof, that by this subtill meanes they maye
holde to them the kinge, in whome elles they have but
small truste and affiaunce. Here I saye, where so great
and heyghe matters be in consultation, where so manye
noble and wyse menne counsell theyr kynge onelie to
warre, here yf I selie man shoulde rise up and will them
to tourne over the leafe, and learne a newe lesson, sayinge
that my counsell is not to medle with Italy, but to tarye
styll at home, and that the kyngedome of Fraunce alone is
almooste greater, then that it maye well be governed of
one man: so that the kynge shoulde not nede to studye
howe to gette more; and then shoulde propose unto them
the decrees of the people that be called the Achoriens,
whiche be situate over agaynste the Ilande of Utopia on
the southeaste side.

These Achoriens ones made warre in their kinges quarrell

for to gette him another kingdome, whiche he laide claime unto, and avaunced hymselfe ryghte inheritoure to the crowne thereof, by the tytle of an olde aliaunce.

At the last when they had gotten it, an[d] sawe that they hadde even as muche vexation and trouble in kepynge it, as they had in gettynge it, and that either their newe conquered subjectes by sundrye occasions were makynge daylye insurrections to rebell against them, or els that other countreis were continuallie with divers inrodes and forragynges inuadynge them: so that they were ever fighting either for them, or agaynste them, and never coulde breake up theyr campes: seyng them selves in the meane season pylled and impoverished; their money caried out of the realme: their own men killed to maintaine the glorye of an other nation: when they had no warre, peace nothynge better then warre, by reason that their people in war had so inured themselves to corrupte and wicked maners, that they had taken a delite and pleasure in robbinge and stealing: that through manslaughter they had gathered boldnes to mischiefe: that their lawes were had in contempte, and nothing set by or regarded: that their king beynge troubled with the charge and governaunce of two kingdomes, could not nor was not hable perfectlie to discharge his office towardes them both: seing againe that all these evelles and troubles were endles: at the laste layde their heades together, and like faithfull and lovinge subjectes gave to their kynge free choise and libertie to kepe styll the one of these two kingdomes whether he would: alleginge that he was not hable to kepe both, and that they were mo then might well be governed of halfe a king: forasmuche as no man woulde be content to take him for his mulettour, that kepeth an other mans moyles besydes his. So this good prince was constreyned to be content with his olde kyngedome and to geve over the newe to one of his frendes. Who shortelye after was violentlie driven out. Furthermore if I shoulde declare unto them, that all this busie preparaunce to warre, wherby so many

141

nations for his sake should be broughte into a troublesome
hurlei-burley, when all his coffers were emptied, his treasures wasted and his people destroied, should at the length
through some mischance be in vaine and to none effect:
and that therfore it were best for him to content him selfe
with his owne kingedome of Fraunce, as his forfathers and
predecessours did before him; to make much of it, to
enrich it, and to make it as flourisshing as he could, to
endevoure him selfe to love his subjectes, and againe to
be beloved of them, willingly to live with them, peaceably
to governe them, and with other kyngdomes not to medle,
seinge that whiche he hath all reddy is even ynoughe for
him, yea, and more then he can well turne hym to: this
myne aduyse, maister More, how thinke you it would be
harde and taken?

So God helpe me not very thankfully, quod I.

Wel let us procede then, quod he. Suppose that some
kyng and his counsel were together whettinge their wittes,
and devisinge what subtell crafte they myght invente to
enryche the kinge with great treasures of money. First one
counselleth to rayse and enhaunce the valuation of money
when the kinge must paye anye: and agayne to calle
downe the value of coyne to lesse then it is worthe, when
he muste receive or gather any. For thus great sommes
shal be payde wyth a lytyl money, and where lytle is due
muche shal be received. Another counselleth to fayne
warre, that when under this coloure and pretence the kyng
hath gathered greate aboundaunce of money, he maye,
when it shall please him, make peace with great solemp-
nitie and holye ceremonies, to blinde the eyes of the poore
communaltie, as taking pitie and compassion forsothe upon
mans bloude, lyke a loving and a mercifull prince. Another
putteth the kynge in remembraunce of certeine olde and
moughteeaten lawes, that of longe tyme have not bene put
in execution, whych because no man can remembre that
they were made, everie man hath transgressed. The fynes
of these lawes he counselleth the kynge to require: for

there is no waye so proffitable, nor more honorable, as the whyche hathe a shewe and coloure of justice. Another advyseth him to forbidde manye thinges under greate penalties and fines, specially suche thinges as is for the peoples profit not be used, and afterwarde to dispence for money with them, whyche by this prohibition substeyne losse and damage.

For by this meanes the favour of the people is wonne, and profite riseth two wayes. First by takinge forfaytes of them whome covetousnes of gaynes hath brought in daunger of this statute, and also by sellinge privileges and licences, whyche the better that the prince is, forsothe the deerer he selleth them: as one that is lothe to graunte to any private persone anye thinge that is againste the proffite of his people. And therefore maye sel none but at an exceding dere pryce. Another giveth the kynge counsel to endaunger unto his grace the judges of the realme, that he maye have them ever on his side, and that they maye in everye matter despute and reason for the kynges right. Yea and further to call them into his palace and to require them there to argue and discusse his matters in his owne presence. So there shal be no matter of his so openlye wronge and unjuste, wherein one or other of them, either because he wyl have sumthinge to allege and objecte or that he is ashamed to saye that whiche is sayde alreadye, or els to pike a thanke with his prince, wil not fynde some hole open to set a snare in, wherewith to take the contrarie parte in a trippe. Thus whiles the judges cannot agree amonges them selfes, reasoninge and arguing of that which is playne enough, and bringinge the manifest trewthe in dowte: in the meane season the kinge maye take a fyt occasion to understand the lawe as shal moste make for his advauntage, whereunto all other for shame, or for feare wil agree. Then the judges may be bolde to pronounce on the kynges side. For he that geveth sentence for the king, cannot be without a good excuse. For it shal be sufficient for him to have equitie on his part, or the bare wordes of

143

the lawe, or a wrythen and wrested understandinge of the same, or els (whiche with good and just judges is of greater force then all lawes be) the kynges indisputable prerogatiue.

To conclude, al the counsellours agre and consent together with the ryche Crassus, that no abundance of gold can be sufficient for a prince, which muste kepe and maynteyne an armie: furthermore that a kynge, thoughe he would, can do nothinge unjustlye. For all that all men haue, yea also the men them selfes be all his. And that euery man hath so much of his owne, as the kynges gentilnes hath not taken from hym. And that it shal be moste for the kinges aduantage, that his subjectes haue very lytle or nothinge in their possession, as whose sauegarde doth herein consiste, that his people doe not waxe wanton and wealthie through riches and libertie, because where these thinges be, there men be not wonte patiently to obeye harde, unjuste and unlawefull commaundementes; whereas on the other part neade and pouertie doth holde downe and kepe under stowte courages, and maketh them patient perforce, takynge from them bolde and rebellynge stomakes. Here agayne if I shoulde ryse up, and boldelye affirme that all these counselles be to the kinge dishonoure and reproche, whose honoure and safetye is more and rather supported and upholden by the wealth and ryches of his people, then by hys owne treasures: and if I should declare that the comminaltie chueseth their king for their owne sake and not for his sake: to the intent, that through his laboure and studie they might al liue wealthily sauffe from wronges and injuries: and that therfore the kynge ought to take more care for the wealthe of his people, then for his owne wealthe, euen as the office and dewtie of a shepehearde is in that he is a shepherde, to feede his shepe rather then himselfe. For as towchinge this, that they thinke the defence and mayntenaunce of peace to consiste in the pouertie of the people, the thing it selfe sheweth that they be farre out of the waye. For where shal a man finde more

144

wrangling, quarrelling, brawling, and chiding, then among beggers? Who be more desierous of newe mutations and alterations, then they that be not content with the present state of their lyfe? Or finallye who be bolder stomaked to bringe all in a hurlie-burlye (therby trustinge to get some windfal) then they that have nowe nothinge to leese? And yf any kyng were so smally regarded and so lightly estemed, yea so behated of his subjectes, that other wayes he could not kepe them in awe, but onlye by open wronges, by pollinge and shavinge, and by bringinge them to beggerie, sewerly it were better for him to forsake his kingedome, then to holde it by this meanes: whereby though the name of a king be kepte, yet the maiestie is lost. For it is againste the dignitie of a kynge to have rule over beggers, but rather over ryche and welthie men. Of this mynde was the hardie and couragius Fabrice, when he sayde, that he had rather be a ruler of riche men, then be ryche himselfe. And verelye one man to live in pleasure and wealth, whyles all other wepe and smarte for it, that is the parte, not of a kynge, but of a jayler.

To be shorte as he is a folyshe phisition, that cannot cure his patientes disease, onles he caste him in an other syckenes, so he that cannot amend the lives of his subjectes, but be taking from them the wealthe and commoditie of lyfe, he muste nedes graunte that he knoweth not the feate how to governe men. But let him rather amende his owne lyfe, renounce unhonest pleasures, and forsake pride. For these be the chiefe vices that cause hym to runne in the contempte or hatred of his people. Let him lyve of hys owne, hurtinge no man. Let him doe cost not above his power. Let him restreyne wyckednes. Let him prevente vices, and take awaye the occasions of offenses by well orderynge hys subjectes, and not by sufferynge wickednes to increase afterward to be punyshed. Let hym not be to hastie in callynge agayne lawes, whyche a custome hathe abrogated: specially suche as have bene longe forgotten, and never lacked nor neaded. And let hym never under

145

the cloke and pretence of transgression take suche fynes
and forfaytes, as no judge wyll suffre a private persone to
take, as unjuste and ful of gile.

Here if I should brynge forth before them the lawe of
the Macariens, whiche be not farre distaunt from Utopia:
whose kynge the daye of hys coronation is bounde by a
solempne othe, that he shall never at anye time have in
hys treasure above a thousande pounde of golde or sylver.
They saye a verye good kynge, whiche toke more care for
the wealthe and commoditye of his countrey, then for
thenriching of him selfe, made this lawe to be a stop and a
barre to kinges from heaping and hording up so muche
money as might impoveryshe their people. For he forsawe
that this som of treasure woulde suffice to supporte the
kynge in battaile against his owne people, if they shoulde
chaunce to rebell: and also to maintein his warres againste
the invasions of his forreyn enemies. Againe he perceived
the same stocke of money to be to litle and unsufficient to
encourage and enhable him wrongfullye to take away other
mens goodes: whyche was the chiefe cause whie the lawe
was made. An other cause was this. He thought that by this
provision his people shoulde not lacke money, wherewith
to mayneteyne their dayly occupieng and chaffayre. And
seynge the kynge could not chewse but laye out and bestowe al that came in above the prescript some of his
stocke, he thought he woulde seke no occasions to doe his
subjectes injurie. Suche a kynge shal be feared of evel
men, and loved of good men. These, and suche other informations, yf I shoulde use among men wholye inclined
and geven to the contrarye part, how deaffe hearers thinke
you shoulde I have?

Deaffe hearers douteles (quod I) and in good faith
no marveyle. And to be plaine with you, truelye I can not
allowe that suche communication shal be used, or suche
counsell geven, as you be suere shall never be regarded nor
receaved. For howe can so straunge informations be profitable, or how can they be beaten into their headdes, whose

146

myndes be allredye prevented with cleane contrarye persuasions? This schole philosophie is not unpleasaunte amonge frendes in familiare communication, but in the counselles of kinges, where great matters be debated and reasoned with greate authoritiye, these thinges have no place.

That is it whiche I mente (quod he) when I sayde philosophye hadde no place amonge kinges.

In dede (quod I) this schole philosophie hath not, whiche thinketh all thinges mete for every place. But there is an other philosophye more civile, whyche knoweth, as ye wolde say, her owne stage, and thereafter orderynge and behavinge hereselfe in the playe that she hathe in hande, playethe her parte accordingelye with comlyenes, utteringe nothinge oute of dewe ordre and fassyon. And this is the philosophye that you muste use. Or els whyles a commodye of Plautus is playinge, and the vyle bondemen skoffynge and tryffelinge amonge them selfes, yf you shoulde sodenlye come upon the stage in a Philosophers apparrell, and reherse oute of Octavia the place wherein Seneca disputeth with Nero: had it not bene better for you to have played the domme persone, then by rehersynge that, whych served neither for the tyme nor place, to have made suche a tragycall comedye or gallymalfreye? For by bryngynge in other stuffe that nothinge apperteynethe to the presente matter, you muste nedes marre and pervert the play that is in hand, thoughe the stuffe that you bringe be muche better. What part soever you have taken upon you, playe that as well as you can and make the best of it: And doe not therefore disturbe and brynge oute of ordre the whole matter, bycause that another, whyche is meryer and better, cummethe to your remembraunce. So the case standeth in a common wealthe, and so it is in the consultations of kynges and prynces. Yf evel opinions and noughty persuasions can not be utterly and quyte plucked out of their hartes, if you can not, even as you wolde, remedy vices, which use and custome hath confirmed: yet for this

147

cause you must not leave and forsake the common wealthe: you muste not forsake the shippe in a tempeste, because you can not rule and kepe downe the wyndes. No, nor you muste not laboure to dryve into their heades newe and straunge informations, whyche you knowe wel shal be nothinge regarded wyth them that be of cleane contrary mindes. But you must with a crafty wile and a subtell frayne studye and endevoure youre selfe, as muche as in you lyethe, to handle the matter wyttelye and handesome-lye for the purpose, and that whyche you can not turne to good, so to order it that it be not verye badde. For it is not possible for al thinges to be well, onles all men were good. Whych I thinke wil not be yet thies good many yeares.

By this meanes (quod he) nothing elles wyl be brought to passe, but whyles that I goe aboute to remedye the madnes of others, I shoulde be even as madde as they. For if I wolde speake suche thinges that be trewe I must neades speake suche thinges; but as for to speake false thinges, whether that be a philosophers parte or no I can not tel, truelye it is not my part. Howebeit this communication of mine, thoughe peradventure it maye seme un-plesaunte to them, yet can I not see why it shoulde seme straunge, or folishelye newfangled. If so be that I should speake those thinges that Plato faynethe in his weale pub-lique: or that the Utopians doe in theires, these thinges thoughe they were (as they be in dede) better, yet they myghte seme spoken oute of place. Forasmuche as here amonges us, everye man hathe his possessions several to him selfe, and there all thinges be common. But what was in my communication conteyned, that mighte not, and oughte not in anye place to be spoken? Savynge that to them whyche have thoroughlye decreed and determined with them selfes to runne hedlonges the contrary waye it can not be acceptable and pleasaunt, because it calleth them backe, and sheweth them the jeopardies. Verilye yf all thynges that evel and vitiouse maners have caused to seme inconveniente and noughte should be refused, as thinges unmete and reprochefull, then we must among Christen people wynke at the moste parte of al those thinges, whych Christ taught us, and so streitly forbad them to be winked at, that those thinges also whiche he whispered in the eares of his disciples he commaunded to be proclaimed in open houses.

And yet the most parte of them is more dissident from the maners of the worlde nowe a dayes, then my communication was. But preachers, slie and wilie men, followynge youre counsel (as I suppose) bicause they saw men evel willing to frame theyr manners to Christes rule, they have wrested and wriede his doctryne, and like a rule of leade have applyed it to mennes manners: that by some meanes at the leaste waye, they myghte agree together. Whereby I can not see what good they have done: but that men may more sickerlye be evell. And I truelye shoulde prevaile even as litle in kinges counselles. For either I muste saye otherwayes then they saye, and then I were as good to saye nothinge, or els I muste saye the same that they saye, and (as Mitio saieth in Terence) helpe to further their madnes. For that craftye wyle, and subtil traine of yours, I can not perceave to what purpose it serveth, wherewith you wolde have me to study and endevoure my selfe, yf all thinges can not be made good, yet to handle them wittily and handsomely for the purpose, that as farre forth as is possible they may not be very evel. For there is no place to dissemble in, nor to wincke in. Noughtye counselles muste be openlye allowed and verye pestilent decrees muste be approved. He shal be counted worse then a spye, yea almoste as evel as a traytour, that with a faynte harte doth prayse evel and noyesome decrees. Moreover a man canne have no occasion to doe good, chaunsinge into the companye of them whych wyl soner perverte a good man, then be made good them selfes: through whose evel company he shal be marred, or els if he remayne good and innocent, yet the wickednes and follye of others shal be

149

imputed to hym, and layde in his necke. So that it is impossible with that craftye wyele and subtel trayne to turne anye thinge to better. Wherefore Plato by a goodlye similitude [11] declareth, why wise men refraine to medle in the common wealthe. For when they see the people swarme into the stretes, and daily wet to the skinne with rayne, and yet can not persuade them to goe out of the rayne and to take their houses, knowynge wel, that if they shoulde goe out to them, they should nothinge prevayle, nor wynne ought by it, but with them be wette also in the raine, they do kepe them selfes within their houses, being content that they be saffe them selves, seinge they cannot remedye the follye of the people.

Howe be it doubtlesse, maister More, (to speke truelye as my mynde geveth me) where possessions be private, where money bearethe all the stroke, it is harde and almoste impossible that there the weale publique maye justeleye be governed, and prosperouslye floryshe. Onles you thinke thus: that justyce is there executed, where all thinges come into the handes of evell men; or that prosperitye there florysshethe, where all is divided amonge a fewe; whyche fewe neverthelesse doe not leade theire lives very wealthely, and the resydewe lyve myserablye, wretchedlye and beggerlye. Wherefore when I consyder with my selfe and weye in my mynde the wyse and godlye ordinaunces of the Utopians, amonge whome with verye fewe lawes all thinges be so wel and wealthelye ordered, that vertue is had in pryce and estimation, and yet, all thinges beinge there common, everye man hath aboundaunce of everye thinge. Againe on the other part, when I compare with them so manye nations ever makinge newe lawes, yet none of them all well and sufficientlye furnysshed with lawes; where everye man calleth that he hathe gotten, his owne proper and private goodes; where so many newe lawes daylye made be not sufficiente for everye man to enjoye, defend, and knowe from an other mans that whych he calleth his owne; which thinge the infinite controversies in the lawe, dayle rysynge, never to be ended, playnly declare to be trewe.

These thinges (I say) when I consider with me selfe, I holde wel with Plato, and doe nothinge marveille, that he woulde make no lawes for them, that refused those lawes, whereby all men shoulde have and enjoye equall portions of welthes and commodities. For the wise man did easely foresee, this to bee the one and onlye waye to the wealthe of a communaltye, yf equalitye of all thinges should be broughte in and stablyshed. Whyche I thinke is not possible to be observed, where everye mans gooddes be proper and peculiare to him selfe. For where everye man under certeyne tytles and pretences draweth and plucketh to himselfe as much as he can, so that a fewe devide among them selfes all the whole riches, be there never so muche abundaunce and stoore, there to the residewe is lefte lacke and povertye. And for the moste parte it chaunceth, that this latter sorte is more worthye to enjoye that state of wealth, then the other be: bycause the ryche men be covetous, craftye and unprofitable. On the other parte the poore be lowly, simple and by theire daylye laboure more profitable to the common welthe then to them selfes. Thus I doe fullye persuade me selfe, that no equall and juste distribution of thinges can be made, nor that perfecte wealthe shall ever be among men, onles this propriety be exiled and bannished. But so long as it shal continew, so long shal remaine among the most and best part of men the hevy and inevitable burden of poverty and wretchednes. Whiche, as I graunte that it maye be sumwhat eased, so I utterly denye that it can wholy be taken away. For if there were a statute made, that no man should possesse above a certeine measure of grounde, and that no man shoulde have in his stocke above a prescripte and appointed some of money: if it were by certein lawes decreed, that neither the kinge shoulde be of to greate power, neither the people to haute and wealthy, and that offices shoulde not be obteined by inordinate suite, or by brybes and gyftes: that they shoulde neither be bought nor sold, nor that it shoulde be nedeful for the officers, to be at any cost or charge in their offices: for so occasion is geven to theym by fraude and ravin to gather up their money againe, and by reason of giftes and bribes the offices be geven to rich men, which shoulde rather have bene executed of wise men: by such lawes I say, like as sicke bodies that be desperat and past cure, be wont with continual good cherissing to be kept and botched up for a time: so these evels also might be lightened and mitigated. But that thei may be perfectly cured, and brought to a good and up-ryght state, it is not to be hoped for, whiles every man is maister of his owne to him selfe. Yea, and whyles you goe aboute to doe youre cure of one parte, you shall make byg-ger the sore of an other parte, so the healpe of one causeth anothers harme: forasmuche as nothinge can be geven to annye one, onles it be taken from an other.

But I am of a contrary opinion (quod I) for me thinketh that men shal never there live wealthelye, where all thinges be commen. For howe can there be abundaunce of gooddes, or of any thing, where every man withdraweth his hande from labour? Whome the regard of his owne gaines driveth not to worke, but the hope that he hath in other mens tra-vayles maketh him slowthfull. Then when they be pricked with povertye, and yet no man can by any lawe or right defend that for his owne, which he hathe gotten with the laboure of his owne handes, shal not there of necessitie be continual sedition and blodeshed? Speciallye the authori-tye and reverence of magistrates beinge taken awaye, whiche, what place it maye have with such men amonge whome is no difference, I cannot devise.

I marvel not (quod he) that you be of this opinion. For you conceave in youre minde either none at al, or els a verye false image and similitude of this thing. But yf you had bene with me in Utopia and had presently sene theire fasshions and lawes, as I dyd, whyche lived there v. years and moore, and wolde never have commen thence, but onlye to make that newe lande knowen here: then doubtles you wolde graunt, that you never sawe people wel ordered, but onlye there.

Surely (quod maister Peter) it shal be harde for you to make me beleve, that there is better order in that newe lande, then is here in these countryes, that wee knowe. For good wittes be as wel here as there: and I thinke oure commen wealthes be auncienter than theires; wherin long use and experience hath found out many thinges commodious for mannes lyfe, besides that manye thinges heare amonge us have bene found by chaunce, whiche no wytte coulde ever have devysed.

As touchinge the auncientnes (quod he) of common wealthes, than you might better judge, if you had red the histories and cronicles of that land, which if we may beleve, cities were there, before men were here. Nowe what thinge soever hetherto by witte hath bene devised, or found by chaunce, that myght be as wel there as here. But I thinke verily, though it were so that we did passe them in witte: yet in study, in travaile, and in laboursome endevoure they farre passe us. For (as theire chronicles testifie) before our arrival there, they never hard any thing of us, whome they cal the ultraequinoctialles: saving that ones about M.CC. yeares ago, a certeine shyppe was lost by the ile of Utopia whiche was driven thether by tempest. Certeine Romaines and Egyptians were cast on lande. Whyche after that never wente thence. Marke nowe what profite they tooke of this one occasion through delygence and earneste travaile. There was no crafte nor scyence within the impire of Rome, wherof any proffite could rise, but they either lerned it of these straungers, or els of them taking occasion to searche for it, founde it oute. So greate proffite was it to them that ever anye wente thyther from hence. But yf annye like chaunce before this hath brought anye man from thence hether, that is as quyte out of remembraunce, as this also perchaunce in time to come shalbe forgotten, that ever I was there. And like as they

153

quickelye, almoste at the first meting, made theire owne what soever is amonge us wealthelye devised: so I suppose it wolde be long before we wolde receave anythinge that amonge them is better instituted then amonge us. And this I suppose is the chiefe cause whie theire common wealthes by wyselyer governed, and doe flourish in more wealthe, then ours, though we neither in wytte nor riches be their inferiours.

Therefore gentle maister Raphael (quod I) I praye you and beseche you describe unto us the ilande. And study not to be shorte: but declare largely in order their groundes, their rivers, their cities, theire people, theire manners, their ordinaunces, their lawes, and to be short, al thinges, that you shal thinke us desierous to knowe. And you shal thinke us desierous to know what soever we knowe not yet.

There is nothing (quod he) that I wil doe gladlier. For all these thinges I have freshe in mind. But the matter requireth leasure.

Let us go in therfore (quod I) to dinner, afterward we wil bestowe the time at our pleasure.

Content (quod he) be it.

So we went in and dyned. When dinner was done, we came into the same place again, and sate us downe upon the same benche, commaunding oure servauntes that no man should trouble us. Then I and maister Peter Giles desiered maister Raphael to performe his promise. He therefore seing us desirous and willing to harken to him, when he had sit stil and paused a litle while, musing and bethinkinge himselfe, thus be began to speake.

The end of the Firste boke.

THE SECONDE BOKE

of the communication of

RAPHAEL HYTHLODAYE,

concernyng the best state of a common wealthe conteyninge the discription of Utopia, with a large declaration of the politike gouernement, and of all the good lawes and orders of the same ilande.

THE iland of Utopia, conteynethe in breadthe in the middel parte of it (for there it is brodest) CC. miles. Which bredthe continueth throughe the moste part of the lande, saving that by litle and litle it commeth in, and waxeth narrower towardes both the endes. Which fetching about a circuite or compasse of V. C. miles, do fasion the whole iland like to the new mone. Betwene these two corners the sea runneth in, dividyng them a sonder by the distaunce of xi. miles or there aboutes, and there surmountethe into a large and wyde sea, which by reason that the land on every side compassethe it about, and shiltreth it from the windes, is not roughe, nor mounteth not with great waves, but almost floweth quietlye, not muche unlike a greate standinge powle: and maketh welnieghe all the space within the bellye of the lande in maner of a haven: and to the greate commoditie of the inhabitauntes receaveth in shyppes towardes everye parte of the

155

lande. The forefrontes or frontiers of the ii. corners, what with fordes and shelves, and what with rockes be verye jeoperdous and daungerous. In the middle distaunce betwene them bothe standeth up above the water a greate rocke, which therfore is nothing perillous bycause it is in sight. Upon the top of this rocke is a faire and a strong tower builded, which they holde with a garrison of men. Other rockes there be lyinge hidde under the water, which therfore be daungerous. The channelles be knowen onely to themselfes. And therfore it seldome chaunceth that anye straunger oneles he be guided by an Utopian can come in to this haven. In so muche that they themselfes could skaselye entre withoute jeoperdie, but that theire way is directed and ruled by certaine lande markes standing on the shore. By turninge, translatinge, and removinge thies markes into other places they maye destroye theire enemies navies, be they never so many. The out side or utter circuite of the land is also ful of havens, but the landing is so suerly fenced, what by nature, and what by workemanshyp of mans hand, that a fewe defenders maye dryve backe many armies. Howbeit as they saye, and as the fassion of the place it selfe dothe partly shewe, it was not ever compassed about with the sea. But kyng Utopus, whose name, as conquerour the iland beareth (for before his tyme it was called Abraxa) which also broughte the rude and wild people to that excellent perfection in al good fassions, humanitye, and civile gentilnes, wherin they nowe goe beyond al the people of the world: even at his firste arrivinge and enteringe upon the lande, furthwith obteynynge the victory, caused xv. myles space of uplandyshe grounde, where the sea had no passage, to be cut and dygged up.

And so brought the sea rounde aboute the lande. He set to this worke not only the inhabitauntes of the ilande (because they should not thinke it done in contumelye and despyte) but also all his owne soldiours. Thus the worke beyng divided into so greate a numbre of workemen, was with excedinge marvelous spede dyspatched. In so muche that the borderers, whiche at the firste began to mocke, and to jeste at this vaine enterpryse, then turned theire derision to marveyle at the successe, and to feare. There be in the ilande liiii. large and faire cities, or shiere townes, agreyng all together in one tonge, in lyke maners, institucions and lawes. They be all set and situate alyke, and in al poyntes fashioned alyke, as farforthe as the place or plotte sufferethe.

Of these cities they that be nigheste together be xxiiii. myles asonder. Againe there is none of them distaunte from the nexte above one dayes jorneyeye a fote. There com yearly to Amaurote out of every cytie iii. old men wyse and well experienced, there to entreate and debate, of the common matters of the land. For this citie (because it standeth juste in the middes of the ilande, and is therefore moste mete for the ambassadours of all partes of the realme) is taken for the chiefe and heade cetye. The precinctes and boundes of the shieres be so commodiously appoynted oute, and set fourthe for the cities, that none of them all hathe of anye syde lesse then xx. myles of grounde, and of some syde also muche more, as of that part where the cities be of farther distaunce asonder. None of the cities desire to enlarge the boundes and limites of theire shieres. For they counte them selfes rather the good husbandes, then the owners of theire landes. They have in the country in all partes of the shiere houses or fermes builded, wel appointed and furnyshed with all sortes of instrumentes and tooles belongynge to husbandrye. These houses be inhabited of the citezens, whyche come thether to dwelle by course. No howsholde or ferme in the countrey hath fewer then xl. persones men and women, besydes two bondmen, whyche be all under the rule and order of the good man, and the good wyfe of the house, beinge bothe verye sage, discrete and aunciente persones. And every xxx. fermes or families have one heade ruler, whyche is called a philarche, being as it were a head baylyffe. Out of every one of these families or fermes commeth

157

everye yeare into the citie xx. persones whiche have continewed ij. yeres before in the countreye. In theire place so manye freshe be sent thether oute of the citie, whoe, of them that have bene there a yeare all readye, and be therefore expert and conninge in husbandry, shal be instructed and taughte. And they the nexte yeare shall teache other. This order is used for feare that either skarsnes of victualles, or some other like incommoditie should chaunce throughe lacke of knowledge, yf they should be altogether newe, and freshe, and unexperte in husbandrie. This maner and fassion of yearelye chaunging and renewinge the occupiers of husbandrye, though it be solempne and customablye used, to thintent that no man shall be constrayned againste his wil to contynewe longe in that harde and sharpe kynde of lyfe, yet manye of them have suche a pleasure and delyte in husbandrye, that they obteyne a longer space of yeares. These husbandmen plowe and til the ground, and breede up cattel, and provide and make ready woode, whyche they carrye to the citie either by lande, or by water, as they maye moste convenyently.

They brynge up a greate multitude of pulleyne, and that by a mervaylouse policye. For the hennes dooe not sytte upon the egges: but by keepynge theym in a certayne equall heate they brynge lyfe into them, and hatche theym. The chykens, as sone as they be come oute of the shel, follow men and women in steade of the hennes. They brynge up verye fewe horses: nor none, but very fearce ones: and that for none other use or purpose, but onlye to exercyse theire youthe in rydynge and feates of armes. For oxen be put to all the laboure of plowyng and drawinge. Whiche they graunte to be not so good as horses at a sodeyne brunte, and (as we saye) at a deade lifte, but yet they holde opinion that oxen wil abide and suffre muche more laboure, payne and hardnes, then horses wil. And they thinke that oxen be not in daunger and subject unto so many diseases, and that they be kepte and mainteined with muche lesse coste and charge: and finallye that they

be good for meate, when they be past laboure. They sowe corne onelye for breade. For their drinke is eyther wyne made of grapes, or els of apples, or peares, or els it is cleare water. And many times meathe made of honey or licouresse sodde in water, for thereof they have great store. And though they knowe certeynlie (for they knowe it perfectly in dede) how muche vitailes the citie wyth the whole countreye or shiere rounde aboute it doeth spende: yet they sowe muche more corne, and bryed up muche more cattell, then serveth for their owne use, partynge the overplus among their borderers. What soever necessarie thinges be lacking in the countrey, all suche stuffe they fetch out of the citie: where without any exchaunge they easelye obteyne it of the magistrates of the citie. For every moneth manie of them go into the citie on the holy daye. When theyr harvest day draweth neare and is at hande, then the philarches, which be the head officers and bailifes of husbandrie, send worde to the magistrates of the citie what numbre of harvest men is nedefull to be sent to them oute of the citie. The whiche companye of harvest men
beynge readye at the daye
appoynted, almost in one
fayre daye dispacheth
all the harvest
woorke.

' '

,

Of the Cities and Namely of Amaurote.

As for their cities, who so knoweth one of them, knoweth them all: they be al so like one to an other, as farfurthe as the nature of the place permitteth. I will describe therefore to you one or other of them, for it skilleth not greatly which: but which rather then Amaurote? [12] Of them all this is the worthiest and of most dignitie. For the resideu knowl-

edge it for the head citie, because there is the counsell
house. Nor to me anye of them all is better beloved, as
wherin I lived five whole yeares together. The citie of
Amaurote standeth upon the side of a lowe hill in fashyon
almost foure square. For the breadth of it beginneth a litle
beneth the toppe of the hill, and still continueth by the
space of two miles, untill it come to the ryver of Anyder.
The length of it, which lieth by the ryvers syde, is sumwhat more. The river of Anyder riseth four and twentie
myles above Amaurote out of a litle springe. But beynge
increased by other smale rivers and broukes that runne
into it, and amonge other two sumwhat bygge ons, before
the citie it is half a mile broade, and farther broader. And
fortie myles beyonde the citie it falleth into the Ocean
sea. By all that space that liethe betwene the sea and the
citie, and certen myles also above the citie the water ebbeth
and floweth six houres together with a swift tide. Whan
the sea floweth in, for the length of thirtie miles it filleth all
the Anyder with salte water, and driveth backe the freshe
water of the ryver. And sumwhat further it chaungeth the
swetenes of the freshe water with saltnes. But a litle beyonde that the river waxeth swete, and runneth foreby the
citie freshe and pleasaunt. And when the sea ebbeth, and
goeth backe againe, the freshe water foloweth it almooste
even to the verie fal into the sea. Ther goeth a bridge
over the river made not of piles or of timber, but of stone-
warke with gorgious and substancial arches at that part of
the citie that is farthest from the sea: to the intent that
shippes maye passe alonge forbie all the side of the citie
without let.

They have also an other river which in dede is not verie
great. But it runneth gently and pleasauntly. For it riseth
even oute of the same hill that the citie standeth upon,
and runneth downe a slope through the middes of the
citie into Anyder. And because it riseth a litle withoute the
citie, the Amaurotians have inclosed the head springe of it,
with strange fences and bulwarkes, and so have joyned it

to the citie. This is done to the intente that the water shoulde not be stopped nor turned away, or poysoned, if their enemies should chaunce to come upon them. From thence the water is derived and conveied downe in cannels of bricke divers wayes into the lower partes of the citie. Where that cannot be done, by reason that the place wyll not suffer it, there they gather the raine water in great cisternes, whiche doeth them as good service. The citie is compassed aboute with a heighe and thicke stone walle full of turrettes and bulwarkes. A drie diche, but deape, and brode, and overgrowen with bushes, briers and thornes, goeth aboute thre sides or quarters of the city. To the fourth side the river it selfe serveth for a ditche. The stretes be appointed and set furth very commodious and handsome, both for carriage, and also againste the windes.

The houses be of faire and gorgious building, and on the strete side they stande joyned together in a long rowe through the whole streate without any partition or separation. The stretes be twentie foote brode. On the backe side of the houses through the whole length of the streete, lye large gardens inclosed rounde aboute wyth the backe part of the streetes. Everye house hathe two doores, one into the streete, and a posterne doore on the backsyde into the garden. These doores be made with two leaves, never locked nor bolted, so easie to be opened, that they wil followe the least drawing of a fynger, and shutte againe alone. Whoso will, may go in, for there is nothinge within the houses that is private, or anie mans owne. And every tenth yeare they chaunge their houses by lot. They set great store by their gardeins. In them they have vineyardes, all maner of fruite, herbes and flowres, so pleasaunt, so well furnished and so fynely kepte, that I never sawe thynge more frutefull, nor better trimmed in anye place. Their studie and deligence herin commeth not onely of pleasure, but also of a certen strife and contention that is betwene strete and strete, concerning the trimming, husbanding and furnisshing of their gardens: everye man for his owne parte. And verelye you shall not lightelye finde in all the citie anye thinge, that is more commodious, eyther for the profite of the citizens, or for pleasure. And therfore it maye seme that the first founder of the citie mynded nothing so much, as these gardens.

For they saye that kinge Utopus him selfe, even at the first beginning appointed and drewe furth the platte fourme of the citie into this fashion and figure that it hath nowe, but the gallant garnishinge, and the beautifull settinge furth of it, wherunto he sawe that one mannes age would not suffice: that he left to his posteritie. For their cronicles, whiche they kepe written with all deligente circumspection, conteinynge the historie of M. vii. C. lx. yeares, even from the firste conquest of the ilande, recorde and witnesse that the houses in the beginning were very low, and like homely cotages or poore sheppard houses, made at all adventures of everye rude pece of tymber, that came firste to hande, with mudde walles and ridged rooffes, thatched over with strawe. But nowe the houses be curiouslye buylded after a gorgious and gallante sorte, with three storyes one over another. The outsides of the walles be made either of harde flynte, or of plaster, or els of bricke, and the inner sydes be well strengthened with tymber work. The roofes be plaine and flat, covered with a certen kinde of plaster that is of no coste, and yet so tempered that no fyre can hurt or perishe it, and withstandeth the violence of the wether better then any leade. They kepe the winde oute of their windowes with glasse, for it is ther much used, and somhere also with fine linnen cloth dipped in oyle or ambre, and that for two commodities.

For by thys meanes more lighte
commeth in, and the winde
is better kepte
oute.

Of the magistrates.

EVERYE thirtie families or fermes, chuese them yerely an officer, which in their olde language is called the syphograunte, and by a newe, name the philarche. Every ten syphograuntes, with al their thirtie families be under an officer which was ones called the tranibore, nowe the chiefe philarche. Moreover as concerninge the election of the prince, all the syphogranntes, which be in number 200. first be sworne to chuese him whom they thinke mooste mete and expediente. Then by a secrete election, they name prince one of those iiij. whome the people before named unto them. For oute of the iiij. quarters of the citie there be iiij. chosen, oute of every quarter one, to stande for the election; Whiche be put up to the counsell. The princes office continueth all his life tyme, oneles he be deposed or put downe for suspition of tirannie. They chuese the tranibores yearly, but lightlie they chaunge them not. All the other officers be but for one yeare. The tranibores everye thyrde daye, and sumtimes, yf nede be, oftener come into the counsell house with the prince. Their counsell is concerninge the common wealthe. If there be any controversies amonge the commoners, whiche be verye fewe, they dis-- patch and ende them by and by. They take ever ij. siphograuntes to them in counsel, and everi dai a new coupel. And it is provided, that nothinge touchinge the common wealthe shal be confirmed and ratified, onlesse it have bene reasoned of and debated thre daies in the counsell, before it be decreed.

It is deathe to have anye consultation for the common wealthe oute of the counsell, or the place of the common election. This statute, they saye, was made to the entent that the prince and tranibores might not easilye conspire together to appresse the people by tyrannie, and to chaunge the state of the weale publik. Therfore matters of great weight and importance be broughte to the election house of the siphograuntes, which open the matter to their families. And afterwarde, when they have consulted amonge themselves, they shew their devise to the counsell. Somtime the matter is brought before the counsel of the whole ilande. Furthermore this custome also the counsel useth, to dispute or reason of no matter the same daye that it is firste proposed or put furthe, but to deffere it to the nexte syttinge of the counsell. Because that no man when he hath rashely there spoken that commeth to his tonges ende, shall then afterwarde rather studye for reasons wherwith to defende and mainteine his first folish sentence, than for the commoditie of the common wealth: as one rather willing the harme or hindraunce of the weale publike then any losse or diminution of his owne existimation. And as one that would be ashamed (which is a verie folishe shame) to be counted anye thing at the firste oversene in the matter. Who at the first ought to have

spoken rather wyselye,

then hastely, or

rashlye.

Of Sciences, Craftes and Ocupations.

HUSBANDRIE is a science common to them all in generall, bothe men and women, wherein they be all experte and cunning. In this they be all instructe even from their youth: partelie in their scholes with traditions and preceptes, and partlie in the countrey nighe the citie, brought up as it were in playinge, not onely beholding the use of it, but by occasion of exercising their bodies practising it also. Besides husbandrie, whiche (as I saide) is common to them all, everye one of them learneth one or other several and particular science, as his owne proper crafte. That is most commonly either clothworking in wol or flaxe, or masonrie, or the smithes craft, or the carpenters science. For there is none other occupation that any number to speake of doth use there. For their garmentes, which throughoute all the ilande be of one fashion, (savynge that there is a difference betwene the mans garmente and the womans, betwene the maried and the unmaried) and this one continueth for evermore unchaunged, semely and comelie to the eye, no lette to the movynge and weldynge of the bodye, also fytte both for wynter and summer: as for these garmentes (I saye) every familie maketh their owne. But of the other foresaide craftes everye man learneth one. And not onely the men, but also the women. But the women, as the weaker sort, be put to the easier craftes: as to worke wolle and flaxe. The more laborsome sciences be committed to the men. For the mooste part every man is broughte up in his fathers crafte. For moste commonlye they be naturallie therto bente and inclined. But yf a mans minde stande to anye other, he is by adoption put into a familye of that occupation, which he doth most fantasy. Whome not onely his father, but also the magistrates do diligently loke to, that he be put to a discrete and an honest householder. Yea, and if anye person, when he hath learned one crafte, be desierous to learne also another, he is likewyse suffred and permitted.

When he hathe learned bothe, he occupieth whether he wyll: onelesse the citie have more neade of the one, then of the other. The chiefe and almooste the onelye offyce of the syphograuntes is, to see and take hede, that no manne sit idle: but that everye one applye hys owne craft with earnest diligence. And yet for all that, not to be wearied from earlie in the morninge, to late in the evenninge, with continuall worke, like labouringe and toylinge beastes.

For this is worse then the miserable and wretched condition of bondemen. Whiche nevertheles is almooste everye where the lyfe of workemen and artificers, saving in Utopia. For they dividynge the daye and the nyghte into xxiiii. juste houres, appointe and assigne onelye sixe of those houres to woorke before noone, upon the whiche they go streighte to diner: and after diner, when they have rested two houres, then they worke iii. houres and upon that they go to supper. Aboute eyghte of the cloke in the eveninge (countinge one of the clocke at the firste houre after noone) they go to bedde: eyght houres they geve to slepe. All the voide time, that is betwene the houres of worke, slepe, and meate, that they be suffered to bestowe, every man as he liketh best him selfe. Not to thintent that they shold mispend this time in riote or slouthfulness: but beynge then licensed from the laboure of their owne occupations, to bestow the time well and thriftelye upon some other science, as shall please them. For it is a solempne custome there, to have lectures daylye early in the morning, where to be presente they onely be constrained that be namelye chosen and appoynted to learninge. Howbeit a greate multitude of every sort of people, both men and women go to heare lectures, some one and some an other, as everye mans nature is inclined. Yet, this notwithstanding, if any man had rather bestowe this time upon his owne occupation, (as it chaunceth in manye, whose mindes rise not in the contemplation of any science liberall) he is not letted, nor prohibited, but is also praysed and commended, as profitable to the common wealthe.

After supper they bestow one houre in playe: in summer in their gardens: in winter in their commen halles: where they dine and suppe. There they exercise themselves in musike, or els in honest and wholsome communication. Diceplaye, and suche other folishe and pernicious games they know not. But they use ij. games not much unlike the chesse. The one is the battell of numbers, wherein one numbre stealethe awaye another. The other is wherin vices fyghte with vertues, as it were in battel array, or a set fyld. In the which game is verye properlye shewed, bothe the striffe and discorde that vices have amonge themselfes, and agayne theire unitye and concorde againste vertues. And also what vices be repugnaunt to what vertues: with what powre and strength they assaile them openlye: by what wieles and subtelty they assaulte them secretelye: with what helpe and aide the vertues resiste and overcome the puissaunce of the vices: by what craft they frustrate their purposes: and finally by what sleight or meanes the one getteth the victory.

But here least you be deceaved, one thinge you muste looke more narrowly upon. For seinge they bestowe but vi. houres in woorke, perchaunce you maye thinke that the lacke of some necessarye thinges hereof maye ensewe. But this is nothinge so. For that smal time is not only enough but also to muche for the stoore and abundaunce of all thinges that be requisite, either for the necessitie, or commoditie of life. The which thinge you also shall perceave, if you weye and consider with your selfes how great a parte of the people in other contreis lyveth ydle. First almost all women, whyche be the halfe of the whole numbre: or els if the women be somewhere occupied, there most comonlye in their steade the men be ydle. Besydes this how greate, and howe ydle a companye is there of preystes, and relygious men, as they cal them? put thereto al ryche men, speciallye all landed men, which comonlye be called gentilmen, and noble men. Take into this numbre also theire servauntes: I meane all that flocke of stoute bragging russhe bucklers. Joyne to them also sturdy and valiaunte beggers, clokinge their idle lyfe under the coloure of some disease or sickenes. And trulye you shal find them much fewer then you thought, by whose labour all these thinges are wrought, that in mens affaires are now daylye used and frequented. Nowe consyder with youre selfe, of these fewe that doe woorke, how fewe be occupied, in necessarye woorkes. For where money beareth all the swinge, there many vayne and superfluous occupations must nedes be used, to serve only for ryotous superfluite, and unhonest pleasure. For the same multitude that now is occupied in woork, if they were devided into so fewe occupations as the necessarye use of nature requyreth; in so great plentye of thinges as then of necessity woulde ensue, doubtles the prices wolde be to lytle for the artifycers to maynteyne theire livinges.

167

But yf all these, that be nowe busied about unprofitable occupations, with all the whole flocke of them that lyve ydellye and slouthfullye, whyche consume and waste everye one of them more of these thinges that come by other mens laboure, then ij. of the workemen themselfes doo: yf all these (I saye) were sette to profytable occupatyons, you easelye perceave howe lytle tyme would be enoughe, yea and to muche to stoore us with all thinges that maye be requisite either for necessitie, or for commoditye, yea or for pleasure, so that the same pleasure be trewe and natural. And this in Utopia the thinge it selfe makethe manifeste and playne. For there in all the citye, with the whole contreye, or shiere adjoyning to it scaselye 500. persons of al the whole numbre of men and women, that be neither to olde, nor to weake to worke, be licensed and discharged from laboure. Amonge them be the siphograuntes (whoe thoughe they be by the lawes exempte and privileged from labour) yet they exempte not themselfes: to the intent that they may the rather by their example provoke other to worke. The same vacation from labour do they also enjoye, to whome the people persuaded by the commendation of the priestes, and secrete election of the siphograuntes, have geven a perpetual licence from laboure to learninge. But if any one of them prove not accordinge to the expectation and hoope of him conceaved, he is forthwith plucked backe to the company of artificers. And contrarye wise, often it chaunceth that a handicraftes man doth so earnestly bestowe his vacaunte and spare houres in learninge, and throughe diligence so profyteth therin, that he is taken from his handy occupation, and promoted to the company of the learned.

Oute of this ordre of the learned be chosen ambassadours, priestes, tranibores, and finallye the prince him selfe. Whome they in theire olde tonge cal Barzanes, and by a newer name, Adamus. The residewe of the people being neither ydle, nor yet occupied about unprofitable exercises, it may be easely judged in how fewe houres how muche good woorke by them may be doone and dispatched, towardes those thinges that I have spoken of. This commodity they have also above other, that in the most part of necessarye occupations they neade not so much work, as other nations doe.

For first of all the buildinge or repayringe of houses asketh everye where so manye mens continual labour, bicause that the unthrifty heire suffereth the houses that his father buylded in contyneuaunce of tyme to fall in decay. So that which he myghte have upholden wyth lytle coste, hys successoure is constreyned to buylde it agayne a newe, to his great charge. Yea manye tymes also the howse that stoode one man in muche moneye, another is of so nyce and soo delycate a mynde, that he settethe nothinge by it. And it beynge neglected, and therefore shortelye fallynge into ruyne, he buyldethe uppe another in an other place with no lesse coste and chardge. But amonge the Utopians, where all thinges be sett in a good ordre, and the common wealthe in a good staye, it very seldom chaunceth, that they cheuse a newe plotte to buyld an house upon. And they doo not only finde spedy and quicke remedies for present faultes: but also prevente them that be like to fall. And by this meanes their houses continewe and laste very longe with litle labour and smal reparations: in so much that this kind of woorkmen somtimes have almost nothinge to doo. But that they be commaunded to hewe timbre at home, and to square and trimme up stones, to the intente that if anye woorke chaunce, it may the spedelier rise.

Now, syr, in theire apparell, marke (I praye you) howe few woorkmen they neade. Fyrste of al, whyles they be at woorke, they be covered homely with leather or skinnes, that will last vii. yeares. When they go furthe abrode they caste upon them a cloke, whych hydeth the other homelye apparel. These clookes through out the whole iland be all of one coloure, and that is the natural coloure of the wul. They therefore do not only spend much lesse wullen clothe then is spente in other contreis, but also the same standeth them in muche lesse coste. But lynen clothe is made with lesse laboure, and is therefore hadde more in use. But in lynen cloth onlye whytenesse, in wullen only clenlynes is regarded. As for the smalnesse or finenesse of the threde, that is no thinge passed for. And this is the cause wherfore in other places iiii. or v. clothe gownes of dyvers coloures, and as manye silke cootes be not enoughe for one man. Yea and yf he be of the delicate and nyse sorte x. be to fewe: whereas there one garmente wyl serve a man mooste commenlye ij. yeares. For whie shoulde he desyre moo? Seinge yf he had them, he should not be the better hapte or covered from colde, neither in his apparel anye whitte the comlyer. Wherefore, seinge they be all exercysed in profitable occupations, and that fewe artificers in the same craftes be sufficiente, this is the cause that plentye of all thinges beinge among them, they doo sometymes bringe forthe an innumerable companye of people to amend the hyghe wayes, yf anye be broken. Many times also, when they have no suche woorke to be occupied aboute, an open proclamation is made, that they shall bestowe fewer houres in worke. For the magistrates doe not exercise theire citizens againste theire willes in unneadefull laboures. For whie in the institution of that weale publique, this ende is onelye and chiefely pretended and mynded, that what time maye possibly be spared from the necessarye occupacions and affayres of the commen wealth, all that the citizeins shoulde withdrawe from the bodely service to the free libertye of the minde, and garnisshinge of the same. For herein they suppose the felicitye of this liffe to consiste.

Of theire liuinge and mutual conuersation together.

BUT NOWE wil I declare how the citizens use them selfes one towardes another: what familiar occupieng and enterteynement there is amonge the people, and what fassion they use in the distribution of every thing. Firste the city consisteth of familles, the families most commonlye be made of kinredes. For the women, when they be maryed at a lawefull age, they goo into theire husbandes houses. But the male children with al the whole male ofspringe continewe still in their owne family and be governed of the eldest and auncientest father, onles he dote for age: for then the next to him in age is placed in his rowme.

But to thintent the prescript number of the citezens shoulde neither decrease, nor above measure increase, it is ordeined that no familie which in every citie be vi. thousand in the whole, besydes them of the contrey, shall at ones have fewer children of the age of xiiii. yeares or there about then x. or mo then xvi. for of children under this age no numbre can be prescribed or appointed. This measure or numbre is easely observed and kept, by putting them that in fuller families be above the number into families of smaller increase. But if chaunce be that in the whole citie the stoore increase above the just number, therewith they fil up the lacke of other cities. But if so be that the multitude throughout the whole ilande passe and excede the dewe number, then they chuese out of every citie certein citezens, and build up a towne under their owne lawes in the next land where the inhabitauntes have muche waste and unoccupied ground, receaving also of the same countrey people to them, if they wil joyne and dwel with them. They thus joyning and dwelling together do easelye agre in one fassion of living, and that to the great wealth of both the peoples. For they so bringe the matter about by theire

171

lawes, that the ground which before was neither good nor
profitable for the one nor for the other, is nowe sufficiente
and fruteful enoughe for them both. But if the inhabitauntes
of that lande wyl not dwell with them to be ordered by
their lawes, then they dryve them out of those boundes
which they have limited, and apointed out for them selves.
And if they resiste and rebel, then they make warre agaynst
them. For they counte this the moste juste cause of warre,
when anye people holdethe a piece of grounde voyde and
vacaunt to no good nor profitable use, kepyng other from
the use and possession of it, whiche notwithstandyng by
the lawe of nature ought thereof to be nouryshed and re-
lieved. If anye chaunce do so muche diminishe the number
of any of theire cities, that it cannot be fylled up agayne,
without the diminishynge of the just numbre of the other
cyties (whiche they say chaunced but twyse synce the
beginnyng of the lande throughe a greate pestilente plage)
then they fulfyll and make up the numbre with cytezens
fetched out of theire owne forreyne townes, for they had
rather suffer theire forreyne townes to decaye and peryshe,
then any cytie of theire owne ilande to be diminished.
But nowe agayne to the conversation of the cytezens
amonge themselfes.

The eldeste (as I sayde) rulethe the familye. The wyfes
bee ministers to theire husbandes, the children to theire
parentes, and to bee shorte the yonger to theire elders.
Every cytie is devided into foure equall partes or quarters.
In the myddes of every quarter there is a market place of
all maner of thinges. Thether the workes of every familie
be brought into certeyne houses. And everye kynde of thing
is layde up severall in bernes or store houses. From hence
the father of everye familye, or every housholder fetchethe
whatsoever he and his have neade of, and carieth it away
with him without money, without exchaunge, without any
gage, pawne, or pledge. For whye shoulde any thing be
denyed unto him? Seynge there is abundaunce of all
thinges, and that it is not to bee feared, leste anye man

wyll aske more then he neadeth. For whie should it be thoughte that that man woulde aske more then anough which is sewer never to lacke? Certeynely in all kyndes of lyvinge creatures either feare of lacke dothe cause covetousnes and ravyne, or in man only pryde, which counteth it a glorious thinge to passe and excel other in the superfluous and vayne ostentation of thinges. The whyche kynde of vice amonge the Utopians can have no place.

Nexte to the market places that I spake of, stande meate markettes: whether be brought not only all sortes of herbes, and the fruites of trees, with breade, but also fishe, and all maner of iiii. footed beastes, and wilde foule that be mans meate. But first the fylthynes and ordure therof is clene washed awaye in the renninge ryver without the cytie in places appoynted mete for the same purpose. From thence the beastes be brought in kylled, and cleane wasshed by the handes of theire bondemen. For they permitte not their frie citezens to accustome them selfes to the killing of beastes, through the use whereof they thinke clemencye, the genteleste affection of oure nature, by lytle and lytle to decaye and peryshe. Neither they suffer anye thinge that is fylthye, lothesom, or unclenlye, to be broughte into the cytie, least the ayre by the stenche therof infected and corrupte, shoulde cause pestilente diseases. Moreover everye strete hath certeyne great large halles sett in equal distaunce one from another, everye one knowen by a severall name. In these halles dwell the syphograuntes. And to everye one of the same halles be apoynted xxx. families, on either side xv. The stewardes of everye halle at a certayne houre come in to the meate markettes, where they receyve meate accordinge to the number of their halles.

But first and chieflie of all, respect is had to the sycke, that be cured in the hospitalles. For in the circuite of the citie, a litle without the walles, they have iiii. hospitalles, so bigge so wyde, so ample, and so large, that they may seme iiii. litle townes, which were devised of that bignes partely to thintent the sycke, be they never so many in numbre, shuld not lye to thronge or strayte, and therefore uneasely and incommodiously: and partly that they which were taken and holden with contagious diseases, suche as be wonte by infection to crepe from one to another, myght be layde apart farre from the company of the residue. These hospitalles be so wel appointed, and with al thinges necessary to health so furnished, and more over so diligent attendaunce through the continual presence of cunning phisitians is geven, that though no man be sent thether against his will, yet notwithstandinge there is no sicke persone in al the citie, that had not rather lye there, then at home in his owne house.

When the stewarde of the sicke hath received suche meates as the phisitians have prescribed, then the beste is equallye devided among the halles, according to the company of every one, saving that there is had a respect to the prince, the byshop, the tranibours, and to ambassadours and all straungers, if there be any, which be verye fewe and seldome. But they also when they be there, have certeyne severall houses apointed and prepared for them. To these halles at the set houres of dinner and supper commeth all the whole siphograuntie or warde, warned by the noyse of a brasen trumpet: except suche as be sicke in the hospitalles, or els in their owne houses. Howbeit no man is prohibited or forbid, after the halles be served, to fetch home meate out of the market to his own house, For they knowe that no man wyl doe it without a cause reasonable. For thoughe no man be prohibited to dyne at home, yet no man doth it willyngly: because it is counted a pointe of smal honestie. And also it were a follye to take the payne to dresse a badde diner at home, when they may be welcome to good and fyne fare so neighe hande at the hall. In this hal al vile service, all slavery, and drudgerie, with all laboursome toyle, and base busines is done by bondemen. But the women of every family by course have the office and charge of cookerie for sethinge and dressinge the meate, and orderinge all thinges thereto belongyng.

They sit at three tables or moe, accordinge to the numbre of their company. The men sitte upon the bench next the wall, and the women againste them on the other side of the table, that yf anye sodeyne evyll should chaunce to them, as many tymes happeneth to women with chylde, they maye rise wythoute trouble or disturbaunce of anye bodie, and go thence into the nurcerie. The nurceis sitte severall alone with theyr younge suckelinges in a certaine parloure appointed and deputed to the same purpose, never withoute fire and cleane water, nor yet without cradels, that when they wyll they maye laye downe the younge infantes, and at theyr pleasure take them oute of their swathynge clothes, and holde them to the fire, and refreshe them with playe. Every mother is nource to her owne childe, onles either death, or sycknes be the let. When that chaunceth, the wives of the syphograuntes quyckelye provyde a nource. And that is not harde to be done. For they that can doo it, profer themselves to no service so gladlye as to that. Because that there thys kinde of pitie is muche praysed: and the chylde that is nourished, ever after taketh his nource for his owne naturall mother. Also amonge the nourceis sytte all the children that be under the age of v. yeares. All the other chyldren of bothe kyndes, as well boyes as girles, that be under the age of maryage, do eyther serve at the tables, or else if they be to yonge therto, yet they stand by with marvailous silence. That whiche is geven to them from the table they eate, and other several dynner tyme they have none.

The siphograunte and his wife sitte in the myddes of the high table, forasmuch as that is counted the honorablest place, and bicause from thence all the whole companie is in their sight. For that table standeth over wharte the over ende of the hall. To them be joyned two of the auncientest and eldest. For at everye table they sit foure at a meesse. But yf there be a church standing in that syphograuntie or warde, then the priest and his wife sitteth with the siphograunt, as chiefe in the company. On both sydes of them

sit yonge men, and nexte unto them againe olde men. And
thus through out all the house equall of age be sette together, and yet be mixt and matched with unequal ages.
This, they say, was ordeyned, to the intent that the sage
gravitie and reverence of the elders should kepe the yongers
from wanton licence of wordes and behavioure. Forasmuch
as nothynge can be so secretlye spoken or done at the table,
but either they that sit on the one side or on the other muste
nedes perceave it. The dishes be not set down in order
from the first place but all the olde men (whose places be
marked with some speciall token to be knowen) be first
served of their meate, and then the residue equally. The
old men devide their deinties as they think best to the
yonger on eche syde of them.

   Thus the elders be not defrauded of their dewe honoure,
and neverthelesse equall commoditie commeth to every one.
They begin everye dinner and supper of redinge sumthing
that perteneth to good maners and vertue. But it is shorte,
because no man shal be greved therwith. Hereof thelders
take occasion of honest communication, but neither sadde
nor unpleasant. Howbeit they do not spende all the whole
dinertime themselves with longe and tedious talkes: but
they gladly heare also the yonge men: yea, and purposelye
provoke them to talke, to thintent that they may have a
profe of every mans wit, and towardnes, or disposition to
vertue, which commonlie in the libertie of feasting doth
shew and utter it self. Their diners be verie short: but
their suppers be sumwhat longer, because that after dyner
foloweth laboure, after supper slepe and natural reste,
whiche they thinke to be of more strength and efficacie to
wholsome and healthfull digestion. No supper is passed
without musicke. Nor their bankettes lacke no conceytes
nor jonketes. They burne swete gummes and spices or per-
fumes, and pleasaunt smelles, and sprinckle aboute swete
oyntementes and waters, yea, they leave nothing undone
that maketh for the cheringe of the companye. For they be
muche enclined to this opinion: to thinke no kinde of

pleasure forbydden, wherof commeth no harme. Thus therfore and after this sort they live togethers in the citie, but in the countrey they that dwell alone farre from any neighboures, do dyne and suppe at home in their owne houses. For no familie there lacketh any kinde of victualles, as from whom commeth all that the citezens eate and lyve by.

Of their journeyng or trauayling abrode, with diuers other matters cunninglye reasoned, and wyttilye discussed.

BUT if any be desierous to visite either theyr frendes dwelling in an other citie, or to see the place it selfe: they easelie obteyne licence of their siphograuntes and tranibores, onless there be some profitable let. No man goeth out alone but a companie is sente furth together with their princes letters, which do testifie that they have licence to go that journey, and prescribeth also the day of their retourne. They have a wageyn geven them, with a common bondman, which driveth the oxen, and taketh charge of them. But onles they have women in their companie, they sende home the wageyn againe, as an impediment and a let. And thoughe they carye nothynge furth with them, yet in all their jorney they lack nothing. For whersoever they come, they be at home. If they tary in a place longer then one daye, than there every one of them falleth to his owne occupation, and be very gentilly enterteined of the workemen and companies of the same craftes. If any man of his owne heade and without leave, walke out of his precinct and boundes, taken without the princes letters, he is broughte againe for a fugitive or a runaway with great shame and rebuke, and is sharpely punished. If he be taken in that faulte againe, he is punished with bondage. If anye be desirous to walke abrode into the feldes, or into the countrey that belongeth to the same citie that he dwelleth in, obteininge the good wil of his father, and the consente of his wife, he is not prohibited. But into what part of the contrei soever he commeth he hath no meat geven him until he have wrought out his forenones taske, or dispatched so muche work, as there is wont to be wrought before supper. Observing this law and condition, he may go whether he wil within the boundes of his own citie. For he shal be no les profitable to the citie, then if he were within it. Now you se how litle liberte they have to loiter: howe they can have no cloke or pretence to ydlenes. There be neither winetavernes, nor ale houses, nor stewes, nor anye occasion of vice or wickednes, no lurkinge corners, no places of wycked counsels or unlawfull assembles. But they be in the presente sighte, and under the eies of every man. So that of necessitie they must either apply their accustomed labours, or els recreate themselves with honest and laudable pastimes.

This fashion and trade of life, being used amonge the people, it cannot be chosen, but that they muste of necessitie have store and plentie of all thinges. And seyng they be all therof parteners equallie, therefore can no man there be poore or nedie. In the counsell of Amaurot, whether, as I said, every citie sendeth three men a pece yearly, as sone as it is perfectly knowen of what thinges there is in every place plentie, and againe what thinges be skant in any place: incontinent the lacke of the one is perfourmed and filled up with the aboundance of the other. And this they do frely without anye benefite, taking nothing againe of them, to whom the thinges is given, but those cities that have geven of their store to any other citie that lacketh, requiring nothing againe of the same citie, do take suche thinges as they lacke of an other citie, to the which they gave nothinge. So the whole ylande is as it were one familie, or housholde.

But when they have made sufficient provision of store for themselves (which they thinke not done, until they have provided for two yeres folowinge, because of the uncertentie of the next yeares proffe) then of those thinges, wherof they have abundaunce, they carie furth into other countreis great plentie: as grayne, honnie, wulle, flaxe, woode, madder, purple died felles, waxe, tallowe, lether, and lyvinge beastes. And the seventh parte of all these thynges they geve franckelye and frelie to the pore of that countrey. The residewe they sell at a reasonable and meane price. By this trade of traffique or marchaundise they bring into their own contrey, not only great plenty of golde and silver, but also all suche thynges as they lacke at home, whiche is almoste nothinge but iron. And by reason they have longe used this trade, nowe they have more aboundaunce of these thinges, then anye man wyll beleve. Nowe therfore they care not whether they sell for readye money, or els upon truste to be payed at a daye, and to have the mooste parte in debtes. But in so doynge they never followe the credence of privat men: but the assuraunce or warrauntise of the whole citie, by instrumentes, and writinges made in that behalfe accordingly. When the daye of paiement is come and expired, the citie gathereth up the debte of the private debtoures, and putteth it into the common boxe, and so longe hath the use and profite of it, untill the Utopians their creditours demaunde it. The mooste parte of it they never aske. For that thynge whiche is to them no profite to take it from other, to whom it is profitable: they thinke it no righte nor conscience.

But if the case so stand, that they must lende part of that money to an other people, then they require theyr debte: or when they have warre. For the whiche purpose onelye they kepe at home all the treasure, whiche they have, to be holpen and socoured by it either in extreame jeopardyes, or in suddeine daungers. But especiallye and chiefelie to hiere therewith, and that for unreasonable great wayges, straunge soldiours. For they hadde rather put straungers in

179

jeopardie, then theyr owne countreyemen: knowynge that
for money ynoughe, their enemyes themselves many times
may be boughte or solde, or elles throughe treason be sette
togethers by the eares amonge themselves. For this cause
they kepe an inestimable treasure. But yet not as a treasure:
but so they have it, and use it, as in good faythe I am
ashamed to shewe: fearinge that my woordes shall not be
beleved. And this I have more cause to feare, for that I
knowe howe difficultlie and hardelye I meselfe would have
beleved an other man tellinge the same, if I hadde not
presentlye sene it with mine owne eyes.

For it muste neades be, that howe farre a thynge is
dissonaunt and disagreing from the guise and trade of the
hearers, so farre shall it be out of their belefe. Howebeit, a
wise and indifferent estimer of thynges will not greatlye
marveill perchaunce, seynge all theyr other lawes and
customes do so muche differre from oures, yf the use also
of gold and sylver amonge them be applied, rather to their
owne fashyons than to oures. I meane in that they occupie
not money themselves, but kepe it for that chaunce, whiche
as it maye happen, so it maye be that it shall never come
to passe. In the meane time golde and sylver, wherof money
is made, they do so use, as none of them doethe more
esteme it, then the verye nature of the thing deserveth. And
then who doeth not playnelye se howe farre it is under
iron: as without the whiche men can no better lyve then
without fiere and water. Whereas to golde and silver nature
hath geven no use, that we may not well lacke: if that the
follye of men hadde not sette it in higher estimation for
the rarenesse sake. But of the contrarie parte, nature as a
mooste tender and lovynge mother, hathe placed the beste
and mooste necessarie thinges open abroade: as the ayere,
the water and the yearth it selfe. And hathe removed and
hyd farthest from us vayne and unprofitable thinges. Therefore if these metalles amonge them shoulde be faste locked
up in some tower, it might be suspected, that the prince
and the counsell (as the people is ever foolishelie ymaginin-

inge) intended by some subtiltie to deceave the commons, and to take some profite of it to themselves. Furthermore if they shold make therof plate and such other finelie and cunninglie wroughte stuffe: if at anye time they should have occasion to breake it, and melte it againe, therewith to paye their souldiers wages, they see and perceave verye well, that men woulde be lothe to parte from those thinges, that they ones begonne to have pleasure and delite in.

To remedie all this they have founde oute a meanes, whiche, as it is agreeable to all their other lawes and customes, so it is from ours, where golde is so much set by and so diligently kept, very farre discripant and repugnaunt: and therfore uncredible, but onelye to them that be wise. For where as they eate and drinke in earthen and glasse vesselles, whiche in dede be curiouslye and properlie made, and yet be of very small value: of golde and sylver they make commonly chaumber pottes, and other vesselles, that serve for moste vile uses, not onely in their common halles, but in every mans private house. Furthermore of the same mettalles they make greate chaines, fetters, and gieves wherin the[y] tie their bondmen. Finally whosoever for anye offense be infamed, by their eares hange rynges of golde, upon their fyngers they weare rynges of golde, and aboute their neckes chaines of golde, and in conclusion their heades be tied aboute with gold.

Thus by al meanes possible thei procure to have golde and silver among them in in reproche and infamie. And these mettalles, which other nations do as grevously and sorowefullye forgo, as in a manner their owne lives: if they should altogethers at ones be taken from the Utopians, no man there would thinke that he had lost the worth of one farthing. They gather also pearles by the sea side, and diamondes and carbuncles upon certen rockes, and yet they seke not for them: but by chaunce finding them, they cut and polish them. And therwith thei deck their yonge infauntes. Whiche like as in the first yeres of their childhod, they make muche and be fonde and proude of such ornamentes, so when they be a litle more growen in yeares and discretion, perceiving that none but children do weare such toies and trifels: they lay them awaye even of their owne shamefastenesse, wythoute anye byddynge of their parentes: even as oure chyldren, when they waxe bygge, doo caste awaye nuttes, brouches, and puppettes. Therfore these lawes and customes, whiche be so farre differente from al other nations, howe divers fantasies also and myndes they doo cause, dydde I never so playnelie perceave, as in the ambassadoures of the Anemolians.

These ambassadoures came to Amaurote whiles I was there. And because they came to entreate of great and weightie matters, those three citizens a pece oute of everie citie were comen thether before them. But all the ambassadours of the nexte countreis, whiche had bene there before, and knewe the fashions and maners of the Utopians, amonge whom they perceaved no honoure geven to sumptuous apparell, silkes to be contemned, golde also to be infamed and reprochful, were wont to come thether in verie homelye and simple araie. But the Anemolianes, because they dwell farre thence and had very litle aquaintaunce with them, hearinge that they were all apparelled a like, and that verie rudely and homely: thinkinge them not to have the thinges whiche they did not weare: being therfore more proude, then wise: determyned in the gorgiousness of their apparel to represente verye goddes, and wyth the brighte shyninge and glisterynge of their gay clothing to dasell the eyes of the silie poore Utopians. So there came in iii. ambassadours with c. servauntes all apparelled in chaungeable colours: the moste of them in silkes: the ambassadours themselves (for at home in their owne countrey they were noble men) in cloth of gold, with great cheines of gold, with golde hanginge at their eares, with gold ringes upon their fingers, with brouches and aglettes of gold upon their cappes, which glistered ful of peerles and precious stones: to be short, trimmed and adourned with al those thinges, which among the Utopians were either the punishement of bondmen, or the reproche of infamed persones, or elles trifels for yonge children to playe withal.

Therefore it wolde have done a man good at his harte to have sene howe proudelye they displeyed theire pecockes fethers, howe muche they made of theire paynted sheathes, and howe loftely they set forth and advaunced them selfes, when they compared their gallaunte apparrell with the poore rayment of the Utopians. For al the people were swarmed forth into the stretes. And on the other side it was no lesse pleasure to consider howe muche they were deceaved, and how farre they missed of their purpose, being contrary wayes taken then they thought they should have bene. For to the eyes of all the Utopians, excepte very fewe, which had bene in other countreys for some resonable cause, all that gorgeousness of apparel semed shamefull and reprocheful. In so muche that they most reverently saluted the vilest and most abject of them for lordes: passing over the ambassadoures themselfes without any honour: judging them by their wearing of golden cheynes to be bondmen. Yea you shoulde have sene children also, that had caste away their peerles and pretious stones, when they sawe the like sticking upon the ambassadours cappes, digge and pushe theire mothers under the sides, sainge thus to them. Loke, mother, how great a lubbor doth yet were peerles and precious stoones, as though he were a litel child stil. But the mother, yea and that also in good earnest: peace, sone, saithe she: I thinke he be some of the ambassadours fooles. Some founde faulte at theire golden cheines, as to no use nor purpose, being so smal and weake, that a bondeman might easely breake them, and agayne so wyde and large, that when it pleased him, he myght cast them of, and runne awaye at libertye whether he woulde. But when the ambassadoures hadde bene there a daye or ii. and sawe so greate abundaunce of gold so lyghtely esteimed, yea in no lesse reproche, then it was with them in honour: and besides that more golde in the cheines and gieves of one fugitive bondman, then all the costelye ornaments of them iii. was worth: they beganne to abate their courage, and for very shame layde away al that gorgyouse arraye, wherof they were so proud. And specyally when they had talked familiarlye with the Utopians, and had learned al theire fassions and opinions.

For they marveyle that any men be so folyshe, as to have delite and pleasure in the doubteful glisteringe of a lytil tryffelynge stone, which maye beholde annye of the starres, or elles the sonne it selfe. Or that anye man is so madde, as to count him selfe the nobler for the smaller or fyner threde of wolle, which selfe same wol (be it now in never so fyne a sponne threde) a shepe did ones weare: and yet was she all that time no other thing then a shepe. They marveile also that golde, whych of the owne nature is a thinge so unprofytable, is nowe amonge all people in so hyghe estimation, that man him selfe, by whome, yea and for the use of whome it is so much set by, is in muche lesse estimation, then the golde it selfe. In so muche that a lumpyshe blockehedded churle, and whyche hathe no more wytte then an asse, yea and as ful of noughtynes as of follye, shall have nevertheles manye wyse and good men in subjectyon and bondage, only for this, bycause he hath a greate heape of golde. Whyche yf it should be taken from hym by anye fortune, or by some subtyll wyle and cautele of the lawe, (whyche no lesse then fortune dothe bothe raise up the lowe and plucke downe the highe) and be geven to the moste vile slave and abject dryvell of all his housholde, then shortely after he shall goo into the service of his servaunt, as an augmentation or overplus beside his money. But they muche more marvell at and detest the madness of them, whyche to those riche men, in whose debte and daunger they be not, do give almost divine honoures, for none other consideration, but bicause they be riche: and yet knowing them to bee suche nigeshe penny fathers, that they be sure as longe as they live, not the worthe of one farthinge of that heape of gold shall come to them.

These and such like opinions have they conceaved, partely by education, beinge brought up in that common wealth, whose lawes and customes be farre different from these kindes of folly, and partely by good litterature and learning. For though there be not many in every citie, which be exempte and discharged of all other laboures, and appointed only to learning; that is to saye, suche in whome even from theire very childhode they have perceaved a singular towardnes, a fyne witte, and a minde apte to good learning: yet all in their childhode be instructe in learninge. And the better parte of the people, bothe men and women throughe oute all their whole lyffe doo bestowe in learninge those spare houres, which we sayde they have vacante from bodelye laboures. They be taughte learninge in theire owne natyve tong. For it is bothe copious in woordes, and also pleasaunte to the eare, and for the utteraunce of a mans minde very perfecte and sure. The mooste parte of all that syde of the worlde useth the same langage, savinge that amonge the Utopians it is fyneste and pureste, and accordinge to the dyversytye of the countreys it is dyverslye alterede.

Of all these philosophers, whose names be heare famous in this parte of the worlde to us knowen, before oure cummynge thether not as muche as the fame of annye of them was cumen amonge them. And yet in musike, logike, arythmetyke, and geometrye they have founde oute in a manner all that oure auncient philosophers have tawghte. But as they in all thinges be almoste equal to oure olde auncyente clerkes, so oure newe logiciens in subtyl inventions have farre passed and gone beyonde them. For they have not devysed one of all those rules of restrictions, amplifications and suppositions, verye witelye invented in the small logicalles, whyche heare oure children in every place do learne. Furtheremore they were never yet hable to fynde out the seconde intentions: insomuche that none of them all coulde ever see man himselfe in commen, as they cal him, thoughe he be (as you knowe) bygger than ever was annye gyaunte, yea and poynted to of us even wyth our fynger.[14]

But they be in the course of the starres, and the movynges of the heavenly spheres verye expert and cunnynge. They have also wittely excogitated and devised instrumentes of divers fassions: wherein is exactly comprehended and conteyned the movynges and situations of the sonne, the mone, and of al the other starres, which appere in theire horizon. But as for the amityes and dissentions of the planettes, and all that deceyteful divination by the starres, they never as much as dreamed thereof. Raynes, windes, and other courses of tempestes they knowe before by certeine tokens, which they have learned by long use and observation. But of the causes of al these thinges and of the ebbinge, flowinge and saltenes of the sea, and finallye of the original begynnynge and nature of heaven and of the worlde, they holde partelye the same opinions that oure olde philosophers hold, and partely, as our philosophers varye among themselfes, so they also, whiles they bringe newe reasons of thinges, do disagree from all them, and yet among themselfes in all poyntes they doe not accorde. In that part of philosophie, which intreateth of manners and vertue, theire reasons and opinions agree with ours. They dispute of the good qualityes of the sowle, of the body and of fortune. And whether the name of goodnes maye be applied to all these, or onlye to the endowementes and giftes of the soule.

They reason of vertue and pleasure. But the chiefe and principall question is in what thinge, be it one or moe, the felicitye of man consistethe. But in this poynte they seme almooste to muche geven and enclyned to the opinion of them, which defende pleasure, wherein they determine either all or the chiefyste parte of mans felicitye to reste.[15] And (whyche is more to bee marveled at) the defense of this soo deyntye and delicate an opinion they fetche even from theire grave, sharpe, bytter and rygorous religion. For they never dispute of felicity or blessednes, but they joine unto the reasons of philosophye certeyne principles taken oute of religion: wythoute the whyche to the investigation of trewe felicitye they thynke reason of it selfe weake and unperfecte.

Those principles be these and such lyke. That the soule is immortal, and by the bountiful goodnes of God ordeined to felicitie. That to our vertues and good deades rewardes be appointed after this life, and to our evel deades punish-mentes. Though these be perteyning to religion, yet they thincke it mete that they shoulde be beleved and graunted by profes of reason. But yf these principles were con-dempned and dysannuled, then without anye delaye they pronounce no man to be so folish, whiche woulde not do all his diligence and endevoure to obteyne pleasure be ryght or wronge, onlye avoydnge this inconvenience that the lesse pleasure should not be a let or hinderaunce to the bigger: or that he laboured not for that pleasure, whiche would bringe after it displeasure, greefe and sorrow. For they judge it extreame madnes to folowe sharpe and pein-ful vertue, and not only to bannishe the pleasure of life, but also willingly to suffer griefe, without anye hope of proffit thereof ensuinge. For what proffit can there be, if a man, when he hath passed over all his lyfe unpleasauntly, that is to say, miserablye, shall have no rewarde after his death?

But nowe, syr, they thinke not felicitie to reste in all pleasure, but only in that pleasure that is good and honeste, and that hereto, as to perfet blessednes our nature is allured and drawen even of vertue, whereto onlye they that be of the contrary opinion do attribute felicitie. For they define vertue to be life ordered according to nature, and that we be hereunto ordeined of God. And that he dothe followe the course of nature, which in desiering and refusinge thinges is ruled by reason. Furthermore that reason doth chiefely and principallye kendle in men the love and veneration of the devine majestie. Of whose goodnes it is that we be, and that we be in possibilitie to attayne felicite. And that sec-ondarely it bothe stirrethe and provoketh us to leade our

187

lye oute of care in joy and mirth, and also moveth us to
helpe and further all other in respecte of the societe of
nature to obteine and enjoye the same. For there was never
man so earnest and paineful a follower of vertue and hater
of pleasure, that wold so injoyne you laboures, watchinges
and fastinges, but he would also exhort you to ease, lighten
and relieve, to your powre, the lack and misery of others,
praysing the same as a dede of humanitie and pitie.

Then if it be a poynte of humanitie for man to bring
health and comforte to man, and speciallye (which is a
vertue moste peculiarlye belonging to man) to mitigate and
assuage the greife of others, and by takyng from them the
sorowe and hevynes of lyfe, to restore them to joye, that is
to saye, to pleasure: whie maye it not then be sayd, that
nature doth provoke everye man to doo the same to himselfe? For a joyfull lyfe, that is to say, a pleasaunt lyfe is
either evel, and if it be so, then thou shouldest not onlye
helpe no man therto, but rather, as much as in the lieth,
withdrawe all men frome it, as noysome and hurteful, or els
if thou not only mayste, but also of dewty art bound to
procure it to others, why not chiefely to the selfe? To
whome thou art bound to shew as much favoure and gentel-
nes as to other. For when nature biddeth the to be good
and gentle to other she commaundeth the not to be cruell
and ungentle to the selfe. Therefore even very nature (saye
they) prescribeth to us a joyful lyfe, that is to say, pleasure
as the ende of all oure operations. And they define vertue to
be lyfe ordered accordynge to the prescripte of nature. But
in that that nature dothe allure and provoke men one to
healpe another to lyve merily (which suerly she doth not
without a good cause, for no man is so farre above the
lotte of mans state or condicion, that nature dothe carke and
care for hym onlye, whiche equallye favourethe all that be
comprehended under the communion of one shape forme
and fassion) verely she commaundeth the to use diligent
circumspection, that thou do not so seke for thine owne
commodities, that thou procure others incommodities.

Wherefore theire opinion is, that not only covenauntes and bargaynes made amonge private men ought to be well and faythefullye fulfilled, observed and kepte, but also commen lawes, whiche either a good prince hath justly publyshed, or els the people neither oppressed with tyrannye, neither deceaved by fraude and gyell, hath by theire common consent constituted and ratifyed, concerninge the particion of the commodities of lyfe, that is to say, the matter of pleasure. These lawes not offended, it is wysdome, that thou looke to thine own wealthe. And to doe the same for the common wealth is no lesse then thy duetie, if thou bearest any reverent love, or any naturall zeale and affection to thy native countreye. But to go about to let an other man of his pleasure, whiles thou procurest thine owne, that is open wrong. Contrary wyse to withdrawe somethinge from the selfe to geve to other, that is a pointe of humanitie and gentilnes: whiche never taketh awaye so muche commoditie, as it bringethe agayne. For it is recompensed with the retourne of benefytes; and the conscience of the good dede, with the remembraunce of the thankefull love and benevolence of them to whom thou hast done it, doth bringe more pleasure to thy mynde, then that whiche thou hast withholden from thy selfe could have brought to thy bodye. Finallye (which to a godly disposed and a religious mind is easy to be persuaded) God recompenseth the gifte of a short and smal pleasure with great and everlastinge joye. Therfore the matter diligently weyede and considered, thus they thinke, that all our actions, and in them the vertues themselfes, be referred at the last to pleasure, as their ende and felicitie.

Pleasure they call every motion and state of the bodie or mynde wherin man hath naturally delectation. Appetite they joyne to nature, and that not without a good cause. For like as, not only the senses, but also right reason coveteth whatsoever is naturally pleasaunt, so that it may be gotten without wrong or injurie, not letting or debarring a greater pleasure, nor causing painful labour, even so those thinges that men by vaine ymagination do fayne against nature to be pleasaunt (as though it laye in their power to chaunge the thinges, as they do the names of thinges) al suche pleasures they beleve to be of so small helpe and furtheraunce to felicitie, that they counte them a great let and hinderaunce. Because that in whom they have ones taken place, all his mynde they possesse with a false opinion of pleasure. So that there is no place left for true and naturall delectations. For there be many thinges, which of their owne nature conteyne no plesauntnes: yea the moste parte of them muche griefe and sorrowe. And yet throughe the perverse and malicyous flickeringe inticementes of lewde and unhoneste desyres, be taken not only for speciall and sovereigne pleasures, but also be counted amonge the chiefe causes of life.

In this counterfeat kinde of pleasure they put them that I spake of before; whiche the better gownes they have on, the better men they thinke them selfes. In the which thing they doo twyse erre. For they be no lesse deceaved in that they thinke theire gowne the better, than they be, in that they thinke themselfes the better. For if you consider the profitable use of the garmente, whye should wulle of a fyner sponne threde, be thougt better, than the wul of a course sponne threde? Yet they, as though the one did passe the other by nature, and not by their mistakyng, avaunce themselfes, and thinke the price of their owne persones thereby greatly encreased. And therefore the honour, which in a course gowne they durste not have loked for, they require, as it were of dewtie, for theyr fyner gownes sake. And if they be passed by without reverence, they take it displeasauntly and disdainfullye. And agayne is it not lyke madnes to take a pryde in vayne and unprofitable honours? For what naturall or trewe pleasure doest thou take of an other mans bare hede, or bowed knees? Will this ease the paine of thy knees, or remedie the phrensie of thy hede? In this ymage of counterfeite pleasure, they be of a marvelous madnesse, whiche

for the opinion of nobilitie, rejoyse muche in their owne
conceyte. Because it was their fortune to come of suche
auncetoures, whose stocke of longe tyme hathe bene
counted ryche (for nowe nobilitie is nothing elles) speciallye riche in landes. And though their auncetours left
them not one foote of lande, yet they thinke themselves
not the lesse noble therfore of one heare.

In this number also they counte them that take pleasure
and delite (as I said) in gemmes and precious stones, and
thynke themselves almoste goddes, if they chaunce to gette
an excellente one, speciallye of that kynde, whiche in that
tyme of their own countre men is had in hyghest estimation. For one kynde of stone kepeth not his pryce styll in
all countreis and at all times. Nor they bye them not, but
taken out of the golde and bare: no nor so neither, untyll
they have made the seller to sweare, that he will warraunte
and assure it to be a true stone, and no counterfeit gemme.
Suche care they take lest a counterfeite stone should deceave their eyes in steade of a ryghte stone. But why
shouldest thou not take even as muche pleasure in beholdynge a counterfeite stone, whiche thine eye cannot discerne
from a righte stone? They shoulde bothe be of lyke value
to thee, even as to the blynde man.

What shall I saye of them, that kepe superfluous riches,
to take delectation only in the beholdinge, and not in the
use or occupiynge thereof? Do they take trew pleasure,
or elles be thei deceaved with false pleasure? Or of them
that be in a contrarie vice, hidinge the gold whiche they
shall never occupye, nor peradventure never se more? And
whiles they take care leaste they shall leese it, do leese it
in dede. For what is it elles, when they hyde it in the
ground, takyng it bothe frome their owne use, and perchaunce frome all other mennes also? And yet thou, when
thou haste hydde thy treasure, as one out of all care,
hoppest for joye. The whiche treasure, yf it shoulde chaunce
to bee stolen, and thou ignoraunt of the thefte shouldest
dye tenne years after: all that tenne yeares space that thou

191

lyvedest after thy money was stoolen, what matter was it to thee, whether it hadde bene taken awaye or elles safe as thou lefteste it? Trewlye both wayes like profytte came to thee.

To these so foolyshe pleasures they joyne dicers, whose madnesse they knowe by hearsay and not by use. Hunters also, and hawkers. For what pleasure is there (say they) in castinge the dice upon a table. Which thou hast done so often, that if there wer any pleasure in it, yet the oft use might make thee werie thereof? Or what delite can there be, and not rather dyspleasure in hearynge the barkynge and howlynge of dogges? Or what greater pleasure is there to be felte, when a dogge followeth an hare, then when a dogge followeth a dogge? for one thinge is done in bothe, that is to saye, runnynge, yf thou haste pleasure therin. But yf the hope of slaughter and the expectation of tear-ynge in peces the beaste doth please thee: thou shouldest rather be moved with pitie to see a selye innocente hare murdered of a dogge, the weake of the stronger, the feare-full of the fearce, the innocente of the cruell and unmercy-full. Therefore all thys exercyse of huntynge, as a thynge unworthye to be used of free men, the Utopians have rejected to their bouchers, to the whiche crafte (as we sayde before) they appointe their bondemen. For they counte huntynge the lowest, the vyleste and mooste abjecte part of boucherie, and the other partes of it more profitable and more honeste, as bryngynge muche more commoditie, in that they kyll beastes onely for necessitie. Whereas the hunter seketh nothinge but pleasure of the seeyle and wofull beastes slaughter and murder. The whiche pleasure in beholdinge deathe, they thinke doeth rise in the very beastes, either of a cruel affection of mind, or els to be chaunged in continuaunce of time into crueltie, by longe use of so cruell a pleasure. These therfore and all suche like, whiche be innumerable, though the common sorte of people doth take them for pleasures, yet they, seing there is no natural pleasauntnes in them, do playnly determine them to have no affinitie with trew and right pleasure. For as touchinge that they do commonlye move the sense with delectation (whiche semeth to be a woorke of pleasure) this doeth nothynge diminishe their opinion. For not the nature of the thing, but their perverse and lewde custome is the cause hereof, whiche causeth them to accept bitter or sowre thynges for swete thynges.

They make divers kindes of pleasures. For some they attribute to the soule, and some to the body. To the soule they geve intelligence and that delectation that commethe of the contemplation of trewth. Hereunto is joyned the pleasaunte remembraunce of the good lyfe paste. The pleasure of the bodye they devide into ii. partes. The first is when delectation is sensibly felt and perceaved. The seconde parte of bodely pleasure, they say, is that which consisteth and resteth in the quiete and upryghte state of the bodye. And that trewlye is everye mannes owne propre health entermingled and disturbed with no griefe. For this, yf it be not letted nor assaulted with no greif, is delectable of it selfe, thoughe it be moved with no externall or outwarde pleasure. For though it be not so plain and manyfeste to the sense, as the gredye luste of eatynge and drynkynge, yet neverthelesse manye take it for the chiefeste pleasure. All the Utopians graunt it to be a right sovereigne pleasure, and as you woulde saye, the foundation and grounde of all pleasures, as whiche even alone is hable to make the state and condition of life delectable and pleasaunt. And it beyng once taken awaye, there is no place lefte for any pleasure. For to be without greife not havinge health, that they call unsensibilitie, and not pleasure.

The Utopians have long ago rejected and condempned the opinion of them whiche sayde that stedfaste and quiete healthe (for this question also hathe bene diligently debated amonge them) oughte not therfore to be counted a pleasure, bycause they saye it can not be presentlye and sensiblye perceaved and felte by some outwarde motion.

But of the contrarie parte nowe they agree almooste all in this, that healthe is a moost soveraigne pleasure. For seynge that in sycknesse (saye they) is greiffe, whiche is a mortal enemie to pleasure, even as sicknes is to health, why should not then pleasure be in the quietnes of health? For they say it maketh nothing to this matter, whether you saye that sycknesse is a griefe, or that in sickenes is griefe, for all commethe to one purpose. For whether health be a pleasure it selfe, or a necessary cause of pleasure, as fier is of heate, truelye bothe wayes it foloweth, that they cannot be withoute pleasure, that be in perfect helth. Furthermore whiles we eat (say they) then healthe, whiche beganne to be appayred, fighteth by the helpe of foode againste hunger. In the which fight, whiles health by litle and litle getteth the upper hande, that same procedyng, and (as ye would say) that onwardnes to the wonte strength ministreth that pleasure, wherby we be so refreshed. Health therfore, whiche in the conflict is joyefull, shall it not be mery, when it hath gootten the victorie? But as soone as it hathe recovered the pristinate strength, which thing onely in all the fight it coveted, shal it incontinent be astonied? Nor shall it not know nor imbrace the owne wealthe and goodnes? For where it is said, healthe can not be felt: this, they thinke, is nothing trew. For what man wakyng, say they, feleth not himselfe in healthe, but he that is not? Is there anye man so possessed with stonishe insensibilitie, or with lethargie, that is to say, the sleping sicknes, that he will not graunt healthe to be acceptable to him, and delectable? But what other thinge is delectation, than that whiche by an other name is called pleasure?

They imbrace chieflie the pleasures of the mind. For them they counte the chiefist and most principall of all. The chiefe parte of them they thinke doth come of the exercise of vertue, and conscience of good life. Of these pleasures that the body ministreth, they geve the preeminence to helth. For the delite of eating and drinking, and whatsoever hath any like pleasauntnes, they determyne to be pleasures muche to be desired, but no other wayes than for healthes sake. For suche thinges of their own proper nature be not so pleasaunt, but in that they resiste sickenesse privelie stealing on. Therfore like as it is a wise mans part, rather to avoid sicknes, then to wishe for medicines, and rather to drive away and put to flight carefull griefes, then to call for comfort: so it is muche better not to neade this kinde of pleasure, then thereby to be eased of the contrarie griefe. The whiche kinde of pleasure, yf anye man take for his felicitie, that man must nedes graunt, that then he shal be in most felicitie, if he live that life, which is led in continuall hunger, thurste, itchinge, eatinge, drynkynge, scratchynge and rubbing. The which life how not only foule, and unhonest, but also howe miserable, and wretched it is, who perceveth not? These doubtles be the basest pleasures of al, as unpure and unperfect. For they never come, but accompanied with their contrarie griefes. As with the pleasure of eating is joynd hunger, and that after no very egal sort. For of these ii. the griefe is both the more vehement, and also of longer continuaunce. For it beginneth before the pleasure, and endeth not until the pleasure die with it. Wherefore suche pleasures they thinke not greatlye to be set by, but in that thei be necessari. Howbeit they have delite also in these, and thankfulli knowledge the tender love of mother nature, which with most pleasaunt delectation allureth her children to that, to the necessarie use wherof they must from time to time continually be forced and driven. For how wretched and miserable should our life be, if these dailie greffes of hunger and thurst coulde not be driven awaye, but with bitter potions and sower medicines, as the other diseases be, wherwith we be seldomer troubled?

But beutie, strengthe, nemblenes, these as peculiar and pleasaunt giftes of nature they make muche of. But those pleasures that be receaved by the eares, the eyes and the nose, whiche nature willeth to be proper and peculiar to man (for no other livinge creature doth behold the fairenes and the bewtie of the worlde, or is moved with any respecte of savours, but onely for the diversitie of meates, neither perceaveth the concordaunte and discordant distaunces of soundes and tunes) these pleasures, I say, they accept and alowe as certen pleasaunte rejoysinges of life. But in all thinges this cautel they use, that a lesse pleasure hinder not a bigger, and that the pleasure be no cause of displeasure, whiche they thinke to folow of necessitie, if the pleasure be unhoneste. But yet to dispise the comlines of bewtie, to wast the bodelie strength, to turne nimblenes into slough-ishnesse, to consume and make feble the bodie with fast-inge, to do injurie to healthe, and to rejecte the pleasaunte motions of nature; onles a man neglecte these commodities, whiles he dothe with a fervent zeale procure the wealthe of others, or the commen profite, for the whiche pleasure for-borne, he is in hoope of a greater pleasure at Goddes hande; elles for a vaine shaddow of vertue, for the wealth and profite of no man, to punishe himselfe, or to the intente he maye be hable courragiouslie to suffer adversitie, whiche perchaunce shall never come to him; this to do they thinke it a point of extreame madnes, and a token of a man cruel-lye minded towardes himselfe, and unkind towardes nature, as one so disdaining to be in her daunger, that he re-nounceth and refuseth all her benefites.

This is their sentence and opinion of vertue and pleasure. And they beleve that by mans reason none can be found trewer then this, onles any godlyer be inspired into man from heven. Wherin whether they beleve well or no, neither the time doth suffer us to discusse neither it is nowe neces-sarie. For we have taken upon us to shewe and declare their lores and ordinaunces, and not to defende them. But this thynge I beleve verely, howe soever these decrees be, that there is in no place of the world, neyther a more excellent people, neither a more flourishynge commen wealth. They be lyghte and quicke of bodie, full of activitie and nimblenes, and of more strength then a man woulde judge them by their stature, which for all that is not to

lowe. And thoughe theyr soyle be not verie frutefull, nor
their aier very wholsome, yet againste the ayer they so
defende them with temperate diete, and so order and
husbande their grounde with diligente travaile, that in no
countrey is greater increase, and plentye of corne and
cattell, nor mens bodies of longer lyfe, and subject or
apte to fewer diseases. There therfore a man maye see well
and diligentlie exploited and furnished, not onely those
thinges whiche husbandemen do commenly in other countreis, as by craft and cunninge to remedie the barrennes
of the grounde; but also a whole wood by the handes of
the people plucked up by the rootes in one place, and set
againe in an other place. Wherein was had regard and
consideration, not of plenty, but of commodious carriage,
that wood and timber might be nigher to the sea, or the
rivers, or the cities. For it is lesse laboure and businesse
to carrie grayne farre by land, than wood. The people be
gentle, merie, quickie, and fyne witted, delitinge in quietnes, and when nede requireth, hable to abide and suffer
much bodelie laboure. Els they be not greatly desirous and
fond of it; but in the exercise and studie of the mind they
be never wery.

When they had herd me speak of the Greke literature
or lerning (for in Latin there was nothing that I thought
they would greatly alow, besides historiens and poetes)
they made wonderfull earneste and importunate sute unto
me that I would teach and instructe them in that tonge
and learninge. I beganne therfore to reade unto them, at
the first truelie more bicause I would not seme to refuse
the laboure, then that I hooped that they would any thing
profite therein. But when I had gone forward a litle, I
perceaved incontinente by their diligence, that my laboure
should not be bestowed in vaine. For they began so easelie
to fashion their letters, so plainlie to pronounce the woordes,
so quickelie to learne by hearte, and so suerlie to rehearse
the same, that I marvailed at it, savinge that the most parte
of them were fine and chosen wittes and of ripe age, piked

oute of the companie of the learned men, whiche not
onelie of their owne free and voluntarie will, but also by
the commaundemente of the counsell, undertoke to learne
this langage. Therefore in lesse then thre yeres space there
was nothing in the Greke tonge that they lacked. They
were hable to rede good authors withoute anie staye, if the
booke were not false. This kynde of learninge, as I suppose, they toke so muche the sooner, bycause, it is sumwhat allyaunte to them. For I thinke that this nation tooke
their beginninge of the Grekes, bycause their speche, which
in al other poyntes is not much unlyke the Persian tonge,
kepeth dyvers signes and tokens of the Greke langage in
the names of their cityes and of theire magistrates. They
have of me (for when I was determyned to entre into my
iiii. voyage, I caste into the shippe in the steade of marchandise a prety fardel of bookes, bycause I intended to
come againe rather never, than shortly) they have, I saye,
of me the moste parte of Platoes workes, more of Aristotles,
also Theophrastus of plantes, but in divers places (which
I am sorye for) unperfecte. For whiles we were a ship-
borde, a marmoset chaunced upon the booke, as it was
negligentlye layde by, which wantonlye playinge therewyth
plucked oute certeyne leaves, and toore them in pieces.

Of them that have wrytten the grammer, they have
onelye Lascaris. For Theodorus I caried not wyth me, nor
never a dictionayre but Hesichius, and Dioscorides. They
sett great stoore by Plutarches bookes. And they be delyted wyth Lucianes mery conceytes and jestes. Of the
poetes they have Aristophanes, Homer, Euripides, and
Sophocles in Aldus [16] small prynte. Of the historians they
have Thucidides, Herodotus, and Herodian. Also my companion, Tricius Apinatus, caried with him phisick bokes,
certein smal woorkes of Hippocrates and Galenes Micro-
techne. The whyche boke they have in great estimation.
For thoughe there be almost no nation under heaven that
hath lesse nede of phisicke then they, yet this notwithstandyng, phisicke is no where in greater honour. Bycause

198

they counte the knowledge of it among the goodlyeste and most profytable partes of philosophie. For whyles they by the helpe of this philosophie searche oute the secrete mysteryes of nature, they thinke themselfes to receave therby not onlye wonderfull greate pleasure, but also to obteine great thankes and favour of the autour and maker therof. Whome they thinke, according to the fassion of other artificers, to have set furth the marvelous and gorgious frame of the world for man with great affeccion intentively to beholde. Whom only he hath made of witte and capacitie to considre and understand the excellencie of so great a woork. And therefore he beareth (say they) more goodwil and love to the curious and diligent beholder and vewer of his woork and marvelour at the same, then he doth to him, which like a very brute beaste without witte and reason, or as one without sense or moving, hathe no regarde to soo greate and soo wonderfull a spectacle. The wittes therefore of the Utopians, inurede and exercised in learnynge, be marveilous quycke in the invention of feates helpinge annye thinge to the advantage and wealthe of lyffe. Howbeit ii. feates theye maye thanke us for. That is, the scyence of imprinting, and the crafte of makinge paper. And yet not onelye us but chiefelye and principallye themselfes.

For when we shewede to them Aldus his print in bookes of paper, and told them of the stuffe wherof paper is made, and of the feate of graving letters, speaking sumwhat more, then we colde plainlye declare (for there was none of us, that knewe perfectlye either the one or the other) they furthwith very wittely conjectured the thinge. And where as before they wrote onely in skinnes, in barkes of tryes, and in rides, nowe they have attempted to make paper, and to imprint letters. And thoughe at the first yt proved not all of the beste, yet by often assayinge the same they shortelye got the feate of bothe. And have so broughte the matter aboute, that yf they had copyes of Greeke authores, they coulde lacke no bookes. But nowe they have

199

no moore then I rehearsed before, savinge that by pryntynge of bookes they have multiplyed and increased the same into manye thousandes of copies. Whosoever cummethe thether to see the lande, beinge excellent in anye gifte of wytte, or througe muche and longe journienge wel experiensed and sene in the knoweledg of many countreies (for the whyche cause wee were very welcome to them) him they receyve and interteyne wonders gentilly and lovinglye. For they have delite to heare what is done in everye lande, howbeit verye fewe merchaunte men come thether. For what shoulde they bring thether, onles it were iron, or els gold and silver, whiche they hadde rather carrye home agayne? Also such thinges as are to be caryed oute of theire lande, they thinke it more wysedome to carry that

gere furthe themselfes, then that other

shoulde come thether to fetche it,

to thentente they maye the bet-

ter knowe the out landes on

everye syde of them, and

kepe in ure the feate

and knowledge

of sailinge.

Of Bondemen, Sicke Persons, Wedlock, and Divers Other Matters.

THEY neither make bondemen of prisoners taken in battayle, oneles it be in battaylle that they foughte them selfes,[17] nor of bondmens children, nor to be short, of anye suche as they canne gette out of forreine countries, though he were theire a bondman. But either suche as amonge themselfes for heinous offences be punyshed with bondage, or elles suche as in the cities of other landes for great tres-passes be condempned to deathe. And of this sort of bonde-men they have mooste stoore.

For manye of them they bringe home sumtimes payinge very lytle for them, yea mooste commonlye gettynge them for gramercye. These sortes of bondemen they kepe not onely in continual woorke and labour, but also in bandes. But their oune men they handle hardest, whom they judge more desperate, and to have deserved greater punisshe-mente, bycause they being so godlye broughte up to vertue in soo excelente a common wealth, could not for all that be refreined from misdoing. An other kinde of bondemen they have, when a vile drudge being a poore laborer in an other country doth chuese of his owne free wyll to be a bond-man among them. These they intreate and order honestly, and enterteine almoste as gentellye as theire owne free cytyzeins, savynge that they put them to a lyttle more laboure, as thereto accustomed. Yf annye suche be disposed to departe thens (whiche seldome is seene) they neither holde him againste his wyll, neither sende him away with emptye handes. The sycke (as I sayde) they see to with great affection, and lette nothing at al passe concerninge either phisyche or good diete, whereby they may be re-stored againe to their health.

Such as be sicke of incurable diseases they comforte with sittinge by them, with talkinge with them, and to be shorte, with all maner of helpes that may be. But yf the disease be not onelye uncurable, but also full of contynuall payne and anguishe; then the priestes and the magistrates exhort the man, seinge he is not hable to doo anye dewtye of lyffe, and by overlyvinge his owne deathe is noysome and irkesome to other, and grevous to himselfe, that he wyl determine with himselfe no longer to cheryshe that pestilent and peineful disease. And seinge his lyfe is to him but a tormente, that he wyl not bee unwillinge to dye, but rather take a good hope to him, and either dispatche himselfe out of that payneful lyffe, as out of a prison, or a racke of tormente, or elles suffer himselfe wyllinglye to be rydde oute of it by other. And in so doinge they tell him he shall doo wysely, seing by his deathe he shall lose no commoditye, but ende his payne. And bycause in that acte he shall followe the counsel of the pryestes, that is to saye, of the interpreters of Gooddes wyll and pleasure, they shewe him that he shall do lyke a godly and a vertuous man. They that be thus persuaded, finyshe theire lives willynglye, either with hunger, or elles dye in theire sleape without anye fealing of deathe. But they cause none suche to dye agaynste his wyll, nor they use no lesse dilygence and attendaunce aboute him, belevinge this to be an honorable deathe. Elles he that killeth himself before that the pryestes and the counsel have allowed the cause of his deathe, him as unworthy either to be buryed, or with fier to be consumed, they caste unburied into some stinkinge marrish. The woman is not maried before she be xviii. yeres olde. The man is iiij. yeres elder before he marye.

And matrymoneie is there never broken, but by death; excepte adulterye breake the bonde, or els the intollerable wayewarde maners of either partye. For if either of them finde themselfe for any such cause greved, they maye by the license of the counsel chaunge and take another. But the other partie lyveth ever after in infamye and out of wedlocke. Howebeit the husbande to put away his wife for no other faulte, but for that some myshappe is fallen to her bodye, this by no meanes they wyll suffre. For they judge it a great poynt of crueltie, that anye body in their moste nede of helpe and comforte, shoulde be caste of and forsaken, and that olde age, whych both bringeth sicknes with it, and is a sychenes it selfe, should unkindly and unfaythfullye be delte withal. But nowe and then it chaunseth, where as the man and the woman cannot well agree betw[e]ne themselfes, both of them fyndinge other, with whome they hope to lyve more quietlye and merylye, that they by the full consente of them bothe be divorsed asonder and maried againe to other. But that not without the authoritie of the counsell. Whiche agreeth to no divorses, before they and their wyfes have diligently tried and examyned the matter. Yea and then also they be lothe to consent to it, bycause they know this to be the next way to break love betwene man and wyfe, to be in easye hope of a new marriage.

Breakers of wedlocke be punyshed with mooste grevous bondage. And if both the offenders were maried, then the parties whiche in that behalfe have sufferede wrong, beinge divorsed from the avoutrers,[18] be maried together, if they wille, or els to whom they lust. But if either of them both do styl continewe in love towarde so unkinde a bed-fellowe, the use of wedlocke is not to them forbidden, if the partye faulteles be disposed to followe in toylinge and drudgerye the person which for that offence is condempned to bondage. And very ofte it chaunceth that the repent-aunce of the one, and the earneste diligence of the other, dothe so move the prince with pytie and compassion, that he restoreth the bonde person from servitude to libertie and fredom again. But if the same partie be taken eftsones in that faulte there is no other waye but death. To other trespaces no prescript punishmente is appoynted by anye lawe. But accordinge to the heynousenes of the offense, or contrarye, so the punishmente is moderated by the discre-tion of the counsell. The husbandes chastice theire wyfes, and the parentes theire children, oneles they have done anye so horryble an offense, that the open punyshemente thereof maketh muche for the advauncemente of honeste maners.

But moste commenlye the moste heynous faultes be punyshed with the incommoditie of bondage. For that they suppose to be to the offenders no lesse griefe, and to the common wealth more profit, then yf they should hastely put them to death, and so make them quite out of the waye. For there cummeth more profit of theire laboure, then of theire deathe, and by theire example they feare other the longer from lyke offenses. But if they beinge thus used, doo rebell and kicke againe, then forsothe they be slayne as desperate and wilde beastes, whom neither prison nor chaine coulde restraine and kepe under. But they whiche take theire bondage pacientlye be not lefte all hopeles. For after they have bene broken and tamed with long miseries, if then thei shewe such repentaunce, as therebye it maye bee perceaved that they be soryer for theire offense then for their punyshemente, sumtymes by the prynces prerogatyve, and sumtymes by the voyce and consent of the people, theire bondage either is mitigated, or els cleane released and forgeven. He that moveth to advoutreye is in no lesse daunger and jeoperdie then yf he hadde committed advoutrye in dede. For in all offenses they counte the intente and pretensed purpose as evel as the acte or dede it selfe, thinking that no lette oughte to excuse him that did his beste to have no lette.

They have singular delite and pleasure in foles. And as it is a greate reproche to do anye of them hurte or injury, so they prohibite not to take pleasure of foolyshnes. For that, they thinke, dothe muche good to the fooles. And if any man be so sadde and sterne, that he cannot laughe neither at their wordes, nor at their dedes, none of them be committed to his tuition; for feare least he would not intreate them gentilly and favorably enough, to whom they should brynge no delectation (for other goodnes in them is none) muche lesse anye proffite shoulde they yelde him. To mocke a man for his deformitie, or for that he lacketh anye parte or lymme of his bodye, is counted greate dishonestye and reproche, not to him that is mocked, but to him that mocketh. Which unwysely doth imbrayde anye man of that as a vice, that was not in his powre to eschewe. Also as they counte and reken verye litell witte to be in him, that regardeth not naturall bewtie and comlinesse, so to helpe the same with payntinges, is taken for a vaine and a wanton pride, not withoute greate infamie. For they knowe, even by very experience, that no comelinesse of bewtye doethe so hyghelye commende and avaunce the wives in the conceite of their husbandes, as honest conditions and lowlines. For as love is oftentimes wonne with bewty, so it is not kept, preserved and continued, but by vertue and obedience.

They do not onely feare their people from doyng evil by punishmentes, but also allure them to vertue with rewardes of honoure. Therfore they set up in the markette place the ymages of notable men, and of such as have bene great and bounteful benefactors to the commen wealth, for the perpetual memorie of their good actes, and also that the glory and renowme of the auncetors maye styrre and provoke their posteritie to vertue. He that inordinatly and ambitiously desireth promotions is left al hopeles for ever atteining any promotion as long as he liveth. They lyve together lovinglye. For no magistrate is eyther hawte or fearfull. Fathers they be called, and lyke fathers they use themselves. The citezens (as it is their dewtie) willynglye exhibite unto them dew honour without any compulsion. Nor the prince himselfe is not knowen from the other by princely apparell, or a robe of state, nor by a crown or diademe roial, or cap of maintenaunce, but by a litle sheffe of corne caried before him. And so a taper of wax is borne before the bishop, wherby onely he is knowen.

They have but few lawes. For to people so instructe and institute very fewe do suffice. Yea this thing they chiefely reprove among other nations, that innumerable bokes of lawes and expositions upon the same be not sufficient. But they think it against all right and justice that men shoulde be bound to those lawes, which either be in number mo then be hable to be read, or els blinder and darker, then that anye man can well understande them. Furthermore they utterlie exclude and banishe all attorneis, proctours, and sergeauntes at the lawe; whiche craftelye handell matters, and subtelly dispute of the lawes. For they thinke it moste meete, that every man should pleade his own matter, and tel the same tale before the judge that he wold tell to his man of law. So shal there be lesse circumstaunce of wordes, and the trueth shal soner come to light, whiles the judge with a discrete judgement doethe waye the woordes of him whom no lawyer hath instructe with deceit, and whiles he helpeth and beareth out simple wittes against the false and malicious circumventions of craftie children. This is harde to be observed in other countreis, in so infinite a number of blinde and intricate lawes. But in Utopia every man is a cunning lawier. For (as I said) they have very few lawes; and the plainer and grosser that anye interpretation is, that they allowe as most juste. For all lawes (saie they) be made and publyshed onely to the intente that by them every man shoulde be put in remembraunce of his dewtie. But the craftye and subtill interpretation of them (forasmuche as few can atteyne thereto) canne put verye fewe in that remembraunce, where as the simple, the plaine and grosse meaninge of the lawes is open to everye man.

Elles as touchinge the vulgare sort of the people, whiche be bothe mooste in number, and have moste nede to knowe their dewties, were it not as good for them, that no law were made at all, as when it is made, to bringe so blynde an interpretation upon it, that without greate witte and longe arguynge no man can discusse it? To the fyndynge oute whereof neyther the grosse judgemente of the people can attaine, neither the whole life of them that be occupied in woorkinge for their livynges canne suffice thereto. These vertues of the Utopians have caused their nexte neiboures and borderers, whiche live fre and under no subjection (for the Utopians longe ago, have delivered manye of them from tirannie) to take magistrates of them, some for a yeare, and some for five yeares space. Which when the tyme of their office is expired, they bringe home againe with honoure and praise, and take new againe with them into their countrey. These nations have undoubtedlye very well and holsomely provided for their common wealthes. For seynge that bothe the makinge and marringe of the weale publique doeth depende and hange upon the maners of the rulers and magistrates, what officers coulde they more wyselye have chosen, then those which can not be ledde from honestye by bribes (for to them that shortly after shal depart thens into their own countrey money should be unprofitable) nor yet be moved eyther with favoure, or malice towardes any man, as beyng straungers, and unaquainted with the people? The whiche two vices of affection and avarice, where they take place in judgementes, incontinente they breake justice, the strongest and suerest bonde of a common wealth. These peoples whiche fetche their officers and rulers from them, the Utopians cal their fellowes. And other to whome they have bene beneficiall, they call their frendes.

As touching leagues, which in other places betwene countrey and countrey be so ofte concluded, broken and renewed, they never make none with anie nation. For to what purpose serve leagues? say they. As thoughe nature had not set sufficient love betwene man and man. And who so regardeth not nature, thinke you that he will passe for wordes? They be brought into this opinion chiefelye, because that in those partes of the worlde, leagues betwene princes be wont to be kepte and observed very sklenderly. For here in Europa, and especiallye in these partes where the faith and religion of Christe reigneth, the majestie of leagues is everye where estemed holy and inviolable, partlie through the justice and goodnes of princes, and partly at the reverence and motion of the head bishops. Which like as they make no promisse themselves but they do verye religiouslye perfourme the same, so they exhorte all princes in any wise to abide by their promisses, and them that refuse or denye so to do, by their pontificall powre and authoritie they compell thereto. And surely they thinke well that it might seme a verye reprochefull thing, yf in the leagues of them which by a peculiare name be called faithful, faith should have no place.

But in that newe founde parte of the world, which is scaselie so farre frome us beyond the line equinoctiall, as our life and maners be dissident from theirs, no trust nor confidence is in leagues. But the mo and holier ceremonies the league is knitte up with, the soner it is broken by some cavillation founde in the wordes, which many times of purpose be so craftelie put in and placed, that the bandes

can never be so sure nor so stronge, but they will find some
hole open to crepe out at, and to breake both league and
trueth. The whiche craftye dealing, yea the whiche fraude
and deceite, if they should know it to be practised among
private men in their bargaines and contractes, they would
incontinent crie out at it with an open mouth and a sower
countenaunce, as an offense moste detestable, and worthye
to be punnyshed with a shamefull deathe: yea even very
they that avaunce themselves authours of lyke counsell
geven to princes. Wherfore it may wel be thought, either
that al justice is but a basse and a low vertue, and which
avaleth it self farre under the highe dignitie of kynges;
or at the least wise, that there be two justices, the one
meete for the inferiour sorte of the people, goynge afote
and crepynge lowe by the grounde, and bounde down on
every side with many bandes bycause it shall not run at
rovers; the other a princelye vertue, which like as it is of
much hygher majestie, then the other pore justice, so also
it is of muche more libertie, as to the which nothing is
unlawfull that it lusteth after.

These maners of princes (as I said) whiche be there so
evell kepers of leagues, cause the Utopians, as I suppose,
to make no leagues at al, which perchaunce would chaunge
their minde if they lived here. Howbeit they thinke that
thoughe leagues be never so faithfullye observed and
kepte, yet the custome of makynge leagues was very
evell begon. For this causeth men (as though nations
which be seperat asondre, by the space of a litle hil or a
river, were coupled together by no societie or bonde of
nature) to thinke themselves borne adversaries and enemies
one to another, and that it were lawfull for the one to seke
the death and destruction of the other, if leagues were not:
yea, and that after the leagues be accorded, friendship doth
not grow and encrease; but the licence of robbing and stealing doth styll remaine, as farfurth as for lack of forsight and
advisement in writing the wordes of the league, any sentence or clause to the contrarie is not therin sufficientlie

comprehended. But they be of a contrarye opinion. That is, that no man oughte to be counted an enemye, whiche hath done no injurye. And that the felowshippe of nature is a stronge league; and that men be better and more surely knit togethers by love and benevolence, then by covenauntes of leagues; by hartie affection of minde, then by wordes.

Of Warfare.

WARRE or battel as a thing very beastly, and yet to no kinde of beastes in so muche use as to man, they do detest and abhorre. And contrarie to the custome almooste of all other nations, they counte nothynge so much against glorie, as glory gotten in warre. And therefore thoughe they do daylie practise and exercise themselves in the discipline of warre, and not onelie the men, but also the women upon certen appointed daies, lest they should be to seke in the feate of armes, if nede should require, yet they never go to battell, but either in the defence of their owne countrey, or to drive out of their frendes lande the enemies that have invaded it, or by their power to deliver from the yocke and bondage of tirannye some people, that be there-with oppressed. Which thing they do of meere pitie and compassion. Howbeit they sende helpe to their frendes; not ever in their defence, but sometymes also to requite and revenge injuries before to them done. But this they do not onlesse their counsell and advise in the matter be asked, whiles it is yet newe and freshe. For if they finde the cause probably, and if the contrarie part wil not restoore agayne suche thynges as be of them justelye demaunded, then they be the chiefe autours and makers of the warre. Whiche they do not onlie as ofte as by in-rodes and invasions of soldiours praies and booties be driven awaye, but then also muche more mortally, when

209

their frendes marchauntes in anie lande, either under the pretence of unjuste lawes, or elles by the wrestinge and wronge understandinge of good lawes, do susteine an unjust accusation under the colour of justice.

Neither the battell whiche the Utopians fought for the Nephelogetes against the Alaopolitanes a litle before oure time was made for any other cause, but that the Nephelogete marchaunt men, as the Utopians thought, suffred wrong of the Alaopolitanes, under the pretence of righte. But whether it were righte or wronge, it was with so cruel and mortal warre revenged, the countreis rounde about joyninge their helpe and powre to the puisaunce and malice of bothe parties, that moste florishing and wealthy peoples, being some of them shrewedly shaken, and some of them sharpely beaten, the mischeves wer not finished nor ended, until the Alaopolitanes at the last were yelded up as bondemen into the jurisdiction of the Nephelogetes. For the Utopians fought not this war for themselves. And yet the Nephelogetes before the warre, when the Alaopolitanes flourished in wealth, wer nothing to be compared with them.

So egerlye the Utopians prosequute the injuries done to their frendes, yea, in money matters; and not their owne likewise. For if they by conveyne or gile be wiped beside their goodes, so that no violence be done to their bodies, they wreake their anger by absteininge from occupieng with that nation, until they have made satisfaction. Not forbicause they set lesse stoore by their owne citizeins, then by their frendes; but that they take the losse of their frendes money more hevelie then the losse of their own. Bicause that their frendes marchaunte men, forasmuche as that they leise is their own private goods, susteine great dammage by the losse. But their owne citizeyns leise nothing but of the commen goods, and of that whiche was at home plentifull and almost superfluous, els had it not bene sent furth. Therfore no man feleth the losse. And for this cause they thinke it to cruell an acte, to revenge that

losse with the deathe of manie, the incommoditie of the
which losse no man feeleth neither in his lyfe, nor yet in
his living.

But if it chaunce that any of their men in any other
countrey be maimed or killed, whether it be done by a
commen or a private counsel, knowyng and trying out the
trueth of the matter by their ambassadours, onlesse the
offenders be rendered unto them in recompence of the
injurie, they will not be appeased; but incontinent they
proclaime warre against them. The offenders yelded, they
punishe either with death or with bondage.

They be not only sory, but also ashamed to atchieve the
victorie with bloudshed, counting it greate folie to bie
precious wares to dere. They rejoyse and avaunt themselves, if they vanquishe and oppresse their enemies by
craft and deceite. And for that act they make a generall
triumph, and as yf the matter were manfullye handeled,
they set up a pyller of stone in the place where they so
vanquished their enemies, in token of the victorie. For then
they glorie, then they boaste and cracke that they have
plaied the men in deede, when they have so overcommen,
as no other living creature but onely man could; that is to
saye, by the mighte and puisaunce of wit. For with bodily
strength (say they) beares, lions, boores, wulfes, dogges
and other wild beastes do fight. And as the moste part
of them do passe us in strength and fierce courage, so in
wit and reason we be much stronger then they all.

Their chief and principall purpose in warre, is to obteine
that thynge, whiche if they had before obteined, they
woulde not have moved battell. But if that be not possible,
they take so cruell vengeaunce of them whiche be in the
faulte, that ever after they be aferde to do the like. This
is their chiefe and principall intent, whiche they immediatlie
and first of al prosequute, and set forwarde. But yet so,
that they be more circumspecte in avoidinge and eschew-
ynge jeopardies, then they be desierous of prayse and
renowne.

Therefore immediatlye after that warre is ones solemnelie denounced, they procure many proclamations signed with their owne commen seale to be set up privilie at one time in their enemies lande, in places moste frequented. In these proclamations they promisse greate rewardes to hym that wil kill their enemies prince, and some what lesse giftes, but them verye greate also, for everye heade of them, whose names be in the saide proclamations conteyned. They be those whom they count their chiefe adversaries, next unto the prince. Whatsoever is prescribed unto him that killeth any of the proclaimed persons, that is dubled to him that bringeth anye of the same to them alive; yea, and to the proclaimed persones themselves, if they wil chaunge their mindes and come in to them, taking their partes, they profer the same greate rewardes with pardone and suertie of their lives. Therefore it quickely commeth to passe that their enemies have all other men in suspicion, and be unfaithfull and mistrusting among themselves one to another, living in great feare, and in no lesse jeopardie. For it is well knowen, that divers times the most part of them (and speciallie the prince him selfe) hathe bene betraied of them, in whom they put their moste hope and trust. So that there is no maner of act nor dede that giftes and rewardes do not enforce men unto.

And in rewardes they kepe no measure. But remembring and considering into how great hasarde and jeopardie they cal them, endevoure themselves to recompence the greatnes of the daunger with like great benefites. And therefore they promise not only wonderful great abundaunce of golde, but also landes of great revenues lieng in most saffe places among theire frendes. And theire promisses they perfourme faythfully withoute anye fraude or covyne. This custome of byinge and sellynge adversaryes among other people is dysallowed, as a cruel acte of a basse and a cowardyshe mynde. But they in this behalfe thinke themselfes muche prayse woorthy, as who lyke wyse men by this meanes dispatche great warres withoute anny battell or skyrmyshe.

Yea they counte it also a dede of pytye and mercye, bicause that by the deathe of a fewe offenders the lyves of a greate numbre of innocentes, as wel of theire oune men as also of theire enemies, be raunsomed and saved, which in fighting shoulde have bene sleane. For they doo no lesse pytye the basse and common sorte of theire enemies people, then they doo theire owne; knowing that they be driven and enforced to warre againste their willes by the furyous madnes of theire princes and heades.

Yf by none of these meanes the matter goo forwarde as they woulde have it, then they procure occasyons of debate and dissention to be spredde amonge theire enemies. As by bringinge the princes brother, or some of the noble men, in hoope to obtayne the kingedome. Yf this waye prevayle not, then they reyse up the people that be nexte neygheboures and borderers to theire enemyes, and them they sette in theire neckes under the coloure of some olde tytle of ryghte, such as kynges doo never lacke. To them they promysse theire helpe and ayde in theire warre. And as for moneye they gyve them abundaunce. But of theire owne cytyzeins they sende to them fewe or none. Whome they make so much of and love so intierlye, that they would not be willing to chaunge anye of them for their adversaries prince. But their gold and silver, bycause they kepe it all for thys only purpose, they laye it owte frankly and frely; as who shoulde lyve even as wealthely, if they hadde bestowed it everye pennye. Yea and besydes theire ryches, whyche they kepe at home, thei have also an infinite treasure abrode, by reason that (as I sayde before) manye nations be in their debte.

Therefore they hiere soldiours oute of all countreis and sende them to battayle, but cheifly of the Zapoletes.[19] This people is 500. myles from Utopia easterwarde. They be hideous, savage and fyerce, dwellynge in wild woodes and high mountaines, where they were bredde and brought up. They be of an harde nature, hable to abide and susteine heate, colde and labour, abhorrynge from all delicate deintyes, occupyenge no husbandrye nor tyllage of the

ground, homelye and rude both in buildinge of their houses
and in their apparrel, geven unto no goodnes, but onely
to the breedinge and bringynge up of cattel. The moste
parte of theire lyvinge is by huntynge and stealynge. They
be borne onelye to warre, whyche they diligentlye and
earnestelye seke for. And when they have gotten it, they be
wonders glad thereof. They goo furthe of theire countreye
in greate companyes together, and whosoever lackethe
souldyours, there they proffer theire service for small wages.
This is onelye the crafte they have to gette theire livynge
by. They maynteyne theire lyfe by sekinge theire deathe.
For them whomewyth they be in wayges they fyghte hardelye, fyerslye and faythefullye. But they bynde themselfes
for no certeyne tyme. But upon this condition they entre
into bondes, that the nexte daye they wyll take parte with
the other syde for greatter wayges, and the nexte daye
after that, they wyll be readye to come backe agayne for a
lytle more moneye. There be fewe warres thereawaye,
wherin is not a greate numbre of them in bothe partyes.
Therefore it dayelye chauncethe that nye kynsefolke,
whyche were hiered together on one parte, and there verye
frendelye and familiarlye used themselfes one wyth another,
shortely after beinge separate in contrarye partes, runne
one againste another envyouslye and fyercelye, and for-
gettinge bothe kindred and frendeshype, thruste theire
swordes one in another. And that for none other cause, but
that they be hyered of contrarye prynces for a lytle moneye.
Whyche they doo so hyghle regarde and esteame, that they
will easelye be provoked to chaunge partes for a halfepenye
more wayges by the daye. So quyckelye they have taken a
smacke in covetesenes. Whyche for all that is to them no
proffyte. For that they gette by fyghtynge, immedyatelye
they spende unthryftelye and wretchedlye in ryotte.

This people fyghteth for the Utopians agaynste all nations, bycause they geve them greatter wayges, then annye
other nation wyll. For the Utopians lyke as they seke good
men to use wel, so they seke these evell and vicious men

214

to abuse. Whome, when neade requirethe, with promisses of greate rewardes they putte forthe into great jeopardyes. From whens the mooste parte of them never cummeth againe to aske their rewardes. But to them that remaine alive they paye that which they promissed faithfully, that they maye be the more willinge to put themselfes in like daunger another time. Nor the Utopians passe not how many of them they bring to destruction. For they beleve that they should doo a verye good deade for all mankind, if they could ridde out of the worlde all that fowle stinking denne of that most wicked and cursed people.

Next unto thies they use the soldiours of them for whom they fighte. And then the helpe of their other frendes. And laste of all, they joyne to theire oune citizens. Emong whome they give to one of tried vertue and prowes the reule, goovernaunce and conduction of the whole armye. Under him they appoynte ij. other, whyche, whyles he is sauffe, be bothe private and oute of offyce. But yf he be taken or slayne, the one of the other ij. succedeth hym, as it were by inherytaunce. And if the seconde miscarrye, then the thirde taketh his rowme, leaste that (as the chaunce of battell is uncerteine and doubtful) the jeopardye or deathe of the capitaine shoulde brynge the whole armye in hasarde.

They cheuse soldyours, out of every citye those whych putte furthe themselffes wyllyngelye. For they thruste no man forthe into warre agaynste his wyll. Bycause they beleve, yf annye man be fearefull and fainte harted of nature, he wyll not onely doo no manfull and hardy acte hym selfe, but also be occasyon of cowardenes to his fellowes. But if annye battel be made agaynste theire owne countreye, then they putt these cowardes (so that they be stronge bodyed) in shyppes amonge other bolde harted men. Or elles they dyspose them upon the walles, from whens they maye not flye. Thus what for shame that theire enemies be at hande, and what for bycause they be without hope of runninge awaye, they forgette all feere. And manye

times extreame necessitye turnethe cowardnes into prowes
and manlynes. But as none of them is thrust forthe of his
countrey into warre againste his wyll, so women that be
wyllynge to accompany theire husbandes in times of warre
be not prohibited or letted. Yea they provoke and exhorte
them to it with prayses.

And in set fylde the wyves doo stande everye one by
theire owne husbandes syde. Also every man is compassed
next aboute with his owne children, kinsfolkes and aliaunce.
That they, whom nature chiefely moveth to mutual suc-
coure, thus standynge together, maye healpe one another.
It is a great reproche and dishonesty for the husband to
come home without his wiffe, or the wyffe withoute her
husbande, or the sonne without his father. And therfore if
the other part sticke so harde by it that the battel come to
their handes, it is fought with great slaughter and blod-
shed, even to the utter destruction of both partes. For as
they make all the meanes and shyftes that maye be to kepe
themselfes from the necessitye of fyghtinge, or that they
may dispatche the battell by their hiered soldyours; so
when there is no remedy, but that they muste neades
fight themselfes, they do as corragiouslye fall to it, as
before, whyles they myght, they did wiselye avoyde and
refuse it. Nor they be not most fierce at the first bront.
But in continuance by litle and lytle theire fierce courage
encreaseth, with so stubborne and obstynate myndes, that
they wyll rather dye then gyve back an ynche. For that
suertye of lyvinge, whiche everye man hath at home beinge
joyned with noo carefull anxietye or remembraunce how
theire posterite shall lyve after them (for this pensifnes
oftentymes breakethe and abateth couragious stomakes)
maketh them stowte and hardye, and disdaineful to be
conquered. Moreover theire knowledge in chevalrye and
feates of armes putteth them in a good hope.

Finally the wholesome and vertuous opinions, wherin
they were brought up even from theire childhode, partely
through learnynge, and partelye throughe the good ordi-

naunces and lawes of theire weale publique, augmente and encrease theire manfull courage. By reason wherof they neither set so litle store by their lives, that they will rassh-elye and unadvisedlye caste them away: nor they be not so farre in lewde and fond love therewith, that they will shamefullye covete to kepe them, when honestie biddeth leave them. When the battel is hottest and in al places most fierce and fervent, a bende of chosen and picked yong men, whiche be sworne to live and dye togethers, take upon them to destroye theire adversaries capitaine. Whome they invade, now with privy wieles, now by open strength. At him they strike both nere and farre of. He is assayled with a long and a continuall assaulte, freshe men styll commynge in the weried mens places. And seldome it chaunceth (onles he save hymselfe by flying) that he is not either slayne, or els taken prisoner and yelded to his enemies alive.

If they wynne the fyelde, they persecute not theire enemies with the violent rage of slaughter. For they had rather take them alive then kyl them. Neither they do so follow the chase and pursute of theire enemies, but they leave behinde them one parte of theire hoste in battaile arraye under their standardes. In so muche that if al their whole armie be discumfeted and overcum saving the rere-warde, and that they therewith athcieve the victory, then they had rather lette al their enemies scape, then to fol-lowe them out of array. For they remembre, it hath chaunced unto themselfes more then ones; the whole powre and strength of their hoste being vanquished and put to flight, whiles their enemies rejoysing in the victory have persecuted them flying some one way and some another; a small companye of theire men lying in an ambushe, there redy at all occasions, have sodainelye rysen upon them thus dispersed and scattered oute of arraye, and through presumption of safety unadvisedly pursuing the chase, and have incontinent changed the fortune of the whole bat-tayll, and spite of their tethes wrestinge oute of their handes the sure and undouted victorye, being a litle before conquered, have for their parte conquered the conquerers.

It is hard to say whether they be craftier in layinge an ambushe, or wittier in avoydinge the same. You would thinke they intende to flye, when they meane nothing lesse. And contrarye wyse when they go about that purpose, you wold beleve it were the leaste parte of their thought. For if they perceave themselfes either overmatchd in numbre, or closed in too narrowe a place, then they remove their campe either in the night season with silence, or by some pollicie they deceave theire enemies, or in the day time they retiere backe so softelye, that it is no lesse jeoperdie to medle with them when they geve backe, then when they preese on. They fence and fortifie their campe sewerlye with a deape and a brode trenche. The earth therof is cast inward. Nor they do not set drudgeis and slaves aworke about it. It is doone by the handes of the souldiours them selfes. All the whole armye worketh upon it, excepte them that kepe watche and warde in harneis before the trenche for sodeine aventures. Therefore by the labour of so manye a large trenche closinge in a greate compasse of grounde is made in lesse tyme then anye man woulde beleve.

Theire armoure or harneys, whiche they weare, is sure and strong to receave strokes, and handsome for all movinges and gestures of the bodye, insomuche that it is not unweldye to swymme in. For in the discipline of theire warefare amonge other feates thei learne to swimme in harnes. Their weapons be arrowes aloufe, whyche they shote both strongely and surelye, not onelye fotemen, but also horsemen. At hande strokes they use not swordes but pollaxes, whiche be mortall, as wel in sharpenes, as in weyghte, both for foynes and downe strokes. Engines for warre they devyse and invent wonders wittelye. Whiche when they be made they kepe verye secret, leaste yf they shoulde be knowen before neade requyre, they should be but laughed at and serve to no purpose. But in makynge them, hereunto they have chiefe respecte, that they be both easy to be caried, and handsome to be moved and turned about.

Truce taken with their enemies for a shorte time they do so firmelye and faythfullye keape, that they wyll not breake it; no, not though they be thereunto provoked. They doe not waste nor destroye theire enemies lande with forraginges, nor they burne not up their corne. Yea, they save it as muche as may be from being overrunne and troden downe either with men or horses, thinkinge that it growethe for theire owne use and proffit. They hurt no man that is unarmed, onles he be an espiall. All cities that be yelded unto them they defende. And suche as they wynne by force of assaulte, they neither dispoyle nor sacke, but them that withstode and dyssuaded the yeldynge up of the same, they put to deathe; the other souldiours they punnyshe with bondage. All the weake multitude they leave untouched. If they knowe that annye citezeins counselled to yealde and rendre up the citie, to them they gyve parte of the condemned mens goods. The resydewe they distribute and give frelye amonge them, whose helpe they had in the same warre. For none of them selfes taketh anye portion of the praye.

But when the battaile is finished and ended, they put theire frendes to never a penny coste of al the charges that they were at, but laye it upon theire neckes that be conquered. Them they burdeine with the whole charge of theire expenseis, whiche they demaunde of them partelye in moneie to be kept for like use of battayll, and partelye in landes of great revenues to be payde unto them yearelye for ever. Suche revenues they have now in manye countreis. Whiche by litle and litle rysinge of dyvers and sondry causes be increased above vij. hundrethe thousand ducates by the yere. Thether they sende forth some of their citezeins as lieuetenauntes, to live there sumptuously like men of honoure and renowne. And yet, this not withstandinge, muche moneye is saved, which commeth to the commen treasory; onles it so chaunce, that they had rather trust the countrey with the money. Which many times they do so long, until they have nede to occupie it. And it seldome happeneth that thei demaund al. Of these landes they assigne parte unto them which, at their request and exhortacion, put themselfes in such jeoperdies as I spake of before. If anye prince stirre up warre agaynste them, intending to invade theire lande, they mete hym incontinent oute of theire owne borders with greate powre and strengthe. For they never lyghtely make warre in their owne countrei. Nor they be never broughte into so extreme necessitie as to take helpe out of forreyne landes into their owne ilande.

Of the Religions in Utopia.

THERE be divers kindes of religion not only in sondrie partes of the ilande, but also in divers places of every citie. Some worship for God, the sonne; some, the mone; some, some other of the planettes. There be that give worship to a man that was ones of excellente vertue or of famous glory, not only as God, but also as the chiefest and hyghest God.

But the moste and the wysest parte (rejectynge al these) beleve that there is a certayne godlie powre unknowen, everlastinge, incomprehensible, inexplicable, farre above the capacitie and retche of mans witte, dispersed throughoute all the worlde, not in bignes, but in vertue and power. Him they call the father of al. To him alone they attribute the beginninges, the encreasinges, the procedinges, the chaunges and the endes of al thinges. Neither they geve any divine honours to any other then to him. Yea al the other also, though they be in divers opinions, yet in this pointe they agree all togethers with the wisest sorte, in beleving that there is one chiefe and principall

God, the maker and ruler of the whole worlde: whome
they all commonlye in their countrey language call
Mythra.[20] But in this they disagree, that among some he
is counted one, and amonge some another. For every
one of them, whatsoever that is whiche he taketh for the
chief God, thinketh it to be the very same nature, to whose
only divine mighte and majestie, the summe and soveraintie
of al thinges by the consent of al people is attributed and
geven.

Howbeit they all begyn by litle and litle to forsake and
fall from this varietie of superstitions, and to agre togethers
in that religion whiche semethe by reason to passe and
excell the residewe. And it is not to be doubted, but all
the other would long agoo have bene abolished, but that
whatsoever unprosperous thynge happened to anie of them,
as he was mynded to chaunge his religion, the fearful-
nesse of people did take it, not as a thinge comminge by
chaunce, but as sente from GOD out of heaven. As thoughe
the God whose honoure he was forsakynge would revenge
that wicked purpose against him. But after they hearde us
speake of the name of Christe, of his doctrine, lawes,
myracles, and of thee no lesse wonderful constancie of so
manye martyrs, whose bloude wyllinglye shedde broughte
a great numbre of nations throughoute all partes of the
worlde into their sect; you will not beleve with howe
gladde mindes, they agreed unto the same: whether it
were by the secrete inspiration of GOD, or elles for that
they thought it nieghest unto that opinion, which among
them is counted the chiefest. Howbeit I thinke this was
no smale helpe and furtheraunce in the matter, that they
harde us say, that Christ instituted among his, al thinges
commen; and that the same communitie doth yet remaine
amongest the rightest Christian companies.

Verely howsoever it came to passe, manye of them consented togethers in our religion, and were wasshed in the
holy water of baptisme. But because among us foure (for
no mo of us was left alive, two of our companye beyng

221

dead) there was no priest; which I am right sorie for;
they beynge entered and instructed in al other pointes of
our religion, lacke onely those sacramentes, whiche here
none but priestes do minister. Howbeit they understand
and perceive them and be very desierous of the same. Yea,
they reason and dispute the matter earnestly among themselves, whether without the sending of a Christian bishop,
one chosen out of their own people may receave the ordre
of priesthod. And truely they were minded to chuese one.
But at my departure from them they had chosen none.

They also which do not agree to Christes religion, feare
no man from it, not speake against any man that hath received it. Saving that one of our company in my presence
was sharpely punished. He as soone as he was baptised
began against our willes, with more earneste affection then
wisedome, to reason of Christes religion; and began to
waxe so hote in his matter, that he did not onlye preferre
our religion before al other, but also did utterly despise and
condempne all other, calling them prophane, and the
folowers of them wicked and develish and the children
of everlastinge dampnation. When he had thus longe reasoned the matter, they laide holde on him, accused him
and condempned him into exile, not as a despiser of religion, but as a sedicious person and a raiser up of dissention amonge the people.

For this is one of the auncientest lawes among them;
that no man shall be blamed for resoninge in the maintenaunce of his owne religion. For kyng Utopus, even at
the firste beginning, hearing that the inhabitauntes of the
land wer, before his comming thether, at continuall dissention and strife amonge themselves for their religions; perceyving also that this common dissention (whiles every
severall secte tooke several partes in fighting for their
countrey) was the only occasion of his conquest over them
al, as sone as he had gotten the victory; firste of all he
made a decree, that it should be lawfull for everie man
to favoure and folow what religion he would, and that he

mighte do the best he could to bring other to his opinion, so that he did it peaceablie, gentelie, quietly and soberlie, without hastie and contentious rebuking and invehing against other. If he could not by faire and gentle speche induce them unto his opinion yet he should use no kinde of violence, and refraine from displeasaunte and seditious woordes. To him that would vehemently and ferventlye in this cause strive and contende was decreed banishment or bondage. This lawe did kynge Utopus make not only for the maintenaunce of peace, which he saw through continuall contention and mortal hatred utterly extinguished; but also because he thought this decrie should make for the furtheraunce of religion. Wherof he durst define and determine nothing unadvisedlie, as douting whether God desiering manifolde and diverse sortes of honour, would inspire sondry men with sondrie kindes of religion. And this suerly he thought a very unmete and folish thing, and a point of arrogant presumption, to compell all other by violence and threateninges to agre to the same that thou belevest to be trew.

Furthermore thoughe there be one religion whiche alone is trew, and al other vaine and superstitious, yet did he wel foresee (so that the matter were handeled with reason, and sober modestie) that the trueth of the own powre would at the last issue out and come to lyghte. But if contention and debate in that behalfe should continuallye be used, as the woorste men be mooste obstinate and stubbourne, and in their evyll opinion mooste constante; he perceaved that then the beste and holyest religion woulde be troden underfote and destroyed by most vaine supersticions, even as good corne is by thornes and weedes overgrowen and chooked.

Therfore all this matter he lefte undiscussed, and gave to everye man free libertie and choise to beleve what he woulde. Savinge that he earnestelye and straitelye charged them, that no man should conceave so vile and baase an opinion of the dignitie of mans nature, as to think that the soules do die and perishe with the bodye; or that the world runneth at al aventures governed by no divine providence. And therfore thei beleve that after this life vices be extreamelye punished and vertues bountifully rewarded. Hym that is of a contrary opinion they counte not in the numbre of men, as one that hathe avaled the heighe nature of hys soule to the vielnes of brute beastes bodies, muche lesse in the numbre of their citizens, whose lawes and ordenaunces, if it were not for feare, he wold nothing at al esteme. For you maye be suer that he will studie either with craft prively to mocke, or els violently to breake the commen lawes of his countrey, in whom remaineth no further feare then of the lawes, nor no further hope then of the bodye. Wherfore he that is thus minded is deprived of all honours, excluded from all offices and reject from all common administrations in the weale publique. And thus he is of all sortes despised, as of an unprofitable and of a base and vile nature. Howbeit they put him to no punishment, because they be persuaded that it is in no mans power to beleve what he list. No nor they constraine hym not with threatninges to dissemble his minde and shew countenaunce contrarie to his thought. For deceit and falshod and all maners of lies, as nexte unto fraude, they do mervelouslie deteste and abhorre. But they suffer him not to dispute in his opinion, and that onelye amonge the commen people. For els aparte amonge the priestes and men of gravitie they do not onelye suffer, but also exhorte him to dispute and argue, hoping that at the last, that madnes will geve place to reason.

There be also other, and of them no small numbre, which be not forbidden to speake theyr mindes, as grounding their opinion upon some reason, beyng in their living neither evell nor vicious. Their heresie is much contrarie to the other. For they beleve that the soules of brute beastes be immortall and everlasting. But nothynge to be compared with oures in dignitie, neither ordeined nor predestinate to like felicitie.

224

For al they beleve certeinly and sewerly that mans blesse shal be so great, that they do mourne and lament every mans sicknes, but no mans death, oneles it be one whome they see depart from his life carefullie and agaynst his will. For this they take for a verye evel token, as thoughe the soule beynge in dispaire and vexed in conscience, through some privie and secret forefeiling of the punishement now at hande were aferde to depart. And they thinke he shall not be welcome to God, which, when he is called, runneth not to him gladlye, but is drawen by force and sore against his will. They therfore that see this kinde of deathe do abhorre it, and them that so die they burie with sorow and silence. And when they have praied God to be mercifull to the soule and mercifully to pardon the infirmities therof, they cover the dead coorse with earth. Contrariewise all that departe merely and ful of good hope, for them no man mourneth, but followeth the heerse with joyfull synging, commending the soules to God with great affection.[21] And at the last, not with mourning sorrow, but with a great reverence they bourne the bodies. And in the same place they sette up a piller of stone, with the dead mans titles therin graved. When they be come home they reherse his vertuous maners and his good dedes. But no part of his life is so oft or gladly talked of as his meri deth.

They thinke that this remembraunce of the vertue and goodnes of the dead doeth vehemently provoke and enforce the living to vertue. And that nothing can be more pleasaunt and acceptable to the deade. Whom they suppose to be present among them, when they talke of them, though to the dull and feble eiesight of mortall men they be invisible. For it were an unconvenient thinge that the blessed shoulde not be at libertie to goo whether they woulde. And it were a pointe of greate unkindnes in them to have utterly cast awaye the desire of visitinge and seing their frendes, to whome they were in their life time joyned by mutuall love and amitie. Whiche in good men after their deathe they counte to be rather increased then diminished.

They beleve therefore that the deade be presentlye con-
versaunt amonge the quicke, as beholders and witnesses of
all their wordes and dedes. Therfore they go more cor-
ragiously to their busines as having a trust and affiaunce
in such overseers. And this same belefe of the present conversation of their forefathers and auncetours among them
feareth them from all secrete dishonestie.

They utterly despise and mocke sothsayinges and divinations of thinges to come by the flighte or voices of birdes,
and all other divinations of vaine superstition, whiche in
other countreis be in greate observation. But they highlye
esteme and worshyppe miracles that come by no healpe of
nature, as woorkes and witnesses of the presente power of
God. And suche they saye do chaunce there verye often.
And sometimes in great and doubtefull matters, by commen intercession and prayers, they procure and obteine
them with a sure hope and confidence, and a stedfast
belefe.

They thinke that the contemplation of nature and the
prayse thereof comminge, is to God a very acceptable
honoure. Yet there be many so earnestlye bent and affec-
tioned to religion, that they passe no thing for learning,
nor geve their mindes to any knowledge of thinges. But
ydelnes they utterly forsake and eschue, thinking felicitie
after this life to be gotten and obteined by busie labors
and good exercises. Some therfore of them attende upon
the sicke, some amende high waies, clense ditches, repaire
bridges, digge turfes, gravell and stones, fel and cleave
wood, bring wood, corne and other thinges into the cities
in cartes, and serve not onelye in commen woorkes, but
also in private laboures as servauntes, yea, more then
bondmen. For what so ever unpleasaunt, harde and vile
worke is anye where, from the whiche labour, lothsomnes
and desperation doth fray other, al that they take upon
them willingly and gladly, procuring quiete and rest to
other, remaininge in continual woorke and labour themselves, not embraidinge others therewith. They neither re-

prove other mens lives, nor glorie in theire owne. These
men the more serviceable they behave themselves, the more
they be honoured of all men.

Yet they be divided into two sectes. The one is of them
that live single and chast, absteining not onely from the
companie of women, but also from eating of fleshe, and
some of them from all maner of beastes. Whiche utterly
rejecting the pleasures of this present life as hurtfull, be all
wholye set upon the desier of the lyfe to come by watch-
ynge and sweatynge, hoopinge shortly to obtaine it, being
in the meane season merie and lustie. The other secte is
no lesse desirous of laboure, but they embrace matrimonye,
not despisynge the solace therof, thinking that they can
not be discharged of their bounden duties towardes nature
without labour and toyle, nor towardes their native countrey without procreation of children. They abstaine from
no pleasure that doeth nothinge hinder them from laboure.
They love the flesh of foure footed beastes, bicause they
beleve that by that meate they be made hardier and
stronger to woorke. The Utopians counte this secte the
wiser, but the other the holier. Which in that they preferre
single life before matrimony, and that sharp life before an
easier life, if herein they grounded upon reason they would
mock them. But now forasmuch as they say they be led to
it by religion, they honor and worship them. And these be
they whom in their language by a peculier name, they cal
Buthrescas, the which woord by interpretation signifieth
to us men of religion or religious men.

They have priestes of exceding holines, and therefore
very few. For there be but xiij. in every citie accordinge to
the number of their churches, savyng when they go furthe
to battell. For than vij. of them goo furth with the armie;
in whose steades so manie newe be made at home. But
the other at their retourne home againe reentre every one
into his owne place, they that be above the numbre, untill
suche time as they succede into the places of the other at
their dyinge, be in the meane season continuallie in com-

panie with the bishoppe. For he is the chiefe heade of them al. They be chosen of the people, as the other magistrates be, by secrete voices for the avoydinge of strife. After their election they be consecrate of their own companie. They be overseers of al divine matters, orderers of religions, and as it wer judges and maisters of maners. And it is a great dishonestie and shame to be rebuked or spoken to by any of them for dissolute and incontinent living. But as it is their office to geve good exhortations and counsel, so is it the dutie of the prince and the other magistrates to correct and punishe offenders, saving that the priestes, whome they find exceading vicious livers, them they excommunicate from having anye interest in divine matters. And there is almoste no punishement amonge them more feared. For they runne in verye great infamie, and be inwardly tormented with a secret feare of religion, and shall not long scape free with their bodies. For unlesse they by quicke repentaunce approve the amendement of their lives to the priestes, they be taken and punished of the counsel, as wicked and irreligious.

Both childhode and youth is instructed and taught of them. Nor they be not more diligente to instructe them in learning, then in vertue and good maners. For they use with verie great endeavour and diligence to put into the heades of their children, whiles they be yet tender and pliaunte, good opinions and profitable for the conservation of their weale publique. Which when they be once rooted in children, do remayne with them al their life after, and be wonders profitable for the defence and maintenaunce of the state of the commen welth. Whiche never decaieth but throughe vices risinge of evill opinions.

The priestes, onles they be women (for that kinde is not excluded from priesthoode, howbeit fewe be chosen, and none but widdowes and old women) the men priestes, I saye, take to their wifes the chiefest women in all their countreye. For to no office among the Utopians is more honour and preeminence geven. In so much that if they commit any offence, they be under no commen judgement, but be left only to God and themselfes. For thei thinke it not lawful to touch him with mannes hande, be he never so vitious, which after so singular a sort was dedicate and consecrate to God, as a holly offering. This maner may they easelye observe, bicause they have so fewe priestes, and do chuse them with such circumspection. For it scasely ever chaunceth that the moste vertuous amonge vertuous, which in respect only of his vertue is avaunced to so high a dignity, can fal to vice and wickednes. And if it should chaunce in dede (as mans nature is mutable and fraile) yet by reason they be so fewe and promoted to no might nor powre, but only to honoure, it were not to be feared that anye great dammage by them should happen and ensue to the commen wealthe. They have so rare and fewe priestes, least if the honour were communicated to many, the digniti of the ordre, which among them now is so highly estemed, should rune in contempt. Speciallye bicause they thincke it hard to find many so good as to be meet for that dignity, to the execution and discharge whereof it is not sufficiente to be endued with meane vertues.

Furthermore these priestes be not more estemed of their owne countrey men, then they be of forrein and straunge countreis. Which thinge maye hereby plainly appere. And I thinke also that this is the cause of it. For whiles the armies be fighting together in open feld they a litle beside, not farre of, knele upon their knees in their hallowed vestimentes, holding up their handes to heaven, praing first of all for peace, nexte for vyctory of their owne parte, but to neyther part a bluddy victory. If their host gette the upper hand, they runne in to the mayne battayle and restrayne their owne men from sleying and cruelly pursuinge theire vanquyshed enemies. Whyche enemyes, yf they doo but see them and speake to them, it is ynoughe for the savegarde of theire lyves. And the touching of theire clothes defendeth and saveth al their gooddes from ravine and spoyle. This thinge hathe avaunced them to so greate

229

wourship and trewe majesty among al nations, that manye
times they have as wel preserved theire own citizens from
the cruel force of their enemies, as they have theire enemies from the furyous rage of theire owne men. For it is
well knowen, that when theire owne army hathe reculed
and in dyspayre turned backe and runne away, their enemies fyerslye pursuing with slaughter and spoyle, then the
priestes cumming betwene have stayed the murder, and
parted bothe the hostes. So that peace hath bene made and
concluded betwene bothe partes upon equall and indifferent conditions. For there was never any nation, so fierce,
so cruell and rude, but they hadde them in suche reverence,
that they counted their bodyes hallowed and sanctified,
and therefore not to be violentlye and unreverentlye
touched.

They kepe hollye the firste and the laste daye of every
moneth and yeare, divydinge the yeare into monethes,
whyche they measure by the course of the moone, as they
doo the yeare by the course of the sonne. The fyrste dayes
they call in theire language Lynemernes and the laste
Trapemernes, the whyche woordes may be interpreted,
primifeste and finifest, or els in our speache, first feaste and
last feast. Their churches be verye gorgious and not onelye
of fine and curious workemanship, but also (which in the
fewenes of them was necessary) very wide and large, and
hable to receave a great company of people. But they be
al sumwhat darke. Howbeit that was not donne through
ignoraunce in buildinge, but as they say, by the counsel
of the priestes. Bicause they thought that over much light
doth disperse mens cogitations, whereas in dimme and
doubtful lighte they be gathered together, and more earnestly fixed upon religion and devotion; which bicause it is
not there of one sort among all men, and yet all the kindes
and fassions of it, thoughe they be sondry and manifold,
agre together in the honour of the divine nature, as goyng
divers wayes to one ende; therefore nothing is sene nor
heard in the churches, but that semeth to agre indefferently
with them all.

If there be a distinct kind of sacrifice peculiar to anye several secte, that they execute at home in their owne houses. The common sacrifices be so ordered, that they be no derogation nor prejudice to anye of the private sacrifices and religions. Therefore no ymage of annye god is seene in the churche, to the intente it maye bee free for every man to conceive God by their religion after what likenes and similitude they will. They call upon no peculiar name of God, but only Mithra, in the which word they all agree together in one nature of the divine majesti whatsoever it be. No prayers bee used but suche as everye man maye boldelie pronounce withoute the offendinge of anny secte.

They come therefore to the churche the laste day of everye moneth and yeare, in the evenynge yet fastinge there to gyve thankes to GOD for that they have prosperouslye passed over the yeare or monethe, wherof that hollye daye is the laste daye. The nexte daye they come to the church earlye in the mornyng, to praye to GOD that they maye have good fortune and successe all the newe yeare or monethe whych they doo begynne of that same hollye daye. But in the holly dayes that be the laste dayes of the monethes and yeares, before they come to the churche, the wives fall downe prostrat before theire husbandes feet at home and the children before the feete of their parentes, confessinge and acknowleginge themselfes offenders either by some actuall dede, or by omission of their deuty, and desire pardon for their offense. Thus yf anye cloude of privy displeasure was risen at home, by this satisfaction it is over-blowen, that they may be presente at the sacrifices with pure and charitable mindes. For they be aferd to come there with troubled consciences. Therefore if they knowe themselfes to beare anye hatred or grudge towardes anye man, they presume not to come to the sacrifices, before they have reconciled themselfes and purged theire con-sciences, for feare of great vengeaunce and punyshe-mente for their offense.

When they come thether, the men goo into the ryghte syde of the churche and the women into the lefte syde.

There they place themselfes in suche ordre, that all they whyche be of the male kinde in every household sitte before the goodman of the house, and they of the female kinde before the goodwyfe. Thus it is forsene that all their gestures and behaviours be marked and observed abrode of them by whose authority and discipline they be governed at home. This also they diligently see unto, that the younger evermore be coupled with his elder, lest children beinge joyned together, they should passe over that time in childish wantonnes, wherin they ought principally to conceave a religious and devoute feare towardes God, which is the chieffe and almost the only incitation to vertu.

They kill no living beast in sacrifice, nor they thinke not that the merciful clemencye of God hath delite in bloude and slaughter, which hath geven liffe to beastes to the intent they should live. They burne franckensence and other sweet savours, and light also a greate numbre of waxe candelles and tapers, not supposinge this geare to be any thing avaylable to the divine nature, as neither the prayers of men. But this unhurtful and harmeles kind of worship pleaseth them. And by thies sweet savoures and lightes, and other such ceremonies men feele themselfes secretlye lifted up and encouraged to devotion with more willynge and fervent hartes. The people wearethe in the churche white apparell. The priest is clothed in chaungeable colours. Whiche in workemanshipe bee excellent, but in stuffe not verye pretious. For theire vestimentes be neither embraudered with gold, nor set with precious stones. But they be wrought so fynely and conningelye with divers fethers of foules, that the estimation of no costely stuffe is hable to countervaile the price of the worke. Furthermore in these birdes fethers, and in the dewe ordre of them, whiche is observed in theire setting, they saye, is conteyned certaine divine misteries. The interpretation whereof knowen, whiche is diligentlye taught by the priestes, they be put in remembraunce of the bountifull benefites of God towarde them; and of the love and honoure whiche of

232

theire behalfe is dewe to God; and also of their deuties one towarde another.

When the priest first commeth out of the vestry thus apparelled, they fall downe incontinent everye one reverentlye to the ground, with so still silence on everye part, that the very fassion of the thinge striketh into them a certayne feare of God, as though he were there personally presente. When they have lien a litle space on the ground, the priest gevethe them a signe for to ryse.

Then they sing prayses unto God, whiche they intermixt with instrumentes of musicke, for the moste parte of other fassions then these that we use in this parte of the worlde. And like as some of ours bee muche sweter then theirs, so some of theirs doo farre passe ours. But in one thinge doubtles they goo exceding farre beyonde us. For all their musike bothe that they playe upon instrumentes, and that they singe with mannes voyce dothe so resemble and expresse naturall affections, the sound and tune is so applied and made agreable to the thinge, that whether it bee a prayer, or els a dytty of gladnes, of patience, of trouble, of mournynge, or of anger; the fassion of the melodye dothe so represente the meaning of the thing, that it doth wonderfullye move, stirre, pearce and enflame the hearers myndes. At the laste the people and the priest together rehearse solempne prayers in woordes, expreslye pronounced, so made that everye man maye privatelye applye to hymselfe that which is commonlye spoken of all.

In these prayers everye man recognisethe and knowledgethe God to be hys maker, hys governoure and the principal cause of all other goodnes, thankynge him for so many benefites receaved at his hande. But namelye that throughe the favoure of God he hath chaunced into that publyque weale, whiche is moste happye and welthye, and hathe chosen that religion, whyche he hopeth to be moste true. In the whyche thinge if he doo anye thinge erre, or yf there be any other better then eyther of them is, being more acceptable to God, he desierethe him that he wyl

of his goodnes let him have knowledge thereof, as one
that is ready too followe what way soever he wyll leade
hym. But yf this fourme and fassion of a commen wealthe
bee beste, and his owne relygion most true and perfecte,
then he desyrethe GOD to gyve hym a constaunte stede-
fastnes in the same, and too brynge all other people to
the same ordre of lyvynge and to the same opinion of
God, onles there bee annye thinge that in this diversitye
of religions dothe delite his unsercheable pleasure. To be
shorte he prayeth hym that after his deathe he maye come
to hym. But how soone or late that he dare not assygne or
determine. Howebeit, if it myght stande with his majesties
pleasure, he woulde be muche gladder to dye a paynefull
deathe and so to goo to God, then by longe lyvyng in
worldlye prosperitye to bee awaye from him. Whan this
prayer is said they fal doune to the ground again and a
lytle after they ryse up and go to dinner. And the resydewe
of the daye they passe over in playes and exercise of
chevalrye.

Nowe I have declared and described unto you, as
truelye as I coulde the fourme and ordre of that commen
wealth, which verely in my judgment is not only the beste,
but also that which alone of good right maye claime and
take upon it the name of a commen wealth or publique
weale. For in other places they speake stil of the commen
wealth, but every man procureth his owne private gaine.
Here where nothinge is private, the commen affaires bee
earnestlye loked upon. And truely on both partes they
have good cause so to do as they do. For in other countreys
who knoweth not that he shall sterve for honger, onles
he make some severall provision for himselfe, though the
commen wealthe floryshe never so muche in ryches? And
therefore he is compelled even of verye necessitie to have
regarde to him selfe, rather then to the people, that is to
saye, to other. Contrarywyse there, where all thinges be
commen to every man, it is not to be doubted that any man
shal lacke anye thinge necessary for his private uses, so that

the commen store houses and bernes be sufficientlye stored. For there nothinge is distributed after a nyggyshe sorte, neither there is anye poore man or begger. And thoughe no man have anye thinge, yet everye man is ryche. For what can be more riche, then to lyve joyfully and merely, without al griefe and pensifenes; not caring for his owne lyving, nor vexed or troubled with his wifes importunate complayntes, nor dreadynge povertie to his sonne, nor sorrowyng for his doughters dowrey? Yea they take no care at all for the lyvyng and wealthe of themselfes and al theirs, of theire wyfes, theire chyldren, theire nephewes, theire childrens chyldren, and all the succession that ever shall followe in theire posteritie. And yet besydes this there is no lesse provision for them that were ones labourers and be nowe weake and impotent, then for them that do nowe laboure and take payne.

Here nowe woulde I see, yf anye man dare bee so bolde as to compare with this equytie, the justice of other nations; among whom, I forsake God, if I can fynde any signe or token of equitie and justice. For what justice is this, that a ryche goldesmythe, or an usurer, or to bee shorte, anye of them which either doo nothing at all, or els that whyche they doo is such that it is not very necessary to the common wealth, should have a pleasaunte and a welthie lyvinge, either by idlenes, or by unnecessarye busines; when in the meane tyme poore labourers, carters, yronsmythes, carpenters and plowmen, by so greate and continual toyle, as drawing and bearinge beastes be skant hable to susteine, and againe so necessary toyle, that without it no commen wealth were hable to continewe and endure one yere, should yet get so harde and poore a lyving, and lyve so wretched and miserable a lyfe, that the state and condition of the labouringe beastes maye seme muche better and welthier? For they be not put to soo continuall laboure, nor theire lyvinge is not muche worse, yea to them muche pleasaunter, takynge no thoughte in the meane season for the tyme to come. But these seilye poore

235

wretches be presently tormented with barreyne and un-frutefull labour. And the remembraunce of theire poore indigent and beggerlye olde age kylleth them up. For theire dayly wages is so lytle, that it will not suffice for the same daye, muche lesse it yeldeth any overplus, that may daylye be layde up for the relyefe of olde age.

Is not this an unjust and an unkynde publyque weale, whyche gyveth great fees and rewardes to gentlemen, as they call them, and to goldsmythes,[22] and to suche other, whiche be either ydle persones, or els onlye flatterers, and devysers of vayne pleasures; and of the contrary parte maketh no gentle provision for poore plowmen, coliars, laborers, carters, yronsmythes, and carpenters: without whome no commen wealthe can continewe? But after it hath abused the labours of theire lusty and flowring age, at the laste when they be oppressed with olde age and syckenes, being nedye, poore, and indigent of all thinges, then forgettyng their so manye paynefull watchinges, not remembring their so manye and so greate benefites, recom-penseth and acquyteth them moste unkyndly with myser-able death. And yet besides this the riche men not only by private fraud, but also by commen lawes, do every day pluck and snatche awaye from the poore some parte of their daily living. So whereas it semed before unjuste to recompense with unkindnes their paynes that have bene beneficiall to the publique weale, nowe they have to this their wrong and unjuste dealinge (which is yet a muche worse pointe) geven the name of justice, yea and that by force of a lawe.

Therfore when I consider and way in my mind all these commen wealthes, which now a dayes any where do florish, so God helpe me, I can perceave nothing but a certein conspiracy of riche men procuringe theire owne com-modities under the name and title of the commen wealth. They invent and devise all meanes and craftes, first how to kepe safely, without feare of lesing, that they have un-justly gathered together, and next how to hire and abuse the worke and laboure of the poore for as litle money as may be. These devises, when the riche men have decreed to be kept and observed under coloure of the comminaltie, that is to saye, also of the pore people, then they be made lawes.

But these most wicked and vicious men, when they have by their unsatiable covetousnes devided among them selves al those thinges, whiche woulde have sufficed all men, yet how farre be they from the welth and felicitie of the Utopian commen wealth? Out of the which, in that all the desire of money with the use thereof is utterly secluded and banished, howe greate a heape of cares is cut away! How great an occasion of wickednes and mischiefe is plucked up by the rotes! For who knoweth not, that fraud, theft, rauine, brauling, quarelling, brabling, striffe, chiding, contention, murder, treason, poisoning, which by daily punishmentes are rather revenged then refrained do dye when money dieth? And also that feare, griefe, care, laboures and watchinges do perish even the very same moment that money perisheth? Yea poverty it selfe, which only semed to lacke money, if money were gone, it also would decrease and vanishe away. And that you may perceave this more plainly, consider with your selfes some barein and unfruteful yeare, wherin manye thousandes of people have starved for honger. I dare be bolde to say, that in the end of that penury so much corne or grain might have bene found in the rich mens bernes, if they had bene searched, as being divided among them whome famine and pestilence then consumed, no man at al should have felt that plague and penuri.

So easely might men gette their living, if that same worthye princesse, lady money, did not alone stop up the waye betwene us and our lyving, which a Goddes name was very excellently devised and invented, that by her the way therto should be opened. I am sewer the ryche men perceave this, nor they be not ignoraunte how much better it were too lacke noo necessarye thing, then to abunde with overmuche superfluite; to be ryd oute of innumerable cares and troubles, then to be beseiged and encombred with great ryches. And I dowte not that either the respecte of every mans private commoditie, or els the authority of oure savioure Christe (which for his great wisdom could not but know what were best, and for his inestimable goodnes could not but counsel to that which he knew to be best) wold have brought all the worlde longe agoo into the lawes of this weale publique, if it wer not that one only beast, the princesse and mother of all mischiefe, pride, doth withstande and let it. She measurethe not wealth and prosperity by her owne commodities, but by the miserie and incommodities of other; she would not by her good will be made a goddesse, yf there were no wretches left, over whom she might, like a scorneful ladie, rule and triumph, over whose miseries her felicities mighte shyne, whose povertie she myghte vexe, tormente and encrease by gorgiouslye settynge furthe her richesse. Thys hellhounde creapeth into mens hartes, and plucketh them backe from entering the right pathe of life, and is so depely roted in mens brestes, that she can not be plucked out.

This fourme and fashion of a weale publique, which I would gladly wish unto al nations, I am glad yet that it hath chaunced to the Utopians, which have folowed those institutions of life, whereby they have laid such foundations of their common wealth, as shal continew and last not only wealthely, but also, as far as mans wit may judge and conjecture, shall endure for ever. For, seyng the chiefe causes of ambition and sedition with other vices be plucked up by the rootes and abandoned at home, there can be no jeopardie of domisticall dissention, whiche alone hathe caste under foote and brought to noughte the well fort[i]fied and stronglie defenced wealthe and riches of many cities. But forasmuch as perfect concorde remaineth, and wholsome lawes be executed at home, the envie of al forein princes be not hable to shake or move the empire, though they have many tymes long ago gone about to do it, beyng evermore driven backe.

Thus when Raphaell hadde made an ende of his tale,

though many thinges came to my mind, which in the maners and lawes of that people semed to be instituted and founded of no good reason, not onely in the fashion of their chevalry, and in their sacrifices and religions, and in other of their lawes, but also, yea and chiefly, in that which is the principal foundation of al their ordinaunces, that is to say, in the communitie of their life and livynge, withoute anye occupieng of money, by the whiche thinge onelye all nobilitie, magnificence, wourshippe, honour and maiestie, the true ornamentes and honoures, as the common opinion is, of a common wealth, utterlye be overthrowen and destroied; yet because I knew that he was wery of talking, and was not sure whether he coulde abyde that anye thynge shoulde be sayde againste hys mynde; speciallye remembrynge that he had reprehended this faulte in other, which be aferde lest they should seme not to be wise enough, onles they could find some fault in other mens inventions; therfore I praising both their institutions and hys communication, toke him by the hand, and led him in to supper; sayinge that we woulde chuese an other time to waye and examine the same matters, and to talke with him moore at large therin. Whiche woulde God it might ones come to passe. In the meane time, as I can not agree and consent to all thinges that he saide, beyng else without doubt a man singularly well learned, and also in all worldelye matters exactly and profoundly experienced, so must I nedes confesse and graunt that many thinges be in the Utopian weale publique, whiche in our cities I maye rather wishe for, then hope after.

¶ Thus endeth the afternoones talke of Raphael Hythlodaye concerning the lawes and institutions of the Ilande of Utopia

THE BOOK

OF

THE COURTIER

Baldassare Castiglione

CHIEF SPEAKERS IN THE DIALOGUES

OF

THE COURTIER

·

ELISABETTA GONZAGA, *wife of* Guidobaldi di Montefeltro, *Duke of Urbino*

LADY EMILIA PIA, *friend and companion of the Duchess, and widow of the Duke's half-brother*

MARGARITA GONZAGA, *young niece and companion of the Duchess*

COSTANZA FREGOSO, *young half-niece of the Duke*

FRANCESCO MARIA DELLA ROVERE* ("THE LORD GENERALL"), *young nephew and adopted heir of the Duke*

FEDERICO FREGOSO (SIR FREDERICK), *half-nephew of the Duke, afterwards made a cardinal*

OTTAVIANO FREGOSO (LORD OCTAVIAN), *elder brother of* Costanza *and* Federico, *afterwards a Doge of Genoa*

COUNT LUDOVICO DA CANOSSA (COUNT LEWIS), *a kinsman of* Castiglione, *afterwards Bishop of Bayeux*

GIULIANO DE' MEDICI ("MY LORD MAGNIFICO"), *son of* Lorenzo the Magnificent; *close friend of* Castiglione; *afterwards Duke of Nemours*

BERNARDO DOVIZI (BIBBIENA), *an adherent of the Medici, afterwards a cardinal*

CESARE GONZAGA, *kinsman of the Duchess, cousin and close friend of* Castiglione

BERNARDO ACCOLTI, *better known as* UNICO ARETINO, *"the unique Aretine," a courtier-poet*

LORD GASPAR PALLAVICINO, *the young man who is the Benedick to Lady Emilia Pia's Beatrice*

PIETRO BEMBO, *Venetian scholar and poet, afterwards a cardinal*

242

Epistle of the Author

AFTER the Lorde Guidubaldo of Montefeltro Duke of Urbin was departed out of this life, certein other Gentilmen and I that had bine servauntes to him, continued in servyce wyth Duke Francescomaria Della Roveré hys heire and successor in the state: and whyle the savour of the vertues of Duke Guidubaldo was fresh in my mynde, and the great delite I took in those yeeres in the loving companie of so excellent Personages as then were in the Court of Urbin: I was provoked by the memorie therof to write these bookes of the *Courtier*. The which I accomplished in a fewe dayes,[1] myndinge in time to amende those faultes that spronge of the desire that I had speedilie to paye this debt. But fortune now manie yeeres hath alwayes kept me under in suche continuall travayles, that I coulde never gete leyser to bringe it to the passe that my feeble judgement might be throughlie satisfied withall. At such time therfore as I was in Spayne, being advertised out of Italy how the Lady Vittoria Colonna Marquesse of Pescara, unto whom in foretime I had graunted a Copie of this booke, contrarie to her promise, had made a great part of it to be copied out: it greeved me somwhat whether I would or no, standinge in doubt of the sundrie inconveniences that in the like cases may happen. Yet had I a hope that the witt and wis-

243

dome of that Lady (whose troth I have alwaies had in reverence, as a matter from above) was sufficient to provide, not to be harmfull unto me my beeinge obedient to her commaundement. At last I hard an yncklinge that part of the booke was rief in Naples in many mens handes: and as men are alwayes desirous of noveltie, it was thought that they attempted to imprint it. Wherfore I, amased at this mischaunce, determined wyth my self to overlooke by and by that litle in the booke that time served me therto, with entent to set it abrode, thinking it lesse hurtful to have it somwhat corrected with mine owne hande, then much mangled with an other mannes. Therfore to have this my pourpose take effect, I tooke in hande to reade it over afresh, and sodeinlie at the first blush by reason of the title, I tooke no litle grief, which in proceadinge forward encreased much more, remembringe that the greater part of them that are brought in to reason, are now dead. For beside those that are mentioned in the Proheme of the last booke, M. Alphonsus Ariosto him self is dead, unto whom the booke was dedicated, a noble yonge Gentilman, discreete, full of good condicions, and apt unto every thing meete for one livinge in court. Likewise Duke Julian de Medicis, whose goodnesse and noble Courtesy deserved to have bene a longer time enjoyed of the world. Also M. Bernard, Cardinall of S. Maria in Portico, who for his livelie and pleasant promptnes of witt, was most acceptable unto as manie as knew him, and dead he is. The Lord Octavian Fregoso is also dead, a man in oure tymes verie rare, of a most noble courage, of a pure lief, full of goodnesse, witt, wisdome and Courtesie, and a verie frende unto honour and vertue, and so worthy prayse, that his verie ennemies could say none other of hym, then what sounded to his renoume: and the mishappes he hath borne out with great steadinesse, were sufficient inoughe to geve evidence, that fortune, as she hath alwayes bene, so is she in these dayes also an enemie to vertue. There are dead in like maner manie other that are named in this boke, unto whom a man wold have thought that nature had promised a verie longe lief. But the thinge that should not be rehersed wythout teares is, that the Dutchesse she is also dead. And if my minde be troubled with the losse of so manye frindes and good Lordes of myne, that have left me in this lief, as it were in a wildernes full of sorow, reason would it should with much more grief beare the heavinesse of the Dutchesse death, then of al the rest, bicause she was more woorth then all the rest, and I was much more bounde unto her then unto all the rest. Therfore for leesinge time to bestowe that of dutye I ought upon the memorye of so excellent a Ladye, and of the rest that are no more in lief, provoked also by the jeopardye of the booke, I have made him to be imprinted, and setforth in such sort, as the shortnes of time hath served me. And bicause you had no acqueintance, neither with the Dutches, nor with any of the rest that are dead, saving only with Duke Julian, and with the Cardinal of S. Maria in Portico, while they lived, therfore to the entent, in what I can do, you may have acqueintance with them after their death, I send unto you this booke, as a purtraict in peinctinge of the Court of Urbin: not of the handiwoorke of Raphael, or Michael Angelo, but of an unknowen peincter, and that can do no more but draw the principall lines, without settingfurth the truth with beawtifull coulours, or makinge it appeere by the art of Prospective that it is not. And wher I have enforced my self to setfurth together with the communication the propreties and condicions of such as are named in it, I confesse I have not only not fully expressed, but not somuch as touched the vertues of the Dutchesse. Bicause not onlye my stile is unsufficient to express them, but also mine understanding to conceive them. And if in this behalf, or in anie other matter woorthy reprehention (as I know well there want not manie in the booke) fault be found in me, I will not speake against the truth. But bicause men somtime take such delite in finding fault, that they find fault also in that deserveth not reproof, unto some that blame me bicause I have not folowed Boccaccio, nor bound my self to the maner of the Tuscane speach used nowadayes, I will not let to say, for all Boccaccio was of a fine witt, according to those times, and in some part writt with great advisement and diligence: yet did he write much better whan he lett him self be guided with witt and his owne naturall inclination, without anie other maner studie or regarde to polish his writinges, then whan with al travaile and bent studye he enforced him self to be most fine and eloquent. For his verie favourers affirme that in his own matters he was far deceived in judgement, litle regarding such thinges as have gotten him a name, and greatlye esteaminge that is nothing woorth. Had I then folowed that trade of writing which is blamed in him by such as praise him in the rest, I could not have eschewed the verye same reprooffes that are laied to Boccaccio himself as touching this. And I had deserved somuch the more, for that his errour was then, in beleavyng he did well, and mine should be nowe, in knowinge I do amisse. Again if I had folowed that trade which is reckened of many to be good, and was litle regarded of him, I should appeere in folowing it to disagree from the judgement of him whom I folowed: the which thing (in mine opinion) were an inconvenience. And beeside yf this respect had not moved me, I could not folowe him in the matter, forsomuch as he never wrott any thing in treatise like unto these bookes of the *Courtier*: and in the tunge, I ought not in mine advise, bicause the force or rule of speach doeth consist more in use, then in anye thinge els: and it is alwayes a vice to use woordes that are not in commune speach. Therfore it was not meete I should have used many that are in Boccaccio, which in his time were used, and now are out of use emonge the Tuscanes them selves. Neyther would I binde my self to the maner of the Tuscane tunge in use nowe a dayes, bicause the practising emonge sundrye Nations, hath alwayes bene of force to transport from one to an other (in a maner) as merchaundise, so also new woordes, which afterward remaine or decaye, according as they are admitted by custome or refused. And this beside the record of auntient writers, is to be evidently seene in Boccaccio, in whom there are so manie woordes French, Spanish, and provincial, and some perhappes not well understood of the Tuscanes in these dayes, that whoso woulde pick them out, should make the booke much the lesser. And bicause (in mine opinion) the kinde of speach of the other noble Cities of Italy, where there resorte men of wisdome, understandinge and eloquence, which practise great matters of government of states, of letters, armes, and diverse affayres, ought not altogether to be neglected for the woordes whiche in these places are used in commune speach: I suppose that they maye be used welinough, writing such as have a grace and comlynesse in the pronuntiation, and communly counted good and of propre signification, though they be not Tuscane, and have also their origion out of Italy. Beeside this in Tuscane they use many woordes cleane corrupte from the Latin, the which in Lumbardye and in the other partes of Italy remaine wholl and without any chaunge at al, and they are so universallye used of everye man, that of the best sorte they are allowed for good, and of the commune people understood with out difficulty. Therfore I thinke I have committed no errour at all, yf in writing I have used any of these, and rather taken the wholl and pure woord of mine owne Countrey, then the corrupt and mangled of an other. Neyther doeth that rule seeme good unto me, where many say the vulgar tung, the lesse it is like unto the Latin, the more beawtiful it is: and I can not perceive why more authoritie should consist in one custome of speach, then in an other. For if Tuscane be sufficient to authorise corrupt and mangled Latin woordes, and to geve them so greate a grace, that mangled in such sort everye man may use them for good (the which no man denieth) should not Lumbardy or any other countrey have the authoritye to allow the very Latin woordes that be pure, sounde, propre and not broken in any part so, but they may be well borne: and assuredly as it may be called a rash presumption to take in hand to forge new wordes, or to set up the olde in spite of custome: so is it no lesse, to take in hande against the force of the same custome to bring to naught, and (as it were) to burye alive such as have lasted nowe many yeeres, and have ben defended from the malice of the time with the shield of use, and have preserved their estimation and dignitye, whan in the warres and turmoiles of Italy, alterations were brought up both of the tunge, buildinges, garmentes and maners. And beeside the hardnesse of the matter, it seemeth to be (as it were) a certein wickednesse. Therfore where I have not thought good in my writing to use the wordes of Boccaccio which are used no more in Tuscane, nor to binde my self to their law that think it not lawful to use them that the Tuscanes use not nowadayes, me thynke I ought to be held excused. But I suppose both in the matter of the booke and in the tunge, forsomuch as one tung may help an other, I have folowed Authores asmuch woorthie praise, as Boccaccio. And I beleave it ought not to be imputed unto me for an errour, that I have chosen to make my self rather knowen for a Lumbard, in speaking of Lumbard, then for no Tuscan, in speaking of tomuch Tuscan. Bicause I wil not do as Theophrastus did, which for speaking tomuch the meere Athenian tunge, was of a simple olde woman knowen not to be of Athens. But bycause in thys point there is sufficyent talke in the first booke, I will make no more a do. And to avoid al contention I confesse to my fault-finders, that I have no knowleage in this their Tuscan tunge so hard and secrete: and I say that I have written it in mine owne, and as I speak, and unto such as speake as I speake: and so I trust I have offended no man. For I beleave it is forbed no man that is, to wryte and speake in his owne tunge, neyther is anye man bound to reade or heare that contenteth hym not. Therfore if they will not reade my *Courtier*, they shall offende me nothing at all. Other say, bicause it is so hard a matter and (in a maner) unpossible to finde out a man of such perfection, as I would have the Courtier to be, it is but superfluous to write it: for it is a vaine thing to teach that can not be learned. To these men I answere, I am content, to err with Plato, Xenophon, and M. Tullius, leaving apart the disputing of the intelligible world and of the Ideas or imagined fourmes: in which number, as (according to that opinion) the Idea or figure conceyved in imagination of a perfect commune weale, and of a perfect king, and of a perfect Oratour are conteined: so is it also of a perfect Courtier. To the image wherof if my power could not draw nigh in stile, so much the lesse peynes shall Courtiers have to drawe nigh in effect to the ende and marke that I in writing have set beefore them. And if with all this they can not compasse that perfection, such as it is, which I have endevoured to expresse, he that cummeth nighest shall be the most perfect: as emong many Archers that shute at one marke, where none of them hitteth the pinn, he that is nighest is out of doubt better then the rest. Some again say that my meaning was to facion my self, perswading my self that all suche qualities as I appoint to the Courtier are in me. Unto these men I will not cleane deny that I have attempted all that my mynde is the Courtier shoulde have knowleage in. And I thinke who so hath not the knowleage of the thinges intreated upon in this booke, how learned so ever he be, he can full il write them. But I am not of so sclender a judgment in knowing my self, that I wil take upon me to know what soever I can wish. The defence therfore of these accusations and peraventure of many mo, I leave for this once, to the judgement of the commune opinion: bicause for the most part the multytude, though they have no perfect knowleage, yet do they feele by the instinct of nature a certein savour of good and ill, and can geve none other reason for it: one tasteth and taketh delite, an other refuseth and is against his stomake.

Therfore if the book shall generally please, I wil count him good, and think that he ought to live: but if he shall displease, I will count him naught, and beleave that the memorye of him shall soone perish. And if for all this mine accusers will not be satisfied with this commune judgemente, let them content them selves with the judgement of time, which at length discovereth the privie faultes of every thing: and bicause it is father to truth and a judge without passion, it accustometh evermore to pronounce true sentence of the life or death of writynges.

THE COURTIER

FIRST BOOK

The First Booke of The Courtier of Counte Baldesser Castilion, unto Maister Alfonsus Ariosto

I HAVE a long time douted with my self (moste loving M. Alphonsus) whiche of the two were harder for me, either to denie you the thing that you have with such instance many times required of me, or to take it in hand: because on the one side mee thought it a verie hard matter to denie any thing, especially the request being honest, to the person whom I love dearely, and of whom I perceive my selfe dearly beloved. Againe, on the other side, to undertake an enterprise which I doe not know my selfe able to bring to an ende, I judged it uncomly for him that weyeth due reproofes so much as they ought to bee weyed.

At length, after much debating, I have determined to proove in this behalfe, what ayde that affection and great desire to please can bring unto my diligence, which in other things is woont to encrease the labour of men.

You then require me to write, (what is to my thinking) the trade and maner of courtiers, which is most convenient for a gentleman that liveth in the Court of Princes, by the which he may have the knowledge how to serve them perfitely in every reasonable matter, and obtaine therby favour of them, and praise of other men.

Finally of what sort hee ought to bee that deserveth to be called so perfit a Courtier, that there be no want in him:

Wherefore I considering this kinde of request (say) that in case it shoulde not appeare to my selfe a greater blame, to have you esteeme me to be of small friendship, than all other men of little wisdom, I would have ridde my hands of this labour, for feare least I should be counted rash of al such as knowe, what a hard matter it is, among such diversitie of maners, that are used in the Courts of Christen-dome, to picke out the perfectest trade and way, and (as it were) the floure of this Courtiership. Bicause use maketh us many times to delite in, and to set little by the selfe same things: whereby sometime it proceedeth that maners, garments, customes, and fashions, which at somtime have ben in price, become not regarded, and contrariwise, the not regarded, become of price.

Therefore it is manifestly to be discerned, that use hath greater force than reason, to bring up new inventions among us, and to abolish the olde, of the which who so goeth about to judge the perfection, is oftentimes deceived.

For which consideration, perceiving this and many other lettes, in the matter propounded for me to write upon, I am constreined to make a peece of an excuse, and to open plainely that this error (if it may be termed an errour) is common to us both, that if any blame happen to me about it, it may be partned with you. For it ought to bee reckned a no lesse offence in you, to lay upon me a burthen that passeth my strength, than in me to take it upon me.

Let us therefore at length settle our selves to beginne that that is our purpose and drift, and (if be it possible) let us fashion such a Courtier, as the Prince that shall be worthie to have him in his service, although his state be but small, may notwithstanding be called a mighty Lord.

We wil not in these books follow any certaine order or rule of appointed preceptes, the which for the most part is woont to bee observed in teaching of any thing whatsoever it bee: But after the manner of men of olde time, renuing a gratefull memorie: we will repeate certaine reasonings that were debated in times past, betweene men very excellent for that purpose. And although I was not there present,[2] but at the time when they were debated, it was my chaunce to be in Englande, yet soone after my returne, I heard them of a person that faithfully reported them unto me. And I will endevour my selfe, for so much as my memory will serve me, to call them particularly to remembrance, that you may see, what men worthy great commendation, and unto whose judgement a man may in every point give an undoubted credite, have judged and beleeved in this matter.

Neither shall we swarve from the purpose to arrive in good order at the ende, unto the which all our communication is directed, if we disclose the cause of the reasonings that hereafter follow.

As every man knoweth, the little Citie of Urbin is situated upon the side of the Appennine (in a manner) in the middes of Italy, towards the Goulfe of Venice. The which for all it is placed among hilles, and those not so pleasant as perhappes some other that we behold in many places, yet in this point the Element hath beene favourable unto it, that all about, the Countrey is verie plentifull and full of fruites: so that beside the holesomnes of ayre, it is verie aboundant and stored with all thinges necessarie for the life of man. But among the greatest felicities that man can reckon to have, I count this the chiefe, that now a long time it hath alwaies bene governed with very good princes, in the common calamities of the wars of Italie it remained also a season without any at all.

But without searching further of this, we may make a

good proofe with the famous memorie of Duke Fridericke,[3] who in his daies was the light of Italy. Neither do wee want true and very large testimonies yet remaning of his wisedome, courtesie, justice, liberalitie, of his invincible courage and policy of warre. And of this doe his so manye victories make proofe, chiefly his conquering of places impugnable, so sodaine readines in setting forward to give battaile, his putting to flight sundrie times with a small number, very great and puissant armies, and never sustained losse in anye conflict. So that we may, not without cause, compare him to many famous men of olde time.

This man among his other deedes praise-worthie, in the hard and sharpe situation of Urbin buylt a Palace, to the opinion of many men, the fairest that was to bee found in all Italie, and so furnished it with all necessarie implementes belonging thereto, that it appeared not a Palace, but a Citie in forme of a Palace, and that not onelye with ordinarye matters, as Silver plate, hangings for Chambers of very rich cloth of Golde, of Silke and other like, but also for sightlines: and to decke it out withall, placed there a wondrous number of auncient Images of Marble and Mettall, very excellent paintings and Instruments of Musicke of all sortes, and nothing would he have there but what was most rare and excellent.

To this with verie great charges hee gathered together a great number of most excellent and rare bookes, in Greeke, Latin, and Hebrue, the which all hee garnished with gold and silver, esteeming this to be the chiefest ornament of his great Palace.

This Duke then following the course of nature, when he was threescore and five yeares of age, as he had lived, so did he end his lyfe with glorie. And left Duke after him a child of ten yeres having no more male, and without mother, who hight Guidubaldo.

This childe, as of the state, so did it appeare also that he was heire of all his fathers vertues: and sodainly with a marveilous towardnes, began to promise so much of him-

selfe, as a man would not have thought possible to bee
hoped of a man mortall. So that the opinion of men was,
that of all Duke Frederickes notable deedes, there was
none greater than that he begat such a sonn. But fortune
envying this so great vertue, with all her might gainstood
this so glorious a beginning, in such wise that before Duke
Guidubaldo was xx. yeares of age, he fell sicke of the goute,
the which encreasing upon him with most bitter paines,
in a short time so nummed him of all his members, that hee
coulde neither stand on foote, nor move himselfe. And in
this manner was one of the best favoured, and towardliest
personages in the world, deformed and marred in his greene
age. And beside, not satisfied with this, fortune was so contrarie to him in al his purposes, that verye seldome he
brought to passe any thing to his mind. And for all hee
had in him most wise counsaile, and an invincible courage,
yet it seemed that whatsoever he tooke in hand, both in
feats of armes, and in everye other thing small or great, it
came alwaies to ill successe.

And of this make proofe his manye and diverse calamities,
which hee alwaies bare out with such stoutnesse of courage,
that vertue never yeelded to fortune. But with a bold
stomacke despising her stormes, lived with great dignitie
and estimation among all men: in sicknesse, as one that
was sounde, and in adversitie, as one that was most fortunate. So that for all hee was thus diseased in his bodie
he served in time of warre with most honourable entertainement under the most famous kings of Naples, Alphonsus and Ferdinande the yonger. Afterward with Pope
Alexander the sixt, with the Lordes of Venice and Florence.

And when Julius the second was created Pope, hee was
then made General Capitaine of the Church: at which time
proceeding in his accustomed usage, hee set his delight
above all thinges to have his house furnished with most
noble and valiant Gentlemen, with whom hee lived verie
familiarly, enjoying their conversation.

Wherein the pleasure which hee gave unto other men

was no lesse, than that he received of other, because hee was verie well seene in both toongs, and togither with a loving behaviour and pleasantnesse hee had also accompanied the knowledge of infinite things. And beside this, the greatnesse of his courage so quickned him, that where hee was not in case with his person to practise the feates of Chivalrie, as he had done long before, yet did he take verie great delight to beholde them in other men, and with his wordes sometime correcting, and otherwhile praising every man according to his deserts, he declared evidently how great a judgement hee had in those matters.

And upon this at Tilt, at Tourney, in playing at all sorts of weapon, also in inventing devices in pastimes, in Musicke, finally in all exercises meete for noble Gentlemen, every man strived to shew himselfe such a one, as might deserve to bee judged worthie of so noble assembly.

Therefore were all the houres of the day divided into honourable and pleasant exercises, as well of the bodie, as of the minde. But because the Duke used continually, by reason of his infirmitie, soone after Supper to goe to his rest, everie man ordinarily, at that houre drew where the Dutchesse was, the Ladie Elizabeth Gonzaga, where also continually was the Ladie Emilia Pia, who for that shee was indued with so lively a wit and judgement, as you know, seemed the maistresse and ringleader of all the company, and that everie man at her received understanding and courage.

There was then to bee heard pleasant communications and merie conceites, and in everie mans countenance a man might perceive painted a loving jocundnesse. So that this house truely might wel be called the very Mansion place of mirth and joy. And I beleeve it was never so tasted in other place, what manner a thing the sweete conversation is that is occasioned of an amiable and loving company, as it was once there.

For leaving apart what honour it was to all us to serve such a Lorde, as hee whom I declared unto you right now, everye man conceived in his minde an high contentation every time we came into the Dutchesse sight. And it appeared that this was a chaine that kept all linked together in love, in such wise that there was never agreement of wil or hartie love greater betweene brethren, than there was betweene us all.

The like was betweene the woman with whom we had such free and honest conversation, that everye man might commune, sitte, dallye, and laugh with whom hee had lusted.

But such was the respect which we bore to the Dutchesse will, that the selfe same libertie was a very great bridle. Neither was there any that thought it not the greatest pleasure he could have in the world, to please her, and the greatest griefe to offend her.

For this respect were there most honest conditions coupled with wondrous great libertie, and devises of pastimes, and laughing matters tempred in her sight, beside most witty jestes, with so comely and grave a Majestie, that the verye sober moode and greatnes that did knit together all the actes, woordes and gestures of the Dutchesse in jesting and laughing, made them all that had never seene her in their lyfe before, to count her a verie great Ladie.

And all that came in her presence, having this respect fixed in their breast, it seemed shee had made them to her becke.

So that everie man enforced himselfe to followe this trade, taking (as it were) a rule and ensample of faire conditions at the presence of so great and so vertuous a Ladie. Whose most excellent qualities I entend not now to expresse, for it is neither my purpose, and againe they are well ynough knowne to the world, and much better than I am able either with tongue, or with pen to indite.

And such as would perhaps have lien hid a space, fortune, as shee that wondreth at so rare vertues, hath thought good with manye adversities and temptations of miseries to disclose them, to make triall thereby that in the tender breast of a woman, in companie with singular beautie, there can dwel wisedome, and stoutnes of courage and all other vertues that in grave men themselves are most seldome.

But leaving this apart, I say that the maner of the gentlemen in the house was immediately after supper to assemble together where the Dutchesse was. Where among other recreations, musicke and dauncing, which they used continually, sometime they propounded feate questions, otherwhile they invented certayne wittye sportes and pastimes at the device sometime of one sometime of another, in the which under sundry coverts oftentimes the standers by opened subtilly their immaginations unto whome they thought best.

At other times there arose other disputations of divers matters, or else jeastings with prompt inventions. Many times they fell into purposes, (as we now a daies terme them) where in this kinde of talke and debating of matters, there was wonderous great pleasure on al sides: Because (as I have said) the house was replenished with most noble wittes. Among which (as you know) were most famous the Lord Octavian Fregoso, Sir Friderick his brother, the Lord Julian de Medicis, M. Peter Bembo, the Lord Cesar Gonzaga, Counte Lewis of Canossa, the Lord Gasper Pallavicin, the Lorde Lodovicus Pius, Maister Morello of Ortona, Peter of Naples, Maister Robert of Bari, and infinite of other most worthy knights and gentlemen.

Beside these, there were many that for all ordinarilye they dwelled not there, yet spent they most of all their time there, as Maister Bernard Bibiena, Unico Aretino, John Christopher Romano, Peter Mount, Therpander, Maister Nicholas Phrisio, so that thither ran continually Poets, Musitions, and all kind of men of skill, and the excellentest in every faculty that were in all Italy.

After Pope Julius the second had with his owne presence by the ayde of the Frenchmen brought Bolonia to the obedience of the Apostolique sea againe, in the yeare a thousande five hundred and sixe, in his returne toward Rome he took Urbin in his way, where hee was received as honorably as was possible, and with as sumptuous and costly preparation, as could have bene in any other City of Italie whatsoever it be. So that beside the Pope, all the Cardinals and other Courtiers thought themselves thorowly satisfied.

And some there were that provoked with the sweetnes of this company, after that the Pope and the Court was departed, continued many daies together in Urbin. At which time they did not onely proceede in their accustomed trade of disporting and ordinarye recreations, but also every man set to his helping hande to augment them somewhat, and especially in pastimes, which they had up almost every night.

And the order thereof was such, that as soone as they were assembled where the Dutchesse was, every man sat him downe at his will, or as it fell to his lot, in a circle together, and in sitting were devyded a man and a woman, as long as there was women, for alwaies lightly, the number of men was far the greater.

Then were they governed as the dutchesse thought best, which many times gave this charge unto the Ladye Emilia.

So the day after the Pope was departed, the companye being gathered to the accustomed place, after much pleasant talke, the Dutchesse pleasure was that the Ladye Emilia shoulde begin these pastimes.

And she after a little refusing of that charge, said in this manner: Sith it is your pleasure [Madame] I shall be she that must give the onset in our pastimes this night, because I ought not of reason disobey you, I thinke meete to propound a pastime, whereof I suppose shall ensue little blame, and lesse travaile.

And that shall be to have every man, as nigh as he can, propound a device not yet heard of, then shal we choose out such a one as shall be thought meete to be taken in hand in this company.

And after she had thus spoken, she turned her to the
Lord Gaspar Pallavicin, willing him to propound his: who
immediately made answere.

But first (Madame) you must begin to propound yours.
Then said the Ladye Emilia:

I have already done. But your grace must commande
him (Madame) to be obedient.

Then the dutchesse laughing, to the intent (quoth she)
every man shall obey you, I make you my Deputie, and
give unto you all mine authority.

It is surely a great matter, answered the Lord Gaspar,
that it is alwaies lawful for women to have this priviledge,
to be exempt and free from paines taking.

And truely reason woulde we should in any wise know
why. But because I will not be he that shall give example
to disobey, I shall leave this untill an other time, and will
speake of that I am now charged withall, and thus I begin.

Mine opinion is, that our mindes, as in other thinges, so
also in loving are diverse in judgement, and therefore it
chaunceth often times, that the thing which is most acceptable unto one, is most abhorred of an other. Yet for all that
they alwaies agree in that everye man counteth most deare
the wight beloved. So that many times the overmuch affection in lovers doth deceive their judgment, that they weene
the person whom they love, to be so garnished with al
excellent vertues and without fault, that he hath no peere
in the world.

But because the nature of man doth not admit such full
perfections, and there is no man that hath not some default
or want in him, it can not be said that such as these be,
are not deceyved, and that the lover doth not become blind
as touching the beloved.

I would therefore our pastimes should be this night to
have everye man open what vertues he would principally
the person he loved should be indued withall. And seeing
it is so necessarily that we al have some sport, what vice
he would also have in him: to see who can find out most

praise-worthy and manly vertues, and most tollerable vices, that should be least hurtfull both to him that loveth, and to the wight beloved.

After the L. Gaspar had thus spoken, the L. Emilia made a signe unto the Lady Constaunce Fregosa, because she was next in order, to follow: who was now about to speake when the Dutchesse solemnly saide.

Seeing the L. Emilia will not take the paines to finde out some pastime, reason willeth that the other Ladies should be partakers of the same privilege, and bee also free from this burden for this night, especially seeing there are so many men in place, for assure your selfe wee shall want no pastime.

So shall we doo, answered the L. Emilia, and putting the L. Constance to silence, turned her to the L. Cesar Gonzago that sat next her, commaunding him to speake, and thus began.

Who so will diligently consider all our dooing, hee shall finde alwaies in them sundry imperfections. And that happeneth, because nature doth vary, as well in this, as in all other things. Unto one she hath given the light of reason in one thing, and unto an other, in an other thing.

Therefore it commeth to passe, where one man knoweth that an other knoweth not, and is ignorant in the thing that the other hath understanding in, eche man doth easily perceive the errour of his fellow, and not his owne, and wee all thinke our selves to bee verie wise, and paradventure in that point most, wherin we are most foolish.

So that we have seene by experience in this house many men which at the beginning were counted most wise, in processe of time were knowne to bee most foolish, which hath proceeded of no other thing but of our owne diligence.

Like as it is said to be in Pulia, of them that are bitten with a Tarrantula, about whom men occupy many instruments of musicke, and with sundry sounds go searching out, untill the humour that maketh this disease, by a certain concordance it hath with some of those soundes, feeling it, do sodenly moove, and so stirreth the pacient, that by that stirring he recovereth his health againe. In like maner wee, when wee have felt some privie operation of folly, we provoke it so subtilly, and with such sundry persuasions, and so divers waies, that at length wee understand whether it tended.

Afterward the humour knowne, we so stir it, that alwaies it is brought to the perfection of open folly. And some is wexed foolish in verses, some in musicke, some in love, some in daucing, some in making antiques,[4] some in riding, some in playing at fence, everie man according to the mine of his mettall: wherby hath ensued (as you know) marvellous great pastime.

I hold therfore for certaine, that in every one of us there is some seede of folly, the which beeing stirred may multiply (in a maner) infinite.

Therefore I would this night our pastime were to dispute upon this matter: and that everie man might say his mind, seeing I must be openly foolish, in what sort of folly I am foolish, and over what matter, judging it the issue for the sparkles of folly that are daily seene to proceede from mee. And let the like be said of all the rest, keeping the order of our devises.

And let every man doe his best to grounde his opinion upon some sure signe and argument, and so by this our pastime shall everie one of us get profite, in that we shall know our defaults, and then shall we the better take heede.

And in case the vaine of folly which wee shall discover, be so ranke that it shall appeare to us past remedie, we shall set thereto our helping hand, and according to the doctrine of Frier Marian, wee shall gaine a soule, which shall be no smal gain.

At this devise there was much laughing, and none could refraine from speaking.

One saide, I should bee found foolish in imagining. An other, in viewing. An other said, he was already become foolish for love: and such like matters.

Then Frier Seraphin, after his manner, laughing. This (quoth he) should bee too tedious a matter. But if you will have a pretie pastime, let everie man tell his opinion, how it commeth that (in a maner) all women abhorre rattes, and love serpents, and you shall see that none will hit upon it, but I, that know this misterie by a straunge meane. And now began hee to enter into his trifling tales, but the L. Emilia commanded him to siléce, and overskipping the Ladie that sat there, made a signe to Unico aretino that was next in order, and hee went without looking for anie more bidding.

I (quoth he) would gladly bee a judge of authoritie, that I might with all kinde of torment boult out the truth of offenders: and that, to discover the deceits of an ungrate woman, who with the eyes of an angell, and heart of a Serpent, never agreeth her toong with her minde, and with a fained deceivable compassion, purposeth nothing els but to make Anatomie of hearts.

Neither is there in all the sandie country of Libia to be found so venimous a serpent that is so desirous of mans bloud, as is this false creature. Which not onely for the sweetenesse of voice and pleasant sound of words, but also for her eyes, for her laughing, for her countenance, and for all her gestures is a most perfect Marmaide.

Therefore seeing it is not lawfull for me, as I would, to use chaines, ropes, or fire, to understand a matter of trueth, my desire is to compasse the knowledge of it with a merry pastime, which is this: That everie man should expresse his fansie what the S. doth signifie that the Dutchesse carieth in her forehead.

For although this be also an artificiall covert, the better to beguile, perhaps there may bee an interpretation which she never thought upon. And who knoweth whether fortune, with pitie beholding y[e] torments of men, hath stirred her with his small token, to discover against her will the inwarde desire she hath to slea and bury alive in calamitie him that honoureth and serveth her.

The Dutchesse laughed, and Unico perceiving shee would have excused her selfe of this interpretation, no (quoth hee) speake you not, madam, for it is not your turne to speake now.

The L. Emilia then turned her and said: M. Unico there is none of us all here that giveth not place to you in everie thing, and especially in knowing the disposition of the Dutchesse. And as you by your divine wit know her better than all the rest, so doe you love her better than all the rest, which like birds of feeble sight, that cannot looke stedfastly into the circle of the Sun, cannot so well perceive the perfection of it.

Therefore all labour were in vaine in clearing of this doubt, saving your judgement alone.

This enterprise then is reserved onely to you, as unto him that alone can bring it to an end, and none other.

Unico, after he had pawsed a while, being still called upon to say his fansie, at length rehearsed a rime upon the foresaid matter, expounding what signified the letter S., the which manie judged to be made at the first sight. But because it was more wittie and better knit than a man would have believed the shortnes of time required, it was thought he had prepared it before.

So after mens favourable voice given in the prayse of this rime, and after sufficient talke, the L. Octavian Fregoso, whose turne was then next, began in this sorte smyling.

My Lordes, if I shoulde say unto you that I never felt passion of love in my dayes, I am sure the Dutchesse and the L. Emilia, although they believe it not in deede, yet would they make semblance to believe it, and would say that it proceeded because I mistrusted I should never frame any woman to love me.

The which truely I have not hetherto proved with such instance, that of reason I should dispaire to obtaine it once. Neither have I forborne the doing of it, because I set so much by my selfe, and so litle by women, that I thinke none worthie to bestow my love and service upon. But rather amased at the continuall bewailing of some lovers, that with their palenesse, sorrow, and silence, it appeareth they have evermore their owne discomfort painted in their eyes. And if they speake accompanying every worde with certaine treblefolde sighes, they reason of nothing else but of teares, of torments, of desperations, and of longing for death. So that whensoever any sparke of love hath begonne to kindle in my brest, I have by and by enforced my selfe with all diligence to quench it: not for any hatred that I have conceived against women (as these Ladies suppose) but for mine owne health.

On the other side, I have knowne some other cleane contrarie to these sorrowful, which do not onely advance and content them selves, with the chearefull lookes, loving wordes, and sweete countenances of their Ladies, but also sauce their sorrowes with sweetnes, so that they count debates, the angers, and the disdaines of them, most sweete.

Therefore these men seeme unto mee to bee much more than happie: for whereas they finde so much sweetnesse in the amorous disdaines, which some mē recken much more bitter than death, I believe in loving gestures they should feele that woonderfull blisse, which we seeke for in vaine in this world.

Therefore would I our pastime were this night, to have every man shew, where there must bee a disdaine against him in the person beloved, what the cause should be that should make the person conceive this disdeine. For if there be any here that have proved those sweet disdaines, I am sure they will desire for courtesie one of these causes that make them so sweete. And perhaps I shall with a better will proceede somewhat farther in love, in hope that I shall also finde this sweetnesse, where as some finde bitternesse.

And so shall not these Ladies give me any more this slanderous report, that I am not in love.

This pastime was much praised, and therfore did every man settle himselfe to reason upon this matter. But ye L.

Emilia holding her peace, M. Peter Bembo that sat next in order, spake in this maner:

My Lords, this pastime that the L. Octavian hath propounded, hath raised no smal doubt in my minde, where he hath reasoned of the disdaines of love, the which though they be sundry, yet unto me have they alwaies beene most bitter.

Neither do I believe, that I can learne any sauce that shall bee sufficient to sweeten them.

But peradventure they are the more and the lesse bitter, according to the cause whereof they arise. For I have in my daies (I remember) seene the woman whom I served, stirred against me, either upon a vaine suspition that shee conceived her selfe of my trustinesse, or els upon some other false opinion that had been put into her head by some mens report to my hinderance, so that I beleeved no griefe might be compared to mine.

And me thought that the greatest sorrow I felt, was to suffer without deserving, and to susteine this affliction, not for any offence of mine, but for the small love that was in her.

At other times I saw her disdainful for some oversight of mine, and knew that her anger proceeded of mine offence, and at that instant I judged the former vexation to be very light, in comparison to that which I felt then. And me thought to be in displeasure, and that for mine owne trespasse, with the person whom onely I coveted, and with such diligence sought to please, was the greatest torment of all other.

Therefore would I our pastime were to have everie man declare his opinion, where there must be a disdaine against him in the person beloved, of whom hee would the cause of this disdaine should have his beginning, whether of her, or of himselfe: to know which is greater griefe, either to displease the wight beloved, or to receive displeasure of the wight beloved.

Every man looked what the L. Emilia woulde make

265

answere to this, but without any word speaking to Bembo, she turned her, and made a signe to sir Fridericke Frigoso to shew his devise. And hee incontinently beganne thus.

Madame, I woulde it were lawfull for me, as the maner is many times, to remit me to the judgement of an other, for I for my part would with all my heart allow some of the pastimes that have been alreadie propounded by these Lords, because indeed mee thinke they would be worth the hearing. Yet least I should breake the order, this I say: who so would take in hand to praise our Court, leaving apart the deserts of the Dutchesse, which ghostly spirit with hir influence is sufficient to draw from the earth up into heaven the simplest wits in the world, he might well doe it without suspition of flatterie. For peradventure in all Italy a man shall have much a do to find out so many Gentlemen and noble personages that are so worthie, and beside the principall profession of Chivalrie so excellent in sundrie things, as are presently here.

Therefore if in any place men may bee found that deserve ye name of good Courtiers, and can judge what belongeth to the perfection of Courtiership, by reason a man may believe them to be here.

To disgrace therfore many untowardly Asseheades, that through malapartnesse thinke to purchase them the name of a good Courtier, I would have such a pastime for this night, that one of the company might bee picked out, who should take it in hand to shape in wordes a good Courtier, specifying all such conditions and particular qualities, as of necessitie must bee in him that deserveth this name.

And in such thinges as shall not appeare necessarie, that it may bee lawfull for everie man to reply against them, as the maner of Philosophers schooles is against him that keepeth disputations.

Sir Fredericke proceeded still forwarde in his talke, when the L. Emilia interrupting him, said: If it be my Ladie the Dutchesse pleasure, this shall be our pastime for this once. The dutchesse answered: I am well pleased.

266

Then (in maner) all the company began to say both to the Dutchesse and among themselves, that this was the trimmest pastime they could have.

And without looking for answere the one of the other, they craved upon the L. Emilia, to appoint who should first begin. Who turning toward the Dutchesse said.

Command you, madame, whom shall please you to take this enterprise in hand, for I will not by choosing more one than another, declare my selfe to judge in this behalfe, whom I thinke to be better skilled than the rest, and so do wrong to some.

The Dutchesse answered: make you this choise your selfe, and take heede that in disobeying, you be not a president to the rest to bee disobedient.

Then the L. Emilia saide laughing unto Lewis Count of Canosse: therfore for leesing anye more time, you (Counte) shalbe he that shal take this enterprise upon him in forme and manner as sir Fredericke hath declared. Not for that wee know ye are so good a Courtier, that ye have at your fingers ends that belongs therto: but because in repeating everie thing arsiversie, as we hope ye wil, we shal have so much the more pastime, and everie one shall be able to answere you.

Where if an other more skilfull than you should take it in hand, there should bee nothing said against him for telling the truth, and so should we have but a cold pastime.

The Counte answered by and by: we need not feare (Madame) that wee shall want contrarying in words against him that telleth the truth, as long as you be here.

And after they had laughed a while at this answere, he proceeded on: but truely I would with all my heart be rid of this burthen, for it is too hard for mee. And I know that to be most true in me, which you have spoken in jest: namely, that I have no understanding in that belongeth to a good Courtier. And this doe I not seeke to prove with any other triall: for seeing I do not ye deedes,

267

a man may judge I understand it not, and I believe I am the lesse to bee blamed. For out of doubt, it is a worse matter not to do wel, than not to understand how to do it. Yet seeing your pleasure is, that I shall take the charge upon me, I cannot, nor will refuse it, for withstanding your order and judgement, the which I know is much better than mine.

Then the L. Cesar Gonzaga. Because it is now (quoth hee) well forward in night, and we have here readie for us other sortes of pastimes, peradventure it shuld not be amisse to deferre this reasoning untill to morrow, and the Counte shall have leisure to thinke better upon that he hath to say: for in verie deed, to entreat upon such a matter at the first sight, it is a hard thing.

Then answered the Counte: I will not do as he did, that stripped himselfe into his doublet, and leaped lesse ground than he did before in his Coate. And me thinke my lucke is good that it is late, because the shortnesse of time shall make me use fewe words, and the sodainesse of the matter shall so excuse me, that it shall be lawfull for me to speake without blame, whatsoever commeth first to minde.

Because I will not therfore carry this burthen of duetie any longer upon my shoulders, this I say: in everie thing it is so hard a matter to know the true perfection, that it is almost unpossible, and that by reason of the varietie of judgemēts.

Therfore many there are, that delight in a man of much talke, and him they call a pleasant fellow. Some wil delight more in modestie, some other will fancie a man that is active and alwaies dooing: other, one that sheweth a quietnesse and a respect in everie thing. And thus doth everie man praise or dispraise according to his fancie, alwaies covering a vice with the name of the next vertue to it, and a vertue with the name of the next vice: as in calling him that is sawcie, bold: him that is sober, dry: him that is seelie, good: him that is unhappie, wittie: and likewise in the rest.

Yet doe I thinke that eche thing hath his perfection, although it be hid, and with reasonable discourses, might be judged of him that hath knowledge in that matter.

And for as much as the truth (as I have said) is often-times hid, and I take not upon me to have this knowledge, I can not praise, but that kinde of Courtiers which I set most by, and allow that which seemeth unto me most nigh the truth, in my small judgement. The which you shall follow if ye thinke it good, or els sticke to your owne, if it shall varie from mine. Neither will I (for all that) stand stiffe that mine is better than yours, for not onely one thing may seeme unto you, and an other to me.

But also unto my selfe it may appeare sometime one thing, sometime an other.

I wil have this our Courtier therefore to bee a gentleman borne and of a good house. For it is a great deale lesse dispraise for him that is not borne a gentleman to faile in the actes of vertue, then for a gentleman. If he swerve from the steps of his ancestors, hee staineth the name of his familie.

And doth not onely not get, but looseth that is alreadie gotten. For noblenesse of birth, is as it were a cleare lampe that sheweth forth and bringeth into light, workes both good and bad, and inflameth and provoketh unto vertue, as well with the feare of slaunder, as also with the hope of praise.

And whereas this brightnesse of noblenesse doth not dis-cover the workes of the unnoble, they have a want of provocation and of feare of slaunder, and they reckon not them selves bound to wade any further than their ancestors did before them, whereas the noble of birth counte it a shame not to arrive at the least at the bounds of their pre-decessors set forth unto them.

Therefore it chanceth alwaies in a manner, both in armes and in all other vertuous acts, that the most famous men are Gentlemen. Because nature in every thing hath deeply sowed that privie seed, which giveth a certaine force and propertie of her beginning, unto whatsoever springeth of it, and maketh it like unto her selfe.

As we see by example, not onely in the race of horses and other beastes, but also in trees, whose slippes and graftes alwaies for the most part are like unto the stocke of the tree they came from: and if at any time they grow out of kinde, the fault is in the husbandman. And the like is in men, if they be trained up in good nurture, most commonly they resemble them from whom they come, and often times passe them, but if they have not one that can well traine them up, they growe (as it were) wilde, and never come to their ripenesse.

Truth it is, whether it be through the favor of the Starres or of nature, some there are borne indued with such graces, that they seeme not to have beene borne, but rather fashioned with the verie hand of some God, and abound in all goodnes both of bodie and minde. As againe we see some so unapt and dull, that a man will not believe, but nature hath brought them into the world for a spite and mockerie.

And like as these with continuall diligence and good bringing up for the most part can bring small fruit: even so the other with litle attendance climbe to the full perfection of all excellencie.

And to give you an example, marke me the Lord Hyppolitus da Este Cardinall of Ferrara, he hath had so happie a birth, that his person, his countenance, his words, and all his gestures are so fashioned and compact with this grace, that among the most ancient prelates (for all he is but young) he doth represent so grave an authoritie, that a man would weene he were more meete to teach, than needful to learne.

Likewise in companie with men and women of al degrees, in sporting, in laughing, and in jesting, he hath in him certaine sweetnes, and so comely demeanours, that who so speaketh with him, or yet beholdeth him, must needes beare him an affection for ever.

But returning to our purpose, I say, that betwene this excellent grace, and that fond foolishnes, there is yet a meane, and they that are not by nature so perfectly furnished, with studie and diligence may polish and correct a great part of the defaults of nature.

The Courtier therefore, beside noblenesse of birth, I will have him to bee fortunate in this behalfe, and by nature to have not onely a wit, and a comely shape of person and countenance, but also a certaine grace, and (as they say) a hewe, that shall make him at the first sight acceptable and loving unto who so beholdeth him.

And let this bee an ornament to frame and accompany all his acts, and to assure men in his looke, such a one to be worthie the companie and favour of everie great man.

Here without any longer tarrying the L. Gasper Pallavicin said: that our pastime may have the forme and maner agreed upon, and least it should appeare, that we litle esteeme the authoritie given us to contrary you, I say (in mine advise) that this noblenesse of birth is not so necessarie for the Courtier. And if I wist that any of you thought it a strange or a new matter, I would alledge unto you sundry, who for all they were borne of most noble bloud, yet have they been heaped full of vices: and contrariwise, many unnoble that have made famous their posteritie.

And if it be true that you said before, that the privie force of the first seede is in everie thing, we should all bee in one maner condition, for that we had all one selfe beginning, and one should not be more noble than an other.

But beside the diversities and degrees in us of high and low, I believe there be many other matters, wherein I judge fortune to bee the chiefe, because we see her beare a stroke in all worldly things, and (as it were) take a pastime to exalte manie times whom pleaseth her without any desert at al, and bury in the bottomles depth the most worthie to be exalted.

I confirme your saying as touching the happinesse of

them that are borne abounding in all goodnesse both of minde and bodie: but this is seene as well in the unnoble, as in the noble of birth, for nature hath not these so subtile distinctions: yea (as I have said) we see many times in persons of most base degree, most hie gifts of nature.

Therefore seeing this noblenes is gotten neither with wit, force, nor art, but is rather a praise of our ancestors than our owne, me thinke it a strange opinion that the parents of our Courtier being unnoble, his good qualities should be defaced, and those other good conditions which you have named shuld not be sufficient to bring him to the top of all perfection: that is to say, wit, beautie of phisnomy, disposition of person, and the grace which at the first sight shall make him most acceptable unto al men.

Then answered Counte Lewis, I denie not, but in men of base degree may raign the very same vertues that are in Gentlemen. But to avoide rehearsall of that wee have alreadie said, with many other reasons that might be alleaged in commendation of noblenes, the which is evermore honored of all men, because it standeth with reason, that good should spring of good: for so much as our intent is to fashion a Courtier without any maner default or lack in him, and heaped with all praise, me thinke it a necessary matter to make him a Gentleman, as well for many other respects, as also for the common opinion, which by and by doeth leane to noblenes.

For where there are two in a noble mans house, which at the first have given no proofe of themselves with workes good or bad, as soone as it is knowne that the one is a Gentleman borne, and the other not, the unnoble shall be much lesse esteemed with everie man, than the Gentleman, and he must with much travell and long time imprint in mennes heades a good opinion of himselfe, which the other shall get in a moment, and onely for that he is a Gentleman: and how waightie these imprintings are, everie man may easilie judge.

For to speak of our selves, we have seene men come to

this house, which for al they were fooles and dulwitted, yet had they a report through al Italy of great Courtiers, and though at length they were discovered and knowne, yet many daies did they beguile us, and maintained in our mindes that opinion of themselves, which at the first they found there imprinted, although they wrought according to their small skill.

Wee have seene other at the first in verie small estimation, and afterward in the ende, have acquitted themselves marvellous well. And of these errors there are divers causes, and among other the obstinateness of Princes, which to prove maistries, oftentimes bend themselves to favour him, that to their seeming, deserveth no favor at all.

And many times in deede they are deceived: but because they have alwaies many that counterfaite them, a verie great report dependeth upon their favor, the which most commonly the Judges follow. And if they finde any thing that seemeth contrary to the common opinion, they are in doubt for deceiving them selves, and alwaies looke for some matter secretly, because it seemeth, that these generall opinions ought to bee founded upon a troth, and arise of reasonable causes.

And forasmuch as our mindes are verie apte to love and to hate: as in the sights of combates and games, and in all other kinde of contention, where the lookers on are affectionate without manifest cause unto one of the two parties, with a greedy desire to have him get the victorie, and the other the losse.

Also as touching the opinion of mens qualities, the good or ill report at the first brunt moveth our minde to one of these two passions.

Therefore it commeth to passe, that for the most part we judge with love, or els with hatred.

You see then of what importance this first imprinting is, and how he ought to endevour him selfe to get it good at first, if hee entend to be set by, and to purchase him the name of a good Courtier.

But to come to some particularitie, I judge the principall and true profession of a Courtier ought to bee in feates of armes, the which above all I will have him to practise lively, and to bee knowne among other of his hardines, for his atchieving of enterprises, and for his fidelitie towarde him whom he serveth. And hee shall purchase himselfe a name with these good conditions, in doing the deedes in every time and place, for it is not for him to fainte at any time in this behalfe without a wondrous reproch.

And even as in women honestie once stained doth never returne againe to the former estate: so the fame of a gentleman that carrieth weapon, if it once take a foyle in anye litle point through dastardlinesse or any other reproch, doth evermore continue shamefull in the world and full of ignorance.

Therefore the more excellent our Courtier shall be in this arte, the more shall he be worthie praise: albeit I judge not necessarie in him so perfect a knowledge of things and other qualities that is requisite in a Captaine. But because this is overlarge a scope of matters, we wil holde our selves contented, as wee have saide, with the uprightnesse of a well meaning mind, and with an invincible courage, and that he alwaies shew himself such a one.

For many times men of courage are sooner knowne in small matters than in great. Often times in dangers that stand them upon, and where many eyes be, ye shal see some that for all their hart is dead in their bodie, yet pricked with shame or with the company, goe forwarde, as it were, blindfield and doe their duetie. And God knoweth both in matters that litle touch them, and also where they suppose that without missing they may convey them selves from danger, how they are willing inough to sleepe in a whole skinne.

But such as thinke them selves neither marked, seene, nor knowne, and yet declare a stoute courage, and suffer not the least thing in the world to passe that may burthen them, they have that courage of spirite which we seeke to have in our Courtier. Yet will wee not have him for all that so lustie to make braverie in wordes, and to bragge that hee hath wedded his harnes for a wife, and to threaten with such grimme lookes, as wee have seene Berto [5] doe often times.

For unto such may well be said, that a worthie gentle woman in a noble assemblie spake pleasantly unto one, that shall bee namelesse for this time, whom she to shew him a good countenance, desired to daunce with her, and hee refusing it, and to heare musicke, and many other entertainements offered him, alwaies affirming such triffes not to be his profession, at last the gentlewoman demaunding him, what is then your profession? he answered with a frowning looke, to fight.

Then saide the Gentlewoman: seeing you are not now at the warre nor in place to fight, I would think it best for you to bee well besmered and set up in an armory with other implements of warre till time were that you should be occupied, least you waxe more rustier than you are. Thus with much laughing of the standers by, she left him with a mocke in his foolish presumption.

He therefore that we seeke for, where the enimies are, shall shew him selfe most fierce, bitter, and evermore with the first. In everie place beside, lowly, sober, and circumspect, fleeing above all things, bragging and unshamefull praysing himselfe: for therewith a man alwaies purchaseth himselfe the hatred of the hearers.

And I, answered the L. Gasper, have known few excellent in any thing whatsoever it be, but they praise them selves. And me thinke it may wel be borne in them: for he y[t] is of skill, when he seeth that hee is not knowne for his workes of the ignorant, hath a disdaine, that his cunning should be buried, and needes must be open one way, least he should bee defrauded of the estimation that belongeth to it, which is the true rewarde of vertuous travailes.

Therefore among auncient writers, he that much excelleth doth seldome forbeare praysing himselfe.

They in deed are not to be borne withall, that having no skill in them will praise themselves: but we wil not take our Courtier to be such a one.

Then the Count, if you have well understood (quoth he) I blamed the praysing of a mans selfe impudently, and without respect. And surely (as you say) a man ought not to conceive an ill opinion of a skilfull man that praiseth himselfe discretely, but rather take it for a more certaine witnes, than if it came out of an other mans mouth.

I agree well that hee, which in praysing him selfe falleth not into error, nor purchaseth himselfe lothsomnes or hatred of the hearers, is most discreete: and beside the prayses which he giveth himselfe, deserveth the same of other men also, because it is a verie hard matter.

Then the L. Gasper, this (quoth he) must you teach us.

The Counte answered: among the auncient writers there hath not also wanted that hath taught it. But in mine opinion, all doth consist in speaking such thinges after a sorte, that it may appeare that they are not rehearsed to that end: but that they come so to purpose, that he can not refraine telling them, and alwaies seeming to flee his owne prayse, tell the truth. But not as those lustie lads doe, that open their mouth and thrust out wordes at a venture they care not how. As within these few dayes one of our company, being pusshed through the thigh with a pike at Pysa, thought that it was the byting of a flie. And an other saide that hee occupied no looking glasse in his chamber, because in his rage hee was so terrible to behold, that in looking upon his owne countenance he should put himselfe into much feare.

At this every one laughed. But the L. Cesar Gonzaga saide unto them: at what laugh you?

Know yee not that the great Alexander, hearing a certaine philosophers opinion to be that there were infinite worlds, fel in weeping: And when he was asked the

276

question why hee wept, hee answered: Because I have not yet one in hand, as though his mind was to have them all.

Doe you not thinke that this was a greater braverie, than to speake of a flie byting?

So was Alexander a greater person than hee that so saide, aunswered the Count.

But excellent men in verie deed are to be held excused, when they take much upon them, because hee that undertaketh great enterprises, must have a boldnesse to doe it, and a confidence of himselfe, and not a bashfull or cowardly minde, but yet sober in wordes: shewing as though he tooke lesse uppon him than he doth in deede, so that his taking uppon him doe not extend unto rashnes.

Here the Count respecting a while, M. Bernard Bibiena said merely: I remember you saide before, that this our Courtier ought of nature to have a faire comelinesse of phisnomy and person, with the grace that ought to make him so amiable.

As for the grace and beautie of phisnomy, I thinke not the contrarie but they are in me, and therefore doe so many women burne for the love of me, as you know. But for the comelines of person, I stand somewhat in doubt, and especially by reason of my legges here, for me thinke in deede they are not so well made as I could wish they were: the body and the rest is metely well.

Therfore declare somewhat more particularly this comelinesse of person, what it should be, that I may be out of this doubt, and set my hart at rest.

When they had a while laughed at this, the Count saide: Certes, the grace of the Phisonomy may well bee saide to bee in you without any lye. And no other example doe I alledge but this, to declare what maner thing it should be: for undoubtedly wee see your countenance is most acceptable and pleasant to behold unto every man, although the proportion and draughts of it be not verie delicate, but it is manly and hath a good grace withall.

And this qualitie have many and sundry shapes of visages.

And such a countenance as this is, will I have our Courtier to have, and not so soft and womanish as many procure to have, that doe not onely courle the haire, and picke the browes, but also pampre them selves in everie point like the most wanton and dishonest women in the world: and a man would thinke them in going, in standing, and in all their gestures so tender and faint, that their members were readie to flee one from an other, and their wordes they pronounce so drawningly, that a man woulde weene they were at that instant yeelding up the ghost: and the higher in degree that men are they talke withall, the more they use such fashions.

These men, seeing nature (as they seeme to have a desire to appeare and to be) hath not made them women, ought not to bee esteemed in place of good women, but like common Harlots to bee banished, not onely out of princes courtes, but also out of the company of gentlemen.

To come therefore to the qualitie of the person, I say he is well, if he bee neither of the least, nor of the greatest size. For both the one and the other hath with it a certaine spitefull woonder, and such men are marvelled at, almost as much as men marvel to behold monstrous thinges. Yet if there must needes be a default in one of the two extremities, it shall be lesse hurtfull to bee somewhat of the least, than to exceed the common stature of height.

For men so shut up of bodie, beside that many times they are of a dull wit, they are also unapt for all exercise of nimblenesse, which I much desire to have in the Courtier.

And therefore wil I have him to bee of a good shape, and well proportioned in his lims, and to shew strength, lightnesse and quicknesse, and to have understanding in all exercises of the bodie that belong to a man of warre.

And herein I thinke the chiefe point is to handle wel all kinde of weapon, both for footeman and horseman, and to know the vantages in it. And specially to bee skilfull on those weapons that are used ordinarily among Gentlemen.

For beside the use that he shall have of them in warre, where peradventure needeth no great cunning, there happen oftentimes variances betweene one gentleman and an other, whereupon ensueth a combat. And many times it shall stand him in steade to use the weapon that he hath at that instant by his side, therefore it is a very sure thing to be skilfull.

And I am none of them which say, that he forgetteth his cunning when hee commeth to the point: for to abide by, who so looseth his cunning at that time, sheweth that hee hath first lost his heart and his spirites for feare.

I thinke also it will serve his turne greatly, to know the feat of wrastling, because it goeth much together with all weapon on foote.

Againe it is behovefull both for himselfe and for his friendes, that he have a foresight in the quarrels and controversies that may happen, and let him beware of the vantages, declaring alwaies in everie point both courage and wisedom.

Neither let him runne rashly to these combats, but when he must needes to save his estimation withall: for beside the great daunger that is in the doubtful lot, he that goeth headlong to these thinges, and without urgent cause, deserveth great blame, although his chaunce bee good.

But when a man perceiveth that he is entred so far that hee can not draw backe without burthen, hee must both in such thinges as hee hath to doe before the combate, and also in the combate, be utterly resolved with him selfe, and alwaies shew a readinesse and a stomacke. And not as some doe, passe the matter in arguing and points.

And having the choise of weapon, take such as have neither point nor edge. And arme themselves as though they should goe against the shotte of a Cannon.

And weening it sufficient not to be vanquished, stand alwaies at their defence and give ground, in so much that they declare an extreame faint hart, and are a mocking stocke to the verie children.

As those two of Ancona: that a while agoe fought a combate beside Perugia, and made them to laugh that looked on.

And what were they, quoth the L. Gasper Pallavicin? The L. Cesar answered: Cousins Germains of two sisters. Then saide the Count: at the combat a man would have thought them naturall bretheren: then hee went forwarde.

Also men occupy their weapon oftentimes in time of peace about sundrie exercises, and gentlemen are seene in open shewes in the presence of people, women and princes.

Therefore will I have our Courtier a perfect horseman for everie saddle. And beside the skill in horses, and in whatsoever belongeth to a horseman, let him set all his delight and diligence to wade in everie thing a little farther than other men, so that he may be knowne among all men for one that is excellent.

As it is redde of Alcibiades, that hee excelled all other nations wheresoever hee came. And everie man in the thing hee had most skill in. So shall this our Courtier passe other men, and everie man in his owne profession.

And because it is yᵉ peculiar praise of us Italians to ride well, to manage with reason, especially rough horses, to runne at the Ring, and at Tilt, he shall be in this esteemed among the best Italians.

At Tournament in keeping a passage, in fighting at Barriers, he shall be good amongst the best Frenchmen.

At *Joce di canne*,[6] running at Bull, casting of Speares and Dartes, hee shall bee among the Spaniards excellent. But principally let him accompanie all his motion with a certaine good judgement and grace, if hee will deserve that generall favor which is so much set by.

There be also many other exercises, the which though they depend not throughly upon Armes, yet have they a great agreement with them, and have in them much manly activitie. And of them me thinke, hunting is one of the chiefest.

For it hath a certaine likenesse with warre, and is truely a pastime for great men, and fit for one living in Court. And it is found that it hath also beene much used among them of olde time.

It is meete for him also to have the arte of swimming, to leape, to runne, to cast the stone: for beside the profit that he may receave of this in the warres, it happeneth to him many times to make proofe of him selfe in such thinges, whereby hee getteth him a reputation, especially among the multitude, unto whom a man must sometim apply him selfe.

Also it is a noble exercise, and meete for one living in Court to play at Tenise, where the disposition of the bodie, the quicknes and nimblenesse of everie member is much perceived, and almost whatsoever a man can see in all other exercises.

And I reckon vauting [7] of no lesse praise, which for all it is painefull and hard, maketh a man more light and quicker than any of the rest.

And beside the profit, if that lightnes bee accompanied with a good grace, it maketh (in my judgement) a better shew than any of the rest.

If our Courtier then bee taught these exercises more than indifferently well, I believe he may set aside tumbling, climing upon a cord, and such other matters that tast somewhat of Jugglers craft, and doe litle beseeme a gentleman.

But because wee can not alwaies endure among these so painefull doings, beside that the continuance goeth nigh to give a man his fill, and taketh away the admiration that men have of thinges seldom seene, wee must continually alter our life with practising sundrie matters.

Therefore will I have our Courtier to descend many times to more easie and pleasant exercises. And to avoide envie, and to keepe company pleasantly with every man, let him doe whatsoever other men doe: so hee decline not at any time from commendable deedes, but governeth him selfe with that good judgement that will not suffer him to enter into any folly: but let him laugh, dally, jest, and daunce, yet in such wise that he may alwaies declare him selfe to be wittie and discreete, and every thing that hee doth or speaketh, let him doe it with a grace.

Truely, saide then the Lord Cesar Gonzaga, the course of this communication shoulde not bee stopped: but if I should holde my peace, I should not satisfie the libertie which I have to speake, nor the desire that I have to understand one thing. And let me be pardoned, if where I ought to speake against, I demaund a question: because I suppose I may lawfully doe it after the example of M. Bernard, who for the too great desire he had to bee counted a well favored man, hath offended against the lawes of our pastime, in demaunding without speaking against.

Behold I beseech ye, said then the Dutchesse, how one error bringeth in a great sort. Therefore who so offendeth and giveth evil example, as M. Bernard hath done, deserveth to bee punished, not onely for his owne offence, but for other mens also.

Then answered the Lord Cesar: Therefore must I (Madame) escape punishment, for that M. Bernard ought to be punished for his owne offence and mine both.

Nay (quoth the Dutchesse) you ought both, to have double punishment. He for his offence, and for being an occasion for you to commit the like: and you for your offence, and for taking him for a president that did offend.

I have not hetherto offended Madam, answered the Lord Cesar. Therefore because I will leave the whole punishment for M. Bernard I will keepe silence.

And now hee helde his peace, when the Ladie Emilia answered: say what pleaseth you, for (by the Dutchesse leave) I pardon this fault, and whosoever shall offend in so small a trespasse.

Upon that the Dutchesse saide: I am well pleased. But take ye heede you deceive not your selfe thinking peradventure to be better reported of for mercy than for justice. For in pardoning the offender too much, ye doe wrong to him that doth not offend.

Yet will not I have my rigour at this time in accusing your mercy to bee the cause that we shall loose the hearing of this the Lord Cesars demaund. So he, after the Dutchesse and the Ladie Emilia had made a signe to him, saide by and by.

If I doe well beare in minde, me thinke (Count Lewis) you have this night often times repeated, that the Courtier ought to accompany all his doings, gestures, demeaners: finally all his motions with a grace.

And this, me thinke, ye put for a sauce to everie thing, without the which all his other properties and good conditions were litle worth.

And I believe verily that every man would soone bee perswaded therein, for by the vertue of the word a man may say, that who so hath grace, is gracious.

But because you have saide sundry times that it is the gift of nature and of the heavens, and againe, where it is not so perfect, that it may with studie and diligence be made much more: they that be borne so happie and so welthie with such a treasure (as some that wee see) me thinke therein they have litle neede of any other teacher, because the bountifull favor of heaven doth (as it were) in spite of them, guide them higher than they covet, and maketh them not onely acceptable but marvellous unto all the world.

Therefore I doe not reason of this, because the obtaining of it of our selves lyeth not in our power.

But such as by nature have onely so much, that they be apt to become gracious in bestowing labour, exercise, and diligence, I would faine know with what arte, with what learning, and by what meane they shall compasse this grace, as well in the exercises of the bodie (wherein ye thinke it so necessarie a matter) as in al other things that they doe or speake.

Therefore as you have, in praysing this qualitie to us engendred (I believe) in al a fervent thyrst to come by it, by the charge ye receyved of the Ladie Emilia, so with teaching it us, ye are bound to quench it.

Bound I am not (quoth the Count) to teach you to have good grace, nor any thing els, saving onely to shew you what a perfect Courtier ought to be.

Neither wil I take upon me to teach you this perfection, since a while agoe, I said, that the Courtier ought to have the feate of wrastling and vauting, and such other thinges, the which how should I bee able to teach them, not having learned them my selfe, I am sure ye know it all?

It sufficeth, that as a good souldier can speake his mind to an Armourer, of what fashion, of what temper and goodnes hee will have his harnesse, and for all that can not teach him to make it, nor to hammer or temper it: So perhaps I am able to tell you what a perfect courtier ought to be, but not to teach you how he should doe to be one.

Notwithstanding to fulfill your request in what I am able, although it bee (in maner) in a proverbe, that Grace is not to be learned, I say unto you, who so mindeth to be gracious, or to have a good grace in the exercises of the bodie, (presupposing first that he be not of nature unapt) ought to beginne betimes, and to learne his principles of cunning men.

The which thing how necessarie a matter Philip king of Macedonie thought it, a man may gather in that his will was, that Aristotle so famous a Philosopher, and perhaps the greatest that ever hath beene in the world, shoulde bee the man that should instruct Alexander his sonne, in the first principles of letters.

And of men whom wee know now adaies, mark how well and with what a good grace Sir Galliazzo Sanseverino maister of the horse to the French king, doth all exercises of the bodie, and that because, beside the naturall disposition of person that is in him, he hath applyed all his studie to learne of cunning men, and to have continually excellent men about him, and of everie one to choose the best of that they have skill in.

For as in wrastling, in vauting, and in learning to handle sundrie kind of weapons, he hath taken for his guide our maister Peter Mount, who (as you know) is the true and onely maister of all artificiall force and sleight: So in ryding, in justing, and in everie other feate, he hath alwaies had before his eyes, the most perfectest that hath beene knowne to be in those professions.

He therefore that will bee a good scholler, beside the practising of good thinges must evermore set all his diligence to be like his maister, and (if it were possible) chaung him selfe into him.

And when hee hath had some entrie, it profiteth him much to behold sundrie men of that profession: and governing himselfe with that good judgement that must alwaies be his guide goe about to picke out, sometime of one, and sometime of an other, sundrie matters.

And even as the Bee in greene medowes fleeth alwaies about the grasse, choosing out flowers: So shall our Courtier steale his grace from them that to his seeming have it, and from eche one, that parcell that shall be most worthie prayse. And not to do as a friend of ours, whom you all know, that thought he resembled much Ferdinande the younger of Aragon, and regarded not to resemble him in any other point, but in the often lifting up of his heade, wrything therewithall a part of his mouth, the which custome the king had gotten by infirmitie.

And many such there are that thinke that they doe much, so they resemble a great man in somewhat, and take many times the thing in him that worst becommeth him.

But I, imagining with my selfe often times how this grace commeth, leaving apart such as have it from above, finde one rule that is most generall, which in this part (me thinke) taketh place in all things belonging to a man in word or deede, above all other. And that is to eschue as much as a man may, and as a sharpe and daungerous rocke, too much curiousnesse, and (to speake a new word) to use in everye thing a certaine disgracing to cover arte withall, and seeme whatsoever he doth and saith, to doe it without paine, and (as it were) not minding it.

And of this doe I believe grace is much derived, for in rare matters and well brought to passe, every man knoweth the hardnesse of them, so that a readinesse therein maketh great wonder.

And contrariwise to use force, and (as they say) to hale by the haire, giveth a great disgrace, and maketh everie thing how great so ever it bee, to be litle esteemed.

Therefore that may bee saide to be a verie arte, that appeareth not to be arte, neither ought a man to put more diligence in any thing than in covering it: for in case it be open, it looseth credite cleane and maketh a man litle set by.

And I remember that I have redde in my dayes, that there were some most excellent Orators, which among other their cares, enforced themselves to make everie man believe, that they had no sight in letters, and dissembling their cunning, made semblant their Orations to be made verie simply, and rather as nature and truth ledde them, than studie and arte, the which if it had beene openly knowne, would have put a doubt in the peoples minde, for feare least hee beguiled them.

You may see then, how to shew arte, and such bent studie taketh away the grace of every thing.

Which of you is it that laugheth not when our maister Peterpaul daunceth after his owne fashion, with such fine skippes, and on tipto, without moving his heade, as though hee were all of wood, so heedfully, that truly a man woulde weene hee counted his paces. What eye is so blind, that perceiveth not in this the disgrace of curiositie, and in many men and women here present, the grace of that not regarded agility and slight conveyance (for in the motions of

286

the bodie many so terme it) with a kind of speaking or smyling, or gesture, betokening not to passe upon it, and to minde any other thing more than that, to make him beleeve that looketh on, that he can not doe amisse.

Here maister Bernard Bibiena not forbearing any longer, said: you may see yet that our maister Robert hath found one to praise his maner of dauncing, though the rest of you set litle by it. For if this excellencie doth consist in disgracing and in shewing not to passe upon, and rather to minde any other thing than that a man is in hand withall, maister Robert hath no peere in the world. For that men should well perceive that hee litle mindeth it, many times his garments fal from his back, and his slippers from his feete, and daunceth on still without taking up againe any of both.

Then answered the Count: Seeing you will needs have me speake, I will say somewhat also of our vices.

Doe you not marke, this that you call in maister Robert disgracing, is a verie curiositie? for it is well knowne that hee enforceth himselfe with all diligence possible to make a shew not to minde it, and that is to minde it too much.

And because hee passeth certaine limits of a meane, that disgracing of his is curious, and not comely, and is a thing that commeth cleane contrary to passe from the drift, (that is to wit) to cover arte.

Therefore I judge it no lesse vice of curiositie to be in dispraysing (which in it selfe is praise worthie) in letting a mans clothes fall off his backe, than in Precisenesse (which likewise of it selfe is praise worthie) to carrie a mans heade very stedfast for feare of ruffling his haire, or to keepe in the bottom of his cappe a looking glasse, and a combe in his sleeve, and to have alwaies at his heeles up and downe the streetes a Page with a Spunge and a Brush.

For this maner of Precisenesse and curiousnesse is too much in extremitie, which is alwaies a vice, and contrarie to that pure and amiable simplicitie, which is so acceptable to mens mindes.

Marke what an ill grace a man at Armes hath, when he enforceth him selfe to goe so bolt upright, setled in saddle (as we use to say after the Venetian phrase [8]) in comparison of an other that appeareth not to minde it, and sitteth on horsebacke so nimbly and close as though hee were on foote.

How much more doe we take pleasure in a Gentleman that is a man at armes, and how much more worthy praise is he if he bee modest, of few wordes, and no bragger, than an other that alwaies craketh of himselfe, and blaspheming with a braverie seemeth to threaten the world.

And this is nothing els, but a curiositie to seem to be a roister.

The like happeneth in all exercises, yea in everie thing in the world that a man can doe or speake.

Then said the L. Julian: this in like maner is verified in musicke: where it is a verie great vice to make two perfect cocordes, the one after the other, so that the verie sense of our hearing abhorreth it, and oftentimes delyteth in a second or in a seventh, which in it selfe is an unpleasant discorde, and not tollerable: and this proceedeth because the countenance in the perfect tunes engendreth irkesomnesse, and betokeneth a too curious harmony, the which in mingling therewithall the unperfect is avoided, with making (as it were) a comparison, whereby our eares stand to listen and greedely attend and tast the perfect, and are otherwhile delited with the disagreement of the second or seventh, as it were with a thing litle regarded.

Behold ye then, answered the Count, that curiousnes hurteth in this, as well as in other things.

They say that also, it hath been a proverbe among some most excellent painters of olde time, that Too much diligence is hurtfull, and that Appeles found fault with Protogenes, because he could not keepe his handes from the table.

Then saide the Lord Cesar. The verie same fault (me thinke) is in our Frier Seraphin, that hee can not keepe his handes from the table, especially as long as there is any meate stirring.

The Count laughed, and went forwarde: Apelles meaning was, that Protogenes knew not when it was well, which was nothing els but to reprehend his curiousnes in his workes.

This vertue therefore contrarie to curiositie, which we for this time terme Recklesnesse, beside that it is the true fountaine from the which all grace springeth, it bringeth with it also an other ornament, which accompanying any deede that a man doth, how litle so ever it be, doth not onely by and by open the knowledge of him that doth it, but also many times maketh it to bee esteemed much more in effect than it is, because it imprinteth in the mindes of the lookers on, an opinion, that who so can so sleightly doe well, hath a great deale more knowledge than in deede he hath: and if he will apply his studie and diligence to that he doth, he might do it much better.

And to repeate even the verie examples, marke a man that taketh weapon in hand: If going about to caste a darte, or holding in his hand a sword or any other waster, he setleth him selfe lightsomly (not thinking upon it) in a ready aptnesse, with such activitie, that a man would weene his bodie and all his members were naturally setled in that disposition, and without any paine, though he doth nothing else, yet doth he declare him selfe unto every man to be most perfect in that exercise.

Like wise in dauncing, one measure, one motion of a bodie that hath a good grace, not being forced, doth by and by declare the knowledge of him that daunceth.

A musition, if in singing he rolle out but a plain note, ending in a double relise with a swete tune, so easily that a man would judge hee did it at a venture, in that point alone he doth men to understand, that his knowledge is farre greater than it is in deede.

Oftentimes also in painting, one line not studied upon, one draught with the Pensell sleightly drawne, so it appeareth the hand without the guiding of any studie or art, tendeth to his marke, according to the Painters purpose, doth evidently discover the excellencie of the workeman, about the opinion whereof every man afterwarde contendeth, according to his judgement.

The like happeneth also, in a maner, about everie other thing. Therefore shall our Courtier be esteemed excellent, and in everie thing he shall have a good grace, and especially in speaking, if he avoide curiositie: into which error many men run, and sometime more than other, certaine of our Lumbardes, which after a yeares travaile abroad, come home and beginne by and by to speake the Romane tongue, sometime ye Spanish tongue or the French, and God woteth how.

And all this proceedeth of an over great desire to shew much knowledge: and in this wise a man applyeth his studie and diligence to get a most odious vice.

And truely it were no small travaile for me, if I should use in this communication of ours, those auncient Tuskane wordes, that are not in use among the Tuskanes now adaies: and beside that, I believe every man would laugh at me.

Then spake Sir Fredericke. In deede reasoning together as we now doe, peradventure it were not well done to use those auncient Tuskane wordes: for (as you say) they woulde bee a loathsomnesse both to the speaker and to the hearer, and of many they shoulde not be understood without much a doe.

But he that should write, I would thinke he committed an errour in not using them: because they gave a great grace and authoritie unto wrytings, and of them is compact a tongue more grave, and more full of majestie, than of the new.

I know not, answered the Count, what grace and authoritie those wordes can give unto wrytings that ought to be eschued, not only in the manner of speach that wee now use (which you your selfe confesse) but also in any other maner that can be imagined. For if any man, of how good

a judgement so ever hee were, had to make an Oration of
grave matters in the verie Councell Chamber of Florence,
which is the heade of Tuskane: or els to comune privately
with a person of estimation in that Citie about waightie
affaires: or also with the familiarest friend hee hath about
pleasant matters: or with women or Gentlemen about matters of love, either in jeasting or dallying, banketing, gaming, or where ever else: or in any time or place, or purpose,
I am assured he would flee the using of those auncient
Tuskane words, and in using them, beside that he would be
a laughing stocke, hee would bring no small loathsomnesse
to him that heard them.

Therefore me thinke it a straunge matter to use those
words for good in wryting, that are to bee eschewed for
naughtie in every manner of speach: and to have that
which is never proper in speach, to bee the properest way
a man can use in wryting.

Forsomuch as (in mine opinion) wryting is nothing els,
but a maner of speach, that remaineth still after a man
hath spoken, or (as it were) an image, or rather the life
of the wordes. And therefore in speache, which as soone
as the sound is pronounced, vanisheth away, peradventure
some things are more to be borne withall, than in writing.
Because wryting keepeth the wordes in store, and referreth
them to the judgement of the Reader, and giveth time to
examine them deepely.

And therefore reason willeth, that greater diligence
should bee had therein, to make it more trimme and better
corrected: yet not so, that the written wordes should be
unlike the spoken, but in wryting to choose out the fairest
and proprest of signification that be used in speaking.

And if that should be lawfull in writing which is not
lawfull in speaking, there should arise an inconvenience of
it (in my judgement) verie greate: namely, that a man
might use a greater libertie in the thing, where he ought
to use most diligence, and the labour he bestoweth in
writing, in steade of furtherance should hinder him.

Therefore it is certaine, whatsoever is allowed in wryting, is also allowed in speaking: and that speach is most beautifull, that is like unto beautifull wrytings.

And I judge it much more behovefull to be understood in wryting than in speaking, because they that write are not alwaies present with them that reade as they that speake with them that speak.

Therefore would I commend him, that beside the eschewing of many auncient Tuskane words, would apply him selfe also to use both in wryting and speaking, such as now adaies are in use in Tuskane and in other partes of Italy, and that have some grace in pronunciation.

And (in my minde) who so followeth any other trade, is not assured not to runne into that curiositie so much blamed, which we have spoken of before.

Then spake Sir Fredericke: I can not deny you, Count Lewis, that wryting is not a maner of speaking. But this I say, if the words that are spoken have any darkenesse in them, that communication pierceth not the minde of him that heareth: and passing without being understood, waxeth vaine and to no purpose: the which doth not happen in writing.

For if the words that the writer useth bring with them a litle (I will not say difficultie) but covered subtiltie, and not so open, as such as be ordinarily spoken, they give a certaine authoritie to writing, and make the Reader more heedefull to pause at it, and to ponder it better, and he taketh a delyte in the wittinesse and learning of him that wryteth, and with a good judgement, after some paines taking, he tasteth the pleasure that consisteth in hard thinges.

And if the ignorance of him that readeth bee such, that he can not compasse that difficultie, there is no blame in the writer, neither ought a man for all that to thinke that tongue not to bee faire.

Therefore in wryting, I holde opinion it is necessarie for a man to use the Tuskan wordes, and onely such as have beene used among the auntient Tuskanes: for it is a great testimoniall, and approved by time, that they be good and of a pithie signification, in that they be applyed to. And beside this, they have that grace and majestie that antiquitie giveth not onely to wordes, but unto buildinges, images, paintings, and to everie thing that is of force to preserve it. And many times with this onely brightnesse and dignitie, they make the forme of sentences verye faire, and through the vertue and elegancie thereof, every matter how base so ever it be, may be so decked out, that it may deserve very great commendation.

But this your custome, that you make so much a doe off, appeareth unto me very daungerous, and many times it may be naught. And if any vice of speech be taken up of many ignorant persons, me thinke for all that it ought not to be received for a rule, nor followed of other.

Besides this, customes be many and diverse, and yee have not a notable Citie in Italie, that hath not a diverse maner of speach from al the rest.

Therefore if ye take not the paines to declare which is the best, a man may as well give him selfe to the Bergamaske tongue, as to the Florentine, and to follow your advise, it were no errour at all.

Me seemeth then, who so will be out of doubt and wel assured, it is requisite for him to determine with him selfe to follow one, that by all mens accorde is judged good, and to take him for a guide alwaies, and for a shield, against such as will goe about to find fault, and that I thinke ought to be none other, (I meane in the vulgar tongue) but Petrarca and Boccacio: and who so swarveth from these two, goeth at all adventure, as he that walketh in the darke without light, and therefore many times strayeth from the right way.

But we are so hardy now adayes, that wee disdaine to doe as other good men of ancient time have done: that is to say, to take diligent heede to following, without the which, I judge no man can write well. And mee thinke

Virgill declareth a great tryall of this, who for all that with his so divine a witte and judgement, hee tooke all hope from his posterite for any to follow him at any time, yet would he follow Homer.

Then the Lorde Gasper Pallavicin, This disputation (quoth he) of wryting in verie deede is worth the hearing: yet were it more to our purpose, if you woulde teach in what sorte the Courtier ought to speake, for me thinke hee hath more neede of that, and he serveth his turne oftner with speaking than with wryting.

The Lord Julian answered: there is no doubt, but so excellent and perfect a Courtier hath neede to understand both the one and the other: and without these two qualities, peradventure all the rest shoulde not bee much worthie praise.

Therefore if the Count will fulfill his charge, hee shall teach the Courtier not onely to speake, but also to write well.

Then said the Count: I will not (my Lord) undertake this enterprise, for it should bee a great folly for me to teach an other that I understand not my self. And though I were skilfull in it, yet can I not see howe I should thinke to do the thing in so few wordes, which great Clarkes have scarse done with such great studie and diligence, unto whose wrytinges I would remit our Courtier, if it were so, that I were bound to teach him to write and to speake.

The Lord Cesar then said: the Lorde Magnifico meaneth the speaking and wryting of the vulgar tongue, and not Latin, therfore those wrytings of great Clarkes are not for our purpose.

But you must shew us in this behalfe as much as you know, and for the rest yee shall be held excused.

I have alreadie saide, answered the Count. But in reason-ing upon the Tuskan tongue, perhaps it were rather the Ladie Julians parte, than any mans els to give judgement in it.

The L. Magnifico saide: I can not, nor of reason ought to

speake against him, that saith the Tuskane tongue is fairer then all the rest.

Truth it is, there are many wordes in Petrarca, and Boccaccio, worne out of use now adaies: and such would I never use, neither in speaking, nor in wryting, and peradventure they themselves, if they were now alive, woulde use them no more.

Then spake Sir Fredericke: no doubt but they would use them still. And you Lordes of Tuskane ought to renew your tongue, and not to suffer it decay, as you doe: for a man may say now, that there is lesse knowledge in Florence, than in many other places of Italie.

Then answered maister Bernard: those words that are no more in use in Florence, doe still continue among the men of the Countrie, and are refused of the Gentlemen for wordes corrupt and decayed by antiquitie.

Then the Dutches, let us not swarve (quoth shee) from our first purpose, but let us marke Count Lewis, teach the Courtier to speake and to write well, bee it Tuskane, or what ever els.

The Count answered: I have alreadie spoken (Madame) what I know. And I suppose the verie same rules that teach the one, may also serve to teach the other. But since you commaund me: I will make answere unto Sir Fredericke what commeth in my head, for I am of a contrarie opinion to him.

And peradventure I shal be driven to answere somewhat more darkely than will be allowed, but it shall be as much as I am able to say.

And first I say, that (to my judgement) this our tongue which we name the vulgar tongue, is tender and new, for all it hath beene now used a long while. For in that Italie hath beene, not onely vexed and spoiled, but also inhabited a long time with barbarous people, by the great resorte of those nations the Latin tongue was corrupted and destroyed, and of that corruption have sprong other tongues. The which like the Rivers that departe from the

toppe of the Appennine, and runne abroad towarde the
two seas: so are they also divided, and some dyed with the
Latin speach have spredde abroad sundrie waies, some
into one parte, and some into an other, and one dyed with
barbarousnesse hath remained in Italy.

This then hath a long time beene among us out of order,
and diverse, because there was none that would bestow
diligence about it, nor write in it, ne yet seeke to give it
brightnesse, or any grace: yet hath it beene afterwarde
brought into better frame in Tuskane, than in the other
partes of Italie.

And by that it appeareth, that the flower of it hath remained there ever since those first times, because that
Nation hath kept proper and sweete accents in the pronunciation, and an order of Grammer, where it was meete,
more than the other. And hath had three noble writers,[9]
which wittily both in wordes and tearmes, that custome
did allow in their time, have expressed their conceites, and
that hath happened (in my minde) with a better grace to
Petrarca, in matters of love, than to any of the other.

Where there arose afterwarde from time to time, not
onely in Tuskane, but in all Italy, among gentlemen brought
up in Court, in armes and in letters, some studie, to speake
and to write more finely than they did in that first rude
age, when the turmoile of the miseries that rose through
barbarous nations, was not as yet quieted, many words have
beene left out, as well in Florence it selfe, and in all Tuskane, as in the residue of Italie, and other brought in, in
their steade, and made in this behalfe the alteration that
happeneth in all worldlye thinges: the which also hath
evermore chaunced in other tongues.

For in cause these auncient Latin writinges had lasted
hetherto, we shoulde see that Evander and Turnus, and the
other Latins in those dayes, spake otherwise than did afterwarde the last kings of the Romans, and the first Con-
sules.

You may see the verses sung by the Salii were scantly

understood of their posteritie: but because it was so ordeined by the first inventers of it, they were not altered
for reverence of religion.

So from time to time Orators and Poets forsooke many
wordes that had beene used among their predecessors: for
Antonius, Crassus, Hortensius, and Cicero, eschued many
that Cato had used, and Virgill many of Ennius and so
did the rest. For albeit they had antiquitie in great reverence, yet did they not esteeme them so much, that they
would be so bound to them, as you will have us now. Yea,
where they thought good, they spake against them, as
Horace, that saith his predecessors did foolishlye praise
Plautus, which would that we should have the authoritie
to bring up new wordes. And Cicero in many places reprehendeth manie of his predecessors.

And to blame S. Gibda, he saith that his Orations smelled
of antiquitie. And affirmeth that Ennius also in some pointes
set litle by his predecessors, so that if wee will follow
them of old time, we shall not follow them.

And Virgill that you say followed Homer, followed him
not in the tongue.

Therefore would I (for my parte) alwaies shunne the
use of those auncient wordes, except it were in certaine
clauses, and in them verie seldom. And (in my judgement)
hee that useth them otherwise, committeth a no lesse
error, than who so would, to follow them of old time, feede
upon maste, where he hath now aboundance of corne
found out.

And because you say, the auncient wordes onely with
the brightnesse of antiquitie, decke out so highly every
matter, how base so ever it be, that it may make it worthie
great commendation: I say unto you, that not of these
auncient words onely, but of those that bee good in deede,
I make no small account, that I suppose without the juice
of faire sentences, they ought of reason to be litle set by.
For to divide the sentences frõ the words, is the deviding
of the soule from the bodie, the which can not bee done,

297

neither in the one nor in the other, without destruction ensue upon it.

That therefore which is the principall matter and necessarie for a Courtier to speake, and write well, I believe is knowledge. For he that hath not knowledge and the thing in his minde that deserveth to bee understood, can neither speake nor write it.

Then must hee couch in a good order that hee hath to speake or to write, and afterwarde expresse it well with wordes: the which (if I bee not deceived) ought to bee apt, chosen, cleare, and well applyed, and (above all) in use also among the people: for very such make the greatnesse and gorgeousnesse of an Oration, so he that speaketh have a good judgement and heedfulnesse withall, and the understanding to picke such as be of most proper signification, for that he intendeth to speake and commend, and tempering them like waxe after his owne minde, applyeth them in such part and in such order, that at the first shew they may set forth and doe men to understand the dignitie and brightnesse of them, as tables of painting placed in their good and naturall light.

And this doe I say, as well of writing as of speaking, wherein certain things are requisite that are not necessarie in writing, as a good voice, not too subtill or soft, as in a woman: nor yet so boistrous and rough, as in one of the countrie, but shril, cleare, sweete and well framed with a prompt pronunciation, and with fit maners, and gestures, which (in my minde) consist in certaine motions of all the bodie, not affected nor forced, but tempred with a manerly countenance and with a moving of the eyes that may give a grace and accorde with the wordes, and (as much as he can) signifie also with gestures, the intent and affection of the speaker.

But all these things were in vaine and of small account, if the sentences expressed by the wordes should not be faire, wittie, subtill, fine and grave according to the matter.

I doubt, saide the L. Morello, if this Courtier speake

with such finenesse and gravitie among us, there will be some that will not understand him.

Nay, every one shall understand him, answered the Count, for finenes hindreth not the easinesse of understanding.

Neither will I have him to speake alwaies in gravity, but of pleasant matters, of mery conceites, of honest devises, and of jestes according to the time, and in all notwithstanding after a pithy maner, and with readinesse and varietie without confusion, neither shall hee in anie part shew vanitie or childish follie.

And when hee shall then commune of a matter that is darke and hard, I will have him both in words and sentences well pointed, to expresse his judgement, and to make every doubt cleare and plaine after a certaine diligent sorte without tediousnesse.

Likewise (when hee shall see time) to have the understanding to speake with dignitie and vehemencie and to raise those affections which our mindes have in them, and to inflame or stirre them according to the matter: sometime with a simplicitie of such meekenesse of minde, that a man would weene nature her selfe spake to make them tender and (as it were) dronken with sweetnes: and with such conveyance of easinesse, that who so heareth him, may conceive a good opinion of him selfe, and thinke that he also with verie litle adoe, might attaine to that perfection, but when hee commeth to the proofe, shall finde him selfe farre wide.

I would have our Courtier to speake and write in that sorte, and not onely choose gorgeous and fine wordes out of every part of Italie, but also I woulde judge him worthie praise to use some of those termes both French and Spanish, which by our custome have beene admitted.

Therefore it shoulde not mislike me, falling so to purpose, to say *vauntcourrour*, to say, to ascertaine, to aventure, to say, to pearce through a bodie with talke, meaning thereby to use a familiaritie with him, and grope him to get of him some perfect knowledge: to say, a royall gentleman, a neat man to be about a prince, and such other tearmes, so hee may thinke to be understood.

Sometime I would have him take certaine wordes in an other signification than that is proper to them, and wrasting them to his purpose (as it were) graffe them like a graffe of a tree in a more luckie stocke, to make them more sightly and faire, and (as it were) draw the matters to the sense of the verie eyes, and (as they say) make them felt with hande, for the delite of him that heareth, or readeth.

Neither would I have him to sticke to forge new also, and with new figures of speach, deriving them featly from the Latins, as the Latins in old time derived from the Grecians.

In case then of such learned men both of good witte and judgement, as now adayes may be picked out among us, there were some that would bestow their travell to write after the maner that we have spoken off, in this tongue things worth the reading, we should soone see it in good frame, and following with termes and good phrases, and so copious that a man might as well write in it, as in any other tongue: and though it were not the mere auncient Tuskane tongue, yet shoulde it be the Italian tongue, commune, plentifull, and variable, and (as it were) like a delicious garden full of sundrie flowers and fruites.

Neither should this bee a new matter: for of the foure tongues, that were in use among the Greeke writers, picking out of everie word, moodes and rules as they thought meete, they raised thereby an other, which was named ye Commune tongue, and afterwarde all five they called with one name the Greeke tongue.

And albeit the Athenian tongue was more fine, pure, and eloquenter than the rest, yet did not the good writers that were not of Athens borne, so affect it, but in the stile of writing, and (as it were) in the smacke and propertie of their naturall speach they were wel inough knowne:

neither were they any whit the lesse regarded for all that, but rather such as would appeare over mere Athenians were blamed for it.

Among the Latin wryters in like case many there were in their dayes much set by that were no Romanes, although there appeared not in them that proper and peculiar purenesse of the Romane tongue, which men of an other nation can verie seldome attaine.

In times past, Titus Livius was not neglected, although some one saide hee found in him mere Padowan: Nor Virgill, for that he was reprehended that hee spake not Romane.

And (as you know) there were also read, and much set by in Rome, many writers of barbarous nations.

But wee more precise a great deale than they of old time, doe binde our selves with certaine new lawes out of purpose: and having the broad beaten way before our eyes, seeke through gappes to walke in unknowne pathes. For in our owne tongue, whose office is (as all others) to expresse well and clearely the conceites of the minde, we delite in darknesse, and calling it the vulgar tongue, will use in it wordes, that are not onely not understood of the vulgar people, but also of the best sorte of men, and those men of learning, and are not used in any part, not regarding that all good writers of olde time blamed such wordes as were refused of custome, the which you (in my mind) do not wel know: forsomuch as you say, if any vice of speach be taken up of any ignorant persons, it ought not to bee called a custome, nor received for a rule of speach.

And (as at other times I have heard you say) ye will have againe in stead of Capitolio, we should say Campidoglio: gor Ieronymo, Girolamo: Aldace, for Audace: and for Patrono, padrone: and such corrupt and mangled wordes, because they have bin found so written by some ignorant Tuscane of olde time, and bicause the men of the Countrie speak so in Tuscane now a daies.

The good use of speech therfore I beleeve, ariseth of men that have witte, and with learning and practise have gotten a good judgement, and with it consent and agree to receive the wordes that they thinke good, which are knowen by a certaine naturall judgement, and not by art or any manner rule.

Doe you not knowe, that figures of speech which give such grace and brightnesse to an Oration, are all the abuse of Grammer rules, but yet are received and confirmed by use, because men are able to make no other reason but that they delite, and to the verie sense of our eares it appeareth, they bring a life and a sweetnes.

And this believe I is good custome, which the Romanes, the Neapolitans, the Lumbards, and the rest are as apt to receive, as the Tuskanes. Truth it is, in everie tongue some things are alwaies good, as easiness to be understood, a good order, varietie, picked sentences, clauses well framed: and on the other side Affectation, and the other contrary to these, are to bee shunned.

But of words some there are that last a good time, and afterwarde waxe stale and cleane lose their grace: other some take force and creepe into estimation.

For as the seasons of the yeare make leaves and fruites to fall, and afterwarde garnish the trees a fresh with other: even so, doth time make those first wordes to fall, and use maketh other to spring a fresh, and giveth them grace and estimation, until they in like sorte consumed by litle and litle with the envyous byting of time, come to their end, because at the last both wee and whatsoever is ours, are mortall.

Consider with our selves, that we have no more knowledge of the Osca tongue. The Provinciall tongue, that (a man may say) the last day was renowmed of noble writers, now is it not understoode of the inhabitants of the Countrey.

I believe therefore (as the Lorde Magnifico hath saide) that were Petrarca and Boccaccio at this present in life, they woulde not use many words that we see in their writings. Therefore (in mine opinion) it is not wel done to follow them therein.

Yet doe I much commend them that can follow that ought to be followed: but notwithstanding I believe it be possible inough to write well without following, and especially in this our tongue, wherein we may bee helped by custome, the which I wil not take upon me in the Latin.

Then Sir Fredericke, why, will you (quoth hee) custome should bee more apprised in the vulgar tongue, than in the Latin?

Nay, both in the one and the other (answered the Count) I judge custome ought to bee the mistresse. But for so much as those men, unto whom the Latin tongue was as proper, as is the vulgar tongue now to us, are no more in the world, we must learne of their writinges that they learned by use and custome: neither doth auncient speach signifie any thing els but an auncient custome of speach: and it were a fond matter to love the auncient speach for nothing els but to speake rather as men did speake, than as men doe speake?

Did not they then of olde time follow, answered Sir Fredericke?

I believe, (quoth the Count) many did follow, but not in every point.

And if Virgill had altogether followed Hesiodus, hee should not have passed him, nor Cicero Crassus, nor Ennius his predecessors.

Behold Homer, who is so ancient that he is thought of many to be the first heroicall Poete, as well of time, as also of excellencie of phrase: and whom will you have him to have followed?

Some other, answered Sir Fredericke, more auncient than he was, which wee heare not of, by reason of antiquitie.

Whom will you say then Petrarca and Boccaccio followed, said the Count, which (a man may say) were but three dayes agoe in the world?

303

I know not, answered Sir Fredericke, but it is to bee thought they in like wise bent their minde to following, though we know not of whom.

The Count answered: a man may believe that they that were followed, were better than they that did follow: and it were too great a wonder that their name and renowne, if they were good, should so soone bee cleane lost. But I believe their verie maister was witt, and their owne naturall inclination and judgement. And thereat no man ought to wonder, for (in a manner) alwaies a man by sundrie waies may climbe to the top of all perfection.

And there is no nature, that hath not in manye things of like sorte unlike the one to the other, which for al that among themselves deserve a like praise.

Marke me musike, wherein are harmonies sometime of base sound and slow, and otherwile verie quicke and of new devises, yet doe they all recreate a man, but for sundrie causes, as a man may perceive in the manner of singing that Bidō useth, which is so artificiall, cunning, vehement, stirred, and such sundrie melodies, that the spirites of the hearers move all and are inflamed, and so listing, a man would weene they were lift up into heaven.

And no lesse doth our Marchetto Cara move in his singing, but with a more soft harmony, that by a delectable way and full of mourning sweetenes maketh tender and perceth the mind, and sweetly imprinteth in it a passion full of great delite.

Sundrie thinges in like manner doe equally please our eyes so much that a man shall have much a doe to judge in which they most delite.

Behold in painting Lenard Vincio, Mantegna, Raphael, Michelāgelo, George of Castelfranco: they are all most excellent doers, yet are they in working unlike, but in any of them a man would not judge that there wanted ought in his kinde of trade: for everie one is knowne to bee of most perfection after his manner.

The like is of many Poets both Greeke and Latin, which being diverse in writing are alike in prayse.

Orators also have alwaies had such a diversitie among them, as (in a manner) every age hath brought forth and set by one sorte of Orators peculiar for that time, which have beene unlike and disagreeing not onely to their predecessors and followers but also among them selves. As it is written among the Grecians of Isocrates, Lysias, Eschines, and many other excellent, but yet like unto none saving themselves.

And among the Latins, Carbo, Lælius, Scipio Affricanus, Galba, Sulpitius, Cotta, Graccus, Marcus Antonius Crassus, and so many that it should be long to repeate them, all good and most divers one from another. So that who so could consider al the Orators that have beene in the world, he should finde so many Orators, so manie kindes of speach.

Me thinke I remember also that Cicero in a place bringeth in Marcus Antonius to say unto Sulpitius that there are many that follow no man, and yet climbe they to a high degree of excellencie.

And speaketh of certaine that had brought up a new stile and phrase of speaking faire, but not used of Orators of that time wherein they followed none but themselves.

Therefore he affirmeth also that maisters should consider the nature of their scholers, and taking it for their guide, direct and prompt them in the way that their wit and naturall inclination moveth them unto.

For this cause therefore, Sir Fredericke, doe I believe if a man have not an inclination unto some author whatsoever he bee, it were not well done to force him to follow him. Because the vertue of that disposition of his soone fainteth, and is hindred, by reason that it is to stray out of the way in which he would have profited, had he not beene stopped in it.

I know not then how it will stand well, in steade of enriching this tongue, and of giving it majestie and light, to make it poore, slender, bare and darke, and to seeke to

305

shut it up into so narrow a roome, that everye man should bee compelled to follow onely Petrarca and Boccaccio, and that we should not also in that tongue, credite Politian, Laurēce de Medicis, Francis Diaceto, and certain other that notwistanding are Tuskanes, and perhaps of no lesse learning and judgement than Petrarca and Boccaccio.

And truely it should bee a great miserie to stop without wading any further than almost the first that ever wrote: and to dispaire, that so many and so noble wits shall never finde out any moe than one good manner of speach in the tongue that unto them is proper and naturall.

But now adaies there be some so scrupulous, that (as it were) with a religion and high mysteries of this their Tuskan tongue, put as many as heareth in such dread, that they bring in like case many gentlemen and learned men in such awe, that they dare not open their mouth: and confesse plainely, that they can not speake the tongue which they have learned of their nourses, even from their cradle.

But in this point (me think) we have spoken too much. Therefore let us now proceede in our communication of the Courtier.

Then answered Sir Fredericke: but first I will say this litle, which is, that I deny not but the opinions and writers of men are diverse among them selves: neither doe I judge it comely for one that is vehement and quicke of nature to take in hand to write of soft and quiet matters. Nor yet for an other that is severe and grave to write of mery conceites. For in this point, me think, it is reason every man should apply him selfe to his own proper inclination. And of this I believe spake Cicero, when he said that maisters should have a consideration to the nature of their scholars, least they should do like the ill husband-man, that sometime in a soyle that is good onely for vines, will sowe graine.

But it will not sinke into my heade why in a peculiar tongue, that is not so proper unto all men, as are discourses

and conceites, and many other operations, but an invention contained under certaine termes, a man may not with
more reason followe them that speake best, than speake at
all aventure. And that, as in the Latin tongue a man ought
to apply himselfe to be in the tongue like unto Virgill and
Cicero rather than Silius and Cornelius Tacitus, so in the
vulgar tongue why it were not better to follow the tongue
of Petrarca and Boccaccio than any mans else: and therein
expresse well his owne conceites, and so apply himselfe as
(Cicero saith) to his own naturall inclination. And thus
shall the difference which you say is betweene the good
Orators, be found to consist in the senses and not in the
tongue.

Then the Count, I feare me (quoth he) wee shall enter
into a large sea, and leave our first purpose of the courtier.
But I would knowe of you, wherein consisteth the goodness
of this tongue?

Sir Fredericke answered: in keeping well the propertie
of it, and in taking it in the signification (using the same
stile and measure) that all such have done as have written well.

I would know then, quoth the Count, whether this stile
and measure which you speake of, arise of the sentences
or of the wordes?

Of the wordes, answered Sir Fredericke. Doe you not
thinke then, quoth the Count, that the wordes of Silius and
Cornelius Tacitus, are the verie same that Virgill and Cicero
use? and taken in the same signification? Sir Fredericke
aunswered: they are the very same in deede, but some ill
applyed and diversly taken.

The Count answered: in case a man should picke out
of a booke of Cornelius and of Silius, all the wordes placed
in other signification than is in Virgill and Cicero, (which
shoulde bee very few) would you not then say that
Cornelius in the tongue were equall with Cicero, and Silius
with Virgill?

Then the Ladie Emilia, me thinke (quoth she) this your

disputation hath lasted too long, and hath beene very
tedious, therefore it shall be best to deferre it untill an
other time.

Sir Fredericke begun stil to make answere, but the Ladie
Emilia alwais interrupted him.

At last the Count saide, many will judge of styles: and
talke of numbers and measures, and of following, but they
can not doe mee to understand what manner a thing stile
and measure is, and wherein following consisteth: Nor why
thinges taken out of Homer or any other, are so well
couched in Virgill, that they appeare rather amplified than
followed, and peradventure the occasion thereof is, that
I am not able to conceive it.

But because a great argument that a man understandeth
a thing, is the understanding that hee hath to teache it,
I feare mee they themselves have small understanding in
it, and praise Virgill and Cicero, because they heare them
praysed of many, not for that they know the difference
betwene them and others, which out of peradventure consisteth not in the observation of two or three, or of ten
wordes used after a diverse manner from other.

In Salust, in Cesar, in Varro, and in other good writers,
there are founde some termes applyed otherwise than
Cicero applyeth them, and both the one and the other doe
well inough. Because in so trifling a matter the goodnesse
and perfection of a tongue doth not consist, as Demosthenes
answered Eschines well, that had taken him up, demaunding him of certaine wordes which he had used and yet
were not auncient, what monsters, or woondrous matters
they were? whereat Demosthenes laughed and answered
him, that the fortunes of Greece dependeth not upon them.

Even so woulde I passe full litle, if a Tuskane should
reprehend mee for speaking rather *Satisfatto* then *Sodis-
fatto*: and *Honorevole*, than *Horrevole*: and *Causa*, than
Cagione: and *Populo*, than *Popolo*, and such other matters.

Then arose Sir Fredericke upon his feete and saide: I
beseech ye give the hearing of these few words.

308

The Ladie Emilia answered laughing, upon my displeasure I forbid any of you to talke anye more in this matter, for I will have you to breake it of until an other night.

But you Count, proceede you in your communication of the Courtier, and let us see how good a memory you have: for I believe if you can knit it againe where you brake of, you shall not doe a litle.

Madam, answered the Count, me thinke the threed is broken in sunder, but if I be not deceived, I trow wee saide that pestilent curiositie doth alwaies give an evill grace unto all thinges: and contrariwise simplicitie and Rechlesnesse a marvailous good grace. In commendation whereof and in dispraise of curiositie, manye other thinges might be saide, yet will I alledge but one moe, and then have done.

All women generally have a great desire to be, and when they can not be at the least to appeare beawtifull.

Therefore where nature in some part hath not done her devoir, therein they endevour them selves to supply it with arte. Of this ariseth the trimming of the face, with such studie and many times paines, the pilling of the browes and forehead, and the using of all those manner waies, and the abyding of such lothsomnesse that you women believe are kept very secrete from men, and yet doe all men know them.

The Ladie Constance Fregosa laughed at this and saide: you should doe much better to goe forwarde in your communication, and declare how a man may attaine a good grace, and speak of Courting, than to discover the faultes of women without purpose.

Nay it is much to purpose, answered the Count, because these faultes that I talke of, take this grace from you: for they proceede of nothing els, but of curiousnesse, whereby ye discover openly unto every man the over great desire that yee have to be beawtifull.

Doe you not marke how much more grace is in a woman,

309

that if she doth trimme her selfe, doth it so scarcely and so litle, that who so beholdeth her, standeth in doubt whether she bee trimmed or no: than in an other so bedawbed, that a man would wene she had a viser on her face, and dareth not laugh for making it chappe: nor at any time changeth her colour, but when she apparaileth her selfe in the morning and all the rest of the day standeth like an image of woode without moving, shewing her selfe onely in torche light, as craftie marchantmen doe their clothes in their darke lights.

How much more then doth a man delite in one, I meane not foule, that is manifestly seene she hath nothing upon her face, though shee bee not white nor so redde, but with her naturall colour somewhat wan, sometime with blushing, or through other chaunce dyed with a pure rednesse, with her haire by happe out of order and ruffled, and with her simple and naturall gestures, without shewing her selfe to bestow diligence or studie to make her faire?

This is that not regarded purenesse which best pleaseth the eyes and mindes of men, that stand alwaies in awe to be deceived by arte.

White teeth is a good sight in a woman, for since they are not so in open sight as is the face, but most commonly are hid, a man may thinke she bestoweth not so much labour about them, to make them white, as shee doth in the face.

Yet who so should laugh without cause purposely to shew them, shoulde discover the arte, and for all their faire whitenesse shoulde appeare unto all men to have a verie ill grace, as Egnatius in Catullus.

The like is in the hands, which being delicate, smooth and faire, if they be shewed bare at any time when occasion is to occupie them, and not of purpose to shew the beawtie of them, they leave a very great desire of them selves, and especially after they are covered with gloves againe, for a man woulde judge that in putting them on again she passeth not and litle regardeth whether they be in sight or no, and that they are so faire rather by nature, than by any studie or diligence.

Have ye not had an eye otherwhile, when either in the streetes going to Church, or in any other place, or in sporting, or by any other chaunce it happeneth that a woman lifteth up her clothes so high, that she sheweth her foote, and sometime a litle of her pretie legge un-wittingly?

And seemeth she not to you to have a verie good grace, if ye behold her then with a certaine womanly disposition, cleanely and precise, with her shoes of velvet, and her hose sitting cleane to her legge?

Truely it delyteth mee much, and I believe all of you: for every man supposeth that precisenesse in so secrete a place and so seldom seene, to be unto that woman rather naturall and proper, than forced, and that thereby she thinketh to get her no commendation at all.

In such sorte is curiousnesse avoided and covered, the which you may now conceive how contrarie it is, and taketh away the grace of everie operation and deed, as well of the bodie as of the minde, whereof hetherto we have spoken but litle, and yet ought it not to bee omitted, for as the minde is much more worthie than the body, so deserveth it also to be better decked and polished.

And how that ought to be in our Courtier (leaving apart the precepts of so manie wise Philosophers that write in this matter, and define the vertues of the mind, and so subtilly dispute of the dignitie of them) we will expresse in fewe wordes, applying to our purpose, that it is sufficient he bee (as they terme it commonly) an honest man and well meaning: for in this is comprehended the goodnesse, the wisedom, the manlinesse and the temperance of the mind, and all other qualities that belong to so worthie a name. And I recken him onely a true morall Philosopher that will be good, and to that he needeth few other pre-cepts than that will of his.

And therefore saide Socrates well, that he thought his

instructions had brought forth good fruite, when by them hee had provoked any one to apply his will to the knowledge and learning of vertue. For they that are come to the point that they covet nothing more than to be good, doe easily attaine the understanding of all that belongeth thereto: therefore herein wil we make no more adoe.

But beside goodnesse the true and principall ornament of the minde in every man (I believe) are letters, although ye Frenchmen know onely the noblenes of armes, and passe for nothing beside: so that they doe not onely set by letters, but they rather abhorre them, and all learned men they doe count very rascalles, and they thinke it a great villany when any one of them is called a Clarke.

Then answered the Lord Magnifico, you say verye true, this error in deed hath longe raigned among the Frenchmen. But if Monseigneur de Angoulesme [10] have so good luke that he may (as men hope) succede in the Crowne, the glory of armes in France doth not so florish nor is had in such estimation, as letters will be, I believe.

For it is not long sins I was in France, and saw this Prince in the Court there, who seemed unto mee beside the handsomnesse of person and bewtie of visage, to have in his countenance so great a majestie, accompanied neverthelesse with a certaine lovely courtesie, that the realme of Fraunce shoulde ever seeme unto him a small matter.

I understood afterwarde by many gentlemen both French and Italian, verie much of the most noble conditions, of the greatnesse of courage, prowesse and liberalitie that was in him: and among other things, it was tolde me, that hee highly loved and esteemed letters, and had in very great reputation all learned men, and blamed the Frenchmen themselves that their mindes were so far wide from this profession, especially having at their doores so noble an universitie as Paris is, where all the world resorteth.

Then spake the Count: It is great wonder that in these tender yeares, onely by the provocation of nature, contrarie to the manner of the countrie, he hath given him selfe to so good a way. And because subjectes follow alwaies the conditions of the higher powers, it is possible that it may come to passe (as you say) that ye Frenchmen will yet esteeme letters to be of that dignitie that they are in deede. The which (if they will give eare thereto) they may soone bee perswaded.

Forsomuch as men ought to covet of nature nothing so much, and nothing is more proper for them, than knowledge: which thing it were a great folly to say or to holde opinion that it is not alwaies good.

And in case I might commune with them, or with other that were of a contrary opinion to me, I would doe my diligence to shew them, how much letters (which undoubtedlye have beene graunted of God unto men for a soveraigne gift) are profitable and necessarie for our life and estimation. Neither should I want the examples of so many excellent captaines of old time, which all joyned the ornament of letters with prowesse of armes.

For (as you know) Alexander had Homer in such reverence, that hee laide his *Ilias* alwaies under his beds heade: and hee applyed diligently not these studies onely, but also the speculations of Philosophy under the discipline of Aristotle.

Alcibiades encreased his good conditions, and made them greater with letters, and with the instructions of Socrates.

Also what diligence Cesar used in studie, those thinges which hee had so divinelye writen him selfe, make triall.

It is saide that Scipio Affricanus carried alwaies in his hand the bookes of Xenophon, wherein under the name of Cyrus he instructeth a perfect king.

I coulde recite unto you Lucullus, Sylla, Pompeius, Brutus, and many other Romanes and Grecians, but I woulde doe no more but make mention of Hannibal, which being so excellent a Captaine (yet for all that of a fierce nature and voide of all humanity, an untrue dealer, and a despiser of men and of the Gods) had also understanding in letters, and the knowledge of the Greeke tongue.

313

And if I bee not deceived (I trow) I have redde in my time, that he left a booke behinde him of his own making in the Greeke tongue. But this kinde of talke is more than needeth: for I knowe all you understand how much the Frenchmen be deceived in holding opinion letters to doe any hurt to armes.

You know in great matters and adventures in wars the true provocation is glory: and who so for lucres sake or for any other consideration taketh it in hande (beside that hee never doth any thing worthie prayse) deserveth not the name of a gentleman, but is a most vile marchant.

And every man may conceive it to be true glory, that is stored up in the holy treasure of letters, except such unluckie creatures as have no taste thereof.

What minde is so fainte, so bashfull, and of so base a courage, that in reading the actes and greatnes of Cesar, Alexander, Scipio, Annibal, and so many other, is not incensed with a most fervent longing to be like them: and doth not preferre the getting of that perpetuall fame, before the rotten life that lasteth two dayes? Which in despite of death maketh him live a great deale more famous than before.

But hee that favoureth not the sweetnes of letters, can not know how much is the greatnesse of glory, which is a long while preserved by them, and onely measureth it with the age of one or two men, for further hee beareth not in minde. Therefore can be not esteeme this short glory so much as he would doe that, which (in a manner) is everlasting, if by his ill happe hee were not barred from the knowledge of it. And not passing upon it so much, reason perswadeth, and a man may well believe hee will never hazard himselfe so much to come by it, as hee that knoweth it.

I woulde not now some one of the contrarie parte should alledge unto mee the contrarie effectes to confute mine opinion with all: and tell mee how the Italians with their knowledge of letters have shewed small prowesse in armes from a certaine time hetherto, the which neverthelesse is too true: but in very deed a man may well say that the offence of a few, hath brought (beside the great damage) an everlasting reproch unto all other, and the verie cause of our confusion, and of the neglecting of vertue in our mindes (if it bee not cleane deade) proceeded of them. But it were a more shamefull matter unto us to publish it, than unto the Frenchmen the ignorance in letters.

Therefore it is better to passe that over with silence that cannot bee rehearsed without sorrow, and leaving this purpose into the which I am entred against my wil, returne againe unto our Courtier, whom in letters I will have to be more than indifferently well seene, at the least in those studies, which they call Humanitie and to have not onely the understanding of the Latin tongue, but also of the Greek, because of the many and sundrie things that with great excellencie are written in it.

Let him much exercise him selfe in Poets, and no lesse in Oratours and Historiographers, and also in writing both rime and prose, and especially in this our vulgar tongue. For beside the contentation that hee shall receive thereby him selfe, hee shall by this meanes never want pleasant intertainements with women which ordinarily love such matters.

And if by reason either of his other businesse beside, or of his slender studie hee shall not attaine unto that perfection that his writings may bee worthy much commendation, let him bee circumspect in keeping them close, least he make other men to laugh at him. Onely hee may shew them to a friende whom he may trust.

For at the least wise hee shall receive so much profit, that by that exercise hee shall be able to give his judgement upon other mens doinges. For it happeneth very seldome, that a man not exercised in writing, how learned soever he be, can at any time know perfectly the labour and toile of writers, or tast of the sweetnesse and excellency of styles, and those inner observations that often times are founde in them of olde time.

And beside that, those studies shal make him copious, and (as Aristippus answered a Tirant) bold to speake upon a good ground with every man.

Notwithstanding I will have our Courtier to keepe fast in his minde one lesson, and that is this, to bee alwaies warie both in this and in everie other point, and rather fearefull than bolde, and beware that hee perswade not himselfe falsly, to know the thing he knoweth not in deede.

Because we are of nature all the sort of us much more greedy of prayse than is requisite, and better do our eares love the melodie of wordes sounding to our praise, than any other song or sound that is most sweete. And therefore many times like the voyces of Marmaidens, they are the cause of drowning of him that doth not well stoppe his eares at such deceitfull harmony.

This daunger being perceived, there hath beene among the auncient wise men that have writen bookes, how a man should knowe a true friend from a flatterer. But what availeth it? If there bee many of them (or rather infinite) that manifestly perceive they are flattered, and yet love him that flattereth them, and hate him that telleth them the troth.

And oftentimes (standing in opinion that he that prayseth them is too scarce in his wordes) they them selves helpe him forwarde, and utter such matters of themseves, that the most impudent flatterer of all is ashamed of.

Let us leave these blinde buzzards in their owne errour, and make our Courtier of so good a judgement, that he will not bee given to understand blacke for white, nor presume more of himselfe than what he knoweth very manifestly to be true, and especially in those thinges, which (if yee beare well in minde) the Lorde Cesar rehearsed in his devise of pastimes, that we have many times used for an instrument to make many become foolish. But rather that hee may be assured not to fall into any error, where he knoweth those prayses that are given him to be true, let him not so openly consent to them, nor confirme them so without resistance, but rather with modestie (in a manner) deny them cleane, shewing alwaies and counting in effect, armes to bee his principall profession, and all the other good qualities for an ornament thereof.

And principally among Souldiers, least hee bee like unto them that in learning will seeme men of warre, and among men of warre, learned.

In this wise, for the reasons we have said, he shall avoide curiousnesse, and the meane thinges which he taketh in hand, shall appeare very great.

Here M. Peter Bembo answered: I know not (Count Lewis) how you will have this Courtier, being learned, and of so many other vertuous qualities, to count every thing for an ornament of armes, and not armes, and the rest for an ornament of letters. The which without other addition, are in dignitie so much above armes, as the mind is above the bodie: because the practising of them belongeth properly to the minde, even as the practising of armes doth the bodies.

The Count answered then: nay the practising of armes belongeth as well to the minde as to the bodie. But I would not have you (maister Peter) a judge in this cause, for you would be too partiall to one of the partes.

And for so much as this disputation hath alreadie beene tossed a long time by most wise men, we need not to renue it, but I count it resolved upon armes side, and wil have our Courtier (since I have the fashioning of him at my will) thinke thus also.

And if you be of a contrarie opinion, tarrie till you heare a disputation, where it may bee as well lawfull for him that taketh part with armes, to use his armes, as they that defend letters, use in the defence the verie same letters, so that if each helpe them selves with their instruments, you shall see that letters shall loose.

Oh (quoth maister Peter) you rebuked the Frenchmen

317

before for setting litle by letters, and declared what a great light of glory they shew unto men, and how they make them immortall: and now it seemeth you are in an other opinion.

Doe you not remember that such verses are taken out of Petrarch?

The great Macedo, when he proched neare
   Fierce Achylles famous tomb thus saide and sight:
O happie Prince that found a trumpe so cleare,
   And happie he that praisde so worthie a wight.

And if Alexander envied Achilles, not for his deedes, but for his fortune that gave him so great lucke to have his actes renowmed by Homer, a man may gather hee esteemed more the letters of Homer, than the armes of Achilles.

What other judge then, or what other sentence looke you for, as touching the dignitie of armes and letters, than that which was given by one of the greatest Captaines that ever were?

The Count answered: I blame the Frenchmen because they think letters hurt the profession of armes: and I holde opinion that it is not so necessary for any man to be learned, as it is for a man of warre.

And these two points linked together, and aided the one by the other (which is most fit) will I have to bee in the Courtier. Neither do I thinke my selfe for this to be in an other opinion, but (as I have said) I will not dispute, which of them is most worthie prayse.

It sufficeth that learned men take not in hand at anie time to praise any but great men and glorious actes, which of them selves deserve praise by their proper essentiall vertues from whence they arise.

Beside that, they are a most noble Theme for writers, which is a great ornament, and partly the cause of continuance of writinges, that peradventure shoulde not be so much read, and set by, if there wanted in them noble matter, but counted vaine and of small reputation.

And if Alexander envied Achilles, because hee was praised of him that did it, yet doth it not consequently follow, that he esteemed letters more than armes. Wherein he had knowne him selfe so farre wide from Achilles, as in writing hee thought all they would be from Homer that shoulde goe about to write of him, I am sure hee would much sooner have desired well doing in himselfe, than well speaking in an other.

Therefore think I that this was a close praise of him selfe, and a wishing for that he thought he had not, namely the high excellencie of a writer, and not for that hee thought with him selfe hee had alreadie obtained, that is to say, the prowesse of armes, wherein hee counted not Achilles any whit his superior, wherefore he called him happie, as it were signifying, where his fame aforetime was not so renowmed in the worlde, as was the fame that by so divine a Poeme was cleare and excellent, it proceeded not for that his prowesse and deserts were not such, and worthie so much praise: but it arose of fortune, that had before hand prepared for Achilles, that miracle of nature for a glorious renowne and trumpet of his acts.

And peradventure againe he minded thereby to stirre up some noble witt to write of himselfe, declaring thereby how acceptable it would be to him, forsomuch as hee loved and reverenced the holy monuments of letters: about the which we have spoken sufficient.

Nay more than sufficient, answered the Lord Lodovicus Pius, for I believe there is never a vessell in the world possible to be found so bigge, that shall bee able to receive all the thinges that you will have in this Courtier.

Then the Count, abide yet a while (quoth hee) for there be many other thinges to be had in him yet.

Peter of Naples answered: after this manner Crassus de Medicis shall have a great advantage of M. Peter Bembo.

At this they all laughed. And the Count beginning a fresh, my Lords (quoth he) you thinke I am not pleased with yͤ Courtier, if he be not also a Musition, and beside his understanding and cunning upon the booke, have skil in like manner on sundry instruments. For if wee weigh it well, ther is no ease of the labors, and medicines of feeble mindes to be found more honest and more praise worthie in time of leisure than it. And principally in Courtes, where (beside the refreshing of vexations that musike bringeth unto eche man) many things are taken in hand to please women withall, whose tender and soft breastes are soone pierced with melodie, and filled with sweetnesse.

Therefore no marvell, that in olde times and now adayes they have alwaies beene inclined to Musitions, and counted this a most acceptable food of the minde.

Then the L. Gasper, I believe musick (quoth he) together with many other vanities is meet for womē, and peradventure for some also that have the likenesse of men, but not for them that be men in deede: who ought not with such delicacies to womanish their mindes, and bring them selves in that sort to dread death.

Speake it not, answered the Count. For I shall enter in a large sea of the praise of Musicke, and call to rehearsall how much it hath alwaies beene renowmed among them of olde time, and counted a holy matter: and how it hath beene the opinion of most wise Philosophers, that the worlde is made of musike, and the heavens in their moving make a melodie, and our soule is framed after the verie same sort and therefore lifteth up it selfe, and (as it were) reviveth the vertues and force of it selfe with Musicke.

Wherefore it is written that Alexander was so fervently stirred with it, that (in a manner) against his will hee was forced to arise from bankets and runne to weapon, afterward the Musition chaunging the stroke, and his manner of tune, pacified him selfe again, and returned from weapon to banketing.

And I shall tell you that grave Socrates when he was

well stricken in yeares, learned to play upon the harpe. And I remember I have understoode that Plato and Aristotle will have a man that is wel brought up, to be also a Musition: and declare with infinite reasons the force of musicke to bee to very great purpose in us, and for many causes (that should be too long to rehearse) ought necessarily to be learned from a mans childhood, not onely for the superficiall melodie that is heard, but to be sufficient to bring into us a new habite that is good, and a custome inclining to vertue, which maketh the minde more apt to the conceiving of felicitie, even as bodely exercise maketh the bodie more lustie, and not onely hurteth not civil matters and warrelike affaires, but is a great stay to them.

Also Lycurgus in his sharp lawes allowed musicke. And it is read that the Lacedemoniãs, which were valiant in armes, and the Cretenses used harpes, and other soft instruments: and many most excellent Captaines of olde time (as Epaminondas) gave themselves to musicke: and such as had not a sight in it (as Themistocles) were a great deale the lesse set by.

Have you not reade, that among the first instructions which the good olde man Chiron taught Achilles in his tender age, whom he had brought up from his nurse and cradle, musicke was one? And the wise maister woulde have those handes that should shedde so much Troyan bloud, to bee often times occupied in playing upon the Harpe?

What souldier is there (therefore) that will thinke it a shame to follow Achilles, omitting many other famous Captaines that I could alledge?

Doe ye not then deprive our Courtier of Musicke, which doth not onely make sweete the mindes of men, but also many times wilde beastes tame: and who so savoureth it not, a man may assuredly thinke him not to be well in his wits.

Behold I pray you what force it hath, that in times past

allured a fish to suffer a man to ride upon it through the tempestuous sea.

We may see it used in the holy temples, to render laud and thankes unto God, and it is a credible matter that it is acceptable unto him, and that he hath given it unto us for a most sweete lightning of our travailes and vexations.

So that many times the boysterous labours in the fields, in the heat of the sun, beguile their paine with rude and carterly singing.

With this the unmannerly countrie woman, that ariseth before day out of her sleepe to spinne and carde, defendeth her selfe and maketh her labour pleasant.

This is the most sweete pastime after raine, winde and tempest, unto the miserable marriners.

With this doe the verie Pilgrimes comfort themselves in their troublesome and long voyages. And oftentimes prisoners, in adversitie, fetters and in stockes.

In like manner for a greater proofe, that the tunablenesse of musick (thought it be but rude) is a verie great refreshing of all worldlye paines and griefes, a man woulde judge that nature hath taught it unto nurses for a speciall remedie to the continuall waylings of sucking babes, which at the sound of their voice fall into a quiet and sweete sleepe, forgetting the teares that are so proper to them, and given us of nature in that age, for a gesse of the rest of our life to come.

Here the Count pausing a while, the L. Julian said: I am not of the Lorde Gaspers opinion, but I believe for the reasons you alledge, and for many other, that musicke is not only an ornament, but also necessarie for a Courtier.

But I would have you declare, how this and the other qualities which you appoint him, are to bee practised, and of what time, and in what sort. Because many thinges that of themselves be worthie praise, oftentimes in practising them out of reason seeme most foolish. And contrariewise, some thinges that appeare to bee of small moment, in the well applying them, are greatly esteemed.

Then said the Count: before we enter into this matter, I will talke of an other thing, which for that it is of importance (in my judgement) I believe our Courtier ought in no wise to leave it out. And that is the cunning in drawing, and the knowledge in the verie arte of painting.

And wonder ye not if I wish this feate in him, which now adayes perhappes is counted an handicraft and full litle to become a gentleman, for I remember I have reade that the men of olde time, and especially in all Greece, would have gentlemens children in the scholes to apply painting, as a matter both honest and necessarie. And this was received in the first degree of liberall artes, afterwarde openly enacted not to bee taught to servants and bondmen.

Among the Romanes in like manner it was in verie great reputation, and thereof sprung the sirname of the most noble family of Fabii, for the first Fabius was sirnamed Pictor, because in deed he was a most excellent Painter, and so addicted to painting, that after hee had painted the walles of the temple of Health, hee writte therein his name, thinking with him selfe, that for all he was borne in so noble a familie, which was honoured with so many titles of Consulshippes and triumphes, and other dignities, and was learned and well seene in the law, and reckoned among orators, to give also an increase of brightenesse, and an ornament unto his renowne, by leaving behind him a memorie that he had beene a Painter.

There have not in like manner wanted many other of notable families that have beene renowned in this arte, of the which (beside that in it selfe it is most noble and worthie) there ensue many commodities, and especially in warre, to draw out Countries, Platformes, Rivers, Bridges, Castels, Holdes, Fortresses, and such other matters, the which though a man were able to keepe in minde (and that is a hard matter to doe) yet can he not shew them to others.

And in verie deed who so esteemeth not this arte, is (to my seeming) farre wide from all reason: for somuch as

323

the ensigne of the world that we behold with a large skye, so bright with shining starres, and in the middest, the earth, environed with the seas, severed in partes with hilles, dales, and rivers, and so decked with such divers trees, beautifull flowers and herbes, a man may say it to be a noble and great painting, drawne with the hand of nature and of God: the which who so can follow, in mine opinion he is worthie much commendation. Neither can a man attaine to this, without the knowledge of many thinges, as he well knoweth that tryeth it.

Therefore had they of old time in very great estimation, both the arte and the artificers, so that it came to the toppe of all excellencie.

And of this may a man gather a sufficient argument at the auncient Images of Marble and mettall, which at this day are to bee seene. And though painting bee a diverse matter from carving, yet doe they both arise of one selfe fountaine (namely) of a good patterne.

And even as the Images are divine and excellent, so it is to be thought paintinges were also, and so much the more, for that they containe in them a greater workemanship.

Then the Ladie Emilia turning her unto John Christopher Romano, that sate there among the rest, howe thinke you (quoth she) to this judgement, will you graunt that painting containeth in it a greater workemanshipe, than carving?

John Christopher answered: in my minde carving is of more travaile, of more arte, and of more dignitie than painting.

Then saide the Count, Because Images are more durable, perhaps a man may say that they are of a more dignitie. For sith they are made for a memorie, they better satisfie the effect why they be made, than painting.

But beside memorie, both painting and carving are made also to set out a thing, and in this point hath painting a great deale the upper hand, the which though it be not so long lasting (to terme it so) as carving is, yet doth it for all that endure a long time, and for the while it lasteth, is much more sightly.

Then answered John Christopher: I believe verily you think not as you speake, and all this doe you for your Raphaelles sake.

And peradventure too, you judge the excellencie you know to bee in him in painting, to be of such perfection, that carving in Marble can not come to that degree. But waigh with your selfe, that this is the prayse of the artificer, and not of the arte.

Then he proceeded: and I judge also both the one and the other, to bee an artificiall following of nature. But yet I knowe not how you can say, that the truth and property that nature maketh, can not bee followed better in a figure of Marble or Mettall, wherein the members are all rounde proporcioned and measured as nature her selfe shapeth them, than in a Table, where men perceive nothing but the outwarde sight, and those colours that deceive the eyes: and say not to me, that being, is not nigher unto the truth than seeming.

Againe, I judge carving in Marble much harder, because if yee make a faulte, it can not be amended againe, for marble can not be joyned together, but ye must be driven to make a new Image.

The whiche happeneth not in painting, for a man may alter, put to, and diminish, alwaies making it better.

The Count saide laughing: I speake not for Raphaelles sake, neither ought you to think me so ignorant a person, but I understand the excellencie of Michaelangelo, of you your selfe, and of other men in carving of Marble, but I speake of the arte, and not of the Artificers.

And you say well, that both the one and the other is following of nature. But for all that, it is not so, that painting appeareth and carving is: for although images are all rounde like the lively patterne, and painting is onely seene in outwarde apparance, yet want there many things in images, that want not in paintinges, and especially lights

325

and shadowes, for flesh giveth one light, and Marble another, and that doth the Painter naturally follow with cleare and darke, more and lesse, as he seeth occasion, which the graver in marble can not doe.

And when the Painter maketh not his figure round he maketh the muscules and members in round wise, so that they goe to meete with the partes not seene, after such a manner, that a man may very well gather the Painter hath also a knowledge in them, and understandeth them.

And in this point he must have an other craft that is greater to frame those members, that they may seeme short, and diminish according to the proportion of the sight by the way of prospective, which by force of measured lines, colours, lights, and shadowes, discover unto you also in the outwarde sight of an upright wall the plainesse and fairenesse, more and lesse as pleaseth him.

Thinke you it againe a trifling matter to counterfeite naturall colours, flesh, cloth, and all other coloured thinges.

This can not nowe the graver in marble doe, ne yet expresse the grace of the sight that is in the blacke eyes, or in azure with the shining of those amorous beames.

Hee can not shew the colour of yellow haire, nor the glistring of armor, nor a darke night, nor a sea tempest, nor those twincklings and sparkes, nor the burning of a Citie, nor the rysing of the morning in the colour of Roses, with those beames of purple and golde. Finally hee can not shewe the skye, the sea, the earth, hilles, woodes, medowes, gardens, rivers, Cities, nor houses, which the Painter doth all.

For this respect (me thinke) painting is more noble, and containeth in it a greater workmanship than graving in Marble. And among them of olde time, I believe it was in as high estimation as other thinges, the which also is to be discerned by certain litle remnants that are to be seene yet, especially in places under ground in Roome.[11]

But much more evidently may a man gather it by olde wrytings, wherein is so famous and so often mention both of the worke and workemen, that by them a man may understande in what high reputation they have beene alwaies with Princes and common weales.

Therefore it is read, that Alexander loved highly Apelles of Ephesus, and so much, that after he had made him draw out a woman of his naked, whome hee loved most dearely, and understanding that this good Painter, for her marvellous beautie was most fervently in love with her, without any more adoe, hee bestowed her upon him. Truely a worthie liberallitie of Alexander, not to give onely treasure and states, but also his owne affections and desire, and a token of verie great love towarde Appelles, not regarding (to please him withall) the displeasure of the woman that he highly loved, who it is to be thought was sore agreeved to chaunge so great a king for a painter.

There bee many other signes rehearsed also of Alexanders good will towardes Apelles, but he shewed plainly in what estimation he had him, when hee commanded by open Proclamation no other Painter should bee so hardie to drawe out his picture.

Here could I repeat unto you the contentions of many noble Painters, with the greatest commendation and marvaile (in a manner) in the world.

I coulde tell you with what solemnitie the Emperours of olde time decked out their triumphes with paintinges, and dedicated them up in haunted places, and how deare it cost them, and that there were some painters that gave their workes freely, seeming unto them no golde nor silver was enough to value them: And how a table of Protogenes was of such estimation, that Demetrius lying encamped before Rhodes, where hee might have entred the Citie by setting fire to the place, where hee wist this table was, for feare of burning it, stayed to bid them battaile, and so he wunne not the Citie at all.

And how Metrodorus a Philosopher and a most excellent Painter, was sent out of Athens to Lord Paulus, to bring up his children, and to decke out his triumph he had to make.

And also many noble writers have written of this arte, which is a token great inough to declare in what estimation it hath beene. But I will not wee proceede any farther in this communication.

Therefore it sufficeth onely to say that our Courtier ought also to have a knowledge in painting, since it was honest and profitable, and much set by in those dayes when men were of more prowesse than they are now. And though hee never get other profit or delite in it (beside it is a helpe to him to judge of the excellencie of Images both olde and new, of vessels, buildings, old coines, cameses,[12] gravings, and such other matters) it maketh him also understand the beautie of lively bodies, and not onely in the sweetnesse of the Phisiognomie, but in the proportion of all the rest, as well in men as other living creatures.

See then how the knowledge in painting is cause of verie great pleasure. And this let them thinke that doe enjoy and view the beautie of a woman so throughly, that they thinke themselves in Paradise, and yet have not the feate of painting: the which if they had, they would conceive a farre greater contentation, for then shoulde they more perfectly understand the beauty that in their brest ingendreth such hearts ease.

Here the Lorde Cesar laughed and saide: I have not the arte of painting, and yet I knowe assuredly I have a farre greater delite in beholding a woman in the world, than Apelles himselfe that was so excellent, whom ye named right now, coulde have if he were now in life againe.

The Count answered: this delite of yours proceedeth not wholy of beautie, but of the affection which you perhaps beare unto the woman. And if you will tell the truth, the first time that you beheld that woman, yet felt not the thousandeth part of the delite which you did afterwarde, though her beautie were the verie same.

Therefore you may conceive how affection beareth a greater stroke in your delite than beautie.

I deny not that (quoth the Lord Cesar:) but as delite

ariseth of affection, so doth affection arise of beautie, therefore a man may say for all that, that beautie is the cause of delite.

The Count answered: there be many other thinges also, that beside beautie oftentimes inflame our minds as manners, knowledge, speach, gestures, and a thousand moe (which peradventure after a sorte may be called beautie too) and above all, the knowing a mans selfe to be beloved: so that without the beautie you reason of, a man may bee most fervently in love:

But those loves that arise onely of the beautie which we discerne superficially in bodies, without doubt will bring a farre greater delite to him that hath a more skill therein, than to him that hath but a litle.

Therefore returning to our purpose, I believe Apelles conceived a farre greater joye in beholding the beautie of Campaspes, than did Alexander, for a man may easily believe, that the love of them both proceeded of that beautie, and perhaps also for this respect Alexander determined to bestow her upon him, that (in his mind) could know her more perfectly than he did.

Have you not reade of the five daughters of Croton, which among the rest of that people, Zeusis the Painter chose to make of all five one figure that was most excellent in beautie, and were renowned of many Poets, as they that were allowed for beautifull of him that ought to have a most perfect judgement in beautie?

Here the Lorde Cesar declaring him selfe not satisfied, nor willing to consent by any meanes, that anie man could tast of the delite that he felt in beholding the beautie of a certain woman, but hee him selfe began to speake, and then was there heard a great scraping of feet in the flore, with a cherme of loud speaking, and upon that every man turning him selfe about, saw at the chamber doore appeare a light of Torches, and by and by after entred in the Lord Generall [13] with a great and noble traine, who was then returned from accompanying the Pope a peece of the way.

And at the first entrie into the Palace, demaunding what the Dutches did, hee was certified what kinde of pastime they had in hande that night, and howe the charge was committed to Count Lewis, to entreat of courting. Therefore he hasted him as much as he could to come betime to heare somwhat.

And so soone as hee had saluted the Dutches, and setled the rest that were risen up at his comming, he sat him downe in the circle among them, and certaine of the chief of his traine, among which were the Marques Phebus of Ceva and Ghirardin brethren, Maister Hector of Rome, Vincent Calmeta, Horace Floridus, and many other. And when all was whist, the Lord Generall said.

My Lordes, my comming should bee too hurtfull if I shoulde hinder such good communication as I gesse was even now among you.

Therefore doe you me not this injurie, to deprive both your selves and mee of this pleasure.

Then answered Count Lewis, I believe (my Lord) silence ought rather to please all parties than speaking. For seeing it hath beene my lot this night before all other to take this travaile in hand, it hath now wearied me in speaking, and I weene all the rest in hearing, because my talke hath not beene worthie of this company, nor sufficient inough for the waightinesse of the matter I have beene charged withall, wherein since I have litle satisfied my selfe, I recken I have much lesse satisfied others.

Therefore (my Lorde) your lucke hath beene good to come at the latter end, and now shall it be well done to give the entreprise of that is behinde to an other that may succeede in my rowme. For whosoever hee be, I knowe well he will much better acquite him selfe than I should do, if I went forward with it, being thus wearie as I am.

This will I in no wise permit, answered the Lorde Julian, to be deceived of the promise ye have made. And I know well the Lorde Generall will not be against the understanding of that point.

And what promise was that, quoth the Count? The Lord Julian answered: To declare unto us in what sort the Courtier ought to use those good conditions and qualities which you say are meete for him.

The Lorde Generall, although he were but a childe in yeares, yet was hee wise and discrete, more than a man would thinke belonged unto those tender yeares of his, and in every gesture hee declared with a greatnesse of mind, a certaine quicknesse of wit, which did sufficiently prognosticate the excellent degree of honor and vertue, whereunto afterwarde he ascended.

Wherefore he saide incontinently: if all this be behind yet to bee spoken of (mee thinke) I am come in good season. For understanding in what sort the Courtier must use his good conditions and qualities, I shall know also what they are, and thus shall I come to the knowledge of all that have beene spoken hitherto.

Therefore sticke not (Count) to pay this debt, being alreadie discharged of one part thereof.

I should not have so great a debt to discharge, answered the Count, if the paines were equally devided, but the fault hath beene in giving a Ladie authoritie to command, that is too partiall: and so smyling he beheld the Ladie Emilia, which said immediately.

You ought not to complaine of my partialitie, yet since you doe it against reason, we will give one part of this honour, which you call paines, unto an other: and turning her unto Sir Fredericke Fergoso.

You (quoth she) propounded this devise of the Courtier, therefore reason willeth ye should say somewhat in it: and that shall be to fulfill the Lord Julians request, in declaring in what sort, manner and time the Courtier ought to practise his good conditions and qualities, and those other thinges which the Count hath saide are meete for him.

Then Sir Fredericke, Madame (quoth he) where ye will sever the sort, the time, and the manner of good conditions and qualities, and the well practising of the Courtier, ye will sever that can not be sundred: for it is these thinges that make the conditions and qualities good, and the practising good.

Therefore since the Count hath spoken so much and so well, and also saide somwhat of these circumstances, and prepared for the rest in his minde that he had to say, it were but reason he should go forwarde untill hee came to the end.

The Ladie Emilia answered: Set the cause you were the Count your selfe, and spake that your mind giveth you he would doe, and so shal all be well.

Then said Calmeta, my Lordes, since it is late, least Sir Fredericke should finde a scuse to utter that hee knoweth, I believe it were well done to defere the rest of the communication untill to morrow, and bestow the small time that remaineth about some other pastime without ambition.

The which being agreed upon of all hands, the Dutchesse willed the Lady Margaret and the Ladie Constance Fregosa, to shew them a daunce.

Wherefore Barletta immediately, a very pleasant Musition, and an excellent dauncer, who continually kept all the Court in mirth and joy, began to play upon his Instruments, and they hand in hand shewed them a daunce or two, with a very good grace and great pleasure to the lookers on.

That done, because it was farre in night, the Dutchesse arose upon her feete, and so every man taking his leave reverently of her, departed to his rest.

SECOND BOOK

The Second Booke of the Courtier, of Count Baldesser Castilion, unto Maister Alfonsus Ariosto

Not without marvel manie a time and often have I considered with my selfe, how one errour shoulde arise, the which because it is generallye seene in olde men, a man may beleve it is proper and naturall unto them: and that is, how (in a manner) al of them commend the times past, and blame the times present: dispraysinge our doings and maners, and whatsoever they did not in their youth:

Affirming moreover every good custome and good trade of living, every vertue, finally each thinge to decline alwaies from evil to worse.

And in good sooth it seemeth a matter verie wide from reason, and worthie to be noted, that ripe age which with long practise is wont to make mens judgements more perfect in other things, should in this behalfe so corrupt them, that they shoulde not discerne, y^t if the world waxed worse and worse, and the fathers were generally better than the children, we shoulde long ere this time have beene come to that utmost degree of ill that can not waxe worse. And yet doe we see not onely in our dayes, but also in times past that this hath alwaies beene the peculiar vice of that age.

The which is to be manifestly gathered by the wrytings of many most auncient authors, and especially Comedie writers, which expresse better than the rest, the trade of mans life.

The cause therfore of this false opinion in olde men, I

believe (in mine opinion) is, for that, yeares wearing away, carry also with them many commodities, and among other take away from the bloud a great part of the lively spirites that altereth the complexion, and the instruments waxe feeble, whereby the soule worketh her effects.

Therefore the sweete flowers of delyte vade away in that season out of our harts, as the leaves fall from the trees after harvest, and in steade of open and cleare thoughts, there entreth cloudie and troublous heavinesse accompanied with a thousand heart griefes: so that not onely the bloud, but the minde is also feeble: neither of the former pleasures receiveth it any thing els but a fast memorie, and the print of the beloved time of tender age, which when wee have upon us, the heaven, the earth, and each thing to our seeming rejoyceth and laugheth alwaies about our eyes, and in thought (as in a savorie and pleasant Garden) flourisheth the sweete spring time of mirth, so that peradventure it were not unprofitable, when now in the colde season, the Sunne of our life (taking away from us our delites) beginneth to draw towarde the West, to lose in like case therewithall the mindfulnes of them, and to finde out (as Themistocles saith) an arte to teach us to forget: for the senses of our bodies are so deceivable, that they beguile many times also the judgement of the minde.

Therefore (me thinke) olde men be like unto them, that sayling in a vessell out of an haven, beholde the ground with their eyes, and the vessell to their seeming standeth still and the shore goeth: and yet is it cleane contrarie, for the haven, and likewise the time and pleasures continue still in their estate, and we with the vessel of mortalitie fleing away, go one after another through the tempestuous sea, that swalloweth up and devoureth all thinges, neither is it graunted us at any time to come on shore againe, but alwaies beaten with contrarie windes, at the ende wee breake our vessell at some rocke.

Because therefore the minde of old age is without order subject to many pleasures, it can not taste them: and even as to them that bee sicke of a Fever, when by corrupt vapours they have lost their taste, all wines appeare most bitter, though they be precious and delicate in deede: so unto olde men for their unaptnesse, (wherein notwithstanding desire faileth them not) pleasures seeme without tast and cold, much differing from those that remember they have proved in foretime, although the pleasures in themselves be the selfe same.

Therefore when they feele them selves voide of them, it is a griefe, and they blame the time present for ill, not perceiving that this chaunce proceedeth of them selves, and not of the time.

And contrariwise, when they call to minde the pleasures past, they remember therewithall the time they had them in, and therefore commend it for good, because to their weening it carrieth with it a savour of it, which they felt in them when it was present.

By reason that in effect our mindes conceive an hatred against all thinges that have accompanied our sorrowes, and love such as have accompanied our pleasures.

Upon this it commeth, that unto a lover it is most acceptable, sometime to beholde a windowe though it be shut, because otherwhiles it may be his chaunce to see his maistresse there: in like manner to see a ring, a letter, a garden, or any other place, or what ever other thing he supposeth hath beene a witting testimoniall of his pleasures.

And contrariwise, oftentimes a faire trimmed and well decked Chamber is abhorred of him that hath been kept prisoner in it, or abidden therin any other sorrow.

And in my dayes I have knowne some that will never drinke of a cup like unto that wherein in their sicknes they had taken a medicine. For even as that window, ring, or letter, doth bring to the minde a sweete remembrance unto the one, that so much pleaseth him, for that he imagineth it was a parcell of his pleasures, so unto the other the chamber or cup seemeth to bring with the memorie, his sicknesse or imprisoning againe.

The verie same cause (I believe) moveth olde men to prayse the times past, and discommend the present.

Therefore as they talke of other thinges, so doe they also of Courtes, affirming such as have beene in their memory to be much more excellent and farre better furnished with notable men, than we see them to bee that are now adayes.

And immediately when they enter into this kinde of talke, they beginne to extoll with infinite prayses the Courtiers of Duke Philip, of Duke Borso, and declare the sayings of Nicholas Piccininus, and rehearse that in those times a man shoulde verie soldome have heard of a murther committed, and no combates, no crafts nor deceites, but a certaine faithfull and loving good meaning among all men, and an upright dealing. And in Courtes at that time there raigned such good conditions, and such honestie, that the Courtiers were (in a manner) religious folke: and woe unto him that shoulde have spoken an evil word of an other, or made but a signe otherwise than honestie to a woman.

And on the other side, they say in these dayes every thing is cleane contrary, and not onely that brotherly love and manerly conversation is lost among Courtiers, but also in Courtes there raigneth nothing els but envy and malice, ill manners, and a most wanton life in every kinde of vice: the women enticefull, past shame, and the men womanish.

They dispraise also the apparrell to be dishonest and too soft. To be short, they speake against infinit things, among the which many in very deede deserve to be discommended, for it can not be excused, but there are many evil and naughtie men among us, and this our age is much more full of vices, than was that which they commend.

But (me thinke) they do ful ill scanne the cause of this difference, and they be fonde persons, because they would have all goodnesse in the world without any ill, which is unpossible.

For since ill is contrarie to good, and good to ill, it is (in a manner) necessarie by contrarietie and a certaine counterpeise the one shoulde underproppe and strengthen the other, and where the one wanteth or encreaseth, the other to want or increase also: because no contrarie is without his other contrarie.

Who knoweth not that there should bee no justice in the worlde, were it not for wronge? no stoutnesse of courage, were there not faint harted? nor continencie, were there not incontinencie? nor health, were there not sicknesse? nor truth, were there not lyes? nor happinesse were there not mischaunces?

Therefore Socrates saith well in Plato, that hee marvaileth that Esope made not an Apologus or fable, wherin he might have fained that God, since hee coulde never couple pleasure and sorrow together, might have knit them with an extremitie, so that the beginning of the one should have beene the end of the other. For wee see no pleasure can delite us at any time if sorrow goeth not before.

Who can love rest well, unlesse hee have first felt the griefe of wearinesse? Who favoureth meate, drinke, and sleepe, if hee have not first felt hunger, thirst, and watching?

I believe therefore passions and diseases are given to men of nature, not principally to make them subject to them, for it were not meete that she which is the mother of all goodnesse, shoulde by her owne purposed advise give us so many evils, but since nature doth make health, pleasure and other goodnesse, consequently after these, were joyned diseases, sorrowes and other evils.

Therefore since vertues were graunted to the world for favor and gift of nature, by and by were vices by that linked contrarietie necessarily accompanied with them: so that the one encreasing or wanting, the other must in like manner encrease or want.

Therefore when our olde men prayse the Courtes of times past because there were not in them so vitious men, as some that are in ours, they do not know that there were not also in them so vertuous men, as some that are in ours.

The which is no wonder, for no ill is so evil, as that which ariseth of the corrupt seede of goodnesse.

And therefore where nature nowe bringeth forth much better wittes than she did tho, even as they that be given to goodnesse doe much better than did those of their time, so also they that bee given to ill doe much worse.

Therefore it is not to bee saide, that such as abstained from doing ill, because they knewe not how to doe it, deserve in that case any prayse: for although they did but a litle ill, yet did they the worst they knew.

And that the wittes of those times were generally much inferiour to these now adayes, a man may judge by all that hath proceeded from them, as letters, painting, statutes, buildings and all other things.

Againe these olde men discommend many things in us, which of them selves are neither good nor badde, onely because they did them not: and say it is no good sight to see yong men on horsebacke about the streetes, and especially upon Mules, nor to weare furres nor side garments in winter, nor to weare a cappe befor a man bee at the least eighteene yeares of age, and such other matters, wherein truely they be much deceived. For these fashions (beside that they be commodious and profitable) are brought up by custome, and generally men delite in them, as at that time they were contented to goe in their jacket, in their breechlesse hose, and in their lowe shoes with latchets, and (to appeare fine) carry all daye long a Hauke upon their fist, without purpose, and daunce without touching a womans hand, and used many other fashions, the which as they are now stale, so were they at that time much set by.

Therefore may it be lawfull for us also to follow the custome of our times, without controlement of these olde men, which going about to prayse themselves, say.

When I was twentie yeares olde I lay with my mother and sisters, nor a great while after wist I what women ment: and now children are not so soone crept out of the shell, but they know more naughtinesse, than they that were come to mans state did in those dayes.

Neither be they aware in so saying, that they confirme our children to have more wit than their old men.

Let them leave therefore speaking against our times, as full of vices: for in taking away them, they take also away the vertues. And let them remember that among the good men of auntient time, when as the glorious wits florished in the world, which in very deede were of most perfection in every vertue, and more than manly, there were also many most mischievous, which if they had still lived, shoulde have excelled our ill men so much in ill, as those good men in goodnes: and of this doe all Histories make full mention.

But unto these olde men I weene I have made a sufficient answere. Therefore we will leave apart this discourse, perhaps too tedious, but not altogether out of purpose: and being sufficient to have declared that the Courtes of our time are worthie no lesse praise than those that old men commend so much, we will attend to our communication that was had about the Courtier, whereby a man may easily gather in what degree the Court of Urbin was among the rest, and what manner a Prince and Ladie they were that had such noble wittes attending upon them, and how fortunate all they might call them selves that lived in that familiar fellowship.

When the day following therefore was come, there was great and sundrie talke betweene the gentlemen and Ladies of the Court upon the disputation of the night before: which arose a great part of it, upon the Lorde Generalles greedy desire, to understand as much as had beene said in the matter, who had enquired it almost of every man: and (as it is alwaies wont to come to passe) it was reported unto him sundrie waies, for some praysed one thing, some an other.

And also among many, there was a contention of the Countes own meaning, for every man did not so fully beare in mind the matters that had been spoken. Therefore almost the whole day was spent about talking in this, and as soone as night drew on, the Lord Generall commanded meat to bee set on the borde, and tooke all the Gentlemen with him.

And immediately after supper hee repayred to the Dutchesse chamber: who, beholding so great a company assembled sooner than they had done at other times, saide.

Me thinke, it is a great waight, Sir Fredericke, that is laide upon your shoulders, and a great expectation that you must satisfie.

Here not tarrying for Sir Frederickes aunswere, and what great waight (I beseech ye) is it, saide then Unico Aretino:

Who is so foolish that when he can doe a thing, wil not doe it in a fitte and due time? Reasoning in this wise about the matter everie man sat him downe in his wonted place and manner with very heedfull expectation of the propounded talke.

Then Sir Fredericke turning him to Unico, doe you not thinke then M. Unico (quoth he) that I am laden this night with a great and painefull burden, since I must declare in what sorte, manner and time, the Courtier hath to practise his good conditions and qualities, and to use those other things that are alreadie saide to bee meete for him?

Me thinke it is no great matter, answered Unico: and I believe a good judgement in the Courtier is sufficient for all this, which the Count saide well yesterday night that he ought to have: and in case be so, without any other precepts, I suppose hee may practise wel inough the thing that hee knoweth, in due time and after a good sorte.

The which to bring more particularly into rule, were too hard a matter, and perhaps more than needeth, for I know not who is so fond to goe about his fence, when the rest bee in their musicke: or to goe about the streetes dancing the morisco, though he could doe it never so well: or going about to comfort a mother that had buried her childe, to begin to talke with her of pleasant matters and merie conceites. I believe surely no gentleman will doe this, unlesse hee were cleane out of his wits.

Me thinke (M. Unico) quoth sir Fredericke then, ye harpe too much upon your extremities. For it happeneth otherwhile, a man is so fond, that hee remembreth not him selfe so easily, and oversights are not all alike.

And it may be, that a man shall abstaine from a common folly which is too manifest, as that is you speake of, to goe daunce the Morisco in the market place, and yet shall he not refraine from praysing him selfe out of purpose, from using a noysome sawsinesse, from casting out otherwhile a word thinking to make men laugh, which for that it is spoken out of time will appeare colde and without grace.

And these oversights oftentimes are covered with a certaine veile that suffereth a man not to forget who doth them, unlesse hee take no heede to them.

And although for many causes our sight discerneth but litle, yet for ambitions sake it is darkened in especiall, for every man willingly setteth forth him selfe in that he perswadeth himselfe he knoweth whether this perswasion of his be true or false.

Therefore the well behaving of a mans selfe in this case (me thinke) consisteth in certaine wisedome and judgement of choice, and to know more and lesse what encreaseth or diminisheth in thinges, to practise them in due time, or out of season.

And for all the Courtier bee of so good a judgement that he can discerne these differences, yet shall he the sooner compasse that he seeketh, if this imagination be opened with some rule, and the waies shewed him, and (as it were) the places where he should ground himselfe uppon, than if hee should take him selfe only to the generallitie.

For so much as therefore the Count yesterday night entreated upon Courtiership so copiously and in so good a manner, hee hath made me (truely) conceive no small feare and doubt that I shall not so throughly satisfie this noble audience in the matter that lyeth upon me to discourse in, as he hath doone in that was his charge. Yet to make my selfe partener in what I may of his praise, and to be sure not to erre (at the least in this parte) I will not contrarie him in any point.

Wherefore agreeing to his opinions, and beside the rest, as touching noblenesse of birth, wit and disposition of person, and grace of countenance, I say unto you that to get him worthie prayse and a good estimation with all men, and favour with such great men as he shal attend upon, me thinke it is behoveful he have the understanding to frame all his life and to set forth his good qualities generally in company with all men without purchasing him selfe envy.

The which how hard a matter it is of it selfe, a man may consider by the seldomnesse of such as are seene to attaine to that point: because we are all the sorte of us in very deede more inclined of nature to dispraise faultes, than to commend thinges well done. And a man would thinke that many by a certaine rooted malice, although they manifestly discerne the goodnesse, enforce them selves with all studie and diligence to finde in things either a fault, or at the least the likenesse of a fault.

Therefore it behoveth our Courtier in all his doings to be charie and heedfull, and what so he saith or doth to accompany it with wisedom, and not onely to set his delite to have in him selfe partes and excellent qualities, but also to order the tenor of his life after such a trade, that the whole may be answerable unto these parts, and see the selfe same to bee alwaies and in every thing such, that it disagree not from it selfe, but make one bodie of these good qualities, so that every deede of his may bee compact and framed of all the vertues, as the Stoikes say the duetie of a wise man is: although notwithstanding alwaies one vertue is the principall, but all are so knit and linked one to another, that they tende to one end, and all may be applyed and serve to every purpose.

Therefore it behoveth hee have the understanding to set them forth, and by comparison, and (as it were) contrarietie of the one, sometime to make the other better knowne: as the good painters with a shadow make the lights of high places to appeare, and so with light make low the shadowes of plaines, and meddle divers colours together, so that through that diversitie both the one and the other are more sightly to beholde, and the placing of the figures contrarie the one to the other is a helpe to them to doe the feate that the painters mind is to bring to passe.

So that lowlinesse is much to be commended in a gentleman that is of prowesse and well seene in armies: and as that fiercenesse seemeth the greater when it is accompanied with sober mood, even so doth sober moode encrease and shew it selfe the more through fiercenesse.

Therefore litle speaking, much doing, and not praysing a mans owne selfe in commendable deedes, dissembling them after an honest sorte, doth encrease both the one vertue and the other in a person that can discretely use this trade: and the like is to be saide in all the other good qualities.

Therefore will I have our Courtier in that he doth or saith to use certaine generall rules, the which (in my minde) containe briefly as much as belongeth to mee to speake.

And for the first and chiefe let him avoid (as the Count saide well in that behalfe yesternight) above all thinges curiositie.

Afterwarde let him consider well what the thing is he doth or speaketh, the place where it is done, in presence of whom, in what time, the cause why he doth it, his age, his profession, the end wherto it tendeth, and the meanes that may bring him to it: and so let him apply him selfe discreetly with these advertisements to what soever hee mindeth to doe or speake.

After Sir Fredericke had thus saide, he seemed to stay a while. Then saide M. Morello of Ortona: mee thinke these your rules teach but litle. And I for my part am as skilfull now as I was before you spake them, although I remember I have heard them at other times also of ye Friers with whom I have beene in confession, and I ween they terme them circumstances.

Then laughed Sir Fredericke and saide: if you doe well beare in minde, the Count willed yesternight that the chiefe profession of the Courtier shoulde bee in armes, and spake very largely in what sort he should doe it, therefore will we make no more rehearsall thereof.

Yet by our rule it may bee also understood, that where the Courtier is at skirmish, or assault, or battaile upon the lande, or in such other places of enterprise, he ought to worke the matter wisely in separating him selfe from the multitude, and undertake notable and bolde feates which hee hath to doe, with as litle company as he can, and in the sight of noble men that be of most estimation in the campe, and especially in the presence and (if it were possible) before the very eyes of his king or great personage he is in service withall: for in deede it is meete to set forth to the shew things wel done.

And I believe even as it is an evil matter to seeke a false renowne, and in the thing he deserveth no prayse at all, so is it also an ill matter to defraud a mans selfe of his due estimation, and not to seeke that prayse, which alone is the true rewarde of vertuous enterprises.

And I remember I have knowne of them in my time, that for all they were of prowesse, yet in this point they have shewed them selves but grosse headed, and put their life in as great hazarde to goe take a flocke of sheepe, as in being the formost to scale the walles of a battered towne, the which our Courtier will not doe if hee beare in mind the cause that bringeth him to warre, which ought to be onely his estimation.

And if he happen moreover to be one to shew feates of Chivalrie in open sights, at tilt, turney, or *Joco di canne*, or in any other exercise of the person, remembering the place where he is, and in presence of whom, hee shall provide before hand to be in his armour no lesse handsom and sightly than sure, and feede the eyes of the lookers on with all thinges that hee shall thinke may give a good grace, and shall doe his best to get him a horse set out with faire harnesse and sightly trappings, and to have proper devises, apt posies, and wittie inventions that may draw unto him the eyes of the lookers on as the Adamant stone doth yron.

He shall never be among the last that come forth into the listes to shew themselves, considering the people, and especially women take much more heede to the first than to the last: because the eyes and mindes that at the beginning are greedy of that noveltie, note every lite matter, and printe it: afterwarde by continuance they are not onely full, but wearie of it.

Therefore was there a noble Stageplayer in olde time that for this respect would alwaies be the first to come forth to play his part.

In like manner also if our Courtier doe but talke of armes, he shall have an eye to the profession of them hee talketh withall, and according to that frame himselfe, and use one maner of talke with men, and an other with women: and in case hee will touch any thing sounding to his owne praise, he shall doe it so dissemblingly as it were a chaunce and by the way, and with the discretion and warinesse that Count Lewis shewed us yesterday.

Doe you not now thinke (M. Morello) that our rules can teach somewhat? Trow you not that that friend of ours I tolde you of a few daies ago had cleane forgotten with whom hee spake, and why? When to entertaine a gentle woman whom he never saw before, at his first entring in talke with her, he began to tell how many men he had slaine, and what a hardie felow hee was, and how hee coulde play at two hand sword.

And had never done until he had taught her how to defend certaine strokes with a Pollaxe being armed, and how unarmed, and to shew how (in a mans defence) to laye hand upon a dagger, so that the poore gentlewoman stood upon thornes, and thought an houre a thousand yeare till she were got from him, for feare least he would goe nigh to kill her as hee had done those other.

Into these errours runne they that have not an eye to the circomstances which you say you have heard of Friers.

Therefore I say of the exercises of the bodie, some there are that (in a manner) are never practised but in open shew, as running at tilt, barriers, *Joco de canne*, and all the rest that depende uppon Armes.

Therefore when our Courtier taketh any of these in hand, first he must provide to bee so well in order for Horse, harnesse, and other furnitures belonging thereto, that he want nothing. And if he see not him selfe throughly furnished in all pointes, let him not meddle at all. For if he be not well, it can not be excused that it is not his profession.

After this, he ought to have a great considerataion in presence of whome hee sheweth him selfe, and who be his matches. For it were not meet that a gentleman should be present in person and a doer in such a matter in the countrey, where the lookers on and the doers were of a base sorte.

Then said the Lorde Gasper Pallavicin. In our countrey of Lumbardy these matters are not passed upon, for you shall see the yong gentleman upon the holy dayes come daunce all the day long in the sunne with them of the countrey, and passe the time with them in casting the barre, in wrastling, running and leaping. And I believe it is not ill done. For no comparison is there made of noblenesse of birth, but of force and sleight, in which thinges many times the men of the countrey are not a whit inferiour to gentlemen, and it seemeth this familiar conversation conteyneth in it a certaine lovely freenesse.

This daunzing in the sunne, answered Sir Fredericke, can I in no case away with all: and I can not see what a man shall gaine by it.

But who so will wrastle, runne and leape with men of the countrey, ought (in my judgement) to doe it after a sorte:

to prove himselfe and (as they are wont to say) for courtisie, not to try maistry with them: and a man ought (in a manner) to be assured to get the upper hand, else let him not meddle withall, for it is too ill a sight and too foule a matter and without estimation, to see a gentleman overcome by a carter, and especially in wrastling.

Therefore I believe it is well done to abstaine from it, at the least wise in presence of many, because if hee overcome his gaine is small, and his losse in being overcome very great.

Also they play at tenise (in manner) alwaies in open sight, and this is one of the common games, which the multitude with their presence much set forth.

I will have our Courtier therefore to doe this and all the rest beside handling his weapon, as a matter that is not his profession: and not to seeme to seeke or looke for any prayse for it.

Nor yet will I have him to be acknowne that he bestoweth much studie or time about it, although he doe it excellently well. Neither shall he bee like unto some that have a delite in musicke, and in speaking with whom soever, alwaies when he maketh a pause in their talke, beginne in a voice as though he would sing. Other walking in the streetes or in the Churches, goe alwaies dansing. Other meeting in the market place or wheresoever any friend, make a gesture as though they would play at fence, or wrastle according as their delite is.

Here saide the Lord Cesar Gonzaga, we have in Rome a young Cardinall that doth better than so, which feeling him selfe lustie of person, leadeth as many as come to visite him (though hee never saw them before) into a garden, and is very instant uppon them to strip themselves into their doublet to leape with him.

Sir Fredericke laughed, afterwarde hee proceeded on. There be some other exercises that may be done both openly and privately, as dancing: and in this I believe the Courtier ought to have a respect, for if he daunceth in the

presence of many, and in a place full of people, he must
(in my minde) keepe a certaine dignitie, tempered notwithstanding with a handsome and sightly sweetenesse of
gestures.

And for all he feeleth him selfe very nimble and to have
time and measure at will, yet let him not enter into that
swiftnesse of feet and doubled footinges, that we see are
very comely in our Barletta, and peradventure were unseemely for a gentleman: although privately in a chamber
together as we be now, I will not say but hee may doe both
that, and also dance the Morisco, and braulles,[14] yet not
openly unlesse hee were in a maske.

And though it were so that all men knew him, it skilleth
not, for there is no way to that, if a man will shew him
selfe in open sights about such matters, whether it be in
armes, or out of armes. Because to be in a maske bringeth
with it a certaine libertie and licence, that a man may
among other thinges take upon him the forme of that he
hath better skill in, and use bent studie and precisenesse
about the principall drift of the matter wherein he will shew
himselfe, and a certaine recklessnesse about that is not of
importance, which augmenteth the grace of the thing, as it
were to disguise a yong man in an olde mans attier, but so
that his garments be not a hindrance to him to shew his
nimblenesse of person. And a man at armes in forme of a
wilde shepheard, or some other such kinde of disguising,
but with an excellent horse and well trimmed for the purpose, because the minde of the lookers on runneth forthwith to imagin the thing that is offered unto the eyes at the
first shew, and when they behold afterwarde a far greater
matter to come of it than they looked for under that attire,
it delyteth them, and they take pleasure at it.

Therefore it were not meete in such pastimes and open
shewes, where they take up counterfeiting of false visages,
a prince should take upon him to bee like a prince in deede,
because in so doing, the pleasure that the lookers on receive
at the noveltie of the matter shoulde want a great deale, for

it is no noveltie at all to any man for a prince to bee a prince. And when it is perceyved that beside his being a prince, he will also beare the shape of a prince, he loseth the libertie to doe all those things that are out of dignitie of a prince.

And in case there any contentiō happen especially with weapon in these pastimes, he might easily make men believe that he keepeth the person of a prince because hee will not be beaten but spared of the rest: beside that, doing in sporte the verie same hee should doe in good earnest when neede required, it would take away his authoritie in deede, and would appeare in like case to be play also.

But in this point the prince stripping himselfe of the person of a prince, and mingling him selfe equally with his underlinges (yet in such wise that hee may bee known) with refusing superioritie, let him chalenge a greater superioritie, namely, to passe other men, not in authoritie, but in vertue, and declare that the prowesse is not encreased by his being a prince.

Therefore I say that the Courtier ought in these open sights of armes to have the selfe same respect according to his degree.

But in vauting, wrastling, running and leaping, I am well pleased he flee the multitude of people, or at the least be seene very seldome times. For there is no thing so excellent in the world, that the ignorant people have not their fil of, and smally regard it in often beholding it.

The like judgement I have to Musicke: but I woulde not our Courtier should doe as many doe, that as soone as they come to any place, and also in the presence of great men with whome they have no acquaintance at all, without much entreating set out them selves to shew as much as they know, yea and many times that they know not, so that a man would weene they came purposely to shewe themselves for that, and that it is their principall profession.

Therefore let our Courtier come to shew his musick as a thing to passe the time withall, and as he were enforced to

349

doe it, and not in the presence of noble men, nor of any great multitude.

And for all hee be skilfull and doth well understand it, yet will I have him to dissemble the studie and paines that a man must needes take in all thinges that are well done. And let him make semblance that he esteemeth but litle in himselfe that qualitie, but in doing it excellently well, make it much esteemed of other men.

Then saide the Lord Gasper Pallavicin. There are many sortes of musicke, as well in the brest [15] as upon instruments, therefore would I gladly learne which is the best, and at what time the Courtier ought to practise it.

Me thinke then answered Sir Fredericke, pricksong is a faire musicke, so it be done upon the booke surely and after a good sorte. But to sing to the lute is much better, because all the sweetnes consisteth in one alone, and a man is much more heedfull and understandeth better the feat manner, and the aire or veyne of it, when the eares are not busied in hearing any moe than one voice: and beside every litle errour is soone perceived, which happeneth not in singing with company, for one beareth out an other.

But singing to the lute with the dittie (me thinke) is more pleasant than the rest, for it addeth to the wordes such a grace and strength, that it is a great wonder.

Also all Instrumentes with freats are full of harmony, because the tunes of them are very perfect, and with ease a man may doe many thinges upon them that fill the mind with sweetnesse of musicke.

And the musicke with a sette of Violes doth no lesse delite a man: for it is verie sweet and artificiall.

A mans brest giveth a great ornament and grace to all these instruments, in the which I will have it sufficient that our Courtier have an understanding. Yet the more cunninger he is upon them, the better it is for him, without medling much with the instruments that Minerva and Alcibiades refused, because it seemeth they are noysome.

Now as touching the time and season when these sortes

of musicke are to bee practised: I believe at all times when a man is in familiar and loving company, having nothing else adoe. But especially they are meete to be practised in the presence of women, because those sights sweeten the mindes of the hearers, and make them the more apt to bee pierced with the pleasantnesse of musicke, and also they quicken the spirits of the very doers.

I am well pleased (as I have saide) they flee the multitude, and especially of the unnoble.

But the seasoning of the whole must be discretion, because in effect it were a matter unpossible to imagine all cases that fall. And if the Courtier bee a righteous judge of him selfe, hee shall apply him selfe well inough to the time, and shall discerne when the hearers minds are disposed to give eare and when they are not. He shall know his age, for (to say the truth) it were no meete matter, but an ill sight to see a man of any estimation being old, hore-headed and toothlesse, full of wrinkles, with a lute in his armes playing upon it, and singing in the middest of a company of womē, although he coulde doe it reasonably well. And that because such songes containe in them wordes of love, and in olde men love is a thing to be jested at: although otherwhile he seemeth among other miracles of his to take delite in spite of yeares to set a fire frosen heartes.

Then answered the Lord Julian: doe you not barre poore olde men from this pleasure (Sir Fredericke) for in my time I have knowne men of yeares have very perfect brestes and most nimble fingers for instruments, much more than some yong men.

I goe not about (quoth Sir Fredericke) to barre old men from this pleasure, but I wil barre you and these Ladies from laughing at that follie.

And in case olde men will sing to the lute, let them doe it secretely, and onely to rid their mindes of those troublesome cares and grievous disquieting that our life is full of: and to taste of that excellencie which I believe Pythagoras and Socrates savoured in musicke.

And set case they exercise it not at all: for that they have gotten a certaine habite and custome of it, they shall favour it much better in hearing, than he that hath no knowledge in it: For like as the armes of a Smith that is weake in other thinges, because they are more exercised, bee stronger than an other bodies that is sturdie, but not exercised to worke with his armes: even so the armes that bee exercised in musicke, doe much better and sooner discerne it, and with much more pleasure judge of it, than other, how good and quicke soever they be, that have not beene practised in ye variety of pleasant musicke: because those musical tunes pearce not, but without leaving any tast of themselves passe by ye eares not accustomed to heare them, although the verie wilde beastes feele some delite in melodie.

This is therefore the pleasure meete for olde men to take in musicke.

The selfe same I say of dauncing, for in deede these exercises ought to be left off before age constraineth us to leave them whether we will or no.

It is better then, answered here M. Morello halfe chafed, to except all old men, and to say that onely yong men are to be called Courtiers.

Then laughed Sir Fredericke and saide: Note (maister Morello) whether such as delite in these matters, if they bee not yong men, doe not studie to appeare young, and therefore dye their haire and make their bearde grow twice a weeke, and this proceedeth upon that nature saith to them in secrete, that these matters are not comely but for yong men.

All these Ladies laughed, because they knewe these wordes touched maister Morello, and he seemed somwhat out of patience at the matter.

Yet are there other entertainements with women, saide immediatly Sir Fredericke, meete for olde men.

And what be these (quoth maister Morello) to tell fables?

352

And that too, answered Sir Fredericke. But every age (as you know) carrieth with him his thoughts, and hath some peculiar vertue and some peculiar vice. And olde men for all they are ordinarilye wiser than yong men, more continent, and of a better foresight, yet are they withall more lavish in wordes, more greedy, harder to please, more fearefull, alwaies chafing in the house, sharpe to their children, and wil have every man wedded to their will.

And contrariwise, yong men are hardy, easie to be entreated, but more apt to brawling and chiding, wavering and unstedfast, that love and unlove all at a time: given to all their delites, and enimies to them that tell them of their profit.

But of all the other ages, mans state is most temperate, which hath now done with the curst prankes of youth, and not yet growne to auncientnes.

These then that bee placed (as it were) in the extremities, it is behovefull for them to know how to correct the vices with reason, that nature hath bredde in them.

Therefore ought old men to take heede of much praysing them selves, and of the other vices, that wee have saide are proper to them, and suffer the wisedom and knowledge to beare stroke in them that they have gottē by long experience, and to be (as it were) Oracles, to the which every man should haunt for counsaile, and have a grace in uttering that they know, applying it aptly to the purpose, accompanying with grace of yeares a certaine temperate and merry pleasantnesse.

In this wise shall they be good Courtiers, and be well entertained with men and women, and every man will at all times be glad of their company, without singing or dauncing: and when need requireth they shall shewe their prowesse in matters of waight.

The very same respect and judgement shall yong men have, not in keeping the fashion of olde men (for what is meete for the one, were not in all pointes so fit for the other: and it is a common saying, To much gravitie in yong men is an ill signe) but in correcting the naturall vices in them.

Therefore delight I in a yong man, and especially a man at armes, if hee have a certaine sagenesse in him and few wordes, and somewhat demure, without those busie gestures and unquiet manners which we see so many times in that age: for they seeme to have a certaine gift above other yong men.

Beside that, this milde behaviour containeth in it a kind of sightly fiercenesse, because it appeareth to be stirred, not of wrath but of judgement, and rather governed by reason than appetite: and this (in manner) alwaies is knowne in all men of stomacke.

And we see it likewise in brute beastes, that have a certaine noble courage and stoutnesse above the rest: as the Lion and the Egle: neither is it voide of reason, for so much as that violent and sodaine motion without wordes or other token of choler which with all force bursteth out together at once (as it were the shot of a gunne) from quietnes, which is contrarie to it, is much more violent and furious, than that which increaseth by degrees and waxeth hotte by litle and litle.

Therefore such going about some enterprise, are so full of wordes, they so leape and skip and can not stand still, that it appeareth they be ravished in those matters, and (as our maister Peter Mount saith well) they doe like children, that going in the night sing for feare, as though y^t singing of theirs should make them plucke up their spirits to bee the bolder.

Even as therefore in a yong man a quiet and ripe youth is to be commended, because it appeareth that lightnesse (which is the peculiar vice of that age) is tempred and corrected: even so in an olde man a greene and lively old age is much to be esteemed, because it appeareth that the force of the mind is so much, that it heateth and giveth a certaine strength to that feeble and colde age, and maintaineth it in that middle state, which is the better parte of our life.

But in conclusion all these good qualities shall not suffise our Courtier to purchase him the generall favour of great men, gentlemen and Ladies, if he have not also a gentle and loving behaviour in his dayly conversation.

And of this I believe verily it is a hard matter to give any manner rule, for the infinite and sundrie matters that happen in practising one with an other: for so much as among all men in the worlde, there are not two to be found that in every point agree in minde together.

Therefore he that must be plyable to bee conversant with so many, ought to guide himselfe with his own judgement. And knowing the difference of one man and an other, every day alter, fashion and manner according to the disposition of them he is conversant withall.

And for my part I am not able in this behalfe to give him other rules than the aforesaide, which one maister Morello learned of a childe in confessing himselfe.

Herein L. Emilia laughed and saide, you would ridde your hands of paines taking (Sir Fredericke) but you shall not escape so, for it is your part to minister talke untill it be bedtime.

And what if I have nothing to say (madam) how then, answered Sir Fredericke?

The Ladie Emilia saide: we shall now trye your wit. And if all be true I have hearde, there have beene men so wittie and eloquent, that they have not wanted matter to make a booke in the prayse of a flie, other in the praise of a quartaine Fever, an other in the prayse of baldnesse: doth not your hart serve you to finde out somewhat to say for one night of Courting?

We have alreadie, answered Sir Fredericke, spoken as much as will goe nigh to make two bookes. But since no excuse shall serve, I will speake until you shall thinke I have fulfilled though not my dutie, yet my power.

I suppose the conversation which ye Courtier ought

chiefly to bee plyable unto, with all diligence to get him favor, is the very same that he shall have with his prince. And although this name of conversation bringeth with it a certaine equalitie, that a man would not judge can raigne betweene the maister and the servant, yet will we so terme it for this once.

· I will have our Courtier therefore (beside that he hath and doth dayly give men to understand that he is of the prowesse which wee have said ought to be in him) to turne all his thoughts and force of minde to love, and (as it were) to reverence the prince hee serveth above all other thinges, and in his wil, manners and fashions, to bee altogether plyable to please him.

Here without any longer stay, Peter of Naples said: of these Courtiers now adayes ye shall finde ynow, for (me thinke) in few words ye have painted us out a joly flatterer.

You are farre deceived, answered Sir Fredericke, for flatterers love not their Lordes, nor their friendes, the which I say unto you I will have principally in our Courtier.

And to please him, and to obey his commandements whom he serveth, may bee done without flatterie, for I meane the commandements that are reasonable and honest, or such as of themselves are neither good nor bad, as in gamming and pastime, and giving him selfe more to some one exercise than to an other. And to this will I have the Courtier to frame him selfe, though by nature he were not enclined to it: so that whensoever his Lord looketh upon him, hee may thinke in his minde that hee hath to talke with him of a matter that he wil be glad to heare. The which shall come to passe if there bee a good judgement in him to understande what pleaseth his prince, and a wit and wisedom to knowe how to apply it, and a bent will to make him pleased with the thing which perhaps by nature should displease him.

And having these principles, he shall never be sadde before his prince, nor melancholy, nor so soleyn as many, that a man would weene were at debate with their Lordes, which is truely a hatefull matter.

He shal not be ill tongued, and especially against his superiours which happeneth oftentimes: for it appeareth that there is a storme in courtes that carrieth this condition with it, that alwaies looke who so receiveth most benefits at the Lordes hands, and is promoted from very base degree to high estate, hee is evermore complayning and reporteth worst of him: which is an uncomely thing, not onely for such as these be, but even for such as be ill handled in deed.

Our Courtier shall use no fond saucinesse. He shall be no carrier about of tryfling newes. He shall not be overseene in speaking otherwhile wordes that may offend, where his intent was to please.

He shall not be stubborne and full of contention, as some busie bodies that a man would weene had none other delyte but to vexe and stirre men like flies, and take upon them to contrarie every man spitefully without respect. He shall be no babler, not given to lightnesse, no lyar, no boaster, nor fond flatterer, but sober, and keeping him alwaies within his boundes, use continually, and especially abroad, the reverence and respect that becommeth the servant toward the maister.

And shall not doe as many that meeting a prince how great soever he be, if they have once spoken with him before come towarde him with a certaine smyling and friendlye countenance, as though they would make of one their equall, or shew favour to an inferiour of theirs.

Very seldom or (in manner) never shall he crave any thing of his Lorde for him selfe, least the Lorde having respect to deny it him for him selfe, should not graunte it him without displeasure, which is farre worse. Againe, in suing for others, he shall discretely observe the times, and his sute shall bee for honest and reasonable matters, and he shal so frame his sute, in leaving out those points that he shall knowe will trouble him, and in making easie after a comely sort the lettes, that his Lorde wil evermore graunt it him and though he deny it, hee shall not thinke to have offended him whom he meant not to doe, for because great men oftentimes after they have denyed a request to one that hath sued to them with great instance, think the person that laboured to them so earnestly for it, was verie greedy of it, and therefore in not obtaining it, hath cause to beare him ill will that denyed him it, and upon this suspition they conceive an hatred against that person and can never afterwarde brooke him nor afforde him good countenance.

He shal not covet to presse into the chamber or other secrete places where his Lord is withdrawne, unlesse hee be bid, for all he bee of great authoritie with him: because great men oftentimes when they are privately gotten alone, love a certaine libertie to speake and doe what they please, and therefore will not bee seene or heard of any person that may lightly deeme of them, and reason willeth no lesse.

Therefore such as speake against great men for making of their chamber persons of no great qualitie in other thinges, but in knowing how to attend about their person (me thinke) commit an error: because I can not see why they should not have the libertie to refresh their mindes, which we our selves would have to refresh ours.

But in case the Courtier that is inured with waightie affaires, happen to be afterwarde secretly in chamber with him, he ought to change his coate, and to deferre grave matters till an other time and place, and frame him selfe to pleasant communication, and such as his Lord will be willing to give eare unto, least hee hinder that good moode of his. But herein and in all other thinges, let him have an especiall regarde, that he bee not combrous to him.

And let him rather looke to have favour and promotion offered him, than crave it so openly in the face of the world, as many doe, that are so greedie of it, that a man would weene, the not obtaining it greeveth them as much as the losse of life: and if they chaunce to enter into any displeasure, or els see other in favour, they are in such anguish of mind, that they can by no meanes dissemble the malice, and so make all men laugh them to scorne, and many times they are the cause that great men favour some one, onely to spite them withall.

And afterwarde if they happen to enter into favor, then passing a meane, they are so dronken in it, that they know not what to doe for joy: and a man would weene that they wist not what were become of their feete and handes, and (in a manner) are readie to call company to behold them, and to rejoyce with them, as a matter they have not been accustomed withall. Of this sorte I will not have our Courtier to be.

I woulde have him to esteeme favour and promotion, but for all that not to love it so much, that a man should thinke hee coulde not live without it. And when he hath it, let him not shew him selfe new or straunge in it, nor wonder at it when it is offered him.

Nor refuse it in such sort as some, that for very ignorance receive it not, and so make men believe that they acknowledge themselves unworthie of it.

Yet ought a man alwaies to humble him selfe somewhat under his degree, and not receive favor and promotions so easily as they be offered him, but refuse them modestly, shewing he much esteemeth them, and after such a sort, that he may give him an occasion that offereth them, to offer them with a great deale more instance.

Because the more resistance a man maketh in such manner to receive them, the more doth he seeme to the prince that giveth them to be esteemed, and that the benefit which hee bestoweth is so much the more, as he that receiveth it, seemeth to make of it, thinking him selfe much honoured thereby.

And these are the true and perfect promotions, that make men esteemed of such as see them abroad: because when they are not craved, every man conjectureth they arise of true vertue, and so much the more, as they are accompanied with modestie.

Then saide the Lord Cesar Gonzaga, me thinke ye have this clause out of the Gospel, where it is writen: When thou art bid to a mariage, goe and sit thee down in the lowest roome, that whē he commeth that bid thee, he may say, Friend come higher and so it shall bee an honour for thee in the sight of the guestes.

Sir Fredericke laughed and saide: it were too great a sacriledge to steale out of the Gospel. But you are better learned in scripture than I was aware of: then he proceeded.

See into what daunger they fall sometime, that rashly before a great man enter into talke unrequired, and many times that y^t Lord, to scorne them withall, maketh no answere, and turneth his head to the other hand: and in case hee doth make answere, every man perceiveth it is done full scornefully.

Therefore to purchase favour at great mens handes, there is no better way than to deserve it. Neither must a man hope when he seeth an other in favor with a prince, for whatsoever matter, in folowing his steps to come to the same, because every thing is not fitte for every man. And ye shall finde otherwhile some one that by nature is so readie in his mery jestes, that what ever he speaketh, bringeth laughter with it, and a man would weene that he were borne onely for that: and if another that hath a grave fashion in him, of how good a wit soever he be, attempt the like, it will be very cold and without grace, so that hee will make a man abhore to heare him, and in effect will be like the Asse, that to counterfeite the dogge, would play with his maister.

Therefore it is meete eche man know him selfe, and his owne disposition, and apply him selfe thereto, and consider what thinges are meete for him to follow, and what are not.

Before you goe any further, saide here maister Vincent

Calmeta, if I have well marked, me thought ye saide right now, that the best way to purchase favour, is to deserve it: and the Courtier ought rather to tarry til promotions be offred him, than presumptuouslye to crave them.

I feare me least this rule be litle to purpose, and mee thinke experience doth us manifestly to understand the contrary: because now adaies very few are in favour with princes, but such as be malapert. And I wote well you can be a good witnesse of some, that perceiving themselves in small credite with their princes, are come up onely with presumption.

As for such as come to promotion with modestie, I for my part know none, and if I give you respite to bethinke your selfe, I believe ye will find out but few.

And if you marke the French court which at this day is one of the noblest in all Christendom, ye shal find that all such as are generally in favor there, have in them a certaine malapertnesse, and that not onely one with an other, but with the king him selfe.

Doe you not so say, answered Sir Fredericke, for in Fraunce there are very modest and curteous gentlemen. Truth it is, that they use a certaine libertie and familiaritie without ceremonies, which is proper and natural unto them, and therfore it ought not to bee termed malapertnesse. For in that manner of theirs, although they laugh and jeast at such as be malapert, yet doe they set much by them that seeme to them to have any prowesse or modestie in them.

Calmeta answered: marke the Spaniards that seeme the very maisters of Courtly fashions, and consider how many ye find that with women and great men are not most malapert, and so much worse than the Frenchmen, in that at the first shew they declare a certaine modestie? And no doubt but they bee wise in so doing, because (as I have said) the great men of our time doe all favour such as are of these conditions.

Then answered Sir Fredericke: I can not abide (maister

Vincent) that yee should defame in this wise the great
men of our time, because there be many notwithstanding
that love modestie: the which I doe not say of it selfe is
sufficient to make a man esteemed.

But I say unto you, when it is accompanied with great
prowesse, it maketh him much esteemed that hath it.
And though of it selfe it lye still, the worthie deedes speake
at large, and are much more to be wondred at, than if they
were accompanied with presumption or rashnesse.

I will not now deny, but many Spaniards there bee full
of malapertnesse: but I say unto you, they that are best
esteemed, for the most part are very modest.

Againe some other there be also so cold, that they flee
the company of men too out of measure, and passe a certaine degree of meane: so that they make men deeme
them either too fearefull, or to high minded. And this do
I in no case allowe, neyther would I have modestie so drie
and withered, that it should become rudenesse. But let
the Courtier, when it commeth to purpose, bee well spoken,
and in discourses upon states, wise and expert: and have
such a judgement that he may frame him selfe to the
manners of the Countrey where ever hee commeth.

Then in lower matters, let him be pleasantly disposed,
and reason well upon every matter, but in especiall tende
alwaies to goodnesse. No envious person, no carrier of an
evil tongue in his head: nor at any time given to seeke
preferment or promotion any naughtie way, nor by the
meane of any subtill practise.

Then saide Calmeta: I will assure you all, the other
waies are much more doubtfull and harder to compasse,
than is that you discommend: because now adayes (to
rehearse it againe) great men love none but such as be of
that condition.

Doe you not so say, answered then Sir Fredericke, for
that were too plaine an argument, that the great men of
our time were all vicious and naught, which is untrue, for
some there be that be good.

But if it fell to our Courtiers lot to serve one that were vicious and wicked, as soone as he knoweth it, let him forsake him, least hee tast of the bitter paine that all good men feele that serve the wicked.

We must pray unto God, answered Calmeta, to helpe us to good, for when we are once with them, wee must take them with all their faultes, for infinite respectes constraine a gentleman after he is once entred into service with a Lord, not to forsake him. But the ill lucke is in the beginning: and Courtiers in this case are not unlike unluckie foules bred up in an ill vale.

Me thinke, quoth Sir Fredericke, duetie ought to prevaile before all other respects, but yet so that a gentleman forsake not his Lord at the warre, or in any other adversitie, and be thought to doe it to follow fortune, or because hee seemed then to want the meane to profitte by: at all other times I believe hee may with good reason, and ought to forsake that service that among good men shall put him to shame, for all men will imagine that he that serveth the good, is good, and he that serveth the ill is ill.

I woulde have you to cleare me of one doubt that I have in my head, quoth then the Lorde Lodovicus Pius, namely whether a gentleman be bound or no, while he is in his princes service, to obey him in all thinges which he shall commaund, though they were dishonest and shameful matters.

In dishonest matters we are not bound to obey any bodie, answered Sir Fredericke.

And what? (replyed the Lord Lodovicus Pius) if I be in service with a prince who handleth me well, and hopeth that I will doe any thing for him that may bee done, and he happen to command me to kill a man, or any other like matter, ought I to refuse to doe it?

You ought, answered Sir Fredericke, to obey your Lord in all thinges that tend to his profit and honour, not in such matters as tende to his losse and shame.

363

Therefore if he shoulde command you to conspire treason, ye are not onely not bound to doe it, but yee are bound not to doe it, both for your owne sake, and for being a minister of the shame of your Lord.

Truth it is, many things seeme at the first sight good, which are ill: and many ill, that notwithstanding are good.

Therefore it is lawful for a man somtime in his Lords service, to kill not one man alone, but ten thousand, and to doe many other thinges, which if a man waigh them not as he ought, wil appeare ill, and yet are not so in deede.

Then answered the Lord Gasper Pallavicin. Ah by your faith talke somewhat in this case, and teach us howe wee may discerne things good in deede, from such as appeare good.

I pray you pardon mee, quoth Sir Fredericke, I wil not at this time enter into that, for there were too much to be saide in it: but all is to be referred to your discretion.

Cleare ye me at the least of an other doubt, replyed the Lord Gasper. And what doubt is that, quoth Sir Fredericke?

This answered the Lorde Gasper: I woulde knowe where I am charged by my maister in expresse wordes in an enterprise of businesse what ever it bee, what I have to doe therein: if I, at the deed doing thinking with my selfe in doing it more or lesse, or otherwise than my commission, to bring it more prosperously to passe, and more for his profit that gave mee that commission, whether ought I to governe my selfe according to the first charge, without passing the bounds of the commission, or els doe the thing that I judge to be best?

Then answered Sir Fredericke: in this point I would give you the judgement with the example of Manlius Torquatus, which in that case for over much affection slue his sonne, if I thought him worthie great prayse, (which to saye the truth) I doe not: although againe I dare not discommend him, contrarie to the opinion of so many hundred yeares. For out of doubt, it is a daungerous matter to swarve from the commandements of a mans superiors, trusting more in his owne judgement than in theirs, whom of reason he ought to obey.

Because if his imagination faile him, and the matter take ill successe, he runneth into the error of disobedience, and marreth that hee hath to doe, without any manner of excuse or hope of pardon. Againe, in case the matter come well to passe according to his desire, he must thanke his fortune, and no more adoe. Yet in this sorte a custome is brought up, to set litle by the commandement of the superior powers. And by his example that bringeth the matter to good passe, which peradventure is a wise man, and hath discoursed with reason and also aided by fortune, afterwarde a thousande other ignorant persons, and light headed, will take a stomacke to doe after their owne way, and to appeare wise and of authoritie, will swarve from the commission of their heads, which is a very ill matter, and oftentimes the cause of infinit errors.

But I believe in this point, the person whom the matter toucheth, ought to skanne it deeply, and (as it were) put in a balance the goodnesse and commoditie that is like to ensue unto him in doing contrarie to that he is charged, admitting his purpose succeed according to his hope.

And counterpeise on the other side the hurt and discommoditie that ariseth, if in doing otherwise than hee is cōmanded, the matter chance to have ill successe: and knowing that the hurt may bee greater and of more importance, if it succeed ill, then the profit, if it happen well, hee ought to refraine, and in every point to observe his commission.

And contrariwise, if the profit be like to bee of more importance, if it succeed well, than the hurt, if it happen amisse, I believe he may with good reason take in hande to doe the thing that reason and judgement shall set before him, and leave somewhat aside the very forme of the commission, after the example of good merchant

365

men, that to gaine much, adventure a litle, and not much, to gaine a litle.

I allow well that he have a regarde to the nature of the Lord he serveth, and according to that, frame himselfe. For in case he be rigorous (as many such there are,) I woulde never counsaile him, if he were my friend, to vary in any parcell from the appointed order, least it happen unto him, as a maister Inginner of Athens was served, unto whom P. Crassus Mutianus, being in Asia, and going about to batter a towne, sent to demaund of him one of ye two shipmastes that he had seene in Athens to make a Ram to beat downe the walles, and saide, hee woulde have the greater.

This Inginner, as he that was very cunning in deede, knew the greater would not very well serve for this purpose, and because the lesser was more easie to be carried, and also fitter to make that ordinance, he sent that to Mutianus. And after he had understood how the matter passed, he sent for the poore Inginner, and asked him why he obeyed him not, and not admitting any reason he could alledge for himselfe, made him to be stripped naked, beaten and whipped with rods, so that he dyed, seeming to him in steade of obeying him, he would have counsailed him: therefore with such rigorous men, a man must looke well to his doings.

But let us leave a part now this practise of the superiours, and come downe to the conversation that a man hath with his equalles or somewhat inferiors, for unto them also must a man frame himselfe, because it is more universally frequented, and a man findeth himselfe oftner among them, than among his superiors.

Although there be some fond persons, that being in company with the greatest friende they have in the world, if they meete with one better apparrelled, by and by they cleave unto him: and if an other come in place better than he, they doe the like altogether unto him.

And againe when the prince passeth through the market

place, through Churches or other haunted places, they make all men give them roome with their elbowes, till they come to their heeles, and though they have nothing to say to him, yet will they talk with him, and keepe him with a long tale, laugh, clappe the handes, and nod the heade, to seeme to have waightie businesse, that the people may see they are in favour.

But because these kind of men vouchsafe not to speake but with great men, I will not we should vouchsafe to speake of them.

Then the Lorde Julian, Since ye have (quoth he) made mention of these that are so readie to felowshippe themselves with the wel appareled, I would have you to shew us in what sort the Courtier shoulde apparrell himselfe, what kinde of garment doth best become him, and how he should fit himself in all his garments about his bodie: because we see infinit varietie in it.

And some are araied after the French fashion, some after the Spanish attyre, another will seeme a Dutchman. Neither want we of them also that will clothe themselves like Turkes: Some weare beardes, other doe not.

Therefore it were a good deed in this varietie, to shew how a man should choose out the best.

Sir Fredericke saide: In very deede, I am not able to give any certaine rule about rayment, but that a man should frame himselfe to the custome of the most. And since (as you say) this custome is so variable, and Italians are so desirous to take up other mens fashions, I believe every man may lawfully apparrell him selfe at his pleasure.

But I know not by what destinie it commeth, that Italie hath not as it was wont to have, a fashion of attire, known to be the Italian fashion: for although the bringing up of these new fashions maketh the first to appeare very grosse, yet were they peradventure a token of libertie, where these have beene a prognosticate of bondage, the which (me thinke) now is plainely inough fulfilled.

And as it is writtē, when Darius, the yeare before hee

fought with Alexander, had altered his sword he wore by his side, which was a Persian blade, into the fashion of Macedonie, it was interpreted by the Soothsayers, how this signified, that they into whose fashion Darius had altered the forme of his Persian blade, shoulde become rulers of Persia: even so where wee have altered our Italian fashions into straunge, me thinke it signified, that all they into whose fashions ours were chaunged, should come in to overcome us: the which hath beene too true: for there is not now a nation left that hath not left us their pray, so that there remaineth litle behinde to pray upon, and yet for all that cease they not to pray still.

But I will not enter into communication of sorrow: therefore it shall be well to speake of the raiment of our Courtier, the which so it be not out of use, nor contrary to his profession, in the rest (I thinke) it will doe well inough, so as the wearer be satisfied withall.

Truth it is, that I would love it the better, if it were not extreme in any part, as the Frenchman is wont to be sometime over long, and the Dutchman over short, but as they are both the one and the other amended and brought into better frame by the Italians.

Moreover I will holde alwaies with it, if it bee rather somewhat grave and auncient,[16] than garish. Therfore me thinke a blacke colour hath a better grace in garments than any other, and though not throughly blacke, yet somewhat darke, and this I meane for his ordinarie apparrell.

For there is no doubt, but upon armor it is more meete to have sightly and merrie colours, and also garments for pleasure, cut, pompous and rich.

Likewise in open shewes about triumphes, games, maskeries, and such other matters, because so appointed there is in them a certain livelinesse and mirth, which in deede doth well set forth feates of armes and pastimes.

But in the rest I coulde wish they should declare the solemnitie that the Spanish nation much observeth, for outwarde matters many times are a token of the inwarde.

Then said the Lord Cesar Gonzaga, I would not stick much at this, for so a gentleman be of worthinesse in other matters, his garments neither encrease nor minish reputation.

Sir Fredericke answered: ye say true. Yet which of us is there, that seeing a gentleman goe with a garment upon his backe quartered with sundrie colors, or with so many pointes tied together, and all about with laces and fringes set overthwart, will not count him a verie dizarde, or a common jeaster?

Neither dizard, quoth maister Peter Bembo, nor a jeaster would a man count him, that had lived any while in Lumbardy, for there they goe all so.

Why then, answered the Dutchesse smyling, if they goe all so, it ought not to be objected to them for a vice, this kinde of attire being as comely and proper to them, as it is to the Venetians, to weare their long wyde sleeves, and to the Florentines their hoodes.

I speake no more of Lombardy quoth sir Fredericke, than of other places, for in every nation yee shall finde both foolish and wise.

But to speake that I thinke is most requisite as touching apparell, I will have the Courtier in all hys garmentes handsome and cleanely, and take a certaine delight in modest precisenes, but not for all that after a womanish or light manner, neyther more in one poynte than in another, as wee see many so curious about their haire, that they forget all the rest.

Other delite to have their teeth faire: other in their beard: other in buskins: other in caps: other in coiffes. And so it commeth to passe, that those few things which they have clenly in them, appeare borrowed ware, and all the rest which is most fond, is knowne to be their owne. But this trade will I have our Courtier to flie by my counsaile, with an addition also, that he ought to determine with him selfe what he will appeare to be, and in such sort as he

369

desireth to be esteemed, so to apparrel himselfe, and make his garments helpe him to bee counted such a one, even of them that heare him not speake, nor see him doe any manner thing.

I thinke it not meet, quoth the Lord Pallavicin, neither is it used amongst honest men, to judge mens conditions by their garments, and not by their wordes and deeds, for many a man might bee deceived: and this proverbe ariseth not without cause: The habite maketh not The Monke.

I say not, answered Sir Fredericke, that men shoulde give a resolute judgement by this alone, of mens conditions, and that they are not knowne by words and deedes, more than by the garments. But I say that the garment is withal no small argument of the fancy of him that weareth it, although otherwhile it appeare not true. And not this alone, but all the behaviour, gestures and manners, beside wordes and deeds, are in a judgement of inclination of him in whom they are seene.

And what things be those, answered the Lorde Gasper, that you finde we may give judgement upon, that are neither wordes nor deeds?

Then saide Sir Fredericke: You are too subtill a Logitian, but to tell you as I meane, some operations there are that remaine after they are done, as building, writing, and such other: some remaine not, as these that I meane now. Therefore doe I not count in this purpose, going, laughing, looking, and such matters to bee operations, and notwithstanding outwardly doe give many times a knowledge of that in writing.

Tell me, did you not give your judgement upon that friend of ours we communed off this morning past, to be a foolish and light person, as soone as you saw he wryed his head, and bowed his bodie, and invited with a chearefull countenance the company to put off their caps to him.

So in like manner, when you see one gaze earnestly w^h his eies abashed, like one that hath litle wit: or that laugheth so fondly as doe those dumbe men, with the great wennes in their throat, that dwell in the mountaines of Gergamo, though hee neither speake ne doe any thing els, will you not count him a very foole?

Ye may see then, that these behaviours, manners, and gestures, which I minde not for this time to terme Operations, are a great matter to make men knowne.

But me thinke there is an other thing that giveth and diminisheth much reputation: namely, the choise of friends, with whom a man must have inwarde conversation. For undoubtedly reason willeth, that such as are coupled in strayte amitie, and unspeakable company, should be also alike in will, in minde, in judgement, and inclination.

So that who so is conversant with the ignorant or wicked, he is also counted ignorant and wicked. And contrariwise, he that is conversant with the good, wise, and discrete, hee is reckened such a one. For it seemeth by nature, that every thing doeth willingly felowshippe with his like.

Therefore I believe that a man ought to have respect in the first beginning of these friendships, for of two neare friendes, who ever knoweth the one, by and by he imagineth the other to bee of the same condition.

Then answered maister Peter Bembo: To be bound in friendship with such agreement of minde as you speake of, me thinke in deede a man ought to have great respect, not onely for getting or loosing reputation, but because now adayes ye finde verie few true friendes.

Neither doe I believe that there are any more in the world, those Pylades and Orestes, Theseus and Perithous, nor Scipio and Lælius, but rather it happeneth dayly, I wote not by what destinie, that two friendes, which many yeares have lived together with most hartie love, yet at the ende beguile one an other, in one manner or other, either of malice or envy, or for lightnesse, or some other ill cause: and each one imputeth the fault to his fellow, of that which perhaps both the one and the other deserveth.

Therefore because it hath happened to mee more than once to be deceived of him whom I loved best, and of whom I hoped I was beloved above any other person, I have thought with my selfe alone otherwhile to bee well done, never to put a mans trust in any person in the worlde, nor to give him selfe so for a pray to friende how deare and loving soever he were, that without stoppe a man should make him partaker of all his thoughts, as he would his owne selfe: because there are in our mindes so many dennes and corners, that it is unpossible for the wit of man to know the dissimulations that lye lurking in them.

I believe therefore that it is well done to love and beare with one more than an other, according to their deserts and honestie: but not for all that so to assure a mans selfe, with this sweete baite of friendship, that afterward it should bee too late for us to repent.

Then Sir Fredericke, Truely (quoth he) the losse should be much more than the gaine, if that high degree of friendship should be taken from the fellowship of man, which (in mine opinion) ministreth unto us al the goodnesse contained in our life: and therefore will I in no case consent to you, that it is reasonable, but rather I can finde in my hart to conclude, and that with most evident reasons, that without this perfect friendship, men were much more unluckie than all other living creatures.

And albeit some wicked and prophane taste of this holy name of friendship, yet is it not for all that to bee so rooted out of mens mindes, and for the trespasse of the ill, to deprive the good of so great a felicitie. And I believe verily for my part, there is here among us moe than one couple of friends, whose love is indissoluble and without any guile at all, and to endure untill death, with agreement of will, no lesse than those men of old time, whom you mentioned right now. And so is it alwaies, when beside the inclination that commeth from above, a man chooseth him a friende like unto him selfe in conditions. And I meane the whole to consist among the good and vertuous men, because the friendshippe of the wicked, is no friendship.

I allow well that this knot, which is so strayte, knit or

binde no moe than two, els were it in hazarde: for (as you know) three Instrumentes of musicke are hardlier brought to agree together than two.

I would have our Courtier therefore to finde him out an especiall and hartie friend, if it were possible, of that sorte wee have spoken off. Then according to their deserts and honestie, love, honour and observe all other men, and alwaies doe his best to fellowshippe himselfe with men of estimation that are noble and knowne to bee good, more than with the unnoble and of small reputation, so he bee also beloved and honoured of them. And this shall come to passe, if he be gentle, lowly freeharted, easie to bee spoken to, and sweete in companie, humble and diligent to serve, and to have an eye to his friendes profit and estimation, as wel absent as present, bearing with their naturall defaults that are to be borne withall, without breaking with them upon a small ground, and correcting in himselfe such as lovingly shall bee tolde him, never preferring himselfe before other men in seeking the highest and chiefe roomes of estimation, neither in doing as some that a man would weene despised the worlde, and with a noysome sharpenesse will tell every man his duetie, and beside that they are full of contention in every tryfling matter, and out of tune, they controll whatsoever they do not themselves, and alwaies seeke cause to complaine of their friendes, which is a most hatefull thing.

Here when Sir Fredericke had made a stay, the Lorde Gaspar Pallavicin saide: I would have you to expresse somewhat more particularly this cõversatiõ with friends, than you doe, for in deede you keepe your selfe too much in the general, and touch unto us things (as it were) by the way.

How by the way? answeryd Sir Fredericke, Would you have me to tell you also the very wordes that a man must use? Suppose you not then we have sufficiently communed of this?

I thinke yea, answered the Lord Gasper. Yet doe I desire to understande also some particular point of the manner of entertainement among men and women, which (me thinke) is very necessarie matter, considering the most part of mans time is spent therein in Courtes, and if it were alwaies after one manner wise, a man would soone waxe wearie of it.

Me thinke, answered Sir Fredericke, we have given the Courtier a knowledge in so many thinges, that hee may well varie his conversation, and frame himselfe according to the inclination of them he accompanieth him selfe withall, presupposing him to be of a good judgemēt, and otherwhile to guide him selfe. And according to the time otherwhile, have an eye to great matters, and sometime to pastimes and games.

And what games, quoth the Lord Gasper?

Sir Fredericke answered: let us aske counsaile of Frier Seraphin that dayly inventeth new.

But in good earnest, replyed the Lorde Gasper, doe you not thinke it a vice in the Courtier to play at Dice and Cardes?

I thinke it none, quoth Sir Fredericke, unlesse a man apply it too much, and by reason of that, setteth aside other thinges more necessarie, or els for none other intent but to get money and to beguile his fellow, and in his losse fume and take on so, that it might bee thought a token of covetousnesse.

The Lord Gasper answered: and what say you to the game at Chests?

It is truly an honest kind of entertainment and wittie, quoth Sir Fredericke. But me thinke it hath a faulte, which is, that a man may be too cunning at it, for who ever will bee excellent in the play of Chests, I believe he must bestow much time about it, and apply it with so much studie, that a man may as soone learne some noble science, or compasse any other matter of importance, and yet in the ende in bestowing all that labour, hee knoweth no more but a game.

374

Therefore in this I believe there happeneth a verie rare thing, namely, that the meane is more commendable, than the excellencie.

The Lord Gasper answered: there be many Spaniards excellent at it, and in many other games, which for all that bestow not much studie upon it, nor yet lay aside the compassing of other matters.

Believe not the contrarie answered Sir Fredericke, but they bestow much studie upon it, although fainingly.

As for those other games ye speake of beside Chestes, peradventure they are like many which I have seene that serve to small purpose, but onely to make the common people wonder.

Therefore (in mine opinion) they deserve none other praise or rewarde, than the great Alexander gave unto him, that standing a far off, did so well broch Chiche peason upon a needle.

But because fortune, as in many other thinges, so in the opinion of men seemeth to beare a great stroke, it is sometime seene that a gentleman how well conditioned soever he be, and endewed with many qualities, shall be litle set by of a great man, and (as they say) groweth not in favour with him, and without any cause why, that a man may discerne.

Therefore when he commeth into his presence without any acquaintance before hand, with the rest about him, though he be wittie and readie in his answeres, and sheweth himselfe handsomely in his behaviors, in his conditions and wordes, and in what ever belongeth unto him, yet will that Lord set light by him, and rather give him an ill countenance, than esteeme him: and of this will arise that the rest immediately will frame themselves to their Lords minde, and it shall seeme unto every man that he is litle worth, neither will any man regard him, or make of him, or laugh at his pleasant sayings, or set anie thing by him, but will begin all to serve him sluttish pranckes, and make him a Cousin.

Neither shall good answeres suffise the poore soule, nor yet the taking of thinges as spoken in jeast, for even the very Pages will bee at him, so that were he the fairest conditioned man in the world, he can not choose but bee thus baited and jeasted at.

And contrariwise, if a prince be inclined to one that is most ignorant, that can neither do nor say any thing, his manners and behaviors, (be they never so fonde and fool-ish) are many times commended with acclamation and wonder of all men, and it seemeth that all the Court be-holdeth and observeth him, and every man laugheth at his boording and certaine carterly jestes, that shoulde rather move a man to vomit than to laugh: so addicted and stiffe men be in the opinions that arise of the favorers and dis-favorers of great men.

Therefore will I have our Courtier the best he can (beside his worthinesse) to helpe himselfe with wit and arte, and when ever he hath to goe where he is straunge and not knowne, let him procure that there goe first a good opinion of him, before he come in person, and so worke, that they may understand there, how he is in other places with Lordes, Ladies, and gentlemen in good estima-tion: because that fame, which seemeth to arise of the judgements of many, engendreth a certaine assured con-fidence of a mans worthiness, which afterwarde finding mens mindes so setled and prepared, is easily with deedes maintained and encreased, beside that a man is eased of the trouble that I feele, when I am asked the question Who I am, and what is my name.

I can not see what this can helpe, answered maister Bernard Bibiena, for it hath sundrie times happened unto me, and I believe to many moe, after I had grounded in my mind by report of many men of judgement a matter to be of great perfection before I had seene it, when I had once seene it, I fainted much, and I was much de-ceived in mine imagination, and this proceeded of nothing els, but of giving too much credit to fame and report, and of conceiving in my minde so great an opinion, that measuring it afterwarde with the truth, the effect, though it were great and excellent, yet in comparison of that I had imagined of it, seemed very slender unto me.

Even so (I feare me) may also come to passe of that Courtier. Therefore I can not see how it were wel done to give these expectations, and to send that fame of a man before: because our mindes many times fashion and shape thinges, which is unpossible afterwarde to answere to and fulfill, and so doth a man lose more than he gaineth by it.

Here Sir Fredericke said: Thinges that come to you and many moe being lesse in effect than the fame is of them, are for the most part of that sorte, that the eye at the first sight may give a judgement of them. As if you have never beene at Naples or at Rome, when you heare men commune of it, you imagine much more of it, than perhaps you finde afterwarde in sight. But in the conditions of men it is not alike, because that you see outwardly is the least part.

Therefore in case the first day you heare a gentleman talke, you perceive not the worthinesse in him that you had before imagined, you doe not so soone lose the good opinion of him, as you do in the thinges wherein your eye is by and by a judge. But you will looke from day to day, to have him disclose some other hid vertue, keeping notwithstanding alwaies the stedfast imprinting which you have risen by the words of so many.

And this man then being (as I set case our Courtier is) of so good qualities, hee will every houre strengthen you more and more, to give credence to that fame, for that with his doinges hee shall give you a cause, and you will ever surmise somewhat more to be in him, than you see.

And certainly it can not be denied, but these first imprintinges have a very great force, and a man ought to take much heede to them.

And that you may understand of what waight they be, I say unto you, that I have knowne in my dayes a gentleman, who albeit hee was of sufficient mannerly behaviour and modest conditions and well scene in armes, yet was he not in any of these qualities so excellent, but there were many as good and better.

Notwithstanding (as lucke served him) it befell that a gentlewoman entred most fervently in love with him, and this love dayle encreasing through declaration that the yong man made to agree with her in that behalfe, and perceiving no manner meane howe they might come to speake together, the gentlewoman provoked with too great passion opened her desire unto another gentlewoman, by whose meane she hoped upon some commoditie: this woman neither in bloud nor in beautie was a whit inferior to the first.

Upon this it came to passe, that she perceyving her talke so effectually of this yong man, whom she never sawe, and knowing how that gentlewoman, whom she wist well was most discrete and of a very good judgement, loved him extremely, imagined forthwith that hee was the fairest, the wisest, the discreetest, and finally the worthiest man to be beloved that was in the worlde: and so without seeing him, fell so deepe in love with him, that she practised what she coulde come by to him, not for her friend, but for her own selfe, and to make him answerable to her in love, the which she brought to passe without any great adoe, for (to say the truth) she was a woman rather to be sought upon than to seeke upon others.

Now heare a pretie chance. It happened not long time after, that a letter which this last gentlewoman writ unto her lover, came to the hands of an other, that was a noble woman of excellent qualities and singular beautie, who being (as the most part of women are) inquisitive and greedy to understande secrets, and especially of other women, opened the letter, and in reading it, perceived it was written with an extreme affection of love.

And the sweete words full of fire that shee read, first moved her to take compassion on that Gentlewoman: for she knew verye well from whom the letter came, and to whom it went.

Afterwarde they had such force, that scanning them in her minde, and considering what manner a man this was like to bee, that coulde bring that woman into such love, by and by she fell in love with him, and that letter was more effectuall to worke in this case, than peradventure it woulde have beene if it had beene sent her from the yong man him selfe.

And as it chanceth sometime, poyson prepared in a dish of meate for some great man, killeth him that tasteth first of it, so this poore gentlewoman because she was too greedy, dranke of the amorous poison that was ordained for another.

What shall I say to you? the matter was verie open, and spred so abroad that many women beside these, partly in despite of the other, and partly to doe as the other did, bent all their studie and diligence to enjoy his love, and for a season played as children doe at Chopcherie, and the whole proceeded of the first opinion which that woman conceived that heard him so praysed of an other.

Now the Lorde Gasper Pallavicin answered her smiling. You to confirme your judgement with reason, alleage unto me womens doinges, which for the most part are voide of all reason. And in case you woulde tell all, this good fellow so favored of so many women was some doult, and a man in deede not to be regarded, because the manner of them is alwaies to cleave to the worst, and like sheepe to doe that they see the first doe, bee it well or ill.

Beside that, they be so spitefull among themselves, that if he had beene a monstrous creature they would surely have stolen him one from another.

Here many beganne and (in manner) all, to speake against the Lord Gasper, but the Dutchesse made them all to holde their peace. Afterwarde she said smyling.

If the ill which you speak of women were not so farre wide from the truth, that in speaking it, it hurteth and

shameth rather the speaker than them, I woulde suffer you
to be answered. But I will not have you, in speaking against
you with a number of reasons, forsake this your ill custome,
because you may bee sharpely punished, for this offence
of yours: which shall be with the ill opinion that all they
will conceive of you that heare you talke in this wise.

Then answered Sir Fredericke: Say not, my Lord Gasper,
that women are so void of reason, though sometime they
apply them selves to love more through the judgement of
others than their owne.

For great men and many wise men, doe often times the
like. And if it be lawful to tell the truth, you your selfe
and all wee here have many times, and doe at this present
credite the opinion of others, more than our owne.

And that it is true, not long agoe there were certain
verses shewed here, that bore the name of Senazarus, and
were thought of every body very excellent, and praysed out
of reason, afterwarde when they were certainely knowne
to be an other mans doing, they lost by and by their reputation, and seemed worse than meane.

And where there was song in the Dutchesse presence
here a certaine Antheme, it never delyted nor was reckned
good, until it was knowne to be the doing of Josquin de
Pris.

But what token wil you have more plainer of opinion?
Doe you not remember where you your selfe dranke of one
selfe wine, sometime ye said it was most perfect, and
another time, without all taste? and that because you had
beene perswaded they were two sortes, the one of the
coast of Genua, and the other of this soile.

And when the error was opened, by no meanes you
would believe it: that false opinion was grounded so stifly
in your head, which arose notwithstanding of other mens
words.

Therfore ought the Courtier diligently to apply in the
beginning to give a good opinion of him selfe, and consider
what a harmefull and deadly thing it is, to run in the con-

trarie. And in this danger more than other men doe they stand, that will make profession to bee very pleasant and with this their merry fashion, purchase them a certaine libertie, that lawfully they may say and doe what commeth in their minde, without thinking upon it.

For such men many times enter into certaine matters, which when they can not get out againe, will afterwarde helpe them selves with raising laughter, and it is done with so ill a grace, that it will in no wise frame, whereby they bring a very great lothsomnesse upon as many as see or heare them, and they remaine very colde and without any grace or countenance.

Sometime thinking therby to be subtill witted and full of jestes, in the presence of honourable women, yea, and oftentimes to themselves, they thrust out filthy and most dishonest wordes: and the more they see them blush at it, the better Courtiers they recken themselves and still they laugh at it, and rejoyce among them selves at this goodly vertue they thinke they have gotten them.

But they practise this beastlinesse for none other cause, but to be counted good fellowes.

This is the name alone which they deeme worthie praise, and which they brag more of, than of any thing els, and to get it them, they speake the foulest and shamefullest villanies in the world.

Many times they shoulder one an other downe the stayers, and hurle billets and brickes, one at anothers heade.

They hurle handfuls of dust in mens eyes. They cast horse and man into ditches, or downe on the side of some hill.

Then at table, potage, sauce, gelies, and what ever commeth to hand, into the face it goeth. And afterward laugh: and who so can doe most of these tricks, he counteth him selfe the best and gallantest Courtier, and supposeth that he hath wonne great glory.

And in case otherwhile they get a Gentleman in their

pleasaunt pastimes, that will not give himselfe to such horse play, they say by and by: He is too wise, we shall have him a Counseller, he is no good fellow.

But I will tell you a worse matter. Some there be that contend and lay wager, who can eate and drinke more unsaverie and stinking thinges, and so abhorring and contrarie to mans senses, that it is not possible to name them without very great lothsomnesse.

And what thinges bee those, quoth the Lord Lodovicus Pius?

Sir Fredericke answered: Let the Marquesse Phebus tell you, for hee hath often seene it in Fraunce, and peradventure felt it.

The Marquesse Phebus answered: I have seene none of these thinges done in Fraunce more than in Italie. But looke what good things the Italians have in their garments, in feasting, in banketing, in feates of armes and in every other thing that belongeth to a Courtier, they have it all of the Frenchmen.

I deny not answered Sir Fredericke, but there are also among the Frenchmen very honest and sober gentlemen, and for my part I have knowne many (without peradventure) worthie all prayse. But yet some there are of litle good manner. And to speake generally (me thinke) the Spaniardes agree more with Italians, in conditions, than Frenchmen: because (in my minde) the peculiar quiet gravitie of the Spaniardes is more agreeable to our nature than the quicke livelinesse that is perceived in the French nation almost in everie gesture: which is not to be discommended in them, but is rather a grace, for it is so naturall and proper to them, that there is no manner affection or curiositie in it.

There are many Italians that woulde faine counterfaite their fashion, and can doe nought els but shake the heade in speaking, and make a legge with an ill grace, and when they come out of their doores into the Citie, goe so fast that good footemen can scant overtake them, and with

THE COURTIER

these manners they weene them selves good Frenchmen,
and to have of that libertie: which (I wis) chaunceth very
seldome saving to such as are brought up in Fraunce, and
have learned that fashion from their childhood.

The like is to be saide in the knowledge of sundrie
tongues, which I commend much in our Courtier, and
especially Spanish and Frēch, because the entercourse of
both the one nation and the other is much haunted in
Italy, and these two are more agreeable unto us than unto
any of the rest, and those two Princes for that they are
very mightie in warre and most royall in peace, have their
Court alwaies furnished with valiant gentlemen, which
are dispersed throughout the worlde, and againe we must
needes practise with them.

I will not now proceede to speake any more particularlye
of matters too well knowne, as that our Courtier ought not
to professe to be a glutton nor a drunkard, nor riotous and
unordinate in any ill condition, nor filthie and unclenly in
his living, with certaine rude and boysterous behaviors that
smell of the plough and cart a thousand mile off, for hee
that is of that sorte, it is not onely not to be hoped that he
will make a good Courtier, but he can be set to no better
use than to keepe sheepe.

And to conclude, I say that (to doe well) the Courtier
ought to have a perfect understanding in that wee have
saide is meete for him, so that every possible thing may be
easie to him, and all men wonder at him, and hee at no
man: meaning notwithstanding in this point that there be
not a certaine loftie and unmannerly stubbornesse, as some
men have that shew themselves not to wonder at the
things which other men doe, because they take upon them
that they can doe them much better: and with their silence
doe commend them as unworthy to bee spoken of, and will
make a gesture (in a manner) as though none beside were
(I will not say their equal) but able to conceive the understanding of the prowesse of their cunning.

Therfore ought the Courtier to shunne these hatefull

383

manners, and with gentlenesse and courtesie prayse other mens good deedes.

And though hee perceive himselfe excellent and farre above others, yet shew that he esteemeth not himselfe for such a one.

But because these so full perfections are very seldome found in the nature of man, and perhaps never, yet ought not a man that perceiveth himselfe in some part to want, to lay aside his hope to come to a good passe, though he can not reach to that perfect and high excellencie which hee aspireth unto.

Because in every arte there bee many other places beside the best, all praise worthie, and he that striveth to come by the highest, it is seldome seene that hee passeth not the meane.

I will have our Courtier therefore, if he finde himselfe excellent in any thing beside armes, to set out himselfe, and get estimation by it after an honest sorte, and be so discrete and of so good a judgement, that he may have the understanding after a comely manner, and with good purpose to allure men to heare or to looke on that hee supposeth himselfe to be excellent in, making semblant alwaies to doe it, not for a bragge and to shewe it for vaine glory, but at a chance, and rather praied by others, than comming of his owne free will.

And in every thing that he hath to doe or to speake, if it be possible, let him come alwaies provided and thinke on it before hand, shewing notwithstanding the whole to be done *ex tempore*, and at the first sight.

As for the things he hath but a meane skill in, let him touch them (as it were) by the way, without grounding much upon them, yet in such wise that a man may believe he hath a great deale more cunning therein, than he uttereth: as certaine Poets sometime that harped upon very subtil pointes of Philosophie, or rather sciences, and peradventure had small understanding in the matter.

And in that hee knoweth himselfe altogether ignorant

in, I will never have him make any profession at all, nor seeke to purchase him any fame by it: but rather when occasion serveth, confesse to have no understanding in it.

This, quoth Calmeta, woulde Nicholetto never have done, which being a very excellent Philosopher, and no more skilfull in the lawe than in fleeing, when a governour of Padoa, was minded to give him one of the Lectures in ye law, he would never yeeld at the perswasion of many scholers, to deceive the opinion which the governour had conceived of him, and confesse that he had understanding in it: but said still that he was not in this point of Socrates opinion, for it is not a Philosophers part to say at any time, that he hath no understanding.

I say not, answered Sir Fredericke, that the Courtier should of himselfe goe say hee hath no understanding, without it be required of him: for I allow not this fondnesse to accuse and debase him selfe. Againe I remember some otherwhile that in like sorte do willingly disclose some matters, which although they happened perhaps without anie fault of theirs, yet bring they with them a shadow of slander, as did a gentleman (whom you al know) which alwaies when he heard any mention made of the battaile beside Perna against king Charles, he would by and by declare how he fled away, and a man would weene that hee saw or understood nothing els in that journey.

Afterwarde talking of a certaine famous justing, he re-hearsed still how hee was overthrowne: and manye times also hee seemed in his talke to seeke howe hee might bring into purpose to declare that upon a night as hee was going to speake with a gentlewoman, hee was well beaten with a cudgel.

Such trifling follies I will not have our Courtier to speake off. But me think when occasion is offered to shew his skill in a matter he is altogether ignorant in, it is well done to avoide it. If necessitie compel him, let him rather confesse plainely his lacke of understanding in it, than hazarde him-selfe, and so shall he avoide a blame that many deserve now adayes, which I wote not through what corrupt inwarde motion or judgement out of reason, doe alwaies take upon them to practise the thing they know not, and lay aside that they are skilfull in.

And for a confirmation of this, I know a very excellent musition, which leaving his musicke a part hath wholy given himselfe to versifying, and thinketh himselfe a great clarke therin, but in deede he maketh every man to laugh him to scorne, and now hath he also cleane lost his musicke.

An other, one of the chiefest painters in the worlde,[17] neglecting his arte wherein he was very excellent, hath applied himself to learn Philosophy, wherein he hath such straunge conceits and monstrous fansies, that withall the painting he hath he can not paint them.

And such as these there be infinite. Some there be that knowing themselves to have an excellencie in one thing, make their principall profession in an other, in which notwithstanding they are not ignorant, but when time serveth to shew themselves in that they are most skilfull in, they doe it alwaies very perfectly: and otherwhile it commeth so to passe, that the company perceiving them so cunning in that which is not their profession, they imagine them to bee much better in that they professe in deed.

This arte in case it bee coupled with a good judgement, discontenteth me nothing at all.

Then answered the Lord Gasper Pallavicin. I thinke not this an arte, but a very deceite, and I believe it is not meet for him that will be an honest man to deceive at any time.

This quoth Sir Fredericke, is rather an ornament that accompanieth the thing he doth, than a deceite: and though it be a deceite, yet it is not to be disalowed.

Will you not say also, that he that beateth his fellow, where there be two playing at fence together, beguileth him, and that is because hee hath more arte than the other.

And where you have a jewell that unset seemeth faire, afterwarde when it commeth to a goldsmithes handes that in well setting it maketh it appeare much more fairer, will you not say that the goldsmith deceiveth the eyes of them that looke on it? And yet for that deceite, deserveth he prayse, for with judgement and arte a cunning hand doth many times adde a grace and ornament to Ivorie, or to silver, or to a stone that is faire in sight, setting it in gold.

We say not then that this arte or deceite (in case you will so terme it) deserveth any manner blame.

Also it is not ill for a man that knoweth himselfe skilfull in a matter, to seeke occasion after a comely sorte to shew his feate therein, and in like case do cover the partes hee thinketh scant worthie prayse, yet notwithstanding after a certaine warie dissimulation.

Doe you not remember how king Ferdinande without making any shew to seek it, tooke occasion very well to strippe himselfe sometime into his doublet? and that because he knew he was very well made and nimble withall. And because his handes were not all of the fairest, he seldom plucked of his gloves, and (in manner) never. And few there were that tooke heede to this warinesse of his.

Me thinke also I have reade, that Julius Cæsar ware for the nonce a garland of Laurell, to hide his baldnesse withall. But in these matters a man must be very circumspect and of a good judgement, least he passe his boundes: for to avoide one errour oftentimes a man falleth into an other, and to get him prayse, purchaseth blame.

Therefore the surest way in the world, is, for a man in his living and conversation to governe himselfe alwaies with a certaine honest meane, which (no doubt) is a great and most sure shield against envie, the which a man ought to avoid in what he is able.

I will have our Courtier also to take heede he purchaseth not the name of a lyar, nor of a vaine person, which happeneth many times, and to them also that deserve it not. Therefore in his communicatiō let him be alwaies heedfull not to goe out of the likelihood of truth, yea and not to speake too often those truthes that have the face of a lye, as many do that never speake, but of wonders, and will bee of such authoritie, that every incredible matter must bee believed at their mouth.

Other, at the first entring into friendship with a new friend, to get favor with him, the first thing that they speake, sweare that there is not a person in the worlde whom they love better, and they are willing to jeoparde their life for his sake, and such other matters out of reason, and when they part from him, make wise to weepe, and not to speake a word for sorrow. Thus because they would be counted to be loving wormes, they make men count them lyers, and fond flatterers.

But it were too long a matter and tedious to recken up all vices that may happen in conversation. Therefore, for that I desire in ye Courtier, it sufficeth to say (beside the matters rehearsed) that he bee such a one that shall never want good communication and fitte for them hee talketh withall, and have a good understanding with a certaine sweetnesse to refresh the hearers minds, and with merry conceites and jestes to provoke them to solace and laughter, so that without being at any time lothsome or satiate, he may evermore delite.

Now I hope my Ladie Emilia will give me leave to holde my peace, which in case she deny me, I shall by mine owne wordes be convicted not to be ye good Courtier I have told you of: for not onely good communication, which neither at this time nor perhaps at any other ye have heard in me, but also this I have, such as it is, doth cleane faile me.

Then spake the Lord Generall: I will not have this false opinion to sticke in the heade of any of us, that you are not a very good Courtier: for (to say the truth) this desire of yours to hold your peace proceedeth rather because you would be ridde of your paine, than for that ye want talke.

Therefore that it may not appeare in so noble assembly as this is, and in so excellent talke, any parcel be left out, say you not nay to teach us how wee shoulde use these jestes you have made mention of, and shew us the arte that belongeth to all this kinde of pleasant speach to provoke laughter and solace after an honest sorte, for (in mine opinion) it is verie necessarie and much to purpose for a Courtier.

My Lord, answered Sir Fredericke, jestes and merrie conceites are rather a gift, and a grace of nature, than of arte, but yet there are some nations more redier in it than other some, as the Tuscanes, which in deed are very subtill.

Also it appeareth proper to the Spaniardes to invent merry conceits. Yet are there many notwithstanding both of this nation and other also, that in too much babling passe sometime their boundes and were unsavery and fond, because they have no respect to the condition of the person they commune withal, to the place where they bee, to the time, to the great gravitie and modesty which they ought to have in themselves.

Then aunsweared the L. Generall: You deny that there is any arte in jeastes, and yet in speaking against such as observe them not with modestie and gravitie, and have not respect to the time and to the person they commune withall, me thinke ye declare that this may also be taught and hath some doctrine in it.

These rules my Lord, answered Sir Fredericke, be so generall, that they may bee applyed to every matter, and helpe it forwarde. But I have saide there is no arte in jeastes, because (me thinke) they are onely of two sortes: whereof the one is enlarged in communication that is long and without interruption: as is seene in some men that with so good an utterance and grace and so pleasantly declare and expresse a matter that happened unto them or that they have seene and heard, that with their gesture and wordes they set it before a mans eyes, and (in manner) make him feele it with hand, and this peradventure for want of an other terme we may call Festivitie or els Civilitie.

The other sorte of jeastes is verie briefe, and consisteth onely in quicke and subtill sayinges, as many times there are heard among us, and in nickes: neither doth it appeare that they are of any grace, without some litle byting, and these among them of olde time were also called Sayinges, now some terme them Privie tauntes.

I say therefore in the first kind, which is a merry manner of expressing, there needeth no arte, because very nature her selfe createth and shapeth men apt to expresse pleasantly, and giveth them a countenance, gestures, a voice, and wordes for the purpose to counterfeite what they lust.

In the other of Privie tauntes, what can arte doe? Since that quippe ought to be shot out and hit the pricke before a man can discerne that he that speaketh it can thinke upon it, els it is colde and litle worth.

Therefore (thinke I) all is the worke of witte and nature.

Then tooke maister Peter Bembo the matter in hand, and said: The Lord Generall denieth not that you say: namely that nature and wit beare not the chiefest stroke, especially as touching invention, but it is certaine that in each mans minde, of how good a wit soever he be, there arise conceites both good and bad, and more and lesse, but then judgement and arte both polish and correct them, and chooseth the good and refuseth the bad.

Therefore laying aside that which belongeth to wit, declare you unto us that consisteth in arte: that is to wit of jeasts and merry conceites that move laughter, which are meete for ye Courtier and which are not: and in what time and manner they ought to bee used: for this is that the Lord Generall demaundeth of you.

Then Sir Frederick saide smiling: there is never a one of us here that I will not give place unto in everie matter, and especially in jeasting, unlesse perhaps follies, which make men laugh many times more than wittie sayings, were also to be allowed for jeastes.

And so turning him to Count Lewis and to maister Bernard Bibiena, hee saide unto them. These bee the maisters of this facultie, of whom in case I must speak of merry sayings, I must first learne what I have to say.

Count Lewis answered: me thinke you begin now to practise that you say yee are not skilfull in, which is, to make these Lordes laugh in mocking maister Bernarde and me, because every one of them woteth well that the thing which you prayse us for, is much more perfectly in you.

Therefore in case you be wearie, it is better for you to sue to the Dutchesse that it would please her to deferre the remnant of our talke till to morrow, than to goe about with craft to ridde your handes of paines taking.

Sir Fredericke began to make answere, but the Ladie Emilia interrupted him immediatly and saide: It is not the order that the disputation should be consumed upon your prayse, it sufficeth yee are verie well knowne all. But because it commeth in my minde that you (Count) imputed to me yesternight, that I devided not ye paines taking equally, it shall bee well done that Sir Fredericke rest him a while and the charge of speaking of jeastes wee will commit to maister Bernarde Bibiena, for we doe not onely know him very quicke witted in talking without intermission, but also it is not out of our memory that hee hath sundrie times promised to write of this matter. And therefore we may thinke he hath very wel thought upon it all this while, and ought the better to satisfie us in it. Afterwarde when there shal be sufficiently spoken of jeastes, Sir Fredericke shall proceed forwarde againe with that he hath yet behinde concerning the Courtier.

Then saide Sir Fredericke: Madam, I know not what I have left behinde any more, but like a travailer on the way now wearie of the painefulnesse of my long journey at noone tide, I will rest me in maister Bernardes communication at the sowne of his wordes, as it were under some faire tree that casteth a goodly shadow at the sweete roaring of a plentifull and living spring: afterwarde (may happe) being somewhat refreshed, I may have somewhat els to say.

Maister Bernarde answered laughing: If I shew you the

toppe,[18] ye shall see what shadow may be hoped for at the leaves of my tree.

To heare the roaring of the lively spring ye speake of, it may happen be your chance so to doe, for I was once turned into a spring: not by anie of the Goddes of olde time, but by our Frier Marian. And from that time hetherto I never wanted water.

Then began they all to fall in a laughing, because this pleasant matter which maister Bernard ment happened to him in Rome in the presence of Galeotto Cardinall of S. Petro in Vincula, was well knowne to them all.

After they had ceased laughing, the Ladie Emilia saide: Leave now making us laugh with practising of jeastes, and teach us how we should use them, and whence they are derived, and whatever els ye know in this matter. And for losing any more time, beginne out of hand.

I doubt me, quoth maister Bernard, it is late, and least my talke of pleasant matters should seeme unpleasant and tedious, perhaps it were good to deferre it till to morrow.

Here incontinently many made answere that it lacked yet a good deale of the houre when they were wont to leave of reasoning.

Then maister Bernarde turning to the Dutchesse and the Ladie Emilia. I will not refuse this labour (quoth he) although I be wont to marvell at the boldnesse of them that dare take upon them to sing to the Lute, when our James Sansecondo standeth by, even so ought not I in the presence of hearers that have much better understanding in that I have to say, than I my selfe, take upon me to entreat of jeastes. Neverthelesse least I should shew a president to any of these Lordes to refuse that they shall bee charged withall, I will speake as briefly as I can possible what commeth in my minde as touching matters that cause laughter, which is so proper to us, that to describe a man, the common saying is, He is a living creature that can laughe: because this laughing is perceived onely in a man, and (in manner) alwaies is a token of a certaine jocondnesse and merry moode that he feeleth inwardly in his minde, which by nature is drawne to pleasantnesse, and coveteth quietnesse and refreshing.

For which cause we see men have invented manie matters, as sportes, games and pastimes, and so many sundrie sortes of open shewes.

And because wee beare good will to such as are the occasion of this recreation of ours, the manner was among the kings of olde time, among the Romanes, the Athenians and many other, to get the good will of the people withall, and to feede eyes and mindes of the multitude, to make great Theaters, and other publike buildinges, and there to shew new devices of pastimes, running of horses and Charets, fightinges of men together, straunge beastes, Comedies, Tragedies, and daunces of Antique. Neither did the grave Philosophers shun these sights, for manie times both in this manner and at bankets they refreshed their wearisome mindes, in those high discourses and divine imaginations of theirs.

The which in likewise all sortes of men are willing to doe, for not onely Ploughmen, Mariners, and all such as are inured with hard and boysterous exercises with hand, but also holy religious men and prisoners that from houre to houre waite for death, goe about yet to seeke some remedie and medicine to refresh themselves.

Whatsoever therfore causeth laughter, the same maketh the mind jocunde and giveth pleasure, nor suffereth a man in that instant to mind the troublesome griefes that our life is full off.

Therefore (as you see) laughing is very acceptable to all men, and hee is much to be commended that can cause it in due time and after a comely sort.

But what this laughing is, and where it consisteth, and in what manner, sometime it taketh the veines, the eyes, the mouth and the sides, and seemeth as though it would make us burst, so that what ever resistance we make, it is not possible to keepe it, I will leave it to be disputed of

Democritus, the which also in case he would promise us, hee shoulde not performe it.

The place therefore and (as it were) the head spring that laughing matters arise of, consisteth in a certaine deformitie, or ill favourednesse, because a man laugheth onely at those matters that are disagreeing in themselves, and (to a mans seeming) are in ill plight, where it is not so in deed. I wote not otherwise how to expound it.

But if you will bethinke your selfe, ye shall perceive the thing that a man alwaies laugheth at, is a matter that soundeth not well, and yet is it not in ill sitting.

What kind of waies therefore those be that the Courtier ought to use in causing laughter, and of what scope, I will assay in what I can to utter unto you as farre as my judgement can give me, because to make men laugh alwaies is not comely for the Courtier, nor yet in such wise as frantike, dronken, foolish and fond men and in like manner common jeasters doe: and though to a mans thinking, Courtes can not be without such kind of persons, yet deserve they not the name of a Courtier, but each man to be called by his name, and esteemed such as they are.

The scope and measure to make men laugh in taunting, must also be diligently considered: who he is that is taunted, for it provoketh no laughter to mocke and scorne a sillie soule in miserie and calamitie, nor yet a naughtie knave and common ribauld, because a man would thinke that these men deserved to be otherwise punished, than in jeasting at. And mens minds are not bent to scoffe them in miserie, unlesse such men in their mishappe bragge and boast of themselves, and have a proud and hautie stomacke.

Againe, a respect must be had to them that are generally favoured and beloved of every man, and that beare stroke, because in mocking and scorning such a one, a man may sometime purchase himselfe daungerous enimitie. Therefore it is not amisse to scoffe and mocke at vices that are in persons not of such miserie that it should move compassion, nor of such wickednesse that a man would thinke they deserved not to goe on the ground, nor of such authoritie, that any litle displeasure of theirs may be a great hinderance to a man.

You shall understande moreover, that out of the places jeasting matters are derived from, a man may in like manner picke grave sentences to praise or dispraise. And otherwhile with the selfe same words, as to praise a liberall man that partaketh his goods in common with his friendes, the common saying is, That he hath, is none of his owne.

The like may bee saide in dispraise of one that hath stolen or compassed that hee hath by other ill meanes. It is also a common saying, She is a woman of no small price, when a man will prayse her for the vertues, for her wisedom and goodnesse. The verie same may be saide of a woman that looketh to be kept sumptuously.

But it commeth oftner to purpose, that a man in this case serveth his turne with the selfe same places, than with the selfe same wordes. As within these few dayes three gentlemen standing at masse together in a Church where was a gentlewoman one of the three was in love withall, there came a poore begger and stood before her requiring her almes, and so with much instance and lamenting with a groning voice repeated many times his request: yet for all that did she not give him her almes, nor deny it him in making signe to depart in Gods name, but stood musing with her selfe as though she minded an other matter.

Then saide the gentleman that loved her, to his two companions, see what I may hope for at my mistresse hands, which is so cruel, that she will neither give the poore naked soule dead for hunger, that requireth her with such passion and so instantly, her almes, ne yet leave to depart, so much she rejoyceth to behold with her eyes one that is brought lowe with miserie, and that in vaine requireth her rewarde.

One of the two answered: it is no crueltie, but a privie admonition for you to doe you to wit, that your mistresse is not pleased with him that requireth her with much instance.

The other answered: Nay, it is rather a lesson for him, that although she give not that is required of her, yet she is willing inough to be sued to.

See here, because the gentlewoman sent not the poore man away, there arose one saying of great dispraise, one of modest praise, and another of nipping boord.[19]

To returne therefore to declare the kindes of jeastes appertaining to our purpose, I say (in mine opinion) there are of three sortes, although Sir Fredericke hath made mention but of two. The one a civill and pleasant declaration without interruption, which consisteth in the effect of a thing. The other a quick and subtil readinesse, which consisteth in one saying alone.

Therefore will we adde a third sorte to these, which we call Boordes or merrie Pranckes, wherein the processe is long, and the sayings short, and some deedes withall.

The first therefore that consisteth in communication without interruption, are in that sorte (in a maner) as though a man would tell a tale. And to give you an example, when Pope Alexander y[e] sixt dyed and Pius the third was created, being then in Rome, and in the Palaice, your Sir Anthonie Agnello of Mantua, my Ladie Dutchesse, and communing of the death of the one, and creation of the other, and therein making sundrie discourses with certaine friends of his, he saide.

Sirs, in Catullus time, gates began to speake without tongues, and to heare without eares, and in that sorte discovered Advouteries.

Now although men bee not of such worthinesse as they were in those dayes, yet perhaps the gates that are made, a great sort of them especially here in Rome, of aunciemt Marble, have the same vertue they had then.

And for my part I believe that these two will cleare us of all our doubtes, in case wee will aske counsaile of them.

Then those Gentlemen mused much at the matter, and attended to see to what end it would come, when sir Anthony following on still up and down lift up his eies, as at a sodaine, to one of the two gates of the Hall where they walked: and staying a while, with his finger hee shewed his company the inscription over it, which was Pope Alexanders name, and at the end of it was V, and I, because it should signifie (as ye know) the sixt.

And said: See here, this gate saith Alexander Papa VI., which signifieth, he hath beene Pope through the force he hath used, and hath prevailed more thereby than with right and reason.

Now let us see if we may of this other understand any thing of the new Bishop: and turning him as at adventure to the other gate, pointed to the inscription of one N, two P P, and one V, which signifieth Nicolaus Papa quintus, and immediately he said.

Good Lord, ill newes, see here this gate saith *Nihil Papa valet*.

See now how this kinde of jeastes is proper and good, and how fitting it is for one in Court, whether it be true or false a man saith, for in this case it is lawfull to feigne what a man lusteth without blame: and in speaking the truth, to set it forth with a feate lye, augmenting or diminishing according to the purpose.

But the perfect grace and very pith of this, is to set forth so well and without paine, not onely in wordes, but in gestures, the thing a man purposeth to expresse, that unto the hearers he may appeare to doe before their eyes the thinges he speaketh of.

And this expressed manner in this wise hath such force, that otherwhile it setteth forth and maketh a matter delite very much, which of it selfe is not very merrie nor wittie.

And although these protestations neede gestures, and the earnestnesse that a lively voice hath, yet is the force of them knowne also otherwhile in writing.

Who laugheth not when John Boccaccio in the eight journey of his hundreth tales declareth how the Priest of Varlungo strained himselfe to sing a Kyrie and a Sanctus, when he perceived Belcolore was in the Church.

There be also pleasant declarations in his tales of Calandrino, and manie other.

After the same sort seemeth to be the making of a man laugh in counterfeiting or imitating (how ever wee list to terme it) of a mans manners, wherein hetherto I have seene none passe our maister Robert of Bari.

This were no small praise quoth maister Robert, if it were true, for then woulde I surely goe about to counterfeite rather the good than the bad: and if I could liken my selfe to some I know, I would thinke my self a happie man. But I feare me I can counterfeite nothing but what maketh a man laugh, which you saide before consisteth in vice.

Maister Bernard answered. In vice in deede, but that that standeth not in ill plight. And weete ye well that this counterfeiting yee speake of, can not be without wit, for beside the manner to apply his wordes and his gestures, and to set before the hearers eyes the countenance and manners of him he speaketh of, he must bee wise, and have great respect to the place, to the time and to the persons with whom hee talketh, and not like a common jeaster passe his boundes, which thinges you wonderfully well observe, and therefore I believe yee are skilfull in all.

For undoubtedly it is not meete for a gentleman to make weeping and laughing faces, to make soundes and voices, and to wrastle with him selfe alone, as Berto doth, to apparrel himselfe like a lobbe of the Countrie, as doth Strascino, and such other matters, which doe well become them, because it is their profession.

But we must by the way and privily steale this counterfeiting, alwaies keeping the estate of a gentleman, without speaking filthie wordes, or doing uncomely deedes, without making faces and antiques, but frame our gestures after a certaine manner, that who so heareth and seeth us, may by our wordes and countenances imagine much more than he seeth and heareth, and upon that take occasion to laugh.

He must also in this counterfeiting take heede of too

much taunting in touching a man, especially in the ill favourednesse of visage, or ill shape of bodie. For as the mishaps and vices of the bodie minister many times ample matter to laugh at, if a man can discretely handle it, even so the using of this manner too bytingly, is a token not onely of a common jeaster, but of a plaine enimie.

Therefore must a man observe in this point (though it be hard) the fashion of our maister Robert, as I have saide, which counterfeiteth all men, and not without touching them in the matters wherein they be faultie, and in the presence of them selves, and yet no man findeth himselfe agreeved, neither may a man thinke that he can take it in ill part. And of this I will give you no example, because we all see infinite in him dayly.

Also it provoketh much laughter (which neverthelesse is contained under declaration) when a man repeateth with a good grace certaine defaults of other men, so they be meane and not worthie greater correction: as foolish matters sometime simply of them selves alone, sometime annexed with a litle readie nipping fondnesse. Likewise certaine extreame curious matters. Otherwhile a great and well forged lye: as few dayes agoe our maister Cesar declared a pretie foolish matter, which was, that being with the Maior of this Citie, hee saw a Countrieman come to him, to complaine that hee had an asse stolen from him, and after he had tolde him of his povertie, and how the thiefe deceived him, to make his losse the greater he saide unto him.

Sir if you had seene mine Asse you should have known what a cause I have to complaine, for with his pad on his backe a man would have thought him verie Tully him selfe.

And one of our traine meeting a herde of Goates before the which was a mightie great Ram Goate, he stayed, and with a marvellous countenance saide: Marke me the Goate, he seemeth a Saint Paul.

The Lord Gasper saith, he knew an other, which for that

he was an olde servant to Hercules Duke of Ferrara, did offer him two pretie boyes which he had, to be his pages, and these two died both before they came to his service. The which when the Duke understood, he lamented lovingly with the father, saying that he was verie sorie, bycause when he sawe them upon a time, hee thought them handsome and wittie children. The father made answere.

Nay my Lord, you sawe nothing, for within these few daies they were become much more handsome and of better qualities than I woulde ever have thought: and song together like a couple of Haukes.

And one of these dayes a Doctour of ours beholding one that was judged to bee whipped about the market place, and taking pittie upon him, because the poore soules shoulders bledde sore, and went so soft a pace, as though he had walked about for his pleasure to passe the time withall, he saide to him: Goe on a pace poore fellow, that thou maist be the sooner out of thy paine.

Then he turning about, and beholding him that so saide (in a manner) with a wonder, staied a while without any word, afterwarde he saide: When thou art whipped, goe at thy pleasure, for now will I goe as I shall thinke good.

You may remember also the foolish matter that not long agoe the Duke rehearsed of the Abbot, that being present upon a day when Duke Fredericke was talking where he shoulde bestow the great quantitie of rubbish that was cast up to lay the foundation of this Pallace, working dayly uppon it saide: My Lorde, I have well bethought mee where you shall bestow it, let there be a great pitte digged, and into that may you have it cast without any more adoe.

Duke Fredericke answered him not without laughter: And where then shall be bestowe the quantitie of earth that shall be cast out of that Pitte? The Abbot saide unto him: Let it be made so large, that it may wel receive both the one and the other. And so for all the Duke repeated sundrie times the greater the Pitte was, the more earth should be cast out of it, yet could he never make it sinke into his braine, but it might be made so large, that it might receive both the one and the other: and he answered him nothing else, but, make it so much the larger. Now see what a good forecast this Abbot had.

Then saide maister Peter Bembo: And why tell you not that, of your great Captaine of Florence, that was beseeged of the Duke of Calabria within Castellina? Where there were founde upon a day in the towne certaine quarels poysoned, that had beene shotte out of the campe, hee wrote unto the Duke, if the warre shoulde proceede so cruelly, he would also put a medicine upon his Gunstones, and then he that hath the worst, hath his mendes in his hands.

Maister Bernarde laughed and saide: If you holde not your peace (maister Peter) I will tell whatsoever I have seene my selfe, and heard of your Venetians, which is not a litle, and especially when they play the ryders.

Doe not I beseech ye, answered maister Peter, for I will keepe to my selfe two other verie pretie ones that I know of your Florentines.

Maister Bernarde saide: They are rather of the Seneses, for it often happeneth among them. As within these few dayes one of them hearing certaine letters read in the Councell Chamber, in which for avoiding too often repetition of his name y^t was spoken of, this tearme was many times put in, *il Prelibato,* (which signifieth the aforenamed) he saide unto them that read them: soft, stay there a litle, and tell me this Prelibato what is he? A friende to our Communaltie?

Maister Peter laughed: then he proceeded: I speake of Florentines, and not of Seneses. Speake it hardly, quoth the Ladie Emilia, and bash not for that matter.

Maister Peter saide, when the Lords of Florence were in warre against the Pisanes they were otherwhile out of money, by reason of their great charges and laying their heades together upon a day in the councell chamber, what

way were best to make provision to serve their turne withall, after manie devises propounded, one of the auncientest
Citizens saide.

I have found two waies, whereby without much travell
we may in a small while come by a good portion of money.
Whereof the one is (because we have no readier rent than
the custome at the gates of Florence) where we have XI.
gates, let us with speede make a XI. moe, and so shall we
double our revenue.

The other way is to set up a Mint in Pistoia, and an
other in Prato, no more nor lesse than is here within Florence, and there doe nothing els day and night but coine
money, and all Ducats of golde: and this devise (in mine
opinion) is the speedier and lesse chargeable.

They fell a laughing a pace at the subtil device of the
Citizen, and when laughing was ceased, the Ladie Emilia
said: Will you (maister Bernarde) suffer maister Peter
thus to jeast at Florentines without a revenge?

Maister Bernarde answered smiling: I pardon him this
offence, for where hee hath displeased me in jeasting at
Florentines, he hath pleased me in obeying of you, the
which I would alwaies doe my selfe.

Then saide the Lord Cesar: I heard a Brescian speak a
joly grosse matter, which being this yeare in Venice at
the feast of the Ascension, rehearsed in a place where I
was to certaine mates of his, the goodly matters hee had
seene there, what sundrie marchandise, what plate, what
sortes of spices, and what cloth and silke there was, then
how the Signoria issued out with a great pompe in the
Bucentoro to wedde the Sea, in which were so many
gentlemen well apparayled, so manye sortes of instruments and melodies, that a man would have thought it a
Paradise.

And when one of his companions demaunded him what
kinde of Musicke did please him best of all that he had
hearde there, hee saide: All were good, yet among the
rest I saw one blow on a straunge Trumpet, which at every

push thrust it into his throate more than two handfull, and then by and by drew it out againe, and thrust it in a fresh, that you never saw a greater wonder.

Then they all laughed, understanding the fond imagination of him that thought the blower thrust into his throat that part of yᵉ Shagbut that is hid in putting it backe againe.

Then maister Bernarde went forwarde: Those affections and curiosities that are but meane, bring a lothsomnesse with them, but when they bee done out of measure, they much provoke laughter. As otherwhile when some men are heard to speake of their auncientrie and noblenesse of birth: some time women of their beautie and handsomnesse.

As not long ago a gentlewoman did, which at a great feast being verie sad, and musing with her selfe, it was demanded of her what she thought upō, that should make her so sad. And she made answere, I thought upon a matter, which as oft as it commeth into my mind doth much trouble me, and I can not put it out of my hart: which is, where in the day of generall judgement, all bodies must arise againe and appeare naked before the judgement seat of Christ, I can not abide the griefe I feele in thinking that mine must also be seene naked.

Such affectations as these be, because they passe the degree, doe rather provoke laughter than lothsomnesse.

Those feate lyes now that come so well to purpose, how they provoke laughter yee all know.

And that friend of ours that suffereth us not to want, within these fewe dayes rehearsed one to me that was verie excellent.

Then saide the Ladie Julian, What ever it were, more excellenter it can not be, nor more subtiler, than one that a Tuskane of ours, which is a merchant man of Luca, affirmed unto me the last day for most certaine.

Tell it us, quoth the Dutchesse. The Lord Julian saide smyling: This merchant man (as he saith) being upon a

403

time in Polonia, determined to buye a quantitie of Sables, minding to bring them into Italie, and to gaine greatly by them. And after much practising in the matter, where he could not himselfe goe into Moscovia, because of the warre betwixt the king of Polonia, and the Duke of Moscovia, he tooke order by the meane of some of the Countrie, that upon a day appointed, certain merchant men of Moscovia should come with their Sables into the borders of Polonia, and he promised also to be there himselfe to bargaine with them.

This merchant man of Luca travailing then with his company toward Moscovia, arrived at the river of Boristhenes, which he found hard frozen like a marble stone, and saw the Moscovites which for suspicion of the warre were in doubt of the Polones, were on the other side, and nearer came not than the breadth of the river.

So after they knew the one the other, making certain signes, the Moscovites beganne to speake aloude, and tolde the price howe they would sell their Sables, but the colde was so extreme, that they were not understood, because the wordes before they came on the other side where this merchant of Luca was and his interpreters, were congeled in the ayre, and there remained frozen and stopped. So that the Polones that knew the manner, made no more adoe, but kindled a great fire in the middest of the river (for to their seeming that was the point whereto the voyce came hote before the frost tooke it) and the river was so thicke frozen, that it did well beare the fire.

When they had thus done, the wordes that for space of an houre had beene frozen, beganne to thaw, and came downe, making a noyse as doth the snow frō the mountaines in May, and so immediately they were well understood: but the men on the other side were first departed: and because he thought that those wordes asked too great a price for the Sables, he woulde not bargaine, and so came away without.

Then they laughed all. And maister Bernard, Truely

(quoth hee) this that I will tell you is not so subtill, yet is it a pretie matter, and this it is.

Where talke was a few dayes agoe of the Countrie or world newly found out by the Mariners of Portugal, and of straunge beastes and other matters brought from thence, that friende I tolde you of, affirmed that he had seene an Ape, very divers in shape from such as wee are accustomed to see that plaied excellently well at Chestes.

And among other times upon a day before the king of Portugal the gentleman that brought her plaied at Chestes with her, where the Ape shewed some draughtes very subtil, so that she put him to his shifts, at length she gave him Checkemate. Upon this the gentleman being somewhat vexed (as commonly they are all that lose at the game) toke the king in his hand which was good and bigge (as the fashion is among the Portugales) and reached ye Ape a great knocke on the heade. She forthwith leaped aside complaining greatly, and seemed to require justice at the kinges handes for the wrong done her.

The gentleman afterward called her to play with him again, the which with signes she refused a while, but at last was contented to playe another game, and as she had done the other time before, so did she now drive him to a narrow point.

In conclusion: the Ape perceiving she could give the gentleman the mate, thought with a new devise she would be sure to escape without any moe knockes, and privily conveyed her right hand without making semblant what her intent was, under the gentlemans left elbowe, leaning for pleasure upon a litle taffata coushin, and snatching it slightly away, at one instant gave him with her left hand a mate with a paune, and with her right hand cast the coushing upon her head to save her from strokes: then she made a gamboll before the king joyfully, in token (as it were) of her victory. Now see whether this Ape were not wise, circumspect, and of a good understanding.

Then spake the Lord Cesar Gonzaga: It must needs be

that this Ape was a doctour among other Apes, and of much authoritie: and I believe the common weale of the Apes of India sent her into Portugal to get a name in a straunge Countrie.

At this every man laughed, both for the lye and for the addition made to it by the Lord Cesar: so proceeding on in this talke, maister Bernard saide: you have understood therefore what jeastes are that be of effect and communication without interruption as much as commeth to minde: therefore it shall be well now we speake of such as consist in one saying alone, and have a quick sharpnesse that lyeth briefly in a sentence or in a worde. And even as in the first kinde of merrie talke a man must in his protestation and counterfeiting take heede that hee be not like common jeasters and parasites, and such as with fond matters move men to laugh, so in this briefe kinde the Courtier must be circumspect that he appeare not malicious and venemous, and speake tauntes and quippes onely for spite and to touch the quicke, because such men oftentimes for offence of the tongue are chastised in the whole bodie.

Of those readie jeastes therefore that consist in a short saying, such are most lively that arise of doubtfulnesse, though alwaies they provoke not laughing: for they bee rather praysed for wittie, than for matters of laughter. As few dayes it is that our maister Anniball Palleotto saide to one that appointed him a maister to teach his children the Grammer, and after that hee had praysed him, to be a man very well learned, coming to wages, saide, that besides the money he would have a chamber furnished to dwell and sleepe in, for that he had not *letto*, that is a bedde.

Then maister Anniball answered presently: and how can he be learned, if he have not *letto*, this is, read.

See how well he tooke a vantage at the diverse significacion of *haver letto* (which is interpreted both to have a bedde, and to have read.) But because those doubtfull wordes have a pretie sharpenesse of wit in them, being taken in a contrarie signification to that all other men take them, it appeareth (as I have saide) that they rather provoke a man to wonder than to laugh, except when they be joyned with other kindes of sayinges.

The kinde therefore of wittie sayinges that is most used to make men laugh, is when we give eare to heare on thing, and he that maketh answere, speaketh an other, and is alledged contrarie to expectation, and in case a doubt be annexed therewithall, then it is verie wittie and pleasant. As the last night disputing to make a faire *mattonato,* that is, paviment in the chamber of the Ladie Dutchesse, after many wordes. You maister John Christopher saide, If we could have the bishop of Potentia, and make him flat, it should be very fit, for that he is the fairest *matto nato,* that is naturall foole, that ever I did see.

Every one laughed greatlye for that dividing that worde *matto nato* you made the doubt, afterwarde saying that if they had to make flat a bishop and place him for pavement of a chamber it was farre from the opinion of the hearers, thus the sentence came to bee verie sharpe and worthie the laughing.

But of doubtfull wordes there be many sortes, therefore must a man bee circumspect, and choose out termes very artificiall, and leave out such as make the jeast colde, and that a man would weene were haled by the haire, or els (as wee have saide) that have too much bitternesse in them. As certain cōpanions being in a friends house of theirs, who had but one eye, after he had desired the companie to tarrie dinner with him, they departed all saving one, that saide.

And I am well pleased to tarrie, for I see a voide roome for one, and so with his finger pointed to the hole where his eye had beene.

See how bitter and discourteous this is passing measure, for he nipped him without a cause, and without being first pricked himselfe: and he saide the thing that a man might speake against blinde men. Such generall matters delite not, because it appeareth they are thought upon of purpose.

And after this sorte was the saying to one without a nose: And where dost thou fasten thy spectacles? Or wherewithall doest thou smell Roses at the time of the yeare?

But among other merry sayings, they have a verie good grace, that arise when a man at the nipping talke of his fellow, taketh the verie same words in the selfe same sense, and returneth them backe againe, pricking him with his owne weapon. As an Attorney in the law, unto whom in the presence of the Judge his adversarie saide, what barkest thou? Forthwith he answered: Because I see a thiefe.

And of this sorte was also, when Galeotto of Narni passing through Siena stayed in a streete to enquire for an Inne, and a Senese seeing him so corpulent as he was, saide laughing: Other men carrie their Bougettes behind them, and this good fellow carrieth his before him. Galeotto answered immediately: So must men doe in the Countrie of theeves.

There is yet an other sorte called in Italian *Bischizzi* and that consisteth in chaunging or increasing, or diminishing of a letter or sillable. As he that said: Thou shouldest be better learned in the Latin tongue than in the Greeke.

And to you (madam) was written in the superscription of a letter, To the Ladie Emilia Impia.

It is also a merrie devise to mingle together a verse or moe, taking it in an other meaning than the Author doth, or some other common saying. Sometime in the verie same meaning, but altering a worde, as a gentleman that had a foule and scouling wife: when he was asked the question how hee did, he answered.

Thinke thou thy selfe, for *Furiarum maxima juxta me cubat.*[20]

And maister Hierom Donato going a visiting the Stations of Rome in Lent in companie with many other gentlemen, met with a knotte of faire Romane Ladies, and when one of these gentlemen had said:

Quot cœlum stellas, tot habet tua Roma Puellas.[21]

By and by he added:

Pascua quotque hædos, tot habet tua Roma cinædos.[22]

Shewing a rout of yong men that came on the other side.

And Marcantonio della Torre said after the manner to the bishop of Padoa, Where there was a Nunrie in Padoa, under the charge of a religious person, much esteemed for his good life and learning, it happened that this Father haunting much to the Nunrie very familiarly, and confessing often the sisters, begatte five of them with childe, where there were not passing five mo in all. And when the matter was knowne, the Father would have fledde, and wist not how.

The bishoppe caused him to be apprehended, and upon that, he confessed that he had gotten those five Nunnes with childe through y᷎e temptations of the divel, so that the bishoppe was fully bent to chastice him sore. And because this man was learned, hee had made manie friendes, which altogether assayed to helpe him, and among the rest there went also maister Marcontonio, to entreate for him.

The bishop woulde in no wise give eare to them. At length they being instant upon him, and commending the guiltie, and excusing him through the commoditie of place, frailtie of man, and many other causes, the bishop saide.

I will doe nothing for you, because I must make account unto God of this. And when they had replied againe, the bishop said: what answere shall I make unto God at the day of judgemēt, when he shall say unto me, *Redde rationem villicationis tuæ?* [23]

Maister Marcantonio answered him immediatelye: Mary my Lorde, the verie same that the Gospel saith: *Domine quinque talenta tradidisti mihi, ecce alia quinque superlucratus sum.*[24]

Then could not the bishop abstaine laughing, and hee asswaged much his anger and the punishment that hee had ordained for the offender.

It is likewise verie pretie to allude to names and to faine somewhat, wherfore he y^t the talke is of is so called, or els because he doth some thing: as not long since the provost of Luca (which as you know is one merrilie disposed) asking the bishoprik of Caglio, the Pope answered him.

Dost thou not know that Caglio, in ye Spanish tongue is as much to say as, I holde my peace, and thou art a great prater. Therefore it were unfitting for a bishop at any time in naming his title to make a lye, now Calia, hold thy peace then.

To this ye provost gave an answere, the which although it were not in this sorte, yet was it no lesse pretie than this. For after he had often put him in remembrance of this his sute and saw it of none effect, at last hee saide, Holy father, in case your holinesse doe give me this bishop-rike, it shall not be without profit to you, for then will I surrender two offices into your hands.

And what offices hast thou to surrender into my handes, quoth the Pope? the provost answered: I shall surrēder unto you *Officium principale* and *Officium beatæ Mariæ.*

Then could not the Pope though he were a very grave person, abstaine from laughing. An other also in Padoa saide, Calphurnius was so named because he was wont to heate furnaces.

And upon a day when I asked Phedra how it happeneth, where prayer is made in the Church upon good Fryday not onely for Christians, but also for Paganes and for Jewes, there was no mention made of the Cardinalles, as there was of bishops and other prelates. He answered me, that the Cardinalles were contained in the Collect, *Oremus pro hæreticis et Schismaticis.*

And our Count Lewis saide, that I reprehended a ladie of love for occupying a certaine kinde of lye that shined much, because when she was trimmed therewithall, I might see my selfe in her face, and for that I was ill favoured I could not abide to looke upon my selfe.

In this manner was that maister Camillo Paleotto said unto maister Anthonio Porcaro, which reasoning of a companion of his that under confession had saide unto the Priest that he fasted with all his hart, and went to Masse and to holy service, and did all the good deedes in the world, saide: This fellow in stead of accusing praiseth him selfe. Unto whom maister Camillo answered nay, he rather confesseth him selfe of these matters, because he reckoneth the doing of them great sinne.

Doe you not remember how well the Lord Generall saide the last day, when John Thomas Galeotto wondred at one that demaunded two hundred Ducats for a horse? for when John Thomas said that he was not worthie a farthing, because among other ill properties he had, he coulde not abide weapons, neither was it possible to make him come nigh where he saw any, the Lord Generall saide (willingly to reprehend him of cowardise) if the horse hath this propertie that hee can not abide weapons, I marvell hee asketh not a thousand Ducates.

Also sometime a man speaketh the very same word, but to another ende than the common use is. As, when the Duke was passing over a verie swift river, he saide to the trumpter: goe on. The trumpter turned him backe with his cappe in his hand and after a reverent manner, saide: It shall bee yours my Lord.

It is also a pleasant manner of jeasting, when a man seemeth to take the wordes and not the meaning of him that speaketh. As this yeare a Dutchman in Rome meeting in an evening our maister Phillip Beroaldo whose scholler he was, saide unto him *Domine magister, Deus det vobis bonum sero*. And Beroaldo answered incontinently *Tibi malum cito*.[25]

And another Spaniard sitting at the table with the great Captaine, Diego de Chignognes saide, *Vino dios* (calling for wine) Diego answered him againe. *Vino, y no lo conocistes,*[26] to nip him for a chesnut.[27]

Also maister James Sadoleto saide unto Beroaldo, that had tolde him how hee would in any wise goe to Bolonia, what is the cause that maketh you thus to leave Rome where there are so many pleasures, to goe to Bolonia, full of disquietnesse?

Beroaldo answered: I am forced to goe to Bolonia for three Counts. And now he had lift up three fingers of his left hand to alledge three causes of his going, when maister James sodainly interrupted him and saide: The three countes that make you goe to Bolonia are, Count Lewis da San Bonifacio, Count Hercules Rangon and the Count of Pepoli.

Then they all laughed because these three Countes had been Beroaldoes scholers and were proper young men and applyed their studie in Bolonia.

This kinde of merry jeasting therfore maketh a man laugh much, because it bringeth with it other manner answeres than a man looketh for to heare, and our own errour doth naturally delite us in these matters, which when it deceiveth us of that we looke for, wee laugh at it.

But the termes of speach and figures that have any grace and grave talke, are likewise (in a manner) alwaies comely in jeastes and merrie pleasantnesse.

See how wordes placed contrariwise give a great ornament, when one contrarie clause is set against an other.

The same manner is oftentimes verie merrie and pleasant. As a Genuese that was verie prodigall and lavish in his expences being reprehended by an usurer, who was most covetous that saide unto him: And when wilt thou leave casting away thy substance? Then answered he: when thou leavest stealing of other mens.

And because (as we have alreadie saide) of the places that wee derive jeastes from, that touch a man, wee may many times from the very same take grave sentences to praise and cõmend: It is a very comely and honest manner both for the one and the other purpose, when a man consenteth to and confirmeth the selfe same thing that the other speaketh, but interpreteth it otherwise thã he meaneth.

As within these few daies a Priest of the countrie saying Masse to his parishioners, after he had told them what holy dayes they should have that weeke, he beganne the generall confession in the name of all the people, and saide: I have sinned in ill doing, in ill speaking, in ill thinking, and the rest that followeth, making mention of all the deadly sins. Then a Gossippe of his and one that was very familiar with the Priest to sporte with him, saide to the standers by.

Beare recorde, Sirs, what he confesseth with his owne mouth he hath done, for I entend to present him to the bishop for it.

The very same manner used Sallazza della Pedrad to honour a Ladie withall, with whom entring in talk, after he had praysed her, beside her vertuous qualities, for her beautie also, she answered him that she deserved not that praise, because she was now well striken in yeares. And he then saide to her: That is in you of age, is nothing els but to liken you unto the Angels which were first, and are the auncientest creatures that ever God made.

Also merry sayinges are much to the purpose to nippe a man, as well as grave sayinges to praise one, so the metaphors be well applyed, and especially if they be answered, and he that maketh answere continue in the selfe same metaphor spoken by the other.

And in this sorte was answered to M. Palla Strozzi, which banished out of Florence, and sending thither one of his about certaine affaires, saide unto him after a threatening manner.

Tel Cosmus de Medicis in my name, that the henne sitteth a brood. The messenger did the errand to him, as hee was willed. And Cosmus without any more deliberation, answered him immediately.

413

Tell maister Palla in my name againe, that Hens can full ill sit a brood out of the nest.

With a metaphor also maister Camillo Parcaro commended honorably the Lord Marcantonia Colonna, who understanding that maister Camillo in an Oration of his had extolled certaine noble men of Italy that were famous in marciall prowesse, and among the rest had made most honourable mention of him, after rendring due thankes, he saide to him: you (maister Camillo) have done by your friendes as some marchant men play by their money, which finding a counterfeite Ducate, to dispatch him away, cast him into a heape of good ones and so utter him.

Even so you, to honour me withall, where I am litle worth, have set me in companie with so excellent and vertuous personages, that through their prowesse, I may peradventure passe for a good one. Then maister Camillo made answere.

They that use to counterfeite Ducates, gylt them so that they seeme to the eye much better than the good: therefore if there were to be found counterfeiters of men, as there be of Ducates, a man might have a just cause to suspect you were false, being (as you are) of much more faire and brighter mettall than anie of the rest.

You may see that this place is common both for the one and the other kinde of jeastes, and so are many moe, of the which a man might give infinite examples, and especially in grave sayinges. As the great captaine saide, (which being set at table and every roome filled) saw two Italian gentlemen standing by that had done him verie good service in the warre, sodainly he start up and made all the rest to arise to give place to those two, and saide.

Make roome Sirs for the gentlemẽ to sit at their meat, for had not they beene, wee shoulde not have had now wherewithall to feede our selves. He saide also to Diego Garzia that perswaded him to remove out of a dangerous place that lay open upon gunshot: Since God hath not put feare into your minde, put not you it into mine.

414

And king Lewis, which is now French king, where it was saide unto him soone after his creation, that then was the time to be even with the enimies that had done him much injurie while hee was Duke of Orleans. Hee made answere: That the French king hath nothing adoe to revenge the wronges done to the Duke of Orleans.

A man toucheth also in jeast manie times with a certaine gravitie without moving a man to laugh. As Gein Ottomani brother to the great Turke, when hee was prisoner in Rome, he saide: Justing (as wee used it in Italie) seemed to him over great a daliance, and a trifle to that should be in deede.

And he saide, when it was told him that king Ferdinande the younger was nimble and quicke of person in running, leaping, vauting, and such matters, in his countrey slaves used these exercises, but great men learned from their childhood liberalitie, and were renowmed for that.

And in a manner after that sorte, saving it had a litle more matter to laugh at, was that the Archbishop of Florence saide unto Cardinall Alexandrino, That men have nothing but Substance, a bodie and a soule. Their Substance is at Lawiers disposing, their bodie at Phisitions, and their soule at Divines.

Then answered the Lord Julian: A man might adde unto this ye saying of Nicholetto: which is, that it is seldom seene a Lawier to goe to law, nor a Phisition take medicin, nor a Divine a good Christian.

Maister Bernarde laughed, then hee proceeded: Of this there bee infinite examples spoken by great Princes and very grave men. But a man laugheth also many times at comparisons. As our Pistoia wrote unto Seraphin: I send thee backe againe thy great male which is like thy selfe. If ye remember well Seraphin was much like a male.

Againe, there be some that have a pastime to liken men and women to horses, to dogges, to birdes, and often times to coffers, to stooles, to cartes, to candelstickes, which sometime hath a good grace, and otherwhile very stale.

415

Therefore in this point a man must consider the place, the time, the persons, and the other thinges wee have so manie times spoken of.

Then spake the Lord Gasper Pallavicin: The comparison that the Lorde John Gonzaga made of Alexander the great to maister Alexander his sonne, was very pleasant. I wote not what it was, answered maister Bernarde.

The Lord Gasper saide: The Lord John was playing at dice (as his use is) and had lost a number of Ducats and was still on the losing hand, and maister Alexander his sonne, which for all hee is a childe, deliteth no lesse in play than his Father, stoode very still to behold him, and seemed very sad.

The Count of Pianella, that was there present with manie other gentlemen, said: See (my Lord) maister Alexander is verie heavie for your losse, and his hart panteth waiting when lucke wil come to you that he may get some of your winninges: therfore rid him of his griefe, and before yee lose the rest, give him at least one Ducate that he may goe play him too, among his companions.

Then saide the Lord John: You are deceived, for Alexander thinketh not upon such a trifle, but as it is writen of Alexander the great while he was a childe, understanding that Philip his father had discomfitted a great armie, and conquered a certaine kingdom, he fell in weeping, and when he was asked the question why he wept, hee answered, because he doubted that his father woulde conquere so many Countreyes, that he woulde have none left for him to conquere: Even so now Alexander my sonne is sory and readie to weepe in seeing me his father lose, because he doubted that I shall lose so much, that I shall leave him nothing at all to lose. When they had a while laughed at this, maister Bernarde went forwarde.

A man must take heed also his jesting be not wicked, and that the matters extend not to appeare quicke witted, to blaspheme, and studie therein to invent new waies.

Least herein, where a man deserveth not onely blame,

but also sharpe punishment, he should appeare to seeke a prayse, which is an abhominable matter. And therefore such as these be, that goe about to shew their pregnant witte with small reverence to Godwarde, deserve to bee excluded out of everie gentlemans company.

And no lesse, they that be filthie and baudie in talke, and that in the presence of women have no manner respect, and seeme to take none other delite, but to make women blush for shame, and uppon this go seeking out merrie and jeasting words.

As this yeare in Ferrara at a banket in presence of many Ladies, there was a Florentine and a Senese, which for the most part (as you know) are enimies together. The Senese saide to nip the Florentine: We have marryed Siena to the Emperour and given him Florence to dowrie. And this he spake because the talke was abroad in those dayes, that the Seneses had given a certaine quantitie of money to the Emperour, and he tooke the protection of them upon him.

The Florentine answered immediately: But Siena shall be first ridden (after the French phrase, but hee spake the Italian word) and then shall the dowrie afterwarde be pleaded for at good leasure.

You may see the taunt was wittie, but because it was in presence of women, it appeared bawdie and not to be spoken.

Then spake the Lord Gasper Pallavicin: Women have none other delite but to heare of such matters, and yet will you deprive them of it. And for my part I have beene readie to blush for shame at wordes which women have spoken to mee oftner than men.

I speake not of such women as these be, quoth maister Bernard, but of the vertuous that deserve to be reverenced and honoured of all gentlemen.

The Lorde Gasper saide: It were good we might find out some pretie rule how to know them, because most commonly the best in apparance are cleane contrarie in effect.

Then saide maister Bernard smiling: were not the Lorde

Julian here present, that in every place is counted the protector of women, I would take upon me to answere you, but I will not take his office from him.

Here the Ladie Emilia in like manner smyling, saide: Women neede no defender against an accuser of so small authoritie. Therefore let the Lorde Gasper alone in this his forward opinion, risen more because he could never finde woman that was willing to looke upon him, than for any want that is in women, and proceed you in your communication of jeastes.

Then maister Bernarde, truely Madam (quoth hee) me thinke I have named unto you many places, out of the which a man may picke pleasaunt and wittie sayinges, which afterwarde have so much the more grace, as they are set forth with a comelye protestation.

Yet may there bee alleaged manie other also, as when to increase or diminish, thinges be spoken that uncredibly passe the likelihood of truth. And of this sorte was that Marius de Volterra saide by a prelate that thought him selfe so tall a person, that as he went into Saint Peters, hee stouped for hitting his heade against the great beame over the porch.

Also the Lord Julian here saide, that Golpino his servant was so leane and drye, that in a morning as he was blowing the fire to kindle it, the smoke bore him up the chimney unto the fonnel, and had gone away with him had he not stuck on the crosse at one of the holes above.

And maister Augustine Bevazzano tolde, that a covetous man which woulde not sell his corne while it was at a high price, when he saw afterwarde it had a great fall, for desperation hee hanged him selfe upon a beame in his chamber, and a servant of his hearing the noise, made speede, and seeing his maister hang, forthwith cut in sunder the rope and so saved him from death: afterwarde when the covetous man came to him selfe, hee would have had his servant to have paide him for his haulter that he had cut.

Of this appeareth to bee also that Laurence de Medicis saide unto a colde jeaster: thou shouldest not make me to laugh if thou tickledst me. The like he answered unto an other foolish person, who in a morning had found him in bed very late, and blamed him for sleeping so much, saying unto him: I have now beene in the newe and olde market place, afterwarde I went out at the gate of San Gallo to walke about the walles, and have done a thousand other matters, and you are yet in bedde. Then saide Laurence: that I have dreamed in one houre, is more worth, than all that you have done in foure.

It is also pretie when one reprehendeth a thing which a man would not thinke hee minded to reprehend. As the marquesse Fredericke of Mantua our Dutchesse father being at table with many gentlemen, one of them after he had eaten up his dish of broth, saide: by your leave my Lorde marquesse. And when he had so saide, he began to suppe up the rest that remained in the dish. Then saide the marquesse by and by: Aske leave of the swine, for thou doest me no wrong at all.

Also maister Nicholas Leonicus saide, to touch a noble man that was falsly reported to be liberall: Gesse you what liberalitie is in him, that doth not onely give away his owne good but other mens also.

That is in like manner an honest and comely kinde of jeasting, that consisteth in a certaine dissimulation, when a man speaketh one thing and privily meaneth another. I speake not of the manner that is clean contrarie, as if one shoulde call a dwarfe a giant: and a blacke man, white: or one most ill favored, beawtifull: because they be too open contraries, although otherwhile also they stirre a man to laugh. But when with a grave and drie speach in sporting a man speaketh pleasantly that hee hath not in his mind.

As when a gentleman tolde maister Augustine Folietto a loud lye and earnestly did affirme it, because he thought he scarse believed it. At last maister Augustine saide: Gentleman, if you will ever doe me pleasure, be so good to me as to quiet your selfe in case I doe not believe any thing you say.

Yet when he replyed againe and bound it with an oth to be true, at length hee saide: Since you will have me, I am content to believe it for your sake, for to say the truth I would doe a greater thing for you than this commeth too.

In a manner after the same sorte Don Giovanni di Cardona saide of one that woulde forsake Rome: in mine opinion this fellow is ill advised, for hee is so wicked, that in abiding in Rome it may be his chaunce in time to be made a Cardinall.

Of this sorte is also that Alfonsus Santocroce saide, which a litle before having certaine injuries done him by the Cardinall of Pavia, and walking without Bolonia with certaine gentleman nigh unto the place of execution, and seeing one newly hanged there, turned him that way with a certaine heavie looke, and saide so loude that everie man might heare him: Thou art a happie man that hast nothing adoe with the Cardinall of Pavia.

And the kinde of jesting that is somewhat grounded upon scoffing seemeth verie meete for great men, because it is grave and wittie and may be used both in sporting matters and also in grave.

Therefore did many of olde time and men of best estimation use it: As Cato, Scipio Affricanus minor. But above all they say Socrates the Philosopher excelled in it. And in our time king Alphonsus the first of Aragon: which upon a time as he went to dinner tooke many rich jewels from his fingers, for wetting them in washing his handes, and so gave them to him that stood next him as though hee had not minded who it was. This servant had thought sure the king marked not to whom he gave them, and because his heade was busied with more waighty affaires, woulde soone forget them cleane, and thereof hee tooke the more assurance when hee saw the king asked not for them againe. And when that matter was passed certaine dayes, weekes, and monthes without hearing any worde of it, he thought surely he was safe.

And so about the yeares end after this matter had happened, an other time as the king was in like manner going to dinner, he stepped forth and put out his hand to take the kinges ringes. Then the king rounding him in the eare, saide: The first is well for thee, these shal be good for another.

See this taunt how pleasant, wittie, and grave it is, and worthie in verie deede for the noble courage of an Alexander.

Like unto this manner grounded upō scoffing there is also an other kinde, when with honest wordes, a man nameth a vicious matter or a thing that deserveth blame. As the great Captaine saide unto a gentleman of his, that after the journey of Cirignola and when all things were alreadie in safetie, met him as richly armed as might be, readie to fight. Then the great Captaine turning him to Don Ugo di Cardona, saide: Feare ye not now any more Sea tempest, for S. Hermus hath appeared. And with this honest worde hee gave him a nicke. Because you know Saint Hermus doth alwaies appeare unto Mariners after a tempest, and giveth a token of calme.

And the meaning of the great Captaine was, that when this gentleman appeared, it was a signe the daunger was alreadie cleane past.

Againe maister Octavian Ubaldino being in Florence in companie with certaine of the best Citizens, and reasoning together of souldiers, one of them asked him whether he knew Antonello da Forli which was then fledde out of the state of Florence. Maister Octavian answered: I have no great knowledge of him, but I have heard him alwaies reported to be a quicke souldier. Then saide an other Florentine, It appeareth he is quicke, for he tarried not so long as to aske leave to depart.

They be also pretie taunts when a man of the very communication of his fellow taketh that he would not, and my

421

meaning is in that sort, as our Duke answered the Captaine that lost Saint Leo. When this state was taken by Pope Alexander, and given to Duke Valentin.

The Duke being in Venice at that time I speake of, many of his subjects came continually to give him secrete information how the matters of state passed, and among the rest, thither came also the Captaine: which after hee had excused himselfe the best he coulde, laying the fault in his unluckinesse, hee saide.

My Lord doubt ye not, my hart serveth mee yet to worke a mean that Saint Leo may be recovered again. Then answered the Duke: trouble not thy self any more about it, for in losing it thou hast wrought a meane that it may be recovered againe.

Certaine other sayinges there are, when a man that is knowne to be wittie speaketh a matter that seemeth to proceede of follie. As the last day maister Camillo Paleotto saide by one: that foole, as soone as hee began to waxe rich, died.

There is like unto this matter a certaine wittie and kinde dissimulation, when a man (as I have saide) that is wise maketh semblant not to understand that hee doth understand.

As the marquesse Fredericke of Mantua, which being sued to by a prating felow that complained upon a certaine of his neighbours taking the Pigions of his Dovehouse with snares, and held one continually in his hand hanging by the foote in a snare, which he had found so deade, hee answered him that there would be a remedie for it.

This fellow never satisfied, not once but many a time repeated unto him his losse, shewing alwaies the Pigion so hanged, and saide still: But I beseech you, how think ye (my Lorde) what shoulde a man doe in this matter?

The marquesse at length saide: By mine advise the Pigion ought in no wise to be buried in the Church, for since he hath so hanged him selfe, it is to be thought that he was desperate.

In a manner after the same sorte was that Scipio Nasica saide unto Ennius. For when Scipio went unto Ennius house to speake with him and called to him in the streete, a maiden of his made him answere that he was not at home. And Scipio heard plainely Ennius him self speak unto his maiden to tell him that he was not at home, so he departed.

Within a while after Ennius came unto Scipioes house, and so likewise stoode beneath, and called him. Unto whom Scipio himselfe with a loude voice made answere, that hee was not at home.

Then saide Ennius: What, doe not I know thy voice? Scipio answered: Thou hast small courtesie in thee, the last day I believed thy maiden, that thou wast not at home, and now wilt not thou believe me my selfe?

It is also pretie when one is touched in the verie same matter that he hath first touched his fellow.

As Alonso Carillo being in the Spanish Court, and having committed certaine youthfull partes, that were of no great importance, was by the kings commandement carried to prison, and there abode for one night. The next day he was taken out againe, and when he came to the pallace in the morning, he entred into the chamber of presence, that was full of gentlemen and Ladies, and jeasting together at this his imprisonment, maistresse Boadilla saide.

Maister Alonso, I tooke great thought for this mishap of yours, for all that knew you were in feare lest the king would have hanged you.

Then saide immediatly Alonso: In deede maistresse, I was in doubt of the matter my selfe too, but yet I had a good hope that you would have begged me for your husband.

See how sharpe and wittie this is. Because in Spaine (as in many other places also) the manner is when a man is lead to execution, if a common harlot will ask him for her husband, it saveth his life.

In this manner also Raphaell the painter answered two Cardinals (with whom he might be familiar) which to make him talke, founde fault in his hearing with a table he had made, where S. Peter and S. Paule were: saying, that those two pictures were too redde in the face. Then saide Raphael by and by.

My Lordes, wonder you not at it, for I have made them so for the nonce, because it is to be thought that S. Peter and S. Paule are even as red in Heaven as you see them here, for very shame, that their Church is governed by such men as you be.

Also those jeasts are pleasant that have in them a certaine privy semblāt of laughter. As when a husband lamented much and bewailed his wife that had hanged her selfe upon a figge tree, an other came to him and plucking him by the sleeve, saide.

Friende, may I receive such pleasure as to have a graffe of that figge tree to graffe in some stocke of mine Orchard?

There be certaine of other jeastes that bee patient and spoken softly with a kinde of gravitie. As a man of the Countrie carrying a coffer upon his shoulders, chaunced therewithall to give Cato a hard push, and afterwarde saide: Give roome: Cato answered: hast thou any thing upon thy shoulders beside that coffer?

It is also a matter of laughter when a man hath committed an errour, and to amend it speaketh a matter purposely that appeareth foolish, and yet is applyed to the end that he hath appointed, and serveth his turne therewithal that he seeme not out of countenance and dismayed.

As not longe since two enemies being together in the counsel chamber of Florence, (as it happeneth often in those Common weales) the one of them which was of the house of Altoviti, slept, and he that satte next unto him for a sport, where his adversarie that was of the house of Alamanni, had saide nothing neither then nor before, stirring him with his elbow made him awake, and saide unto him: Hearest thou not what such a one saith? make answere, for the Lords aske for thine advise.

Then did Altoviti all sleepie arise upon his feete and

without any more deliberation saide: My Lordes, I say the cleane contrarie to that Alamanni hath spoken.

Alamanni answered, what? I have saide nothing: Altoviti saide immediatly: To that thou wilt speake.

In this manner also did your maister Seraphin the Phisition here in Urbin say unto a man of the Countrie, which had received such a stroke upon the eye, that in very deede it was out, yet thought he best to goe seeke to maister Seraphin for remedie. When hee saw it, though he knew it was past cure, yet to plucke money out of his handes as that blow had plucked the eye out of his heade, he promised him largely to heale it. And so he was in hand with him every daye for money, putting him in comfort that within sixe or seven dayes, he should beginne to see with it againe.

The poore Countrie man gave him the litle he had, but when he saw him so prolong the matter, he began to finde himselfe agreeved with the Phisition, and saide that he was nothing the better, neither coulde he see any more with that eye, than if he had none at all in his head.

At length maister Seraphin perceiving there was no more to be gotten at his handes, saide: Brother mine, thou must have patience, thou hast cleane lost thine eye, and no remedie is there for it, pray God thou lose not thine other withall.

The Countrie man seeing this, fell in weeping, and lamented much, and saide, maister mine, you have pilled me and robbed me of my money, I will complaine to the Duke, and made the greatest outcries in the world.

Then saide maister Seraphin in a rage, and to cleare himselfe: ah thou villaine knave: thou wouldest then have two eyes as Citizens and honest men have, wouldest thou? Get thee hence in the divels name. And those words were thrust out with such fury, that the poore sillie man was dismayed, and held his peace, and soft and faire departed in Gods name, thinking that hee himselfe had beene in the wrong.

It is also pretie when a man declareth or interpreteth a matter merrily. As in the Spanish Court in a morning there came into the palace a knight who was very ill favoured, and his wife, that was verye beautifull, both apparrelled in white Damaske, and the Queene saide unto Alonso Carillo, How thinke yee Alonso by these two?

Madam, answered Alonso, me thinke the Ladie is the Dame, and he the Aske, which signifieth a foule person and uglesome. Also when Raphael de Pazzi saw a letter that the Priour of Messina had writen to a maistresse of his, the superscription whereof was: *Esta carta s' ha dar a qui en causa mi penar,* that is, This letter be given to the cause of my griefe: me thinke (quoth he) this letter is directed to Paul Tholossa.

Imagine you howe the standers by laughed at it, for they all knew that Paule Tholossa had lent ten thousand Ducates to the Priour of Messina, and because he was verie lavish in his expences, he coulde finde no way to pay his debt.

It is like unto this, when a man giveth familiar admonition in manner of counsel, but dissemblingly. As Cosmus de Medicis saide unto a friend of his that had more riches than witte, and by Cosmus meanes had compassed an office without Florence, and at his setting forth asking Cosmus what way he thought best for him to take to execute this office well.

Cosmus answered him: Apparel thy selfe in scarlet, and speake litle. Of this sort was that Count Lewis saide unto one that woulde passe for an unknowne person in a certaine daungerous place, and wist not how to disguise him selfe, and the Count being demaunded of his advise therein, answered: Apparrell thy selfe like a Doctor, or in some other raiment that wise men use to weare.

Also Jannotti de Pazzi saide unto one that minded to make an arming coate of as many divers colours as might be invented: Take the wordes and deedes of the Cardinall of Pavia.

426

A man laugheth also at certaine matters disagreeing. As one saide the last day unto maister Antony Rizzo of a certaine Forlivese.

Gesse whether he be a foole or no, for his name is Bartholomew. And an other: Thou seekest a rider and hast no horses. And this man wanteth nothing but good and a horse.

And at certaine other that seeme to agree. As within these few dayes where there was a suspition that a friend of ours had caused a false advousion of a benefice to bee drawne out, afterward when an other Priest fell sicke, Antony Torello saide unto him: What dost thou linger the matter? Why dost thou not send for thy Clarke and see whether thou canst hit upon this other benefice?

Likewise at certaine that doe not agree. As the last day when the Pope had sent for maister John Luke of Pontremolo and maister Dominick da la Porta, which (as you know) are both crookebacked, and made them Auditours, saying that hee intended to bring the Rota into a right frame. Maister Latin Juvenal saide: Our holy father is deceived, if he thinke that he can bring the Rota into a right frame with two crooked persons.

Also it provoketh laughter, when a man graunteth the thing that is tolde him and more, but seemeth to understand it otherwise. As Captaine Peralta being brought into the lists to fight the combat with Aldana, and Captaine Molart that was Aldanas patrone, requiring Peralta to sweare, whether he had about him any Saint Johns Gospel or charme and inchauntment, to preserve him from hurt. Peralta swore that he had about him neither Gospel nor inchantment, nor relike, nor any matter of devotion wherein he had any faith.

Then saide Molart, to touch him to be a Marrane: Well no mo wordes in this, for I believe without swearing that you have no faith also in Christ.

It is pretie moreover to use metaphors at a time in such purposes. As our maister Marcantonio that saide to Botton

427

de Cesena, who had vexed him with wordes: Botton, Botton, thou shalt one day be the button, and the haulter shall be the buttonhole.

And also when Marcantonio had made a Comedy which was very long and of sundrie actes, the very same Botton saide in like manner to Marcantonio: to play your Comedie ye shall neede for preparation as much woode as is in Sclavonia. Maister Marcantonio answered, and for preparation of thy Tragedie three trees [28] is inough.

Againe a man speaketh a word many times wherein is a privie signification farre from that appeareth hee would say. As the Lord Generall here being in companye where there was a communication of a Captaine that in deede all his life time for the more part had received the overthrow, and as then by a chaunce wan the victorie: and when hee that ministred this talke saide: When he made his enterie into that towne he was apparelled in a very faire crimosin velvet coate, which he wore alwaies after his victories. The Lord Generall saide, Belike it is verie new.

And no lesse doth it provoke laughter, when otherwhile a man maketh answere unto that which the other he talketh withall hath not spoken: or els seemeth to believe he hath done that which he hath not done, and should have done it.

As Andrew Cosia, when he went to visit a gentleman that discourteously suffered him to stand on his feete and he himselfe sate, saide: Since you commande me Sir, to obey you, I will sit, and so sate him downe.

Also a man laugheth when one accuseth himself of some trespasse. As the last day when I saide to the Dukes Chaplaine, that my Lordes grace had a Chaplaine that could say masse sooner than he: He answered me, it is not possible. And rounding mee in the eare, saide. You shall understand that I say not the third part of the secretes.

Also Biagin Crivello, when a Priest was slaine at Millane, he required his benefice of the Duke, the which he was minded to bestow upon another. At length Biagin perceiving no other reason would prevaile, and what (quoth he) if I were the cause of his death, why will you not give me his benefice?

It hath also many times a good grace to wish those thinges that can not be. As the last day one of our company beholding all these gentlemen here playing at fence, and he lying upon a bedde, saide: O what a pleasure it were, were this also a valiant mans and a good souldiers exercise.

In like manner it is a pretie and wittie kinde of speaking, and especially in grave men and of authoritie, to answere contrarie to that he woulde with whom he talketh, but drily and (as it were) with a certaine doubting and heedfull consideration.

As in times past Alphonsus the first king of Aragon, giving unto a servant of his, horse, harnesse and apparrell, because he told how the night before he had dreamed that his highnesse had given him all those kinde of matters, and not long after, the verie same servant saide againe how he dreamed that night, that he had given him a good sorte of royalles, hee answered him: Henceforth believe dreames no more, for they are not alwaies true.

In this sorte also did the Pope answere the Bishop of Cervia, that to grope his mind saide unto him: Holy father, it is noysed all Rome over and in the Palace too, that your holinesse maketh me governour.

Then answered the Pope: Let the knaves speake what they lust, doubt you not, it is not true I warrant you. I coulde (my Lordes) beside these gather many other places, from which a man maye draw merrie and pleasant jeastes, as matters spoken with feare, with marvaile, with threatnings out of order, with overmuch furiousnesse: Beside this, certaine newly happened cases provoke laughter: sometime silence with a certaine wonder: at other times verie laughter it selfe without purpose. But me thinke I have now spoken sufficient: for the jeastes that consist in wordes (I believe) passe not these boundes we have reasoned of.

As for such as be in operation, though there be infinite partes of them, yet are they drawne into few principles.

But in both kindes the chiefe matter is to deceive opinion, and to answere otherwise than the hearer looketh for: and (in case the jeast shall have any grace) it must needs be seasoned with this deceite, or dissimulation, or mocking, or rebuking, or comparison, or what ever other kinde a man will use.

And although all kinde of jeastes move a man to laugh, yet doe they also in this laughter make diverse effects. For some have in them a certaine cleannesse and modest pleasantnesse. Other bite sometime privily, otherwhile openly. Other have in them a certaine wantonnesse. Other make one laugh as soone as he heareth them. Other the more a man thinketh upon them. Other in laughing make a man blush withall. Other stirre a man somewhat to anger. But in all kindes a man must consider the disposition of the mindes of the hearers, because unto persons in adversity oftentimes merry toyes augment their affliction: and some infirmities ther be, that the more a mã occupieth medicine about them, the worse they waxe.

In case therefore the Courtier in jesting and speaking merry conceites have a respect to the time, to the persons, to his degree, and not use it too often (for pardye it bringeth a lothsomnesse if a man stand evermore about it all day in all kinde of talke and without purpose) hee may be called pleasant and feate conceited. So hee be heedfull also that he be not so bitter and byting, that a man might conjecture hee were an envious person, in pricking without a cause, or for plaine malice, or men of too great authoritie (which is lacke of discretion) or of too much miserie (which is crueltie) or too mischievous (which is vanitie) or els in speaking matters that may offend them whom he would not offend (which is ignorance.) For some there bee that thinke they are bound to speake and to nip without regarde, as often as they can, how ever the matter goe afterwarde.

And among these kinde of persons are they, that to speake a word which should seeme to come of a redines of wit, passe not for staining of a worthie gentlewomans honestie, which is a verie naughtie matter and worthy sore punishment. Because in this point women are in the number of sillie soules and persons in misery, and therefore deserve not to be nipped in it, for they have not weapon to defend themselves.

But beside these respects, he that will be pleasant and full of jeasting, must be shaped of a certaine nature apt to all kinde of pleasantnesse, and unto that frame his fashions, gestures, and countenance, the which the more grave, steadie and set it is, so much the more maketh it the matters spoken to seeme wittie and subtil.

But you (Sir Frederick) that ought to rest your selfe under this my tree without leaves, and in my withered reasonings, I believe you have repented your selfe, and you recken ye are entred into a bayting place [29] of Montefiore.

Therefore it shall be well done for you like a wel practised Courtier (to avoid an ill hosterie) to arise somewhat before your ordinarie houre and set forwarde on your journey.

Nay, answered Sir Fredericke, I am come to so good an hosterie, that I minde to tarrie in it longer than I had thought at y\e first. Therefore I will rest mee yet a while, untill you have made an end of al the talke ye have begun withall. Whereof ye have left out one parcel that ye named at the beginning: which is merrie pranckes, and it were not well done to deceive the companie of it.

But as you have taught us many pretie matters concerning jeastes, and made us hardie to use them through example of so many singular wittes, great men, Princes, Kinges and Popes, I suppose ye will likewise in merie pranckes so bolden us, that we may take a courage to practise some against your selfe.

Then saide maister Bernarde smyling: you shall not be the first, but perhaps it will not be your chaunce, for I have so many times beene served with them, that it maketh me looke well about me: As dogs, after they have

431

beene once scaulded with hote water, are afeard of the colde.

Howbeit since you will save me to speake somewhat of this too, I believe I may rid my handes of it in fewe wordes.

And in mine opinion a merie prancke is nothing els, but a friendly deceite in matters that offend not at al or very litle. And even as in jeasting to speake contrarie to expectation moveth laughter, so doth in merrie pranckes, to doe contrarie to expectation. And these doe so much the more delite and are to be practised, as they be wittie and modest. For he that will worke a merrie prancke without respect, doth many times offend, and then arise debates and sore hatred.

But the places that a man may derive merrie pranckes from, are (in a manner) the verie same that be in jeasts. Therefore to avoid repetition of them, I will say no more but that there bee two kindes of merrie pranckes every one of which may afterward be devided into moe partes.

The one is, when any man whosoever he be, is deceived wittily, and after a feate manner and with pleasantnesse. The other, when a man layeth (as it were) a nette, and sheweth a peece of a baite so, that a man runneth to bee deceived of himselfe.

The first is such, as the merrie prancke was, that within these few dayes was wrought unto a couple of great Ladies (whom I will not name) by the meane of a Spaniarde called Castilio.

Then the Dutchesse, and why, (quoth she) will you not name them? maister Bernarde answered: because I would not have them to take it in ill part.

Then saide the Dutchesse againe, smyling: it is not against good manner sometime to use merrie pranckes with great men also. And I have heard of many that have beene played to Duke Fredericke, to king Alphonsus of Aragon, to Queene Isabel of Spaine, and to many other great Princes, and not onely they tooke it not in ill part, but rewarded verie largely them that played them those partes.

Maister Bernarde answered: neither upon this hope doe I entende to name them. Say as pleaseth you, quoth the Dutchesse. Then proceeded maister Bernarde and saide: Not manie dayes since in the Court that I meane, there arrived a man of the Countrey about Bergamo, to be in service with a gentleman of the Court: which was so well set out with garments and so finely clad, that for all his bringing up was alwaies in keeping oxen and could doe nothing els, yet a man that had not heard him speake woulde have judged him a worthie gentleman.

And so when those two Ladies were enformed that there was arrived a Spaniarde, servant to Cardinall Borgia whose name was Castilio, a very wittie man, a musition, a dauncer, and the best Courtier in all Spaine, they longed verie much to speake with him, and sent incontinently for him, and after they had received him honourably, they caused him to sit down, and began to entertaine him with a very great respect in the presence of all men, and few there were present that knew him not to be a Bergamaske Cowheard.

Therefore seeing those Ladies entertaine him with such respect, and honour him so much, they fell all in a laughing, the more because the sillie fellow spake still his native language the mere Bergamaske tongue.

But the gentlemen that devised this prancke, had first tolde those Ladies that among other thinges he was a great dissembler, and spake all tongues excellently well, and especially the Countrie speach of Lumbard, so that they thought he fained, and many times they beheld the one the other with certaine marvellings, and saide: what a wonderfull matter is this, how he counterfaiteth this tongue?

In conclusion, this communication lasted so long, that every mans sides aked for laughing, and he coulde not choose him selfe but utter so many tokens of his noblenesse of birth, that at length those Ladies (but with much adoe) beiieved hee was the man that he was in deed.

Such merrie pranckes we see dayly, but among the rest they be pleasant that at the first make a man agast, and after that, end in a matter of suretie, because he that was deceived laugheth at himselfe when he perceiveth he was afeard of nothing.

As lying upon a time in Paglia, there chanced to be in the verie same Inne three other good fellowes, two of Pistoia and one of Prato, which after supper (as the manner is for the most part) fell to gaming. And not long after, one of the Pistoians losing his rest, had not a farthing left him to blesse him selfe, but beganne to chafe, to curse, and to banne and to blaspheme terribly, and thus tearing of God he went to bedde. The other two after they had played a while, agreed to worke a merrie prancke with him that was gone to bed.

And when they perceived that he was fallen in sleepe, they blewe out the candels and raked up the fire and beganne to speake aloud, and to make the greatest hurly burly in the world, making wise to contend together about their game. The one saide: Thou tookest the card underneath. The other denying it saide: Thou hast vied upon flush, let us mount: and such other matters, with such noise, that he that slept awoke, and hearing them at play and talking even as though they had seene the cardes, did a litle open his eyes: when hee saw there was no manner light in the chamber, he saide: What a divel meane you to cry thus all night?

Afterwarde hee laide him downe againe to sleepe. The other two companions gave him no manner answere: but still continued in their purpose untill he awoke better, and much wondred, and when he sawe for certaintie that there was neither fire nor any kinde of light, and perceived they played still and fell in contention, he said.

And how can ye see the cardes without light? The one of the two answered, I weene thou hast lost thy sight as well as thy money. Seest thou not that wee have here two candles?

He that was in bedde lift up himselfe upō his elbowes, and in a manner angred, said: Either I am dronken or blinde, or els you make a lye. The two arose and went to yᵉ bed darkelong, laughing and making wise to believe that he went about to mocke them. And he againe saide to them: I tell you truth I see you not. At length the two began to wonder much, and the one said to the other. By good Lord, I believe he speaketh in good earnest, reach me the candle, and let us see lest perhaps hee have some impediment in his sight.

Then thought the poore wretch surely that hee had beene blinde, and weeping downe right, saide: oh sirs, I am blind, and forthwith hee beganne to call upon our Ladie of Loreto and to beseech her to pardon him his blasphemies and cursing for the losse of his money.

But his two companions put him in good comfort and saide: it is not possible but thou shouldest see us. It is some fancie that thou hast conceived in thine head. Oh good Lorde answered the other, it is no fancie, nor I see no more than if I had never had eyes in my head. Thy sight is cleare inough, quoth the two. And the one saide to the other.

Marke how well he openeth his eyes: and how faire they be to looke to: and who would believe but he coulde see? The pore soule wept faster, and cryed God mercie.

In conclusion they saide unto him: see thou make a vow to goe devoutly to our Ladie of Loreto barefooted and bare legged, for that is the best remedie that may be had. And in the mean space we will goe to Aquapendente and the other townes here about to seeke for some Phisition, and will helpe thee in what we can.

Then did the sillie soule kneele upon his knees in the bed, and with aboundance of teares and very bitter repentance for his blaspheming, made a solemne vow to goe naked to our Ladie of Loreto and to offer unto her a paire of eyes of silver, and to eate no flesh upon the wednesday, nor egges upon Friday, and to fast breade and water every Saterday in worship of our Ladie, if she give him the grace to receive his sight againe.

The two companions entring into an other chamber, lighted a candel, and came with the greatest laughter in the world before this poore soule, who for all he was rid of so great an anguish as you may thinke he had, yet was he so astonied with his former feare, that he could not only not laugh, but not once speake a word, and the two companions did nothing else but stur him, saying that hee was bounde to perfourme all those vowes, for that hee had received the grace he asked.

Of the other kinde of merrie pranckes when a man deceiveth himselfe, I will give you none other example, but what happened unto me my selfe not long since. For this shroftide that is past, my Lordes grace of Saint Peter ad vincula, which knoweth full well what a delite I have when I am in maskerie to playe merrie prankes with Friers, having first given order as hee devised the matter, came uppon a day with my Lorde of Aragon and certaine other Cardinals, to ye windowes, making wise to stand there to see maskers passe to and fro, as the manner of Rome is.

I being in maskerie passed by, and when I behelde on the one side of the streete a Frier standing (as it were) in a studie with himselfe, I judged I had found that I sought for, and forthwith ranne to him, like a greedie hauke to her pray, and when I had asked him and he told me who hee was, I made semblant to knowe him, and with many wordes beganne to make him believe that the marshall went about to seeke him for certaine complaintes against him, and perswaded him to goe with me to the Chauncerie and there I would save him.

The Frier dismaied and all trembling seemed as though he wist not what to doe, and saide that he doubted taking, in case he shoulde goe farre from Saint Celso. Stil I put him in good comfort, and said so much to him, that he leaped up behind me, and then me thought my devise was fully accomplished. And I beganne to ride my horse by and by up and downe the merchants streete, which went kicking and winsing.

Imagine with your selves now what a faire sight it was to beholde a Frier on horsebacke behind a masker, his garments flying abroad, and his head shaking too and fro, that a man would have thought he had been alwaies falling.

With this faire sight, the gentlemen began to hurle egges out at the windowes, and afterwarde all the bankers and as many as were there, so that the haile never fell with a more violence from the skye, than there fell egges out from ye windowes, which for the most part came all upô me. And I for that I was in maskerie, passed not upon the matter, and thought verily that all the laughing had beene for the Frier and not for me, and upon this went sundrie times up and downe the bankes, alwaies with that furie of hel behind me. And though the Frier (in manner) weeping besought mee to let him goe downe, and not to shew such shame to the weede, yet did the knave afterwarde privily cause egs to be given him by certaine Lackies set there for the nonce, and making wise to gripe me hard for falling, squised them in my bosom, and many times on my heade, and otherwhile on my forehead, so that I was foule arrayed.

Finally, when every man was wearie both of laughing and throwing egges, he leaped downe from behinde me, and plucking his hoode backwarde, shewed a great bush of haire, and saide: maister Bernarde I am a horsekeeper in the stable of Saint Peter ad vincula, and am hee that looketh to your Mulet.

Then wist I not which prevailed most in me, griefe, anger, or shame. Yet for the lesse hurt, I fled toward my lodging, and the next morning I durst not shew my heade abroad. But the laughing at that merrie prancke did not endure the day following onely, but also lasteth (in man-

ner) untill this day. And so when they had a while renewed the laughing at rehearsing this againe, maister
Bernard proceeded.

It is also a good and pleasant kinde of merrie prancks,
from whence in like manner jeastes are derived, when one
believeth that a man will doe a matter which he will not
in deed.

As when I was in an evening after supper upon the
bridge of Leo, and going together with Cesar Beccadello
sporting one with another, we beganne to take holde fast
the one of the others armes, as though we would have
wrastled, because then wee perceived no man about the
bridge, and being in this manner together, there came two
French men by, which seeing us thus striving, demaunded
what the matter meant, and staied to part us, thinking we
had beene at debate in good earnest.

Then said I incontinently: Helpe sirs, for this poore
gentleman at certaine times of the Moone is frantike, and
see now how he striveth to cast himselfe off the bridge
into the river.

Then did the two runne and laide hand upon Cesar with
me and held him straight. And he (saying alwaies that I
was out of my wit) struggled the more to winde himselfe
out of their handes, and they griped him so much the
harder. At this the people assembled to beholde our ruffling together, and everie man ran, and the more poore
Cesar laide about him with his handes and feete (for he
beganne now to enter into choller) the more resort of the
people there was, and for the great strength he put, they
believed verily that hee would have leaped into the river,
and therefore held they him the straiter, so that a great
throng of people carried him to the Inne above ground,
all turmoiled and without his cappe, pale for wrath and
shame, that nothing hee spake coulde prevaile, partly because those Frenchmen understood him not, and partly
because I also carrying him to the Inne did alwaies bewaile
the poore soules ill lucke, that was so waxed out of his wit.

Now (as we have saide) of merrie prancks a man may talke at large, but it sufficeth to repeat that the places whence they are derived bee the verie same which wee have saide of jestes.

As for examples, we have infinite which wee see dayly and among the rest there are many pleasant in the tales of Boccaccio, as those that Bruno and Buffalmacco plaied [30] to their Calandrino, and to maister Symon: and many other of women, which in verie deede are wittie and pretie.

I remember also I have knowne in my dayes many that have beene merrily disposed in this manner, and among the rest a scholer in Padoa borne in Sicilia, called Pontius, which seeing upon a time a man of the Countrie have a couple of fat Capons, faining himselfe to buye them, was at a point with him for the price, and bid him come with him to his lodging, for beside his price hee woulde give him somewhat to breake his fast withall. And so brought him to a place where was a steeple that stood by him selfe alone severed frō the Church, that a man might goe round about him, and directly over against one of the foure sides of the steeple was a lane.

Here Pontius, when he had first bethought himself what he had to doe, saide unto the man of the Countrie: I have laide these Capons on a wager with a fellow of mine, who saith that this Toure compasseth fortie foote, and I say no, and even as I met with thee, I had bought this packthreed to measure it.

Therefore before we goe to my lodging, I will trye which of us hath wonne the wager. And in so saying, he drew the pacthreed out of his sleeve, and put the one end of it into the man of the Countries hand, and saide: give here, and so tooke the Capons: and with the other end he began to goe about the bell toure, as though hee would have measured it, making first the man of the Countrie to stand still, and to holde the pacthreed directly on the contrarie side of the toure to that, that was at the head of the lane, where as soone as he came, he drove a naile into the wall, to the which hee tyed the packthreede, and leaving it so, went his wayes without any more adoe downe the lane with the Capons.

The man of the countrey stood still a good while, all-wayes lookinge when hee would have done measuring. At length after hee had sayde many times, what do you so long? he thought hee would see, and founde that Pontius held not the line, but a naile that was drivē into the wal, which onelye remayned for payment of his Capons.

Of this sorte Pontius played many Merry Pranckes. And ther have bene also manye other pleasaunt men in this maner, as Gonella Meliolo in those dayes, and now our Frier Seraphin and Frier Marian here, and many well knowen to you all. And in very deede this kind is to bee praysed in men that make profession of nothinge els. But the merry prankes that the Courtier oughte to use, must (by myne advise) bee somewhat wide from immoderate jesting.

He ought also to take heed that his mery prankes turne not to pilferinge, as wee see many naughty packes, that wander about the worlde with divers shifts to get money, fayninge now one matter, now another. And that they be not yet bitter, and above all that hee have respect and reverence, as well in this, as in all other thinges, to women, and especially where the stayninge of their honesty shall consist.

Then the L. Gaspar, truely, M. Bernard (quoth hee) you are too partiall to these women. And why will you that men shoulde have more respect to women than women to men? Set not you as much by your honestye, as they do by theirs?

Thinke you thē that women ought to nip men both with wordes and mockes, in everye matter without anye regard, and men should stand with a flea in their eare, and thanke them for it?

M. Bernard aunsweared: I say not the contrary, but women in their Jestes and merry prankes, ought to have the respectes to menne which wee have spoken of. Yet I say, with more liberty may they touch men of small honesty, then men may them. And that beecause wee our selves have established for a law, that in us wanton life is no vice, nor default, nor any slaunder, and in women it is so great a reproach and shame, that shee that hath once an ill name, whether the reporte that goeth of her be true or false, hath lost her credite for ever.

Therefore since talking of womens honesty is so daungerous a matter to offende them sore. I say that wee ought to touch them in other matters, and refraine from this. For when the Jest or merry prancke, nippeth too sore, it goeth out of ye bounds which we have allready said is fit for a gentleman.

Here M. Bernard making a little stop, the L. Octavian Fregoso saide smyling: My L. Gaspar can make you an aunsweare to this law, which you alledge that wee our selves have made, that it is not perchance so out of reason, as you thinke. For since women are so unperfit creatures, and of litle or no worthinesse in respect of men, it behoved for that they were not apt to worke any vertuous deede of themselves, that they should have a bridle put upon them with shame and feare of infamie, that should (in manner) by force bring into them some good condition. And continencie was thought more necessarie in them than any other, to have assurance of children.

So that verie force hath driven men with all inventions, pollicies, and waies possible, to make women continent, and (in manner) graunted them in all thinges beside to be of small worthinesse, and to doe the cleane côtrarie alwaies to that they ought to doe.

Therefore since it is lawfull for them to swarve out of the way in al other things without blame, if we should touch them in those defaults, wherein (as we have saide) they are to be borne withall, and therefore are not unseemely in them, and passe full litle upon it, we shoulde never move laughter. For you have alreadie saide, that laugh-

ter is provoked with certaine thinges that are disagreeing.

Then spake the Dutchesse: speake you (my Lord Octavian) of women thus, and then complaine that they love
you not?

The Lorde Octavian answered: I complaine not of it,
but rather I thanke them for it, since in not loving of me,
they binde not me to love them. Neither doe I speake after
mine owne opinion, but I say that the Lorde Gaspar might
alleage these reasons.

Maister Bernarde saide: truely women should make a
good bargaine, if they could make attonements with such
two great enimies as you and the Lord Gasper be.

I am not their enimie answered the Lord Gasper, but
you are an enimie to men. For in case you wil not have
women touched in this honestie of theirs, you ought as well
to appoint them a law not to touch men, in that which
is as much shame to us, as incontinencie to women.

And why was it not as meete for Alonso Carillo to make
the answere which hee gave mistresse Boadilla of the hope
that hee had to save his life, in that she would take him
to husband, as it was for her to say first: All that knew him
thought the king woulde have hanged him? [31]

And why was it not as lawfull for Richard Minutoli to
beguile Phillippellos wife, and to traine her to that baite,
as it was for Beatrice to make Egano her husband arise
out of his bedde, and Anichin to beswadele him with a
cudgell, after she had lyen a good space with him?

And the other that tyed the packthreede to her great
toe, and made her owne husband believe that hee was not
himselfe, since you saye those merrie pranckes of women
in Boccaccio are so wittie and pretie?

Then saide maister Bernarde smiling: my Lordes, for so
much as my part hath beene to entreate onely of jeastes,
I entend not to passe my boundes therein, and I suppose
I have alreadie shewed why I judge it not meete to touch
women neither in worde nor deede above their honestie,

442

and I have also given them a rule not to nip men where it greeveth them.

But I say, that those merrie pranckes and jeastes which you (my Lord Gasper), aleage, as that Alonso saide unto maister Boadilla, although it somewhat touch honestie: yet doth it not discontent mee, because it is set farre inough, and is so privie, that it may be seemely understood, so, that hee might have dissembled the matter, and affirmed that he spake it not to that end.

He spake an other (in mine opinion) verie unseemely, which was: when the queene passed by maister Boadillas house, Alonso saw painted with coales all the gate over such kind of dishonest beasts, as are painted about Innes in such sundrie wise, and comming to the Countesse of Castagneto saide unto her.

See (madam) the heads of the wilde beasts that maister Boadilla killeth every day in hunting. Marke you this, though it were a wittie metaphor, and borrowed of hunters, that count it a glorie to have many wilde beastes heades nailed at their gates, yet is it dishonest and shamefull jeasting. Beside that, it was not in answering, for an answere hath much more courtesie in it, because it is thought that a man is provoked to it, and it must needes bee at a sodaine.

But to returne to our matter of the merrie pranckes of women, I say not that they doe well to beguile their husbands: But I say that some of the deceites which Boccaccio reciteth of women, are pretie and wittie inough, and especially those you have spoken of your selfe.

But in mine opinion the prancke that Richard Minutoli wrought, doth passe the boundes, and is much more bitterer than that Beatrice wrought. For Richard Minutoli tooke much more from Philippellos wife, than did Beatrice from Egano her husband: because Richard with that privie pollicie enforced her, and made her to doe of her selfe that she woulde not have done: And Beatrice deceived her husband to doe of her selfe that she lusted.

Then saide the Lorde Gasper: for no other cause can a man excuse Beatrice but for love, which ought to be allowed as well in men as in women.

Then answered maister Bernard: Truely the passions of love bring with them a great excuse of everie faulte, yet judge I (for my part) that a gentleman that is in love, ought as well in this point as in all other thinges, to be voide of dissimulation, and of an upright meaning. And if it be true that it is such an abhominable profit and trespasse to use tradiment against a mans verie enimie. Consider you how much more hainous that offence is against a person whom a man loveth. And I believe each honest lover sustaineth such veines, such watchinges, hazardeth him selfe in such dangers, droppeth so many teares, useth so many meanes and waies to please the woman whom he loveth, not chiefely to come by her body, but to win the fortresse of that minde, to breake in peeces those most hard Diamonds, to heate that colde yce, that lye manie times in the tender breasts of these women.

And this doe I believe is the true and sound pleasure, and the end whereto the intent of a noble courage is bent. And for my part truely (were I in love) I would like it better to know assuredly that she whom I loved and served, loved me againe with hart, and had bent her minde towarde me, without receiving any other contentation, than to enjoy her, and to have my fill of her against her owne wil, for in that case I shoulde thinke my selfe maister of a deade carkase.

Therefore such as compasse their desires by the meane of these merrie prăcks, which may perhaps rather be termed Tradiments [32] than merrie pranckes, doe injurie to other, and yet receive they not for all that the contentation which a man shoulde wish for in love, possessing the bodie without the will.

The like I say of certaine other that in love practise enchantments, sorceries, and otherwhile plaine force, sometimes meanes to cast them in sleepe and such like matters. And know for a sooth, that gifts also diminish much the pleasures of love, because a man may stande in doubt whether he be beloved or no, but that the woman maketh a countenance to love him, to fare the better by him.

Therefore ye see that the love of Ladies and great women is esteemed, because it appeareth that it can arise of none other cause, but of perfect and true love: neither is it to be thought that a great Ladie will at any time shew to beare good will to her inferiour, unlesse she love him in verie deede.

Then answered the Lord Gasper: I denye not that the intent, the paines and daungers of lovers ought not principally to have their end directed to the victorie rather of the minde than of the bodie of the woman beloved. But I say, that these deceites which you in men terme Tradiments, and in women merrie pranckes, are a verie good meane to come to this end, because alwaies he that possesseth the bodie of women, is also maister of the minde: And if you bethinke you well, Philippellos wife after her great lamentation for the deceite wrought her by Richard, knowing how much more savorie the kisse of a lover were than her husbands, turning her rigour into tender affection towarde Richard, from that day forwarde loved him most dearely.

You may perceive now that his continual haunting, his presents, and his so many other tokens, which had beene so long a proofe of his good will towards her, were not able to compasse that, that his being with her a small while did. Now see this merrie prancke or Tradiment (how ever you will terme it) was a good way to win the fortresse of that minde.

Then maister Bernarde, you (quoth he) make a surmise, which is most false, for in case women shoulde alwaies give their minde to him that possesseth their bodie, there shoulde bee none found that woulde not love their husbandes more than any person in the world beside, where it is seene not to be so. But John Boccaccio was (as you bee) without cause an enimie to women.

The Lord Gasper answered: I am no enimy of theirs,

but (to confesse the truth) few men of worthinesse there bee that generally set anie store by women, although otherwhile, to serve their turne withall, they make wise to the contrarie.

Then answered maister Bernard: You doe not onely injurie to women, but to all men also that reverēce them. Notwithstãding (as I have saide) I will not swarve from my first purpose of merrie pranckes, and undertake such an enterprise so hard, as is the defence of women against you that are a valiant Champion.

Therefore I will end this my cōmunication which perhaps hath beene longer than needed, but out of peradventure not so pleasant as you looked for. And since I see the Ladies so quiet, and beare these injuries at your handes so paciently as they doe, I will henceforth believe that some part of that which the Lord Octavian hath spoke is true: namely, That they passe not to be evil reported of in every other matter, so their honestie be not touched.

Then a great part of the women there, for that the Dutchesse had beckoned to them so to doe, arose upon their feete, and ran all laughing toward the Lord Gasper, as they would have buffeted him, and done as the wood women did to Orpheus, saying continually: Now shall you see whether we passe to be ill spoken off or no.

Thus partly for laughing, and partly for the rising of every one from his seate, it seemed the sleepe that now beganne to enter into the eyes and heade of some of them departed, but the Lord Gasper saide.

See I pray you where they have not reason on their side, they will prevaile by plaine force, and so end the communication, giving us leave to depart with stripes.

Then answered the Ladie Emilia: No (quoth she) it shall not be so: for when you perceived maister Bernarde was wearie of his long talk, you began to speake so much ill of women, thinking you shoulde finde none to gainesay you. But wee will set into the field a fresher knight that shall fight with you, because your offence shall not bee long unpunished. So turning her to the Lord Julian, that hetherto had saide litle, she saide unto him.

You are counted the protector of the honour of women, therefore it is now high time to shew that you come not by this name for nothing, and in case yee have not beene worthily recompensed at any time for this professiō hetherto, now must you thinke that in putting to flight so bitter an enimie, you shall binde all women to you much more, and so much, that where they shall doe nothing els but reward you, yet shall the bondage still remaine fresh, and never cease to be recompensed.

Then answered the L. Julian: me thinke (madam) you shew great honour to your enimie, and verie litle to your defender: for undoubtedly the Lorde Gasper hath saide nothing against women, but it hath beene fully answered by maister Bernard. And I believe every one of us knoweth, that it is meete the Courtier beare verie great reverence towarde women, and a discrete and courteous person ought never to touch their honestie neither in jeast, nor in good earnest. Therefore to dispute of this so open a truth, were (in manner) to put a doubt in manifest matters.

I thinke well that the Lorde Octavian passed his boundes somewhat in saying that women are most unperfect creatures, and not apt to worke any vertuous deede, and of litle, or no worthinesse in respect of men. And because many times credite is given to men of great authoritie, although they speake not the ful truth, and when they speake in jeast, the Lord Gasper hath suffered himselfe to be led by the Lord Octavians words, to say that men of wisedom set no store by them, which is most false. For I have knowne few men of worthinesse at any time that doe not love and observe women, the vertue and consequently the worthinesse of whom I deeme not a jotte inferiour to mens.

Yet if we should come to this contention, the cause of women were like to quaile greatly, because these Lords have shaped a Courtier that is so excellent and of so many devine qualities, that who so hath the understanding to consider him to bee such a one as he is, will imagine that the deserts of women can not attaine to that point. But in case the matter should bee equally devided, we shall first neede of so wittie and eloquent a person as is Count Lewis and Sir Fredericke, to shape a gentlewoman of the Pallace with all perfections due to a woman, as they have shaped the Courtier with the perfections belonging to a man. And then if he that defended their cause were any thing wittie and eloquent, I believe (because the truth will be a helpe to him) hee may plainely shew that women are as full of vertues as men be.

The Ladie Emilia answered: Nay a great deale more, and that it is so, ye may see, vertue is the female, and vice the male. The Lord Gasper then laughed, and turning him to maister Nicholas Phrisio, what is your judgement Phrisio (quoth he.)

Phrisio answered: I am sorie for the Lord Julian that he is so seduced with the promises and flattering wordes of the Ladie Emilia to runne into an errour to speake the thing which for his sake I am ashamed of.

The Ladie Emilia answered smiling: you will surely bee ashamed for your owne sake when you shall see the Lord Gasper after he is convicted, confesse his owne errour, and yours too, and demaund that pardon which we will not graunt him.

Then spake the Dutchesse: Because it is verie late, I will wee deferre the whole untill to morrow, the more for that I think it well done we follow the Lorde Julians counsel, that before he come to this disputation we may have a gentlewoman of the Palace so fashioned in all perfections, as these Lordes have fashioned the perfect Courtier.

Madam, quoth the Ladie Emilia then, I pray God it fall not to our lotte, to give this enterprise to any confederate with the Lord Gasper, least he fashion us for a gentlewoman of the Court, one that can doe naught els but looke to the kitchin and spin.

Then saide Phrisio: In deed that is an office fit for her. Then the Dutchesse, I have a good hope in the Lord Julian (quoth she) who will (for the good wit and judgement I know he is of) imagin the greatest perfection that may be wished in a woman, and in like manner expresse it well in wordes, and so shall we have somewhat to confound the Lorde Gaspers false accusation withall.

Madam, answered the L. Julian, I wot not whether your devise be good or no, to commit into my handes an enterprise of so great waight, for (to tell you the truth) I thinke not my selfe able inough. Neither am I like the Count and Sir Fredericke, which with their eloquence have shaped such a Courtier as never was: nor I believe ever shall be. Yet if your pleasure be so, that I shall take his burden upon me, let it be at the least with those conditions that the other have had before me: namely that everie man, where hee shall thinke good, may reply against mee, and this shall I reckon not overthwarting, but aide, and perhaps in correcting mine errours wee shal finde the perfectiō of a gentlewomā of the palace which we seeke for.

I trust, answered the Dutchesse, your talke shall be such, that litle may be saide against you. Therefore settle your minde to thinke upon onely this, and fashion us such a gentlewoman, that these our adversaries may be ashamed to say, that she is not equall with the Courtier in vertue: of whom it shall be well done Sir Fredericke speake no more, for he hath but too well set him forth, especially since we must compare a woman to him.

I have (madam) answered Sir Fredericke, litle or nothing now left to speake of the Courtier, and that I did thinke upon maister Bernardes jestes have made mee forget.

If it be so, quoth the Dutchesse, assembling together to morrow betimes, wee shall have leisure to accomplish both the one and the other. And when she had so saide, they arose all upon their feet, and taking their leave reverently of the Dutchesse, every man withdrew him to his lodging.

THIRD BOOK

The Thirde Booke of the Courtier, of Count Baldesser Castilion, unto Maister Alfonsus Ariosto

IT is read that Pythagoras verie wittily and after a subtill manner found out the measure of Hercules bodie, in that he knew that the space where every five yeares they kept the games or prises of Olympus in Achaia nigh unto Elis before Jupiter Olympicus Temple, was measured by Hercules himselfe: and appointed a furlong of ground there of six hundreth and five and twentie of his own feete: and the other furlongs which after his time were cast out in diverse partes of Greece by his successors, were also of six hundreth and five and twentie of their feete, but for all that somewhat shorter than his. Pythagoras knew forthwith by that proportion how much Hercules foot was bigger than all the other mens feete, and so the measure of his foote once known, he gathereth that all Hercules bodie proportionally in greatnesse exceeded all other mens, so much, as that furlong, all other furlongs.

You may then (gentle maister Alphonsus) by the verie same reason easily gather by this least part of all the rest of the bodie how farre the Court of Urbin excelled all the other in Italy. For if the sportes and pastimes (that are used to none other end but to refresh the wearisom mindes after earnest labours) farre passed all such as are commonly used in the other Courts of Italy.

What (gesse you) were all the other vertuous practises, whereunto all men had their mindes bent, and were fully and wholy addicted. And of this I may be bolde to make my vaunt, nothing mistrusting but to be credited therin, considering I goe not about to prayse so auncient antiquities wherein I might, if I were disposed, faine what I lusted: but of this I speake, I am able to bring forth many men of worthie credence, for sufficient triall, which as yet are in life, and have themselves seene and marked well the living and conversation of such as in times past excelled in that Court. And I reckon my selfe bound (for that lyeth in me to doe) to stretch forth my force with all diligence to defend this famous memorie from mortall oblivion, and with my penne to make it live in the mindes of our posteritie.

Whereby perhaps in time to come, there shall not want that will envie this our time. For there is no man that readeth of the wonderfull families of times past, but in his mind hee conceiveth a certaine greater opinion of them that are written upon, than it appeareth those bookes can expresse, though they have beene written with perfection.

Even so doe wee desire, that all the readers of this our travaile (if at the least wise it shall deserve so much favor, that it may come to the sight of noble men and vertuous Ladies) will cast in their minde and thinke for a suretie, that the Court of Urbin hath beene much more excellent and better furnished with notable men, than wee are able to expresse in writing. And in case so much eloquence were in mee, as there was prowesse in them, I should need none other testimonie to make such give full credence to my wordes, as have not seene it.

When therefore the companie was assembled in the accustomed place, the daye following at the due houre, and set with silence, every man turned his eyes to Sir Fredericke and to the Lorde Julian, waiting when the one of them woulde beginne to speake his minde.

Wherefor the Dutchesse, after she had beene still a while, my Lord Julian (quoth she) every mans desire is to see this your gentlewoman wel set forth, and if you shew us her not in such manner, that all her beauties may bee

451

discerned, wee will suspect that you are jealous over her.

The Lord Julian answered: Madam, if I reckoned her beautiful, I would shew you her without any other setting forth, and in such wise as Paris did beholde the three goddesses. But in case these Ladies bee not a helpe to me to trim her (who can doe it right well) I doubt me, that not onely the Lord Gasper and Phrisio, but all the other Lordes here shall have a just cause to speake ill of her.

Therefore since she is yet in some part deemed beautifull, perhaps it shall be better to keepe her close and see what Sir Fredericke hath yet behinde to speake of the Courtier, which (no doubt) is much more beautifull than my woman can be.

That I had in minde, answered Sir Fredericke, is not so necessarie for ye Courtier, but it may be left out, and no hurt done: yea, it is a contrarie matter almost to that hetherto hath beene reasoned of.

And what matter is it then, quoth the Dutchesse? Sir Fredericke answered, I was purposed in what I could, to declare the causes of these companies and orders of knights brought up by great Princes, under divers standers, as is that of Saint Michael in the house of Fraunce, the order of the Garter under the title of Saint George in the house of England, the golden Fleece in the house of Burgony, and how these dignities be given, and in what sorte they that deserve are disgraded from them, how they first came up, who were the founders of them, and to what end they were ordained, because we see that these knights in great Courtes are alwaies highly esteemed.

I minded also, if time had sufficed me, beside the diversitie of manners used in the Courtes of christian Princes in feasting and appearing in open shewes, to speak somewhat also of the great Turke, but much more particularly of the Sophy king of Persia.

For when I understood by merchant men a long time trafficked in that countrie, the noble men there be verie full of prowesse and well mannered, and use in their conversation one with another, and in womens service, and in all their practisinges much courtesie and great sobrietie, and when time serveth, in martiall feates, in sportings, and undertaking enterprises, much sumptuousnesse, great liberalitie and braverie: I delited to know what order they take in these thinges which they set most store by, wherein their pomps consist, and braveries of garments and armour, wherein they differ from us, and wherein we agree, what kinde of entertainement their women use, and with what sober moode they shew favour to who so is in their love service, but to say the truth, it is no fit time now to enter into this talke, especiallye since there is other to be said, and much more to our purpose than this.

Yes, quoth the Lorde Gasper, both this and many other things bee more to the purpose, than to fashion this gentlewoman of the pallace, forsomuch as the verie same rules that are given for the Courtier, serve also for the woman, for as well ought she to have respect to times and places, and to observe (as much as her weakenesse is able to beare) all the other properties that have beene so much reasoned upon, as the Courtier.

And therefore in stead of this it were not perhaps amisse to teach to me particular points that belong to the service about a Princes person: for no doubt the Courtier ought to knowe them, and to have a grace in doing them. Or els to speake of the way that hee ought to take in the bodily exercises, how to ride, to handle weapon, and wrastle, and wherein consisteth the hardnes of these feates.

Then spake the Dutchesse, smiling: Princes are not served about their persons with so excellent a Courtier as this is. As for the exercises of bodie and strength, and slightnesse of person, we will leave them for maister Peter Mount here to take charge to teach them when he shall thinke most meet, for presently the Lorde Julian hath nothing els to speake of, but of this womã, whom (me thinke) you now begin to have a feare of, and therefore would bring us out of our purpose.

Phrisio answered: certaine it is, that now it is needles and out of purpose to talke of women, especiall being yet behinde somewhat to be spoken of the Courtier, for the one matter ought not to be mingled with the other.

You are in a great errour, answered the Lorde Cesar Gonzaga: for like as no Court, how great soever it be, can have any sightlinesse or brightnesse in it, or mirth without women, nor any Courtier can bee gracious, pleasant or hardie, nor at any time undertake any galant enterprise of Chivalrie, unlesse he be stirred with the conversation and with the love and contentatiō of women, even so in like case, the Courtiers talke is most unperfect evermore, if the entercourse of women give them not a part of the grace wherwithall they make perfect and decke out their playing the Courtier.

The Lorde Octavian laughed and saide: Beholde a peece of the baite that bringeth men out of their wits. Then the Lorde Julian turning him to yᵉ Dutchesse, Madam (quoth he) since it is so your pleasure, I will speak that commeth to mind, but with verie great doubt to satisfie. And I wis a great deale lesse paine it were for mee to fashion a Ladie that shoulde deserve to bee Queene of the world, than a perfect gentlewoman of the Court, for of her I wot not where to fetch any patterne, but for a Queene I shoulde not neede to seeke farre, and sufficient it were for me onely to imagine the heavenly conditions of a Ladie whom I know, and through seeing them, direct all my thoughts to expresse plainelye with wordes the thing, that many see with their eyes, and where I coulde doe no more, yet should I fulfill my duetie in imagining her.

Then saide the Dutchesse: Passe not your bounds (my Lord Julian) but minde the order taken, and fashion the gentlewoman of the pallace, that this so worthie a maistresse may have him that shall so worthily serve her.

Then the Lord Julian proceeded: for a proofe therefore (Madam) that your commandement may drive me to assay to doe, yea the thing I have no skill in, I will speake of this excellent woman, as I woulde have her. And when I have fashioned her after my minde, and can afterwarde get none other, I will take her as mine owne, after the example of Pigmalion.

And whereas the Lorde Gasper hath said, that the verie same rules that are given for the Courtier serve also for the woman. I am of a contrarie opinion. For albeit some qualities are common and necessarie as well for the woman as the man, yet are there some other more meete for the woman than for the man, and some again meete for the man, that she ought in no wise to meddle withall.

The verie same I say of the exercises of the bodie: But principally in her fashions, manners, wordes, gestures and conversation (me thinke) the woman ought to be much unlike the man. For right as it is seemely for him to shew a certaine manlinesse full and steadie, so doth it well in a woman to have a tendernesse, soft and milde, with a kinde of womanlye sweetenesse in every gesture of hers, that in going, standing, and speaking what ever she lusteth, may alwaies make her appeare a woman without anye likenesse of man.

Adding therefore this principle to the rules that these Lords have taught the Courtier, I thinke well, she may serve her turne with manie of them, and be endued with verie good qualities, as the Lorde Gasper saith. For many vertues of the minde I reckon be as necessarie for a woman, as for a man.

Likewise noblenesse of birth, avoiding affectation or curiositie, to have a good grace of nature in all her doings, to be of good conditions, wittie, foreseeing, not haughtie, not envious, not ill tongued, not light, not contentious, not untowardly, to have the knowledge to winne and keepe the good will of her Ladie and of all others, to doe well and with good grace the exercises comely for a woman.

Me thinke well beautie is more necessary in her than in the Courtier, for (to say the truth) there is a great lacke in the woman that wanteth beautie.

She ought also to be more circumspect, and to take better heede that she give no occasion to bee ill reported of, and so behave her selfe, that she be not onely not spotted with any fault, but not so much as with suspition. Because a woman hath not so manie waies to defend her selfe from slanderous reportes, as hath a man.

But for somuch as Count Lewis hath verie particularly expressed the principal profession of the Courtier, and willeth it to bee in Martiall feates, me thinke also behovefull to utter (according to my judgement) what the gentlewoman of the Palace ought to be: in which point when I have throughly saisfied, I shal thinke my selfe rid of the greatest part of my duetie.

Leaving therefore a part the vertues of the minde that ought to be common to her with the Courtier, as wisedom, noblenesse of courage, staiednesse, and many moe, and likewise the conditions that are meet for all women, as to be good and discreete, to have the understanding to order her husbands goodes and her house and children when she is married, and all those partes that belong to a good huswife: I say that for her that liveth in Court, me thinke there belongeth unto her above all other thinges, a certaine sweetenesse in language that may delite, wherby she may gently entertain all kinde of men with talke worthie the hearing and honest, and applyed to the time and place, and to the degree of the person she cõmuneth withal. Accompanying with sober and quiet manners, and with the honestie that must alwaies be a stay to her deedes, a readie livelinesse of wit, whereby she may declare her selfe far wide from all dulnesse: but with such a kinde of goodnesse, that she may bee esteemed no lesse chaste, wise and courteous, than pleasant, feate conceited and sober: and therefore muste she keepe a certaine meane verie hard, and (in a manner) derived of contrary matters, and come just to certaine limittes, but not to passe them.

This woman ought not therefore (to make her selfe good and honest) be so squeimish and make wise to abhorre both the company and the talke (though somewhat of the wantonest) if she bee present, to get her thence by and by, for a man may lightly gesse that she fained to be so coye to hide that in her selfe which she doubted others might come to the knowledge of: and such nice fashions are alwaies hatefull.

Neither ought she againe (to shew her selfe free and pleasant) speake wordes of dishonestie, nor use a certaine familiaritie without measure and bridle, and fashions to make men believe that of her that perhaps is not: but being present at such kinde of talke, she ought to give the hearing with a litle blushing and shamefacednesse.

Likewise to eschew one vice that I have seene raigne in many: namely, to speake and willingly to give eare to such as report ill of other women: for such as in hearing the dishonest behaviors of other women disclosed, are offended at the matter, and make wise not to credit and (in manner) to thinke it a wonder that a womā should leade an uncleane life, they make proofe that since this fault seemeth unto them so foule a matter, they commit it not. But those that goe alwaies harking out the loves of others and disclose them so point by pointe, and with such joy, it seemeth that they envy the matter, and that their desire is to have all men knowe it, that the like may not bee imputed them for a trespace.

And so they tourne it to certaine laughters with a kind of gesture, wherby they make men to suspecte at the very same instant that they take great contentation at it. And of this ariseth, that men although to their seeminge they give diligente eare to it, for the most part conceive an ill opinion of them, and have them in very small reputatiō, and (to their weening) with these behaviours are entised to attempt them farther.

And many times afterward they runne so farre at rovers that it purchaseth them worthely an ill name, and in conclusion are so little regarded, that men passe not for their company, but rather abhorre them. And contrarywise, there is no man so shamelesse and high minded, but beareth greate reverence toward them that be counted good and honest, because that gravity tēpered with knowledge and goodnes, is (as it were) a shielde againste the wanton pride and beastlinesse of sawsie merchants. Wherefore it is seene that one worde, a laughter or a gesture of good will (howe litle soever it bee) of an honest woman, is more set by of very man, than all the toyes and wanton gestures of them that so lavishly shew small shamefastnesse. And where they leade not in deede an uncleane life, yet with those wanton countenances, babling, scornfulnes, and such scoffing conditions, they make men to think they doe.

And forsomuch as words that are not grounded upon some pithy foundation, are vain and childish, the gentlewoman of the palace, beside her descretion to understand the condition of him she talketh withall, to entertaine him honestly, must needes have a sight in many things, and a judgement in her communication to picke out such as be to purpose for the condition of him she talketh withall, and be heedfull that she speake not otherwhile where she would not, words that may offend him.

Let her beware of praising her selfe undiscretely, or being too tedious, that she make him not wearie. Let her not go mingle with pleasant and laughing talke matters of gravitie: nor yet with grave jestes and feat conceites.

Let her not foolishly take upon her to know that she knoweth not, but soberly seeke to be esteemed for that she knoweth, avoyding (as is saide) Curiositie in all thinges.

In this manner shall she be indued with good conditions, and the exercises of the bodie comely for a woman shall she do with an exceeding good grace, and her talke shall bee plenteous and full of wisedom, honestie, and pleasantnesse: and so shall she be not onely beloved but reverenced of all men, and perhaps worthy to be compared to this great Courtier, as well for the qualities of the minde as of the bodie.

When the Lord Julian had hetherto spoken, and he held his peace, and setled himselfe as though hee had made an end of his talke. Then saide the Lord Gasper, no doubt my Lord Julian but you have decked gayly out this gentlewoman, and made her of an excellent condition: yet me seemeth that you have gone generally inough to worke, and named in her certaine things, so great, that I think in my mind you are ashamed to expound them, and have rather wished them in her, after the manner of them that sometimes wish for things unpossible and above nature, than taught them.

Therefore would I that you declared unto us a litle better, what exercises of the bodie are meet for a gentlewoman of the Palace, and in what sorte she ought to entertaine, and what those many thinges be, which you say she ought to have a sight in: and whether wisedom, noblenesse of courage, staiednesse, and those many other vertues that you have spoken of, your meaning is should helpe her about the overseeing only of her house, children and housholde (the which nevertheless you wil not have her principall profession) or els to entertaine, and to doe these exercises of the bodie with a good grace: and in good felowshippe take heede yee put not these sillie vertues to so vile an occupation, that they may be ashamed of it.

The Lord Julian laughed, and saide: you can not choose (my Lord Gasper) but still you must utter your ill stomacke against women. But certes, mee thought I had spoken sufficient, and especially before such audience, that I beleeve none here, but understandeth concerning the exercises of the bodie, that it is not comely for a woman to practise feates of armes, ryding, playing at tenise, wrastling, and many other thinges that belong to men.

Then said Unico Aretino: Among them of old time the manner was, that women wrastled naked with men, but wee have lost this good custome together with many moe.

The Lord Cesar Gonzaga replyed to this. And in my time I have seene women play at tenise, practise feates of

459

armes, ride, hunt, and doe (in a manner) all the exercises beside, that a gentleman can doe.

The Lord Julian answered: Since I may fashion this womã after my mind, I will not only have her not to practise these manly exercises so sturdie and boisterous, but also those that bee meete for a woman, I will have her to doe them with heedefulnesse and with the short mildenes that we have saide is comely for her. And therefore in daunsing I would not have her use too swift and violent trickes, nor yet in singing or playing upon instruments those hard and often divisions that declare more cunning than sweetenes. Likewise the instruments of Musicke which she useth (in mine opinion) ought to bee fit for this purpose.

Imagin with your selfe what an unsightly matter it were to see a woman play upon a tabour or drum, or blow in a flute or trumpet, or any like instrument: and this because the boistrousnesse of them doth both cover and take away that sweete mildnesse which setteth so forth everie deede that a woman doth.

Therefore when she commeth to daunce, or to shew any kind of musicke, she ought to be brought to it with suffring her selfe somewhat to be prayed, and with a certain bashfulnesse, that may declare the noble shamefastnesse that is contrarie to headinesse.

She ought also to frame her garments to this entent, and so to apparrell her selfe, that she appeare not fonde and light.

But for so much as it is lawfull and necessarie for women to set more by their beawtie than men, and sundrie kindes of beautie there are, this woman ought to have a judgement to know what manner garments set her best out, and be most fitte for the exercise, that she entendeth to undertake at that instant, and with them to aray her selfe. And where she perceiveth in her a sightly and chearefull beautie, she ought to farther it with gestures, words and apparrel, that all may betoken mirth. In like case an other that feeleth her selfe of a milde and grave disposition, she ought also to accompany it with fashions of the like sorte, to encrease that that is the gift of nature.

In like manner where she is somewhat fatter or leaner than reasonable sise, or wanner, or browner, to helpe it with garments but fainingly as much as she can possible, and keeping her selfe clenly, and handsom, shewing alwaies that she bestoweth no paine nor diligence at all about it.

And because the Lord Gasper doth also aske what these many thinges bee she ought to have a sight in, and how to entertaine, and whether the vertues ought to bee applyed to this entertainement, I say that I will have her to understãd that y^t these Lordes have willed ye Courtier to know: and in those exercises that wee have saide are not comely for her: I will at the least she have that judgement, that men can have of the thinges which they practise not, and this to have knowledge to praise and make of Gentlemenne more and lesse according to their deserts.

And to make a briefe rehersall in few wordes of that is alreadie saide, I will that this woman have a sight in letters, in musicke, in drawing, or painting, and skilfull in dauncing, and in devising sports and pastimes, accompanying with that discrete sober moode, and with the giving a good opinion of her selfe, the other principles also that have beene taught the Courtier.

And thus in conversation, in laughing, in sporting, in jesting, finally in everie thing she shal be had in great price, and shall entertaine accordingly both with jestes, and feate conceites meete for her, every person that commeth in her company.

And albeit stayednesse, noblenesse of courage, temperance, strength of the minde, wisedom, and the other vertues, a man would thinke belonged not to entertaine, yet will I have her endowed with them all, not so much to entertaine (although notwithstanding they may serve thereto also) as to be vertuous: and these vertues to make her

461

such a one, that she may deserve to bee esteemed, and all her doings framed by them.

I wonder then quoth the Lorde Gasper smyling, since you give women both letters, and stayednesse, and noblenesse of courage, and temperance, ye will not have them also to beare rule in cities, and to make lawes, and to leade armies, and men to stand spinning in the kitchin.

The Lord Julian answered in like manner smiling: Perhaps too this were not amisse: then he proceeded. Do you not knowe that Plato (which in deed was not verie friendly to women) giveth them the overseeing of Cities, and all other martiall offices hee appointed to men? Thinke you not there were many to be found that could as well skill in ruling Cities and armies, as men can? But I have not appointed them these offices, because I fashion a waiting gentlewoman of the Court, not a Queene.

I see well you would covertly have up againe the slaunderous report that the Lord Octavian gave women yesterday: namely, that they be most unperfect creatures and not apt to worke any vertuous deede, and of verie litle worthinesse, and of no value in respect of men: But surely both he and you shoulde be in verie great errour if ye thought so.

Then saide the Lord Gasper: I will not have up againe matters alreadie past, but you woulde faine presse me to speake some word that might offend these Ladies mindes, to make them my foes, as you with flattering them falsely will purchase their good will. But they are so wise above other, that they love truth better (although it make not so much with them) than false prayses: Neither take they it in ill part for a man to say, that men are of a more worthines, and they will not let to confesse that you have spoken great wonders, and appointed to the gentlewoman of the Pallace certaine fonde unpossible matters, and so manie vertues, that Socrates and Cato and all the Philosophers in the world are nothing to her.

For to tell you the plaine truth, I marvell you were not

ashamed so much to passe your bounds, where it ought to have suffised ye to make this gentlewoman of the pallace beautifull, sober, honest, well spoken, and to have the understanding to entertaine without running in slaunder, with dauncing, musicke, sportes, laughing, jestes, and the other matters that wee see dayly used in Court. But to goe about to give her the knowledge of all thinges in the world, and to appoint her the vertues that so seldome times are seene in men, yea and in them of olde time, it is a matter that can neither be held withall, nor scantly heard.

Now that women are unperfect creatures, and consequently of lesse worthinesse than men, and not apt to conceive those vertues that they are, I purpose not to affirme it, because the prowes of these Ladies were inough to make me a lyar. Yet this I say unto you, that most wise men have left in writing, that nature, because she is alwaies set and bent to make things most perfect, if she could, would continually bring forth men, and when a woman is borne, it is a slackenesse or default of nature, and contrarie to that she would doe. As it is also seene in one borne blinde, lame, or with some other impediment, and as in trees many fruites that never ripen.

Even so may a woman bee saide to bee a creature brought forth at a chaunce and by happe, and that it is so, marke me the workes of the man and the woman, and by them make your proofe of the perfection of each of them. Howbeit since these defaults of women are the defect of nature that hath so brought them forth, wee ought not for this to hate them, nor faint in having lesse respect to them than is meete: but to esteeme them above that they are, me thinketh a plaine errour.

The Lord Julian looked the Lord Gasper would have proceeded on still, but when he saw now that hee held his peace, he saide.

Of the unperfectnes of women me thinke you have alleaged a verie colde reason, whereunto (albeit may hap it were not now meete to enter into these subtil pointes)

I answere according to the opinion of him that is of skill, and according to the truth, that substance in what ever thing it be, can not receive into it more or lesse: for as no stone can bee more perfectly a stone than an other, as touching the being of a stone: nor one blocke more perfectly a blocke, than an other: no more can one man be more perfectly a man than an other: and consequently the male kinde shall not be more perfect, than the female, as touching his formall substance, for both the one and the other is conteined under the Species of *Homo,* and that wherein they differ is an Accidentall matter and no Essentiall.

In case you will then tell me that the man is mor perfecter than ye woman though not as touching the Essentiall, yet in the Accidents, I answere that these accidents must consist either in the bodie, or in the minde: if in the bodie, because the man is more sturdier, nimbler, lighter, and more able to endure travaile, I say that this is an argument of smal perfection: for among men themselves such as abounde in these qualities above other, are not for them the more esteemed: and in warre, where the greatest part of painefull labours are and of strength, the stoutest are not for all that the most set by.

If in the minde, I say, what ever thinges men can understand, the selfe same can women understand also: and where it pearceth the capacitie of the one, it may in likewise pearce the others.

Here after the Lord Julian had made a litle stoppe, hee proceeded smiling: Doe you not know that this principle is helde in Philosophye, who so is tender of flesh, is apt of minde: Therefore there is no doubt, but women being tenderer of flesh, are also apter of mind, and of a more inclined wit to musings and speculations, than men. Afterwarde he folowed on.

But leaving this apart, because you saide that I should make my proofe of the perfection of eche of them by the workes, I say unto you, if you consider effects of nature, you shall finde, that she bringeth women forth as they be, not at a chaunce, but fitly necessarie for the end. For albeit she shapeth them of bodie not stout and of a milde mind, with manie other qualities contrarie to mens, yet doe the conditions of each of them stretch unto one selfe end, concerning the selfe same profit. For even as through that weake feeblenesse, women are of a lesser courage, so are they also by the verie same more wary. Therefore mothers nourish up children, and fathers instruct them, and with manlines provide for that abroad, that they with carefull diligēce store up in the house which is no lesse praise.

In case you will then consider the auncient histories (albeit men at all times have beene verie sparing in writing the prayses of women) and them of latter daies, ye shall finde that continually vertue hath raigned as well among women as men: and that such there have beene also that have made warre and obtained glorious victories, governed Realmes with great wisedome and justice, and done what ever men have done.

As touching sciences, doe you not remember yee have reade of so many that were well seene in Philosophie? Other that have beene most excellent in Poetrie? Other, that have pleaded, and both accused and defended before Judges most eloquently?

Of handicrafts, long it were to rehearse, neither is it needfull to make any rehersall thereof. If then in Essentiall substance, the man is no more perfect than the woman, nor yet in the Accidents (and of this beside reason, the experiences are seene) I wot not wherein this his perfection should consist.

And because you said that Natures entent is alwaies to bring forth thinges most perfect, and therefore if she could, would alwaies bring forth a man, and that the bringing a woman forth is rather a default and slacknesse of nature, than her entent. I answere you that this is full and wholy to be denyed, neither can I see why you may say that nature entendeth not to bring forth women, without whom mankinde can not be preserved, whereof nature her selfe is more desirous than of any thing els.

Because through ye means of this felowship of male and female she bringeth forth children, that restore the received benefits in their childhood to their fathers in their old dayes, in that they nourish them: afterwarde they renue them, in begetting themselves also other children, of whom they looke in their olde age to receive it, that being young they bestowed upon their fathers: whereby nature (as it were) turning her about in a circle, fulfilleth an everlastingnesse, and in this wise giveth an immortalitie to mortall men.

Since then to this, the woman is as needfull as the man, I can not discerne for what cause the one is made by hap more than the other.

Truth it is, that Nature entendeth alwaies to bring forth matters most perfect, and therefore meaneth to bring forth the man in his kind, but not more male than female. Yea were it so that she alwaies brought forth male, then should it without peradventure bee an unperfectnesse: for like as of the bodie and of the soule there ariseth a copound more nobler than his partes, which is man: Even so of the felowship of male and female there ariseth a compound preserving mankinde, without which the partes were in decay, and therefore male and female by nature are alwaies together, neither can the one be without the other: right so he ought not to bee called the male, that hath not a female (according to the definition of both the one and the other) nor she the female that hath not a male.

And for so much as one kinde alone betokeneth an imperfection, the Divines of olde time referre both the one and the other to God: Wherefore Orpheus saide that Jupiter was both male and female: And it is read in scripture that God fashioned male and female to his likenesse. And the Poets many times speaking of the Gods, meddle the kindes together.

Then the Lord Gasper, I would not (quoth hee) wee

should enter into these subtill pointes, for these women will not understand us. And albeit I answere you with very good reasons, yet will they believe, or at the least make wise to believe that I am in the wrong, and forthwith will give sentence as they list. Yet since wee are entred into them, onely this will I say, (as you know, it is the opinion of most wise men) that man is likened to the Forme, the woman to the Matter, and therefore as the Forme is perfecter than the Matter yea it giveth him his being, so is the man much more perfect than the woman.

And I remember that I have heard (when it was) that a great Philosopher [33] in certaine Problemes of his, saith: Whence commeth it that naturally the woman alwaies loveth the man, that hath been the first to receive of her amorous pleasures? And contrariwise the man hateth the woman that hath beene the first to couple in that wise with him? And adding thereto the cause, affirmeth it to be this: For that in this act, the woman receiveth of the man perfection, and the man of the woman imperfection: and therefore every man naturally loveth the thing that maketh him perfect, and hateth that maketh him unperfect.

And beside this, a great argument of the perfection of the man, and of the imperfection of the woman, is, that generally every woman wisheth she were a man, by a certain provocatiō of nature that teacheth her to wish for her perfection.

The Lorde Julian answered sodainely: The silly poore creatures wish not to bee a man to make them more perfect, but to have libertie, and to be rid of the rule that men have of their owne authoritie chalenged over them. And the similitude which you give of the Matter and Forme, is not alike in everie point: because the woman is not made so perfectly by the man, as is the Matter by yᵉ Forme, for the Matter receiveth his being of the Forme, and can not stand without it.

Yea the more Matter Formes have, the more imperfection they have withall, and severed from it, are most

467

perfect: but the woman receiveth not her being of the man, yea as she is made perfect by the man, so doth she also make him perfect: whereby both the one and the other come together to beget children: the which thing they can not doe any of them by themselves.

The cause then of the continuall love of the woman toward the first that she hath beene with, and of the hatred of the man towarde the first woman, I will not affirme to be that your Philosopher alleageth in his Problemes, but I impute it to the surenesse and stablenesse of the woman, and wavering of the man, and that not without naturall reason: for since the male is naturally hote, by that qualitie he taketh lightnesse, stirring and unstedfastnesse: and contrariwise the woman through colde quietnesse, steadie waightinesse, and more earnest imprintings.

Then the Ladie Emilia turning her to the Lorde Julian, for love of God (quoth she) come once out of these your Matters and Formes and males and females, and speake so that you may bee understood: for we have heard and verie well understood the ill that the Lord Octavian and the Lord Gasper have spoken of us: but since wee understand not now in what sorte you stand in our defence, me thinke therefore that this is a straying from the purpose, and a leaving of the ill imprinting in every mans mind that these our enimies have given of us.

Give us not this name answered the Lorde Gasper, for more meeter it were for the Lord Julian, which in giving women false prayses declareth that there are none true for them.

The Lorde Julian saide then: doubt ye not (madam) all shall be answered to. But I will not raile upon men so without reason, as they have done upon women. And if perchance there were any one here that meant to pen this our talke, I would not that in place where these Matters and Formes were understood, the arguments and reasons which the Lord Gasper alleageth against you should be seene unanswered to.

468

I wote not, my Lord Julian, quoth then the Lorde Gasper, how in this you can deny, that the man is not through his naturall qualities more perfect than the woman, which of complexion is cold and the man hote, and much more nobler and perfecter is heate than colde, because it is active and forth bringing: and (as you know) the element poureth downe here among us onely heate, and not colde, which pearceth not the workes of nature.

And therfore because women are colde of complexion, I thinke it is the cause of their faint-hartednesse and fear-fulnesse.

Will you still, answered the Lord Julian, enter into subtill pointes? You shall perceive your selfe at everie time to come into a greater pecke of troubles: and that it is so, hearken to.

I graunt you, that heate in it selfe is more perfect thã colde, but this followeth not in medled matters and com-pounded, for in case it were so, the bodie that were most hote should be most perfect: which is false, because tem-perate bodies bee most perfect.

I doe you to wete moreover, that the woman is of complexion colde in comparison of the mans, which for overmuch heate is farre wide from temper, but as touching her selfe, she is temperate, or at the least nearer to temper than the man, because she hath that moisture within her of equall portion with the naturall heat, which in the man through overmuch drouth doth sooner melt and consume away.

She hath also such a kind of colde, that it resisteth, and comforteth the naturall heat, and maketh it nearer to temper, and in the man overmuch heate doth soone bring the naturall warmth to the last degree, the which wanting nourishment, consumeth away: and therefore, because men in generation sooner waxe drye than women, it happeneth oftentimes that they are of a shorter life. Wherefore this perfection may also be given to women, that living longer than men they accomplish it, that is the entent of nature more than men.

Of the heate that the element poureth downe upon us, we talke not now, because it is diverse in signification to it which wee entreat upon: the which since it is nourisher of all thinges under the sphere of ye moone, as well hote as colde, it can not be contrarie to colde.

But the fearefullnesse in women although it betokeneth an imperfection, yet doth it arise of a praise worthie cause, namely the subtilnesse and readinesse of the spirits, that convey speedely the shapes to the understanding, and therefore are they soone out of patience, for outwarde matters.

Full well shall you see many times some men that dread neither death nor any thing els, yet are they not for all that to bee called hardie, because they know not the daunger, and goe forth like harebraines where they see the way open, and cast no more with themselves, and this proceedeth of a certaine grossenes of the dulled spirites.

Therefore a fond person can not be saide to be stoute harted, but verie courage in deede commeth of a proper advisement and determined will so to doe, and to esteeme more a mans honestie and duetie, than all the perils in the world, and although he see none other way but death, yet to be of so quiet an hart and minde that his senses be not to seeke nor amazed, but doe their duetie in discoursing and bethinking, even as though they were most in quiet.

Of this guise and manner we have seene, and heard say many great men to be, likewise many women, which both in old time and presently have shewed stoutnesse of courage, and brought matters to passe in the worlde worthie infinite prayse, no lesse than men have done.

Then said Phrisio: these matters began, when the first woman in offending, made others to offend also against God, and for inheritance left unto mankinde death, affections, sorrowes, and all other miseries and calamities, that be felt now a daies in the world.

The Lord Julian answered: Since you will also farther your purpose with entring into scripture, doe you not know that the same offence was in like manner amended by a woman? which hath profited much more than she hindred us, so that that trespasse acquited with so worthie a deede, is counted most happie. But I purpose not now to tell you, how much in dignitie all humane creatures bee inferiour to the virgin our Lady, for meddling holy matters with these our fond reasonings: Nor rehearse how manie women with infinite stedfastnesse have suffered cruel death under Tyrants for the name of Christ: nor them that with learning in disputation have confuted so many Idolaters.

And in case you will answer mee, that this was a miracle and the grace of the holy Ghost, I say unto you that no vertue deserveth more prayse, than that which is approved by the testimony of God.

Many other also of whom there is no talke, you your selfe may looke upon, especially in reading Saint Hierom, which setteth out certaine of his time with such wonderful prayses, that they might suffice the holiest man that can be.

Imagin then how many there have beene of whom there is made no mention at all: because the sillie poore soules are kept close without the pompous pride, to seeke a name of holinesse among the people, that now a daies many men have, accursed Hipocrites, which not minding, or rather setting small store by the doctrine of Christ, that willeth a man when he fasteth, to annoint his face that he may appeare not to fast, and commandeth prayer, almes deedes, and other good works, to be done, not in the market place, nor Sinagogues, but in secrete, so that the left hand know not of the right: they affirme no treasure in the world to be greater, than to give a good example, and thus hanging their heade aside, and fastning their eyes upon the ground, spreading a report about, that they will not once speake to a woman, nor eate any thing but rawe hearbes, smoky, with their side garments all to ragged and torne, they beguile the simple.

But for all that, they abstaine not from falsifying willes, sowing mortall hatred betweene man and wife, and otherwhile poison: using sorcerie, inchauntments, and all kinde of ribaldrie, and afterwarde alleage a certaine authoritie of their own head, that saith: *Si non castè, tamen cautè*, and with this weene to heale every great sore, and with good reason to perswade him that is not heedfull that God forgiveth soone all offences, how hainous soever they be, so they be kept close, and no evil example ariseth of them.

Thus with a veile of holinesse, and this mischievous devise, many times they turn all their thoughtes to defile the chaste mind of some woman, oftentimes to sow variance betweene brethren, to governe states, to set up the one and plucke down the other, to chop off heades, to imprison and banish men, to be the ministers of wickednesse, and (in a manner) the storers and hoorders up of the roberies that manie Princes commit.

Other past shame, delight to seeme delicate and smoth, with their crowne minionly shaven, and well clad, and in their gate lift up their garment to shew their hose sit cleane, and the handsomnesse of person in making curtesie. Other use certaine bylookes and gestures even at masse, which they hold opinion become them well, and make men to behold them: michievous and wicked men, and cleane voide not onely of all religion, but of all good manner. And when their naughtie life is laide to them, they make a jest at it, and give them a mocke that telleth them of it, and (as it were) count their vices as praise.

Then saide the Ladie Emilia. Such delight you have to speake ill of Friers, that are fallen into this talke without all purpose. But you commit a great offence to murmure against religious persons, and without any profit ye burden your conscience: for were it not for them, that they pray unto God for us, we shoulde yet have farre greater plagues than we have.

Then laughed the Lorde Julian, and saide: How gessed you so eaven (madam) that I speake of Friers, since I named them not? But forsooth this that I say is not called murmuring, for I speake it plaine and openly. And I meane not the good, but the bad and wicked, of whom I have not yet spoken the thousandeth part of that I know.

Speake you not now of Friers, answered the Ladie Emilia: for I thinke it (for my part) a grievous offence to give eare to you, and for hearing you any more, I wil get me hence.

I am well pleased, quoth the Lord Julian, to speake no more of this. But to return to the prayses of women, I say that the Lord Gasper shal not finde me out any notable man, but I will finde his wife, or sister or daughter of like merite, and otherwhile above him. Beside that, many have beene occasion of infinite goodnesse to their men, and sometime broken them of many errours.

Therefore since women are (as wee have declared) naturally as apt for the selfe same vertues, as men be, and the proofe thereof hath beene often seene, I wote not why, in giving them that is possible they may have, and sundrie times have had, and still have, I ought to bee deemed to speake wonders, as the L. Gasper hath objected against me: Considering that there have ever beene in the world, and still are, women as nigh the woman of the Pallace, whom I have fashioned, as men nigh the man whome these Lordes have fashioned.

Then saide the Lord Gasper: those reasons that have experience against them (in my minde) are not good. And I wis, if I should happen to aske you what these great women are, or have beene, so worthie praise, as the great men whose wives, sisters, or daughters they have beene, or that have beene occasion of any goodnesse, or such as have broken them of their errors, I believe it woulde comber you shroudly.

Surely answered the Lord Juliã, none other thing could comber me, but the multitude of them. And if time served me, I would tell you to this purpose the Historie of Octavia wife to Marcus Antonius, and sister to Augustus: of Porcia daughter to Cato and wife to Brutus: of Caia Cecilia wife to Tarquinius Priscus: of Cornelia daughter to Scipio, and of infinite other, which are most known. And not onely these of our countrie, but also Barbarians, as that Alexandra, which was wife to Alexander king of the Jewes, who after the death of her husband, seeing the people in an uproare, and alreadie runne to weapon to slea the two children which he had left behinde him, for a revenge of the cruel and straight bondage that their father had alwaies kept them in, she so behaved her selfe, that sodainly she aswaged that just furie, and in a moment, with wisedom made those mindes favourable to the children, which the father in many yeares with infinite injuries, had made their most enimies.

Tell us at the least, answered the Ladie Emilia, how she did. The Lorde Julian saide: she perceiving her children in so great a jeopardie, immediatly caused Alexanders bodie to be cast out into the middest of the market place, afterwarde calling unto her the Citizens, she saide, that she knew their mindes were set on fire with most furie against her husband: for the cruel injuries which he wickedly had done them, deserved it: and even as when he lived, she did her best alwaies to withdrawe him from so wicked a life, so now she was readie to make a tryall thereof, and to helpe them to chastice him even dead, as much as she might, and therefore shoulde take that bodie of his and give it to be devoured of dogs, and rent it in peeces in the cruellest manner they coulde imagine. But she desired them to take pittie upon the innocent children, that could not onely be in no fault, but not so much as weeting of their fathers ill doings.

Of such force were these words, that the raging fury once conceived in all that peoples mindes, was sodenly aswaged, and turned into so tender an affection, that not onely with one accord, they chose those children for their heades and rulers, but also to the deade corps they gave a most honourable buriall.

Here the Lord Julian made a litle pause, afterwarde hee proceeded. Know you not that Mithridates wife and sisters shewed a farre lesse feare of death, than Mithridates himselfe? And Asdruballes wife, than Asdrubal himselfe?

Know you not that Harmonia daughter to Hiero the Siracusan, woulde have died in the burning of her Countrie?

Then Phrisio, where obstinacie is bent, no doubt (quoth he) but otherwhile ye shall find some women that will never chaunge purpose, as she that could no longer call her husband pricklouse, with her handes made him a signe.

The Lord Julian laughed and saide: Obstinacie that is bent to a vertuous ende, ought to bee called stedfastnesse, as in Epicaria a libertine of Rome, which made privie to a great conspiracie against Nero, was of such stedfastnesse, that being rent with all the most cruel torments that could be invēted, never uttered any of the partners: And in like perill many noble gentlemen and Senators, fearefully accused brethren, friendes, and the dearest and best beloved persons to them in the world.

What say you of this other, called Leona? In whose honour the Athenians dedicated before the Castle gate, a Lionesse of mettall without a tongue, to betoken in her the steadie vertue of silence. For she being in like sorte made privie to a conspiracie against Tirants, was not agast at the death of two great men her friendes, and for all she was torne with infinite and most cruel torments, never disclosed any of the conspiratours.

Then said the Ladie Margaret Gonzaga: Me seemeth that you make too briefe rehersall of these vertuous acts done by women. For although these our enimies have heard them and read them, yet they make wise not to know them, and woulde faine the memorie of them were lost. But in case ye will doe us to understand them, they will at the least be honourable to us.

Then answered the Lorde Julian: With a good will. Now will I tell you of one, that did such a deed, as I believe the Lorde Gasper himselfe will confesse that verie few men doe. And began.

In Massilia there was in times past an usage which is thought came out of Greece, and that was, that openly there was poyson laide up meddled with Cicuta, and it was lawfull for him to take it that alledged to the Senate that he ought to bee rid of his life for some discommoditie that hee felt therein, or els for some other just cause: to the entent that who so had suffered too much adversitie, or tasted over great prosperitie, hee might not continue in ye one, or change the other. In the presence therefore of Sextus Pompeius.

Here Phrisio not tarrying to have the Lord Julian proceede further, this mee seemeth (quoth he) is the beginning of some long tale.

Then the Lord Julian turning him to the Ladie Margaret said: See Phrisio will not suffer me to speake. I would have tolde you of a woman, that after she had shewed the Senate that she ought of right to dye, glad and without any feare, tooke in the presence of Sextus Pompeius the poyson with such stedfastnesse of minde, and with such wise and loving exhortations to hers, that Pompeius, and the rest that beheld in a woman such knowledge and steadinesse in the trēbling passage of death, remayned (not wythout teares) astonied wyth great wonder.

Then the L. Gasper smiling, and I againe remember (quoth hee) that I have red an Oration, wherein an unfortunate husband asketh leave of the Senate to dye, and alledgeth that hee hath a just cause, for that he can not abide the continuall wearysomnesse of hys wifes chatting, and had lieffer drinke of that poyson which you say was laid up openly for these respectes, than of his wives scoldinges.

The L. Julian aunsweared: Howe many seely poore women shoulde have a juste cause to aske leave to dye, for abidinge, I will not say the ill wordes, but the most evill deedes of their husbandes? For I know some my selfe, that in this world suffer the paynes which are sayd to bee in hell.

Be there not againe, trow you, aunswered the L. Gasper, many husbandes that are so tormented wyth their wives, that every houre they wish for death?

And what displeasure, quoth the L. Julian, can women do their husbands, that is so wythout remedye, as those are which husbands do their wives? whiche though not for love, yet for feare are obedient to their husbandes.

Sure it is indeede (quoth the L. Gasper) that the little they doo well otherwhile, commeth of feare, for fewe there are in the worlde that secretely in their minde hate not their husbandes.

Nay, cleane contrarie, answered the Lorde Julian: and in case you will remember what you have reade, it is to be seene in all histories, that alwaies (in a manner) wives love their husbandes better than they their wives.

When have you ever seene or red that a husband shewed such a token of love towarde his wife, as did Camma towarde her husband?

I wot not, answered the Lord Gasper, what she was, nor what token she shewed. Nor I, quoth Phrisio.

The Lorde Julian answered: Give eare. And you (my Ladie Margaret) looke ye beare well away. This Camma was a most beautifull young woman, indowed with such modestie, and honest conditions, that no lesse for them, than for her beautie she was to be wondred at: and above other thinges, with all her hart she loved her husband, who had to name Synattus.

It happened that an other gentleman of greater authoritie than Synattus, and (in a manner) heade ruler and Tyrant of the Citie where they dwelled, fell in love with this young woman: and after hee had long attempted by all waies and meanes to compasse her, and all but lost labour, bethinking him selfe that the love she bore her husband, was the onely cause that withstood his desires, hee caused this Synattus to be slaine.

Thus instant upon her afterward continually, other fruite could he never get of her, than what hee had before. Wherefore this love dayly encreasing, hee was fully resolved to take her to wife, for all in degree she was much inferiour to him.

So sute being made to her friendes by Sinoris (for so was the lover named) they tooke in hand to perswade her to bee contented with it: Declaring that to agree thereto, was verie profitable, and to refuse it, perillous for her, and them all. She after she had a while gainesayed them, at length made answere that she was contented.

Her kinsfolke brought this tydfnges to Synoris, which passing measure glad, gave order to have this marriage made out of hand.

After they were then both come for this purpose solemnly into the Temple of Diana, Camma had caused to be brought to her a certaine sweete drinke which she had made, and so before the image of Diana, in the presence of Sinoris she dranke the one moitie. Afterwarde with her owne hand (for this was the usage in marriages) she gave the remaine to the bridegroome, which dranke it cleane up.

Camma as soone as she saw her devise take effect, kneeled her downe very joyfull before the image of Diana, and saide.

Oh Goddesse, thou that knowest the bottom of my hart, bee a good witnesse to me, how hardly after my deare husband deceased, I have refrained from killing my selfe, and what paines I have sustained to endure the griefe to live in this bitter life, in which I have felt none other joy or pleasure, but the hope of the revenge, which I perceive now is come to effect.

Therefore with gladnes and contentation, I goe to finde out the sweete company of that soule, which in life and death I have alwaies more loved than mine owne selfe.

And thou caitife, that weenedst to have beene my husband, in stead of a marriage bed, give order to prepare thee a grave, for of thee doe I here make a sacrifice to the shadow of Synattus.

Synoris amazed at these wordes, and alreadie feeling the operation of the poyson within him, that put him to great paine, proved many remedies, but all prevailed not. And Camma had fortune so favourable on her side, or what ever els, that before she dyed, she had knowledge that Synoris was dead.

When she heard of that, with verie great contentation she laid her upon her bed, with her eyes to heaven, continually calling upon the name of Synattus and saying: O most sweete mate, since now I have bestowed for the last tokens upon thy death, both teares and revenge, and perceive not that I have any thing yet behind to doe for thee here, I flee the world, and this without thee a cruel life, which for thy sake onely in times past was deare to mee. Come therefore and meete me (oh my Lorde) and embrace as willingly this soule, as she willingly commeth to thee.

And speaking these words with her armes spread, as though she would at that instant have embraced him, dyed. Say now Phrisio, what thinke you by this? Phrisio answered.

Me thinke you woulde make these Ladies weepe. But let us set case this was true, I say unto you, that we finde no more such women in the world.

The Lord Julian said: yes, that there be, and that it is so, give eare. In my dayes there was in Pisa a gentleman whose name was maister Thomas, of what house, I remember not, for all I heard my father often times tell it, which was his great friend.

This maister Thomas then, passing upon a day in a litle vessell from Pisa towarde Sicilia about his affaires, was overtakē with certaine foistes [34] of Moores, that were on the backe of him unawares, and before the governours of the vessell had espied them: and for all the men within, defended themselves well, yet because they were but few,

479

and the enimies many, the vessel with as many as were on borde was taken by the Moores, some hurt, some whole, as fell to their lot, and among them maister Thomas, which had plaied the man and slaine with his owne hand a brother of one of the Captains of those foists.

For which matter the Captaine full of wrath, as you may conjecture by the losse of his brother, woulde have him for his prisoner, and beating and buffeting him dayly, brought him into Barbary, where in great miserie hee determined to keepe him alive his captive and with much drudgery.

All the rest, some one way, some another, within a space were at libertie, and returned home, and brought tidinges to his wife, called maistresse Argentine, and children, of the hard life and great afliction which maister Thomas lived in, and was like without hope to live in continually, unlesse God wonderfully helped him. The which matter when she and they understood for a certaintie, attempting certaine other waies for his deliverance, and where he himselfe was fully resolved to end his life, there happened a carefull affection and tender pittie so to quicken the witte and courage of a sone of his called Paule, that he had respect to no kinde of daunger, and determined either to dye, or to deliver his father. The which matter he brought to passe, and with such privie conveyance, that hee was first in Ligurno before it was knowne in Barbary, that he was parted thence.

Here hence maister Thomas (being arived in safety) writte to his wife, and did her to weete his setting at libertie, and where hee was, and how the next day he hoped to see her.

The honest gentlewoman filled with so great and sodaine joy, that she should so shortly aswell through the zeale as prowesse of her sonne, see her husband whom she loved so much, where she once surely believed never to have seene him againe, after she had read the letter, she lifted her eyes to heaven, and calling upon the name of her husband, fell starke dead to the ground, and with no remedie done to her, did the departed soule returne to the bodie againe. A cruel sight, and inough to temper the willes of men and to withdraw them from coveting too fervently superfluous joyes.

Then saide Phrisio smiling: What know you whether she dyed for sorrow or no, understanding her husband was comming home?

The Lord Julian answered: Because the rest of her life was nothing agreeable thereto. But I weene rather the soule could not tarry the lingring to see him with the eyes of her body, and therefore forsooke it, and drawne out thence with coveting, fled by and by where in reading the letter, her thought was fled.

The Lorde Gasper saide: it may be that this woman was over loving, because women in every thing cleave alwaies to the extremitie, which is ill. And see for that she was over loving she did ill to her selfe, to her husband, and to her children, in whom she turned into bitternesse the pleasure of that dangerous and desired libertie of his. Therefore you ought not to alleage her for one of the women that have beene the cause of so great goodnesse. The Lorde Julian answered.

I alleage her for one of them that make tryall that there are wives which love their husbands. For of such as have beene occasion of great profits in the worlde, I could tell you of an infinit number, and rehearse unto you so auncient, that wellnigh a man woulde judge them fables. And of such as among men, have beene the inventers of such kinde of matters, that they have deserved to be deemed Goddesses, as Pallas, Ceres, the Sybilles, by whose mouth God hath so often times spoken and discovered to the world matters to come.

And such as have taught verie great men, as Aspasia and Diotima, the whiche also with sacrifice drove of a plague tenne yeares that shoulde have fallen in Athens.

I could tell you of Nicostrata mother to Evander, which shewed the Latins their letters. And of another woman

481

also that was maistresse to Pindarus Liricus. And of Corinna and Sappho which were most excellent in Poetrie: but I will not seeke matters so far off.

I say unto you, that leaving the rest apart, of the greatnesse of Rome perhaps women were a no lesse cause than men.

This quoth the Lord Gasper, were good to understand. The Lord Julian answered: Hearken to it then. After Troy was wonne, many Trojans, that in so great a destruction escaped, fled some one way, some another: of which, one part, that by many Sea stormes were tossed and tumbled, came into Italy in the coast where the Tever entreth into the sea.

So landing, to provide for their necessaries, began to goe a forraging about the Countrie. The women that tarried behinde in the ships, imagined among themselves a profitable devise, y^t shoulde make an end of their perillous and long sea-wandering, and in stead of their lost countrie recover them a new.

And after they had laide their heades together, in the mens absence, they set fire on the ships, and the first that began this worke was called Roma.

Yet standing in feare of the mens displeasure that were retyring backe againe, they went to meete with them, and embracing, and kissing in token of good will, some their husbandes, some their next a kin, they asswaged that first brunt: Afterwarde they disclosed to them quietly the cause of their wittie enterprise.

Wherefore the Trojans on the one side, for neede, and on the other for being courteously received of the inhabitants, were very wel pleased with that the women had done, and there dwelled with the Latins in the place where afterward was Rome. And of this arose the auncient custome among the Romans, that women meeting their kinsfolke, kissed them. Now ye see what a helpe these women were to give the beginning to Rome.

And the Sabine women were a no lesse helpe to the

encrease of it, than were the Trojane to the first beginning: for when Romulus had purchased him the generall hatred of all his neighbours, for the ravin that he made of their women, hee was assailed with warre on all sides, the which for that he was a valiant man, hee soone rid his handes of with victorie: onely the war with the Sabines excepted, which was verie sore, because Titus Tatius king of the Sabines was verie puisant and wise.

Whereupon after a sore bickering betweene the Romanes and Sabines, with verie great losse on both sides, preparing for a fresh and cruell battaile, the Sabine women clad in blacke, with their haire scattered and haled, weeping, comfortlesse, without feare of weapons now bent to give the onset, came into the middest betweene their fathers and husbands, beseeching them not to sile their hands with the bloud of their fathers in law, and sonnes in law, and in case it were so that they repined at this aliance, they should bend their weapons against them: for much better it were for them to dye, than to live widowes or fatherlesse, and brotherlesse, and to remember that their children had beene begotten of such as had slaine their fathers, or they themselves of such as had slaine their husbands.

With these pitifull wailings many of them carried in their armes their young babes, of whom some began alreadie to lose their tongue, and seemed to call and sport with their grandfathers, unto whom the women shewing forth their nephewes, and weeping saide.

Behold your owne bloud that in such rage ye seeke to shed with your owne hands.

Of such force was in this case the affection and wisedom of the women, that there was not onely concluded betweene the two kinges enimies together, an indissoluble friendship and league, but also (which was a more wonderfull matter) the Sabins came to dwel in Rome, and of two peoples was made one, and so did this accorde much encrease the strength of Rome: thanked be the wise and couragious women which were so rewarded of Romulus, that parting the people into thirtie bandes, gave them the names of the Sabine women.

Here the Lord Julian pausing a while, and perceiving that the Lord Gasper spake not, trow you not (quoth he) that these women were occasion of goodnesse to their men, and helped to the greatnesse of Rome.

The Lord Gasper answered: No doubt, they were worthie much praise. But in case you woulde as well tell the faultes of women, as their well doing, you woulde not have kept hid, that in this warre of Titus Tatius, a woman betrayed Rome, and taught the enimies the way to take the Capitolium, whereby the Romans were well nigh all undone.

The Lorde Julian answered: You mention me one ill woman, and I tell you of infinit good. And beside the afore named, I could apply to my purpose a thousand other examples of the profit done to Rome by women, and tell you why there was once a temple builded to Venus armata, and an other to Venus calva, and how the feast of handmaidens was instituted to Juno, because the hand-maidens once delivered Rome from the guiles of the enimies.

But leaving all these thinges apart, that couragious acte for discovering the conspiracie of Catilina, for which Cicero is so praysed, had it not chiefely his beginning of a common woman, which for this may be saide to have beene the occasion of all the good that Cicero boasteth hee did the common weale of Rome?

And in case I had sufficient time, I woulde (may hap) shew you also, that women have oftentimes corrected men of many vices: but (I feare me) my talke hath alreadie beene overlong and combrous. Therefore since I have ac-cording to my power fulfilled the charge that these Ladies have given me, I meane to give place to him that shall speake more worthier matters to bee heard, than I can.

Then the Ladie Emilia, Doe you not deprive (quoth she) women of the true praises due unto them? And remember though the Lorde Gasper and perchaunce the Lord Octavian too, heare you with noysomnesse, yet do we, and these other Lords harken to you with pleasure.

Notwithstanding the L. Julian would there have ended, but all the Ladies began to entreat him to speake.

Wherefore he said laughing: Least I should provoke my Lord Gasper to bee mine enimie any more than he is, I will but briefly tell you of a certaine that come into my minde, leaving many that I could recite unto you. Afterwarde he proceeded.

When Philip, Demetrius sonne, was about the Citie of Scio, and had laide siege to it, he caused to be proclamed, that what ever bondmen would forsake the Citie and fle to him, he promised them libertie and their maisters wives.

The spite of women for this so shamefull a proclamation was such, that they came to the walles with weapon, and fought so fiercely, that in a small time they drove Philip awaye with shame and losse, which the men could not doe.

These selfe same women being with their husbands, Fathers and brethren that went into banishment, after they came into Leuconia, did an act no lesse glorious, than this was. For the Erythrians that were there with their federates, made warre against these Sciotes, which not able to hold out, came to accord, with composition to depart onely in their doublet and shirt out of the Citie.

The women hearing of this so shamefull a composition, were much offended, reviling them, that leaving their weapons, they woulde issue out like naked men among their enimies. And when they made answere that it was alreadie so condicioned, they willed them to carrie their shield and speare, and leave their clothes, and answere their enimies that this was their aray.

And in so doing, by their womens counsell, they covered a great part of the shame, which they could not cleane avoide.

Likewise when Cirus had discomfited in a battaile the armie of the Persians, as they ranne away, in their fleeing

they met with their women without their gates, who comming to them, said: whither flee ye you cowards? Entend
ye perhaps to hide you in us, from whence ye came? These
and such like words the men hearing, and perceiving how
much in courage they were inferiour to their women, were
ashamed of them selves, and returning backe againe to
their enimies fought with them a fresh, and gave them the
overthrow.

When the Lorde Julian had hetherto spoken, he stayed,
and turning him to the Dutchesse, saide: Now (madame)
you will licence me to hold my peace.

The Lord Gasper answered: it is time to holde your
peace, when you know not what to saye more. The Lorde
Julian saide smyling: You provoke mee so, that ye may
chance bee occupied all night in hearing the prayses of
women. And ye shall understand of many Spartane womē
that much rejoyced at the glorious death of their children:
and of them that forsooke them, or slew them with their
owne hands when they heard they used dastardlinesse.

Againe, how the Saguntine women in the destruction of
their Countrie, tooke weapō in hand against Hanniballes
souldiers. And how the armie of the Dutchmen vanquished
by Marius, their women not obtaining their sute to live
free in Rome in service with the virgins Vestalles, killed
them selves everie one with their young children. And a
thousand moe that all auncient Histories are full of.

Then saide the Lord Gasper: tush (my Lord Julian) God
wotteth how these matters passed, for these times are so
farre from us, that many lyes may be tolde, and none there
is that can reprove them.

The Lord Julian said: In case you will measure in everie
time the worthinesse of women with mens, ye shall finde
that they have never beene, nor yet presently are any whit
inferior to men.

For leaving apart those so auncient, if ye come to the
time when the Gothes raigned in Italy, ye shall finde that
there was a Queene among them Amalasunta, that ruled

a long while with marvellous wisedom. Afterward Theo-
delinda queene of the Longobardes, of singular vertue,
Theodora empresse of Greece. And in Italy among many
other was a most singular Ladie the Countesse Matilda,
whose prayses I leave to be told of Count Lewis, because
she was of his house.

Nay quoth the Count, it is your part, for you know it is
not meete that a man should praise his owne.

The Lord Julian continued on. And how many famous
in times past find you of this most noble house of Montefeltro? How many of the house of Gonzaga, of Este and
Pii? In case wee will then speake of the time present, we
shall not neede to seeke examples far fet, for we have them
in the house.

But I will not serve my purpose with them, whom wee
see in presence, lest yee should seeme for courtesie to
graunt me it, that in no wise ye can deny me. And to goe
out of Italy, remember ye, in our dayes we have seene
Anne French Queene, a verie great Ladie, no lesse in
vertue than in state: and if in justice and mildnesse, liberalitie and holinesse of life, ye lust to compare her to the
kinges Charles and Lewis (which had been wife to both
of them) you shall not find her a jotte inferiour to them.

Behold the Ladie Margaret, daughter to the Emperor
Maximilian, which with great wisedom and justice hetherto
hath ruled, and still doth her state.

But omitting all other, tell me (my Lorde Gasper) what
king or what prince hath there beene in our daies, or yet
many yeares before in Christendom, that deserveth to be
compared to Queene Isabel of Spaine.

The Lord Gasper answered king Ferdinande her husband. The Lorde Julian said: This will I not deny. For
since the Queene thought him a worthie husband for her,
and loved and observed him so much, it can not bee said
nay, but he deserved to be compared to her. And I thinke
well the reputation he got by her, was a no lesse dowrie
than the kingdom of Castilia.

487

Nay, answered the Lorde Gasper, I believe rather of many of king Ferdinandes actes Queene Isabell bore the prayse.

Then saide the Lorde Julian: In case the people of Spaine, the nobles, private persons, both men and women, poore and rich, be not all agreed together to lye in her prayse, there hath not beene in our time in the worlde a more cleare example of true goodnesse, stoutnesse of courage, wisedom, religion, honestie, courtesie, liberalitie: to be briefe, of al vertue, than Queene Isabel. And where the renowne of that Ladie in every place, and in all nations is very great, they that lived with her, and were present at all her doings doe all affirme this renowne to bee sprong of her vertue and deserts.

And who so will waigh her actes, shall soone perceive the truth to be so. For leaving apart infinite thinges that make tryall of this, and might be tolde, if it were our purpose, every man knoweth that in the first beginning of her raigne, she found ye greatest part of Castilia possessed by great estates: yet recovered she the whole again, so justly and in such sort, that they dispossessed themselves, continued in a great good affection, and were willing to make surrender of that they had in possession.

It is also a most knowne thing with what courage and wisedome she alwaies defended her realmes from most puissant enimies. And likewise to her alone may be given the honour of the glorious conquest of the kingdom of Granado, which in so long and sharpe a warre against stubborne enimies, that fought for their livelode, for their life, for their law, and to their weening in Gods quarrell, declared evermore with counsell and with her owne person so much vertue and prowesse, as perhaps in our time few princes have had ye stomacke, not only to follow her steps, but to envy her.

Beside this, all that knew her, report that there was in her such a divine manner of government, that a man would have weened that her will only was almost inough to make everie man without any more businesse, to doe that he ought: so that scarse durst a man in his owne home and in secrete commit any thing that hee suspected would displease her. And of this a great part, was cause the wonderfull judgement which she had in knowing and choosing ministers meete for the offices she entended to place them in.

And so well coulde she joine the rigour of justice with the mildenesse of mercie and liberallitie, that there was no good person in her dayes that could complaine he had beene smally rewarded, ne any ill, too sore punished.

Wherefore among her people towarde her, there sprang a verie great reverence derived of love and feare, which in all mens mindes remaineth still so setled, that a man woulde thinke they looked that she shoulde beholde them from heaven, and there above either prayse or dispraise them.

And therefore with her name, and with the waies which she ordained, those realmes are still ruled, in wise that albeit her life wanteth, yet her authoritie liveth, like a wheele long swinged about with violence, keeping the same course a good while after of it selfe, though no man move it any more.

Consider you beside this (my Lorde Gasper) that in our time al ye men of Spaine renowmed in what ever thing, have beene made so by Queene Isabel.

And the great Captaine Consalve Ferdinando was more set by for it, than for all his famous victories, and excellent and couragious actes, that in peace and war have made him so notable and famous.

That in case fame bee not unkinde, she will for ever spread abroad to the worlde his immortall prayses, and make proofe that in our age we have had few kinges or great Princes, that by him have not beene surmounted in noble courage, knowledge, and all vertue.

To returne therefore to Italy, I say unto you that we have not wanted here most excellent Ladies. For in Naples

489

wee have two Queenes, and not long agoe in Naples likewise dyed the other Queene of Hungarie, as excellent a Ladie as you know any, and to bee compared well inough to the mightie and glorious king Mathew Covin her husband.

Likewise the Dutchesse Isabel of Aragon most worthie sister to king Ferdinande of Naples which as gold in the fire, so in the stormes of fortune hath she shewed her vertue and prowesse.

If you will come into Lumbardie, you shall marke the Ladie Isabel marquesse of Mantua, whose most excellent vertues shoulde receive great wrong in speaking of them so temperately, as who so will speake of them in this place, must be driven to doe.

I am sory morever that you all knew not the Dutchesse Beatrice of Millane her sister, that you might never againe wonder at a womans wit.

And the Dutchesse Elionor of Aragon, Dutchesse of Ferrara, and mother to both these Ladies whom I have named, was such a one, that her most excellent vertues gave a good tryall to all the world, that she was not onely a worthy daughter to a king, but also deserved to be a Queene over a far greater state than all her auncestors possessed.

And to tell you of an other: How many men know you in the world, woulde abide the bitter strokes of fortune so patiently, as Queene Isabel of Naples hath done? Which for all the losse of her kingdome, banishment and death of king Fredericke her husband, and two sonnes, and imprisonment of the Duke of Calabria her eldest, yet still sheweth her selfe a Queene: and so beareth out the miserable inconveniences of wretched poverty, that every man may see, though she hath chaunged fortune, yet hath she not altered condition.

I omit the naming unto you of infinit other great Ladies, and also women of low degree, as many Pisanes that in defence of their countrie against the Florentines, have declared that noble courage without any feare of death, that the most invincible courages could doe that ever were in the world: Wherefore certaine of them have beene renowned by many noble Poets.

I could tell you of certain most excellent in letters, in musicke, in painting, in carving, but I will not anie more goe searching out among these examples, which are most knowne to you all.

It sufficeth, that if in your minds you thinke upon women whom you your selves know, it shal be no hard matter for you to understand, that they are not most commonly in prowesse or worthinesse inferiour to their fathers, brethren, and husbands: and that many have beene occasion of goodnesse to men, and many times broke them of many of their vices. And where presently there are not found in the world those great Queenes that go to conquere farre Countries, and make great buildinges, Piramides and Cities, as Thomiris Queene of Scithia, Artemisia, Zenobia, Semiramis or Cleopatra, no more are there also men like unto Cæsar, Alexander, Scipio, and the other noble Romane Captaines.

Say not so, answered then Phrisio laughing, for presently there are more found like Cleopatra or Semiramis, than ever there were. And though they have not so manye states, powers and riches, yet there wanteth not in them good will to counterfeite them at the least in giving themselves to pleasure, and satisfying all their lusts as much as they may.

The Lorde Julian saide: You will ever Phrisio passe your boundes. But in case there be found some Cleopatres, there want not for them infinite Sardanapalles, which is much worse.

Make not this comparison quoth the Lorde Gasper then, and believe not that men are so incontinent as women be: and where they were so, yet shoulde it not be worse. For of the incontinencie of women arise infinite inconveniences, that doe not of mens. And therefore (as it was well saide yesterday) they have wisely ordained that it may bee law-

full for them to be out of the way without blame in all
other thinges, that they may apply their force to keepe
themselves in this one vertue of chastitie, without the which
children were uncertain, and the bond that knitteth all the
worlde together by bloud, and by the love that naturally each man hath to that is borne him, shoulde be
loosed.

Therefore a wanton life in women is lesse to be borne
withall than in men, that carrie not their children nine
monthes in their bodie.

Then answered the Lorde Julian: Doubtlesse these be
pretie arguments that yee make, I marvel you put them
not in writing. But tell me, for what cause is it ordained
that a wanton life should not be so shamefull a matter in
men, as in women? Considering if they bee by nature
more vertuous and of greater prowesse, they may also the
easier keepe them selves in this vertue of continencie, and
children shoulde be no more or lesse certaine: for if women
were given to wanton living, so men were continent, and
consented not to the wantonnesse of women, they among
themselves and without any other helpe could not beare
children.

But if you will tell the truth, you your selfe know, that
wee have of our owne authoritie claimed a libertie, whereby wee will have the selfe same offences in us very light,
and otherwhile worthie prayse, and in women not sufficiently to bee punished, but with a shamefull death, or
at the least everlasting slaunder.

Therefore since this opinion hath taken roote, me thinketh it a meete matter to punish them in like manner
sharpely, that with lies bring up a slaunder upon women.
And I believe that every worthie gentleman is bound to
defend alwaies with weapon, where neede requireth, the
truth, and especiallye when he knoweth any woman
falsely reported of to be of litle honestie.

And I, answered the Lord Gasper smiling, doe not
onely affirm to bee every worthie gentlemans duetie,

that you say, but also take it for great courtesie and honestie to cover some offence, that by mishap or over-much love a woman is runne into. And thus you may see that I am more on womens side, where reason beareth me out, than you be.

I deny not that men have taken a litle libertie, and that because they know by the common opinion, that to them wanton living is not so slanderous as to women, which through the weaknesse of their kinde, are much more enclined to appetites, than men: and in case they abstaine otherwhile from satisfying their lusts, they doe it for shame, not that will is not most readie in them.

And therefore have men laide upon them feare of slaunder for a bridle, to keepe them (in a manner) whether they will or no in this vertue, without the which (to say the truth) they were litle to be set by: for the worlde hath no profit by women, but for getting of children.

But the like is not of men, which governe Cities, armies, and doe so many other waightie matters, the which (since you will so have it) I will not dispute how women could doe, it sufficeth they doe it not. And when it was meet for men to make tryall of their continencie, as well how they passed women in this vertue as in the rest, although you graunt it not. And about this, will not I rehearse unto you so many Histories or fables, as you have done, I remit you to the continencie onely of two most mightie personages, youthful and upon their victory, which is wont to make hautie men of lowest degree.

And one is, the great Alexander toward the most beautifull women of Darius his enimie and discomfited. The other Scipio, unto whom being twentie and foure yeares of age, and having wonne by force a Citie in Spaine, there was brought a most beautifull and noble Damsel taken among many other. And when Scipio understood that she was affianced to a Lorde of the Countrie, he did not onely abstaine from al dishonest acte toward her, but un-

defiled restored her to her husband, and a large gift withall.

I could tell you of Xenocrates, which was so continent,
that a most beautiful woman lying naked by his side and
dallying with him, and using all the waies she could (in
which matters she was very well practised) she had
never the power to make him once shew the least
signe of wantonnesse, for all she bestowed a whole night
about it.

And of Pericles that did no more but heare one praise
with overmuch earnestnesse the well favourednesse of a
boye, and he tooke him up sharpely for it. And of many
other most continent of their owne free will, and not for
shame or feare of punishment, that compelleth the greatest
part of women to keepe themselves upright in this vertue,
which notwithstanding deserve much praise withall: and
who so falsely bringeth up of them a slaunderous report
of uncleannesse of living, is worthie (as you have saide)
very sore punishment.

Then spake the Lord Cæsar which had held his peace a
good while: judge you in what sort the Lorde Gaspar
speaketh in the dispraise of women, when these are the
matters that hee speaketh in their prayse.

But if the Lorde Julian will give mee leave, that I may
in his stead answere him certaine few matters, as touching where (in mine opinion) he hath falsely spoken against
women, it shall be good for him and mee both. For he
shall rest him a while, and shall afterwarde the better goe
forwarde to speake of some other perfection of the gentlewoman of the pallace, and I shall have a good turne that
I have occasion to execute jointly with him this duety of a
good knight, which is to defend the truth.

Mary I beseech ye, answered the Lord Julian: for me
thinke I have alreadie fulfilled according to my power,
that I ought, and this communication now is out of the
purpose that I went about.

The Lorde Cesar then began: I will not now speake of

the profit that the worlde hath by women beside the bearing of children: for it is well inough declared how necessarie they be, not onely to our being, but also to our well being. But I say (my Lorde Gasper) that in case they be as you affirme, more enclined to appetites, than men, and notwithstanding abstaine more than men (which you your selfe grant) they are so much the more worthie praise, as their kind is lesse able to withstand naturall appetites.

And if you saye they doe it for shame, I can not see but for one vertue you give them two. For in case shame can doe more in them than appetite, and through it refraine from ill doing, I esteeme this shame (which in conclusion is nothing els but feare of slaunder) a most seldome vertue and raigning in verie fewe men. And if I coulde without infinite reproch to men, tell how many of them bee drowned in unshamefastnes, and impudencie (which is the vice contrarie to this vertue) I should infect these devoute eares that heare me. And for most part these kinde of injurious persons both to God and nature, are men well striken in yeares, which professe some priesthood, some Philosophie, some divinitie, and rule common weales with such Catoes gravitie in countenance, that it maketh an outwarde shew of all the honestie in the world, and alwaies alleage womenkinde to be most incontinent, where they at no time finde themselves more agreeved, than at the want of their naturall lustinesse, that they may satisfie their abhominable desires, which still abide in the minde after nature hath taken them from their bodie, and therefore manye tymes finde out waies, where force prevaileth not.

But I will not tell farther. It sufficeth for my purpose ye graunt that women abstaine more from uncleane living, than men. And sure it is, that they are not kept short with any other bridle, than what they put upon themselves. And that it is true, the most part of them that be kept under with over straight looking to, or beaten of their husbands or fathers, are lesse chaste, than they that have some libertie.

But generally a great bridle to women, is the zeale of true vertue, and the desire of good name, which many that I have knowne in my dayes more esteeme, than their owne life. And in case you will tell the truth, every one of us have seene most noble yong men, discreete, wise, of prowesse, and well favoured spend many yeares in loving, sparing for nothing that might entice, tokens, sutes, teares: to bee short whatsoever may bee imagined, and all but lost labour.

And if it might not bee tolde me that my conditions never deserved I shoulde be beloved, I would alleage my selfe for a witnesse, which more than once through the unchaungeablenes and over stedfast honestie of a woman, was nighe deathes doore.

The Lord Gasper answered: marvell you not thereat, for women that are sued to, alwaies refuse to fulfil his request, that sueth to them, but those that are not sued to, sue to others.

The Lord Cæsar saide: I never knew them that have beene sued to by women, but many there be that perceiving they have attempted in vaine, and spent their time fondly, runne to this noble revenge, and say that they had plentie of ye thing which they did but cast in their minde. And to their weening, to report ill, and to studie for inventions how to bring up slaunderous tales of some worthie gentlewoman, is a kinde of Courtiers trade.

But these kinde of persons that knavishly make their vaunt of any woman of price, be it true or false, deserve very sore correction and punishment. And if it be otherwhile bestowed upon them it can not be saide, how much they are to be commended that doe this office.

For in case they tell lyes, what mischiefe can be greater than to take from a worthie woman with guile the thing which she more esteemeth than her life? And no other cause but that ought to make her renowmed with infinite prayses. If againe it bee true they say, what paine can suffise so traiterous a person, that rendreth such ingratitude in recompence to a gentlewoman, which wonne with his false flatterings, fained teares, continuall sutes, bewailings, crafts, deceites, and perjuries, hath suffered her selfe to be led to love overmuch, afterwarde without respect, hath given her selfe unheedfully for a pray to so wicked a spirite?

But to answere you beside this wonderfull continencie of Alexander and Scipio which you have alleaged, I say, that I will not deny, but each of them did a deede worthie much praise. Notwithstanding least yee should say, that in rehearsing to you auncient matters, I tolde you fables, I will alleage a woman of our time of base degree, who notwithstanding shewed a far greater continencie than any of these two great estates.

I say unto you therefore, that I knew once a well favored and tender yong woman, whose name I tell you not, for giving matter to many lewd persons to reporte ill, which as soone as they understand a woman to be in love, make an ill descanting upon it.

She therefore beloved of a worthie and faire condicioned yong gentleman, was bent with heart and minde to love him. And of this not I alone, unto whom of her own accord she uttered trustfully the whole matter, no otherwise than if I had beene, I will not say a brother, but an inwarde sister of hers: but all that beheld her in company of the beloved yong man, were well weeting of her passion.

She thus fervently loving, as a most loving mind could love, continued two yeares in such continencie, that she never made any token to this yong man of the love that she bore him, but such as she coulde not hide from him. At no time she would speake with him, nor receive any letters from him, or tokens, where there never passed day but she was tempted with both the one and the other.

And how she longed for it, that wot I well, for if otherwhile she could privily get any thing that had beene the

yong mans, she was so tender over it, that a man would
have thought that of it had sprong her life and all her joy.
Yet would she never in so long a time content him with
other, than to behold him, and be seene of him againe, and
sometime happening to bee at open feastes, daunce with
him as she did with others.

And because there was no great difference in their
degree, she and the yong man coveted that so great a
love might have a luckie ende, and be man and wife together.

All the men and women in the Citie desired the same,
saving her cruel father, which of a weywarde and straunge
opinion, minded to bestow her upon another more welthie.
And this was not by the unluckie maiden otherwise gaine-
stood, than with most bitter teares.

And after this unfortunate marriage was concluded with
great compassion of the people there, and despairing of
the poore lovers, yet did not this stroke of Fortune serve
to root uppe so grounded a love in the heart of each other,
but lasted afterwarde the terme of three yeares, albeit she
full wisely dissembled it, and sought every way to cut in
sunder those desires, which now were past hope. And in
this while she followed on still in her set purpose of continencie, and perceiving she could not honestly have him,
whom she worshipped in the world, she chose not to have
him at all, and continued in her wont not to accept messages, tokens nor yet his lookes.

And in this resolved determination the seely soule vanquished with most cruell affliction, and waxed through
long passion very fainte, at the three yeares ende, died.
Rather would she forgo her contentations and pleasures so
much longed for, finally her life, than her honestie.

And yet wantede she no meanes nor waies to fulfill her
desire most secretly, and without perill either of slander
or any other losse. And for all that, refrained she from the
thing of her selfe that she so much coveted, and for the
which she was so cõtinually attempted by the person whom

alone in the worlde her desire was to please. And to this was she not driven for feare or any other respect, but onely for the zeale of true vertue.

What will you say of an other that for six monthes almost nightly laye with a most deare lover of his, yet in a garden full of most savorie fruites, tempted with her owne most fervent longing and with the petitions and teares of him that was more deare to her than her owne selfe, refrained from tasting of them. And for all she was wrapped and tyed in the straight chaine of those beloved armes, yet never yeelded she her selfe as vanquished, but preserved undefiled the floure of her honestie.

Trow ye not (my Lorde Gasper) that these bee deedes of continencie alike to Alexanders? Which most fervently inamored, not with the women of Darius, but with this renowne and greatnesse, that pricked him forwarde with the spurres of glory to abide paines and daungers to make himselfe immortall, set at nought not onely other thinges, but his owne life, to get a name above all men? And doe we marvel with such thoughts in his hart that he refrained from a thing which he coveted not greatly? for since he never saw those women before, it is not possible that he should be in love with them at a blush, but rather perhaps abhorred them for Darius, his enimies sake.

And in this case everie wanton acte of his towarde them, had beene an injurie and not love. And therefore no greater matter if Alexander which no lesse with noblenes of courage than martiall prowesse subdued the world, abstained from doing injurie to women.

The continencie in like case of Scipio is doubtlesse much to bee commended, yet if ye consider well, not to be compared to these two womens: for he in like manner also refrained from a thing that he coveted not, being in his enimies countrie, a fresh Captaine, in the beginning of a most waightie enterprise, leaving behinde him in his countrie, such expectation of himself, and having beside to give account to rigorous judges, that oftentimes chastised not onely the great but the least offences of all, and among them hee wist well hee had enimies, knowing also if he had otherwise done, because she was a noble damsell and espoused to a noble man, hee shoulde have purchased him so many enimies and in such sorte, that many woulde have driven off, and perchance have set him cleane besides his victorie.

Thus for so many respects and so waightie, hee abstained from a light and hurtfull appetite, in shewing continencie and freeharted well meaning, the which (as it is written) got him all the hartes of that people: and stood him in stead of another army with favor to vanquish mens harts, which perhaps by force of armes had beene invincible. So that this may rather be termed a warlike pollicie, than pure continencie: albeit beside, the report of this matter is not all of the purest: for some writers of authoritie affirme, that this Damsell was enjoyed of Scipio in the pleasures of love: and of this I tell you, yee may depose upon.

Phrisio saide: Perhaps ye have found it in the Gospell. I have seene it my selfe, answered the Lord Cesar, and therefore I have a much more certaintie of this, than you or any man els can have.

That Alcibiades arose no otherwise from Socrates bed than children doe from their fathers beds: for to say the truth, a straunge place and time was bed and night to view with fixed minde the pure beautie which is saide Socrates loved without any unhonest desire, especially loving better the beautie of the minde, than of the bodie: but in boyes, not in old men, for all they were wiser.

And in good sooth a better example could not have beene picked out to praise the continencie of men, than this is of Xenocrates, which occupied in his studie, fastned and bounde by his profession, which is Philosophie, that consisteth in good manners and not in words, old, cleane spent of his naturall lustinesse, nothing able, no not in making proffer to bee able, refrained from a common haunted woman, which for the names sake might abhorre him.

I would sooner have believed he had beene continēt, if he had declared any token to have beene come to his right senses againe, and in that case have used continencie: or els abstained from the thing which olde men covete more than the battailes of Venus, namely from wine.

But to establish wel continencie in old age, it is written, that hee was full and laden with it. And what can be saide to bee more wider from the continencie of an olde man, than dronkennesse? And in case the shunning of Venus matters in that slow and cold age deserveth so much praise, how much shoulde it deserve in a tender maiden, as those two I have told you of? Of which the one most straightly bridling all her senses, not onely denyed her eyes their light, but also tooke from the hart those thoughts, which alone had beene a most sweete foode a long time to keepe her in life.

The other fervently in love, being so oftentimes alone in the armes of him whom she loved more a great deale than all the world beside, fighting against her own selfe and against him that was more deare to her than her owne selfe, overcame that fervent desire that many times hath and doth overcome so many wise men.

Trow ye not now (my Lorde Gasper) that writers may bee ashamed to make mentiō of Xenocrates in this case, and to reckon him for chaste? where if a man could come by the knowledge of it, I would lay a wager that he slept all that night untill the next day dinner time, like a dead bodie buried in wine: and for all the stirring that woman made, could not once open his eyes, as though he had beene cast into a deade sleepe.

Lord Gasper (quoth she) if you will bethinke your selfe a litle better, I believe you shall finde out some other pretie example of continencie alike unto this.

The Lorde Cesar answered: Is not this other, think ye (Madam) a good example of continencie which he hath

501

alleaged of Pericles? I muse much that hee hath not as well called to rehearsall the continencie and pretie saying that is written of him, that a woman asked too great a summe for one night, and he answered her, that he mineded not to buye repentance so deare.

They ceased not laughing and the Lord Cesar after he had stayed a while, my Lord Gaspar (quoth he) pardon me, if I tell truth. For in conclusion these be the wonderfull continencies that men write of themselves, accusing women for incontinent, in whome are dayly seene infinite tokens of continencie.

And certes if ye ponder it aright, there is no fortresse so impregnable, nor so well fensed that being assaulted with the thousandeth part of the ingins and guiles that are practised to conquere the steadie minde of a woman, would not yeelde up at the first assault.

How many trained up by great estates and enriched through them and advanced to great promotion, having in their hands their fortresses, holdes, and castles, whereupon depended their whole state, their life, and all their goods, without shame or care to be named Traitors, have disloyally given them to whom they ought not?

And would God in our dayes there were such scarcitie of these kinde of persons, that we might not have much more adoe to finde out some one that in this case hath done that hee ought, than to name such as have failed therein.

See you not so many other that dayly wander about to kill men in thickets, and roving by sea, onely to robbe mens money? How many Prelates make marchandise with the goodes of the Church of God? How many Lawiers falsify testaments? What perjuries make they? how many false evidences, onely to get money? How many Phisitions poyson the diseased, onely for it? How many againe for feare of death doe most vile matters? And yet all these so stiffe and hard battailes doth a tender and delicate yong woman gainestand many times: for sundrie there have beene, that have chosen rather to dye than to lose their honestie.

502

Then saide the Lord Gasper: These (my Lord Cesar) be not I believe, in ye world nowadaies.

The Lord Cesar answered: And I will not alleage unto you them of olde time. But this I say, that many might be found out, and are dayly, that in this case passe not for death. And now it commeth into my minde that when Capua was sacked by the Frenchmen (which is not yet so long since but you may full well beare it in mind) a well favored young gentlewoman of Capua, being lead out of her house where she had been taken by a company of Gascoignes, when she came to the river that runneth by Capua, she fained to plucke on her shoe, in so much that her leader let her goe a litle, and she straight way threw her selfe into the river.

What will you say of a poore countrie wench, that not many monthes agoe at Gazuolo beside Mantua, gone into the field a leazing with a sister of hers, sore a thirst entred into a house to drink water, where the good man of the house, that was yong, seeing her meetely well favoured and alone, taking her in his armes, first with faire words, afterward with threateninges attempted to frame her to doe his pleasure, and where she strived stil more obstinatly, at length with many blowes and by force overcame her.

She thus tossed and sobbing, returned into the fielde to her sister: and for all the instance that she made upon her, would never disclose to her what outrage she received in that house, but still drawing homewarde, and shewing her selfe appeased by litle and litle, and to speak without disturbance, she gave her certaine instructions. Afterwarde when she came to the Olio, which is the river that runneth by Gazuolo, keeping her somewhat aloofe from her sister, that knew not, nor imagined that she minded to doe, sodainly cast her selfe into it.

Her sister sorrowfull and weeping, followed downe by the rivers side as fast as she coulde, which carried her a good pace away, and everie time the poore soule appeared above water, her sister threw into her a corde that she had brought with her to bind the corne withall. And for all the corde came to her handes more than once (for she was yet nigh inough the banke) the stedfast and resolved girle alwaies refused it, and pushed it from her. And thus shunning all succour that might save her life, in a short space died. She was neither stirred by noblenesse of bloude, nor by feare of death or slander, but only by the griefe of her lost maidenheade.

Now by this you may gather, how many other women doe deedes most worthie memorie, since (as a man may say) three dayes agoe this hath made such a triall of her vertue, and is not spoken of, ne yet her name knowne.

But had not the death folowed at that time of the bishop of Mantua uncle to our Dutchesse, the banke of the Olio in the place where she cast her selfe in, had now beene garnished with a verie faire sepulture, for a memorie of so glorious a soule, that deserved so much the more cleare renowne after death, as in life it dwelled in an unnoble body.

Here the Lord Cesar tooke respit a while, afterward hee set forwarde: In my dayes also in Rome there happened a like chaunce, and it was, that a fell favoured and well borne yong gentlewoman of Rome, being long followed after of one that shewed to love her greatly, would never please him with any thing, no not so much as a look. So that this fellow by force of money corrupted a waiting woman of hers, who desirous to please him to finger more money, was in hande with her mistresse upon a day, no great holy day, to go visite Saint Sebastianes Church.

And giving the lover intelligence of the whole, and instructing him what he had to doe, lead the yong gentlewoman into one of the dark caves under grounde, that who so goe to Saint Sebastianes are wont to visite. And in it was the yong man first closely hid, which perceiving himselfe alone with her whom hee loved so much, beganne every way to exhort her with as faire language as he coulde, to have compassion upon him, and to chaunge her former rigor into love. But when he saw all his prayers could take none effect, he turned him to threatnings.

And when they prevailed not, he all to beat her. In the ende hee was full and wholy bent to have his purpose, if not otherwise, by force, and therein used the helpe of the naughtie woman that had brought her thither. Yet could he never doe so much as make her graunt to him, but in words and deedes (although her force was but small) alwaies the seely yong woman defended her selfe in what she could possible. So that what for the spite hee conceived when he saw hee coulde not get his will, and what for feare least the matter shoulde come to her kinsfolkes eare, and make him punished for it, this mischievous person with the aide of the woman that doubted ye same, strangled the unluckie yong woman, and there left her, and running his way provided for him selfe for being found out againe.

The waiting woman blinded with her owne offence, wist not to flee, and being taken upon certaine suspitions, confessed the whole matter, and was therefore punished according to her deserts.

The body of the constant and noble gentlewomã with great honour was taken out of the cave and carried to buriall within Rome with a garland of Laurell about her heade, accompanied with an infinite number of men and women: among which was not one that brought his eyes to his home againe without teares. And thus generally of all the people was this rare soule no lesse bewailed than commended.

But to tell you of them that you your selfe know, remember you not that ye have heard tell, as the Ladie Fœlix della Rovere was on her journey to Saona doubting lest certaines sailes that were descried a farre off, had beene Pope Alexanders vessels, that pursued her, was utterly resolved, if they had made toward her, and no remedie to escape, to cast her selfe into the Sea.

And this is not to bee thought that she did upon any

lightnesse, for you as well as any man, doe know with what a wit and wisedom the singular beautie of that Ladie is accompanied.

I can no longer keepe in silence a word of our Dutchesse, who living fifteene yeares in company with her husband, like a widow, hath not onely beene stedfast in not uttering this to any person in the world, but also when she was perswaded by her owne friendes to forsake this widow-head,[35] she chose rather to suffer banishment, povertie, and all other kinde of miserie, than to agree to that, which all other men thought great favour and prosperitie of fortune. And as he still proceeded in talking of this, the Duchesse saide.

Speake of somewhat els, and no more adoe in this matter, for yee have other thinges inough to talke of.

The Lord Cesar followed on. Full well I know that you will not deny mee this (my Lorde Gasper) nor you Phrisio.

No doubtlesse, answered Phrisio: but one maketh no number.

Then saide the Lord Cesar: Truth it is that these so great effectes and rare vertues are seene in few women: Yet are they also that resist the battailes of love, all to be wondred at, and such as otherwhile bee overcome deserve much compassion. For surely the provocations of lovers, the crafts that they use, the snares that they lay in waite are such, and so applyed, that it is too great a wonder, that a tender girle should escape them.

What day, what houre passeth any time that the yong woman thus laide at is not tempted by her lover with money, tokens: and all thinges that he can imagine may please her?

At what time can she ever looke out at a window, but she seeth continually the earnest lover passe by? With silence in wordes, but with a paire of eyes that talke. With a vexed and faint countenance. With those kinled sighes. Oftentimes with most aboundant teares.

When doth she at any time issue out at her doores to

506

Church or any other place, but he is alwaies in the face of her? And at every turning of a lane meeteth her in the teeth, with such heavie passion painted in his eyes, that a man woulde weene that even at the instant hee were readie to dye?

I omit his precisenesse in sundrie thinges, inventions, merrie conceites, undertaking enterprises, sportes, daunces, games, maskeries, justes, tournaments, the which thinges she knoweth all to be taken in hande for her sake.

Againe, in the night time she can never awake, but she heareth musick, or at the least that unquiet spirite about the walles of her house, casting forth sighes and lamentable voices.

If by happe she talketh with one of her waiting women about her, she (being alreadie corrupted with money) hath straight way in a readinesse some pretie token, a letter, a rime, or some such matter, to present in her lovers behalfe and here entring to purpose, maketh her to understand how this seely soule burneth, how he setteth litle by his owne life, to doe her service, and how hee seeketh nothing of her but honestie, and that onely his desire is to speake with her.

Here then for all hard matters are found out remedies, counterfeite keyes, ladders of ropes, waies to cast into sleepe, a trifling matter is painted out, examples are alleaged of others that doe much worse: so that every matter is made so easie, that she hath no more trouble but to say, I am content. And in case the poore soule make resistance but a while, they ply her with such provocations, and finde such meanes, that with continuall beating at, they breake in sunder that is a let to her.

And many there be, that perceiving they can not prevaile with faire wordes, fall to threatnings, and say that they wil tell their husbands, they are that they be not.

Other bargaine boldly with their fathers, and many times with ye husbands, which for promotions sake give their owne daughters and wives for a pray against their will.

Other seeke by inchauntments, and witchcraftes, to take
from them the libertie that God hath graunted to soules,
wherein are seene wonderful conclusions. But in a thousand yeare I coulde not repeat all the crafts that men use
to frame women to their willes, which bee infinite.

And beside them which every man of him selfe findeth
out, there hath not also wanted this have wittily made
bookes,[36] and bestowed great studie to teach how in this
behalfe women are to be deceived.

Now judge you how from so many nets these simple
dooves can be safe, tempted with so sweete a baite. And
what great matter is it then, in case a woman knowing
her selfe so much beloved and worshipped many yeares
together, of a noble and faire cōdicioned yong man, which
a thousand times a day hazardeth his life to serve her,
and never thinketh upon other but to please her. How with
the continuall beating which the water maketh when it
pearceth the most hard marble stone, at length is it
brought to love it? And so she being vanquished by passions, yeeldeth to that whereof you spake, by reason of
the imbecillitie of that sexe, she being by nature more
desirous of that matter than the man that is in love.

Is this (thinke you) so hainous a trespasse, that the
seely poore creature taken with so many entisements, deserveth not, if the worst should fall, the pardon that many
times murtherers, theeves, fellons and traitors have?

Will you have this vice so uncomparable great, that
because one woman is founde to runne into it, all women
kinde should be cleane dispised for it, and generally
counted void of continencie? Not regarding that many are
found most invincible, that against the continuall flickering provocations of love are made of Diamonds, and stiffe
in their infinit stedinesse, more than the rocks, against the
surges of the sea.

Then the Lorde Gasper when the L. Cesar stayed talking, began to make him answere, but the Lord Octavian
smyling: Tush for love of God (quoth he) graunt him the

victory, for I know ye shall doe small good, and me thinke I see you shall not onely make all the women your enimies, but also the more part of the men.

The Lord Gasper laughed and said: Nay, the women have rather great cause to thanke me. For had not I contraried the Lorde Julian and the Lorde Cesar, they should not have come to the knowledge of so many prayses as they have given them.

Then saide the Lord Cesar: The prayses which my Lorde Julian and I have given women, and many mo beside, were most knowne, therefore they have beene but superfluous.

Who woteth not that without women no contentation or delite can be felt in all this life of ours? which (set them aside) were rude, and without all sweetenesse, and rougher than the life of forrest wilde beastes?

Who knoweth not that women rid our harts of all vile and dastardly imaginations, vexations, miseries, and the troublesom heavines that so oftentimes accompanieth them?

And in case we will consider the truth, we shal know moreover, as touching the understanding of great matters, that they doe not stay our wits, but rather quicken them, and in warre make them [past] feare, and hardie passing measure.

And certes it is not possible, that in the hart of man, where once is entred the flame of love, there shoulde at any time raigne cowardlinesse. For he that loveth, alwaies coveteth to make him selfe as lovely as he can, and evermore dreadeth that hee take no foile, that shoulde make him litle set by: and passeth not to goe a thousand times in a day to his death, to declare him selfe worthie of that love.

Therefore who so coulde gather an armie of lovers that should fight in the presence of the Ladies they loved, should subdue the whole world, unlesse against it on the contrarie part there were an other armie likewise in love.

And to abide by, the holding out of Troy tenne yeares against all Greece, proceeded of nothing els but of certaine lovers, which when they entended to issue out abroad to fight, armed them selves in the presence of their Ladies, and many times they helped them, themselves, and at their setting forth rounded them some certaine word, y^t set them on fire and made them more than men.

Afterwarde in fighting they wist well that they were beheld from the walles and towers by the Ladies, wherefore they deemed everie bold enterprise that they undertooke, was commended of them, which was the greatest rewarde to them that they coulde have in the world.

Many there be that holde opinion that the victorie of king Ferdinande and Isabell of Spaine, against the king of Granada was chiefely occasioned by women: for the most times when the armie of Spaine marched to encounter with the enimies, Queene Isabel set forth also with all her Damsels: and there were many noble gentlemen that were in love, who till they came within sight of the enimies, alwaies went communing with their Ladies. Afterwarde echone taking his leave of his, in their presence marched on to encounter with the enimies, with that fiercenesse of courage, that love and desire to shew their Ladies that they were served with valiant men, gave them.

Whereupon it befell many times that a very few gentlemen of Spaine put to flight and slew an infinite number of Moores, thanked be the courteous and beloved women. Therefore I wot not (my Lorde Gasper) what waywarde judgement hath leade you to dispraise women.

Doe you not see that of all comely exercises and which delight the world, the cause is to be referred to no earthly thing, but to women? Who learneth to daunce featly for other, but to please women?

Who applyeth the sweetnesse of musicke for other cause, but for this? Who to write in meeter, at the least in the mother tongue, but to expresse the affections caused by women?

510

Judge you how many most noble Poemes we had beene without both in Greek and Latin had women beene smally regarded of Poets.

But in leaving all other apart, had it not beene a very great losse, in case maister Francis Petrarca, that writte so divinely his loves in this our tongue, had applyed his minde onely to Latin matters: as he would have done had not the love of ye Damsell Laura sometime staied him from it?

I name not unto you the fine wits that are now in the world, and here present, which dayly bring forth some noble fruite, and notwithstanding take their ground only of the vertue and beautie of women. See whether Salomon minding to write mystically verie high and heavenly matters, to cover them with a gracious vaile, did not faine a fervent Dialogue full of the affection of a lover with his woman, seeming to him that he coulde not finde here beneath among us any likenesse more meete and agreeing with heavenly matters, than the love towarde women: and in that wise, and manner, minded to give us a litle of the smacke of that divinitie, which he both for his understanding and for the grace above others, had knowledge of.

Therefore this needed no disputation (my Lorde Gasper) or at the least so many wordes in the matter. But you in gainesaying the truth, have hindred the understanding of a thousand other pretie matters, and necessarie for the perfection of the gentlewoman of the Pallace.

The Lord Gasper answered: I believe there can no more be saide: Yet if you suppose that the Lorde Julian hath not garnished her throughly with good conditions, the fault is not in him, but in him that hath so wrought that there are no moe vertues in the worlde: for all that there be, he hath bestowed upon her.

The Dutchesse saide smiling: Well, you shall see that the Lord Julian wil yet finde out moe beside.

The Lord Julian answered: in good sooth (Madam) me seemeth I have sufficiently spoken. And for my part, I am

511

well pleased with this my woman. And in case these Lordes will not have her as she is, let them leave her to me.

Here when all was whist, Sir Fredericke saide: My Lord Julian, to give you occasion to say somewhat els, I will but aske you a question, as touching that you have willed to bee the principall profession of the gentlewoman of the Pallace. And this it is, that I long to know how she should behave her selfe in a point that (to my seeming) is most necessarie.

For albeit the excellent qualities which you have given her, containe in them discretion, knowledge, jugement, sleight, sober mood, and so many other vertues, whereby of reason she ought to have the understanding to entertaine every man, and in all kind of purpose, yet think I notwithstanding above any other thing, that it is requisite for her to know what belongeth to communication of love.

For even as every honest gentleman for an instrument to obtaine the good will of women, practiseth those noble exercises, precise fashions and good manners which we have named, even so to this purpose applyeth he also his wordes, and not onely when he is stirred thereto by some passion, but oftentimes also to doe honour to the woman he talketh withal, seeming to him that to declare to love her, is a witnesse that she is worthie of it, and that her beawtie and worthinesse is such, that it enforceth everie man to serve her.

Therefore would I know, how this woman in such a case shoulde behave her selfe uprightly, and how to answere him that loveth her in deed, and how him that maketh false semblant: and whether she ought to dissemble the understanding of it, or be answerable, or shun the matter, and how to handle her selfe.

Then said the Lord Julian: It were first needfull to teach her to know them that make semblant to love, and them that love in deede. Afterwarde for being answerable in love or no, I believe she ought not to be guided by any other mans will, but by her owne selfe.

Sir Frederick said: Teach you her then what are the most certaine and surest tokens to discerne false love from true, and what tryall she shall thinke sufficient to content her selfe withall, to be out of doubt of the love shewed her.

The Lord Julian answered smiling: That wote not I, because men bee now a daies so craftie, that they make infinite false semblāts, and sometime weepe, when they have in deede a greater lust to laugh: therefore they should be sent to the constant Ile under the Arch of faithfull lovers. But lest this woman of mine (which is my charge and no mans els, because she is my creature) should runne into these errours which I have seene many other runne into, I woulde say that she shoulde not be light of credence that she is beloved: nor bee like unto some, that not onely make [not] wise they understande him not that cōmuneth with them of love, be it never so farre of, but also at the first word accept all the prayses that be given them: or els deny them after such a sorte, that is rather an alluring for them to love them they commune withall, than a withdrawing of themselves.

Therefore the manner of entertainment in reasoning of love that I will have my woman of the Pallace to use, shal be alwaies to shunne believing that who so talketh of love, loveth her any whit the more. And in case the gentleman be (as many such there are abroad) malaperte, and hath small respect to her in his talke, she shall shape him such an answere, that he shall plainely understand she is not pleased withall. Againe, if he be demure and useth sober fashions and wordes of love covertly, in such honest manner, as I believe the Courtier whom these Lordes have fashioned will doe, the woman shall make wise not to understand him, and shall draw his wordes to another sense, seeking alwaies soberly with the discretion and wisedom that is alreadie saide becommeth her, to stray from that purpose.

But in case the communication bee such that she can not faine not to understand it, she shall take the whole (as it were) for a merrie devise, and make wise that she knoweth it is spoken to her rather to honour her withal, than that it is so in deede, debasing her deserts, and acknowledging at the gentlemans courtesie the prayses which he giveth her: and in this sort she shall be counted discreete, and shall bee on the surer hande for being deceived.

Thus me seemeth the gentlewoman of the Pallace ought to behave her selfe in communication of love.

Then Sir Fredericke. You debate this matter, my Lord Julian (quoth he) as though it were requisite, that all such as speake with women of love, should tell lyes, and seeke to deceive them, the which in case it were so, I woulde say your lessons were good. But if this gentleman that entertaineth, loveth in very deede, and feeleth the passion that so tormenteth mens hearts sometime, consider you not in what paine, in what calamitie and death ye put him in, when at no time you will that the woman shall believe him in any thing hee saith about this purpose?

Shall othes, teares, and so many other tokens then, have no force at all? Take heede (my Lord Julian) least a man may thinke that beside ye naturall crueltie which many of these women have in them, you teach them yet more.

The Lorde Julian answered: I have spoken, not of him that loveth, but of him that entertaineth with communication of love, wherein one of the necessariest points is, that wordes be never to seeke: and true lovers as they have a burning heart so have they a colde tongue, with broken talke and sodaine silence.

Therefore (may hap) it were no false principle to say, He that loveth much, speaketh litle. Howbeit in this I believe there can bee given no certaine rule, by reason of the diversitie of mens manners. And I wot not what I should say, but that the woman be good and heedfull, and alwaies beare in minde, that men may with a great deale lesse daunger declare them selves to love, than women.

The Lorde Gaspar saide laughing: Why (my Lorde

Julian) will not you that this your so excellent a woman shall love againe, at the least when she knoweth certainely she is beloved, considering if the Courtier were not loved againe, it is not likely he would continue in loving her: and so should she want many favours, and chieflye the homage and reverence wherewithall lovers obey, and (in a manner) worship the vertue of the woman beloved.

In this, answered the L. Julian, I will not counsell her. But I say perdee to love, as you now understãd, I judge it not meet, but for unmarried women. For when this love can not ende in matrimonie, the woman must needs have alwaies the remorse and pricking that is had of unlawfull matters, and she putteth in hazard to staine the renowne of honestie, that stãdeth her so much upon.

Then answered Sir Fredericke smyling: Me thinke (my Lord Julian) this opinion of yours is verie soure and crabbed, and I believe you have learned it of some Frier Preacher, of them that rebuke women in love with lay men, that their part may be the more. And me seemeth you set over hard lawes to married women, for many there be that their husbands beare very sore hatred unto without cause, and nippe them at the hart, sometime in loving other women, otherwhile in working them all the displeasures they can imagine.

Some are compelled by their fathers to take olde men full of diseases, uglesome and waywarde that make them leade their life in continuall miserie. And in case it were lawfull for such to bee devorced and severed from them they bee ill coupled withall, perhaps it were not to be allowed that they shoulde love any other than their husband. But when either through the starres, their enimies, or through yᵉ diversitie of complexion, or any other casualtie, it befalleth that in bed, which ought to be the nest of agreement and love, the cursed furie of hell soweth the seede of his venome, which afterwarde bringeth forth disdaine, suspition, and the pricking thornes of hatred, that tormenteth those unluckie soules bound cruelly together

515

in the fast lincked chaine that can not be broken but by
death, why will not you have it lawfull for this woman to
seeke some easement for so hard a scourge, and give unto
another that which her husband not onely regardeth not,
but rather cleane abhorreth?

I hold well, that such as have meete husbands and bee
beloved of them, ought not to doe them injurie: but the
other in not loving him that loveth them doe themselves
injurie.

Nay, they doe themselves injurie in loving other beside
their husband, answered the Lord Julian. Yet since not
loving is not many times in our will, if this mishappe
chaunce to the woman of the Pallace, that the hatred of
her husband or the love of an other bendeth her to love I
will have her to graunt her lover nothing els but the minde:
not at any time to make him any certaine token of love,
neither in worde nor gesture, nor any other way that he
may be fully assured of it.

Then saide maister Robert of Bari smiling, I appeale
(my Lord Julian) from this judgement of yours, and I
believe I shall have many fellowes. But since you will
teach this currishnesse (that I may terme it so) to married
women, will ye also have the unmarried to bee so cruel
and discourteous? and not please their lovers at the least
in somewhat?

In case my woman of the Pallace, answered the Lorde
Julian, be not married, minding to love, I will have her to
love one she may marrie, neither will I thinke it an offence
if she shew him some token of love. In which matter I
will teach her one generall rule in few wordes, and that is,
That she shew him whom she loveth all tokens of love,
but such as may bring into the lovers minde a hope to
obtaine of her any dishonest matter. And to this she must
have a great respect, because it is an errour that infinite
women runne into, which ordinarily covet nothing so much
as to bee beautifull.

And because to have many lovers they suppose is a

testimony of their beautie, they doe their best to winne them as many as they can. Therefore oftentimes they run at rovers in behaviours of small modesty, and leaving the temperate sober moode that is so sightly in them, use certaine wanton countenances, with baudie words and gestures full of unshamefastnesse, holding opinion that men marke them and give eare to them willingly for it, and with these fashions make themselves beloved, which is false.

Because the signes and tokens that bee made them, spring of an apetite moved by an opinion of easinesse, not of love. Therefore will not I that my woman of the Pallace with dishonest behaviours shoulde appeare as though she woulde offer her selfe unto who so will have her, and allure what she can the eyes and affection of who so beholdeth her: but with her deserts and vertuous conditions, with amiablenesse and grace drive into the minde of who so seeth her, the very love that is due unto everie thing worthie to bee beloved, and the respect that alwaies taketh away hope from who so mindeth any dishonest matter.

He then that shall be beloved of such a woman, ought of reason to holde himselfe contented with every litle token, and more to esteeme a looke of hers with affection of love, than to be altogether maister of an other. And to such a woman I wot not what to adde more, but that she be beloved of so excellent a Courtier, as these Lordes have fashioned, and she likewise to love him, that both the one and the other may have full and wholy his perfection.

After the Lord Julian had thus spokē he held his peace, when the L. Gaspar laughing, now (quoth he) you can not complaine that the Lord Julian hath not fashioned this woman of the Pallace most excellent. And if perdee there bee any such to bee found, I say that she deserveth well to bee esteemed equall with the Courtier.

The Ladie Emilia answered: I will at all times be bound to find her, when you finde the Courtier.

Maister Robert said then: Doubtlesse it can not be said nay, but the Lorde Julians woman which he hath fashioned is most perfect. Yet in these her last properties as touching love, mee seemeth notwithstäding that he hath made her somewhat over crabbed, and especially where he will have her in wordes, gestures and countenance to take cleane away all hope from the lover, and settle him as nigh as she can in dispaire.

For (as all men know) the desires of man stretch not to such kinde of matters, whereof there is no hope to bee had. And although at times some women there have beene that perhaps bearing them selves loftie of their beautie and worthinesse: the first worde they have saide to them that communed with them of love hath beene, that they shoulde never looke to come by any thing of them that liked them: yet in countenance, and dalliance together they have beene afterwarde more favourable to them, so that with their gentle deedes they have tempred in part their proude wordes.

But if this woman both in wordes, deedes, and behaviours take hope quite away, I believe our Courtier, if he be wise, will never love her, and so shall she have this imperfection, that she shall be without a lover.

Then the Lord Julian, I will not (quoth he) have my woman of the Pallace to take away the hope of every thing, but of dishonest matters, the which, in case the Courtier bee so courteous and discreete, as these Lordes have fashioned him, he will not onely not hope for, but not once motion.

For if beautie, manners, wit, goodnesse, knowledge, sober moode, and so many other vertuous conditions which wee have given the woman, be the cause of the Courtiers love toward her, the end also of this love must needes be vertuous, and if noblenesse of birth, skilfulnesse in martiall feates, in letters, in musicke, gentlenesse, being both in speech and behaviour indowed with so many graces, be ye meanes wherewithall the Courtier compasseth ye womans love, the ende of that love must needes be of the same condition that the meanes are by the which hee commeth to it. Beside that, as there bee in the world sundrie kindes of beautie, so are there also sundrie desires of men: and therfore it is seene that many, perceiving a woman of so grave a beautie, that going, standing, jeasting, dallying, and doing what she lusteth, so tempreth all her gestures, that it driveth a certaine reverence into who so beholdeth her, are agast and afeard to serve her.

And rather drawne with hope, love those garish and enticefull women, so delicate and tender, that in their wordes, gestures and countenance, declare a certaine passion somewhat feeble, that promiseth to be easily brought and turned into love.

Some to be sure from deceites, love certaine other so lavish both of their eyes, wordes and gestures, that they doe what ever first commeth to minde, with a certaine plainenesse that hideth not their thoughts.

There want not also many other noble courages, that seeming to them that vertue consisteth about hard matters (for it is over sweet a victory to overcome that seemeth to another impregnable) are soone bent to love the beauties of those women, that in their eyes, wordes and gestures, declare a more churlish gravitie than the rest, for a tryall that their prowesse can enforce an obstinate minde, and bend also stubborne willes and rebels against love, to love.

Therefore such as have so great affiance in themselves because they reckon themselves sure from deceite, love also willingly certaine women, that with a sharpenesse of wit, and with arte it seemeth in their beautie that they hide a thousand craftes. Or els some other, that have accompanied with beautie a certaine scornefull fashion, in few wordes, litle laughing, after a sort as though (in a manner) they smally regarded who so ever beholdeth or serveth them.

Againe ther are found certaine other, that vouchsafe not

to love but women that in their countenance, in their speach and in all their gestures have about them all hansomnesse, all faire conditions, all knowledge, and all graces heaped together like one floure made of all the excellencies in the world.

Therefore in case my woman of the Pallace have scarcitie of their loves proceeding of an ill hope, she shal not for this be without a lover: because she shall not want them that shall be provoked through hir desertes and through the affiaunce of the prowesse in themselves, whereby they shall knowe themselves worthie to be loved of her.

Maister Robert still spake against him, but the Dutchesse tolde him that he was in the wrong, confirming the Lord Julians opinion: after that she added: We have no cause to complaine of the L. Julian, for doubtlesse I think that the woman of the Pallace whom hee hath fashioned, may be compared to the Courtier, and that with some advantage: for he hath taught her to love which these Lordes have not done their Courtier.

Then spake Unico Aretino: It is meete to teach women to love, because I never saw any that coulde doe it, for almost continually all of them accompanye their beautie with cruelty and unkindnesse towarde such as serve them most faithfully, and which for noblenesse of birth, honestie and vertue deserved a rewarde for their good wil: and yet many times give themselves for a pray to most blockish and cowardly men and very Asseheades, and which not onely love them not, but abhorre them.

Therefore to shunne these so foule oversights, perhaps it had beene well done first to have taught them to make a choise of him that should deserve to be beloved, and afterwarde to love him. The which is not necessarie in men, for they know it too wel of themselves: and I my selfe can be a good witnesse of it, because love was never taught me, but by the divine beauty and most divine manners of a Ladie, so that it was not in my will not to worship her: and therefore needed I therein no arte nor

520

teacher at all. And I believe that the like happeneth to as many as love truely.

Therefore the Courtier hath more neede to be taught to make him beloved than to love.

Then saide the Ladie Emilia: Doe you now reason of this then, maister Unico?

Unico answered: me think reason woulde that the good will of women shoulde be gotten in serving and pleasing of them. But it, wherein they reckon themselves served and pleased, I believe must bee learned of women themselves, which ofte times covet such straunge matters, that there is no man that would imagin them, and otherwhile they themselves wot not what they shoulde long for.

Therefore it were good you (madam) that are a woman, and of right ought to know what pleaseth women, should take this paine, to doe the world so great a profit.

Then saide the Ladie Emilia: For so much as you are generally most acceptable to women, it is a good likelyhood that you know all the waies how their good will is to be gotten. Therefore is it perdee meete for you to teach it.

Madam, answered Unico, I can give a lover no profitable advise than to procure that you beare no stroke with ye woman whose good will hee seeketh. For the small qualities which yet seemed to the worlde sometime to be in me, with as faithfull a love as ever was, were not of such force to make me beloved, as you to make mee be hated.

Then answered the Ladie Emilia: God save me (maister Unico) for once thinking, and much more for working any thing that should make you be hated. For beside that I shoulde doe that I ought not, I shoulde bee thought of a slender judgement to attempt a matter unpossible. But since ye provoke me in this sort to speak of that pleaseth women, I will speake of it, and if it displease you, lay the fault in your selfe.

I judge therefore, that who so entendeth to be beloved, ought to love and to be lovely: and these two pointes are inough to obtaine the good will of women.

Now to answere to that which you lay to my charge, I say that every man knoweth and seeth that you are most lovely: Mary whether ye love so faithfully, as you say ye doe, I am verie doubtful and perhaps others too. For, your being over lovely, hath beene the cause that you have beene beloved of many women: and great rivers divided into many armes become small brookes: so love likewise scattred into mo than one body hath small force.

But these your continuall complaintes and accusing of the women whom you have served, of unkindnesse (which is not likely, considering so many deserts of yours) is a certaine kinde of discretion, to cloke the favours, contentations and pleasures which you have received in love, and an assurance for the women that love you and that have given themselves for a pray to you, that you will not disclose them. And therefore are they also well pleased, that you should thus openly shew false love to others, to cloke their true.

Wherefore if happly those women that you now make wise to love, are not so light of beliefe, as you would they were, it happeneth because this your arte in love beginneth to bee discovered, and not because I make you to be hated.

Then said maister Unico: I entend not to attempt to confute your words, because me seemeth it is as well my destinie not to be believed in truth, as it is yours to be believed in untruth.

Say hardly maister Unico, answered the Ladie Emilia, that you love not so, as you would have believed ye did. For if you did love, all your desires shoulde bee to please the woman beloved, and to will the selfe same thing that she willeth, for this is the law of love. But your complaining so much of her, betokeneth some deceite (as I have saide) or els it is a signe that you will that, that she willeth not.

Nay (quoth maister Unico) there is no doubt but I will that that she willeth, which is a signe I love her: but it greeveth mee because she willeth not that, that I will, which is a token she loveth not me, according to the very same law that you have alleaged.

The Ladie Emilia answered: he that taketh in hande to love, must also please and apply himselfe full and wholy to the appetites of the wight beloved, and according to them frame his own: and make his owne desires, servants: and his verie soule, like an obedient handmaiden: nor at any time to think upon other, but to chaunge his, if it were possible, into the beloved wightes, and reckon this his chiefe joy and hapinesse, for so doe they that love truely.

My chiefe happinesse were jumpe, answered maister Unico, if one will alone ruled her soule and mine both.

It lyeth in you to doe it, answered the Ladie Emilia. Then spake maister Bernarde interrupting them: Doubtlesse, who so loveth truely, directeth all his thoughtes, without other mens teaching, to serve and please the woman beloved. But because these services of love are not otherwhile well knowne, I believe that beside loving and serving, it is necessarie also to make some other shew of this love, so manifest, that the woman may not dissemble to knowe that she is beloved: yet with such modestie, that it may not appeare that hee beareth her litle reverence.

And therefore you (Madam) that have begun to declare how the soule of the lover ought to be an obedient handmaiden to the beloved, teach us withall, I beseech you, this secrete matter, which mee thinke is most needefull.

The Lorde Cesar laughed and saide: If the lover be so bashfull, that he is ashamed to tell it her, let him write it her.

To this the Ladie Emilia saide: Nay, if he be descreete, as is meete, before he maketh the woman to understande it, hee ought to bee out of doubt, not to offend her.

Then saide the Lorde Gasper: All women have a delite

to be sued to in love, although they were minded to deny that which they are sued unto for.

The Lorde Julian saide, you are much deceived. For I woulde not counsell the Courtier at any time to use this way, except he were sure not to have a repulse.

What should he then doe? quoth the Lord Gasper. The Lorde Julian answered: In case you will needs write or speake to her, doe it with such sober moode, and so warily, that the wordes may first attempt the minde, and so doubtfully touch her entent and will, that they may leave her a way and a certain issue to faine the understanding that those wordes containe love: to the entent if he finde any daunger, hee may draw backe and make wise to have spoken or written it to another ende, to enjoy these familiar cherishinges and daliances with assurance that oftentimes womē shew to such as should take them for friendship, afterwarde denye them as soone as they perceive they are taken for tokens of love.

Wherefore such as bee too rash, and venture so sawcily with certaine furies and plunges, oftentimes lose them, and worthily: for it displeaseth alwaies everye honest gentle-woman, to bee litle regarded of who so without respect seeketh for love at her before he hath served her.

Therefore (in my minde) the way which the Courtier ought to take, to make his love knowne to the woman me think should be to declare them in signes and tokens more than in wordes. For assuredly there is otherwhile a greater affection of love perceived in a sigh, in a respect, in a feare, than in a thousand wordes. Afterwarde, to make the eyes the trustie messengers, that may carrie the ambassades of the hart.

Because they oftentimes declare with a more force what passiō there is inwardly, than can the tongue, or letters, or messages, so that they not onely disclose the thoughts, but also manie times kindle love in the hart of the person beloved. For those lively spirits that issue out at the eyes, because they are engendred nigh the hart, entring in like case into the eyes that they are levelled at, like a shaft

to the pricke, naturally pearce to the hart, as to their resting place and there are at rest with those other spirits: and
with the most subtill and fine nature of bloud which they
carrie with them, infect the bloude about the hart, where
they are come to, and warme it: and make it like unto
themselves, and apt to receive the imprinting of the image,
which they have carried away with them. Wherefore by
litle and litle comming and going the way through the eyes
to the hart, and bringing backe with them the tunder and
striking yron of beautie and grace, these messengers kindle
with the puffing of desire the fire that so burneth, and
never ceaseth consuming, for alwaies they bring some
matter of hope to nourish it.

Therefore it may full wel be saide, that the eyes are a
guide in love, especially if they have a good grace and
sweetnesse in them, blacke, of a cleare and sightly blacke-
nesse, or els gray, merrie and laughing, and so comely and
pearcing in beholding, as some, in which a man thinketh
verily that the waies that give an issue to the spirits are
so deepe, that by them he may see as farre as the hart.

The eyes therefore lye lurking like souldiers in war,
lying in waite in bushment, and if the forme of all the bodie
be well favoured and of good proportion, it draweth unto
it and allureth who so beholdeth it a farre off: untill he
come nigh: and as soone as he is at hand, the eyes shoote,
and like sorcerers bewitch, and especially when by a right
line they send their glistering beames into the eyes of the
wight beloved, at the time when they doe the like, because
the spirites meete together, and in that sweete encounter
the one taketh the others nature and qualitie: as it is seene
in a sore eye, that beholding stedfastly a sound one, giveth
him his disease. Therefore me thinke our Courtier may in
this wise open a great parcell of the love to his woman.

Truth it is, that in case the eyes bee not governed with
arte, they discover many times the amorous desires more
unto whom a man would least: for through them, (in a
manner) visibly shine forth those burning passions, which
the lover minding to disclose onely to the wight beloved,

openeth them many times also unto whom he would most soonest hide them from.

Therefore hee that hath not lost the bridle of reason, handleth himselfe heedfully, and observeth the times and places: and when it needeth, refraineth from so stedfast beholding, for all it be a most savorie foode, because An open love is too hard a matter.

Count Lewis answered: Yet otherwhile to bee open it hurteth not: because in this case many times men suppose that those loves tend not to the end which every lover coveteth, when they see there is litle heede taken to hide them, and passe not whether they be knowne or no: and therefore with denyall a man chalengeth him a certaine libertie to talke openly, and to stand without suspition with the wight beloved. Which is not so in them that seeke to be secrete, because it appeareth that they stand in hope off, and are nigh some great rewarde, which they would not have other men to know.

I have also seene a most fervent love spring in the heart of a woman, towarde one that seemed at the first not to beare him the least affection in the worlde, onely for that she heard say that the opinion of many was, that they loved together. And the cause of this (I believe) was that so generall a judgement seemed a sufficient witnesse, that he was worthie of her love. And it seemed (in a manner) that report brought the ambassade on the lovers behalfe much more truer and worthier to be believed, than he himselfe could have done with letters or wordes, or any other person for him: therefore sometime this common voice not onely hurteth not, but farthereth a mans purpose.

The Lord Julian answered: Loves that have reporte for their messenger, are verie perillous to make a man pointed to with a finger. And therefore who ever entendeth to walke this race warily, needes must he make countenance to have a great deale lesse fire in his stomack, than in deede he hath, and content himselfe with that, that he thinketh a trifle, and dissemble his desires, jealosies, afflictions and pleasures, and many times laugh with mouth when the hart weepeth, and shew himselfe lavish of that he is most covetous of: and these thinges are so hard to be done, that (in a manner) they are unpossible.

Therefore if our Courtier would follow my counsell, I woulde exhort him to keepe his loves secrete.

Then saide maister Bernarde: You must then teach it him, and mee thinke it is much to purpose: for beside privie signes that some make otherwhile so closely, that (in a manner) without any gesture, the person whom they covet, in their countenance and eyes reade what they have in the hart.

I have sometime heard betweene two lovers a long and a large discourse of love, where of yet the standers by could not plainely understand any particular point, nor be out of doubt that it was of love. Such was the discretion and heedfulnesse of the talker: for without making any manner shew that they were not willing to bee heard, they rounded privily the words onely that were most to purpose, and all the rest they spake aloud, which might bee applyed to divers meaninges.

Then spake Sir Frederick: To reason thus in peecemeale of these rules of secretnesse, were a taking of an infinit matter in hand: therefore would I that we speake somewhat rather how the lover should keepe and maintaine his Ladies good will, which mee thinke is much more necessarie.

The Lord Julian answered: I believe, the meanes that serve him to compasse it, serve him also to keepe it: and all this consisteth in pleasing the woman beloved, without offending her at anye time. Therefore it were a hard matter to give any certaine rule, because who so is not discrete, infinite waies cōmitteth oversights, which otherwhile seeme matters of nothing, and yet offend they much the womans minde. And this happeneth more than to other, to such as be maistred with passion: as some that whensoever they have oportunitie to speake with the woman they love, lament and bewaile so bitterly, and covet many times thinges so unpossible, that through their unreasonablenesse they are lothed of them.

Other, if they bee pricked with any jealousie, stomack ye matter so grievously, that without stop they burst out in railing upon him they suspect, and otherwhile it is without trespasse either of him, or yet of the woman.

And will not have her speake with him, nor once turne her eyes on that side where he is. And with these fashions many times, they doe not onely offend the woman, but also they are the cause that she bendeth her selfe to love him. Because the feare that a lover declareth to have otherwhile lest his Ladie forsake him for the other, betokeneth that he acknowledgeth himselfe inferiour in deserts and prowes to the other, and with opinion the woman is moved to love him. And perceiving that to put him out of favour he reporteth ill of him, although it be true, yet she believeth it not, and notwithstanding loveth him the more.

Then saide the Lorde Cesar: I confesse that I am not so wise that I coulde refraine speaking ill of my fellow lover, except you could teach me some other better way to dispatch him.

The Lord Julian answered smyling: it is saide in a proverbe, When a mans enimie is in the water up to the middle, let him reach him his hande, and helpe him from daunger: but when he is up to the chinne, set his foote on his head, and drowne him out of hande. Therefore certaine there bee that play so with their fellow lovers, and untill they have a sure meane to dispatch them, goe dissembling the matter, and rather shew themselves friendes than otherwise. Afterwarde when occasion serveth so fitlie, that they know they may overthrowe them with a sure riddance, reporting all evill of them, be it true or false, they doe it without sparing, with arte, deceite, and all waies that they can imagin.

But because I would not like that our courtier should at any time use any deceite, I would have him to withdraw the good will of his mistresse from his fellow lover with none other arte, but with loving, with serving and with being vertuous, of prowesse, discrete, sober, in conclusion with deserving more than he, and with being in every thing heedfull and wise, refraining from certaine lewd folies, into the which oftentimes many ignorant runne, and by sundrie wayes.

For in times past I have knowne some that in writing and speaking to womē, used evermore the wordes of Poliphilus, and ruffled so in their subtill pointes of Rethoricke, that the women were out of conceite with their owne selves, and reckoned themselves most ignorant, and an houre seemed a thousand yeare to them, to end that talke and to be rid of them. Other bragge and boast too beyond all measure.

Other speake things many times that redound to the blame and damage of themselves, as some that I am wont to laugh at, which make profession to be lovers and otherwhile say in the companie of women.

I never founde woman that ever loved me, and are not witting, that the hearers by and by judge that it can arise of none other cause, but that they deserve neither to be beloved, nor yet so much as the water they drinke, and count them Asseheades, and would not love them for all the good in the worlde: seeming to them that in case they should love them, they were less worthie, than all the rest that have not loved them.

Other, to purchase hatred to some felow lover of theirs, are so fond that in like manner in the company of women they say: Such a one is the luckiest man in ye world, for once, hee is neither well favoured, nor sober, nor of prowes, neither can hee doe or say more than other men, and yet all women love him, and rune after him, and thus uttering the spite they beare him for this good lucke, although neither in countenance nor deedes hee appeareth lovely, yet make they them believe that hee hath some hid matter in him, for the which hee deserveth the love of so many women.

Wherfore the women that heare them talke of him in

this wise, they also upon this beliefe are moved to love him much more.

Then Count Lewis laughed and saide: I assure you our Courtier if he be discret, will never use this blockishnesse, to get the good will of women.

The Lord Cæsar Gonzaga answered: nor yet another that a gentleman of reputation used in my dayes, who shall be namelesse for the honour of men.

The Dutchesse answered: tell us at the least what hee did. The Lord Cesar saide: this man being beloved of a great Ladie, at her request came privily to the towne where she lay. And after he had seene her and communed with her, as long as they thought meete and had time and leasure thereto, at his leave taking, with many biter teares and sighes in witnesse of the extreame griefe he felt for this departing, he required her to bee alwaies mindfull of him. And afterwarde hee added withall, That she would discharge his Inne, for since hee came thither at her request, he thoght meete that hee shoulde not stand to the charges of his being here, himselfe.

Then beganne all the Ladies to laugh, and saide that he was most unworthie of the name of a gentleman: and manie were ashamed with the selfe shame that he himselfe shoulde worthily have felt, if any time he had gotten so much understanding, that he might have perceived so shamefull an oversight.

Then turned the Lord Gasper to the Lorde Cesar and saide: Better it had beene to have omitted the rehersall of this matter for the honour of women, than the naming of him for the honour of men. For you may well imagine what a judgement that great Ladie had in loving so unreasonable a creature. And perhaps too, of many that served she chose him for the most discretest, leaving behind and shewing ill will unto them that hee was not worthie to waite upon.

Count Lewis laughed and saide: Who woteth whether hee was discrete in other thinges or no, and was out of y^e

way only about Innes? But many times for overmuch love men commit great follies. And if you will tell the truth, perhaps it hath beene your chaunce to commit moe than one.

The L. Cesar answeared smiling: Of good fellowship let us not discover our owne oversightes. Yet we must discover them, aunsweared the Lord Gaspar, that wee may know how to amende them: then he proceeded. Now that the Courtier knoweth howe to winne and keepe the good will of his Lady, and take it from his fellow lover, you (my L. Julian) are dettour to teache her to keepe her loves secrete.

The L. Julian answeared: Me thinke I have sufficiently spoken, therefore get you now an other to talke of this secrete matter.

Then M. Bernard and all the rest began a fresh to be in hand with him instantly, and the Lorde Julian saide: you will tempt me. Ye are all the sort of you too great Clarkes in loves. Yet if ye desire to know further, goe and reade Ovid.

And how, quoth maister Bernarde, shall I hope that his lessons are any thing worth in love, when he counselleth and saith that it is very good for a man in the company of his mistresse To faine the drunkarde? See what a goodly way it is to get good will withall. And he alleageth for a pretie devise to make a woman understande that he is in love with her, being at a banket, To dip his finger in wine and write it upon the table.

The Lorde Julian saide smiling: In those dayes it was no fault. And therefore (quoth maister Bernarde) seeing so sluttish a matter was not disalowed of men in those dayes, it is to bee thought that they had not so courtely behaviours to serve women in love, as we have. But let us not omit our first purpose, to teach to kepe love secrete.

Then saide the Lorde Julian: In mine advise to keepe love secrete, the causes are to be shunned that utter it, which are many: yet one principall, namely, To be over

531

secrete and to put no person in trust. Because every lover coveteth to make his passions knowne to be beloved, and being alone, hee is driven to make many moe signes and more evident, than if hee were aided by some loving and faithfull friend. For the signes that the lover himselfe maketh, give a farre greater suspition, than those that he maketh by them that goe in message betweene.

And for so much as men naturally are greedie to understand, as soone as a stranger beginneth to suspect the matter, hee so applyeth it, that he cometh to the knowledge of the truth, and when he once knoweth it, he passeth not for disclosing it, yea sometime he hath a delite to doe it. Which happeneth not to a friend, who beside that hee is a helpe to him with favour and counsel, doth many times remedie the oversights committed by the blinde lover, and alwaies procureth secretenesse, and preventeth manye matters which hee him selfe can not foresee: beside the great comfort that he feeleth, when he may utter his passions and griefes to a hartie friende, and the partening of them likewise encreaseth his contentations.

Then saide the Lord Gasper: there is an other cause that discovereth loves much more than this. What is that, answered the Lord Julian: The Lorde Gasper saide: Vaine greedinesse joyned with the fondnesse and crueltie of women, which (as you your selfe have saide) procure as much as they can to get them a great number of lovers, and (if it were possible) they would have them all to burne and make ashes, and after death to returne to life, to dye againe. And though they love withall, yet rejoyce they at the torment of lovers, because they suppose the griefe, afflictions, and the calling every houre for death, is a true witnesse that they are beloved, and that with their beautie they can make men miserable and happie, and give them life and death, as pleaseth them. Wherefore they feede onely upon this foode, and are so greedy over it, that for wanting it they never throughly content lovers, nor yet put them out of hope.

But to keepe them still in afflictions and in desire, they use a certaine loftie sowernesse of threatnings mingled with hope, and would have them to esteeme a worde, a countenance or a becke of theirs for a chiefe blisse.

And to make men count them chast and honest as wel others as their lovers, they find meanes that these sharp and discourteous manners of theirs, may bee in open sight, for every man to think that they will much worse handle the unworthie, since they handle them so, that deserve to be beloved. And under this beliefe, thinking themselves with this craft safe from slander, oftentimes they lye nightly with most vile men and whom they scarce know. So that to rejoyce at the calamitie and continuall complaintes of some worthie Gentleman, and beloved of them, they barre themselves from those pleasures, which perhaps with some excuse they might come by, and are the cause that the poore lover by very debating of the matter is driven to use waies by the which the thing commeth to light, that with all diligence should have beene kept most secrete.

Certaine other there are, which if with deceite they can bring many in beliefe that they are beloved of them, nourish among them jealousies, with cherishing and making of the one in the others presence. And when they see that he also whom they love best, is now assured and out of doubt that hee is beloved through the signes and tokens that bee made him, many times with doubtfull words and fained disdaines they put him in uncertaintie.

And nip him at the very hart, making wise not to passe for him, and to give them selves full and wholy to the other.

Whereupon arise malice, enimities, and infinite occasions of strife and utter confusion. For needes must a man shew in that case the extreame passion which he feeleth, although it redound to the blame and slander of the woman.

Other, not satisfied with this only torment of jealosie, after the lover hath declared all his tokens of love and

533

faithfull service, and they received the same with some signe to bee answerable in good will, without purpose and when it is least looked for, they beginne to bethinke themselves, and make wise to believe that he is slacked, and faining new suspitions that they are not beloved, they make a countenãce that they will in any wise put him out of their favour.

Wherefore through these incõveniences the poore soule is constrained of verie force to beginne a fresh, and to make her signes, as though he beganne his service but then, and all the day long passe up and downe through the streete, and when the woman goeth forth of her doores to accompany her to Church and to every place where she goeth, and never to turne his eyes to other place.

And here he returneth to weeping, to sighes, to heavie countenances, and when he can talke with her, to swearing, to blapheming, to desperation, and to all rages which unhappie lovers are led to by these wilde beastes, that have greater thirst of bloud than the verie Tygres.

Such sorrowfull tokens as these bee, are too often seene and known, and manie times more of others than of the causer of them: and thus are they in few daies so published, that a step can not be made, nor the least signe that is, but it is noted with a thousand eyes.

It happeneth then, that long before there be any pleasures of love betwixt them, they are gessed and judged of all the worlde. For when they see yet their lover now nigh deathes doore, cleane vanquished with the crueltie and torments they put him to, determineth advisedly and in good earnest to draw back, then begin they to make signe that they love him hartily, and do him all pleasures and give themselves to him, least if that fervent desire should faile in him, the fruite of love should withall be the lesse acceptable to him, and he ken them the lesse thanke for doing all thinges contrarily.

And in case this love bee alreadie knowne abroad, at this same time are all the effects knowne in like manner abroad that come of it, and so lose they their reputation, and the lover findeth that he hath lost time and labour and shortned his life in afflictions without any fruit or pleasure.

Because he came by his desires, not whē they should have beene so acceptable to him that they woulde have made him a most happie creature, but when hee set litle or nothing by them. For his hart was now so mortified with those bitter passions, that he had no more sense to tast the delite or contentation offred him.

Then saide the Lord Octavian smyling: you held your peace a while and refrained from speaking ill of women, but now you have so well hit them home, that it appeared ye waited a time to plucke up your strength, like them that retire backwarde to give a greater push at the enconter. And to say the truth, it is ill done of you, for now mee thinke ye may have done and bee pacified.

The Ladie Emilia laughed, and turninge her to the Dutches she said: See Madam, our enemies beginne to breake and to square one with an other.

Geve me not thys name aunswered the L. Octavian, for I am not your adversary, but this contention hath displeased me, not because I am sory to see the victory upon womens side, but because it hath lead the L. Gaspar to revile them more than hee ought, and the L. Julian and the L. Cesar to praise them perhaps somwhat more than due: beside that through the length of the talke wee have lost the understandinge of many other pretie matters that are yet behind to be said of the Courtier.

See quoth the Ladie Emilia, whether you bee not our adversarie, for the talke that is past greeveth you, and you would not that this so excellent a gentlewoman of the Pallace had beene fashioned: not for that you have any more to say of the Courtier (for these Lordes have spoken alreadie what they know, and I believe neither you, ne any man els can adde ought thereto) but for the malice you beare to the honour of women.

535

It is out of doubt, answered the Lorde Octavian, beside that is alreadie spoken of the Courtier, I coulde wish much more in him. But since every man is pleased that he shall be as he is, I am well pleased too, and would not have him altered in any point, saving in making him somewhat more friendly to women, than the Lorde Gaspar is, yet not perhaps, so much as some of these other Lords are.

Then spake the Dutchesse: In any case we must see whether your witte bee such that it can give the Courtier a greater perfection, than these Lordes have alreadie done.

Therefore dispose your selfe to utter that you have in your minde, els will wee thinke that you also can not adde unto him more than hath alreadie beene saide, but that you minded to diminish the prayses and worthinesse of the gentlewoman of the Pallace, seeing ye judge she is equall with the Courtier, whom by this meane you woulde have believed might be much more perfect than these Lordes have fashioned him.

The Lord Octavian laughed and saide: The prayses and dispraises given women more than due, have so filled the eares and minde of the hearers, that they have left no voide roome for any thing els to stand in: beside that (in mine opinion) it is verie late.

Then said the Dutchesse: If we tarrie till to morrow, we shall have the more time, and the prayses and disprayses, which (you say) are given women on both sides passing measure, in the mean season will we be cleane out of these Lordes mindes, and so shall they bee apt to conceive the truth that you will tell us.

When the Dutchesse had thus spoken, she arose upon her feet, and courteously dismissing them all, withdrew her to her bedchamber, and every man gotte him to his rest.

FOURTH BOOK

The Fourth Booke of the Courtier, of
Count Baldesser Castilion, unto
Maister Alfonsus Ariosto

Thinking to write out the communicatiō that was had the fourth night after the other mentioned in the former bookes, I feele among sundry discourses a bitter thought that gripeth me in my mind, and maketh me to call to remembrance worldly miseries and our deceitful hopes, and how fortune many times in the verie middest of our race, otherwhile nigh the ende disapointeth our fraile and vaine purposes, sometime drowneth them before they can once come to have a sight of the Haven a farre off.

It causeth me therefore to remember that not long after these reasoninges were had, cruell death bereaved our house of three most rare gentlemen, when in their prosperous age and forwardnesse of honour they most flourished.

And of them the first was the Lord Gaspar Pallavicine, who assaulted with a sharpe disease, and more than once brought to the last cast, although his minde was of such courage that for a time in spite of death hee kept the soule and bodie together, yet did he end his natural course long before he came to his ripe age.[37]

A very great losse, not in our house onely, and to his friendes and kinsfolke, but to his Countrie and to all Lumbardie.

Not long after dyed the Lord Cesar Gonzaga, which to all that were acquainted with him, left a bitter and sorrowfull remembrance of his death. For since nature so seldom

537

times bringeth forth such kinde of men, as she doth, meete it seemed that she should not so soone have bereaved us of him. For undoubtedly a man may say that the Lord Cesar was taken from us even at the very time when hee began to shew more than a hope of himselfe, and to bee esteemed as his excellent qualities deserved. For with many vertuous acts he alreadie gave a good testimonie of his worthinesse, and beside his noblenesse of birth, he excelled also in the ornamēt of letters, of marciall prowesse, and of every worthie qualitie. So that for his goodnesse, wit, nature, and knowledge, there was nothing so high, that might not have beene hoped for at his hands.

Within a short while after the death of maister Robert of Bary was also a great heavinesse to yᵉ whole house: for reason seemed to perswade every man to take heavily the death of a yong man of good behaviour, pleasant and most rare in the beautie of physnomie, and in the making of his person, with a luckie and lively towardnes, as a man coulde have wished.

These men therefore, had they lived, I believe woulde have come to passe, that unto who so had knowne them, they woulde have shewed a manifest proofe, how much the Court of Urbin was worthie to bee commended, and how furnished it was with noble knights, which (in a manner) all yᵉ rest have done that were brought up in it.

For truely there never issued out of the horse of Troy so many great men and Captains, as there have come men out of this house for vertue verie singular and in great estimation with all men.

For as you know Sir Frederick Fregoso was made Archbishoppe of Salerno, Count Lewis, bishop of Baious. The Lorde Octavian Fregoso, Duke of Genua: maister Bernarde Bibiena, Cardinall of Sancta Maria in Portico: maister Peter Bembo, Secretarie to Pope Leo. The Lord Julian was exalted to the Dukedome of Nemours, and to the great estate he is presently in. The Lord Francesco Maria della Rovere generall of Rome, he was also made Duke of

Urbin: although a much more prayse may be given to the
house where hee was brought up, that in it he hath proved
so rare and excellent a Lord in all vertuous qualities, (as
a man may behold) than that hee attained unto the Duke-
dom of Urbin.

And no small cause thereof (I thinke) was the noble
companie where in dayly conversatiō he alwaies heard and
saw commendable nourture.

Therefore (mee thinke) whether it bee by happe, or
through the favour of the starres, the same cause that so
long a time hath graunted unto Urbin very good governours, doth still continue and bringeth forth the like effects.
And therefore it is to be hoped, that prosperous fortune
will still encrease these so vertuous doinges, that the happinesse of the house, and of the state shall not onely not
diminish, but rather dayly encrease: And thereof we see
alreadie many evidēt tokens, among which I reckon the
chiefest to bee, that the heaven hath graunted such a Ladie
as is the Ladie Eleonor Gonzaga the new Dutchesse.

For if ever there were coupled in one bodie alone,
knowledge, wit, grace, beautie, sober conversatiō, gentlenesse, and every other honest qualitie, in her they are so
linked together, that there is made thereof a chaine, which
frameth and setteth forth everie gesture of hers, with all
these conditions together.

Let us therefore proceede in our reasoninges upon the
Courtier, with hope that after us there shall not wante such
as shal take notable and worthy examples of vertue at the
present Court of Urbin, as wee now doe at the former.

It was thought therfore (as the L. Gaspar Pallavicin was
wont to rehearse) that the next day after the reasoninges
conteyned in the last booke, the L. Octavian was not muche
seene: for manye deemed that hee had gotten himselfe out
of company to thinke well upon that he had to say without trouble.

Therefore when the company was assembled at the accustomed houre where the Dutchesse was, they made the

L. Octavian to bee diligently sought for, which in a good while appeared not, so that many of the Gentlemen and Damosels of the Court fell to dauncing and to mind other pastimes, supposing for that night they shoulde have no more talke of the Courtier. And now were they all setled about one thing or an other, when the Lorde Octavian came in (almost) no more looked for.

And beholding the Lorde Cesar Gonzaga and the L. Gasper dauncing, after hee had made his reverence to the Dutchesse, he saide smyling: I had well hoped wee should have heard the Lorde Gaspar speak some ill of women this night too, but since I see him daunce with one, I imagine he is agreed withall. And I am glad that the controversie, or (to terme it better) the reasoning of the Courtier is thus ended.

Not ended, I warrant you, answered the Dutchesse, for I am not such an enimie to men, as you be to women, and therefore I will not have the Courtier bereaved from his due honour and the ornaments which you your selfe promised him yesternight.

And when that she had thus spoken, she commanded them all after that dance was ended, to place themselves after the wonted manner, the which was done. And as they stood all with heedfull expectation, the Lord Octavian saide.

Madam, since for that I wished many other good qualities in the Courtier, it followeth by promise that I must entreat upon them, I am well willing to utter my minde: not with opinion that I can speake all that may be saide in the matter, but onely so much as shall suffice to roote that out of your minde, which yesternight was objected to mee: namely that I speak it more to withdraw the prayses from the gentlewoman of the Pallace, in doing you falsely to believe, that other excellent qualities might be added to the Courtier, and with that pollicie preferre him before her, than for that it is so in deede.

Therefore to frame my selfe also to the houre, which is

later than it was wont to be, when wee beganne our reasonings at other times. I will be briefe.

Thus continuing in the talke that these Lordes have ministred, which I full and wholy allow and confirme, I say, that of thinges which we call good, some there bee that simply and of themselves are alwaies good, as temperance, valiant courage, health, and all vertues that bring quietnesse to mens mindes. Other be good for divers respects and for the end they be applied unto, as the lawes, liberallitie, riches, and other like.

I thinke therefore that the Courtier (if he be of the perfection that Count Lewis and Sir Frederick have described him) may indeede bee a good thing and worthy praise, but for all that not simply, nor of himself but for respect of that whereto he may be applied.

For doubtlesse if the Courtier with his noblenes of birth, comely behaviour, pleasantnesse and practise in so manye exercises, shoulde bring foorth no other fruite, but to be such a one for himselfe, I would not thinke to come by this perfect trade of Courtiershippe, that a man should of reason bestow so much studie and paines about it, as who so will compasse it must do. But I would say rather that many of the qualities appointed him, as dauncing, singing, and sporting, were lightnes and vanitie, and in a man of estimation rather to be dispraised than commended.

Because those precise fashions, the setting forth of ones selfe, merry talke and such other matters beloging to entertainement of women and love (although perhaps many other be of a contrarie opinion) doe many times nothing els but womanish the mindes, corrupt youth, and bring them to a most wanton trade of living: whereupon afterwarde ensue these effects, that the name of Italy is brought into slaunder: and few there bee that have the courage, I will not say to jeopard their life, but to enter once into a daunger.

And without peradventure there bee infinite other thinges, that if a man bestow his labour and studie about

them, woulde bring forth much more profit both in peace
and warre, than this trade of Courtiership of it selfe
alone.

But in case the Courtiers doings be directed to the good
ende they ought to be, and which I meane: mee thinke
then they should not only not be hurtful or vaine, but most
profitable, and deserve infinite prayse.

The ende therefore of a perfect Courtier (whereof
hetherto nothing hath beene spoken) I believe is to purchase him, by the meane of the qualities which these
Lordes have given him, in such wise the good will and
favour of the Prince he is in service withall, that he may
breake his minde to him, and alwaies enforme him franckly
of the truth of every matter meete for him to understand,
without fear or perill to displease him. And when hee
knoweth his minde is bent to commit any thing unseemely
for him, to be bold to stand with him in it, and to take
courage after an honest sorte at the favor which he hath
gotten him through his good qualities, to disswade him
from every ill purpose, and to set him in the way of vertue.
And so shall the Courtier, if he have the goodnesse in
him that these Lordes have given him accompanied with
readinesse of wit, pleasantnesse, wisedom, knowledge in
letters, and so many other thinges, understand how to behave himselfe readily in all occurrents to drive into his
Princes heade what honour and profit shall ensue to him
and to his by justice, liberallitie, valiantnesse of courage,
meekenesse, and by the other vertues that belong to a good
prince, and contrariwise what slander, and damage commeth of the vices contrarie to them.

And therefore in mine opinion, as musicke, sportes, pastimes, and other pleasant fashions, are (as a man woulde
say) the floure of Courtlinesse, even so is the training and
helping forwarde of the Prince to goodnesse, and the fearing him from evil, the fruite of it.

And because the prayses of well doing, côsisteth chiefly
in two pointes, whereof the one is, in choosing out an end

that our purpose is directed unto, that is good in deede, the other, the knowledge to finde out apt and meete meanes to bring it to the appointed good ende: sure it is that the minde of him which thinketh to worke so, that his Prince shall not bee deceived, nor lead with flatterers, railers, and lyers, but shall know both the good and the bad, and beare love to the one, and hatred to the other, is directed to a verie good end.

Me thinke againe, that the qualities which these Lords have given the Courtier, may bee a good meanes to compasse it: and that, because among many vices that we see now a dayes in many of our Princes, the greatest are ignorance and selfe liking.

And the roote of these two mischiefes is nothing els but lying, which vice is worthely abhorred of God and man, and more hurtfull to Princes than any other, because they have more scarcitie than of any thing els, of that which they neede to have more plentie of, than of any other thing: namely, of such as should tell them the truth, and put them in mind of goodnesse: for enimies bee not driven of love to doe these offices, but they delight rather to have them live wickedly and never to amend: on the other side, they dare not rebuke them openly for feare they be punished.

As for friendes, few of them have free passage to them, and those few have a respect to reprehend their vices so freely as they doe private mens. And many times to currie favour and to purchase good will, they give themselves to nothing els but to feede them with matters that may delight and content their minde, though they be foule and dishonest. So that of friendes they become flatterers.

And to make a hand [38] by that straight familiaritie, they speake and worke alwaies to please, and for the most part open the way with lyes, which in the Princes minde engender ignorance, not of outwarde matters onely, but also of his owne selfe. And this may be saide to be the greatest and foulest lye of all other, because the ignorant minde deceiveth himselfe, and inwardly maketh lies of himselfe.

543

Of this it commeth, that great men, beside that they never understand the truth of any thing, drunken with the licentious libertie that rule bringeth with it, and with aboundance of delicats drowned in pleasures, are so farre out of the way, and their minde is so corrupted in seeing themselves alwaies obeied, and (as it were) worshipped with so much reverence and praise, without not onely any reproofe at all, but also gainsaying, that through this ignorance they wade to an extreame selfe liking, so that afterwarde they admit no counsell nor advise of others.

And because they believe that the understanding how to rule is a most easie matter, and to compasse it, there needeth neither arte nor learning, but onely stoutnesse, they bend their mind and all their thoughts to the maintenance of that porte they keepe, thinking it the true happinesse to do what a man lusteth.

Therefore doe some abhorre reason and justice, because they weene it a bridle and a certain meane to bring them in bondage, and to minish in them the contentation and hearts ease that they have to beare rule, if they should observe it: and their rule were not perfect nor whole, if they should be compelled to obey unto duetie and honestie, because they have opinion, that Who so obeyeth, is no right Lorde in deede.

Therefore taking these principles for a president, and suffering themselves to bee leade with selfe liking, they waxe lofty, and with a stately countenance, with sharpe and cruell conditions, with pompous garments, golde and jewels, and with comming (in a manner) never abroad to be seene, they thinke to get estimation and authoritie among men and to bee counted (almost) Gods.

But they are (in my judgement) like the Colosses that were made in Rome the last year upon the feast daye of the place of Agone, which outwardly declared a likenesse of great men and horses of triumph, and inwardly were full of towe and ragges.

But the Princes of this sorte are so much worse, as the Colosses by their owne waighty peise stand upright of themselves, and they because they be ill counterpeised, and without line and levell placed upon unequall ground, through their owne waightines overthrow them selves, and from one errour runne into infinite. Because their ignorance being annexed with this false opinion, that they can not erre, and that the port they keepe commeth of their knowledge, leadeth them every way by right or by wrong to lay hand upon possessions boldly, so they may come by them. But in case they would take advisement to know and to worke that that they ought, they would as well strive not to raigne, as they doe to raigne.

Because they should perceive what a naughtie and dangerous matter it were for subjects that ought to be governed, to be wiser than the Princes that should governe.

You may see that ignorance in musicke, in dancing, in riding, hurteth no man, yet he that is no musition is ashamed and afraide to sing in the presence of others, or to daunce, he that can not, or he that sitteth not well a horse to ride.

But of the unskilfulnesse to governe people arise so many evils, deathes, destructions, mischiefes, and confusions, that it may bee called the deadlyest plague upon the earth. And yet some Princes most ignorant in governement, are not bashfull nor ashamed to take upon them to governe, I wil not say in the presence of foure, or halfe a dosen persons, but in the face of the world: for their degree is set so on loft, that all eyes beholde them, and therefore not their great vices onely, but their least faults of all are continually noted.

As it is written, that Cimon was ill spoken of because he loved wine, Scipio, sleepe, Lucullus, banquets. But would God the Princes of these our times would couple their vices with so many vertues, as did they of olde time: which if they were out of the way in any point, yet refused they not the exhortations and lessons of such as they deemed meete to correct those faultes: Yea they sought with great instance to frame their life by the rule of notable personages: As Epaminondas by Lysias of Pythagoras sect: Agesilaus by Xenophon: Scipio by Panetius, and infinite others.

But in case a grave Philosopher shoulde come before any of our Princes, or who ever beside, that would shew them plainly and without anie circumstance the horrible face of true vertue, and teach them good manners, and what the life of a good Prince ought to be, I am assured they woulde abhorre him at the first sight, as a most venemous serpent, or els they woulde make him a laughing stocke, as a most vile matter.

I say therefore, that since now a days Princes are so corrupt through ill usages, ignorance and false selfe liking, and that it is so harde a matter to give them the knowledge of the truth, and to bend them to vertue, and men with lyes and flatterie, and such naughtie meanes seeke to currie favour with them, the Courtier by the meane of those honest qualities that Count Lewis and Sir Fredericke have given him, may soone, and ought to goe about so to purchase him the good will, and allure unto him ye mind of his Prince, that he may make him a free and safe passage to commune with him in every matter without troubling him. And if he be such a one as is saide, hee shall compasse it with small paine, and so may he alwaies open unto him the trueth of every matter at ease.

Beside this, by litle and litle distil into his mind goodnesse, and teach him continencie, stoutnesse of courage, justice, temperance, making him to tast what sweetnesse is hid under that litle bitternesse, which at the first sight appeareth unto him that withstandeth vices, which are alwaies hurtfull, displeasant and accompanied with ill report and shame, even as vertues are profitable, pleasant and prayseable, and enflame him to them with examples of manye famous captaines, and of other notable personages, unto whome they of olde time used to make images of mettall and marble, and sometime of golde, and to set them up in common haunted places, as well for the honour of them, as for an encouraging of others, that with an honest envie they might also endevor themselves to reach unto that glorie.

In this wise may hee leade him through the rough way of vertue (as it were) decking it aboute with boughes to shadow it, and strowing it over with sightlye flowers, to ease the griefe of the painefull jorney in him that is but of a weake force. And sometime with musicke, sometime with armes, and horses, sometime with rymes, and meeter, otherwhile with communication of love, and with all those waies that these Lords have spoken of, continually keepe that minde of his occupied in honest pleasure: imprinting notwithstanding therein alwaies beside (as I have saide) in company with these flickering provocations some vertuous condition, and beguiling him with a holesom craft, as the warie Phisitions doe, who many times when they minister to yong and tender children in their sicknesse, a medicine of a bitter taste, annoint the cup about the brimme with some sweete licour.

The Courtier therefore applying to such a purpose this veile of pleasure, in every time, in every place, and in everie exercise he shall attain to his end, and deserve much more praise and recompence, than for any other good worke that he can doe in the world.

Because there is no treasure that doth so universally profit, as doth a good prince, nor any mischiefe so universally hurt, as an ill Prince. Therefore is there also no paine so bitter and cruel that were a sufficient punishment for those naughtie and wicked Courtiers, that make their honest and pleasant manners, and their good qualities a cloake for an ill end, and by meane of them seeke to come in favour with their Princes for to corupt them, and to cause them to stray from the way of vertue, and to lead them to vice.

For a man may say, that such as these be, doe infect with deadly poyson, not one vessel whereof one man alone

547

drinketh, but the common fountaine that all the people resorteth to.

The Lord Octavian helde his peace, as though hee woulde have saide no more, but the Lord Gaspar, I can not see my Lorde Octavian (saide he) that this goodnesse of mind and continencie, and the other vertues which you will have the Courtier to shew his Lord, may bee learned: but I suppose that they are given the men that have them, by nature and of God.

And that it is so, you may see that there is no man so wicked and of so ill conditions in the world, nor so untemperate and unjust, which if he be asked the question, will confesse himselfe such a one. But every man be he never so wicked, is glad to be counted just, continent and good: which should not be so, in case these vertues might be learned.

Because it is no shame not to know the thing that a man hath not studied, but a rebuke, it is not to have that which wee ought to be endowed withall of nature.

Therefore doth each man seeke to cover the defaultes of nature, as well in the mind, as also in ye bodie: the which is to bee seene in the blinde, lame, crooked and other maimed and deformed creatures. For although these imperfections may be laide to nature, yet doth it greeve each man to have them in himself: because it seemeth by the testimonie of the selfe same nature that a man hath that default or blemish (as it were) for a patent and token of his ill inclination.

The fable that is reported of Epimetheus doth also confirme mine opinion, which was so unskilfull in dividing the giftes of nature unto men, that hee left them much more needy of every thing, than all other living creatures.

Whereupon Prometheus stole the politike wisedome from Minerva and Vulcan that men have to get their living withall. Yet had they not for all that, civil wisedom to gather themselves together into Cities, and the knowledge to live with civilitie, because it was kept in the Castle of

Jupiter by most circumspect overseers, which put Prometheus in such feare that hee durst not approch nigh them. Whereupon Jupiter taking pitie upon the miserie of men, that coulde not fellowship together for lacke of civill vertue, but were torne in peeces by wilde beastes, he sent Mercurie to the earth to carrie justice and shame, that these two things might furnish cities, and gather citizens together.

And willed that they should be given them, not as other artes were, wherein one cunning man sufficeth for many ignorant, as Phisicke, but that they shoulde be imprinted in every man. And ordeined a law, that all such as were without justice and shame, shoulde be banished and put to death as contagious to the Citie.

Behold then (my Lorde Octavian) God hath graunted these vertues to men, and they are not to be learned, but be naturall.

Then the Lord Octavian somewhat smiling: will you then my Lord Gaspar (quoth he) have men to be so unfortunate and of so peevish a judgement, that with policie they have founde out an arte to tame the natures of wilde beastes and beares, wolves, Lions, and may with the same teach a pretie bird to flie as a man list, and returne backe from the wood and from his naturall libertie of his owne accorde to snares and bondage, and with the same policie can not or wil not find out artes wherby they may profit themselves, and with studie and diligence make their minde more perfect?

This (in mine opinion) were like as if Phisitions should studie with all diligence to have the arte onely to heale fellons in fingers, and the red gumme in yong children, and laye aside the cure of fevers, pleurisie and other sore diseases, the which how out of reason it were every man may consider.

I believe therefore that the morall vertues are not in us altogether by nature, because nothing can at any time be accustomed unto it, that is naturally his contrarie: as it is seene in a stone, the which though it bee cast upward ten

549

thousand times, yet will he never accustome to goe up of it selfe.

Therefore in case vertues were as naturall to us, as heavinesse to the stone, wee should never accustome our selves to vice.

Nor yet are vices natural in this sorte, for then should we never be vertuous: and a great wickednesse and folly it were, to punish men for their faults, that came of nature without our offence.

And this errour shoulde the lawes commit, which appoint not punishment to the offenders for the trespasse that is past, because it can not be brought to passe, that the thing that is done, may not be done, but they have a respect to the time to come, that who so hath offended may offend no more, or els with ill president give not a cause for others to offend. And thus yet they are in opinion, that vertues may be learned, which is most true, because we are borne apt to receive them, and in like manner vices.

And therefore there groweth a custome in us of both the one and ye other through long use, so that first we practise vertue or vice, after that, we are vertuous or vitious.

The contrarie is known in the thinges that bee given us of nature, for first wee have the power to practise them, after that wee doe practise: as it is in the senses, for first we can see, heare, feele, after that, we do see, heare and feele: although notwithstanding many of these doinges bee also set out more sightly with teaching.

Whereupon good schoolemaisters doe not onely instruct their children in letters, but also in good nurture, in eating, drinking, talking, and going, with certaine gestures meete for the purpose.

Therefore even as in the other artes, so also in the vertues it is behofefull to have a teacher, that with lessons and good exhortations may stirre up and quicken in us those moral vertues, whereof wee have the seede inclosed and buried in the soule, and like the good husbandman till them and open the way for them, weeding from about them the briers and darnell of appetites, which many times so shadow and choke our mindes, that they suffer them not to budde nor to bring forth the happie fruites, which alone ought to be wished to growe in the harts of men.

In this sorte then is naturally in every one of us justice and shame, which you say Jupiter sent to the earth for all men. But even as a bodie without eyes, how sturdie soever he be, if he remove to any certaine place, ofttimes faileth: so the roote of these vertues that be potentially engendred in our mindes, if it bee not aided with teaching, doth often come to nought. Because if it shoulde bee brought into doing, and to his perfect custome, it is not satisfied (as is saide) with nature alone: but hath neede of a politike usage and of reason, which may clense and scoure that soule, taking away the dim vale of ignorance, whereof arise (in a manner) all the errours of men.

For in case good and ill were well knowne and perceived, every man woulde alwaies choose the good, and shunne the ill. Therefore may vertue be saide to be (as it were) a wisedom and an understanding to choose the good: and vice, a lacke of foresight and an ignorance that leadeth to judge falsely. Because men never choose the ill with opinion that it is ill, but they are deceived through a certaine likenesse of good.

Then answered the Lorde Gaspar: yet are there many that know plainely they doe ill, and doe it notwithstanding, and that because they more esteeme the present pleasure which they feele, than the punishment that they doubt shall fall upon them, as theeves, murtherers and such other.

The Lord Octavian saide: true pleasure is alwaies good, and true sorrow, evil: therefore these be deceived in taking false pleasure for true, and true sorrow for false: whereupon manye times through false pleasures, they run into true displeasures.

The arte therefore that teacheth to discerne this truth from falshood, may in like case be learned: and the vertue by the which wee choose this good in deede, and not that

551

which falsely appeareth to be, may bee called true knowledge, and more available for mans life, than any other, because it expelleth ignorance, of the which (as I have saide) spring all evil.

Then maister Peter Bembo, I wot not my Lord Octavian (quoth hee) how the Lorde Gaspar should graunt you, that of ignorance should spring all evils, and that there be not many which in offending know for certaintie that they doe offend, neither are they any deale deceived in the true pleasure, nor yet in the true sorrow, because it is sure that such as be incontinent, judge with reason and uprightly, and knowe it, whereunto they are provoked by lust contrarie to due, to be ill, and therefore they make resistance and set reason to match greedie desire, whereupon ariseth the battaile of pleasure and sorrow against judgement.

Finally reason overcome by greedy desire, farre the mightier, is cleane without succour, like a ship, that for a time defendeth her selfe from the tempestuous sea-stormes, at the end beaten with the too raging violence of windes, her gables and tacklinges broken, yeeldeth up to be driven at the will of fortune, without occupying helme or any manner helpe of Pilot for her safegarde.

Forthwith therefore commit they the offences with a certaine doubtfull remorse of conscience, and (in a manner) whether they will or no, the which they woulde not doe, unlesse they knewe the thing that they doe to be ill, but without striving of reason would runne wholy headlong after greedie desire, and then should they not be incontinent, but untemperate, which is much worse.

Therefore is incontinencie saide to bee a diminished vice, because it hath in it a part of reason, and likewise continencie an unperfect vertue, because it hath in it part of affection: therefore mee thinke that it can not be said that the offences of the incontinent come of ignorance, or that they bee deceived and offend not, when they know for a truth that they doe offend.

The Lord Octavian answered: Certesse (maister Peter)

your argumēt is good, yet (in my minde) it is more apparant than true. For although the incontinent offend with that doubtfulnesse, and reason in their minde striveth against greedie desire, and that that is ill seemeth unto them to be ill in deed, yet have they no perfect knowledge of it, nor understand it so throughly as need requireth.

Therefore of this, it is rather a feeble opinion in them, than certaine knowledge, whereby they agree to have reason overcome by affection: but if they had in them true knowledge, there is no doubt, but they woulde not offend: because evermore the thing whereby greedy desire overcommeth reason, is ignorance, neither can true knowledge bee ever overcome by affection, that proceedeth from the bodie and not from the minde, and in case that it be well ruled and governed by reason, it becommeth a vertue: if not, it becommeth a vice.

But such force reason hath, that she maketh the sense alwaies to obey, and by wondrous meanes and waies perceth, lest ignorance should possesse that which she ought to have: so that although the spirits and the sinewes and the bones have no reason in them, yet when there springeth in us the motion of minde, that the imagination (as it were) pricketh forwarde, and shaketh the bridle to the spirits, all the members are in a readinesse, the feete to runne, the handes to take or to doe that which the mind thinketh upon.

And this is also manifestly knowne in many, which unwittingly otherwhile eate some lothsom and abhorring meate, so wel dressed that to their taste it appeareth most delicate: afterward understanding what manner thing it was, it doth not onely greeve them and loath them in their mind, but the bodie also agreeth with the judgement of the minde, that of force they cast that meat up againe.

The Lord Octavian followed on still in his talke, but the Lorde Julian interrupting him. My Lord Octavian (quoth he) if I have well understood, you have saide that Continencie is an unperfect vertue, because it hath in it part

553

of affection: and me seemeth that the vertue (where there is in our mind a variance betwen reason and greedie desire) which fighteth and giveth the victory to reason, ought to be reckoned more perfect, than that which overcommeth, having neither greedie desire nor any affectiō to withstand it.

Because (it seemeth) that that minde abstaineth not from ill for vertues sake, but refraineth the doing it, because he hath no will to it.

Then the Lord Octavian, which (quoth he) woulde you esteeme the valianter Captaine, either he that hazardeth himselfe in open fight, and notwithstanding vanquisheth his enimies, or hee that by his vertue and knowledge weakeneth them in bringing them in case not able to fight, and so without battaile or any jeopardie discomfit them?

He (quoth the Lorde Julian) that overcommeth with most suretie, is out of doubt most to bee praised, so that this assured victorie of his proceede not through the slacknesse of the enimies.

The Lorde Octavian answered: you have judged aright. And therefore I say unto you, that continencie may be compared to a Captaine that fighteth manly, and though his enimies bee strong and well appointed, yet giveth he them the overthrow, but for all that not without much ado and danger. But temperance free from all disquieting, is like the Captaine that without resistance overcommeth and raigneth. And having in the mind where she is, not onely aswaged, but cleane quenched the fire of greedy desire, even as a good prince in civil warre dispatcheth the seditious inward enimies, and giveth the scepter and whole rule to reason.

So in like case this vertue not enforcing the mind, but pouring thereinto through most quiet waies a vehement perswasion that may incline him to honestie, maketh him quiet and full of rest, in every part equall and of good proportion: and on every side framed of a certaine agreement with himself, that filleth him with such a cleare calme-nesse, that hee is never out of patience; and becommeth wholy and most obedient to reason, and readie to turne unto her all his motions, and follow her where she lust to leade him, without any resistance, like a tender lambe that runneth, standeth and goeth alwaies by the Ewes side, and moveth onely as he seeth her doe.

This vertue therefore is most perfect, and is chiefely requisite in Princes, because of it arise many other.

Then the Lorde Cesar Gonzaga, I wot not (quoth he) what vertues requisit for princes may arise of this temperance, if it be she that riddeth the minde of affections (as you say) which perhaps were meete for some Monke, or Heremite, but I can not see how it shoulde be requisite for a Prince that is couragious, freeharted, and of prowesse in martiall feats, for whatsoever is done to him, never to have anger, hatred, good will, disdaine, lust, nor any affection in him: nor how without this he can get him authoritie among the people and souldiers.

The Lorde Octavian answered: I have not said that temperance should throughly rid and root out of mens mindes affections: neither should it bee well so to doe, because there bee yet in affections some parts good: but that which in affections is corrupt and striving against honestie, she bringeth to obey unto reason.

Therefore it is not meete, to ridde the troublesom disquietnesse of the minde, to roote up affections cleane, for this were as if to avoide dronkennesse, there shoulde be an acte established, that no man should drinke wine: or because otherwhile in running a man taketh a fall, every man shoulde bee forbid running.

Marke them that breake horses, they breake them not from their running and comming on loft, but they will have them to doe it at the time and obedience of the rider.

The affections therefore that be cleansed and tried by temperance are assistant to vertue, as anger, that helpeth manlinesse: hatred against the wicked helpeth justice, and likewise the other vertues are aided by affections, which in case they were clean taken away, they woulde leave reason very feeble and faint, so that it shoulde litle prevaile, like a shipmaister that is without winde in a great calme.

Marvell ye not then (my Lorde Cesar) if I have saide, that of temperance arise many other vertues: for when a minde is in tune with this harmony, by the meane of reason he easily received afterwarde true manlinesse, which maketh him bold and safe from all daunger, and (in a manner) above worldlye passions. Likewise justice an undefiled virgin, friende to sober mood and goodnesse, Queene of all other vertues, because she teacheth to doe that which a man ought to doe, and to shun that a man ought to shunne, and therefore is the most perfect, because through her the works of the other vertues are brought to passe, and she is a helpe to him that hath her both for himselfe and for others: without the which (as it is commonly saide) Jupiter himselfe could not well governe his kingdom.

Stoutnesse of courage doth also follow after these, and maketh them all the greater, but she can not stand alone, because who so hath not other vertues, can not be of a stout courage.

Of these then wisedom is guide, which consisteth in a certaine judgement to choose well. And in this happie chaine are also lincked liberallitie, sumpteousnesse, the desire to save a mans estimation, meekenesse, pleasantnesse, courtesie in talke, and many other which is now no time to speake of.

But in case our Courtier will doe as we have saide, he shall finde them all in his Princes minde: and dayly he shall see spring such beautifull floures and fruites, as all the delicious gardens in the world have not the like: and he shall feele very great contentation within himself, when he remembreth that he hath given him, not yᵉ things which foolish persons give, which is, golde, or silver, plate, garments, and such matters, whereof he that giveth them hath himselfe very great scarcitie, and he that receiveth them exceeding great store: but that vertue, which perhaps among all the matters that belong unto man is the chiefest and rarest, that is to say, the manner and way to rule and to raigne in the right kinde. Which alone were sufficient to make men happie, and to bring once againe into the world the golden age, which is written to have beene whē Saturnus raigned in the olde time.

Here, when the Lord Octavian had paused a litle as though he woulde have taken respite, the Lorde Gaspar saide: which reckon you (my Lord Octavian) the happiest government and that were most to purpose to bring into the world againe that golden age which you have made mention of, either the raigne of so good a Prince, or the governmēt of so good a common weale?

The Lorde Octavian answered, I woulde alwaies preferre the raigne of a good Prince, because it is a good governement more agreeable to nature, and if it bee lawfull to compare small matters with infinite, more like unto Gods, which one and alone governeth the universall.

But leaving this, ye see that in whatsoever is broght to passe with the pollicie of man, as armies, great sayling vessels, buildinges and other like matters, the whole is committed to one alone, to dispose thereof at his will.

Likewise in our bodie all the members travaile and are occupied as the hart thinketh good. Beside this, it seemeth meete that people should as well bee governed by one Prince, as many other living creatures bee, whom nature teacheth this obedience, as a most soveraigne matter.

Marke ye whether Deere, Cranes, and many other foules, when they take their flight doe not alwaies set a Prince before, whom they follow and obey. And Bees (as it were) with discourse of reason, and with such reverence honour their King, as the most obedientest people in the world can do.

And therefore all this is a verie great argument that the soveraigntie of a Prince is more according to nature, than a common weales.

Then maister Peter Bembo: and me thinke (quoth he)

557

that since God hath given libertie for a soveraigne gift, it is not reason that it should be taken from us: nor that one man should be partner of it more than another, which happeneth under the rule of Princes, who for the most part keepe their people in most straight bondage. But in common weales wel in order this libertie is well kept.

Beside that, both in judgements and in advisements it happeneth oftener that the opinion of one alone is false, than the opinion of many, because troublous affection either through anger, or through spite, or through lust, sooner entreth into the minde of one alone than into the multitudes, which (in a manner) like a great quantitie of water, is less subject to corruption, than a small deale.

I say againe, that the example of the beastes and foules doth not make to purpose, for both Deere and Cranes and the rest doe not alwaies set one and the selfe formost for them to follow and obey, but they stil change and varie, giving this preferment sometime to one, otherwhile to another, and in this manner it becommeth rather the forme of a common weale, than of a kingdom, and this may be called a true and equall libertie, when they that sometime command, obey againe an otherwhile.

The example likewise of the Bees (me thinke) is not alike, because that king of theirs is not of their owne kinde: And therefore he that will give unto men a worthy head in deede, must bee faine to finde him of another kind, and of a more noble nature than mans, if men (of reason) shoulde obey him, as flockes and heardes of cattell that obey, not a beast their like, but a shepeheard and a heardman, which is a man and of a more worthie kinde, than theirs.

For these respects, I think (my Lord Octavian) the government of a cōmon weale is more to be coveted, than of a king.

Then the Lord Octavian, against your opinion, maister Peter (quoth he) I will alleage but one reason: which is, that of waies to rule people well, there be onely three kindes. The one a kingdome. The other, the rule of good men, which they of olde time called Optimates. The third, the government of the people.

And the transgressing (to terme it so) and contrarie vice that every one of these is changed into being appaired and corrupted, is when the kingdome becommeth a Tyranny: and when the governance of good men is chaunged into the handes of a few great men and not good: and when the rule of the people is at the disposition of the communalty, which making a meddlie of the orders, suffereth the governance of the whole at the will of the multitude.

Of these three ill governments (it is sure) the tyranny is the worst of all, as it may be proved by many reasons. It followeth then, that of the three good, the kingdom is the best, because it is contrarie to the worst, for (as you know) the effects of contrarie causes, they be also contrarie among themselves.

Now as touching it, that you have spoken of libertie, I answere, that true libertie ought not to be saide, to live as a man will, but to live according to good lawes. And to obey is no lesse naturall, profitable and necessary, than to command. And some thinges are borne and so appointed and ordained by nature to command, as some other to obeysance.

Truth it is, that there bee two kinds of bearing rule, the one Lordly and forcible, as maisters over slaves, and in this doth the soule command the bodie. The other more milde and tractable, as good Princes by way of the lawes over their subjectes, and in this reason commandeth greedy desire. And eche of these two waies is profitable: because the bodie is created of nature apt to obey the soule, and so is desire, reason.

There be also many men whose doinges bee applyed onely about the use of the bodie: and such as these bee are so farre wide from the vertues, as the soule from the bodie, and yet because they be reasonable creatures, they be so much partners of reason, as they doe no more but know it, for they possesse it not, ne yet have they the use of it.

These therefore be naturally bondmen, and better it is for them, and more profitable to obey, than to beare sway.

Then saide the Lord Gaspar: In what manner wise be they then to bee commanded that be discret and vertuous, and not by nature bound?

The Lorde Octavian answeared: With that tractable commaundement kingly and civill. And to such it is well done otherwhile to committe the bearing of such offices as be meete for them, that they may likewise beare sway and rule over others of lesse wit than they bee, yet so that the principall governement may full and wholy depend upon the chiefe Prince.

And because you have said, that it is an easier matter to corrupt the mind of one, then of a great sort, I say, that it is also an easier matter to find one good and wise, than a great sort. Both good and wise ought a man to suppose a king may be of a noble progeny, inclined to vertue of hys owne naturall motion, and through the famous memorie of his auncestors, and brought up in right good conditions. And though he be not of an other kinde than man, as you have saide is among the Bees, yet if he be helped forwarde with the instructions, bringing up, and arte of the Courtier, whom these Lordes have fashioned so wise and good, he shall bee most wise, most continent, most temperate, most manly, and most just, full of liberallitie, majestie, holinesse, and mercy: finally, hee shall be most glorious and most dearely beloved to God and man: through whose grace hee shall attaine unto that heroicall and noble vertue, that shall make him passe the boundes of the nature of man, and shall rather be called a demy God, than a man mortall. For God deliteth in and is the defender not of those Princes that will follow and counterfeit him in shewing great power, and make themselves to be worshipped of men, but of such as beside power, whereby they are mightie, endevour themselves to resemble him also in

560

goodnesse and wisedom, wherby they may have a will and a knowledge to doe well and to bee his ministers, distributing for the behoufe of man the benefits and gifts that they receive of him.

Therefore even as in the firmament the sunne and the moone and the other starres shew to the worlde (as it were) in a glasse, a certaine likenesse of God: So upon the earth a much more liker image of God are those good Princes that love and worship him, and shew unto the people the cleare light of his justice, accompanied with a shadow of the heavenly reason and understanding.

And such as these be doth God make partners of his true dealing, righteousnesse, justice and goodnesse, and of those other happie benefits which I can not name, that disclose unto the worlde a much more evident proofe of the Godhead, than doth the light of the sunne, or the continuall turning of the firmament with the sundrie course of the starres.

It is God therefore that hath appointed the people under the custody of princes, which ought to have a diligent care over them, that they may make him account of it, as good stewardes doe their Lorde, and love them, and thinke their owne, all the profit and losse that happeneth to them, and principally above all things provide for their good estate and welfare.

Therfore ought the prince not onely to be good, but also to make others good, like the Carpenters square, that is not onely straight and just it selfe, but also maketh straight and just whatsoever it is occupied about.

And the greatest proofe that the Prince is good, is when the people are good: because the life of the prince is a law and ringleader of Citizens, and upon the conditions of him must needes all others depend: neither is it meete for one that is ignorant, to teach: nor for him that is out of order, to give order: nor for him that falleth, to helpe up an other.

Therefore if the Prince will execute these offices aright,

it is requisite that hee apply all his studie and diligence to get knowledge, afterwarde to fashion within himselfe and observe unchangeably in every thing the law of reason, not writtē in papers or in mettall, but graven in his owne minde, that it may be to him alwaies not onely familiar, but inwarde, and live with him as a parcell of him: to the intent it may night and day, in every time and place, admonish him, and speake to him within his hart, ridding him of those troublous affections that untemperate mindes feele, which because on the one side they be (as it were) cast into a most deepe sleepe of ignorance, on the other overwhelmed with the unquietnesse which they feele through their wayward and blinde desires, they are stirred with an unquiet rage, as he that sleepeth otherwhile with straunge and horrible visions.

Heaping then a great power upon their naughtie desire, there is heaped also a great trouble withall. And when the Prince can doe what he will, then is it great jeopardie lest hee will the thing that he ought not.

Therefore said Bias well, that promotiōs declare what men be: for even as vessels while they are empty, though they have some chincke in them it can ill bee perceived, but if they be filled with licour, they shew by and by on what side the fault is, so corrupted and ill disposed mindes seldom discover their vices, but when they be filled with authoritie. For then they are not able to carrie the heavie burden of power, but forsake themselves, and scatter on every side greedy desire, pride, wrath, solemnesse, and such tyrannicall fashions as they have within them.

Whereupon without regard they persecute the good and wise, and promote the wicked. And they can not abide to have friendship, assemblies and conferences among Citizens in Cities. But maintaine spies, promoters, murtherers and cutthroates to put men in feare and make them to become faint harted. And they sow debate and strife to keepe them in division and weake.

And of these manners insue infinite damages and the

utter undoing of the poore people, and oftentimes cruel slaughter, or at the least continuall feare to the Tyrants themselves. For good Princes feare not for themselves, but for their sakes whome they rule over: and Tyrants feare very them whom they rule over.

Therefor the more number of people they rule over, and the mightier they are, the more is their feare, and the more enimies they have.

How fearefull (thinke ye) and of what unquiet minde was Clearcus Tiranne of Pontus every time he went into the market place, or into the theater, or to any banket, or other haunted place? For (as it is written) hee slept shut into a chest. Or Aristodemus of Argos, which of his bed had made to himselfe a prison (or litle better) for in his pallace hee had a litle roome hanging in the aire, and so high that hee should climbe to it with a ladder, and there slept hee with a woman of his, whose mother overnight tooke away the ladder, and in the morning set it to againe.

Cleane contrarie to this therefore ought the life of a good Prince to bee free and safe and as deare to his subjects as their owne: and so framed, that he may have a part of both the doing and beholding life, as much as shall be behoveful for the benefit of the people.

Then the Lorde Gaspar: And which of the two lives, my Lorde Octavian (quoth he) doe you thinke most meete for a Prince?

The Lorde Octavian answered smyling: ye thinke perhaps that I stand in mine owne conceite to be the excellent courtier that ought to know so many matters, and to apply them to the good end I have spoken of. But remember your selfe, that these Lordes have fashioned him with many qualities that be not in me: therefore let us first doe our best to finde him out, for I remit me to him both in this and in all other thinges that belong to a good Prince.

Then the Lorde Gaspar: I thinke (quoth he) that if any of the qualities given the Courtier want in you, it is rather musicke and daunsing and the rest of small account,

563

than such as belong to the instructing of a prince, and to this end of Courtlinesse.

The Lord Octavian answered: They are not of small account all of them that helpe to purchase a man the favour of a prince, which is necessarie (as wee have saide) before the Courtier aventure to teach him vertue, the which (I trow) I have shewed you may bee learned, and profiteth as much as ignorance hurteth, whereof spring all vices, and especially that false liking a man hath of himselfe. Therefore (in mine opinion) I have sufficiently saide, and perhaps more than my promise was.

Then the Dutchesse, wee shall bee so much the more bound (quoth she) to your gentlenesse, as ye shall satisfie us more than promise. Therfore sticke not to speak your fansie concerning the Lord Gaspars request. And of good felowship shew us beside whatsoever you would teach your Prince, if he had neede of instructions.

And set the case that you have throughly gotten his favour, so as it may be lawful for you to tell him frankly what ever commeth in your minde.

The L. Octavian laughed and saide: If I had the favour of some Prince that I know, and should tell him franckly mine opinion (I doubt me) I shoulde soone loose it: Beside that, to teach him, I shoulde neede first to learne my selfe. Notwithstanding, since it is your pleasure that I shall answere the Lorde Gaspar in this point also, I say, that (in my minde) princes ought to give themselves both to the one and the other of the two lives, but yet somewhat more to the beholding: Because this in them is devided into two partes, whereof the one consisteth in knowing well and judging: the other in commanding aright, and in such wise as it shoulde be done, and reasonable matters, and such as they have authoritie in, commanding them to him, that of reason ought to obey, and in time and place accordingly.

And of this spake Duke Fredericke, when he saide, He that can command, is alwaies obeyed. And to commande is evermore the principall office of princes, which notwithstanding ought many times also to see with their eyes, and to be present at the deede doing, and according to the time and the businesse otherwhile also be doing themselves, and yet hath all this a part with action or practise.

But the end of the active or doing life ought to be the beholding, as of war, peace, and of paines, rest. Therefore is it also the office of a good Prince so to trade his people and with such lawes and statutes, that they may live in rest and in peace, without daunger and with increase of wealth, and injoy peaceably this ende of their practises and actions, which ought to be quietnesse. Because there have beene oftentimes many common weales and Princes, that in warre were alwaies most florishing and mightie, and immediately after they have had peace, fell in decay and lost their puissance and brightnesse, like iron unoccupied. And this came of nothing els, but because they had no good trade of living in peace, nor the knowledge to injoy the benefit of ease.

And it is not a matter lawful to be alwaies in war, without seeking at the ende to come to a peace: although some Princes suppose that their drift ought principally to be, to bring in subjection their borders, and therefore to traine up their people in a warlike wildenesse of spoile and murther, and such matters: they wage them to exercise it, and call it vertue.

Whereupon in the olde time it was an usage among the Scythes, that who so had not slaine one enimie of his, coulde not drinke in solemne bankets of the goblet that was carried about to his companions.

In other places the manner was to reare about ones sepulture so many Obeliskes, as he that lay there buried had slaine of his enimies. And all these thinges and many moe, were invented to make men warlike, onely to bring others in subjection, which was a matter (almost) unpossible, because it is an infinite peece of worke, untill all the worlde be brought under obeysance: and not very reasonable, according to the law of nature which will not have, that in others thing shoulde please us, which in our selves is a griefe to us.

Therefore ought Princes to make their people warlike, not for a greedie desire to rule, but to defend themselves the better and their owne people from who so would attempt to bring them in bondage, or to doe them wrong in any point: or els to drive out Tyrants, and to governe the people well that were ill handled. Or els to bring into bondage them that of nature were such, that they deserved to bee made bondmen, with intent to governe them well, and to give them ease, rest, and peace.

And to this ende also ought to be applied ye lawes, and all statutes of justice, in punishing the ill, not for malice, but because there should be no ill, and lest they should bee a hindrance to the quiet living of the good.

Because in very deede it is an uncomely matter and worthie of blame, that in warre (which of it selfe is nought) men shoulde shew themselves stout and wise, and in peace and rest (which is good) ignorant, and so blockish that they wist not how to enjoy a benefit.

Even as therefore in war they ought to bend their people to the profitable and necessarie vertues to come by the end (which is, peace) so in peace, to come by the end thereof also (which is, quietnesse) they ought to bend them to honest vertues, which be the end of the profitable. And in this wise shall the subjects be good, and the Prince shall have many moe to commend and to rewarde, than to chastise. And the rule both for the subjects and for the prince shalbe most happie, not Lordly, as the maister over his bondman, but soft and meeke, as a good father over his good childe.

Then the Lorde Gaspar: gladly (quoth he) woulde I understand what manner vertues these are, that bee profitable and necessarie in warre, and what honest in peace.

The Lorde Octavian answered: All be good and helpe the turne, because they tend to a good end. Yet chiefly in warre is much set by that true manlinesse, which maketh the mind voide from all passions, so that he not onely feareth not perils, but passeth not upon them. Likewise stedfastnesse, and patience, abiding with a quiet and untroubled mind all the strokes of fortune.

It is behovefull likewise in war and at all other times to have all the vertues that belong to honestie, as justice, stayednesse, sober mood: but much more in peace and rest, because oftentimes men in prosperitie and rest, when favourable Fortune fauneth upon them, waxe unrighteous, untemperate, and suffer themselves to bee corrupted with pleasures.

Therefore such as bee in this state have verie greate neede of these vertues, because rest bringeth ill conditions too soone into mens mindes.

Whereupon arose a Proverbe in olde time, that Rest is not to bee given to bondmen: And it is thought that the Pyramides of Egipt were made to keepe the people occupied, because Unto every man, use to abide paines is most profitable.

There be moreover many other vertues, all helpfull, but it sufficeth for this time to have spoken thus much: for if I could teach my prince and traine him in this manner and so vertuous a bringing up (as wee have set forth) in doing it without any more (I would believe) that I had sufficiently well compassed the ende of a good Courtier.

Then the Lorde Gaspar, My Lord Octavian (quoth he) because you have much praysed good bringing up, and seemed (in a manner) to believe that it is the chiefe cause to make a man vertuous and good, I would know whether the Courtiers instructing of his prince, ought to beginne first of use and (as it were) dayly fashions, that unawares to him may make him to accustome himselfe to well doing: or els whether he ought to begin it himselfe in opening unto him with reason the propertie of good and ill, and in making him to perceive before hee take the matter in hand, which is the good way, and to be followed: and which is the ill, and to be shunned: finally, whether into the mind of his, the vertues ought to bee driven and grounded with reason and understanding first, or with custome.

The Lord Octavian said: you bring me into overlong a discourse: yet because you shall not thinke that I will slacke, for that I am not willing to make answere to your requestes, I say, that like as the soule and the bodie in us are two thinges, so is the soule devided into two parts: whereof the one hath in it reason, and the other appetite.

Even as therefore in generation the body goeth before the soule, so doth the unreasonable part of the soule goe before the reasonable: the which is plainely to bee discerned in yong babes, who (in a manner) immediatly after their birth utter anger and fervent appetite, but afterwarde in processe of time reason appeareth.

Therefore first must the bodie bee cherished before the soule: after that, the appetite before reason: but the cherishing of the bodie for a respect to the soule, and of the appetite for a respect to reason. For as the vertue of the minde is made perfect with learning, so is the civill with custome.

Therefore ought there to be a ground made first with custome, which may governe the appetites not yet apt to conceive reason: and with that good use leade them to goodnesse: afterwarde settle them with understanding, the which although she be last to shew her light, yet doth she the more perfectly make the vertues to be injoyed of who so hath his minde well instructed with manners, wherein (in mine opinion) consisteth ye whole.

The Lorde Gaspar saide: Before ye proceede any further, I woulde know how the bodie should be cherished: because you have saide that we must cherish it before the soule.

The Lorde Octavian answered smyling: know of these men that make much of it and are faire and round, as for mine (as you see) it is not halfe well cherished. Yet may there also be much saide in this behalfe: As, the time meete for marriage, that children be neither too nigh nor too farre off from the fathers age: Exercises, and bringing up soone after their birth, and in the rest of their life, to make them handsome, towardly, and lively.

The Lord Gaspar answered: The thing that woulde best please women to make their children handsome and well-favoured (in my minde) were the fellowship that Plato will have of them in his common weale, and in that wise.

Then the Ladie Emilia smyling: It is not in the covenant (quoth she) that ye should a fresh fall to speake ill of women. I suppose answered the Lord Gaspar, that I give them a great prayse, in saying that they shoulde desire to have a custome brought up, which is alowed of so worthie a man.

The Lorde Cesar Gonzaga saide laughing: Let us see whether among the Lorde Octavians lessons (yet I wot not whether hee have spoken all or no) this may take place: and whether it were well done the Prince should establish it for a law or no.

The few that I have spoken, answered the Lord Octavian, may perhaps bee inough to make a good prince as princes goe now a dayes. Although if a man woulde go more narrowly to worke in the matter, there were much more for him yet to say.

Then said the Dutchesse: Since it costeth us nothing but wordes, shew us of good fellowship that, that woulde come in your minde to teach your Prince.

The Lorde Octavian answered: Many other matters I woulde teach him (madam) if I knew them my selfe: and among the rest, that hee shoulde picke out a certaine number of gentlemen among his subjects, of the noblest and wisest, with whom he shoulde debate all matters, and give them authoritie and free leave to utter their minde franckly unto him without respect: and to take such order with them that they may well perceive, that in every thing he would know the truth and abhorre lying.

569

And beside this Counsell of the nobilitie, I woulde perswade him to choose out others among the people of a baser degree, of whom hee should make an honest substantial Councel, that should debate with the Councel of the nobilitie the affaires of the Citie, belonging to the common and private estate. And in this wise should bee made, of the Prince, as of the heade, of the nobilitie and commons, as of the members, one bodie alone knitte together, the governance whereof should chiefly depend upon the Prince, yet should the rest beare a stroke also in it: and so should this state have the forme and manner of the three good governments, which is, a kingdom, men of the best sorte, and the people.

Afterwarde I woulde shew him, that of cares belonging to a Prince, the chiefest is of justice: for maintenance whereof wise and well tryed men shoulde bee chosen out for officers, whose wisedom were very wisedome in deed, accompanied with goodnesse, for els is it no wisedom, but craft. And where there is a want of this goodnesse, alwaies the arte and subtiltie of Lawiers is nothing els but the utter decay and destruction of the lawes and judgements: and the fault of every offence of theirs is to bee laide in him that put them in office.

I woulde tell him how that of justice also dependeth the zeale toward God, which belongeth unto all men, and especially to Princes, who ought to love him above all things, and to direct all their doings unto him, as unto the true end: And (as Xenophon saith) to honour and love him alwaies, but much more in prosperitie, because they may afterwarde lawfully with a more confidence call to him for assistance when they be in any adversitie: for it is not possible to governe either himselfe or others well, without the help of God, who unto the good sendeth otherwhile good fortune for his minister, to helpe them out of great dangers, sometime adversitie, lest they shoulde slumber so much in prosperitie, that they might happen to forget him, or the wisedom of man, which many times redresseth ill fortune, as a good player the ill chaunces of the dice, with cunning play at tables.

I would not forget also to put the Prince in minde to be devoute in deede, not superstitious, nor given to the vanitie of ignorance and prophecies: for in case hee have accompanied with the wisedom of man, a godly zeale of true religion, he shall also have good lucke, and God his defendor, who will alwaies increase his prosperitie both in peace and war.

Beside, I would declare unto him how he should love his Countrie and his people, keeping them not in too much bondage for being hated of them, whereof arise seditions, conspiracies, and a thousand mischiefes beside: nor yet in too much libertie, least he bee set at nought, whereof proceedeth the licentious and riotous living of the people, theft, roberie and murther without anie feare of lawes, oftentimes the decay and utter destruction of Cities and kingdomes.

Moreover how he should love them that bee nighest to him, from one degree to another, observing among them all in certaine matters a like equalitie, as in justice, and liberallitie, and in some matters a reasonable partialitie, as in being liberall, in recompensing, in bestowing promotions and honours according to the unequalnesse of deserts, which ought not alwaies to exceede, but to bee exceeded with recompences. And that in thus doing hee should not onely not be beloved, but (in a manner) worshipped of his subjects, neither shoulde he neede to commit the guarde of his person to straungers, for his owne (for the better safegard and profitte of themselves) would guarde him in their owne person: and each man woulde willingly obey the lawes, when they should see him to obey them himselfe, and be (as it were) an uncorrupted keeper and minister of them.

And so shall he make all men to conceive such an assured confidence of him, that if he should happen otherwhile to goe beyond them in anie point, every one woulde know it were done for a good intent: the selfe same respect and reverence they woulde have to his will, as they have to the lawes. And thus should the Citizens mindes bee tempered in such sorte, that the good would not seeke for more than is requisite, and the bad shoulde not bee able.

Because many times aboundance of wealth is cause of great destruction, as in poore Italy, which hath been and still is, a pray and bootie in the teeth of straunge nations, as well for the ill government, as for the aboundance of riches that is in it.

Therefore the best way were, to have the greater part of the Citizens, neither verie wealthie, nor verye poore: because the overwealthie many time waxe stiffe necked and recklesse, the poore, desperate and picking. But the meane sorte lye not in waite for others, and live with a quiet mind that none lye in waite for them. And where this meane sorte are the greater number, they are withall the mightier. And therfore neither the poore nor rich can worke any conspiracie against the Prince, or against others, nor move sedition.

Wherefore to avoide this evill, the most surest way is universally to maintaine a meane.

I woulde counsell him therefore to use these and many other remedies for the purpose, that in the minde of the subjects there spring not a longing after new matters and alteration of state, which most commonly they doe, either for gaine, or els for promotion that they hope upon, or for losse, or els for some toile that they be afearde of. And these sturres in their mindes be engendred sometime of hatred and despite that maketh them desperate for the wronges and unshamefull dealing that they receive through the covetousnesse, pride and crueltie, or unlawfull lust of the higher powers: otherwhile of a contempt and litle regarde that ariseth in them through negligence and ill handling and lacke of foresight in Princes.

And these two faults must be prevēted with purchasing him the love of the people, and authority, which is done in rewarding and prompting the good, and in finding wisely a remedie, and sometime with rigour, that the evill and seditions waxe not great: the which thing is easier to be stopped before they come to it, than to plucke them down againe after they are once on loft.

And I would say, to restraine the people from running into those inconveniences, there is no better way than to keepe them from ill customes, and especially such as be put in use, and creepe in unawares by litle and litle, because they be secrete infections that corrupt cities before a man can not onely remedie them, but spye them out.

With such meanes I would counsel the Prince to doe his best to preserve his subjects in quiet estate, and to give them the goods of the mind, and of the bodie, and of fortune: but them of the bodie and of fortune, that they exercise them of the minde: which the greater and plentier they be, so much the more profitable be they: that happeneth not in them of the bodie, nor of fortune.

In case therefore the subjects be good and of worthinesse, and well bent to the end of happinesse, that prince shall be a verie great Lorde: for that is a true and a great governmẽt, under the which the subjects be good, well ruled, and well commanded.

Then the Lord Gaspar, I suppose (quoth hee) that he should be but a small Lorde, under whom the subjectes were all good. For in every place there be few good.

The Lorde Octavian answered: In case some certain Circe should turn into wilde beastes all the French kings subjects, woulde not you thinke him a small Lord for all he raigned over so many thousand beastes? And contrariwise, if onely the Cattel that scatter abroad feeding about our mountaines here, might become wise men, and valiant gentlemen, woulde not you thinke that yᵉ heardmen that shoulde governe them and have them obedient to them, of heardmen were become great Lords.

You may see then, that not the multitude of subjectes, but the worthinesse of them maketh princes great.

The Dutchesse, the Ladie Emilia, and all the rest gave very diligent care to the L. Octavians talke for a good while together, but after hee had here made a litle stoppe, as though hee had made an end of his talke, the Lorde Cesar Gonzaga said.

Certesse (my Lord Octavian) it can not be saide, but your lessons be good and profitable: yet should I believe, that if yee instructed your Prince with them, yee deserve rather the name of a good scholemaister than of a good Courtier: and hee of a good governour rather than of a good Prince.

Yet my meaning is not, but that the care of Princes should be to have their people well ruled with justice and good usages, notwithstanding it may be sufficient for them (in my minde) to choose out good ministers to execute these kinde of matters, but the verie office of them is farre higher.

Therfore if I thought my selfe to be the excellent courtier that these Lordes have fashioned, and in my Princes favour, without peradventure I would never encline him to any vitious matter: but to attaine unto the good end you speake of, and the which I confirme ought to be the fruite of the Courtiers travailes and doinges, I would endevour to put into his heade a certaine greatnesse, with that princely sumptuousnesse and readinesse of courage, and unconquered prowesse in armes, that should make him beloved and reverenced of all men, in such wise, that for this in especiall he should be famous and notable to the world.

I would shew him also, that hee ought to accompany with his greatnesse, a familiar gentle behavior, with a soft and lovely kindnesse, and good cast to make much of his subjects and straungers discreetly more and lesse according to their deserts, observing alwaies notwithstanding the majestie meete for his degree, that shoulde not in any point suffer him to diminish his authoritie through overmuch abasing, nor yet purchase him hatred through overmuch rigorousnesse.

That he ought to be full of liberality and sumptuous, and give unto every man without stint, for God (as they say) is the treasurer of freeharted Princes: make gorgeous banquets, feastes, games, people pleasing shewes, keepe a great number of faire horses for profit in warre, and for pleasure in peace: Haukes, houndes, and all other matters that belong to the contentation of great Princes and the people. As in our dayes we have seene the Lorde Francis Gonzaga marquesse of Mantua do, which in these things seemeth rather king of all Italy, than Lord over one Citie.

I would assay also to bring him to make great buildings both for his honour in life, and to give a memorie of him to his posteritie, as did duke Fredericke in this noble pallace, and now doeth Pope July in the temple of Saint Peter, and the way that goeth from the pallace to his house of pleasure Belvedere, and many other buildings, as also the old auncient Romanes did, whereof so many remnants are to be seene about Rome, Naples, Pozzolo, Baie, Civita vecchia, Porto, and also out of Italy, and so many other places, which be a great witnesse of the prowesse of those divine courages.

So did Alexander the great in like manner, which not satisfied with the fame that he got him worthily for subduing the worlde with martiall prowesse, built Alexandria in Egypt, Bucephalia in India, and other Cities in other Countries: and entended to bring the mountaine Athos into the shape of a man, and in the left hand of him to builde a very large Citie, and in the right a great bolle, into the which should gather all the rivers that ranne from it, and thence should fall downe towarde the sea, a purpose in very deed princely and meete for the great Alexander.

These thinges (thinke I) my Lord Octavian, become a noble and a right Prince, and shall make him both in peace and warre most triumphant, and not put him in the head of such particular and small matters, and have a respect to take weapon in hand onely to conquere and vanquish such as deserve to be conquered, or to profit his subjects withall, or to dispossesse them that governe not as they ought.

For in case that the Romanes, Alexander, Hannibal and the rest had had these respects, they shoulde never have reached to the toppe of the glory they did.

The Lorde Octavian answered them smiling: such as had not these respects should have done the better in case they had had them: although if ye consider well, ye shall finde that many had them: especially those auncientest of olde time, as Theseus and Hercules.

And thinke not that Procustes, Scyron, Caccus, Diomides, Antheus, and Gerion were any other than cruell and wicked tyrants, against whom these noble couraged Demigods kept continuall and mortall warre.

And therefore for ridding the world of such intollerable monsters (for tyrants ought not to bee called by other name) unto Hercules were made temples, and sacrifices, and goodly honours given him, because the benefit to roote up tyrants is so profitable to the worlde, that who so doth it, deserveth a farre greater rewarde, than whatsoever is meete for a mortall man.

And of them you have named. Doe you not thinke that Alexander did profitte with his victories the vanquished? since he so traded those barbarous Nations which hee overcame with such good manners, that of wilde beastes he made them men? He built many beautifull Cities in Countries ill inhabited, planting therein civil kinde of living, and (as it were) coupled Asia and Europe together with the bond of amitie and holy lawes, so that the vanquished by him were more happie than the rest.

Because among some hee brought in matrimonie: among other, husbandrie: among other, Religion: among other, not to slay, but to make much of their parents in their old age: among other, the refraining from bedding with their mothers, and a thousand other matters, that might be saide for a witnesse of the profit which his victories brought unto the world.

But leaving aside them of olde time, what enterprise were more noble, more glorious, and also more profitable, than if Christians would bende their force to conquere the infidels: would you not thinke that this war prosperously atchieved, and being the cause of so many a thousand to be brought from the false sect of Mahumet to the light of the Christian truth, it should be a profit as well to the vanquished, as to the subduers?

And undoubtedly, as Themistocles in times past being banished out of his countrie, and embraced of the king of Persia, and much made of, and honoured with infinite and most rich gifts, said unto his traine: Oh sirs, we had beene undone, had wee not beene undone, even so might then the Turkes and the Moores speak the verie same with good cause, for that in their losse should consist their welfare.

This happinesse therefore (I hope) we shall come to the sight of, if God graunt so long life to Monseigneur d'Angoulesme, that he may come to ye croune of Fraunce, who sheweth such a hope of himselfe, as foure nights agoe the Lorde Julian spake of. And to the crowne of England the Lorde Henry prince of Wales, who presently groweth under his most noble father, in all kind of vertue, like a tender Impe under the shadow of an excellent tree, and laden with fruite to renue him much more beautifull and plenteous when the time shall come.

For as our Castilio writeth from thence,[39] and promiseth at his returne to tell us more at the full, a man can judge no lesse, but that nature was willing in this prince to shew her cunning, in one bodie alone so many excellent vertues, as were sufficient to decke out infinit.

Then saide maister Bernard Bibiena: A very great hope of himselfe promiseth also the Lord Charles prince of Spaine, who not yet fully ten yeares of age, declareth now such a wit, and so certaine tokens of goodnesse, wisedom, modestie, noble courage and of every vertue, that if the Empire of Christendom (as it is thought) come to his handes, it is to be reckoned upon, that hee will darken the

577

name of many Emperors of olde time, and in renowne be compared to the most famous that ever were in the world.

The Lorde Octavian proceeded, I believe therefore that God hath sent such and so heavenly Princes upon the earth, and made them one like another in youth, in might-inesse of armes, in state, in handsomnesse and disposition of person, that they may also bee minded alike in this good purpose: and in case any manner envie or strife of matching others arise at anye time among them, it shall be, who shall be the first, and most enclined and most cour-agious in so glorious an enterprise.

But let us leave this kind of talke, and returne unto our owne. Unto you therefore (my Lord Cesar) I say, that such thinges as you would have the Prince to doe, be very great and worthie much praise. But you must understand that if hee be not skilfull in that I have saide hee ought to have a knowledg in, and have not framed his minde in this wise, and bent it to the way of vertue, it shall be hard for him to have the knowledge to be noble couraged, liberal, just, quicke spirited, wise, or to have any other of those qualities that belong unto him: neither woulde I have him to be such a one for any other thing, but to have the understanding to put in use these conditions.

For as they that builde bee not all good workemen: so they that give, be not all liberall: for vertue never hurteth any man: and many there be, that lay hand on other mens goods to give, and so are lavish of an other mans substance. Some give to them they ought not, and leave in wretched-nesse and misery such as they be bound to. Other give with a certaine ill will, and (as it were) with a despite, so that it is knowne they doe it, because they can doe none other. Other doe not onely not keepe it secrete, but they call witnesse of it, and (in a manner) cause their liberalities to bee cryed. Other foolishly at a sodaine empty the foun-taine of liberalitie, so that afterwarde they can use it no more.

Therefore in this point (as in all other matters) hee must

have a knowledge, and governe himselfe with the wisedom that is a companion unto all the other vertues, which for that they are in the middle, be nigh unto the two extremities, that be vices.

Wherefore hee that hath not knowledge rūneth soone into them. For as it is a hard matter in a circle to find out the pricke in the centre, which is the middle, so is it hard to find out the pricke of vertue placed in the middle betweene two extreeme vices, the one for the overmuch, and the other for the over litle.

And unto these we are enclined, sometime to the one, sometime to the other: and this is knowne by the pleasure and griefe that is felt within us, for through the one wee doe the thing that we ought not, and through the other wee leave undone that which we ought to doe: although pleasure bee much more dangerous, because our judgement is soone led by it to be corrupted. But because the perseverance how farre a man is wide from the centre of vertue, is a hard matter, we ought by litle and litle to draw backe of our selves to the contrary parte of this extremitie, which wee know we be enclined unto, as they doe, that make straight crooked staves, for by that means we shall draw nigh unto vertue, which is placed (as I have saide) in that pricke of the meane.

Whereby it commeth that by many waies we be wide, and by one alone we doe our office and duetie: like as Archers by one way alone hitte the marke, and by many misse the pricke. Therefore oftentimes a Prince to be gentle and lowly, doth many thinges contrarie to comelinesse, and so humbleth himselfe that he is nought set by.

Some other to shew a grave majestie with authoritie according, becommeth cruel and untollerable.

Some one, to be counted eloquēt, entreth into a thousand straunge matters and long processes, with curious wordes giving eare to him selfe, so that other men can not for lothsomnesse heare him.

Therefore my (Lord Cesar) doe you not call a small

579

matter any thing that may better a Prince, how small so ever it be. Nor thinke that I judge it to bee in the reproofe of my lessons, where you say, that a good governour might better thus bee formed, than a good Prince.

For perhaps there can not be a greater praise nor more comely for a Prince, than to call him a good governour.

Therefore if it should fall to my lotte to instruct him, he shoulde have a care not onely to governe the matters alreadie spoken of, but also farre lesser, and understand in peecemeale whatsoever belongeth to his people, as much as were possible: and never credit nor trust any officer so much, as to give him the bridle wholy into his hands, and the disposing of the whole government.

For no man is most apt to all things. And much more hurt commeth of the light beliefe of Princes, than of mistrusting, which otherwile doth not onely not hurt, but oftentimes profiteth exceedingly. Yet in this point a good judgement is very necessarie in a Prince, to discerne who deserveth to bee put in trust, and who not.

I would he shoulde have a care to understand the doings, and to bee an overseer of his officers and ministers. To breake and to ende controversies among his subjects. To take up matters betweene them, and to knitte them together in allyance by marriage. To provide so, that the citie may be all joyned together and agreeing in amitie, like a privat house, well peopled, not poore, quiet, and full of good artificers. To shew favour to marchant men, and to helpe them also with stockes. To be liberall and honourable in house keeping toward straungers and religious persons. To temper all superfluous matters, because through the offences committed in these thinges, albeit they appeare but small, Cities many times fall in decay.

Therefore it is reason that the Prince set a stint to the over sumptuous buildinges of private men, banquetings, unmeasurable dowries of women, their riotous excesse, their pompe in jewels and apparell, which is nothing els but a token of their follie.

For (beside that through ambition and malice that one of them beareth another, they many times lavish out their livelode and husbandes substance, otherwhile for some pretie jewell or other matter of fancie) sometime they sell their honestie to him that will buye it.

Then saide maister Bernard Bibiena smiling: You beginne (my Lord Octavian) to take the Lord Gaspars and Phrisios parte.

Then the Lord Octavian answered in like manner, smiling. The controversie is ended, and I entend not now to renue it. Therefore will I speake no more of women, but returne to my Prince.

Phrisio answered: You may now leave him hardly, and bee contented to have him such a one as you have instructed him. For doubtlesse it were an easier matter to find out a woman of the qualities the Lorde Julian hath spoken of, than a prince of the qualities you woulde have in him.

Therefore (I feare me) he is like the common weale of Plato, and wee shall never see such a one, unlesse it bee perhaps in heaven.

The Lorde Octavian answered: thinges possible, though they be hard, yet is it to bee hoped that they may be: therefore may we yet perhaps see him upon the earth in our time.

For although the heavens be so scant in bringing forth excellent princes, that in so many hundred yeares wee doe scantly see one, yet may this good lucke happen to us.

Then saide Count Lewis: I have a good hope of it. For beside the three great ones that wee have named, of whom may be hoped it that belongeth to the high degree of a perfect Prince, there be also now a daies in Italy certaine Princes children, which although they be not like to have such power, may hap will supply it with vertue: and he that among them all declareth a more towardnesse, and promiseth of him selfe a greater hope than any of the rest (me thinke) is the L. Fredericke Gonzaga sonne and heire

581

to the Marquesse of Mantua, and Nephew to our Dutchesse here.

For beside the honest inclination to good nourture, and the discretion that he declareth in those tender yeares, they that have the bringing up of him, reporte such wonderous thinges, as touching his being wittie, desirous of glorie, stoutharted, courteous, freeharted, friendly to justice, so that of so good a beginning, there can not be looked for but a very good ende.

Then Phrisio, well, no more of this (quoth he) we will pray unto God that we may see this your hope fulfilled.

Here the Lorde Octavian turning him towarde the Dutchesse, after a sort as though hee had ended as much as he had to say. You have now heard Madam (quoth he) what I am able to say of the end of ye Courtier, wherein though I have not satisfied in all pointes, it shall suffice me yet, that I have shewed, that some other perfection may be given him beside the matters which these Lordes have spoken of, who (I believe) have left out both this and whatsoever I am able to say, not because they knew it not better than I, but because they were loth to take the paines.

Therefore will I give them leave to goe forwarde, if they have anye thing els left behinde to bee saide.

Then said the Dutchesse: Beside that it is late (for within a while it will bee time for us to make an ende for this night) me thinke, we ought not to mingle any other talke with this, wherein you have gathered together such sundrie and goodly matters, that concerning the end of Courtlinesse, it may be saide, that you are not onely the perfect Courtier whom we seeke for, and able to instruct your Prince well, but also (if fortune be so favourable on your side) ye may be the good prince your selfe, which should not be without great profit to your Countrie.

Then laughed the Lorde Octavian, and said: perhaps (madam) were I in that estate, it would be with me as it is with many others that can better say well, than doe well.

Here after a little debating of the matter to and fro among the company, with certaine contentions tending to the commendation of that that had beene spoken, and agreeing on all hands not yet to be bed time, the Lord Julian saide smyling.

Madam, I am so very an enimie to craft and guile, that needes must I speake against the Lord Octavian: who for that hee is (as I much doubt him) a secret conspiratour with the Lord Gaspar against women, hath overshot him selfe in committing two errors (in mine opinion) very great: whereof the one is, that meaning to prefer the Courtier before the gentlewoman of the pallace, and to make him to passe those bounds, that she is not able to reach to, he hath also preferred him before the Prince, which is most unseemely. The other, that he hath given him such an ende, that it is evermore hard and otherwhile unpossible for him to come by it: and yet when he doth come by it, he ought not to have the name of a Courtier.

I can not see, quoth the Ladie Emilia, how it is hard or unpossible for the Courtier to come by this his end, nor yet how the Lord Octavian hath preferred him before the Prince.

Graunt it him not, answered the Lord Octavian: for I have not preferred ye Courtier before the Prince. And as touching the end of courtlinesse, I dare undertake that I am not overseene in any point.

Then answered the Lorde Julian: You can not say (my L. Octavian) that alwaies the cause, by the which the effect is such as it is, is no more such as the effect is. Therefore needes must the Courtier, by whose instruction the Prince must bee of such an excellencie, bee more excellent than the Prince: and in this wise shall hee be also of a more worthinesse than the Prince himselfe, which is most unfitting.

Then concerning the ende of Courtlinesse, that which you have spoken may follow when there is litle betweene the age of the Prince and the Courtiers: yet very hardly, for where there is small difference of age, it is likely there is also small difference of knowledge. But in case the Prince be olde and the Courtier yong: it is meete that the olde Prince know more than the yong Courtier, and where this followeth not alwaies, it followeth sometime, and then is the end which you have appointed to the Courtier unpossible.

In case againe the Prince be yong, and the Courtier aged, much adoe shall the Courtier have to win him the good will of the Prince with those qualities that you have given him. For (to say the truth) feates of armes and the other exercises belong unto yong men, and be not comely in age: and musicke, dauncing, feastings, sportings, and love, be matters to be laughed at in olde men, and (me thinke) to an instructer of the life and manners of a Prince, who ought to bee a grave person and of authoritie, ripe in years and experience, and if it were possible, a good Philosopher, a good Captaine, and to have the knowledge almost of every thing, it is most seemely.

Wherfore he that instructeth a Prince (I believe) ought not to bee called a Courtier, but deserveth a farre greater and a more honourable name.

Therefore (my Lord Octavian) pardon me, in case I have opened this your craftie conveyance, which I thinke my selfe bound to do, for the honour of my woman, whom you would have to bee of lesse worthinesse than this courtier of yours, and I will none of that.

The L. Octavian laughed and saide: I more prayse it were for the gentlewoman of the pallace (my Lorde Julian) to exalt her so much that she may bee equall with the Courtier, than so much to debase the Courtier that hee shoulde be equall with the gentlewoman of the pallace: for it were not unfit for the woman also to instruct her Ladie, and with her to draw to the same end of Courtlinesse, which I have said is meete for the Courtier with his Prince. But you seeke more to dispraise the Courtier, than to praise the gentlewoman of the pallace.

Therefore shall it become me also to take parte with the Courtier. Nowe to make you aunswere to your objections, you shall understand that I have not sayde, that the instruction of the Courtier ought to be the only cause why the Prince should bee such a one, for in case he be not inclined of nature and apt to be such a one, all diligence and exhortation of ye Courtier were in vaine. As in like maner every good husbandman should labor in vaine, that woulde take in hande to till and sowe wyth good graine the barraine sand of the Sea, because this barrennesse in that place is naturall. But when to the good seede in a fruitfull soyle with the temperatenes of ayre and raine meete for the season of the yere, there is also applied the diligēce of mans husbandinge the grounde, alwayes great aboundaunce of corne is seene to spring plenteously: yet for all this, is it to be said that the husbandman alone is the cause of it, although without hym all the other thinges doe little or nothing helpe the purpose.

There bee therefore many Princes, that would be good in case their minds were wel tilled, and of them speake I, not of such as be like the barraine Countrey, and of nature so farre wide from good conditions, that no teaching wer able to frame their mind to a right trade.

And forsomuch as (as we have already sayde) such customes and properties be ingendred in us, as our doings are, and vertue consisteth in doing and practise, it is not unpossible nor any marvel, that the Courtier shoulde traine his Prince in many vertues, as justice, liberalitie, noble courage, the practising whereof hee through his greatnesse may lightly put in use, and make it custome, which the Courtier can not doe, because he hath no meanes to practise them.

And thus the Prince inclined to vertue by ye Courtier, may become more vertuous than the Courtier: beside that, you must conceive that the whetstone which cutteth not a whit, doth yet make a toole sharpe: therefore although the Courtier instructeth his Prince, yet (me thinke) it is not to be saide that he is of a more worthinesse than his Prince.

That the ende of this Courtier is hard, and sometime unpossible, and that when the Courtier doth come, he ought not to be named a Courtier, but deserveth a greater name, I tell you plainely, that I deny not this hardnesse, because it is no lesse hard to find out so excellent a Courtier, than to come by such an end.

Yet by reason (me thinke) the unpossiblenesse of the matter lyeth not in the point that you have alleaged. For in case the Courtier bee so yong that he hath not understanding in the thing, which he ought to have a knowledge in, it is not to the purpose to speake of him, because he is not the Courtier that we entreat upon, neither is it possible for him that must have a sight in so manye things to be very yong. And if it happen moreover the Prince to bee so wise and good of himselfe, that he needeth no exhortatiõs or councell of others (although it be so hard a matter as every man knoweth) it sufficeth that the Courtier be such a one, as if his prince had need, he coulde make him vertuous: and then may he in effect fulfill the other part, not to suffer him to be deceived, and to worke that evermore he may understand the truth of every thing, and bolster him against flatterers, and railers, and al such as should endevour to corrupt his minde with honest delights. And in this wise shall he yet come by a part of his ende though hee can not practise the whole.

Which can not bee justly laide to him for a fault, since he refraineth the doing of it upon so good a ground. For were an excellent Phisition in place where al were found and in health, a man ought not therefore to say, that the Phisition (although he cured no diseased) wanted of his end.

Wherefore as the Phisitions respect ought to bee the health of men, even so the Courtiers, the vertue of his Prince: and it sufficeth them both to have this ende inwardly graft in them, when the want of uttering it outwardly in practise is occasioned by the subject, to the which this end is directed.

But in case the Courtier were so olde, that it became him not to bee doing in musicke, feastings, sportinges, martiall feates, and the other sleights of the bodie, yet can it not be saide notwithstanding, that it were unpossible for him to enter that way in favour with his Prince: for where his age taketh away the practising of those thinges, it taketh not away the understanding of them, and if he have practised them in his youth, it maketh him to have so much the more perfect judgement in them, and giveth a knowledg to teach them his Prince so much the more perfectly, as yeares and experience bring knowledge of all thinges with them.

And thus shall the aged Courtier, although hee exercise not the qualities that he is endowed withall, come by his end at length, to instruct well his prince. And in case you will not call him a Courtier, it shall nothing offend me: for nature hath not appointed such narrow boundes to the dignities of men, that one may not come up from one to another.

Therefore many times meane souldiers arise to bee Captaines: private men, Kinges: priests, Popes: and scholers, maisters: and so with their degree or dignitie, they take their name accordingly. Wherefore perhaps a man may say, that to become the instructer of a Prince, were the ende of a Courtier, although I perceive not who should refuse this name of a perfect Courtier, which (in my minde) is worthie very great praise.

And I can not see but Homer, as hee fashioned two most excellent personages for example of mans life, the one in practises, which was Achilles, the other in passions and sufferances, which was Ulisses: even so in like manner minded to fashion a perfect courtier (which was Phœnix) who after rehersall of his loves and many other matters of youth, declareth that he was sent to Achilles by his father Peleus, to be in his company, and to teach him to speake, and to doe: which is nothing els but the end that we have appointed for our Courtier.

Neither can I thinke that Aristotle and Plato tooke scorne of the name of a perfect Courtier, because it is plainely to be seene that they practised the deeds of Courtiership, and gave themselves to this end, the one with the great Alexander, the other with the kinges of Sicilia.

And because it is the office of a good Courtier to know the nature and inclination of his Prince, and so according to the businesse, and as occasion serveth with slightnesse to enter in favour with him (as we have saide) by those waies that make him a sure entrie, and afterwarde bend him to vertue. Aristotle so well knew the nature of Alexander, and with slightnesse framed him selfe so well thereafter that he was beloved and honoured of him more than a father.

Wherefore among many other tokens that Alexander shewed him for a witnesse of his good will, he caused Stagira the citie where hee was borne, once destroyed, to bee builded new againe. And Aristotle, beside the directing him to that glorious ende, that was to make the world onely a general countrie, and all men as one people, that should live in amitie and agreement together, under one government and one law, that like the sunne, should generally give light to all, hee instructed him in the natural sciences, and in the vertues of the mind full and wholy, that he made him most wise, most manly, most continent, and a true morall Philosopher, not in wordes onely, but in deedes.

For there can not be imagined a more noble Philosophie, than to bring to a civill trade of living such wilde people as were the inhabitants of Bactria and Caucasus, India, and Scythia, and to teach them matrimony, husbandrie, to honour their fathers, to abstaine from robbing and killing, and from other naughtie conditions, and to builde so many noble cities in strange countries, so that infinite through those lawes were brought from a wilde life to live like men.

And of these thinges in Alexander, the author was Aristotle, in practising the waies of a good Courtier: the which Calisthenes coulde not do, for all Aristotle shewed him the way of it, who because he was a right philosopher, and so sharpe a minister of the bare truth without mingling it with courtlinesse, hee lost his life and profited not, but rather gave a slaunder to Alexander.

With the very same way of Courtlinesse Plato framed Dion the Syracusan. But when he met afterward with Dionysius the tyrant, like a booke all full of faultes and errors, and rather needfull to be cleane blotted out, than altered or corrected, because it was not possible to scrape out of him that blot of tyranny wherewithall he was stained so long together, he would not practise therein the waies of Courtiership, for he thought they shoulde be all in vaine.

The which our Courtier ought to doe also, if his chaunce be to serve a prince of so ill a nature, that by long custome is growne in use with vices, as they that have the consumption of the lunges with their disease. For in this case he ought to forsake his service, lest hee beare the blame of his Lords ill practises, or feele the hartgriefe that all good men have which serve the wicked.

Here when the Lord Octavian had made a stay, the Lorde Gaspar saide: I had not thought our Courtier had beene so worthie a personage. But since Aristotle and Plato be his mates, I judge no man ought to disdaine this name any more.

Yet wote I not whether I may believe that Aristotle and Plato ever daunced, or were Musitions in all their life time, or practised other feates of chivalrie.

The Lorde Octavian answered: almost it is not lawful to thinke that these two divine wits were not skilful in everything, and therefore it is to be presupposed, that they practised what ever belonged to Courtlinesse.

For where it commeth to purpose, they so penne the

matter, that the verie crafts masters themselves know by their writinges, that they understood the whole, even the pith and innermost roots.

Wherefore to a Courtier or instructer of a prince (how ever ye lust to terme him) that tendeth to the good ende which we have spoken of, it is not to be saide, but that all the good qualities which these Lordes have given him doe belong, though he were never so grave a Philosopher or holy in his manners: because they strive not against goodnesse, discretion, knowledge and will, in all age, and in all time and place.

Then the Lorde Caspar, I remember (quoth he) that these Lordes, yesternight reasoning of the Courtiers qualities, did allow him to be a lover, and in making a rehersall of as much as hetherto hath beene spoken, a man may picke out a conclusion, That the Courtier (which with his worthinesse and credit must encline his prince to vertue) must in manner of necessitie bee aged, for knowledge commeth verye seldom times before yeares, and especially in matters that be learned with experience: I can not see, when he is well drawne in yeares, how it will stand well with him to be a lover, considering (as it hath beene saide the other night) Love frameth not with olde men, and the trickes that in yong men be galantnesse, courtesie and precisenesse so acceptable to women, in them are mere follies, and fondnesse to bee laughed at, and purchase him that useth them hatred of women, and mockes of others.

Therefore in case this your Aristotle and olde Courtier were a lover, and practised the feates that yong lovers doe (as some that we have seene in our dayes) I feare me, he would forget to teach his Prince: and peradventure boyes would mocke him behinde his backe, and women would have none other delight in him, but to make him a jesting stocke.

Then saide the Lord Octavian: Since all the other qualities appointed to the Courtier are meete for him, although hee be olde, mee thinke we shoulde not then barre him from his happinesse to love.

Nay rather, quoth the Lorde Gaspar, to take his love from him, is a perfection over and above, and making him to live happily out of miserie and wretchednesse.

Maister Peter Bembo said: remember you not (my Lord Gaspar) that the Lord Octavian declared the other night in his devise of pastimes, although he be not skilfull in love, to know yet that there be some Lovers, which reckon the disdaines, the angers, the debates and torments which they receive of their Ladies, sweete? Whereupon hee required to bee taught ye cause of this sweetnesse.

Therefore in case our Courtier (though he bee olde) were kindled with those loves that bee sweete without any bitter smacke, he should feele no miserie nor wretchednesse at all. And being wise, as we set case he is, he should not be deceived in thinking to be meete for him whatsoever were meete for yong men.

But in loving should perhaps love after a sorte, that might not onely bring him in slaunder, but to much praise and happinesse, without any lothsomnesse at all, the which very seldom or (in a manner) never happeneth to yong men: and so should he neither lay aside the teaching of his Prince, nor yet commit any thing that should deserve the mocking of boyes.

Then spake the Dutchesse: I am glad (maister Peter) that you have not beene much troubled in our reasonings this night, for now we may be the bolder to give you in charge to speake, and to teach the Courtier this so happie a love, which bringeth with it neither slaunder, nor any inconveniencie: for perhaps it shall be one of the necessariest and profitablest qualities that hetherto hath beene given him, therefore speake of good felowship as much as you know therein.

Maister Peter laughed and saide: I would be loath (madam) where I say that it is lawfull for old men to love, it should be an occasion for these Ladies to thinke mee olde: therefore hardly give ye this enterprise to an other.

The Dutchesse answered: you ought not to refuse to be counted old in knowledge, though ye be yong in yeares. Therefore say on, and excuse your selfe no more.

Maister Peter saide: surely (madam) if I must entreate upon this matter, I must first goe aske counsell of my Hermit Lavinello.[40]

The Ladie Emilia saide then halfe in anger: There is never a one in all the company so disobedient as you be (maister Peter) therefore shoulde the Dutchesse doe well to chastice you somewhat for it.

Maister Peter saide smiling: for love of God (madam) be not angry with me, for I will say what ever you will have me. Goe to, say on then, answered the Ladie Emilia.

Then maister Peter after a whiles silence, somewhat setling himselfe as though he should entreat upô a waightie matter, saide thus: My Lordes, to shew that olde men may love not onely without slaunder, but otherwhile more happily than yong men, I must be enforced to make a litle discourse to declare what love is, and wherein consisteth the happinesse that lovers may have. Therfore I beseech you give the hearing with heedefulnesse, for I hope to make you understand, that it were not unfitting for anie man here to bee a lover, in case he were fifteene or twentie yeares elder than M. Morello.

And here after they had laughed a while, M. Peter proceeded. I say therefore that according as it is defined of the wise men of olde time, Love is nothing else but a certaine coveting to enjoy beautie: and for somuch as coveting longeth for nothing, but for things known, it is requisite that knowledge goe evermore before coveting, which of his owne nature willeth the good, but of himselfe is blind, and knoweth it not. Therefore hath nature so ordained that to every vertue of knowledge there is annexed a vertue of longing. And because in our soule there be three manner waies to know, namely, by sense, reason, and understanding: of sense there ariseth appetite or long-ing, which is common to us with brute beastes: of reason ariseth election or choice, which is proper to man: of understanding, by the which man may be partner with Angels, ariseth will.

Even as therefore the sense knoweth not but sensible matters, and that which may be felt, so the appetite or coveting onely deserveth the same: and even as the under-standing is bent but to behold things that bee under-stood, so is that will onely fedde with spirituall goods.

Man of nature indowed with reason, placed (as it were) in the middle betweene these two extremities, may through his choice inclining to sense, or reaching to understanding, come nigh to the coveting sometime of the one, sometime of the other part.

In these sortes therefore may beautie be coveted, the generall name wherfore may be applyed to all thinges, either naturall or artificiall, that are framed in good pro-portion, and due temper, as their nature beareth.

But speaking of the beautie that we meane, which is onely it, that appeareth in bodies, and especially in the face of man, and moveth this fervent coveting which wee call Love, we will terme it an influence of the heavenly bountifulnesse, the which for all it stretcheth over all thinges that be created (like the light of the sunne) yet when it findeth out a face well proportioned, and framed with a certaine lively agreement of several colours, and set forth with lights and shadowes, and with an orderly dis-tance and limits of lines, thereinto it distilleth it selfe and appeareth most welfavored, and decketh out and lightneth the subject where it shineth with a marvellous grace and glistering (like the sunne beames that strike against beau-tifull plate of fine golde wrought and set with precious jewels).

So that it draweth unto it mens eyes with pleasure, and pearcing through them, imprinteth himselfe in the soule, and with an unwonted sweetnesse all to stirreth her and deliteth, and setting her on fire maketh her to covet him.

When the soule then is taken with coveting to enjoy this beautie as a good thing, in case she suffer her selfe to be guided with the judgement of sense, she falleth into most deepe errours, and judgeth the bodie in which beauty is discerned to be the principall cause thereof: whereupon to enjoy it she reckoneth it necessarie to joine as inwardly as she can, with that bodie, which is false.

And therfore who so thinketh in possessing the bodie to enjoy Beautie, he is farre deceived, and is moved to it, not with true knowledge by the choice of reason, but with false opinion by the longing of sense. Whereupon the pleasure that followeth it, is also false and of necesitie full of errors.

And therefore into one of the two vices runne all those lovers that satisfie their unhonest lusts with ye women whom they love: For either as soone as they be come to the coveted ende, they not only feele a fulnesse and lothsomnesse, but also conceive a hatred against the wight beloved, as though longing repented him of his offence, and knowledged the deceite wrought him by the false judgement of sense, that made him believe the ill to be good: or els they continue in the very same coveting and greedinesse, as though they were not in deed come to the end which they sought for. And albeit through the blind opinion that hath made them dronken (to their seeming) in that instant they feele a contentation, as the diseased otherwhile, that dreame they drinke of some cleare spring, yet be they not satisfied, nor leave of so.

And because of possessing coveted goodnesse, there ariseth alwaies quietnesse and satisfaction in the possessors minde, in case this were the true and right ende of their coveting, when they possesse it they would be at quietnes and throughly satisfied which they be not: but rather deceived through that likenesse, they forthwith returne again to unbridled coveting, and with the very same trouble which they felt at the first, they fall againe into the raging and most burning thirst of the thing, that they hope in vaine to possesse perfectly.

These kinde of lovers therefore love most unluckily, for either they never come by their covetings, which is a great unluckinesse: or els if they doe come by them, they come by their hurt, and ende their miseries with other greater miseries: for both in the beginning and middle of this love, there is never other thing felt, but afflictions, torments, griefes, pining, travaile, so that to be wan, vexed with continuall teares and sighes, to live with a discontented minde, to be alwaies dumbe, or to lament, to covet death, in conclusion most unluckie are the properties which (they say) belong to lovers.

The cause therefore of this wretchednesse in mens mindes, is principally Sense, which in youthfull age beareth most sway, because the lustinesse of the flesh and of the bloud, in that season addeth unto him even so much force, as it withdraweth frō reason.

Therefore doth it easily traine the soule to follow appetite or longing, for when she seeth her selfe drowned in the earthly prison, because she is set in the office to governe the bodie, she can not of her selfe understand plainly at the first the truth of spirituall beholding. Wherefore to compasse the understanding of thinges, she must goe begge the beginning at the senses, and therefore she believeth them, and giveth eare to them, and is contented to be lead by them, especially when they have so much courage, that (in a manner) they enforce her.

And because they bee deceitfull, they fill her with errours and false opinions. Whereupon most commonly it happeneth, that yong men be wrapped in this sensuall love, which is a very rebel against reason, and therefore they make themselves unworthie to enjoy the favors and benefits which love bestoweth upon his true subjects, neither in love feele they any other pleasures, than what beastes without reason doe, but much more grievous afflictions.

Setting case therefore this to be so, which is most true, I say, that the contrarie chaunceth to them of a more ripe age. For in case they, when the soule is not now so much wayed downe with the bodily burden, and when the naturall burning aswageth and draweth to a warmth, if they be inflamed with beautie, and to it bend their coveting, guided by reasonable choice, they bee not deceived, and possesse beautie perfectly, and therefore through the possessing of it, alwaies goodnesse ensueth to them: because beautie is good, and consequently the true love of it is most good and holy, and evermore bringeth forth good fruites in the soules of them, that with the bridle of reason restraine the ill disposition of sense, the which olde men can much sooner do than yong.

It is not therefore out of reason to say, that olde men may also love without slander, and more happily, than yong men: taking notwithstanding this name Old, not for the age at the pits brinke, nor when the cannelles of the bodie be so feeble, that the soule can not through them worke her feates, but when knowledge in us is in his right strength.

And I will not also hide this from you: namely, that I suppose, where sensuall love in every age is naught, yet in yong men it deserveth excuse, and perhaps in some case lawfull: for although it putteth them in afflictions, dangers, travels, and the unfortunatnesse that is said, yet are there many that to winne them the good will of their Ladies practise vertuous thinges, which for all they be not bent to a good end, yet are they good of them selves.

And so of that much bitternesse they picke out a litle sweetnesse, and through the adversities which they sustaine, in the ende they acknowledge their errour.

As I judge therefore, those yong men that bridle their appetites, and love with reason, to be godly: so doe I hold excused such as yeelde to sensuall love, whereunto they be so enclined through the weakenesse and frailtie of man: so they show therein meekenes, courtesie, and prowesse, and the other worthie conditions that these Lords have spoken of, and when these youthfull yeares bee gone and past, leave it off cleane, keeping aloofe from this sensuall coveting as frō the lowest step of the stayres, by the which a man may ascend to true love.

But in case after they draw in yeares once, they reserve still in their colde hart the fire of appetites, and bring stoute reason in subjection to feeble sense, it can not be said how much they are to be blamed: for like men without sense they deserve with an everlasting shame to be put in the number of unreasonable living creatures, because the thoughts and waies of sensuall love bee farre unfitting for ripe age.

Here Bembo paused a while as though he woulde breath him, and when all thinges were whist, maister Morello of Ortona saide: And in case there were some olde man more fresh and lustie and of a better complexion than many yong men, why would you not have it lawfull for him to love with the love that yong men love?

The Dutchesse laughed and said: If the love of yong men bee so unluckie, why would you (maister Morello) that olde men should also love with the unluckinesse? But in case you were olde (as these men say you bee) you would not thus procure the hurt of olde men.

Maister Morello answered: the hurt of olde men (me seemeth) maister Peter Bembo procureth, who will have them to love after a sorte, that I for my part understand not: and (me think) the possessing of this beautie which he prayseth so much, without the bodie, is a dreame.

Doe you believe maister Morello, quoth then Count Lewis, that beautie is alwaies so good a thing as maister Peter Bembo speaketh of?

Not I in good sooth, answered maister Morello: But I remember rather that I have seene many beautifull women of a most ill inclination, cruell, and spitefull, and it seemeth that (in a manner) it happeneth alwaies so, for beautie maketh them proud: and pride, cruel.

Count Lewis saide smiling: To you perhaps they seeme cruell, because they content you not with it, that you would have. But cause maister Peter Bembo to teach you in what sorte olde men ought to covet beautie, and what to seeke at their Ladies handes, and what to content themselves withall: and in not passing out of these boundes, ye shall see that they shall bee neither proude nor cruel: and will satisfie you with what you shall require.

Maister Morello seemed then somewhat out of patience, and saide: I will not know the thing that toucheth me not. But cause you to be taught how the yong men ought to covet this beautie, that are not so fresh and lustie as old men be.

Here Sir Fredericke to pacify maister Morello, and to breake their talke, would not suffer Count Lewis to make answere, but interrupting him, saide.

Perhaps maister Morello is not altogether out of the way in saying that beautie is not alwaies good, for the beautie of women is many times cause of infinit evils in the world, hatred, warre, mortalitie, and destruction, whereof the rasing of Troye can be a good witnesse. And beautifull women for the most part bee either proude and cruell (as is saide) or unchast, but maister Morello would finde no fault with that.

There be also many wicked men that have the comlinesse of a beautifull countenance, and it seemeth nature hath so shaped them, because they may bee the readier to deceive, and that this amiable looke were like a baite that covereth the hooke.

Then maister Peter Bembo, believe not (quoth hee) but beautie is alwaies good. Here Count Lewis because he would returne againe to his former purpose, interrupted him and saide.

Since maister Morello passeth not to understand that, which is so necessarie for him, teach it me, and shew me how olde men may come by this happinesse of love, for I will not care to be counted olde, so it may profit me.

Maister Peter Bembo laughed and saide: first will I take the error out of these gentlemens minde: and afterwarde will I satisfie you also. So beginning a fresh: My Lordes (quoth hee) I would not that with speaking ill of beautie, which is a holy thing, any of us as prophane and wicked should purchase him the wrath of God. Therefore to give maister Morello and Sir Frederick warning, that they lose not their sight, as Stesichorus did, a paine most meete for who so dispraiseth beautie. I say that beautie commeth of God, and is like a circle, the goodnesse whereof is the Centre. And therefore, as there can be no circle without a centre, no more can beautie be without goodnesse.

Whereupon doth very seldom an ill soule dwell in a beautifull bodie. And therefore is the outwarde beautie a true signe of the inwarde goodnesse, and in bodies this comelines is imprinted more and lesse (as it were) for a marke of the soule, whereby she is outwardly knowne: as in trees, in which the beautie of the buddes giveth a testimonie of the goodnesse of the fruite. And the very same happeneth in bodies, as it is seene, that Palmestrers by the visage knowe manie times the conditions, and otherwhile the thoughts of men. And which is more, in beastes also a man may discerne by the face the qualitie of the courage, which in the body declareth it selfe as much as it can.

Judge you how plainely in the face of a Lyon, a horse, and an Eagle, a man shall discerne anger, fiercenesse, and stoutnesse: in lambes and doves simplenesse and verie innocencie: the craftie suttletie in foxes and wolves, and the like (in a manner) in all other living creatures.

The soule therefore for the most part bee also evil, and ye beautifull good. Therefore it may be said that beautie is a face pleasant, merrie, comely, and to be desired for goodnesse: and foulenesse a face darke, uglesome, unpleasant, and to bee shunned for ill. And in case you will consider all thinges, ye shall find, that whatsoever is good and profitable, hath also evermore the comelinesse of beautie.

Behold the state of this great Ingin of the worlde, which God created for the health and perservation of every thing that was made. The heaven rounde besette with so many heavēly lights: and in the middle, the earth environed with the Elements, and upheld with the waight of it selfe: the sunne, that compassing about giveth light to the whole, and in winter season draweth to the lowermost signe, afterwarde by litle and litle climbeth againe to the other part: The moone, that of him taketh her light, according as she draweth nigh, or goeth farther from him: And the other five starres, that diverslye keepe the very same course.

These thinges among themselves have such force by the knitting together of an order so necessarily framed, that with altering them any one jotte, they should be all lowsed, and the world would decay. They have also such beautie and comelinesse, that all the wits men have, can not imagin a more beautifull matter.

Thinke now of the shape of man, which may be called a litle world: in whom every parcell of his bodie is seene to be necessarily framed by arte and not by happe, and then the forme altogether most beautifull, so that it were a hard matter to judge, whether the members, as the eyes, the nose, the mouth, the eares, the armes, yᵉ breast, and in like manner the other partes, give either more profit to the countenance and the rest of the bodie, or comelinesse. The like may bee saide of all other living creatures.

Beholde the feathers of foules, the leaves and boughes of trees, which be given them of nature to keepe them in their being, and yet have they withall a very great slightnesse.

Leave nature, and come to arte. What thing is so necessarie in sayling vessels, as the fore part, the sides, the mainyardes, the maste, the sailes, the sterne, oares, ankers, and tacklinges? All these thinges notwithstanding are so well favoured in the eye, that unto who so beholdeth them,

600

they seeme to have beene found out as wel for pleasure, as for profit.

Pillers, and great beames upholde high buildings and pallaces, and yet are they no lesse pleasurefull unto the eyes of the beholders, than profitable to the buildings.

When men began first to builde, in the middle of the temples and houses, they reared the ridge of the roofe, not to make the workes to have a better shew, but because the water might the more commodiously avoide on both sides: yet unto profit there was forthwith adjoyned a faire sightlinesse, so that if under ye skye where there falleth neither haile nor raine a man should builde a Temple without a reared ridge, it is to bee thought, that it coulde have neither a sightly shew nor any beautie.

Beside other things therfore it giveth a great praise to the world, in saying that it is beautifull. It is praysed, in saying, the beautifull heaven, beautifull earth, beautifull sea, beautifull rivers, beautiful woodes, trees, gardens, beautifull cities, beautifull churches, houses, armies. In conclusion this comely and holy beautie is a wondrous setting out of everie thing. And it may bee saide, that Good and beautifull be after a sorte one selfe thing, especially in the bodies of men: of the beautie whereof the nighest cause (I suppose) is the beautie of the soule: the which as a partner of the right and heavenly beauty, maketh sightly and beautiful what ever she toucheth, and most of all, if the bodie, where she dwelleth, be not of so vile a matter, that she can not imprint in it her propertie.

Therefore Beautie is the true monument and spoile of the victory of the soule, when she with heavenly influence beareth rule over martiall and grosse nature, and with her light overcommeth the darkenesse of the bodie.

It is not then to bee spoken that beauty maketh women proude or cruel, although it seeme so to maister Morello. Neither yet ought beautifull women to beare the blame of that hatred, mortalitie, and destruction, which the unbridled appetites of men are the cause of.

601

I will not now deny, but it is possible also to finde in the world beautifull women unchaste, yet not because beautie inclineth them to unchaste living, for it rather plucketh them from it, and leadeth them into the way of vertuous conditions, through the affinitie that beautie hath with goodnesse.

But otherwhile ill bringing up, the cōtinuall provocations of lovers, tokens, povertie, hope, deceites, feare, and a thousand other matters overcome the stedfastnesse, yea of beautifull and good women: and for these and like causes may also beautifull men become wicked.

Then saide the Lord Cesar: In case the Lord Gaspars saying be true of yesternight, there is no doubt, but the faire women be more chaste than the foule.

And what was my saying quoth the Lorde Gaspar? The Lorde Cesar answered: If I do well beare in mind, your saying was, that the women that are sued to, alwaies refuse to satisfie him that sueth to them, but those that are not sued to, sue to others.

There is no doubt but the beautifull women have alwaies more suters, and be more instantly laide at in love, than the foule. Therefore the beautifull alwaies deny, and consequently bee more chaste than the foule, which not being sued to, sue to others.

Maister Peter Bembo laughed and saide: This argument can not be answered to. Afterwarde he proceeded. It chanceth also oftentimes, that as to other senses, so the sight is deceived, and judgeth a face beautifull, which in deed is not beautifull. And because in the eyes, and in the whole countenance of some women, a man beholdeth otherwhile a certaine lavish wantonnesse painted with dishonest flickeringes, many whom that manner delighteth, because it promiseth them an easinesse to come by the thing that they covet, call it beautie: but in deede it is a cloked unshamefastnesse unworthie of so honourable and holy a name.

Maister Peter Bembo held his peace, and those Lordes

still were earnest upon him to speake somewhat more of this love, and of the way to enjoy beautie aright, and at the last.

Me thinke (quoth he) I have shewed plainly inough, that old men may love more happily than yong, which was my drift, therefore it becometh not me to enter any farther.

Count Lewis answered: You have better declared the unluckinesse of yong men, than the happinesse of olde men, whom you have not as yet taught what they must follow in this love of theirs: onely you have saide, that they must suffer themselves to bee guided by reason, and the opinion of many is, that it is unpossible for love to stand with reason.

Bembo notwithstanding sought to make an ende of reasoning, but the Dutchesse desired him to say on, and he beganne thus a fresh.

Too unluckie were the nature of man, if our soule (in the which this so fervent coveting may lightly arise) should bee driven to nourish it with that onely, which is common to her with beasts, and could not turne it to the other noble parte, which is proper to her.

Therefore since it is so your pleasure: I will not refuse to reason upon this noble matter. And because I know my selfe unworthie to talke of the most holy mysteries of love, I beseech him to leade my thought and my tongue so, that I may shew this excellent Courtier how to love contrary to the wonted manner of the common ignorant sorte.

And even as from my childhood I have dedicated all my whole life unto him, so also now that my wordes may bee answerable to the same intent, and to the praise of him.

I say therefore, that since the nature of man in youthfull age is so much enclined to sense, it may be graunted the Courtier, while hee is yong, to love sensually. But in case afterwarde also in his ripe yeares, he chaunce to be set on fire with this coveting of love, hee ought to bee good and circumspect and heedfull, that he beguile not himselfe, to bee lead willfully into the wretchednesse, that in yong men deserveth more to bee pittied than blamed: and contrariwise in old men, more to be blamed than pittied.

Therefore when an amiable countenance of a beautifull woman commeth in his sight, that is accompanied with noble conditions and honest behaviours, so that as one practised in love, hee woteth well that his hew hath an agreement with hers, as soone as hee is aware that his eyes snatch that image and carrie it to the hart, and that the soule beginneth to beholde it with pleasure, and feeleth within her selfe the influence that stirreth her, and by litle and litle setteth her in heate, and that those lively spirits, that twinckle out through the eyes, put continuall fresh nourishment to the fire: hee ought in this beginning to seeke a speedy remedie and to raise up reason, and with her to sense the fortresse of his hart, and to shut in such wise the passages against sense and appetites, that they may enter neither with force nor subtil practise.

Thus if the flame bee quenched, the jeopardie is also quenched. But in case it continue or encrease, then must the Courtier determine (when he perceiveth hee is taken) to shunne throughly al filthinesse of common love, and so enter into the holy way of love, with the guide of reason.

And first consider that the body, where that beautie shineth, is not the fountaine from whence beautie springeth, but rather because beautie is bodilesse, and (as wee have saide) an heavenly shining beame, she loseth much of her honour when she is coupled with that vile subject and full of corruption, because the lesse she is partner thereof, the more perfect she is, and clean sundred from it, is most perfect.

And as a man heareth not with his mouth, nor smelleth with his eares: no more can he also in any manner wise enjoy beautie, nor satisfie the desire that she stirreth up in our mindes, with feeling, but with the sense, unto whom beautie is the very butte to level at: namely, the vertue of seeing.

Let him lay aside therefore the blinde judgement of the

sense, and enjoy with his eyes ye brightnesse, the comelinesse, the loving sparkels, laughters, gestures, and all the other pleasant furnitures of beautie: especially with hearing the sweetnesse of her voice, the tunablenesse of her wordes, the melody of her singing and playing on instruments (in case the woman be loved bee a musitian) and so shall he with most daintie foode feede the soule through the meanes of these two senses, which have litle bodily substance in them, and be the ministers of reason, without entring farther toward the bodie, with coveting unto any longing otherwise than honest.

Afterwarde let him obey, please, and honour with all reverence his woman, and recken her more deare to him than his owne life, and preferre all her commodities and pleasures before his owne, and love no lesse in her the beautie of minde, than of the bodie.

Therefore let him have a care not to suffer her to run into an errour, but with lessons and good exhortations seeke alwaies to frame her to modestie, to temperance, to true honestie, and so to worke that there may never take place in her other than pure thoughts, and farre wide from all filthinesse of vices. And thus in sowing of vertue in the garden of that minde, he shall also gather the fruites of most beautiful conditions, and savour them with a marvellous good relise.

And this shal be the right engendring and imprinting of beautie in beautie, the which some holde opinion to be the end of love. In this manner shall our Courtier bee most acceptable to his Ladie, and she will alwaies shew her selfe towarde him tractable, lowly and sweete in language, and as willing to please him, as to be beloved of him: and the willes of them both shall bee most honest and agreeable, and they consequently shall bee most happie.

Here maister Morello. The engendring (quoth he) of beautie in beautie aright, were the engendring of a beautifull childe in a beautifull woman, and I woulde thinke it a more manifest token a great deale that shee loved her

605

lover, if she pleased him with this, than with the sweet-nesse of language that you speake of.

Maister Peter Bembo laughed, and saide: You must not (maister Morello) passe your boundes. I may tell you, it is not a small token that a woman loveth, when she giveth unto her lover her beautie, which is so precious a matter: and by the wayes that be a passage to the soule, that is to say, the sight and the hearing, sendeth the lookes of her eyes, the image of her countenance, and the voice of her wordes, that pearce into the lovers hart, and give a wit-nesse of her love.

Maister Morello saide: Lookes and wordes may be, and oftentimes are false witnesses. Therefore who so hath not a better pledge of love (in my judgement) he is in an ill assurance. And surely I looked still that you would have made this woman of yours somewhat more courteous and free towarde the Courtier, than my Lorde Julian hath made his: but (me seemeth) ye be both of the propertie of those judges, that (to appeare wise) give sentence against their owne.

Bembo saide: I am well pleased to have this woman much more courteous towarde my Courtier not yong, than the Lorde Julians is to the yong: and that with good reason, because mine coveteth but honest matters, and therefore may ye woman graunt him them all without blame. But my Lorde Julians woman that is not so assured of the modestie of the yong man, ought to graunt him the honest matters onely, and deny him the dishonest.

Therefore more happie is mine, that hath graunted him whatsoever hee requireth, than the other, that hath part graunted, and part denyed.

And because you may moreover the better understand, that reasonable love is more happy than sensuall, I say unto you that selfe same thinges in sensuall ought to be denyed otherwhile, and in reasonable, graunted: because in the one, they bee honest, and in the other dishonest.

Therefore the woman to please her good lover, beside

the graunting him mery countenance, familiar and secret talke, jeasting, dalying, hand in hand, may also lawfully and without blame come to kissing: which in sensual love according to the Lord Julians rules, is not lawfull. For since a kisse is a knitting together both of bodie and soule, it is to bee feared, lest the sensuall lover will be more enclined to the part of the bodie, than of the soule: but the reasonable lover woteth well, that although the mouth be a parcell of the bodie, yet is it an issue for the wordes, that be the interpreters of the soule, and for the inwarde breath, which is also called the soule.

And therefore hath a delite to joyne his mouth with the womans beloved with a kisse: not to stirre him to any dishonest desire, but because hee feeleth that that bonde is the opening of an entrie to the soules, which drawne with a coveting the one of the other, poure them selves by turne the one into the others bodie, and bee so mingled together, that each of them hath two soules.

And one alone so framed of them both ruleth (in a manner) two bodies. Whereupon, a kisse may be saide to be rather a coupling together of the soule, than of the body, because it hath such force in her, that it draweth her unto it, and (as it were) separateth her from the bodie.

For this doe all chaste lovers covet a kisse, as a coupling of soules together. And therefore Plato the devine lover saith, that in kissing, his soule came as farre as his lippes to depart out of the bodie.

And because the separating of the soule from the matters of the sense, and the through coupling her with matters of understanding may be betokened by a kisse, Salomon saith in his heavenly booke of Balates, O that he would kisse me with a kisse of his mouth, to expresse the desire he had that his soule might be ravished through heavenly love to the beholding of heavenly beautie, in such manner, that coupling her selfe inwardly with it, she might forsake the bodie.

They stood all harkening heedfully to Bembo, reasoning,

and after he had staied a while, and saw that none spake, he saide: Since you have made me to beginne to shew our not yong Courtier this happie love, I will leade him yet somewhat farther forwards, because to stand still at this stay were somewhat perillous for him, considering (as we have oftentimes saide) the soule is most inclined to the senses.

And for all reason with discourse chooseth well, and knoweth that beautie not to spring of the bodie, and therefore setteth a bridle to the unhonest desires, yet to behold it alwaies in that bodie, doth oftentimes corrupt the right judgement. And where no other inconvenience insueth upon it, once absence from the wight beloved carrieth a great passion with it.

Because the influence of that beautie when it is present, giveth a wonderous delite to the lover, and setting his hart on fire, quickeneth and melteth certaine vertues in a traunce and congeled in the soule, the which nourished with the heate of love, flow about and goe bubbling nigh the hart, and thrust out through the eyes those spirits which bee most fine vapours made of the purest and clearest part of the bloud, which receive the image of beautie, and decke it with a thousande sundrie furnitures.

Whereupon the soule taketh a delite, and with a certaine wonder is agast, and yet enjoyeth she it, and (as it were) astonied together with the pleasure, feeleth the feare and reverence that men accustomably have towarde holy matters and thinketh her selfe to be in Paradise.

The lover therefore that considereth onely the beautie in the bodie, loseth this treasure and happinesse, as soone as the woman beloved with her departure leaveth the eies without their brightnesse, and consequently the soule as a widdow without her joy. For since beautie is farre off, that influence of love setteth not the hart on fire, as it did in presence.

Whereupon the poares be dryed up and withered, and yet doth the remembrance of beautie somewhat stirre those vertues of the soule in such wise, that they seeke to scatter abroade the spirits, and they finding the wayes closed up, have no issue, and still they seeke to get out, and so with those shootings inclosed, pricke the soule, and torment her bitterly, as yong children, when in their tender gummes they beginne to breed teeth.

And hence come the teares, sighes, vexations and torments of lovers: because the soule is alwaies in affliction and travell and (in a manner) waxeth woode, until the beloved beautie commeth before her once againe, and then is she immediatly pacified and taketh breath, and throughly bent to it, is nourished with most daintie food, and by her will, would never depart from so sweet a sight.

To avoide therefore the torment of his absence, and to enjoy beautie without passion, the Courtier by the helpe of reason must full and wholy call backe againe the coveting of the bodie to beautie alone, and (in what he can) beholde it in it selfe simple and pure, and frame it within in his imagination sundred from all matter, and so make it friendly and loving to his soule, and there enjoy it, and have it with him day and night, in every time and place, without mistrust ever to lose it: keeping alwaies fast in minde, that the bodie is a most diverse thing from beautie, and not onely not encreaseth, but diminisheth the perfection of it.

In this wise shall our not yong Courtier bee out of all bitternesse and wretchednesse that yong men feele (in a manner) continually, as jelousies, suspitions, disdaines, angers, desperations and certaine rages full of madnesse, whereby many times they be ledde into so great errour, that some doe not onely beat ye woman whom they love, but ridde themselves out of their life.

He shall doe no wrong to the husband, father, brethren or kinsfolke of ye woman beloved. He shall not bring her in slander. He shall not be in case, with much a doe otherwhile to refraine his eyes and tongue from discovering his desires to others. He shal not take thought at departure or in absence, because he shall evermore carrie his precious treasure about with him shutte fast within his hart.

And beside, through the vertue of imagination, hee shall fashion with himselfe that beautie much more faire than it is in deede. But among these commodities, the lover shall find another yet farre greater, in case hee will take this love for a stayre (as it were) to climbe up to another farre higher than it. The which he shall bring to passe, if he will goe and consider with himselfe, what a straight bond it is to bee alwaies in the trouble to behold the beautie of one bodie alone. And therefore to come out of this so narrowe a roome, hee shall gather in his thought by litle and litle so many ornaments, that meddling all beautie together, he shal make an universall conceite, and bring the multitude of them to the unitie of one alone, that is generally spred over all the nature of man. And thus shall he beholde no more the particular beautie of one woman, but an universall, that decketh out all bodies.

Whereupon being made dimme with this greater light, he shall not passe upon the lesser, and burning in a more excellent flame, he shall litle esteeme it, that hee set great store by at the first.

This stayre of love, though it be very noble and such as few arive at it, yet is it not in this sorte to be called perfect, forsomuch as where the imagination is of force to make conveyance, and hath no knowledge, but through those beginninges that ye senses helpe her withall, she is not cleane purged from grosse darknesse: and therefore though she do consider that universall beautie in sunder and in it selfe alone, yet doth she not well and clearely discerne it, nor without some doubtfulnesse, by reason of the agreement that the fancies have with the bodie.

Wherefore such as come to this love, are like to yong birdes almost flush, which for all they flitter a litle their tender winges, yet dare they not stray farre from the nest, nor commit themselves to the winde and open weather.

When our Courtier therfore shall bee come to this point, although hee may bee called a good and happie lover, in respect of them that be drowned in the miserie of sensuall love, yet will I not have him to set his hart at rest, but boldly proceede farther, following the high way after his guide, that leadeth him to the point of true happinesse. And thus in steade of going out of his wit with thought, as he must doe that will consider the bodily beautie, hee may come into his wit, to beholde the beautie that is seene with the eyes of the minde, which then begin to be sharpe and throughly seeing, when the eyes of the bodie lose the floure of their sightlinesse.

Therefore the soule ridde of vices, purged with the studies of true Philosophie, occupied in spirituall, and exercised in matters of understanding, turning her to the beholding of her owne substance, as it were raised out of a most deepe sleepe, openeth the eyes that all men have, and few occupie, and seeth in her selfe a shining beame of that light, which is the true image of the Angelike beautie partened with her, whereof she also partneth with the bodie a feeble shadow.

Therefore waxed blinde about earthly matters, is made most quicke of sight about heavenly. And otherwhile when the stirring vertues of the bodie are withdrawne alone through earnest beholding, either fast bound through sleepe, when she is not hindred by them, she feeleth a certaine privie smell of the right Angelike beautie, and ravished with the shining of that light, beginneth to be inflamed, and so greedely followeth after, that (in a manner) she waxeth dronken and beside her selfe, for coveting to couple her self with it, having found (to her weening) the footesteps of God, in the beholding of whom (as in her happie ende) she seeketh to settle her selfe.

And therefore burning in this most happie flame, she ariseth to the noblest part of her which is the understanding, and there no more shadowed with the darke night of earthly matters, seeth the heavenly beautie: but yet doth she not for all that enjoy it altogether perfectly, because she beholdeth it onely in her particular understanding, which can not conceive the passing great universall beautie.

Whereupon not throughly satisfied with this benefit, love giveth unto the soule a greater happinesse. For like as through the particular beautie of one bodie hee guideth her to the universall beautie of all bodies: Even so in the least degree of perfection through particular understanding hee guideth her to the universall understanding.

Thus the soule kindled in the most holy fire of true heavenly love, fleeth to couple her selfe with the nature of Angels, and not onely cleane forsaketh sense, but hath no more neede of the discourse of reason, for being chaunged into an Angell, she understandeth all thinges that may be understood: and without any veil or cloud, she seeth the maine sea of the pure heavenly beautie and receiveth it into her, and enjoyeth the soveraigne happinesse, that can not be comprehended of the senses.

Since therefore the beauties, which we dayly see with these our dimme eyes in bodies subject to corruption, that neverthelesse be nothing els but dreames and most thinne shadowes of beautie, seeme unto us so well favored and comely, that oftentimes they kindle in us a most burning fire, and with such delight, that we reckon no happinesse may bee compared to it, that wee feele otherwhile throughe the onely love which the beloved countenance of a woman casteth at us.

What happie wonder, what blessed abashment may we reckon that to bee, that taketh the soules, which come to have a sight of the heavenly beauty? what sweet flame? What sweete incense may a man believe that to be, which ariseth of the fountaine of the soveraigne and right beautie? Which is the originall of all other beautie which never encreaseth nor diminisheth, alwaies beautifull, and of it selfe, as well on the one part as on the other, most simply, onely like it selfe, and partner of non other, but in such wise beautifull, that all other beautifull thinges be beautifull, because they be partners of the beautie of it.

This is the beautie unseperable from ye high bountie, and not onely to the indowed with understanding giveth understanding, to the reasonable reason, to the sensuall which with her voice calleth and draweth to her al thinges: sense and appetite to live, but also partaketh with plantes and stones (as a print of her self) stirring, and the natural provocation of their properties.

So much therefore is this love greater and happier then others, as the cause that stirreth it, is more excellent. And therefore, as common fire tryeth gold and maketh it fine, so this most holy fire in soules destroyeth and consumeth whatsoever there is mortall in them, and relieveth and maketh beautifull the heavenly part, which at the first by reason of the sense was deade and buried in them.

This is the great fire in the which (the Poets write) that Hercules was buried on the toppe of the mountaine Oeta: and through that consuming with fire, after his death was holy and immortall.

This is the fiery bush of Moses: The devided tongues of fire: the inflamed Chariot of Helias: which doubleth grace and happinesse in their soules that be worthie to see it, when they forsake this earthly basenesse, and flee up unto heaven.

Let us therefore bend all our force and thoughtes of soule to this most holy light, that sheweth us the way which leadeth to heaven: and after it, putting off the affections we were clad at our coming downe, let us climbe up the staires, which at the lowermost steppe have the shadow of sensuall beautie, to the high mansion place where the heavenly, amiable and right beautie dwelleth, which lyeth hidden in the innermost secretes of God, lest unhalowed eyes shoulde come to the sight of it: and there shall wee finde a most happie end for our desires, true rest for our travels, certaine remedie for miseries, a most healthfull medicine for sicknesse, a most sure haven in ye troublesome stormes of the tempestuous sea of this life.

What tongue mortall is there then (O most holy love) that can sufficiently prayse thy worthines? Thou most

613

beautifull, most good, most wise, art derived of the unitie of the heavenly beautie, goodnesse and wisedom, and therein dost thou abide, and unto it through it, (as in a circle) turnest about.

Thou the most sweete bond of the world, a meane betwixt heavenly and earthly thinges, with a bountifull temper bendest the high vertues to the government of the lower, and turning backe the mindes of mortall men to their beginning, couplest them with it.

Thou with agreement bringest the Elements in one, stirrest nature to bring forth, and that which ariseth and is borne for the succession of the life. Thou bringest severed matters into one, to the unperfect givest perfection, to the unlike likenesse, to enimitie amitie, to the earth fruites, to the Sea calmnesse, to the heaven, lively light.

Thou art the father of true pleasures, of grace, peace, lowlinesse, and good will, enimy to rude wildnesse, and sluggishnesse: to be short, the beginning, and end of all goodnesse.

And forsomuch as thou delightest to dwell in the floure of beautifull bodies and beautifull soules, I suppose that thy abiding place is now here among us, and from above otherwhile shewest thy selfe a litle to the eyes and mindes of them that bee not worthie to see thee.

Therefore vouchsafe (Lorde) to hearken to our prayers, pour thy selfe into our harts, and with the brightnesse of thy most holy fire lighten our darkenesse, and like a trustie guide in this blinde mase shew us the right way: correct the falshood of the senses, and after long wandring in vanitie, give us the right and sound joy. Make us to smell those spirituall savours that relieve the vertues of the understanding, and to heare the heavenly harmony so tunable, that no discorde of passion take place any more in us. Make us dronken with the bottomlesse fountaine of contentation, that alwaies doth delight, and never giveth fill, and that giveth a smacke of the right blisse unto who so drinketh of the renuing and cleare water therof. Purge with the shining beames of thy light our eyes from mistie ignorance, that they may no more set by mortall beautie, and well perceive that the thinges which at the first they thought them selves to see, be not in deede, and those that they saw not, to be in effect. Accept our soules, that bee offered unto thee for a sacrifice. Burne them in the lively flame that wasteth all grosse filthinesse, that after they be cleane sundred from the bodie, they may bee coupled with an everlasting and most sweete bond to the heavenly beautie. And wee severed from ourselves, may bee changed like right lovers into the beloved, and after we be drawn from the earth, admitted to the feast of the angels, where fed with immortall ambrosia and nectar, in the end we may dye a most happie and lively death, as in times past died the fathers of olde time, whose soules with most fervent zeale of beholding, thou didst hale from the bodie, and coupledst them with God.

When Bembo had hetherto spoken with such vehemencie, that a man woulde have thought him (as it were) ravished and beside himselfe, hee stood still without once moving, holding his eyes towarde heaven as astonied: when the Ladie Emilia, which together with the rest gave most diligent eare to this talke, tooke him by the plaite of his garment, and plucking him a little said.

Take heede (maister Peter) that these thoughts make not your soule also to forsake the bodie.

Madam, answered maister Peter, it should not be the first miracle that love hath wrought in me. Then the Dutchesse and all the rest began a fresh to bee instant upon maister Bembo that he would proceede once more in his talke, and every one thought he felt in his minde (as it were) a certaine sparkell of that godly love that pricked him, and they all coveted to heare farther: but maister Bembo,

My Lords (quoth hee) I have spoken what the holy furie of love hath (unsought for) indited to me: now that (it seemeth) he inspireth mee no more, I wot not what to say. And I thinke verily that love will not have his secretes

615

discovered any farther, nor that the Courtier should passe the degree that his pleasure is I should shew him, and therefore it is not perhaps lawfull to speake any more of this matter.

Surely, quoth the Dutchesse, if the not yong Courtier be such a one, that he can follow this way which you have shewed him, of right he ought to be satisfied with so great a happinesse, and not to envie the yonger.

Then the Lord Cesar Gonzaga, the way (quoth he) that leadeth to this happinesse is so steepe (in my mind) that (I believe) it will be much adoe to get to it.

The Lord Gaspar saide: I believe it be hard to get up for men, but unpossible for women.

The Ladie Emilia laughed and saide: If ye fall so often to offend us, I promise you, ye shall be no more forgiven.

The Lorde Gaspar answered: It is no offence to you, in saying, that womens soules be not so purged from passions as mens be, nor so accustomed in beholding, as maister Peter hath saide, it is necessary for them to be, that will taste of the heavenly love.

Therefore it is not read that ever woman hath had this grace: but many men have had it, as Plato, Socrates, Plotinus and many other: and a number of our holy fathers, as Saint Francis, in whom a fervent spirite of love imprinted the most holy seale of five woundes.

And nothing but the vertue of love coulde hale up Saint Paule the Apostle to the sight of those secretes, which is not lawfull for man to speake of, nor shewe S. Stephen the heavens open.

Here answered the Lord Julian. In this point men shall nothing passe women, for Socrates himselfe doth confesse that all mysteries of love which he knew, were opened unto him by a woman, which was Diotima. And the Angell that with the fire of love imprinted the five woundes in Saint Francis, hath also made some women worthie of the same print in our age.

You must remember moreover that Saint Marie Magdalen

had many faultes forgiven her, because she loved much: and perhaps with no lesse grace than Saint Paule, was she many times through Angelike love haled up to the third heaven. And many other (as I shewed you yesterday more at large) that for love of the name of Christ have not passed upon life, nor feared torments, nor any other kind of death how terrible and cruel so ever it were. And they were not (as maister Peter will have his Courtier to be) aged, but soft and tender maidens, and in the age, when he saith that sensuall love ought to be borne withall in men.

The Lord Gaspar began to prepare himselfe to speake to the Duchesse. Of this (quoth shee) let maister Peter be judge, and the matter shall stand to his verdite, Whether women be not as meete for heavenlie love as men. But because the plea betweene you may happen be too long, it shall be amis to defer it until to morrow.

Nay, to night, quoth the Lord Cesar Gonzaga. And how can it be to night, quoth the Dutchesse?

The Lord Cesar answered: Because it is day alredy, and shewed her the light that began to enter in at the clifts of the windowes.

Then every man arose upon his feete with much wonder, because they had not thought that the reasonings had lasted longer than the accustomed wont, saving only that they were begon much later, and with their pleasantnesse had deceived so the Lordes mindes, that they wist not of the going away of the houres. And not one of them felt any hevinesse of sleepe in his eies, the which often happeneth when a man is up after his accustomed houre to goe to bed.

When the windowes then were opened on the side of the Pallaice that hath his prospect towarde the high top of Mount Catri, they sawe already in the East a faire morning like unto the colour of roses, and all starres voyded, saving only the sweete Governesse of heaven, Venus which keepeth the boundes of the night and day, from which appeared to blowe a sweete blast, that filling the aire with a biting colde, began to quicken the tunable notes of the

617

prettie birdes, among the hushing woodes of the hils at hand.

Whereupon they all taking their leave with reverence of the Dutchesse, departed toward their lodgings without torche, the light of the day suffising. And as they were nowe passing out of the great Chamber doore, the Lord Generall turned him to the Dutchesse, and said: Madam, to take up the variance betweene the Lord Gasper and the Lord Julian, wee will asemble this night with the judge sooner than we did yesterday. The Lady Emilia answered, upon condition, that in case my Lorde Gasper will accuse women, and give them (as his wont is) some false report, he will also put us in suretie to stand to triall, for I recken him a wavering starter.

NOTES ON *THE PRINCE*

Note
No.   *Note*

1 Machiavelli had treated of republics in his *Commentary on the First Ten Books of Livy.*

2 Roderigo Borgia, the father of Cesare and Lucrezia Borgia, became Pope Alexander in 1492. "Romania" is Romagna.

3 The King of Spain with whom Alexander divided the kingdom of Naples was Ferdinand of Aragon (1452–1516).

4 *Siracusa* = Syracuse

5 *Roan* = Rouen

6 *Amilcar* = Hamilcar

7 *Gracchyes* = Gracchi. Caius and Tiberius Gracchus, brothers, were Roman statesmen of the second century B.C.

8 Giorgi Scali, a Florentine leader of the late fourteenth century, was deserted by his followers and assassinated.

9 Machiavelli is, of course, ironical in this whole passage in his praise of the spiritual, rather than temporal, power of ecclesiastical states.

10 *Sextus* = Sixtus IV, Francesco della Rovere, pope from 1471 to 1484

11 Dacres has *Como* in error for *Conio.*

12 The incident referred to occurred in 1510.

13 Charles VII, King of France from 1422 to 1461, was called "the Victorious."

14 Castiglione, in *The Courtier,* also recommends hunting as training for war. More, in *Utopia,* disapproves of hunting because of his pity for hunted animals.

15 The word *not* is omitted by Dacres, but is required by the Italian text.

16 In present-day English Dacres' *miserable* may be best rendered as *stingy* or *miserly.*

17 Machiavelli's point is that rioting between the opposing factions should have been checked, by cruelty if necessary, in order to save the city of Pistoia. The passage helps to

Note
No.   *Note*

clarify Machiavelli's ideas about the proper employment of cruelty.

18 The unnamed prince is probably Ferdinand of Aragon.

19 The Countess of Furli, or Forli, was Caterina Sforza (1463–1509). Her husband was murdered in 1488, during an insurrection.

20 Cesare Borgia attacked her state in 1499.

21 *Pre'* is an Italian abbreviation for *Prete*, a priest. Dacres' text has, in error, *Peter*.

22 The "present Emperour" was Maximilian I, Holy Roman emperor from 1493 to 1519.

23 The reference is probably to Cesare Borgia.

24 Machiavelli is, of course, referring to the Medici and addressing Lorenzo de' Medici.

NOTES ON *UTOPIA*

1 Peter Giles, a magistrate of Antwerp, one of Erasmus's students and a friend of Sir Thomas More, is one of the several real persons introduced into More's book.

2 John Clement, who was brought up in More's household, afterwards became a famous physician.

3 More's friend Cuthbert Tunstall, Master of the Rolls, later became Bishop of Durham.

4 Raphael Hythloday is, of course, a fictitious character, whom More adroitly introduces among the real persons like Giles, Tunstall, and Cardinal Morton. The details concerning his voyages with Amerigo Vespucci add to the verisimilitude.

5 *geastwise* = as a guest

6 The insurrection referred to was a revolt by Cornish men in 1497 against Henry VII's tax levies. The insurrectionists marched on London, but were defeated at Blackheath.

7 John Morton, in whose household Sir Thomas More lived as a youth, was at that time Archbishop of Canterbury and Lord Chancellor of England. He became a cardinal in 1493.

8 The Polylerites were one of More's several fictitious peoples. Among others, besides the Utopians, were the Macerians and Zapoletes. The name *Polylerites* is derived from the

Note No.	Note

Greek, and means "much nonsense." Cf. *Utopia*, meaning "no where," as an example of More's punning method of indicating that what he describes is imaginary.

9 Helizeus is Elisha, and More's reference is to the account in 2 Kings ii, 23 of the children who ridiculed Elisha for his baldness, and who, in consequence, were cursed by him and torn by bears.

10 The "balde men" referred to here are, of course, the friars, with their shaven crowns.

11 Plato's "goodlye similitude," paraphrased here, occurs in the *Republic*, VI, 496.

12 Topographically, Amaurote resembles London, as Utopia resembles England; but of course Amaurote, with its wide streets, fireproof buildings, and other improvements, is a greatly idealized sixteenth-century London.

13 More meant that the working day was six hours long. Robynson's error in rendering More's Latin "tres ante meridiem" prevents the text from reading as it should: ". . . and assigne onelye sixe of those houres to woorke, three before noone . . . and after diner, when they have rested two houres, then they work iii. houres and upon that they go to supper."

14 In this passage More is ridiculing the abstractness of medieval scholasticism and the finespun categories and terminologies of the schoolmen.

15 More's discussion of the moral philosophy of the Utopians is indebted to Aristotle's *Ethics* and to Cicero's *About the Ends of Goods and Evils*. In a broader sense, it is an effort to reconcile hedonism, stoicism, and Christian ethics. More's argument, which is likely to seem tortuous to the modern reader, is that pleasure should be the chief aim of life, but that true pleasure is also virtue.

16 Aldus Pius Manutius was one of the most famous of the early printers, as well as a famous scholar. From the Aldine Press at Venice in the late fifteenth and early sixteenth centuries came editions of the Greek and Roman authors mentioned by More in the preceding sentences.

17 The distinction that More is making here is that the Utopians did not make bondmen of prisoners taken in

621

*Note
No.*   *Note*

battle if mercenaries fought for the Utopians, but did make the prisoners bondmen if the Utopians themselves had to fight.

[18] *avoutrers* = adulterers

[19] It has been suggested that in his account of the Zapoletes, who served as mercenary soldiers for adjoining countries, More had in mind the Swiss.

[20] Mythra, or Mithras, was the name of the Persian sun god. More had already said that the language of the Utopians was "not much unlyke the Persian tonge."

[21] More followed his own recommendation of a cheerful attitude toward death. No one who has read Roper's *Life of More* will forget his cheerfulness as he awaited his execution, or as he mounted the scaffold with a jest on his lips.

[22] In More's time and for long afterwards, goldsmiths served as bankers.

NOTES ON *THE COURTIER*

[1] Castiglione's claim that the writing of *The Courtier* was "accomplished in a fewe days" is not likely to be accepted as literally true by anybody. It is a good example of the sort of modest and even nonchalant attitude toward one's achievements that was recommended to the courtier.

[2] Actually, Castiglione was at the court of Urbino in early March, 1507, at the time when the dialogues of *The Courtier* took place. He had just returned from an embassy to England. The pretence of not having been present is impelled by courtly modesty.

[3] Duke Federico di Montefeltro (1422–1482) seems to have been indeed "the light of Italy." He was an able military leader, a man of the highest probity, the head of a polished court, and a scholar who built a distinguished library.

[4] The meaning of "making antiques" is devising mimes or dances.

[5] Berto was one of the buffoons at the papal court.

| *Note*
No. | *Notes* |

6 *Joco di canne* was stick-throwing, an equestrian game introduced into Italy by the Spaniards.

7 "Vauting" was vaulting on a horse, somewhat in the manner of circus riders in modern times.

8 Castiglione's "after the Venetian phrase" is an obvious joke. Naturally the people of Venice, who had no opportunity in their city to ride horseback, might be expected to ride badly.

9 The "three noble writers" are Dante, Petrarch, and Boccaccio.

10 Monseigneur D'Angoulême was afterwards King Francis I of France, admirer of the Italian Renaissance and patron of the French Renaissance.

11 The "places under ground in Roome" are, of course the Roman Catacombs.

12 *cameses* = cameos

13 The "Lord Generall" was Francesco Maria della Rovere, a nephew of Pope Julius II. A young hothead, then seventeen years old, he had just lost the city of Bologna to the French and been reprimanded by his uncle for the defeat.

14 "Braulles" were dances similar to a modern cotillon.

15 Here "brest" means voice.

16 The meaning of "auncient" in this phrase is sober, rather than old.

17 The reference, Opdycke points out in his edition of *The Courtier* (New York, 1903), is to Leonardo da Vinci, whose remarkable inventions and plans for devices like steam cannons, paddle-wheel boats, and airplanes were regarded by his contemporaries as absurd.

18 The reference is to Bibbiena's baldness.

19 *nipping boord* = sharp satire

20 "The greatest of the furies is my bedfellow," an adaptation of Virgil's "Furiarum maxima juxta accubat"—*Aeneid*, V, 605–606.

21 "As many stars as heaven has, so many girls has your Rome."

22 "As many kids as the pasture has, so many sodomites has your Rome."

23 "Give an account of thy stewardship."—St. Luke xvi, 2.

24 "Lord, thou deliveredst unto me five talents: behold, I have gained beside them five talents more."—St. Matthew xxv, 20

25 "The pupil obviously used the phrase in its low Latin meaning, 'Master, God give you good evening.' Beroaldo jocosely
accepted it in its classical meaning, 'Master, God give you
good, late.' "—Opdycke's note.

26 In this case also, a play on the possible meanings of words
is involved. The other Spaniard used "vino" in the sense of
"wine," but Diego de Chignognes jestingly took "vino" to
mean "he came." Thus, the dialogue becomes: "Christ
came." "He came, and thou knewest him not."

27 The reading should be "nip him for a heretic." Hoby mis-
took *marrano*, a heretic, for *marrone*, a chestnut.

28 The reference is to a gallows.

29 A "bayting place" refers to a bad inn.

30 The characters mentioned are in the third, sixth, and ninth
tales of the Eighth Day of the *Decameron,* and in the fifth
tale of the Ninth Day.

31 The characters and situations alluded to here are found in
the sixth tale of the Third Day of the *Decameron* and in
the seventh and eighth tales of the Seventh Day.

32 *tradiments* = treacheries

33 Aristotle, *Physics*, I, xviii

34 *foistes* = galleys

35 The allusion is to the impotence of Duke Guidobaldo, which
was the reason for the proposed divorce.

36 The reference is to Ovid's *Ars Amandi*.

37 Lord Gaspar Pallavicino died at the age of twenty-five, in
1511.

38 "to make a hand" = to gain an advantage

39 Castiglione actually had returned from England at the time
of the conversations described in *The Courtier,* but here he
keeps up the pretence of having been absent.

40 "In Book III of Bembo's *Gli Asolani* (1505), a hermit discourses to Lavinello on the beauty of mystical Christian
love. . . . Much of the following disquisition seems to be
drawn from Plato and from Bembo's *Gli Asolani*. As Bembo
is known to have revised *The Courtier* before publication,
we may assume that he was content with the form and
substance of the discourse attributed to him." (Opdycke's
note)